WITHDRAWN

PENGUIN BOOKS

THE PENGUIN HISTORY OF LATIN AMERICA

Edwin Williamson holds the Forbes Chair of Hispanic Studies in the
University of Edinburgh. He has held academic posts at Trinity College,
Dublin, and Birkbeck College, University of London, and has been a
visiting professor at Stanford University, California, and the University
of Sao Paulo, Brazil. Professor Williamson's research and publications
reflect his interest in both Latin America and the Golden Age of Spain.

EDWIN WILLIAMSON

THE PENGUIN HISTORY
OF LATIN AMERICA

PENGUIN BOOKS

For Susan, Louise and Phoebe

PENGUIN BOOKS

Published by the Penguin Group
Penguin Books Ltd, 80 Strand, London WC2R 0RL, England
Penguin Putnam Inc., 375 Hudson Street, New York, New York 10014, USA
Penguin Books Australia Ltd, 250 Camberwell Road, Camberwell, Victoria 3124, Australia
Penguin Books Canada Ltd, 10 Alcorn Avenue, Toronto, Ontario, Canada M4V 3B2
Penguin Books India (P) Ltd, 11 Community Centre, Panchsheel Park, New Delhi – 110 017, India
Penguin Books (NZ) Ltd, Cnr Rosedale and Airborne Roads, Albany, Auckland, New Zealand
Penguin Books (South Africa) (Pty) Ltd, 24 Sturdee Avenue, Rosebank 2196, South Africa

Penguin Books Ltd, Registered Offices: 80 Strand, London WC2R 0RL, England

www.penguin.com

First published by Allen Lane The Penguin Press 1992
Published in Penguin Books 1992
22

Copyright © Edwin Williamson, 1992
All rights reserved

The moral right of the author has been asserted

The author and publishers would like to thank Cambridge University Press
for permission to use information from maps that appear in
James Lockhart and Stuart B. Schwartz, *Early Latin America:
A History of Colonial Spanish America and Brazil*
(Cambridge University Press, 1983)

Printed in England by Clays Ltd, St Ives plc

Contents

===

Preface

The history of Latin America has fascinated observers as much as it has mystified them. There is something apparently alien about the continent, an exoticism that derives perhaps from it having once been perceived as a 'new world', although there survive monuments and relics of ancient societies whose cultures remain poorly understood by us even today. This elusiveness – hinting simultaneously at a former state of grace and some original corruption – has rendered the interpretation of Latin American history peculiarly vulnerable to speculation and myth-making. I have therefore approached my task with caution, not to say trepidation.

The primary aim of this book is to provide a general survey for the non-specialist reader. As far as possible I try to present a dispassionate and, at times, a tentative, account of events, pointing to gaps in our knowledge or to areas of controversy. On the other hand, I wanted to avoid draining all colour from the picture, and so my method is often narrative, focusing occasionally on personalities, and, when discussing literary works, intended to give the reader an insight into the outstanding features of the culture.

Because my principal interest is in Latin, as opposed to pre-Columbian, America, I begin with the story of how the continent came to the notice of southern Europeans and how some of its inhabitants were conquered by the Spaniards. Before going on to discuss the hybrid societies that subsequently emerged, I include a chapter outlining the background of the main Indian peoples as well as that of the Iberian conquerors. For the period after independence, I decided to sacrifice a comprehensive survey of all the republics in favour of a selective approach in the belief that this would provide a better focus for discussing representative developments without overlooking local conditions altogether. The twentieth century presented the most difficult problem of coverage; I finally opted for an introductory overview followed by shorter chapters on a number of individual countries whose experience has been especially significant. The narrative is concluded in 1990, the year the text was completed but also a year which can be said to mark the end of roughly a half-century of state-sponsored nationalism.

In recent decades, Latin American literature has received quite extraordinary attention throughout the world. The historical circumstances in which it was produced are less well known. I have tried, therefore, to set my discussion of literature and culture in a wider historical context. In those chapters, I devote some attention to individual authors because I believe their work can afford important insights into the ideas, images and preoccupations that have shaped the 'mentality' of a period. Conversely, I thought it would be profitable to bring to bear, as far as I could, the findings of recent historical research on issues which have been the subject of cultural and political debate in Latin America for many years.

A book of this nature inevitably draws on the work of many people. I should like to acknowledge my debt to the numerous scholars who have contributed to our knowledge and understanding of the continent's past. More specifically, I wish to record my gratitude to the Research Comittee at Birkbeck College, University of London, for awarding me a grant that allowed a long period of uninterrupted research. I also want to thank a number of people who helped in the making of this book: Monique and John Fa for their hospitality and bibliographical assistance in Mexico City; Ian Williamson and Francine Nahai for lending me their house in Suffolk, where large sections of the book were written; and, not least, my wife, Susan, whose encouragement, advice and support were invaluable, as always.

Edinburgh, May 1991

PART ONE

THE AGE OF EMPIRE

1. Discovery and Conquest

DISCOVERY

The Lure of the Indies

After enduring a long and testing voyage across unknown regions of the Atlantic Ocean, the Genoese mariner Christopher Columbus came within sight of land in the early morning of 12 October 1492. On making shore, he was convinced that a westward sea passage to the mainland of Asia had been found and that the purpose of his exploration could now be realized: to obtain a licence from the rulers of Japan and China to establish a private trade in gold and spices under the auspices of his patrons, the Catholic Monarchs of Spain.

Asia was a fascinating, if mysterious, continent for Europeans. It was known vaguely as the Indies, a name that applied not only to India itself, but also to Malacca, the Spice Islands and even, loosely, to China and Japan. Few Europeans had ventured very far into its fabulous interior, and images of Asia in the West were coloured by the early fourteenth-century chronicle of the Venetian explorer Marco Polo, who described his overland journey across the central Steppes to the realms of Kublai Khan, ruler of Cathay. Columbus's imagination was influenced also by other more fanciful accounts of Asia, such as the famous chronicles of Sir John Mandeville, who, towards the end of the fourteenth century, evoked lands inhabited by monsters and exotic beasts, where gold-mines could be found and the Christian kingdom of Prester John lay isolated among the heathen.

Commercial links between Europe and Asia had, in fact, existed for centuries through a number of trade routes in the eastern Mediterranean, which had been dominated by the Italian republics of Genoa and Venice since the eleventh century. A chain of trading colonies in the Levant afforded access to Egypt and Syria, the gateways to the riches of Arabia, India and the Far East. From these distant lands, by way of desert caravans or coastal shipping, came spices, silks and other luxuries, for which there was a rising demand in late-medieval Europe. Genoa and Venice grew rich on this trade and acquired considerable commercial and navigational expertise. The Italians also produced sugar on plantations worked by slaves in their Mediterranean colonies – for the traffic in slaves was an integral part of the commercial exchange between Europe and Asia.

Italian merchants had traded with northern Europe by travelling across the Alps, but the slowness of this means of communication impelled them to seek better trade routes, and, when in 1277 a Genoese fleet sailed through the Straits of Gibraltar bound for England and Flanders, a direct sea link was established for the first time between the Mediterranean and Atlantic economies. Within a few years, communities of Genoese merchants could be found in Seville, Cadiz and Lisbon, and this Italian presence in the Atlantic seaboard of the Iberian Peninsula would result eventually in the westward transfer of commercial concerns and maritime skills that had been acquired, through long experience of the Indies trade, at the eastern end of the Mediterranean.

Oriental luxuries were paid for with gold and slaves, and the richest source of these commodities was Africa – especially the central and western regions below the Sahara known at the time as the empire of the Sudan. In exchange for European goods the Sudan sent slaves, ivory and gold in caravans across the desert to the ports on the Mediterranean coasts of the Muslim-held Maghreb, from where they reached southern Europe. However, as precious metals came to form the basis of the European monetary economy, the general demand for gold could not be satisfied by slow-moving camel trains across the Sahara. In the course of the fourteenth century there arose what Pierre Chaunu has called a 'gold famine' in Europe, especially in the south.★ Trade with the Orient went into deficit and the system of commerce which had proved so profitable for the Italians found itself in deepening crisis. This decline in trade contributed to the terrible depression in Europe caused by natural disasters, political upheavals and the demographic ravages that between 1347 and 1350 accompanied the Black Death.

Portugal and Spain felt the effects of the depression until about the middle of the fifteenth century. As Chaunu observed, 'gold almost completely disappeared from the Iberian Peninsula. There was a crisis in Portugal between 1383 and 1434, and a similar one in Navarre.'† Portugal, additionally, suffered from a lack of corn: it had a poor harvest every third year or

★ Pierre Chaunu, *European Expansion in the Later Middle Ages* (North-Holland: Amsterdam, New York and London, 1979), p. 103.
† ibid., p. 103.

so and had to import supplies from North Africa. By the early fifteenth century, material requirements, as well as a revival of a spirit of crusade against the Moors, encouraged the Portuguese to seek more direct control of the sources of gold and grain. In 1415 they crossed the Straits of Gibraltar and captured the port of Ceuta, but their conquest of Morocco was checked at Tangier, with the result that the Portuguese would eventually skirt round the Maghreb and establish a sea route to the Atlantic coasts of sub-Saharan Africa.

A crucial intermediate stage in this move down the coast of Africa was the exploitation of the archipelagos of the Azores, Madeira and the Canaries. Their effective discovery in the course of the 1330s and 1340s (there was some awareness of their existence even earlier) shows the extent of the maritime exploration that was being undertaken from the small fishing ports of southern Portugal and south-west Andalusia. However, these Atlantic islands were not colonized until about a century later, when economic crisis acted as a spur to turn them to some advantage: in the 1430s sugar plantations were set up in Madeira and some of the Canary Islands by Iberian settlers. These early ventures into Atlantic waters were to lead to the probing of the African coastline and, once Cape Bojador was rounded in 1434, a sea route was opened for the Portuguese to trade directly in gold and slaves with the Sudan. Within a few decades a number of *feitorias* (trading stations) were founded at strategic points along the seaboard of northern West Africa and islands offshore.

There followed a remarkable period of maritime expansion by the Portuguese, who by the end of the century would establish a sea route to the Indies, rounding Africa and crossing the Indian Ocean to reach the subcontinent itself and the Spice Islands that lay beyond. As the rising power of the Ottoman empire closed off the traditional trade routes to the Orient through the Levant, Portugal would become the principal intermediary in the trading system between Europe, Africa and Asia, taking over by the 1490s many of the economic activities of Venice and Genoa – the cultivation of sugar, the traffic in slaves and the trading of gold and spices for European goods. Still, the presence of Genoese sailors and merchants in the Atlantic ports of the Iberian Peninsula for close on 200 years was a vital factor in the inauguration of the great Portuguese 'enterprise of the Indies'.

The Four Voyages of Christopher Columbus (1492–1504)

It was in the context of the Portuguese expansion towards the Indies that Christopher Columbus, a member of the Genoese trading community in Portugal, had conceived the notion of finding a sea route directly westwards across the Atlantic to the mainland of Asia. This was not in itself an absurd idea at the time: it had been accepted in antiquity that the world was round, so it was possible, at least in theory, to sail west to Cathay, thereby avoiding the long journey round the continent of Africa. The intervening ocean, however, was an unknown quantity, whose immensity deterred sailors from attempting a westward crossing to the fabled regions on the other side of the world.

A seafarer from his youth, Columbus had married into an important Genoese family long established in Madeira: his wife's grandfather had worked with Prince Henry the Navigator, the moving spirit behind the Portuguese explorations of the ocean, and her father had distinguished himself in Portugal's African ventures. Columbus had taken part in at least one expedition to the great *feitoria* at São Jorge da Mina on the Gold Coast of West Africa, where he had seen at first hand the workings of the Portuguese trading system of slaving and barter. He realized that a westward sea passage to the Indies would bring huge commercial rewards, not to mention glory and fame. Furthermore, such a link would facilitate Portugal's strategic and religious aims: it would allow Christians to make contact with the kingdom of Prester John in the East, so enlisting a powerful new ally and outflanking the Muslim enemy; it would also open the way to the conversion of many millions of pagan souls in preparation for the establishment of the universal monarchy that would precede the Second Coming of Christ Himself.

The question that had to be decided was the width of the ocean. Columbus was well acquainted with the theories of ancient and medieval cosmographers, and he knew that the distance separating western Europe from Asia was a subject of some controversy, stemming from the discrepancy between Ptolemy's estimate of the dimensions of the combined land mass of Europe and Asia, and that of Marco Polo. Columbus's contemporary, the great Florentine scholar Paolo Toscanelli, supported Marco Polo's more optimistic estimate, and he encouraged the Genoese mariner to believe that the width of the ocean was much less than was accepted by established opinion. Columbus, moreover, made other miscalculations of his own, which reduced his estimate of the ocean's width even further – to a mere 2,400 nautical miles from the Canary Islands to Japan, thus placing Japan where the West

Indies actually are. If, as was likely, there were undiscovered islands along the way, then a western sea route was very much a practical proposition; it only remained to persuade the king of Portugal to give his backing to this new enterprise of the Indies.

John II of Portugal, however, was not well disposed towards the project Columbus put to him in 1485: its scientific basis was rightly questioned by his own experts, and, in any case, the Portuguese state had already invested too much in the search for a route to the Indies round Africa. The possibility of such a route seemed highly promising at about this time: in 1484 the explorer Diogo Cão had discovered the mouth of the Congo and was in the process of extending the limits of exploration well beyond, planting a marker as far as 21° 47′ south; and in 1488 Bartholomew Dias would at last round the Cape of Good Hope, paving the way for Vasco da Gama's epoch-making passage to India in 1497–8.

In 1485, therefore, Columbus's plan appeared to the Portuguese Crown to be a far-fetched and wasteful diversion from the much more certain prospect of reaching the Indies round Africa. Columbus approached other European princes, including the rulers of Castile, but none was yet willing to embark on such an adventure. By 1492, however, Ferdinand and Isabella, and especially the latter, having obtained the historic surrender of Muslim Granada, were prepared to risk backing Columbus. The Genoese mariner was granted a licence to undertake an enterprise of discovery; the *Capitulaciones de Santa Fe* were extraordinarily generous, bestowing upon Columbus the hereditary titles of Admiral of the Ocean Sea, Viceroy of the Indies and Governor of all the lands he might discover on his voyage, as well as the right to a one-tenth share of all the riches yielded up by these discoveries. Ferdinand and Isabella also advanced him a loan, and commanded the little sea ports around Cadiz to help equip and provision the expedition. If Columbus were successful, the Crown would acquire sovereignty over new territories overseas and Castile might conceivably outdo Portugal in establishing a direct sea link with Asia and in controlling thereby the lucrative commerce with the great kingdoms of the East.

On 3 August 1492 Columbus set sail from the south-western Andalusian port of Palos. He had three ships – a Galician *nao*, the *Santa María* (100 tons), and two locally built Portuguese-style caravels, the *Pinta* (60 tons) and the *Niña* (50 tons). They were manned by a total of eighty-seven men – mostly tough, experienced sailors from the small ports of the region; the most notable were members of the prominent seafaring Pinzón, Niño and Quintero families, without whose help and experience Columbus would not have been able to carry out his project. On this expedition too was the great

Biscayan mariner Juan de la Cosa, master and owner of the *Santa María*, who would gain fame in subsequent years as an explorer and map-maker.

Forced to stop for nearly a month in the Canaries for repairs, the expedition started out on its voyage of exploration proper on 9 September. After a fruitless month at sea, with his men growing restive and fortified only by his determination, Columbus began to notice favourable signs – flocks of birds passing overhead, branches floating by, and then a strange light flickering on the horizon in the dead of night. Finally, two hours after midnight on 12 October, the lookout on the *Pinta* sighted land – white cliffs lit up by the moon. When dawn broke, the vessels found a small bay and Columbus made the shore; he fell to his knees and thanked the Lord for the mercy of having finally reached land. An ocean had indeed been crossed, but this was not Japan; it was rather a small island in the Bahamas, which Columbus chose to call San Salvador, in honour of his Holy Saviour.

On seeing the three alien vessels, the inhabitants of the island swam out to visit them. The Admiral, as he was now called, noted their appearance: they went about completely naked, some had their bodies painted, their weapons were very primitive, and yet they seemed docile enough, and all too eager to exchange their possessions for trinkets proffered by the Spaniards. Still, this was not what he was looking for: he wanted to reach Japan, and these people were too barbarous to be the subjects of a powerful king. Columbus was a man of rather fixed expectations – he had gambled his life and honour on reaching the Orient, and he now stubbornly sought out evidence that would confirm his preconceptions. Moreover, used as he was to the commercial enterprises of the Italians and the Portuguese, he was keen to assess the economic potential of his discovery. Finding little on San Salvador – though the possibility that the natives might be used for the slave trade did cross his mind – he cruised around other islands in the Bahamas, continually struck by the beauty of the scenery, until he heard of larger islands to the south where gold was to be found. He then arrived on the north coast of 'Colba' (later Hispanicized as Cuba), which he hoped might be Japan; however, there was very little gold, though he observed that the natives relaxed by puffing at a large, burning stick of rolled leaves, which they called *tobacos*, a habit the Spaniards would eventually pick up and introduce throughout Europe.

On the eastern end of the island he learned of the aggressive, man-eating Caribs from the gentler Arawak tribes which he had so far encountered, and so he sailed on eastwards. When he came to another large island which he thought resembled Spain, he called it *La Isla Española* (Hispaniola – the island which today comprises Haiti and the Dominican Republic). Here the natives wore plenty of gold ornaments and were very welcoming – the naked women offered themselves freely to the strangers. On the north-western coast Columbus came across an important native chieftain, Guacanagari, who, to his great relief, showed some of the attributes of kingship – for this was taken as evidence that they were drawing closer to civilization and, therefore, to Japan or China. When the natives talked of a place called Cibao, Columbus thought they were referring to Cipangu, the name by which he knew Japan.

On Christmas Day the *Santa María* ran on to a coral reef and had to be abandoned. But Columbus took this disaster as a sign from God that he should found the first Spanish colony there, and with the help of Guacanagari's men the settlement of Navidad (the Nativity) was built using the timbers of the wrecked ship. A group of twenty-one volunteers was left behind, and Columbus, confident now that he had reached the Indies, set off on 4 January aboard the *Niña* on the return voyage to Spain.

Atrocious weather caused the *Niña* to put in first at the Azores and later at Lisbon as well. Nevertheless, John II received the Admiral with courtesy and allowed him to continue his journey to Spain. On 20 April 1493 he arrived before Ferdinand and Isabella at the royal court in Barcelona, accompanied by a retinue which included six natives bearing parrots in cages. Columbus presented himself in triumph as the discoverer of new lands in the Indies, lands which bore gold and could be profitably used for trading by Spain.

The Catholic Monarchs could now look forward to overtaking Portugal in the contest to establish direct trade links with the Indies (the Portuguese would not reach India until 1498). The requisite legitimacy for their enterprise was obtained from Pope Alexander VI, a Spanish Borgia, who issued a series of bulls granting Castile dominion over all lands that might be discovered in the Western Hemisphere. In order to avoid conflict with Portugal, the bulls sought to allocate to each of the rival Iberian powers a section of the undiscovered portion of the globe. A line of demarcation was drawn in 1493 at a longitude 100 leagues west of the Azores and Cape Verde Islands, but at Portugal's request, and with the diplomatic concurrence of Spain, this line was moved a further 270 leagues westwards by the Treaty of Tordesillas in 1494, thereby unwittingly delivering to Portugal the as yet unknown territory that was to become Brazil.

Even before this diplomatic compromise had been agreed, Columbus had set off from Cadiz on 25 September 1493 with a large expedition of seventeen ships and some 1,500 men (there were no women on board), with the intention of founding a permanent colony on the islands he had discovered.

In Hispaniola he found that the natives had destroyed the settlement of Navidad and killed the Spaniards in revenge for their rapacious behaviour. It was an ominous development, which revealed the nature of the men's expectations. These were hard-bitten adventurers, whose basic motives were not so different from Columbus's own, though far more crudely conceived. At considerable personal risk they had come out to these lands to find the kind of wealth and status largely denied to them in their mother country. It was patently not in their interest to settle quietly to a peasant's life tilling the soil or trading peaceably with the natives; there were, after all, great reserves of indigenous manpower that could be put to work to make the Europeans rich enough to live like lords when they got back home to Spain.

Upset by the destruction of Navidad, Columbus sailed eastwards looking for a new site to found a Portuguese-style trading station or *feitoria* like those on the African coast. A colony, which he called Isabela after the queen, was built in a rather ill-chosen place, and from there the Admiral sent expeditions into the Cibao to locate the source of the natives' gold. He then embarked on a reconnaissance which took him to Cuba once more and round Jamaica, returning to Isabela in September 1494 only to find more problems of indiscipline among the Spaniards – a faction of Catalans had rebelled against his brother Diego, whom he had left in charge. Facing a growing tension between, on the one hand, his vocation as an explorer and trader (recognized in his proud title, Admiral of the Ocean Sea) and, on the other, his role as governor of the new Spanish colony (Viceroy of the Indies, as his other great title had it), Columbus tried to satisfy the ambitions of unruly Spaniards who wanted quick rewards from colonization: he authorized more brutal expeditions into the interior to search for gold and made a *repartimiento* (distribution) of captive Indians to work for the Spaniards. He also considered starting a traffic in slaves to improve the economic prospects of his trading colony, and sent off a shipload of about 500 Indians to Spain (some 200 died of cold during the crossing and most of the rest expired shortly after they were put on the market in the Peninsula). The Indian tribes of Hispaniola rose in revolt and marched on Isabela, but they were easily put down by the Spaniards' guns and savage dogs.

In March 1496 Columbus went back to Spain to defend himself against slanders put about by disgruntled colonists who had returned from Hispaniola. His enterprise of the Indies was becoming discredited at court: there seemed little evidence of rich deposits of gold, no contact had been made with the rulers of either Japan or China, and Hispaniola was apparently seething with discontent; furthermore, the pious Queen Isabella was unhappy with the treatment of the Indians, whom she had expressly forbidden to be taken as slaves. Nevertheless, he was relieved to find that the Catholic Monarchs, despite their reservations, still had confidence in him – possibly because they were concerned about the intentions of the Portuguese, who were known to be preparing a fleet of exploration under Vasco da Gama in the hope of finally reaching India.

It took Columbus about eighteen months to put together a new expedition, which was financed this time by the royal treasury under the supervision of the archdeacon of Seville, Juan Rodríguez de Fonseca, an ambitious official who would accumulate over the next two decades immense influence over the direction of the enterprise of the Indies. Columbus set sail in May 1498 and reached the island of Trinidad in July; he then explored the coast of Venezuela, surmising from the strength of the fresh-water currents in the Gulf of Paria and in the delta of the Orinoco that it must form part of a large continent, a *tierra firme*. But obsessed as he was with his quest for the Orient, he did not realize the implications of his discovery of this great land mass, even though he referred to it metaphorically as an 'other world'. It would be another Italian explorer, Amerigo Vespucci, sailing on a Spanish ship along sea routes opened up by Columbus, who would formulate the powerful idea that a continent unconnected with Asia had been discovered: he was the first to call it a *mundus novus*, a 'new world'. Columbus, for his part, never quite lost his medieval cast of mind; he remained ever the apocalyptic visionary, intrigued by the marvels that were being revealed to him, speculating, for instance, that the Orinoco delta might be the four-headed river that, according to Scripture, irrigates the Earthly Paradise.

On reaching Hispaniola, however, the Admiral found the Spaniards in a state of civil war. The town of Santo Domingo, established in his absence by his brother Bartholomew, had become as ungovernable as the Isabela settlement. Although Columbus tried to achieve a compromise between the warring factions, he and his brothers were resented as foreigners, and his failure to bring the situation under control further eroded his authority. Finally, in August 1500 a royal official, Francisco de Bobadilla, arrived with orders from the Crown to investigate the trouble. The Columbus brothers were arrested and Christopher was sent back to Spain in chains.

This high-handed treatment was, of course, a terrible humiliation for the Admiral, but circumstances dictated a revision of Columbus's original enterprise of the Indies. The political problems of Hispaniola had become so intractable because the island could not be turned into a trading station such as Columbus had envisaged. Gold was not obtainable through barter as in the Portuguese *feitorias* on the African coasts; it had to be directly mined, and this required a far more complex operation, including permanent settlement and the organization of a labour supply, an operation which called for the intervention of the state in order to set up an effective apparatus of government. And so Columbus's personal monopoly of the enterprise, as set out in the *Capitulaciones de Santa Fe*, was broken. In February 1502 the Catholic Monarchs of Castile sent out an experienced administrator, Nicolás de Ovando, as the first royal governor of what would become known as the Spanish Indies.

But Columbus was still intent on finding a westward passage to Asia, and he was authorized to make a fourth voyage of exploration across the Atlantic, setting out in May 1502 on an expedition which was to last until November 1504. This voyage greatly extended Spain's knowledge of the newly discovered lands in the Western Hemisphere, for, in trying to find a passage that would lead him to the mainland of Asia, Columbus traced the coastline of Central America along Honduras, Nicaragua, Costa Rica and Panama. When he returned to Spain, he petitioned the Crown for the restoration of some of his privileges, and succeeded, at least, in securing the eventual appointment of his son Diego as governor of Hispaniola with due recognition accorded to the hereditary titles of viceroy and admiral. Christopher Columbus died on 20 May 1506, convinced to the last that he had found the western sea route to the Orient and that the lands he had discovered were islands and peninsulas in Asia.

The troubles afflicting Columbus in his governorship of the earliest Spanish settlements in the Caribbean foreshadowed the immensely complex problems of government that the Spanish state would face in America. The political disorders on Hispaniola were due to a collision between two branches of humanity which were previously unknown to each other and which had incompatible cultural expectations. The Spaniards, like all contemporary Europeans, operated in a monetary economy in which gold was extremely scarce and therefore in tremendous demand; their society, moreover, accorded high status to lordship over a submissive labour force, whether enslaved or nominally free. The people of the islands, by contrast, lived in a subsistence barter economy, in which gold had a purely decorative value and mechanisms of labour service had not been developed. The Spaniards were therefore seeking goods and services which the indigenous societies were simply not equipped to provide.

Neither side understood this conflict of expectations: the Spanish settlers interpreted the Indians' reluctance to work as laziness, while the Indians could not comprehend the Spaniards' lust for gold or their demands for labour. This conflict threatened each side with destruction: without a supply of Indian labour to mine for a tradable commodity like gold the Spanish colony could not survive, but the Spanish demand for gold and labour would itself place intolerable pressures on native societies. It was the management of this conflict of expectations, with all the ethical and economic difficulties it raised, that would become the supreme political task of the Spanish Crown throughout the sixteenth century.

The conflict, of course, was intrinsically unequal. For a start, the Spaniards, though very few in number, had far superior technological resources and a strong motivation to achieve a set of clear objectives. But this was not all: there was a hidden biological dimension, which visited disaster upon the native population and aggravated the clash of cultures. The meeting of two hitherto isolated races led to an exchange of viruses that caused a high toll of death on both sides.

The Spaniards fell victim to tropical diseases: of the 1,500 men that went out with Columbus in 1493 to settle Hispaniola, only about 360 were surviving in 1502, when Nicolás de Ovando arrived with a further 2,500 settlers; a year later about half of the latter had died of mysterious ailments known as the *modorra* and the *baquía*. Those who survived and acclimatized were called *baquianos*, a term that would eventually be applied to the tough old Indies hands who acted as trackers and Indian-fighters on the frontiers of Spanish settlement throughout the colonial period.

The native populations of the islands, on the other hand, would be all but wiped out by smallpox, measles and other Old World diseases, against which they had no immunities because of their complete isolation from other races over millennia. The loss of life from epidemics was clearly appalling, though the extent of the depopulation is still disputed because of the lack of reliable statistics (some authorities believe the population of Hispaniola may have been as large as 8 million; others put it at roughly 50,000).

Disease interacted with economic pressures to create a terrible dynamic of destruction, which took a swift toll of native lives. Most of the Spanish settlers were rough, uneducated peasants from Extremadura and western Andalusia who were quick to mutiny or to disregard authority, for they had come out to the Caribbean islands to make a fortune and then go back home again. Their disregard for Indian welfare was scandalous and would provoke protests from other Spaniards, particularly the clergy. Their frantic demand for Indian manpower led to cruel exploitation, as well as to a flourishing but illicit slave-trade. Driven to exhaustion by punishing work-schedules, vicious treatment and agricultural disruption, the Indians became even more vulnerable to disease, many of them losing the will to live and to procreate.

The need to maintain the supply of Indian labour became a major stimulus to further Spanish exploration and conquest. As manpower fell drastically, Spanish slavers went out in search of more Indians, eventually ranging from one island to another: Puerto Rico was conquered in 1508, Jamaica in 1509, Cuba in 1511. From these islands the Spanish raiders crossed to parts of the mainland, where they established trading posts to barter for slaves, gold and other commodities. Tierra Firme (the northern coast of modern Colombia and Venezuela), discovered by Columbus on his third journey, had by 1509 attracted Spaniards looking to exploit its riches. In 1509 slave-raiders embarked on the conquest of the isthmus of Panama, founding the settlement of Darién; the explorer Ponce de León discovered Florida in 1513, but it was not effectively settled until much later.

The supply of labour, then, posed a vital problem for successive governors of Hispaniola and the islands. It had defeated Columbus because he had been forbidden to enslave the Indians by Queen Isabella. In an effort to stabilize the volatile colony, the next governor, Nicolás de Ovando, adapted a traditional form of labour service, known in Spain as *encomienda*, to the circumstances of Hispaniola: Indian workers were allocated to Spanish settlers on the understanding that they would be cared for, paid decent wages and instructed in the Christian faith in return for their services. Queen Isabella disliked the *encomienda* because it involved coercion and so fell short of the ideal of free wage labour, which the Spanish Crown would always uphold; she was also, like her successors, wary of creating a new class of feudal lords in the Indies who might challenge royal authority. Still, *encomienda* was preferable to slavery, and it had become clear by then that the Indians would not work voluntarily for wages. Though it enshrined forced labour, *encomienda* represented an attempt to regulate and humanize it by introducing an element of feudal responsibility towards Indian workers on the part of the *encomendero*. The system would subsequently have an enormous impact on labour relations throughout the Spanish Indies.

On Hispaniola itself, however, *encomienda* was soon undermined by the rapid Indian depopulation; it therefore failed to eliminate abuses such as overwork and slave-raiding. When in 1509 Ovando was replaced as governor by Columbus's son Diego Colón, the Spanish state redoubled its attempts to impose law and order on its colonies in the Caribbean. In 1511 the first American *audiencia* (royal court of justice) was created at Santo Domingo. A year earlier four Dominican missionaries had arrived on the island to help organize the Christianization of the Indians. They were soon appalled by the way Spanish *encomenderos* treated their Indian workers. In 1511 the Dominican friar Antonio de Montesinos delivered a famous sermon in which he exhorted the *encomenderos* to treat their Indians humanely on pain of damnation. It was the first major effort by Spanish missionaries to defend the rights of the Indians against the interests of the Spanish settlers. One *encomendero* responded dramatically to this call to the Christian conscience: Bartolomé de las Casas renounced his *encomienda* and eventually became a Dominican friar and the moving spirit in the defence of Indian rights for some five decades of his very long life.

The protests of the Dominicans persuaded Ferdinand of Aragon (Queen Isabella had died in 1504) to promulgate the Laws of Burgos in 1512, which set down fair rates of pay and provided for the supervision of *encomienda* arrangements by royal officials. But these laws proved unenforceable in the Caribbean and were generally ignored. In the same year some attempt was made to control the scandalous practice of slave-hunting: the Crown reiterated its view that only Indians taken in a 'just war' could legitimately be enslaved. A Spanish jurist produced a guide to enable conquistadors in the field to determine the conditions for declaring a just war. The Requirement was a document setting out the Spanish monarch's right to sovereignty over the Indies and outlining the elements of the Christian faith. This declaration had to be read out whenever conquistadors encountered Indian tribes, and only the explicit rejection of its terms would constitute grounds for a just war and the consequent slave-taking. The Requirement was, of course, widely abused by professional slave-hunters.

On the death of Ferdinand in 1516 a further attempt was made by the regent, Cardinal Jiménez de Cisneros, who had been Isabella's spiritual adviser, to bring Christian justice to the Caribbean. The government of Hispaniola was entrusted to a group of three Jeronymite friars, but they too failed to eradicate abuses of the *encomienda* system, and, in view of the rapid decline of the Indian population, they permitted the importation of black slaves from Africa to meet the labour requirements of the colony.

These repeated attempts to reconcile economic necessity with Christian principles would continue for the rest of the century. The process of Spanish colonization would, in fact, be accompanied by much official soul-searching – so much so that by the 1550s the Crown would see fit to air all the very complex juridical and ethical issues raised by Spain's presence in America at a great debate held in Valladolid. By then the moral difficulties under which Crown and Church laboured had been magnified by new conquests on the mainland, which completely overshadowed the problems of Hispaniola and the islands. At the same time, Spain's transatlantic objectives had become much clearer: America was to provide the main business of empire. For in 1519 Ferdinand Magellan had passed through the southern straits that now bear his name and had penetrated into the Pacific Ocean, his expedition circumnavigating the globe for the first time. The Spaniards were now in a position to appreciate the fact that there was no easy sea route to Asia, and that Columbus's original ambition would have to be subordinated to the task of exploring and conquering the huge continent which, as they finally realized, lay between the Iberian Peninsula and Japan.

THE CONQUEST OF THE MAINLAND

For over twenty years after Columbus's first crossing of the Atlantic, the Spaniards discovered little of consequence other than Hispaniola and Cuba. What lay beyond these islands was still a matter for conjecture: voyages of exploration had gradually traced the Caribbean coastline of mainland America but the extent of this Tierra Firme, as it became known, was yet to be revealed. As the native populations declined on the islands, Spaniards took to raiding Tierra Firme for slaves, and from slave-raiding thoughts turned to more ambitious expeditions of conquest and settlement to compensate for the waning attractions of the Caribbean.

In 1513 an expedition under Pedrarias Dávila set out from Spain with royal permission to conquer the isthmian region of Central America. On arrival, Dávila came upon another Spaniard, Vasco Núñez de Balboa, the leader of a group of survivors of an abortive mission to Tierra Firme in 1509, who had already created the settlement of Darién in this inhospitable tropical region. By 1513 Balboa had crossed the isthmus and raised the royal standard over the waters of the Pacific Ocean to claim them for the Catholic Monarchs of Castile. What is more, Balboa had heard rumours of a golden kingdom called Birú which appeared to live up to everything a Spanish conquistador could hope for in the Indies. Pedrarias Dávila soon quarrelled with Balboa and had him executed; he then went on to probe the isthmus for gold and slaves, but failed to turn up any loot which significantly improved upon what had been found on the islands. In 1519 he founded the city of Panama and from there he continued his explorations further afield in search of the fabulous kingdom of Birú.

In these restless times there were many other Spaniards who had dreams of conquest and plunder. Between 1517 and 1518 Diego Velázquez, the conqueror of Cuba, had sent out two expeditions to reconnoitre the coasts of the mainland around the areas we now know as the Yucatán peninsula and the Gulf of Mexico. These had brought back evidence of a rich civilization in the interior, so Velázquez set about equipping an expedition with the purpose of setting up a base as a preliminary to further exploration and eventual conquest. Following normal procedure, Velázquez applied to Spain for the requisite authorization from the Crown, but before the royal assent could reach Cuba the commander appointed to lead the expedition stole a march on Velázquez and set sail without permission from the port of Santiago. This upstart was Hernán Cortés, a 33-year-old hidalgo from Medellín in the province of Extremadura who had distinguished himself as a soldier and administrator on Hispaniola and Cuba since he arrived in the Caribbean at the age of nineteen. The expedition he led was modest: in his ships he carried some 600 men, 16 horses, 14 cannon and 13 muskets; yet with these resources he proposed to confront whatever might lie beyond the wall of mountains on the mainland that barred ready access to the riches of the Indies.

From Cuba, Cortés made the short crossing to the island of Cozumel off Yucatán, where he came across a Maya-speaking Spanish castaway called Jerónimo de Aguilar. Further up the coast in Tabasco he was given a woman called Malintzin – Doña Marina to the Spaniards – who spoke Nahuatl as well as the Maya tongue, and who was to serve Cortés faithfully thereafter as interpreter and mistress. With the services of these two speakers of indigenous languages, Cortés was in an excellent position to assess the nature of the opposition he faced and to devise an informed strategy for his campaign of conquest. Indeed, the quality of Cortés's strategic thinking was to prove crucial to his success, for very soon he came under observation by agents of the emperor Montezuma, following reports of the arrival of strange men with white faces who had been borne upon winged towers across the sea.

On Good Friday, April 1519, Cortés founded Veracruz, the 'City of the True Cross', at a place on the coast of the Gulf of Mexico which fell within the jurisdiction of the Aztec emperor. By so doing, he hoped to win some legitimacy for his enterprise, given that he had departed Cuba without royal permission and in defiance of Velázquez's authority. A few days later the first emissaries from Montezuma arrived bearing ritual gifts and advising the Spaniards to turn back. Cortés, however, would do no such thing; instead, he sent all the gold he had so far gathered back to Spain in the hope of appeasing the emperor Charles V and pre-empting any decision to disqualify him from enjoying the fruits of the conquest he was planning. Then he scuttled all his ships. There could now be no turning back: ahead lay the Aztec capital Tenochtitlán, and there was nothing for it but to march on the city and somehow take it.

As the Spaniards advanced towards the seat of Aztec power, Cortés learned of the political divisions within Montezuma's empire, and of the extent to which the Aztecs were resented by subject peoples and by other kingdoms. He determined to exploit these antagonisms while concealing from the Aztecs his true intentions. At Cempoala he was able to enlist the support of the Totonacs, and subsequently, after a ferocious battle, the Spaniards persuaded the Tlaxcalans, who were historic enemies of the Aztecs, to join them in their campaign to topple Montezuma. When they arrived in the kingdom of the Cholulans, the Spaniards made an initial show of friendship to these willing vassals of the Aztecs, but Cortés uncovered what appeared to be a plot to kill him and decided to carry out an exemplary massacre of nobles and priests assembled for a religious festival in the city. According to native sources, such equivocal tactics sowed confusion and dismay among the Aztecs, giving the invaders a psychological edge over the Indians.

Montezuma, for his part, would appear to have decided early on upon a similar strategy of perplexing the Spaniards, by combining ritual diplomacy with unspecified threats and covert attacks. However, it remains unclear what his real intentions could have been in allowing the Spaniards to advance so far into the heart of his realms. Speculation has focused on the apparent weakness of his character and on his alleged belief that Cortés was the god Quetzalcoatl come to reclaim his kingdom, but these suppositions must be treated with caution: Montezuma was not a hereditary monarch; he had been chosen by an aggressive, imperialist people and must therefore have been a man of outstanding qualities of leadership, one who would have been little disposed to give away a whole empire in the belief that a poorly equipped stranger was a visiting god. Rather, it is far more likely that Montezuma simply misread Cortés, amongst other reasons because the ends of war and politics in Middle America were quite different from those of Renaissance Europe. Where Europeans fought to kill, occupy and plunder, the Indians regarded battle as a ritual of dominance and submission, in which it was preferable to take prisoners alive in order to have them ceremoniously sacrificed to their bloodthirsty gods. Because the Spanish invasion ended in disaster for the Aztecs, Montezuma's tactical errors may well have been retrospectively embroidered by Nahuatl poets and Spanish chroniclers into a haunting fable of foreboding and doom.

There is no question, however, but that Montezuma underestimated the depths of Cortés's cunning and resolve. After two days' march from Cholula, the Spaniards arrived within sight of the Aztec capital and advanced towards it despite repeated warnings by friend and foe that Montezuma had laid a trap and was planning to destroy them. As they approached, the majesty of the setting caused great wonderment. Bernal Díaz, a soldier in Cortés's small army, later wrote:

When we saw all those cities and villages built in the water, and other great towns on dry land, and that straight and level causeway leading to Mexico, we were astounded. These great towns and *cues* [temples] and buildings rising from the water, all made of stone, seemed like an enchanted vision from the tale of Amadís. Indeed, some of our soldiers asked whether it was not all a dream.*

When they reached the main causeway into the lake-bound city, the lord of Texcoco came out to greet the Spaniards and invite them to an audience with Montezuma. Even though he realized that he might well be walking into a trap, Cortés led his men into Tenochtitlán, the most densely populated metropolis in the New World. In the event, he was well received by Montezuma, who accommodated Cortés and his force of some 400 men in a complex of large buildings within the city. For about a week the Spaniards lived in constant fear of being set upon and killed despite the overt courtesies that were being shown to them by the emperor and his household. But with his commanders becoming increasingly agitated about the real intentions of Montezuma and his ministers, Cortés finally decided to seize the emperor and hold him hostage in the Spanish quarters, on the pretext that the emperor had treacherously ordered an attack on the Spanish garrison at Veracruz in which a Spanish commander had been killed. In effect, Cortés was attempting a *coup d'état*; with such a small force, it was plainly impossible for him to make a frontal assault on Aztec power. By capturing Montezuma, the trapped Spaniards could play for time and try to manipulate imperial authority to their own advantage. The fate of Mexico would therefore hinge on the outcome of a battle of wits between two men.

However, at a critical stage in the Spanish *coup d'état*, news arrived that Pánfilo de Narváez had landed at Veracruz with a large force of Spaniards from Cuba, with orders from the governor Velázquez to punish Cortés for his initial insubordination. Cortés decided that only he could deal with this untimely threat to his whole enterprise, and so he set off with the greater part of his force to confront Narváez, leaving one of his commanders, Pedro de Alvarado, in charge of guarding Montezuma. Alvarado was faced with a difficult and volatile situation: since the imperial office was elective and not hereditary, the emperor's authority was in danger of becoming discredited the longer he remained a captive. For their coup to succeed, the Spaniards needed to follow up their seizure of Montezuma with further decisive action in order to secure their position. But the arrival of Narváez had removed Cortés at precisely the wrong moment, leaving the depleted Spanish force

* Bernal Díaz, *The Conquest of New Spain* (Penguin Books: Harmondsworth, 1963), p. 214.

in Tenochtitlán at the mercy of Montezuma's aggressive nephews. Alvarado became alarmed when he heard rumours of a plot by the Aztec nobility to attack the Spaniards; he therefore led a pre-emptive assault on an assembly of Indian priests and nobles attending a religious ceremony. The resulting massacre outraged the Aztecs, who rose in rebellion and laid siege to Alvarado in the Spanish quarters.

Meanwhile, Cortés had managed to persuade the bulk of Narváez's army to support his conquest of the Aztec empire rather than make war on fellow Spaniards. But on his return to Tenochtitlán he found the Spaniards at bay and the Aztecs in a belligerent mood. He also lost patience with the captive Montezuma, whom he suspected of having secretly contacted Narváez with an offer to help him against Cortés in return for his release. Montezuma's authority had, in any case, all but evaporated, since he had effectively been replaced as emperor by Cuitlahuac, one of his brothers. He died shortly after Cortés's return, allegedly from wounds received when he was hit by stones thrown by his own people as he went out to appeal for calm before an angry multitude besieging the Spanish quarters.

Montezuma's death left Cortés's strategy in ruins; provisions were running very low and there were many Spaniards dead or wounded. The Spanish commander therefore chose to withdraw from Tenochtitlán. On 30 June 1520 the Spaniards fought their way out of the city, sustaining very heavy casualties and losing in their retreat much of the gold and jewellery they had amassed. The *noche triste*, this 'sorrowful night' of defeat, marked the nadir of Spanish fortunes in Mexico: Cortés's *coup d'état* had failed disastrously and his remaining forces limped back to Tlaxcala to recover.

Having exhausted the ruses of psychological warfare, Cortés's only option was a full-scale assault on Tenochtitlán. For six months the Spanish leader planned his campaign at Tlaxcala; he summoned reinforcements from the Caribbean, recruited thousands of Indian soldiers, and had brigantines built in sections to be hauled over the sierras and reassembled for use on Lake Texcoco. The Spaniards also had a hidden ally they could have known nothing about; this was the smallpox virus, which had been brought over from Cuba to the mainland by one of Narváez's soldiers and was now spreading among the Indians, who had no immunities against this Old World disease. The new Aztec emperor, Cuitlahuac, was an early victim and he was succeeded by Cuauhtemoc, a ruler who could no longer entertain any illusions about Spanish intentions in Mexico and who was therefore prepared to defend his city and empire to the last man against the European invaders.

In December 1520 Cortés marched into the Valley of Mexico and spent a further three months preparing for war. Finally, in April, the Spanish offensive began: Cortés laid siege to Tenochtitlán, using his brigantines to patrol the lake so as to stop food supplies getting to the city. Still, the first direct assaults proved a failure and costly in lives, even though the Spaniards nearly succeeded in taking the central temple. It became clear that fighting in the maze of narrow streets cancelled out the advantage that horses and guns gave the heavily outnumbered Spanish forces. Cortés saw that if he was to take Tenochtitlán at all, he must raze it to the ground; and so, for some four gruelling months of bitter fighting the Spaniards and their Indian allies pulled down, building by building, the city Cortés was to describe as the most beautiful in the world. On 13 August, when barely a quarter of Tenochtitlán was left standing, the emperor Cuauhtemoc, who had led the heroic resistance of the Aztecs, was captured and forced to surrender. Anxious to reward his exhausted troops in the manner they expected, Cortés had Cuauhtemoc tortured in an attempt to discover the whereabouts of the treasure the Spaniards had lost during the *noche triste*.

After his victory Cortés devoted himself to rebuilding Tenochtitlán and unifying the former dominions of the Aztecs under Spanish rule. In this he succeeded brilliantly, becoming a revered figure for the Indian masses and acquiring the charismatic authority of a ruler in his own right. Charles V rewarded him with great estates, the right to receive tribute from thousands of Indians and the noble title of Marquis of the Valley of Oaxaca. Yet the extent of Cortés's personal power in New Spain, as he called the territories he had conquered, was to arouse the envy of rivals and the suspicion of the Crown itself, anxious as it was to curb the political ambitions of the conquistadors in these rich and distant lands. In 1527 Cortés was relieved of the governorship of New Spain and an *audiencia* (a judicial council of royal officials) took over the administration of the kingdom. Cortés saw fit to return to Spain on two occasions to defend himself against detractors at court, and, in fact, died there in 1547. After Cortés the government of New Spain degenerated under the rule of Nuño de Guzmán, president of the first *audiencia*, into a brutish exploitation of the Indians. In 1530 Guzmán was removed and a second *audiencia* restored some measure of order to the turbulent colony. Royal authority was at last firmly established when New Spain was created a viceroyalty in 1535 and placed in the charge of Antonio de Mendoza, one of the greatest administrators of the Spanish empire.

Hernán Cortés's splendid victory accelerated the tempo of Spanish expansion in America and raised the ceiling of individual ambition; it was as if the many Spanish captains in the Indies were in a race with one another to conquer a second Mexico. Cortés himself lost little time in embarking on further explorations, ranging northwards along the Pacific coast to a wild region he called California, after a mythical land of warrior women featured in *Las sergas de Esplandián* ('The Exploits of Esplandián'), a best-selling romance of chivalry of the period, and southwards to the kingdoms of the Maya and thence into Honduras.

In 1524 two of Cortés's captains led expeditions into Central America. Cristóbal de Olid went to Honduras but tried to lay claim to the territory for himself, angering Cortés by making a deal with his old enemy Velázquez, the governor of Cuba. Cortés set off to punish Olid and found himself on a terrible march through swamps and jungles. As it turned out, Olid had been murdered by the time Cortés arrived in Honduras. In fact, the expedition proved to be entirely futile – no new kingdoms of gold were found and Cortés stained his reputation by ordering the death of the captive Aztec emperor, Cuauhtemoc, on suspicion of stirring the Indian soldiers on the expedition to mutiny. Central America was to disappoint the hopes of its first conquerors. Cortés's other captain, Pedro de Alvarado, spent the next ten years in the conquest of Guatemala and El Salvador without coming across anything to rival the riches of the Aztec empire. Pushing down into Nicaragua, he encountered other Spanish expeditions sent up from the isthmus by the rapacious governor of Panama, Pedrarias Dávila.

The Conquest of Peru

Since killing Balboa, Pedrarias Dávila had found nothing to compare with the fruits of Cortés's conquest, despite his brutal scouring of the southern parts of Central America, a region once optimistically known as Castilla del Oro – Golden Castile. However, news of the Spanish success in Mexico had convinced him that he should concentrate on Nicaragua, where the prospects seemed better than in the south, which had so far yielded not much more than fanciful reports of a land of gold called Birú or Peru. Even so, two veterans of the Indies, Francisco Pizarro and Diego de Almagro, obtained permission from Dávila to search for Peru. A first attempt in 1524 proved discouraging, but a second expedition in 1527 reached the city of Tumbes (north-west Peru), and brought back items of gold and silver and other evidence of an advanced civilization. On the strength of these findings, Pizarro went to Spain in 1528 to obtain a *capitulación* or licence from the Crown entitling him to conquer and settle Peru independently of Pedrarias Dávila. When he returned to Panama, Pizarro brought with him a large number of fellow Extremadurans, including his four half-brothers. His partner Almagro had been recruiting men in Panama in preparation for the conquest, and another partner, the priest Hernando de Luque, was responsible for raising capital for the venture from wealthy investors.

Francisco Pizarro and Diego de Almagro were established figures in the colony of Panama, owning profitable estates and rights to Indian tribute, but they were also hardened conquistadors with an extraordinary appetite for adventure: when they set off to conquer Peru, they were both in their fifties, an advanced age for the time. Pizarro had first arrived in the Indies in 1502 and had taken part in several expeditions of conquest. From Hispaniola he had gone to the mainland with Diego de Ojeda in 1509; then he had crossed the isthmus under Núñez de Balboa on the expedition which discovered the Pacific Ocean in 1513; some years later he went over to Pedrarias Dávila and conspired in Balboa's arrest, after which he received land and Indians from the new governor of Panama. Unlike Hernán Cortés, Pizarro was no gentleman: a former swineherd, he was born out of wedlock and remained uneducated and quite possibly illiterate. Almagro was no better: he was a foundling from Castile who had come to the Indies as a fugitive from justice and had managed to climb his way up to a position of lordship over Indians on the isthmus – such were the opportunities for advancement in the treacherous world of Panamanian politics under Pedrarias Dávila.

Although they had been partners in other ventures, the *capitulación* of conquest that Pizarro brought back from Spain disappointed Almagro; he resented the fact that Pizarro had been granted the title of Governor and Captain-General of Peru, while he had only been promised the much less lucrative governorship of the city of Tumbes. Another potential source of friction was Pizarro's reliance upon his half-brothers and friends from Extremadura, who formed a clique within the expeditionary force. Almagro's resentment subsided, but circumstances would later cause it to flare up into open hostility.

In December 1530 Pizarro set sail from Panama with the main expeditionary force, consisting of about 180 men and 27 horses; Almagro was to follow once he had recruited more Spaniards. On reaching the coast of Ecuador, Pizarro landed his troops and set off for Tumbes, a long march that was plagued by setbacks, disease and Indian attacks. When finally they reached Tumbes, the Spaniards learned that the great empire of the Incas, which they hoped to conquer, was in complete turmoil, having been torn apart by a dynastic war of succession caused by the death of the emperor Huayna Capac from smallpox (the mysterious disease had swept down from Mexico and was now ravaging the population of the central Andes).

The succession was being disputed by Huayna Capac's son, Huascar, and his half-brother, Atahuallpa, who had raised a rebellion in the northern provinces near Ecuador. At the time of Pizarro's arrival Atahuallpa had emerged as the victor and was making his way south to the sacred city of Cuzco, the centre of the Inca world, where his troops were holding Huascar prisoner. Pizarro learned that Atahuallpa was at the time encamped not far from Cajamarca, a city which had been abandoned by most of its inhabitants during the civil war.

Freshly reinforced from Panama, Pizarro decided to seek out Atahuallpa and, as Cortés had done with Montezuma, to take the Inca hostage. As had occurred in Mexico, the Indians kept the Spaniards under surveillance as they made their way to Cajamarca, but, again for reasons which are not clear, the native emperor forbore to destroy an invasion force numbering a mere 60 horsemen and some 100 foot-soldiers. In November 1530, nearly two years after he had left Panama, Pizarro reached Cajamarca and installed himself in the city. He then sent a party of Spaniards to invite Atahuallpa to a meeting. The Spanish emissaries sought to impress the Inca with a display of horsemanship, a ploy which appeared to succeed since the horse was completely alien to the Indians. Atahuallpa agreed to come to Cajamarca the following day, but, in the event, appeared in the evening, having been informed by his spies that the Spaniards unsaddled their horses at night and were therefore more vulnerable to attack.

As the sun declined on the evening of Saturday 16 November 1532, Atahuallpa entered the empty square of Cajamarca on a magnificent litter borne by 80 nobles and escorted by 6,000 men; thousands of warriors in full battle order had been drawn up on a plain outside the city awaiting further orders. For his part, Pizarro had hidden his hundred-odd men in the vacant buildings surrounding the square, where they had been waiting for hours in terrified apprehension. Atahuallpa was perplexed by the absence of the Spaniards and took it as a sign of fear at the strength of his army. But then the priest Vicente de Valverde appeared in the square accompanied by only a native interpreter, and commenced to recite the Requirement, a formal request that the heathen submit to the authority of the Pope and the king of Spain and permit the teaching of the Christian religion. Rejection of the Requirement was considered sufficient grounds for declaring a 'just war' on behalf of the Spanish Crown. Atahuallpa, who had never before set eyes on a book, took Valverde's breviary and examined it with curiosity before tossing it to the ground. Valverde then turned away and cried out to the concealed Spaniards that the Inca had repudiated the word of God. Upon an agreed signal Pizarro's men launched their attack: cannon and guns opened fire on the crowded square, horsemen charged out of the buildings and Pizarro tried to drag Atahuallpa from his litter – which he managed to do only after the Inca's bearers had all been cut down by the Spaniards while fiercely resisting the assault on their emperor. The Spanish horsemen and soldiers chased the panic-stricken Indians out of the city, and then turned on the Inca army waiting on the plain outside Cajamarca; between 6,000 and 7,000 Indians lost their lives, and many more were wounded.

Francisco Pizarro had pulled off an astonishing *coup de main*: in one evening he had seized control of an empire, for the rule of the Inca emperor, whose authority was believed to be divine, was absolute and unquestioned. Like Montezuma before him, Atahuallpa had utterly misjudged the Spaniards; he had found it impossible to conceive that so puny a force could presume to attack an empire which he himself had only just won after a bloody civil war. Out of curiosity he had allowed them to reach Cajamarca, and he later admitted that his intention had been to capture Pizarro and kill or enslave his men. What had spared the Spaniards this fate was their ruthlessness in catching the Inca by surprise.

With Atahuallpa as hostage, events began to move in Pizarro's favour. The Inca was still unaware of the ultimate intentions of the Spaniards: he thought it scarcely possible that they would actually want to rule his empire; more likely they were bandits who could be bought off with gold and later destroyed while trying to escape. Atahuallpa therefore ordered his generals not to attack the Spaniards, and instead offered them a huge ransom in pure gold, which Pizarro eagerly accepted with a solemn promise to release Atahuallpa once it had been collected. Atahuallpa also took care to consolidate his political position: he ordered the troops occupying Cuzco to execute his brother Huascar so as to prevent his defeated rival for the throne from taking advantage of his own captivity. For eight months the Spaniards waited with Atahuallpa for the ransom to arrive from Cuzco and other places. Word had been sent back to Panama for reinforcements; yet the dangers of waiting were obvious: the Spaniards were easy prey for Atahuallpa's victorious armies. In Cuzco there were 30,000 troops under the command of Quisquis; in Jauja, halfway between Cuzco and Cajamarca, there was an army of 35,000 under Chalcuchima; and in the north there was another powerful army under Rumiñavi guarding Quito – any one of these generals might decide to move against the tiny Spanish force holding the emperor. In the circumstances the Spaniards' only recourse was guile. Hernando Pizarro, on his return through Jauja from a foray in search of gold, persuaded Chalcuchima to pay a visit to his captive emperor; at Cajamarca this powerful Inca general was taken prisoner, and yet another blow was delivered to the structure of imperial power.

A further setback for Atahuallpa was the arrival of Diego de Almagro in

April 1533 at the head of a company of 150 conquistadors, all of them eager for booty. Finding himself still a captive after all the gold he had promised had been collected and melted down, Atahuallpa must have realized that only military force could rescue him. In fact, the Spaniards were in a quandary over what they should do with the emperor now that they had received their ransom. Rumours reached Pizarro that Rumiñavi's army was advancing from Quito, so he sent out a party of horsemen under Hernando de Soto to verify this information. However, even before De Soto had returned, Almagro and his followers were pressing Pizarro to kill Atahuallpa forthwith. Pizarro finally yielded, since he feared that the Inca might escape or be the cause of a general rebellion if he were taken with them on the long march to Cuzco. And so, the defenceless Atahuallpa was garrotted. It was a cruel and illegal act, regretted by many Spaniards in Peru, who believed the emperor should have been sent into exile instead, and it was subsequently criticized by the Spanish monarch himself, who was anxious to preserve Spain's moral and religious right to rule in the New World.

With Atahuallpa out of the way, the Spaniards prepared to march on Cuzco, the centre of the empire. Their forces were still very small, but circumstances had provided them with the opportunity to divide and conquer. The war of succession had exacerbated the political and tribal divisions in the empire, and Pizarro was able to play off one side against the other. His murder of Atahuallpa was welcomed by Huascar's branch of the Inca royal family, who began to collaborate with the Spaniards in the hope of regaining the throne they had lost to the usurper from Quito. Pizarro naturally seized this chance to present himself to the tribes loyal to Huascar as the restorer of the legitimate Inca line. He had one of Huascar's brothers, Tupac Huallpa, proclaimed emperor so that when the Spaniards arrived in Cuzco they would be seen as liberators come to expel the Quitan army of occupation commanded by Atahuallpa's general Quisquis.

The march from Cajamarca to Cuzco proved difficult: for the first time since their arrival in Peru the Spaniards had to engage Indian armies in open battle. Pizarro's political strategy collapsed when the puppet emperor Tupac Huallpa fell ill and died. Suspecting the captured Quitan general Chalcuchima of having poisoned Tupac Huallpa, Pizarro had him burnt alive for treason. Eventually, another brother of Huascar, the twenty-year-old Manco, was selected as the new puppet ruler. Finally, after a series of battles along the way, the Spaniards decisively defeated Quisquis's army in a bloody engagement in the mountains above Cuzco. On 15 November Pizarro led his men into the royal city of the Incas, where the Spanish conquerors were able to indulge their lust for gold by looting its abundant treasures.

Although the heartlands of the Inca empire had now fallen to Pizarro, the conquest was by no means complete. There remained the northern provinces of Quito (modern Ecuador), where Rumiñavi's army was based and towards which Quisquis's defeated troops were retreating. To the south the territories which today are Bolivia and Chile had yet to be penetrated. More important still, there were certain issues which needed to be clarified before Spanish power could be securely established in Peru. First, Manco Inca was still under the impression that Pizarro was an adventurer and not a conqueror; he nursed the ambition to rule over a restored empire once the Spaniards could be induced to depart. Secondly, Almagro and his men were growing resentful of the dominance of the Pizarro brothers, since they had not been given a share of Atahuallpa's golden ransom and their hunger for the rewards of conquest had yet to be properly satisfied. These unresolved matters would provoke further bloody wars and delay the pacification of Peru for some three decades.

The conquest of the northern provinces of Quito was undertaken by one of Pizarro's lieutenants, Sebastián de Benalcázar. This expedition, however, had to contend with a rival invasion led by one of the conquerors of Mexico, Pedro de Alvarado, who had proceeded unannounced from Guatemala in search of more riches to plunder. The two armies of conquistadors were poised to do battle with each other, but Alvarado finally agreed to be paid off in gold by Diego de Almagro, who had come up to reinforce Benalcázar. The campaign that followed was particularly hard and bloody; yet by the end of 1534 Benalcázar and Almagro had wrested the provinces of Quito from Atahuallpa's surviving generals and the military power of the Inca empire was comprehensively destroyed.

Meanwhile, Francisco Pizarro, now styling himself Governor of Peru, had been busy consolidating the Spanish presence in the central provinces. A Spanish municipality was established in Cuzco itself, but Cuzco was too far inland and too high up in the Andes to be of use to the Spaniards as a capital. Instead, Pizarro chose to build a new capital city near the coast, close to the mouth of the River Rimac. It was officially founded on 6 January 1535 and called the 'City of the Kings' to commemorate the Epiphany, the feast-day of the Three Kings, though it soon became known as Lima, a corruption of Rimac, the river by which it stood. Pizarro had chosen well, for in the conflict that was brewing with his partner Almagro, Lima would give him the advantage of being supplied directly by sea from Panama.

The bone of contention between Pizarro and Almagro was to be the city of Cuzco. In early 1535 the partners had received an order from Charles V granting Pizarro jurisdiction over the northern territories of the Inca empire, while Almagro was to govern those of the south. Yet the royal decree did not make clear who should get the rich prize of Cuzco, which lay at the centre of the empire. The uncertainty produced tension between supporters of Pizarro and Almagro in the city itself; the quarrel was temporarily defused by Pizarro, who persuaded Almagro to lead an expedition of conquest into lands which are now part of Bolivia and Chile; these provinces were unquestionably under Almagro's jurisdiction and promised further riches. Accordingly, Almagro set off on a campaign which lasted two years and turned out to be a complete disaster. Despite inflicting great cruelty on the Indians and enduring horrible privations in crossing the freezing Andes and the torrid wastes of the Atacama desert, Almagro's expedition found little of value. On their return, empty-handed and forlorn, but possessed of a solidarity forged during that brutal episode, Almagro's 'men of Chile' would covet Cuzco more intensely than before, and they were now confirmed enemies of the Pizarro brothers.

While Almagro and his men were away, Gonzalo and Juan Pizarro were left in charge of Cuzco, but, in truth, their stewardship had proved a fiasco which was to put the entire Spanish conquest of the Inca empire in jeopardy. Few restraints had been placed on the greed of the numerous Spanish bounty-hunters who flocked to the holy city. As a result of so many abuses and outrages committed against the Indians, it became obvious to the puppet ruler, Manco Inca, that the rapacious Spaniards had no intention of quitting Peru. Already heavily censured by the Inca elders for his submissiveness, Manco decided in the autumn of 1535 to cease collaborating with the foreigners and to call for a rebellion to drive them out of his realms. By the spring of 1536 Manco had raised a formidable army and was laying siege to Cuzco, where there were only 190 Spaniards – though they were now led by the capable Hernando Pizarro, who had taken over from his irresponsible younger brothers. Another Inca army was besieging Lima, and there Francisco Pizarro, believing all would be lost, appealed for help to the Spaniards of Panama. As supplies and reinforcements came from all over the Spanish Indies, the siege of Lima was soon broken, but Cuzco remained in peril for nearly a year. The city was finally relieved when Almagro's 'men of Chile' returned from their expedition in April 1537 and forced Manco Inca to withdraw. Almagro then entered the exhausted city and arrested the Pizarro brothers before setting off for Lima to confront Francisco. The erstwhile partners failed to resolve their differences, and Peru, which had fallen to the Spaniards as a result of an internecine conflict among the Incas, was plunged into another civil war – this time between the Spanish conquerors themselves, who were unable to agree over the spoils of victory.

The war did not last long, though the bitterness of its legacy was extremely damaging to Spanish interests in Peru. After a number of skirmishes, Hernando Pizarro succeeded in reaching Cuzco, where he inflicted a heavy defeat on the Almagristas at the battle of Las Salinas on 26 April 1538. Diego de Almagro himself was taken prisoner, made to stand trial and, to the horror of many Spaniards, put to death by strangling. The Pizarros were now masters of Peru, but their hold on the conquered empire was precarious. They had to reckon, in the first instance, with a large faction of vengeful Almagristas now led by their murdered leader's half-caste son. Then there was the rebel Manco Inca, who was still at large raising Indian revolts which had to be put down with much bloodshed, thereby delaying the pacification of the country. To add to the turmoil, a stream of Spanish ruffians poured into Peru in search of Inca gold, only to turn into drifting malcontents when their hopes were disappointed. Finally, the Pizarros had to contend with the distaste felt by the Spanish monarch for the way in which Peru had been won on behalf of the Crown. Atahuallpa's death had caused enough disquiet, but now Almagro's execution provoked anger at the imperial court: when Hernando Pizarro came to Spain in 1539 bearing gifts of gold for the emperor, he was imprisoned and held in confinement for the next twenty-two years. For Francisco, the repercussions of Almagro's murder were to be fatal: on 26 June 1541 twenty Almagristas broke into his palace in Lima and hacked him to death. The assassins then proclaimed the young Diego de Almagro governor of Peru.

Once again, Spanish Peru slipped into civil war, but this time the Crown intervened directly to restore order. A royal official, Cristóbal Vaca de Castro, was sent out, and with an army of Pizarro supporters marched against the Almagristas, defeating them at the battle of Chupas on 16 September 1542. Even then the turmoil was not over: within two years the Spanish settlers in Peru rebelled against the viceroy, Blasco Núñez Vela, over his ham-fisted efforts to implement a new royal code regulating the relations between Spaniards and Indians. It was Gonzalo Pizarro who headed the rebellion, and he effectively became the ruler of Peru after Núñez Vela was killed in battle in 1546.

With the death of the viceroy, the surviving Pizarro brothers and their many followers among the Spanish settlers saw an opportunity to declare their independence from Spain by having Gonzalo proclaim himself king of Peru. In order to prevent this, in 1547 a royal army entered the country under the command of Pedro de la Gasca; he suspended the new code to placate the settlers, and then on 9 April 1548 engaged and defeated the Pizarristas at the battle of Sacsahuana outside Cuzco. With the execution of

Gonzalo for treason, the power of the Pizarros was at last broken; royal authority was vigorously asserted without direct challenge by a succession of able viceroys in the course of the 1550s and 1560s, more than twenty years after Francisco Pizarro and his band of warriors had first irrupted into the Inca empire.

There remained, however, one last major obstacle to the pacification of Peru in the survival of the Indian resistance initiated by Manco Inca, who had led major uprisings in 1536–7 and 1538–9. Deep in the virtually impenetrable jungles covering the mountains around the Vilcabamba valley midway between Cuzco and Lima, Manco had set up an independent neo-Inca state, in which the ancestral religion and laws were revived; from here he continued to launch attacks and foment revolts against the Spaniards until 1545, when he was killed by treacherous Almagrista fugitives, to whom he had given refuge from the Pizarro brothers. His successor, Titu Cusi, was careful to maintain relations, albeit fairly strained at times, with the Spaniards – even to the extent of accepting baptism in 1568 and permitting Augustinian friars to enter Vilcabamba to preach Christianity to his subjects. But this attempt to establish a *modus vivendi* was condemned to failure: the Spaniards could not accept the existence of a neo-Inca statelet in the heart of their realms. It was the viceroy, Francisco de Toledo, who perceived the need to break Inca power altogether if Spain was ever to secure its authority over the Indians of the central Andes. At the same time, the Incas abandoned their policy of accommodation when Titu Cusi died in 1571 from a strange illness. The Indians believed that he had been poisoned by a member of the small circle of Spaniards at the Inca's court, and, in retaliation, the new Inca, Tupac Amaru, repudiated Christianity and had a Spanish missionary put to death by torture. Subsequent efforts by the Spanish authorities to re-establish diplomatic relations were cut short by the murder of a Spanish emissary to Vilcabamba. These outrages gave Viceroy Toledo a pretext to order the destruction of the neo-Inca state; in 1572 the jungle enclave was wiped out by Spanish forces and the last free Inca ruler, Tupac Amaru, was executed. However, the memory of Vilcabamba lived on in the submerged folk-culture of the Indians of the central Andes, and Tupac Amaru became a powerful symbol of independence; so much so that in the 1780s an Indian chieftain took the name Tupac Amaru and led a massive uprising against the whites of Peru.

Still, resistance had not been the only Inca response to the Spanish Conquest. The rebel Manco himself began his political life as a collaborator, a policy that his half-brother, Paullu, continued to pursue after Manco had decided to rebel. Convinced that the Spanish presence was a *fait accompli*, Paullu rejected Manco's exhortations to join what he regarded as futile rebellion and decided instead to transfer his allegiance to the Spanish Crown. Considering the abrupt shifts of power that took place in the aftermath of the conquest, Paullu turned out to be immensely gifted in the arts of political survival, happily serving as puppet Inca under whichever set of Spaniards happened to be in charge of Peru, from Francisco Pizarro through Almagristas and Pizarristas to the first viceroys. Much of the Inca royal family and nobility followed Paullu's example, accepting the sovereignty of the king of Spain and receiving pensions and estates from the Crown as rewards for their loyalty.

Other Explorations and Conquests

The conquest of Peru had proved a long, bloody and treacherous affair, in which many of the leading conquistadors lost their lives. But just as the conquest of Mexico had inspired further penetration of the American continent, so did the news of Atahuallpa's ransom spur other Spanish captains to set out in search of yet more kingdoms of gold. In the 1530s and 1540s the pace of exploration and conquest quickened once again. Interest centred initially on the areas north of the Inca empire – namely, modern Ecuador, Colombia and Venezuela. One of Pizarro's captains, Sebastián de Benalcázar, followed up his conquest of the provinces of Quito in 1534 with an excursion into the territory of the Chibcha Indians, where he founded the Spanish settlements of Popayán (1536) and Cali (1537). As he approached Bogotá, the capital of the most powerful Chibcha kingdom, he encountered two other Spanish expeditions, both of which had penetrated the hinterland of Tierra Firme from different points on the Caribbean coast – one was led by Gonzalo Jiménez de Quesada, who had already conquered the Chibcha kingdom of Tunja, the other by Nikolaus Federmann, a German subject of Charles V. Drawn to the upland savannahs of Bogotá by rumours of gold and emeralds – deposits of gold had been found in 1533 by Pedro de Heredia's expedition to western Colombia – the three rival conquistadors decided to avoid an armed confrontation and abide by the arbitration of the Crown. Eventually, Benalcázar was appointed governor of this new frontier territory and the other two commanders withdrew.

But rumours persisted – rumours which Jiménez de Quesada among others evidently believed – that beyond the Andes, in the mysterious interior of the continent, there lay a land so rich in gold that its king covered himself in the precious dust once a year to bathe in a sacred lake. Though nothing ever came of it, the legend of the Man of Gold, El Dorado, whetted the appetite of Spanish adventurers and, together with other tales of fabulous riches, gave an impetus to daring feats of exploration, which, if they did little else, opened up some very difficult regions of the Americas to the Spaniards. For instance, in 1541 Gonzalo Pizarro, then governor of Quito, crossed the Andes eastwards in search of El Dorado and wandered blindly through the rain forests around the tributaries of the Amazon. Desperate for food, he sent out a forage party under Francisco de Orellana, but, though Pizarro eventually returned to Quito, Orellana lost his way and floated down the entire length of the Amazon − a distance of some 2,000 miles − and then sailed to the island of Hispaniola. The great river-system found a European name as a result of attacks on Orellana by female warriors, whom he therefore called Amazons.

In Mexico and the Caribbean Spaniards were seduced by equally fruitless chimeras of wealth and glory, which called forth equally amazing feats of heroic endeavour. The North American counterpart of El Dorado was the legend of the Seven Cities of Cíbola, whose buildings were said to be encrusted with gold and turquoise. This legend grew out of reports of another great Indian empire situated in the far north-west of Mexico; these reports had been brought back by Alvar Núñez Cabeza de Vaca, one of a handful of survivors of an ill-starred expedition of 400 men which had set out under Pánfilo de Narváez to conquer Florida in 1528 and had been ravaged by disease and Indian attacks. For eight years Cabeza de Vaca had journeyed over sea, swamp and desert from Florida to the Gulf of California, crossing the lands of many savage Indian tribes until he finally reached Mexico City in 1536. Four years later he decided to try his luck again on another epic journey of exploration, which took him through the rain forests of the Brazilian interior, and eventually to Paraguay, where he became for a while governor of Asunción.

The quest for the Seven Cities of Cíbola was undertaken in 1540, when the Spanish viceroy in Mexico sent an expedition of 300 Spaniards and several hundred Indians under Francisco Vazquez de Coronado into what is now New Mexico and Arizona. Finding nothing of interest there, Coronado pressed on eastwards, discovered the Grand Canyon and then crossed the Río Grande into Texas. Hearing tales from the Indians about Quivira, yet another kingdom of gold, he embarked on a second quest, which took him as far north as Oklahoma and Kansas. He returned to Mexico having failed to find what he was looking for, though he had extended Spanish claims over immense territories in the northern part of the Americas.

Another of the great explorers of North America was Hernando de Soto, who had distinguished himself with Pizarro in the subjugation of Peru. Hoping to make a conquest of his own, he led a large expedition of some 600 men to Florida in 1539 – the third major Spanish attempt in twenty-five years to exploit that territory. Once again, De Soto found nothing worth conquering; he wandered through Georgia, Alabama and Louisiana, discovering the Mississippi along the way, but died of a fever in 1541. All of these great tracts of land in the northern part of the continent proved barren so far as the Spaniards were concerned – they lacked obvious sources of gold, and the bellicose nomads who lived there were too recalcitrant to settle to agricultural labour. Such areas were to remain dangerous frontier zones, formally incorporated into the Spanish empire, but sparsely populated until the middle of the nineteenth century, when they were taken over by Anglo-Saxon settlers migrating from the Atlantic seaboard.

In South America, too, vast expanses were neglected. The whole area to the east of the Andean chain – the mass of the continent, in fact – was explored and settled only very slowly because, unlike in Peru, the difficulties of climate and geography were not compensated for by economic resources attractive to sixteenth-century Europeans. The huge interior of Brazil, an area of rain forests and sun-baked savannahs, technically Spanish by the Treaty of Tordesillas but later occupied by the Portuguese, remained virgin territory until late in the twentieth century. The pampas of Argentina and the chilly wastes of Patagonia, like the prairies and deserts of North America, were largely shunned by Spanish settlers until the 1870s.

Attempts to settle the fertile land around the river-systems of the Paraguay and the Paraná were unsuccessful until the late sixteenth century. In the early years the great estuary of the River Plate was of interest only inasmuch as it appeared to promise a south-western passage to Asia. Juan Díaz de Solís began explorations in 1516, but fell victim to cannibals. Magellan tried again in 1520 before turning southwards and finding the strait which now bears his name. It was the Venetian explorer Sebastian Cabot, then in the service of Spain, who called the estuary the Río de la Plata, the River of Silver, in the mistaken belief that silver was to be found on its shores. Not until 1535 was any effort made to settle the area of the River Plate; an expedition led by Pedro de Mendoza arrived from Spain and founded the city of Santa María de los Buenos Aires, which, however, was destroyed by Indians in 1541. Mendoza's men moved on up-river to Paraguay, where they founded Asunción, the first permanent Spanish colony east of the Andes and the only one for another two decades.

In fact, by the middle of the 1540s the momentum of the Spanish conquest had begun to slacken: not only were tales of El Dorado and the Seven Cities of Cíbola turning out to be mirages, but several campaigns, initiated with the usual high hopes between 1527 and 1540, had become grim, bloody struggles against Indian peoples who refused to be 'pacified' by Spain. The balance sheet of conquest was becoming distinctly unfavourable to the Spanish: costs in men and materials outweighed returns in either treasure or native labour supply.

The conquest of the Yucatán peninsula was an especially unrewarding business. It was started by Francisco de Montejo in 1527, but by the 1540s the Maya Indians were still unpacified; as late as 1542 they staged a massive insurrection, which had to be put down with appalling violence. Despite evidence of luxurious civilizations in the past, the Yucatán yielded few riches to its Spanish conquerors and it was to remain a marginal area of New Spain. The west and north-west of Mexico were conquered over a long period from 1529 to 1575. In a notoriously vicious campaign, Nuño de Guzmán carved out the kingdom of New Galicia (comprising the modern Mexican states of Michoacán, Jalisco, Nayarit and Sinaloa), but little in the way of gold was found, and in 1541 the Indians of Jalisco rose in a bloody rebellion known as the Mixtón War, which nearly succeeded in overwhelming the Spaniards. Spanish dominion was extended further into the north-west by Francisco de Ibarra, who created Nueva Vizcaya in brutal campaigns which lasted from 1562 until 1575. For the most part, these territories remained underpopulated borderlands, continually raided by Indian tribes from the barbarous north, and eventually given over to large-scale ranching.

In South America the conquest of Chile followed a pattern similar to that of the Yucatán peninsula and the Mexican north-west. In January 1540 Pedro de Valdivia set off from Cuzco with authority from Francisco Pizarro to conquer and settle the southern extremities of the Inca empire, which Diego de Almagro had abandoned after his disastrous Chilean campaign of 1535. It took Valdivia's expedition a whole year to cross the Andes and traverse the Atacama desert. On 12 February 1541 Valdivia founded the city of Santiago, but within six months it was destroyed by Araucanian Indians, one of the most bellicose peoples encountered by the Spaniards; for over two years Valdivia held out at Cerro Santa Lucia on an island in the Mapocho River until he received reinforcements from Peru. After Santiago was re-founded, the Spaniards pushed southwards, establishing the towns of Concepción in 1550, Valdivia in 1552, and other settlements; they were unable to get any further than the Bío-bío River, which became the frontier with the Araucanians, at whose hands Pedro de Valdivia himself died in 1553. The Spaniards came to have great respect for the martial qualities of the Araucanian Indians, qualities which were famously praised in the most accomplished of the Spanish verse epics of the Renaissance, *La Araucana* by Alonso de Ercilla, a veteran of the Chile campaign.

From Chile the Spaniards crossed into what is now Argentina, founding in the 1560s on the eastern foothills of the Andes the towns of Mendoza and San Juan, which became extensions of the Chilean colony. Other towns of the Argentine interior, such as Tucumán and Córdoba, were founded in the 1560s and 1570s by expeditions from Peru. These trans-Andean settlements, as well as those in central Chile, remained outposts of empire, all of them dependent on the Peruvian economy. In fact, for most of the colonial era what is now modern Argentina did not exist as a distinct entity. The city of Buenos Aires, abandoned by the Spanish in 1541, was refounded permanently in 1580 by an expedition from Paraguay. It was to languish until the late eighteenth century as a seaport of little consequence subsisting on an illicit trade in African slaves and Peruvian silver with Portuguese merchants from Brazil.

The process of conquest, on the wane since the 1540s, can be said to have reached its end by the middle of the 1570s. In the half-century that had elapsed since Cortés landed at Veracruz, Spain had explored and dominated an area many times its own size. It is remarkable that such a feat was carried out not by regular armies, but by small groups of adventurers acting against two great empires and a host of Indian tribes in harsh, dangerous and often unpredictable circumstances. What special advantages did the Spaniards possess?

In the first place, they could call upon superior military technology: they had armour, guns and ships. But in many instances the conquistadors were poorly equipped – Cortés had 13 guns and about 15 cannon when he arrived in Mexico – and difficult terrain often nullified this technical superiority. A more versatile resource was the horse, which gave the Europeans physical and tactical advantages in combat. But again Cortés had a mere 16 horses, and Pizarro 27; in neither case could cavalry have constituted a critical factor in the defeat of native rulers capable of fielding armies of thousands.

A more significant Spanish advantage lay in politics and military strategy. The Spaniards were not invincible: battles were lost and many Indian peoples proved impossible to defeat – at least for long periods of time. But the conquistadors skilfully exploited native rivalries and internal conflicts to win allies and weaken the established powers. And here Spanish success was facilitated by the viruses of the Old World, which swept into America with devastating effects – great epidemics depleted native resources and caused acute demoralization. There was no comparable traffic in the other direction –

even syphilis may not have arrived in Europe from the Indies, as was once believed.

Demographic loss aggravated the psychological imbalance that existed between Indian and Spaniard. Though the Spaniards may have been amazed by their discovery of a New World, they knew exactly what they wanted from it, namely gold and power. What is more, in seeking to acquire these goods, the conquistadors firmly believed they were furthering the designs of Heaven. By contrast, the American Indians did not know what to expect from the intruders. By the time the Aztec and Inca leaders had organized their resistance, it was too late – the structure of imperial authority had been undermined and irreparable divisions had appeared among the native peoples. As a result there could be no concerted effort to repulse the European invaders, whose power and motives were in any case still quite impenetrable to most Indian peoples. However, those few who did have the chance to grasp the nature of the European onslaught were able to survive undefeated – in some cases until well into the nineteenth century, as did the Araucanians. These Indians developed an effective resistance by adopting some of their enemy's superior methods – learning to ride horses and handle guns, for instance. Had the Aztecs or the Incas been given a similar opportunity to respond, the Spanish Conquest might not have succeeded at all. In the final analysis the conquerors enjoyed the advantage of surprise: they were self-righteously on the offensive, whereas most of the indigenous peoples of America, having been caught unawares, fell back on inadequate defences.

And yet, even though there is no mystery about the victory of the conquistadors, the Indians explained their defeat in metaphysical terms. The Spanish friar Bernardino de Sahagún collated oral information related to him by the Aztecs concerning portents and prophecies of doom said to have anticipated the arrival of the Spaniards. From Sahagún's record comes, too, the haunting tale of the psychological prostration of Montezuma before Cortés, due allegedly to his belief that the invader was the god Quetzalcoatl come to resume his divine kingship. In Peru, Spanish chroniclers reported similar myths about the god Viracocha, who had once departed across the Pacific promising to return.

This mythologizing of the Conquest, however, is not devoid of truth; it captures in poetic terms the disorientation of people whose historic seclusion was suddenly pierced by beings from an alien sphere, beings whose intrusion into a familiar and circumscribed environment must indeed have made them appear as visitors 'from behind the sky'.

2. Indians and Iberians

INDIANS

The man who was to give his name to the continent discovered by Columbus and conquered by the Spanish and Portuguese was a Florentine explorer, Amerigo Vespucci, who took part in a Spanish expedition in 1499 to the Orinoco delta and the coast of Venezuela, and in 1501–2 sailed with the Portuguese down the coast of Brazil. Vespucci referred to the continent as a *mundus novus* in a letter to his patron Pier Francesco de Medici, and it was this term that caught the imagination of Europeans. In honour of Vespucci, America was the name given by the German geographer Martin Wald-seemüller to the area corresponding to Brazil in a map of the New World published in 1507; subsequently, the entire continent came to be known by that name. The Spaniards, however, continued to refer to these lands as Las Indias, the Indies, a reflection of Columbus's geographical misconception, and, as a result, the natives were called Indians.

From the first, explorers such as Columbus himself and Vespucci, coming into contact with fairly primitive peoples in the Caribbean or on the coasts of Brazil, tended to idealize them as noble savages. Vespucci depicted what he termed a 'terrestrial paradise', where men and women went naked amid the bounty of Nature. Later experience would modify this idyllic picture, particularly after the Spaniards came across the more developed societies of Middle America and the Andes, though it would never entirely dispel the myth of American innocence first propagated after the early contacts between Europeans and the native peoples.

America, of course, was far from being a virgin continent. It was a 'new world' to Europeans because of its previous isolation from other branches of humanity, and in this regard it is appropriate to speak of its discovery by Columbus, for it was this event which brought the Western Hemisphere into world history. As for the original inhabitants, who had lived there for several millennia before the arrival of Columbus and had penetrated every corner of the continent, the conflicts and problems associated with historical change had not passed them by, even though theirs was a world circumscribed by the natural boundaries of the Americas. The arrival of the Europeans was but one more phase in their historical experience; by its very nature it was a traumatic phase, but perhaps not the worst in the history of many of these native peoples.

Moreover, many parts of this 'new world' were quite densely populated. Demographic estimates are still the subject of debate, but the size of the total population of America at the time of first contact with the Europeans has been put at over 57 million people.* This considerable population did not live in uniform societies. In the extremely varied and often difficult geography of the continent, the human inhabitants had adapted to very different ecological environments, with the result that when the Europeans arrived in America they encountered a wide range of societies, from nomadic hunter-gatherers to fully sedentary civilizations with political and social organizations quite as complex as those of the Old World.

Most of the continent was populated by semi-sedentary or nomadic tribes engaged in a limited slash-and-burn agriculture, and these the Europeans found extremely hard to subdue; they were too mobile and belligerent, usually inhabiting extremely harsh or unrewarding terrain such as rain forests or sun-baked plains, and they were unused to the kind of sustained and intensive labour that European economies required. The Spaniards therefore gravitated towards those sedentary societies which possessed both a developed agriculture and the social mechanisms for delivering tribute and labour; they by-passed the semi-sedentary and nomadic tribes except where these occupied lands with valuable resources, as in the case of the silver-bearing regions of north-central Mexico. By contrast, the Portuguese did not come across sedentary native societies in Brazil. After unsatisfactory attempts to get hunter-gatherers and semi-sedentaries to work sugar plantations, a new labour force had to be imported *en masse* from Africa in order to set up the kind of economy favoured by early modern Europeans. It was, therefore, in Middle America and in the Andean regions that interaction between Europeans and Indians was most intense and complex; these areas formed the crucible of the hybrid societies which subsequently emerged.

---

* Such calculations, based on insufficient or inadequate data, vary considerably: the population of Central Mexico, for example, has been reckoned as high as 25 million by some authorities and as low as 4.5 million by others. The problems of demographic calculation are discussed in William M. Denevan (ed.), *The Native Population of the Americas in 1492* (University of Wisconsin Press: Madison, 1976).

The Development of Civilization in Middle America and the Central Andes

The history of Middle America and the Andean regions before the European invasions may be divided into four periods, corresponding to stages of cultural development: Archaic or Pre-Ceramic (7000–2500 BC); Pre-Classic (2500 BC–AD 1); Classic (AD 1–1000); Post-Classic (1000–1500).

The Archaic or Pre-Ceramic period marks the beginnings of agriculture, with small semi-nomadic tribes using simple techniques of tilling such as the digging stick. In forested areas slash-and-burn methods were employed: trees were cleared and staple crops cultivated for short periods of up to three years, when the soil became exhausted and new sites had to be found. A rudimentary pottery is evident towards the end of this period.

In the Pre-Classic period there developed a settled agrarian economy based on kinship groups living in villages. Small tribal states ruled by priestly élites eventually appeared in the later stages of the period. Religion was still animistic, but public ceremonies were performed in temples of wood and thatch erected on mounds of earth. Pottery and weaving had evolved elaborate decorative styles. The most advanced civilization at this time was that of the Olmecs (1500–400 BC), who inhabited the area around Veracruz on the Gulf of Mexico; it possessed stone sculptures, calendrical systems and hieroglyphs. Its early flowering suggests that this is the source of subsequent civilizations in Middle America. In the Andean region, the most advanced culture was based at Chavín (900–500 BC) in central Peru.

The Classic period embraces societies which have more fully developed the ideas, techniques and social organization of their forerunners, but without introducing fundamental changes. The state has become more powerful and is ruled by a king; the priestly caste remains supreme, though with the increase of warfare the status of soldiers is rising. Cities have emerged, while ceremonial centres are built of stone, as are great public buildings and the houses of the aristocracy. Sites of Classic civilizations in Middle America are Teotihuacán (AD 1–*c.* 750), situated roughly thirty miles north of Mexico City, Monte Albán (500 BC–*c.* AD 800) in Oaxaca, and the lowland Mayan centres of the Petén jungle (AD 300–900), covering southern Yucatán and northern Guatemala. Along the Peruvian coast, the Moche civilization emerged in the north and the Nazca in the south (both *c.* 200 BC–AD 600). By AD 600 Classic civilizations were also to be found in the Andean highlands. Tiahuanaco, near Lake Titicaca, spread its power southwards into Bolivia and the north of Chile; the Huari civilization expanded north from Ayacucho to occupy the central Andean area, stretching from the borders of Ecuador south to Lake Titicaca; however, both civilizations appear to have declined by AD 1000.

A dark age separates the Classic from the Post-Classic civilizations, a period of social collapse and cultural disintegration that appears to have affected the whole of ancient America. What exactly happened is uncertain, but this period is generally believed to have been characterized by ecological disasters resulting from excessive deforestation and soil erosion, followed by invasions of barbarian tribes. Cities and ceremonial sites were abandoned and empires crumbled. This dark age appears to have started around AD 750 with the mysterious fall of Teotihuacán in central Mexico. Within a century both Monte Albán and the Mayan sites of the Petén had also been deserted. Decline set in somewhat later in Peru, but by 1000 both Tiahuanaco and the Huari empire had fallen. During this period there was a reversion to smaller and more localized tribal states, which still preserved vestiges of Classic culture.

After the dark age a new and more vigorous imperialist cycle begins, spanning the centuries between *c.* 900 and the arrival of the Spaniards in *c.* 1500. In this Post-Classic age there are no major innovations in productive technology or cultural forms; the most significant developments occur rather in the organization of the state and society – empires grow bigger as powerful ruling classes learn to exploit the resources of conquered tribes through complex political and ideological devices. Aggressive imperialist expansion gives rise to bellicose, militarized cultures, in which the constant waging of war is justified in religious terms by the need to appease the gods through the sacrifice of human victims. An aristocracy of warriors, priests and administrators has separated itself entirely from the toiling masses by a system of seigneurial privileges and material benefits. Power has become highly centralized and is embodied in an absolute ruler invested with divinely ordained authority.

In Middle America the first of the Post-Classic imperial states is that of the Toltecs, whose capital was the city of Tula or Tollan. Originally one of the barbarian Chichimec tribes that swept down from the northern plains into the fertile central highlands, the Toltecs assimilated the religion and culture of Teotihuacán, and by AD 1000 had built up for themselves an empire which is thought to have extended throughout central and southern Mexico. There is also evidence of Toltec influence on Mayan societies of northern Yucatán: at Chichén Itzá there survive traces of Toltec art, architecture and religion. However, the Toltec state, plagued by internal strife, finally disintegrated by about AD 1200. The next two centuries constituted a period of flux in which a multiplicity of city states fought one another in the absence of a unifying imperial power; this turmoil allowed successive invasions by savage tribes from the north. Although there emerged several kingdoms capable of subjugating their neighbours for a time, it was not until the rise in the early fifteenth century of one such tribe of northern barbarians, the Mexica (later to become known also as Aztecs), that another truly imperialist system was created in Middle America. Once again, the new imperialists absorbed the religion and culture of their forebears, linking the Aztec civilization created by the Mexica with the Toltec era and beyond that with the Classic civilization of Teotihuacán.

In the central Andean zone the Post-Classic age saw the emergence of several powerful kingdoms, of which the most extensive was that of Chimú, with its capital at Chan Chan in the north-western coastal region of Peru. However, the strongest imperial power was not to emerge until the fifteenth century; the new conquerors were the Incas, whose homeland was based around the town of Cuzco in the central Andean highlands. Outstripping the territorial conquests of Classic empires such as Tiahuanaco or the Huari, the Incas imposed their rule over a vast area stretching from Quito in the north to modern Santiago de Chile in the south. Theirs was the largest and most cohesive imperial state to appear in pre-Columbian America, yet by the 1530s, when Pizarro and his men entered the scene, there is reason to believe that the Inca state was overstretched and on the brink of dis-memberment after less than a century of power.

Conquest by the Spanish was undoubtedly facilitated by the fact that both the Aztecs in Middle America and the Incas in the Andes had already achieved substantial political and economic integration in their respective spheres of influence. Both imperial states, however, showed signs of internal weaknesses arising from the discontent of their many subject peoples over tribute-payment and other imperialist exactions. The highly military character of both empires also suggests an insecurity, a need to be constantly on guard against the threat of disintegration. In fact, it was not the imperial state, but the ethnic kingdom and its territorial jurisdiction which formed the most stable and enduring political entity in ancient America. Periodically, one such kingdom might succeed in subduing some of its neighbours and go on to acquire a sphere of influence much wider than its original tribal jurisdiction, but imperialist expansion was invariably followed by decline and relapse into ethnic polities.

The increasingly rapid rise and fall of Indian civilizations and, in particular, the economic collapses and mysterious power struggles which characterized the dark age may be manifestations of an underlying stagnation of productive resources in the two regions of America most suited to agriculture. Despite the grandeur of the Post-Classic empires of the Aztecs and the Incas, neither had advanced upon the technical expertise or artistic achievements of their forerunners; what they had developed instead were more effective devices for exploiting the labour and produce of the vanquished tribes. Pre-Columbian America was, after all, a restricted world, a world that lacked iron and the wheel, draught animals and ships, where mathematics was rudimentary and discursive writing had not been invented. Such a world appears to have been incapable of expanding its hard-pressed resources through technological progress. The arrival of the Europeans irrevocably transformed the Amerindian world, but, even so, not everything was destroyed; rather, the alien conquerors built upon much of what was there: change came gradually, and much of indigenous culture survived until modern times.

The Aztecs

The central highlands of Mexico had been the site of civilization in Middle America since the time of Teotihuacán. But the cities of this altiplano were exposed to invasions by nomadic Chichimec tribes from the northern prairies. One such were the Mexica, who, according to their own legends, commenced their long migration from the region of Aztlán in the north-west down into central Mexico in the latter half of the twelfth century. For another hundred years the small Mexican tribe roamed across the central plateau suffering trials and privations, settling for a while near Tula, where they absorbed Toltec influences, and eventually making a home on the hill of Chapultepec on the western shores of Lake Texcoco in the Anáhuac basin (the modern Valley of Mexico). There they merged with the people of the surrounding areas and, without ever losing the core of their tribal identity, they adopted many of the local customs and beliefs, including the tutelary deity Huitzilopochtli. Several decades later they were driven from Chapultepec and taken into captivity by the neighbouring city-state of Culhuacan. The original myth of the Mexica relates their release from this bondage and their quest for a homeland of their own: the tribal god Huitzilopochtli commanded that they should put down roots in the place where an eagle perched on a cactus bush was to be found attacking a serpent (the national emblem of the Republic of Mexico represents this sign). The portent appeared on a large island on Lake Texcoco, and the Mexica built their capital there in the middle years of the fourteenth century, calling it Tenochtitlán, the 'place of the cactus'.

On this marshy terrain the Mexica developed a technique of land reclamation for agriculture, which involved forming soil-beds called *chinampas*, using heaps of earth and sediment held together with wickerwork. *Chinampas* were extremely fertile, permitting year-round cultivation of crops, but these man-made strips of packed earth could not on their own sustain a growing population; and there were other raw materials required for urban living which were not available in the areas surrounding the lake. Lack of space and material resources forced the Mexica to look outside their lakeland territory and this led to a process of expansion that within a century had converted a once despised and errant tribe of barbarians into the makers of a brilliant imperial civilization. At its centre lay Tenochtitlán, by then a kind of Venice of America, a city of canals and causeways with a population of some 200,000 inhabitants, larger than that of any contemporary European metropolis.

The rise to power of the Mexica began in the early fifteenth century (possibly in the year 1427), when the chieftain Itzcoatl rebelled against paying tribute to the city-state of Atzcapotzalco, then the dominant force in the Valley of Mexico and the capital of the Tepanec kingdom. Victory, however, had to be won in alliance with two other neighbours, the city-state of Texcoco on the far north-eastern shore of the lagoon, and the small town of Tlacopán (later known as Tacuba). It was this Triple Alliance that constituted the Aztec Confederation. The term Aztec, though derived from Aztlán, the place of origin of the Mexica tribe, was rarely employed at the time, but it has become a useful name by which to call the alliance of the three city-states of the Anáhuac valley that went on to win an empire. Tenochtitlán was the dominant partner in the alliance: the Aztec emperor was invariably a member of the royal lineage of the Mexica, though he was chosen in consultation with the lords of Texcoco and Tlacopán.

The royal chieftain Itzcoatl led the alliance in the conquest of all the cities and towns that had formerly paid tribute to the Tepanecs. It was his successor, Montezuma I, who carried Aztec power outside the area of Tepanec dominion, pushing south into the region of Oaxaca, home of the Mixtec people. He subdued several of their urban centres, inflicting terrible massacres, and established Aztec colonies in their midst. The next people to be conquered were the Totonacs, whose territory lay in the tropical lowlands around the Gulf of Mexico. Later rulers would carve out Aztec domains on the Pacific coast around Acapulco and further down towards the present-day Guatemalan border at Soconusco. Nevertheless, there were limits to Aztec power. Close to their homeland, for instance, they were unable (or perhaps unwilling) to subjugate the Tlaxcalans, who inhabited a neighbouring valley; attempts to expand towards the north-west were thwarted by the Tarascans, who ruled an emerging 'empire' in the area of modern Michoacán.

Aztec society itself was sharply divided between nobles and commoners. The aristocracy comprised warriors, priests and important state officials, who owned private land and directly profited from the fruits of conquest. The mass of commoners, however, were agricultural labourers, who lived as their forebears had done before the Aztecs embarked on their imperial career. In common with other peoples of Middle America this large lower class was organized into *calpulli*, communal entities which appear to have derived from kinship groups but which developed into clans performing certain social and economic functions. Most *calpulli* were rural, and each inhabited a head town and a few outlying villages. The chiefs of the *calpulli* were intermediaries responsible for channelling goods and services to the Aztec ruling class, either through imperial administrators or through the ethnic lords of subject kingdoms, whom the Aztecs co-opted into the empire and permitted to benefit from the tribute system. In the cities there were *calpulli* which did not own land but were dedicated instead to a particular trade, much like medieval European guilds. These artisans and merchants formed a middle stratum that was able to profit from imperial expansion, yet did not enjoy any special social privileges. A further class of landless *calpulli* were those whose members worked as household servants or on the estates of the aristocracy in a condition similar to serfdom in Europe. There was also a large class of slaves; these were people who had been captured in battle, or simply peasants who had fallen on hard times and could survive only by selling themselves into slavery. Life for the majority of commoners was very poor. Rural labourers eked out a subsistence living tilling the soil; they also had to pay tribute and take their turn to do the *coatequitl* service, which meant performing such obligations as labouring on state lands, working on the construction of public buildings or serving in the army. Land, though held by the community, was allocated for cultivation to individual families, who were not permitted to dispose of their plots but could pass them on to the next generation. The *calpulli*'s affairs were regulated by hereditary chieftains; they formed a council of elders which included local priests and officials such as a record-keeper and a treasurer.

The basis of Aztec dominion was the levying of tribute in the form of goods and labour from tribes defeated in battle. Territory was also expropriated and distributed as private estates to deserving Aztec nobles. To maintain their hegemony, the Aztecs planted colonies in conquered lands and supported these with Aztec garrisons. Tribute-collectors would bring back an abundance of goods to Tenochtitlán, not just staples such as maize or beans but also luxuries and trappings of status that the Aztec aristocracy craved – objects of jade and gold, precious stones, quetzal feathers and jaguar skins. Indeed, Aztec conquests were motivated as much by religious and cultural factors as by purely economic needs. Defeated tribes were forced to add the Aztec deities to their pantheon and to adopt the Nahuatl tongue. A major reason for waging war was the taking of prisoners to be sacrificed upon the altars of the great pyramid at Tenochtitlán. The Aztec gods stimulated belligerence by their unceasing demand for human blood, and it is possible that the purpose of the continual 'wars of flowers' against the neighbouring Tlaxcalans was to ensure a steady supply of sacrificial victims rather than conquest as such.

The Aztec nobility were able to live in great luxury by adapting the traditional customs and institutions of Middle American tribal culture to their own advantage. The most effective of these adaptations was in the field of myth and religion, for it was religion that underpinned the unquestionable authority of the Aztec emperor or *tlatoani* ('he who speaks'), and provided the rationale for conquest and the imposition of tribute. Religion was a particularly effective tool of imperialism because much of the Aztec religion was common to other peoples of Middle America, all of whom could trace their heritage to the Toltecs, the true founders of Nahuatl civilization. Once the Aztecs had started on their imperial expansion, they took pride in styling themselves the heirs of the Toltecs, a claim which served to give their rule a sacred justification.

Nahuatl religion was exceedingly complex and is far from being fully understood. A major difficulty here is the lack of fixed identities in the well-stocked Aztec pantheon of some 126 main gods. Opposite attributes could be given to the same deity, or a quality associated with one god might be assumed intermittently by his enemy. This mutability arose from the dualism which permeated the Aztec mind. For instance, the originator of the universe was the 'dual god', Ometeotl, who had both a male and a female manifestation, 'Two Lord' and 'Two Lady'; through their union four sons were born – the white, black, red and blue 'smoking mirrors' – who were each responsible for the creation of particular worlds and all the creatures that lived in them. But then again these four creator-gods were also characterized as representing different aspects of a single all-seeing and all-powerful deity known as the Smoking Mirror, Tezcatlipoca.

In Aztec cosmogony four worlds, or 'suns', had come into being and each had been successively destroyed. The age in which they lived, the Fifth Sun, was believed to have been inaugurated with the rise of Teotihuacán, the 'city of the gods', and was the special creation of the Sun God himself, whom the

Aztecs self-servingly identified with their own tribal god Huitzilopochtli. In order for the life of this Fifth Sun to be sustained, the Sun God demanded to be nourished on human hearts – hence the need to procure victims through constant warfare. This Fifth Sun was destined to be destroyed, a certainty that burdened the Aztec psyche with a presentiment of doom.

Another important myth – also linked to that of cosmic destruction and renewal, and which the Aztecs turned to imperialistic ends – was the story of Quetzalcoatl, the Plumed Serpent, a god-made-man said to have reigned in Tula and to have brought civilization, law and good government to the Toltecs. The Plumed Serpent was driven out of Tula by his enemies, taking refuge in the East, from where he was supposed to return one day to inaugurate a golden age. Some Spanish chroniclers recorded that when Hernán Cortés appeared out of the East in 1519, the Indians believed him to be Quetzalcoatl. By claiming a kind of apostolic succession to this Toltec redeemer-king and law-giver (priests were called 'successors to Quetzalcoatl'), the Aztecs imbued their imperial rule with a religious authority, for, like all other imperialists, the Aztecs believed they were conferring the benefits of civilization upon the people they conquered.

The Mayas

The other great civilization of Middle America, and the most highly developed in the arts and sciences, was that of the Mayas, whose territory encompassed the Yucatán peninsula, southern Mexico, Guatemala, Belize and parts of Honduras and El Salvador. Its Classic manifestation occurred between AD 300 and 900 in the Petén jungle of northern Guatemala, though it is believed that Maya culture may have originated in around 1000 BC on the coast of the Gulf of Mexico in the area near Veracruz, which also saw the rise of Olmec culture. If so, Maya culture would have been remotely cognate with the Aztec.

Classic Maya society fell victim to the mysterious decline that first afflicted Teotihuacán. By the middle of the eighth century the Classic sites in the Petén had been abandoned. In about AD 900 a Post-Classic Maya culture emerged at the northern tip of the Yucatán peninsula; this was the result of a fusion with elements of central Mexican culture brought to the Yucatán by Toltec invaders, who conquered Yucatán and made their capital at Chichén Itzá, introducing new styles of architecture and art. The power of Chichén Itzá had declined by the thirteenth century and it was succeeded by a new empire, whose centre was at Mayapán, but this too had disintegrated into smaller states by the time the Spaniards arrived.

The economy of the Mayas was based on maize, which was cultivated by slash-and-burn methods that exhausted the soil within a short period. A consequence of this form of agriculture was a tendency for peasants to live in makeshift settlements of pole and thatch rather than in villages. Maya cities were therefore less concentrated than those in central Mexico, and were primarily religious and administrative centres, where the priesthood and the nobility lived, though it appears that there was more residential settlement by the common people than was previously thought, especially in the main cities of northern Yucatán like Chichén Itzá and Mayapán.

Maya kingdoms were ruled by a leader with religious as well as political authority; society was divided into a class of commoners on the one hand and an upper class of priests, warriors and administrators on the other. 'Empires' were created when a kingdom was able to exact tribute and labour from other smaller states. Like the Aztecs, the Mayas believed that a succession of worlds had been created and destroyed, and that the present era would also have an apocalyptic ending. To put off this calamity they sacrificed human beings and practised various forms of expiation. Their concern with the fate of the cosmos produced a complex calendrical system and a well-developed mathematics, which employed the concept of zero several centuries before it was discovered in India. Hieroglyphic writing appears on stelae, on temple walls and doorways, and in a number of codices; otherwise Maya culture was oral and rich in mythology, of which something has been preserved in the Popol Vuh, the sacred book of the Quiché Maya of Guatemala, which was written in the European alphabet from oral sources after the Spanish Conquest. In architecture the Mayas surpassed other Amerindian civilizations; they were highly skilled in stone sculpture and mural painting, as is evidenced by the frescoes at Bonampak in Chiapas.

The Incas

The Incas were originally one of several insignificant tribes that lived in the Cuzco valley in the central highlands of the Andes. Their myths relate how their first ruler, Manco Capac, brought the tribe to that valley either from the shores of Lake Titicaca or, in another version, from the 'windows' or caves at Paccari-Tambo, a place some eighteen miles south-east of Cuzco. Like Quetzalcoatl for the Toltecs and Aztecs, the mythical figure of Manco Capac was revered as the bringer of civilization to the world; he was also worshipped for being a direct descendant of the Sun God, a family connection which gave Inca rulers a quasi-divine status.

In the late fourteenth century the Incas subjugated the other tribes in the Cuzco valley, and their imperial career began in earnest in 1438, when the great conqueror, Yupanqui Inca Pachacuti, 'the Transformer', ascended the throne. Between 1438 and 1463 he extended Inca rule to the region of Lake Titicaca, and thence north-west. Other conquests by both Pachacuti and his son Topa Inca brought northern territories as far as Quito under Inca control. Pachacuti it was who laid the foundations of the well-organized Inca state centred upon Cuzco, a holy city which possessed the imposing Temple of the Sun representing the very source of Inca power. In 1471 Pachacuti was succeeded by Topa Inca, who, having already subdued the great Chimú kingdom in the north, ventured south into present-day Chile, establishing the limit of Inca power at the River Maule in the territory of the Araucanian Indians. From 1493 the next supreme Inca, Huayna Capac, became involved in an extended campaign against rebellious ethnic kingdoms on the northern frontier zones, especially around Quito. Upon Huayna Capac's death some time between 1525 and 1528, his natural son Atahuallpa seized these frontier territories with the help of several important generals and launched a *coup d'état* against the legitimate successor, his half-brother Huascar. It was during the ensuing civil war that Francisco Pizarro happened to arrive in the kingdoms of the Sun.

In less than a hundred years the Incas had built the most formidable empire in the Western Hemisphere. Like that of the Aztecs, their dominion was characterized essentially by the levying of tribute from scores of subject kingdoms and tribes. But the Incas went much further than the Aztecs in developing a centralized bureaucratic state at the service of a supreme ruling class. In this the physical peculiarities of the Andean region were directly influential.

The geography of the area covered by the Inca empire is marked by great contrasts of climate and terrain. Ascending from the rainless deserts of the coast to the snow-capped peaks of the Andes, one passes through sharply varying ecological environments. On the coast, agriculture is possible only in the vicinity of rivers or on land under irrigation; fishing has therefore always been important. In the highlands, altitude determines the kind of crops that can be produced; for instance, maize will grow well up to 11,000 feet, while at higher levels tubers and grains can be cultivated. In the cold, windswept *puna* – steppe-like grasslands just below the snow-line – no agriculture is possible, though pasture is available for the llamas, vicuñas and other ruminants that provide meat and wool. Each level forms an 'ecological tier' yielding a particular range of produce, and yet there is not enough fertile land on any one tier to sustain a large population.

Over the centuries Andean societies developed a way of overcoming this problem by sending out settlers to cultivate crops at different altitudes in order to complement the produce of their native territories. Andean societies were not therefore territorially integrated units, but took rather the form of 'vertical archipelagos' comprising the ancestral homeland – which provided the core of tribal identity – and outlying agrarian settlements on a number of ecological tiers specializing in various types of produce for distribution and exchange among the dispersed branches of the tribe. Geography thus produced a unique economic structure, which, in turn, determined social values and practices. Where fertile land, being scarce, needed to be so carefully husbanded, it is little wonder that its distribution had to be closely regulated by the community and that a spirit of co-operation should be so highly prized among members of the tribe. As a result, the two ruling principles of Andean tribal society were redistribution and reciprocity.

The basic social unit was the *ayllu*, an extended kinship group or clan similar to the *calpulli* in Middle America. Each *ayllu* possessed land which it allocated to heads of families, who could cultivate it for themselves but were not allowed to sell it to others. It was common practice within the *ayllu* for an individual member to work a neighbour's fields in return for similar assistance; he would also render tribute by taking turn to labour for a time in the fields of the *ayllu* headman and the tribal chieftains. Given the intrinsic difficulties of the terrain, the *ayllus* had to join together to perform certain collective tasks, such as the building of terraces to enlarge the area of cultivation and the construction of systems of irrigation. Because of the threat of crop failure in such a fickle climate, a number of public warehouses were used to store grain and other crops for distribution in case of famine. The produce from the different ecological tiers had to be distributed to all the *ayllus* in the tribe. Thus the geography of the Andes dictated a high degree of collective action and central regulation within the tribal communities.

The Incas elaborated upon these traditional practices of communal regulation and reciprocal services in order to build an imperial state. Inca imperialism did not eliminate local identities; rather, it added a higher stratum of authority to the pre-existing tribal hierarchies. Traditional ethnic chieftains, under the supervision of Inca governors and Inca garrisons, were responsible for the collection of tribute from their people for the Inca aristocracy. Tribute was received from subject peoples largely in the form of labour. The local traditions of collective work were taken over by the imperial state and transformed into the *mita*, a system of forced labour by which the colonized *ayllus* took turns to provide manpower for fixed periods. The *mita* was the expression of homage to three authorities – the supreme Inca and his dynasty, the Sun God and the state. In practice, it meant working on the private estates of the royal family and the high nobility, on lands belonging to the ecclesiastical establishment, and on state enterprises such as mining or construction projects. Other kinds of tribute required by the Inca from subject *ayllus* were specified quantities of goods or textiles to equip the army and state employees, and a supply of young able-bodied persons to act as *yanaconas* (permanent servants to the Inca aristocracy).

The Inca state also used the vertical archipelago structure of the traditional agrarian economy as a means of entrenching its imperial power. For the tribal practice of sending out settlers to cultivate different ecological zones was converted into a programme of colonial resettlement, which allowed the Incas to plant *mitimaes* (loyal peasants) in newly conquered territories and to weaken resistance from conquered peoples by relocating *ayllus* from hostile regions in more secure areas.

The cornerstone of the imperial system was the belief that the supreme Inca's authority was of divine origin since it was bequeathed by Manco Capac, the first Inca, who was held to have been the child of the Sun. The Inca nobles were able to share in the sacred roots of political legitimacy because their lineages were connected by blood-ties to the royal dynasty. Cuzco, having been founded by Manco Capac, was the centre of the world. In fact, the name 'Peru' was a Spanish misnomer; the Incas called their empire Tahuantin-suyu, 'the kingdom of the four parts', since the territory was divided into quarters, respectively to the north, south, east and west of Cuzco; each quarter was governed by an *apo*, a close relative of the supreme Inca, who served as a kind of viceroy within his realm and who was also a member of the council of state that advised the Inca on imperial affairs. As well as being the administrative and political metropolis, Cuzco was a holy city and place of pilgrimage by virtue of its supernatural foundation, which was commemorated in the Coricancha, the Golden Precinct, where the great Temple of the Sun was situated.

As a direct descendant of the Sun God, the supreme Inca was an absolute ruler possessed of an awesome majesty. Just as the sun sustained all living things in the natural world, so the Inca was responsible for the well-being of the social order. In return for his dispensation of justice, his subjects would offer up to him their tribute and labour services. The Inca state, in effect, drew upon elementary tribal relations of reciprocity and mutual aid, and converted them into a sophisticated system of ideological control based upon a relationship between the royal patron and his clients which was not essentially different from that which existed between a contemporary European monarch and his subjects. What many modern writers have seen as unique 'socialist' or 'welfare state' features of the Inca empire were in reality manifestations of royal patronage. Thus, for instance, the Inca would allow his peasants to graze their animals on common lands as a reward for their labour services on his personal estates. The bulk of the tribute-goods collected from the peasants would go towards provisioning the army, the bureaucracy and other branches of the imperial state, but a portion was kept back in storehouses and released in times of famine by the generosity of the Inca in order to relieve the hunger of the masses. Similarly, the Inca would redistribute some of the tribute to provide for the old and the sick. In the view of Nathan Wachtel,* 'the peasants felt therefore that they shared in the consumption of the produce they delivered as tribute', though it may be as well to recall that this form of reciprocity rested on the ideological exploitation of peasant labour.

Certainly, there was a sharp divide between the hard grind of a peasant's life in the villages and the leisured circumstances of the Inca nobility and of the *curacas* (tribal lords) who had been co-opted into the imperial ruling class. These aristocrats – called *orejones* or 'big ears' by the Spaniards because of their custom of distending their ear-lobes with gold discs – possessed private estates and material wealth which they would display as a sign of their power. In addition to the finery of their costume and the delicacy of their diet, they were allowed to practise polygamy and concubinage, and to chew the narcotic coca leaf. These special liberties were strictly forbidden to commoners, for, like all aristocratic societies, the Incas were obsessed with status, and perhaps more than most, the Incas succeeded in using religion to justify social privilege.

Inca religion was very much a family affair, since the supreme Inca and his kin possessed the sacred aura of divine descent. This was another example of the Incas' conversion of tribal customs into the tools of imperialism. All Andean peoples worshipped the mythical founders of their tribe, whom they identified with a particular rock, lake or tree and to whose memory they built a *huaca* (shrine). When conquered by the Incas, a tribe would add the ancestors of the Inca dynasty to its pantheon; mummified bodies of Inca rulers were duly venerated, their lands would continue to be cultivated by peasants, and places or objects associated with them acquired the fetishistic status of a *huaca*. To offset the proliferation of ancestor-gods in the expanding Inca realms, the great empire-builder, Pachacuti, instituted a belief in the

* *The Vision of the Vanquished* (Harvester Press: Brighton, 1976), p. 72.

Supreme Being, Viracocha, creator of the universe, from whom all deities were ultimately derived. The doctrine of Viracocha's pre-eminence, however, did not displace the cult of the Sun God. Inca cosmogony, like that of the Aztecs and the Mayas, divided the history of the universe into 'suns', each age having been brought to an end by a cataclysm. The Fifth Sun had been inaugurated by the Inca Manco Capac, and it was his descendants who were charged with ensuring the continuing survival of the world through sacrifice and expiation. Although not as prodigal of human life as the Aztecs, the Incas sacrificed youths, girls and children – all of whom had to be physically perfect – on occasions when the usual sacrifice of llamas was deemed insufficient to save the world from calamity.

The religious establishment was large and influential. A hierarchy of priests, headed by immediate relatives of the Inca himself, served the many temples and *huacas* found throughout the empire: at the Temple of the Sun in Cuzco some 4,000 people were engaged in the ministry of the state religion. Religious communities of 'chosen women', who were recruited as young girls from all parts of the empire, performed a variety of duties: some might be selected for sacrifice to the gods, others as concubines for the Inca and his favourites; the rest would be employed in weaving precious vicuña wool into garments for the royal family, or in preparing food and libations for the frequent ceremonies that were held by priests and nobles.

This very close identification of religion with government afforded enormous power to the Inca state. In the remains of great buildings in Cuzco, in the massive fortress of Sacsahuamán or in the ruined city of Macchu Picchu, all constructed with huge boulders cut to shape and fitted exactly into place, there survive impressive monuments to its extraordinary capacity to mobilize human labour. Perhaps extreme regimentation by the state was necessary to compensate for technical deficiencies in an otherwise sophisticated civilization: without beasts of burden or knowledge of the wheel, the Incas depended crucially on manpower. But their true success lay in the skill with which they built up a polity that transcended by far the limits of the tribe. The business of government was turned into a dynastic monopoly based on privileged knowledge, not just as regards the arcana of religion but also at a more mundane level: the absence of a system of writing restricted important information to a closed oligarchy, who had access to records kept on knotted cords known as *quipus*. Such privileged knowledge increased the possibilities of political control over the passive multitude of commoners whose culture remained entirely oral. So long as belief in the divine origin of the Inca dynasty and in its right to extensive privileges could be upheld, the edifice of state would remain in place. In 1531, however, Francisco Pizarro and his company of infidels found their way into the Inca empire, Tahuantin-suyu, causing that great pyramid of state to collapse when they violated the sacred pinnacle of its authority.

Other Indian Peoples

The Spaniards came into contact with many other Indian peoples, though none with societies as highly developed as those described above. The larger Caribbean islands like Hispaniola, Cuba and Puerto Rico, where Columbus first encountered Amerindians, were inhabited by Arawak peoples, originally from the mainland of South America. Their society was sedentary, but even though it had not reached the complexity of those in Middle America or the Andes, it exhibited similar features: the basic unit was the kinship group or clan residing in villages where several families lived together in large dwellings of pole and thatch. Each clan was ruled by a chieftain called a *cacique* who received tribute from commoners in the form of labour service; there existed a nobility, as well as a special class of servants known as *naborías*, who were functionally equivalent to the *yanaconas* of the Andes.

Sedentary peoples with a relatively complex social structure were to be found also in Central America and north-western South America, in the highlands of modern Colombia, and in Venezuela. These peoples shared many characteristics with the central Andean societies: quasi-divine dynastic chieftains, an aristocracy of priests and warriors, tribute-paying commoners, and a class of slaves. But their temples and buildings were rudimentary, made of wood and mud, while commoners lived in the kind of multi-family structures similar to those of the Arawaks. Urban settlements were generally small, although there were two larger chiefdoms at Bogotá and Tunja with sufficient power to subjugate lesser polities.

In other areas of America the Spaniards came across semi-sedentary or nomadic peoples with a less stratified social structure and fewer devices for extracting tribute in the form of labour or goods. These tribes were therefore of little economic value to the conquistadors, and they were largely ignored or, if hostile, contained by military garrisons, as in the case of the very bellicose Araucanians of southern Chile or the Chichimecs of northern Mexico and what is now the south-western USA. These, however, were precisely the kind of tribes that the Portuguese encountered in Brazil.

The Indians of Brazil

In Brazil, Indian peoples belonged to four main language families – Tupi, Gê, Arawak and Carib. The largest group, the Tupi, may have originated in the areas around the Paraguay and Paraná rivers, but had been moving northwards along the Atlantic coast and were to be found in the southern Amazon basin. The Amazon and its tributaries also provided a habitat for the Arawak and the Caribs. The Arawaks may have originated in this area or may have migrated there from the north-west; they also inhabited the Caribbean islands and parts of Central America. At the time of the arrival of the Iberians, the semi-sedentary Arawaks were under pressure from invasions by the Caribs, who were originally from the Guiana highlands and had moved into the northern Amazon, having already displaced Arawak tribes from the smaller islands of the Antilles. Gê-speaking peoples were to be found in the vast savannahs of the hinterland.

The economy of these peoples combined fishing and hunting with slash-and-burn agriculture on easily exhaustible soil cleared from the forest. Permanent settlement was very difficult in the harsh environment of jungle or torrid plains: even tribes which relied principally on agriculture lived in temporary villages consisting of huts made of grasses and wood. Their societies were generally small and mobile, based on the kinship group living in multi-family units under the leadership of elders and shamans. Tribes engaged in continual warfare against each other, prowess in battle being a source of status. Combat, with bows and clubs, was extremely savage; its object was not land or booty, but captives, who would be killed and eaten in cannibalistic rites. Since there was no durable settlement, the arts and crafts of these Indian peoples were impermanent or movable – they painted their bodies and decorated gourds, ceramics and basketware.

The Portuguese found it difficult to subdue and organize native peoples whose sense of territory was so fluid and who were so fragmented into peripatetic tribes. Interaction between Indians and Europeans was therefore sporadic and mostly hostile, the usual outcome being the enslavement of Indians captured by Portuguese on raids into the bush. A more benign alternative was the enforced settlement of Indians in mission stations, where they would be civilized according to European norms.

IBERIANS

Spain and Portugal were no strangers to conquest and colonization when they reached the New World. Portugal had already occupied the islands of the Azores and Madeira, and was establishing trading colonies on the coasts of West Africa, while Castile had taken the Moorish kingdom of Granada and was on its way to completing the conquest of the Canary archipelago. More important still was the fact that these neighbouring kingdoms owed their independent existence to a struggle over centuries to expel the Muslims from the Iberian Peninsula. This experience of reconquest had deeply marked both Iberian peoples, reinforcing the heritage of language, religion, customs and mentality bequeathed to them by their common origins in Roman Hispania and the Visigothic kingdom that preceded the Muslim invasion of 711.

The Muslims overran virtually the whole of the Iberian Peninsula and were to remain there for some eight centuries, in the course of which they created a powerful Islamic civilization, unified initially, but then fragmented into smaller, warring kingdoms. From a Christian perspective, however, the period was characterized by a piecemeal recovery of territory lost to the infidel by the Visigoths. The Reconquest had its very modest origins in the mountains of Asturias in the extreme north, where surviving Visigoths engaged in periodic skirmishes with Muslim forces. The Muslim defeat at Covadonga in 718 is conventionally regarded as the start of the gradual Christian push southwards. By the middle of the ninth century the Christians were able to occupy the semi-arid lands between the northern mountain ranges and the Duero River, and in the north-east, around Barcelona, the Muslims had been driven back by the Franks. Still, there was only an intermittent sense of religious crusade in this erratic Christian advance, and the small kingdoms that emerged would as soon become embroiled in dynastic and territorial squabbles with one another as join together against the Muslim enemy.

The next major Christian advance was facilitated by the disintegration in the eleventh century of the great caliphate of Al-Andalus into various quarrelling *taifa* kingdoms. The Christians were able to reach the River Tagus with the capture of Toledo in 1085, and then the River Ebro, after the fall of Zaragoza to the Aragonese in 1118. But these gains were not secured until the thirteenth century, for there were frequent Muslim counter-attacks; so, for roughly two centuries, the heartlands of the Peninsula resembled a mosaic of frontier states, Christian as well as Muslim, each trying to exploit the weakness of its neighbours in a scramble for land, slaves and booty.

Even so, the Christians pressed steadily southwards, occupying and settling conquered territory. In these early stages of territorial expansion the frontier wars were conducted by bands of warriors led by an outstanding *caudillo*. These were largely exercises in free enterprise – predatory raids on Muslim kingdoms in search of gold and tribute. However, the Christian kings would encourage such freebooters by promising to grant them jurisdiction over the lands or towns they might take and defend from the Muslims. Ambitious men could thus more readily find wealth and status in military adventure than from working poor and unrewarding land, and so, fluid and un-stable though it was, the frontier society of the Iberian states was funda-mentally aristocratic, given the opportunities that existed for a commoner to become a nobleman, possessing land and rights over vassals. Similar in-centives would in due course act as spurs to adventure for the conquistadors of America.

By the early thirteenth century there were four well-defined and fairly powerful Christian kingdoms – Portugal, Navarre, Aragon and Castile. An army drawn from the last three won a magnificent victory against the Muslims at Las Navas de Tolosa in 1212, after which the balance of power in the Peninsula shifted decisively in favour of the Christians. At about this time too the destinies of the major Christian kingdoms began to diverge. Portugal, which had evolved into an independent state by 1143 from having been a county of Castile with its head town at Oporto (literally, 'the port'), completed the conquest of the Muslim kingdom of Algarve in 1249, achieving her full territorial integrity much earlier than Castile. Isolated by difficult terrain and facing out towards the Atlantic, Portugal would turn to seafaring and maritime commerce. Aragon, which included the county of Barcelona (Catalonia), having conquered the Muslim kingdom of Valencia and ceded to Castile the right to the kingdom of Murcia in 1179, looked northwards beyond the Pyrenees and towards the Mediterranean, where it was eventually to build a maritime empire comprising the Balearic Islands, Sardinia, Sicily, Naples and several colonies in the Levant. It fell to Castile to pursue the crusade against Islam beyond the thirteenth century. Under Ferdinand III, the Castilians captured the key cities of Córdoba (1236) and Seville (1248) and conquered the greater part of Andalusia, but the kingdom of Granada in the south-east survived behind its mountain defences for another 200 years in a state of precarious independence bought by the payment of tribute to the monarchs of Castile, though it was constantly harassed by the frontier raids of Castilian knights. Castile was thus preoccupied with seizing territory from the infidel long after Aragon and Portugal had concluded their reconquests.

The problems of settling and defending great tracts of underpopulated territory, together with the survival of a fierce spirit of religious crusade, were to stamp upon Castilian society and character qualities which would be carried over in due course to the New World. A major problem was the shortage of manpower. The Crown was obliged to devise ways of attracting settlers from the north into the empty lands further south. This it did by granting land and *fueros* (political liberties) to settlers in the towns founded on new territory. Castilian colonization, in fact, was urban-centred, basing itself on *municipios* (municipalities) established according to norms laid down by the Crown. Settler towns were given jurisdiction over an extensive rural area, in which land was allotted to the *vecinos* (citizens) of the town according to wealth or status by a procedure known as *repartimiento* (distribution). Since many of these towns were situated close to the frontier, they retained a military character, being fortified nuclei in which the *vecinos* could find refuge against the hazards of war. This pattern of settlement would serve in time to populate the Indies.

Yet the further south Castile reached, the fewer the settlers who could be found to populate the land, and vast estates (*latifundia*) were delivered to great nobles, or to institutions such as the Church, the monasteries and the military orders. Such concentrations of land stimulated a tendency towards a seigneurial regime in the countryside, particularly in New Castile, Extremadura and Andalusia. The great nobles and military orders found it more convenient to obtain income from tribute and tithes than from engaging directly in agriculture. In any case, the Muslim peasants, where these remained, were obliged to pay tribute, while Christian smallholders, anxious for military protection in the turbulent frontier zones, 'commended' themselves to a lord in exchange for payments or labour services, thereby curtailing their political liberties and instituting a regime which, in effect, came to resemble feudalism.

The dynamics of conquest thus produced a peculiar system of commendation to a lord through tribute-payment, which was to evolve in America into the institution of *encomienda*, the major device for extracting labour and goods from the Indian communities. The Reconquest also gave Castilians the experience of settling defensively among a subject people of a different race and culture. In the conquered Muslim cities, the Christians superimposed their civic and religious institutions on the Islamic base, turning the chief mosques into churches, and setting up their *municipios* among alien communities; in the countryside, Christians preferred to settle in new towns, while the Muslims continued to live in their scattered rural villages, at least in those regions from which they were not expelled.

A sphere of economic activity which greatly attracted the Castilian nobility was stock-raising. In New Castile, Extremadura and especially Andalusia, large herds of cattle were allowed to roam on the open range tended by horsemen called *vaqueros*. It was a style of cattle-rearing found nowhere else in Europe, though it was already current in Spain by the twelfth century. This peculiar ranching economy, with its culture of branding, corrals, lassoing and round-ups, would have an enormous impact throughout Iberian America from the grasslands of the River Plate to the empty spaces of northern Mexico and Texas; in the USA it would eventually be adopted by nineteenth-century Anglo-Saxon migrants and come to shape the cowboy ethos of the West. More important, though, to the economy of medieval Castile was sheep-rearing. A considerable pastoral economy developed, involving huge flocks moving seasonally over great distances for grazing. The mobility of ranching and shepherding well suited the fluctuations of frontier warfare, but it accentuated the tendency away from arable farming and a settled society of small rural proprietors.

In the thirteenth and fourteenth centuries, Castile became a great producer of wool for the European market, a trade that brought prosperity to the northern ports of the Cantabrian coast and the towns of Old Castile. These urban communities jealously guarded their *fueros* and used their representation in the Cortes (parliament) to exercise some influence in the state by virtue of their right to vote revenues to the Crown. But townspeople and merchants never acquired the power to challenge the seigneurial regime of the countryside; at best they could ally themselves with the king to defend their interests against the nobility. Castile, in fact, was to remain a fiercely aristocratic society of conquest, where ownership of a great estate and the practice of lordship over men constituted the social ideal, not just for the large gentry of caballeros and hidalgos, but also for many commoners, who could still aspire to advancement by force of arms in the wars against Muslim Granada, in the conquest of the Canaries or later yet in the unfolding epic of the Indies. And so liberation from rural toil by the wielding of a sword would continue to be a possibility for an ambitious Castilian until virtually the end of the sixteenth century.

The fall of Andalusia opened the Atlantic to Castile along its south-western coastline. At first, sea power was required to patrol the Straits of Gibraltar in order to prevent the Muslims of North Africa from coming to the aid of the Moors of Granada. But trade was important too, for the straits provided a route by which the commerce of the Mediterranean could reach the north

Atlantic ports of Britanny, England and Flanders. Towards the end of the fourteenth century the ports along Castile's Atlantic coast had come to form, with those of southern Portugal, an arc of maritime enterprise, from which a common zest for exploration would carry Portuguese, Castilians and the many Genoese who had settled in those parts ever further into the ocean. As new islands were discovered overseas, the first stirrings of colonial rivalry between the two Iberian kingdoms of Castile and Portugal occurred in the endeavour to conquer and settle them.

The progress of the Reconquest had been plagued by internal divisions among the Christians. States had been formed by a fissiparous tendency to split off from larger polities: Castile herself originated as a county of the kingdom of León; Portugal was born when a dowry of lands south of the River Minho for the king of Castile's daughter was used by her son, Afonso Henriques, as a springboard for his own regal ambitions. The Christian kingdoms of Iberia were the result, therefore, of a process of fission, recomposition and advance at the expense of the Muslim, and these tendencies were not entirely checked even after the major states had crystallized in the thirteenth century, for dynastic politics and the seigneurial regime of the frontier were constantly throwing up men eager to carve out independent domains for themselves. In the fourteenth and fifteenth centuries Castile endured a series of bloody civil wars and baronial revolts which came close to tearing it apart.

In reaction to the constant threat of disintegration clerics and servants of the monarchy elaborated a rudimentary theory of absolutism, which exalted the king's God-given authority above the rights of the nobles and other estates of the realm. This concept of sovereignty had already appeared in the *Siete Partidas*, the great legal code of Castile produced in the 1260s under Alfonso X the Wise, and adopted as the law of the land in 1348:

> Kings are vicars of God, each one in his own kingdom, placed over the people in order to maintain them in justice and truth in temporal matters.*

John II put it more vigorously in 1439 in reply to criticism of royal power by his nobles:

> So great is the king's right of power that all the laws and all the rights are beneath him, and he holds this position not from men but from God, whose place he holds in temporal matters.†

* Quoted in A. Mackay, *Spain in the Middle Ages*, (Macmillan: London, 1977), p. 133.
† Ibid., p. 137.

Yet such a view of kingship was at variance with a more feudalistic concept of a contract between the king and his vassals, which gave the latter a 'right of resistance' against any king who might act as a tyrant by arbitrarily infringing the traditional rights and liberties of his subjects. On this view, which had been theoretically justified by Aquinas and the medieval schol-astics, political authority derived ultimately from a 'pact of submission', by which the subjects of a monarch undertook to obey the royal will so long as the sovereign upheld 'justice and truth' and fostered the 'common weal'. According to Mario Góngora:

> In the Middle Ages and the sixteenth century, there was not only a right to resist 'tyranny' or specific unjust commands, but also commands which ran contrary to the common weal or the welfare of the subjects. Law, justice and the common weal are so closely interconnected in the medieval outlook that the right of resistance resided ubiquitously in all authorities and communities.*

The tension between the absolutist and contractual views of royal authority was never fully resolved in Spain, and it was to surface in times of great crisis. In America, as we shall see, this tension was of the utmost importance, subsisting throughout the colonial period: it would affect the creation of the imperial state in the sixteenth century, when the Crown sought to impose its authority on conquistadors and settlers; two centuries later, the reforms of the Spanish Bourbons would revive it in the Indies; in the 1800s, it would flare up once more and contribute to the acute crisis of royal authority which precipitated the wars of independence.

The middle years of the fifteenth century saw royal authority in Castile sink to a point where nobles and prelates all but rejected it in the course of a bitter dispute over the succession, which eventually came to yet another civil war. The victor in 1479 against forces supported by the king of Portugal, who had claimed the throne for his Castilian bride, was Isabella, half-sister to the deceased Henry IV, and wife to Ferdinand of Aragon, who in the same year acceded to the throne of that kingdom. The marriage of Ferdinand and Isabella brought the two most powerful Iberian kingdoms together in a dual monarchy, which produced an unprecedented strengthening of royal authority and the creation of a state from which baronial factionalism was successfully banished.

The union of Castile with Aragon, however, was in many ways purely nominal, for it was a dynastic alliance which did not much alter the con-stitutional, administrative or fiscal structures of either kingdom. Castile was

---

* Mario Góngora, *Studies in the Colonial History of Spanish America* (Cambridge University Press: Cambridge, 1975), p. 74.

the more unitary state, with laws that applied throughout its several realms (with the partial exception of the Basque provinces) and a parliament that offered representation to them all. The Crown of Aragon, in contrast, was a federated monarchy comprising three autonomous kingdoms – Aragon, Valencia and Catalonia, each with a parliament of its own, as well as overseas dominions with separate administrations in the Balearic Islands, Sardinia, Naples and Sicily. This Aragonese federation had evolved an institution which, in suitably modified form, was to play a vital role in Castile's administration of its American empire: each of the realms of the Crown of Aragon was ruled by a viceroy to whom the monarch delegated authority in his absence.

The marriage settlement of Ferdinand and Isabella, moreover, formally endorsed the separation of Aragon and Castile, a separation which would lead, for instance, to Aragon's exclusion from trade with the Indies. But Aragon, weakened by baronial strife and by commercial decline in the face of Genoa's maritime supremacy, would experience a powerful Castilianization during the reign of Ferdinand, for Castile was to become the dominant partner in the alliance, and the institutional pluralism of the Aragonese federation would be imbued with the spirit of absolutism emanating from its more assertive neighbour.

Castile's union with Aragon generated the great theme that would dominate Spanish statecraft and imperialism for many centuries – the need to maintain a sense of cultural and political unity given the wide diversity of races, cultures and peoples that were subject to the authority of the monarch. The enduring achievement of Ferdinand and Isabella, the Catholic Monarchs as they were to be titled, was to have invented a political system which proved to have an extraordinary capacity to reconcile these two qualities. For without destroying the traditional rights and liberties of its constituent parts, the Catholic monarchy was able to achieve a unity of purpose which triumphed over the centrifugal tendencies that had repeatedly afflicted the kingdoms of Iberia.

How was this sense of unity achieved? Ferdinand and Isabella did not innovate in government so much as gather existing instruments of power in their own hands and employ these to better effect than their predecessors. In the first place, the Catholic Monarchs were able to assert the authority of the Crown against the great nobles and the military orders. The main instrument here was patronage: royal favour in the form of tithes, offices, grants of land and courtly honours enabled the sovereigns to play upon the social ambitions of the nobles and so control them. The power of the monarchy was further strengthened through the setting-up or revitalization of central institutions.

A mounted police force, the Santa Hermandad, secured order in large areas of the country. The councils of state, once the preserve of the aristocracy, were now staffed by *letrados*, educated men of the lesser nobility who owed their position exclusively to royal patronage. The office of *corregidor*, a royal official who sat on municipal councils, was instituted in all the major towns, greatly extending the range of royal intervention in the regions. Finally, the Cortes of Castile were summoned infrequently, and when they did meet, the monarchs' sway over provincial affairs through the *corregidores* ensured the general compliance of the towns' representatives in voting moneys to the Crown.

Yet the overhaul of the apparatus of state does not of itself account for the success of the Catholic Monarchs. This centralization would have been of little enduring value had it not been accompanied by a state ideology of uncommon power. Its basis was the identification of the monarchy with the ends of the Catholic religion; and acting as its catalyst was a crusade launched in 1482 against the infidels of Granada. Religion, then, was to become the vital binding-force in strife-torn Castile, and it was invigorated by reforms designed to end the moral laxity and abuse of privilege which characterized the late medieval Church.

Much of the drive behind these reforms came from the intensely pious Queen Isabella herself, and here she was advised by able clerics like her confessor Hernando de Talavera and the Franciscan Jiménez de Cisneros. Indeed, the reform of the Franciscans and other mendicant orders released enormous reserves of energy, whose effects would be most notable in the missionary effort to convert the American Indians in the coming century. It was an age too of Renaissance humanism and the renovation of learning, promoted largely by the Church: important Italian scholars found patronage at the court; the University of Alcalá was founded by Cisneros, under whose direction the great Polyglot Bible was produced; the recovery of classical texts was accompanied by a new interest in language – Antonio de Nebrija's grammar of Castilian, the first of a modern European language, came out in 1492. Language, as the queen was advised, 'is the perfect instrument of empire' and the cultural prestige of Castilian endured in Europe for some two centuries. This flourishing humanist culture of Castile provided an important stimulus to the study of the languages and societies of the Amerindian peoples by Spanish missionaries in the New World.

The Church itself became the institution that best advanced the centralizing aims of Ferdinand and Isabella. The Catholic Monarchs were successful in winning control of much of the Church's finances and sources of patronage. In due course, they would be granted a series of rights by the papacy to appoint to all major ecclesiastical offices in the conquered kingdom of Granada and in America. This *Patronato Real* gave the imperial state in the Indies an unrivalled control over the Church hierarchy. Early in the reign, the Holy Office, or Inquisition, was founded in Castile and revitalized in Aragon as an institution designed to guard against deviations from religious orthodoxy by a Christian population among whom lived large numbers of Jews and Muslims.

The long-standing anti-semitism of the common people assured the Inquisition of a wide base of popular support, and its tribunals came to be preoccupied above all with monitoring the *conversos* (Jews converted to Christianity), whose allegiance to their new faith was suspect. The decree of 1492 forcing the Jews to convert or be expelled from Spain was motivated by the Monarchs' overriding desire to create an ideologically homogeneous population in lands which had suffered from persistent political turmoil; they feared that the presence of substantial Jewish and Muslim communities would be a perennial temptation for *conversos* to revert to their old religion in secret. However, the Inquisition did not become particularly important in the Indies, though the widespread popular concern with *limpieza de sangre*, the notion that family honour depended on the absence of any taint of Jewish or Muslim blood, passed to America in the form of a prejudice against marrying persons of colour (a prejudice which in no way inhibited having sexual relations with them).

The alliance of Church and state in the Catholic monarchy appeared to be blessed with divine approval in 1492 – the providential year in which Granada fell to the Christians, so bringing to an end 800 years of the reconquest of the Iberian Peninsula, and the year too when Columbus discovered lands across the ocean which promised Castile untold riches from trade with the Orient. Yet the combination of throne and altar was far more than a coincidence of interests; nor did it imply the acquiescence of the Church in its control by the Crown; the relationship was so important because it was vital for the constitution of an ideology of Spanish royal absolutism, the basis for the creation of a proto-modern nation state in Spain. (In this respect, the campaigns to convert both Jews and Muslims to Catholicism, and the expulsion in 1492 of Jews who refused to convert – policies which are so offensive to the modern liberal conscience – may be seen as prerequisites for the construction of the ideology of a Spanish nation state.)

The potency of this invigorated ideology of royal absolutism lay in the fact that the Church legitimized the power of the Crown by resolving the historic tension between the absolutist and contractual views of royal authority – the sovereign's will would not be deemed 'tyrannical' so long as it was seen to further the ends of religion and observe Catholic orthodoxy. Such a formula not only liberated the Crown from the dangers of the contractual view of sovereignty, which might justify direct challenges to its authority by rebellious subjects, but also spared it charges of arbitrariness, since the will of the monarch was implicitly constrained by reasons of religion as interpreted by the Church. From this association with the Church, then, the Catholic monarchy would in time achieve a formidable monopoly of legitimacy within its many and varied realms across the world. In future, the statecraft of successive kings of Spain would be wedded to the cause of the Catholic religion. For in the defence of orthodoxy, Spanish monarchs sought to preserve also the legitimacy of the central power in what was to become a far-flung empire embracing Europe and America. To subsequent political thinkers in Spain, the Church's legitimation of royal power seemed to be the cornerstone of the state, the fundamental guarantee of its political unity and stability.

Indeed, so central was the relationship of throne and altar to the legitimation of the Spanish nation state that a new, theoretical danger arose towards the middle of the sixteenth century: as royal authority was extended to the New World, its relationship with the Church came under particular intellectual scrutiny, and was given a kind of contractual gloss by neo-scholastic theologians, of whom the most eminent was Francisco de Vitoria. Prompted by the conquest of the Aztecs and the Incas, Vitoria and his disciples re-examined the issue of political legitimacy and further refined the theory of Hispanic absolutism: they argued that, in addition to the laws of God, the king's will should be restrained by the Natural Law common to all humanity. This theory was intended to protect the pagan Indians of America against the abuse of power by conquistadors or royal officials, so conserving the claim to legitimacy of royal authority in the New World. But, in effect, it came close to expressing the relationship between monarch and Church in terms of a contract, for Natural Law was a concept derived from scholasticism and its interpreters were inevitably theologians, who, as men of the Church, were the effective supervisors of the legitimacy of the state, and responsible as such for examining the religious and ethical propriety of the Crown's policies.

For this reason the thinking of the School of Salamanca on Natural Law posed an implicit challenge to the absolute power of the Crown; and it was a considerable challenge because it derived from the theoretical construction of Spanish absolutism itself. Indeed, the theologians of Salamanca would argue that Spain had no intrinsic right in Natural Law to conquer the Indian kingdoms or to dispossess the inhabitants of their property: it had a right only to preach Christianity to the people of the New World. On this basis, the Dominican friar Bartolomé de las Casas would go so far as to advocate the cessation of conquest and the withdrawal of Spain from the Indies. It was an extraordinary position for intellectual and religious servants of an imperial monarchy to adopt; and indeed, in the 1550s, rumours that the emperor Charles V was preparing to 'abandon the Indies' spread alarm and anger among the Spanish settlers in America. These, however, were the counsels of theological purists among the clergy, but they reveal the limits that could be placed on Spanish absolutism through the Catholic monarchy's identification with the interests of the Church. And what is more, such counsels did have a practical effect on imperial policy: Las Casas's defence of the Indians at court influenced very substantially, as we shall see, the legal and institutional framework that was created by the Crown to regulate the relations between Spaniards and Indians in the New World.

Despite these inner theoretical tensions, it was the common ground of all Spanish political thinkers that Church and state were interdependent entities within the structure of the Catholic monarchy, forming a kind of mutual compact that guaranteed a monopoly of political legitimacy. The Jesuit Juan de Mariana observed that they should be 'bound together with good will and the fulfilment of mutual obligations towards each other. Thus united in spirit, the churchmen will look after the security of the state and the princes . . . will apply themselves with greater effort to the protection of the established religion.'*

It followed from these ideological arrangements that for the Catholic monarchy to preserve its authority and legitimacy, it should endeavour at all costs to maintain a single religion among its subjects. The toleration of other religions represented a mortal danger to the integrity of the state, for political unity, which had eluded the Iberian kingdoms for centuries, was predicated on the extraordinary consensus between monarch, Church and people which had been forged by Ferdinand and Isabella and which would be confirmed and defended by their successors.

And so, having defeated the Muslims and expelled the Jews, Spain reacted to the spread of Protestantism in Europe with alarm, as much for political as purely religious reasons. After all, the contamination of heresy anywhere within Spain's extensive empire might lead to discord between throne and altar; in which case, the fabric of the Catholic monarchy would unravel,

* Quoted in J. A. Fernández-Santamaría, *Reason of State and Statecraft in Spanish Political Thought, 1595–1640* (University Press of America: Lanham, New York, London, 1983), p. 64.

doubt would be cast on the legitimacy of royal power, and the whole empire, including the Peninsula itself, would surely be plunged into anarchy. As terrible religious strife began to throw Germany, France and England into turmoil during the sixteenth century, the stubborn defence of one religion by the Spanish Crown appeared to be amply vindicated: compared to the kingdoms and principalities of Europe, the Spanish empire was a marvel of peace, stability and good order. As late as 1615, after Spain had been struggling for decades to preserve the religious and territorial integrity of its realms, the royal chaplain, Juan de Santa María, reiterated the cardinal principle of Spanish politics: 'Let the Christian king understand that if he keeps firm in his faith, and sees to it that his subjects do the same, all will obey and fear him; otherwise everything will collapse.'*

After the deaths of Isabella and Ferdinand, the monarchs of Spain would have to pay an ever higher price to prevent everything from collapsing. A major cause of their difficulties lay in the enormous accretion of territories and peoples that followed the accession of Charles V in 1516. The new king, born in Flanders but belonging to the Habsburg dynasty of Austria, brought with him a fabulous inheritance in central and northern Europe; when elected Holy Roman Emperor in 1519, he was pledged to the defence of Christendom across the continent and the Mediterranean. Spain was therefore dragged into the arena of international politics – against the Ottoman empire, France, the Protestant princes of Germany, the Italian states, and even against the papacy itself. In view of the breadth of the empire, what inspired many supporters of Charles, if not the emperor himself, was the essentially medieval notion of the universal monarchy, famously encapsulated by the poet Hernando de Acuña in the lines:

> One fold, one shepherd only on the earth . . .
> One monarch, one empire, and one sword.

This was the vision of Ferdinand and Isabella writ large, too large, probably, to have won their approval.

In fact, Charles nearly undid the work of his grandparents. As a foreigner (he grew up in Flanders speaking French), he was initially insensitive to the internal equilibrium of Castilian politics, provoking a rebellion of the townsmen in 1520. These *comuneros* of Castile protested against the levying of taxes by a foreign and largely absentee king to pay for remote wars that were not obviously in the interests of Spain. The revolt was crushed in 1521, but it represented the revival in practice by the free commoners of Castile

---

*J. A. Fernández-Santamaría, *Reason of State and Statecraft in Spanish Political Thought, 1595–1640*, pp. 81–2.

of the contractual view of monarchy, according to which the people could claim a 'right of resistance' against a king who abused his powers. It was a right the conquistadors of America would also invoke some twenty years later, when Charles tried to impose upon them laws perceived to be contrary to their vital interests. The defeat of the Castilian *comuneros* managed to preserve the integrity of royal absolutism; yet it was, perhaps, the increasingly religious, crusading character of Charles V's foreign policy that saved the Crown from any further erosion of its legitimacy. The monopoly of legitimacy enjoyed by the Catholic monarchy was indeed a formidable asset, but in the very last resort it had to rest on a broad balance of interests, on a fundamental political consensus, between the Crown, the Church and the people.

As the gold and silver of America began to arrive in Seville, Spain, and Spanish arms, assumed a growing importance for the emperor Charles V in the European theatre. Foreign military entanglements, however, would impose too great a strain on the royal treasury, and already under Charles the wealth of America was being mortgaged to foreign bankers. On his abdication in 1556, his dominions were divided between his brother, who became Holy Roman Emperor, and his son, Philip II of Spain. Despite the division, the new Spanish king was still heir to a huge empire; encompassing the American continent, much of Italy, Franche-Comté and the Netherlands; in 1580, on Philip's accession to the throne of Portugal, not only was the Peninsula once more unified under one sovereign but the Portuguese possessions in Brazil, Africa, India and the Far East were also integrated into the imperial domain. Incomparably vaster and more diverse than Ferdinand and Isabella could ever have imagined it, this gigantic polity was to put the principles of the Catholic monarchy to their most challenging test.

It was imperative, by the inner logic of the monarchy, to preserve the one religion as a binding-force for its many realms, and Philip II proved to be the most devout and Catholic king, convinced of his providential mission to restore the Christian world to its unitary faith. In this he failed utterly, and at enormous material cost; his wars against the Protestant rebel provinces of the Netherlands, against the Protestant Elizabeth I of England, against France and the Turk, exhausted Spain and squandered her treasure from the Indies. When Philip II died in 1598, Spain (which, in effect, meant Castile) was bankrupt, crushed by taxes, and ravaged by the combined scourges of inflation, famine and economic depression. Even so, it had not ceded an inch of the empire, and the preservation of its religious and political integrity was the sacred task that Philip passed on to his successors.

Nevertheless, at the turn of the century, shortly after Philip II's death, there was a general awareness of crisis among the educated classes of Castile, a realization that its economic condition was close to collapse and that the imperial burden could not be sustained without reform. Numerous *arbitristas*, self-appointed analysts of the nation's ills, offered their remedies. But reform meant action by the Crown to restructure the system – action was required to stimulate production and revive agriculture, and to staunch the haemorrhage of American silver that went to pay for wars in Europe. Crucially, reform was necessary to relieve the burden of taxes, which was crippling the townsmen and peasants of Castile, by spreading this burden to other parts of the empire and to the swollen, overprivileged ranks of the nobility and the clergy. Furthermore, the Spanish armed forces were clearly over-stretched trying to defend, and even extend, the faith from the Philippines to the Netherlands; a more pragmatic outlook was perhaps needed, a recognition that it was futile to persist in the attempt to save the Low Countries for the Catholic religion, or to resist the spread of Islam in the Pacific. But a compromise with Protestants in the Netherlands would have entailed accepting the triumph of heresy within the realms of the Catholic monarch; this would harm the reputation of Spain as a great power pledged to defend Catholicism throughout the world, and it might alienate important sectors of the Church, driving a wedge between throne and altar, which could lead to the loss of the precious monopoly of legitimacy that gave unity to the empire.

What price pragmatism? Could the Crown act for 'reasons of state' when these might conflict with the ends of the true religion? Once again, at the beginning of the seventeenth century, the issue of royal authority became the focus of political debate. Given the pervasive climate of religious orthodoxy, the debate over pragmatism had to be conducted in veiled terms. The *políticos*, who included men secretly in sympathy with Machiavelli's view that the prince was above ordinary ethical norms and should act for 'reasons of state' alone, advocated a more vigorous royal absolutism (of the kind that Louis XIV would eventually arrogate to himself in France) as regards raising taxes and suspending customary rights for the sake of reform, as well as a more pragmatic outlook in foreign policy. Against them were ranged the defenders of the traditional Hispanic compact between Crown and Church, resolute anti-Machiavellians, for whom any deviation by the king from the laws of God or the interests of the faith would render his policy inherently unethical and invite divine punishment. This was the dilemma of the Catholic monarchy in the seventeenth century: the empire was threatened by economic collapse because of the immense strain of upholding its religious integrity, upon which in turn political unity was thought to depend; and yet, if the hugely expensive war against the Dutch heretics were to be abandoned for pragmatic reasons alone, might not the empire disintegrate anyway as a punishment from Heaven? Was economic recovery possible only by putting political legitimacy in jeopardy? The Crown chose not to risk pragmatism; it sought instead to hold on to the old guarantee of its legitimacy based as it was on its mutual compact with the Church.

In the 1620s and 1630s great efforts were made to raise revenues to prosecute the war against the Dutch and meet the spiralling costs of the global defence of empire. The policy of the Union of Arms conceived by Philip IV's energetic and reform-minded first minister, the Count-Duke of Olivares, was intended to relieve the fiscal pressure on Castile – which had always borne the brunt of the war effort – by increasing the tax-yield from the other realms of the empire; but the effort at internal reform came to grief in 1640, when it provoked armed rebellions in Catalonia, Portugal and the Italian possessions, as subjects of the Catholic monarch in these realms invoked their 'right of resistance' to a policy that rode roughshod over their customary rights and liberties.

Ironically, a policy designed to hold the empire together, and indeed further its political unification, had succeeded only in pushing the Catholic monarchy to the brink of destruction, because it jeopardized the fundamental consensus between Crown, Church and people that sustained the imperial state. The Catalan revolt was eventually put down, as were all the others save the Portuguese. Spain, however, proved incapable of reducing the Dutch after eighty years of war; in 1648 she was compelled to recognize the independence of the Netherlands, and in 1668 Portugal's right to independence was formally accepted. By the late seventeenth century Spain was no longer the supreme power in the world; she was, rather, an exhausted country whose riches had been spent in pursuing the chimera of political and religious unity, in clinging to a form of absolutism that gave the Crown a formidable legitimacy but left it too much under the influence of the Church. By the latter half of the seventeenth century, the Catholic monarchy had become an anachronism, a relic of the late Middle Ages. In rival monarchies, now economically superior to Spain, reasons of state were accorded priority over the interests of religion, as in the France of Louis XIII and Louis XIV. Elsewhere, ideas of constitutionalism were gaining currency, as in the Netherlands and England.

And yet, in spite of its political and economic weakness, Spain managed to hold on to most of its empire. The Catholic monarchy, out of date and virtually paralysed by inertia though it was, still possessed a sacred nimbus of legitimacy in the eyes of its subjects at home and abroad. This was an asset of incalculable value as far as the American colonies were concerned; for the king was able to command the political loyalty of the diverse and often divided peoples of the Indies, acting as a focus of unity and stability in potentially unruly colonies. Paradoxically, the political weakness of the Spanish state may have contributed to the longevity of its American empire; the situation of the Indies in the seventeenth century has been characterized as 'self-rule at the king's command',* for the élites of the colonies, as we shall see, were able to thrive on the inertia of an absolute monarchy that continued to moulder self-righteously across the sea.

The Catholic monarchy founded by Ferdinand and Isabella proved to be an extraordinarily resilient political creature. Long after Spain had declined economically and her power had ebbed away in Europe, she retained her imperial possessions in America virtually intact. The loyalty the Spanish Crown was able to inspire in its American subjects can be attributed to the monopoly of legitimacy it derived from its mutually supportive relations with the Church, a monopoly which the Habsburgs did so much to defend. But Habsburg Spain continued to decline under the unfortunate Charles II, the last of his line; after his death in 1700, the War of the Spanish Succession gave the throne to the French dynasty of the Bourbons. However, when the Bourbons attempted to introduce reforms in the last decades of the eighteenth century, they upset the traditional Spanish balance of throne and altar. In the Indies, the modern, French-style absolutism of the Bourbon monarchy, setting itself as it did over and against the Church, began to erode the Crown's legitimacy, provoking charges of 'tyranny' from sections of the Spanish American clergy and society. Its foundations having been disturbed, the Catholic monarchy of Spain finally collapsed in America when Napoleon's armies invaded the Iberian Peninsula in 1808.

Portugal's experience of the Reconquest and her Iberian cultural heritage made her share many characteristics with her neighbour Castile, their cognate histories frequently crossing and overlapping with each other. As in the case of Castile, the centuries of fighting against the Muslims produced a society in which religion had a crusading quality and was closely associated with the national identity. The system of land tenure was similar to Castile's: in the fertile, well-populated north, there were a large number of smallholders and tenant farmers; in the south the *latifundium* and a seigneurial regime predominated.

---

*J. H. Elliott, *Cambridge History of Latin America*, ed. Leslie Bethell (10 vols., Cambridge University Press: Cambridge, 1984–92), vol. 1, p. 338.

The Portuguese were not particularly given to seafaring. Though fishing was significant, most of the population were actually peasants who worked the land. Still, Portuguese society was motivated by aristocratic and military values, and, with its reconquest concluded some two centuries before Castile's, Portugal's quest for glory and riches was carried abroad to North Africa and into the Atlantic, where the spirit of adventure of a small minority was to lead to remarkable feats of maritime exploration and empire-building. Exploits overseas, however, went hand in hand with commerce, stimulated by the presence of considerable numbers of Genoese merchants and mariners who had settled along the coast, and especially in Lisbon, which was by far the most populous city.

The Portuguese monarchy in the thirteenth and fourteenth centuries was constantly under threat from ambitious nobles, from a powerful Church, and, not least, from dynastic quarrels in which the hand of Castile was invariably suspected, and with good reason. Relations with Spain would remain ambivalent: the larger neighbour exerted a very powerful influence on culture as well as politics, but there would always exist forces of repulsion, and Portuguese foreign policy was chiefly concerned with maintaining national independence from Castile. Portugal's long association with England – starting as a trading relationship in the twelfth century and periodically formalized by a series of treaties – stemmed from the need for a strong ally to counterbalance the perennial threat of incorporation by Spain.

A turning-point came in 1385 at the battle of Aljubarrota, when a new king, John of Aviz, nominated by the Portuguese Cortes and aided by English allies, won a victory against Castile and the Portuguese nobles. The long reign of John I (1385–1433) saw the development of a powerful monarchy capable of creating a stable nation state largely free from baronial challenges and galvanized by a renewal of the crusading spirit, though this was now directed towards Africa: the imperial phase of Portuguese history began with the taking of Ceuta in 1415. A few years later, John's son, Prince Henry the Navigator, established a school of navigation at Sagres on the Algarve and became the patron of the voyages of exploration that would continue long after his death in 1460 and would eventually open Africa, India and the East to the Europeans.

The death of John I was followed by an interlude of aristocratic revolt and dynastic civil wars, the latter overlapping with the wars of succession which put Isabella on the Castilian throne. In Portugal, John II (1481–95) finally imposed order and proceeded, by a combination of murders and executions, to break the power of the nobility and confiscate much of its wealth. It was John II who finally created in Portugal an absolutist nation state resembling the Catholic monarchy of Spain, with the Church playing a crucial role in giving a monopoly of legitimacy to the unifying authority of the Crown.

For eighty years after John's death, Portugal's Catholic monarchy supervised the building of one of the most far-flung empires ever to have been created by Europeans: in 1487 the Cape of Good Hope was rounded by Bartholomew Dias; by 1498 Vasco da Gama had reached India; the year 1500 saw another Portuguese expedition discover a land that would eventually become Brazil; in the course of the sixteenth century the Portuguese established bases and factories in Ceylon, Malacca and the Spice Islands of the Indonesian archipelago; by the 1570s they had won a monopoly of the lucrative trade between China and Japan from a base established at Macao on the Chinese mainland in 1557.

In that year a new king, Sebastian (1557–78), ascended the throne and changed the course of Portuguese history when he engaged in a fanciful attempt to revive the medieval spirit of religious crusade against the Moor by leading a campaign against the emperor of Morocco. The Portuguese army was cut to pieces at the battle of Alcazar-Kebir; Sebastian himself died in the débâcle, which led by a series of dynastic manœuvres to the succession of Philip II of Spain to the Portuguese throne in 1580. However, the Portuguese people refused to accept Sebastian's death, and a Messianic legend arose claiming that he would one day return to his kingdom and lead it to a new golden age, in which the whole world would be united in a universal monarchy under the Crown of Portugal. This legend struck a very deep chord in the people of the Portuguese dominions, from Macao to Pernambuco; it was still thriving in the eighteenth century and, even as late as 1896, it was capable of inspiring a fanatical uprising at Canudos in the backlands of Brazil in support of the monarchy and against the recently proclaimed Brazilian republic.

Sebastianism kept alive the spirit of independence in a country now brought under the sovereignty of the Spanish Crown. Union with Spain, the mightiest power in the world, had its commercial and military advantages, and Philip II promised to respect Portugal's separate institutions. Portuguese affairs were, nevertheless, conducted by a viceroy in Lisbon reporting to a Council of Portugal in Spain (staffed, though, by Portuguese). These years also saw a contest for supremacy in the mission fields of the Far East between Portuguese Jesuits, established for decades in China and Japan, and Spanish friars newly arrived from the Philippines. That religious dispute offered the strange spectacle of the two Iberian neighbours taking up their sporadic quarrels at the other end of the world, in remote, alien corners of the South China Sea, to which Portugal had come by a tortuous eastern route and Spain, eventually, from the west. By the end of the sixteenth century, Spanish hegemony had earned Portugal the aggressive attentions of the Netherlands, a rising power of merchants and seafarers, which was in rebellion against Spain and for whom Portugal's maritime empire, stretching as it did across the entire globe, was to prove an irresistible temptation. In the 1590s Dutch ships rounded the Cape and began the process of stripping Portugal of most of her trading posts in the East. In 1624 the Dutch attacked the sugar plantations of north-eastern Brazil and later, in 1641, they launched an offensive against Portuguese Angola.

The continuing depredations of the Dutch threatened to rob Portugal of every source of its colonial wealth – Oriental spices, Brazilian sugar and African slaves. Since Spain was by the middle of the seventeenth century too enfeebled and overstretched to protect these assets, the Portuguese (and the Brazilians) had to fend for themselves, eventually ousting the Dutch from Angola in 1648 and expelling them from Brazil in 1654, though most of the trading posts in the East were permanently lost. This struggle against the Dutch in the colonies was a major factor in persuading the Portuguese to rebel against Spain in 1640. Under a new king, John IV, Duke of Braganza, Portugal seceded and reinforced its position by concluding a new alliance with England, symbolized by the marriage of Catherine of Braganza to Charles II in 1661, with Tangier and Bombay as dowry.

The Portuguese Catholic monarchy attained its zenith of material splendour in the first half of the eighteenth century, while Spain was barely recovering from a half-century of decline under the Bourbons. The discovery of gold in Brazil fired the religious fervour of John V (1706–50) to heights of gorgeous, archaic extravagance, immortalized in the monastery-palace of Mafra, which was built as a rival to the Escorial and Versailles by a huge army of draft labour over eighteen years. But the golden indulgence of Mafra was a distraction from the fact that the national economy was being eaten away by debt. Moreover, the Methuen Treaty with England of 1703 established a commercial dependence, whereby the Portuguese exchanged their wines and precious metals for English textiles; more important still, the treaty gave the English access to Brazil, a market which would steadily grow through the eighteenth century and engage England ever more deeply in Portugal's imperial trade.

After the death of John V, Portugal's patent economic weakness in relation to England prompted an attempt at comprehensive reform at home and in the colonies, particularly in Brazil, the 'milch cow' of the empire, during the enlightened despotism of Joseph I's chief minister, the Marquis of Pombal (1750–77). Pombal's reforms did not greatly improve Portugal's economic fortunes but, as was to occur with the Bourbon reforms in the Spanish world, their anticlericalism undermined the monopoly of legitimacy of the Catholic monarchy and indirectly produced the first stirrings of republicanism and autonomy in Brazil. Yet, curiously enough, it was the Protestant British who would facilitate the survival of the Catholic monarchy when Napoleon's armies threatened Portugal in 1808. The entire Portuguese court removed to Rio de Janeiro under British naval escort and there laid the basis for the survival of monarchy in Brazil until 1889, in stark contrast to what happened in Spanish America, where the Catholic monarchy collapsed in chaos.

Although the empires of the two Iberian powers would exhibit many similarities in their social, cultural and religious values, there were also important differences. In the first place, Portugal was a unitary kingdom, whereas Spain had to manage a plurality of territories in the Peninsula itself and in Europe, which not only made the task of government more complex but also embroiled her in endless wars against rival powers. Portugal's empire was a trading empire, a collection of fortified commercial entrepôts and coastal enclaves involving little penetration into the hinterland or extensive settlement. The interior of Brazil, for instance, was only opened up very gradually in the late seventeenth century, those of Angola and Mozambique not until the nineteenth; there was nothing to compare with the formidable military, political, juridical and religious problems encountered by the Spanish Crown in its attempt to incorporate under its authority the empires of the Aztecs and the Incas as well as a large number of other Indian kingdoms. Portugal's empire, despite its physical dispersion, was far more integrated politically than Spain's; Portuguese subjects born overseas identified more closely with the interests of the mother country than did the Spanish Americans, for Spain regarded her dominions as kingdoms in their own right, whereas Portugal's possessions were always viewed more strictly as colonies whose purpose was to enrich their metropolis.

Yet, in the final analysis, Portugal and Castile were both economically backward and not very densely populated. Their imperial careers in the sixteenth and seventeenth centuries were in many ways triumphs of the human spirit over material resources. And their success in holding on to those empires long after both countries had sunk into a mire of economic failure owed much to the extraordinary resilience of the political system they had in common. This was the Catholic monarchy, whose monopoly of legitimacy gave it the capacity to reconcile cultural diversity with political unity, keeping distant possessions loyal to the Crown for some 300 years, and in the case of Portugal's African colonies until the twentieth century.

THE MEETING OF TWO WORLDS

What occurred in the sixteenth century was not so much the discovery of a New World as the meeting of two branches of humanity which had previously been unknown to each other. For the Indians of America, who had lived a completely isolated existence, the encounter with aliens was inherently traumatic. The European invasions brought much that was radically new in the realm of ideas and values, in agricultural methods, including new crops and animals, in technology, with the introduction of the wheel, iron, guns, ships, tools, and in the economy, where the use of money, profit-making and trade were far more developed than in Indian societies. All these innovations would change and also disrupt the Indian world.

Even so, in the imperial areas of Middle America and the Andes the break with tradition was not total. In the first place, Indians and Iberians had comparable ideas of political sovereignty: the Catholic monarchs of the Iberian kingdoms derived their legitimacy and absolute authority from a divine source, as did the rulers of the Aztecs and the Incas. In both the European and the Amerindian imperial states the religious establishment was closely involved in the business of government; a priestly caste or a Church hierarchy buttressed the state and received numerous privileges, land and tribute from the people. Both kinds of society were seigneurial: Indian nobles, like their Iberian counterparts, owned large estates worked by tribute-paying peasants; they also headed large households composed of extended families or kinship groups, as well as numerous dependants and servants. Relations within these households and between noble clans replicated the reciprocal relationship between the monarch and his people, based as it was on patriarchy and patronage – a man of power would bestow favours in return for the loyalty of his clients and subordinates. Aristocrats valued honour and glory derived from military exploits, for in America as in Iberia there was long experience of conquering and subjugating alien kingdoms. Indeed, James Lockhart and Stuart Schwartz have remarked on the extent to which the expectations of indigenous Americans 'matched those of the Iberians, whose conquest lore also included notions of tribute imposition,

The Age of Empire

change of religion and allegiance, and manipulation of local rulers, together with at least provisional local autonomy.'[*]

These two worlds – Renaissance Europe and Indian America – met and clashed in the sixteenth century. The consequences of that encounter were manifold and extremely diverse, and, for reasons not wholly attributable to the Iberians, they were destructive for large numbers of Indians. Nevertheless, it has become clear that there existed sufficient political and social similarities between the two worlds, at least in Middle America and in the central Andes, for there to have occurred a fairly rapid process of restructuring and hybridization after the conquest had been completed.

[*] *Early Latin America: A History of Colonial Spanish America and Brazil* (Cambridge University Press: Cambridge, 1984), p. 45.

3. Spain in America

Patterns of Settlement

The conquest and exploration of the New World were carried out on the initiative of groups of men responding to strange and difficult circumstances. Because of their freedom of action, the conquistadors founded societies which had an improvised, incidental quality: there was no systematic programme of colonization co-ordinated by a central agency. The two major determinants of settlement were the conquistadors' desire for precious metals and their need for a supply of labour; both were necessary for the fulfilment of the overriding ambition of sixteenth-century European adventurers – to achieve noble status by acquiring wealth, land and lordship over men.

The conquistadors were therefore attracted to those parts of the New World which would most readily supply the requisites for a seigneurial way of life. The areas of Spanish settlement in the sixteenth century thus coincided broadly with the boundaries of the former Aztec and Inca empires. Outside the Aztec and Inca spheres of influence there was little colonization in the early stages, except in so far as mineral deposits were discovered. In Mexico this was to occur in territory well to the north of the central valley – the future mining region around Zacatecas – which was inhabited by nomadic Indian tribes and which required for a long time a more marginal and defensive type of settlement. Even in Peruvian silver-mining areas, which were closer to Inca centres of population, European settlement remained marginal, because Spaniards found the altitudes of the Andes inhospitable and preferred the climate at lower levels in territory to the west of the Andean chain.

Partly because of their small numbers, but also for military and political reasons, Spaniards tended to concentrate their settlements at strategic points within regions already densely populated by Indians. These early concentrations in Mexico and Peru became the central areas of European influence; only gradually did Spaniards move out from them to found towns further afield. The Spanish presence in America was therefore very uneven: the central areas soon absorbed Spanish influences, and, as other territories such as Guatemala, Chile and New Granada (modern Colombia and Ecuador) became effectively settled, these too would slowly acquire most of the Hispanic features of the original centres. Still, there remained vast areas in which there was scarcely any Spanish presence: in South America virtually the whole of the interior remained unsettled for over four centuries; to the east of the Andean chain there was only a band of settlement running from the eastern slopes of the Andes in northern Argentina through Paraguay and down the river-system of the Paraná to the estuary of the River Plate; the Caribbean coastal strip of Tierra Firme – northern Venezuela and New Granada – saw some Spanish colonization; in Chile, it was the central regions around Santiago that were settled; in North America, practically the entire area to the north of the Valley of Mexico as far as and including California, New Mexico, Arizona, Texas and Florida was only very sparsely inhabited by the Spaniards.

What is more, these huge territories beyond the limits of Inca or Aztec control were populated by Indian tribes whose social development differed widely: there were sedentary tribute-paying communities in New Granada or elaborate Mayan societies in Central America, both of which had many features in common with the pre-Columbian imperial states; semi-nomadic societies, such as the Araucanians of southern Chile or the various Chichimec peoples of northern Mexico; and simple tribes of hunter-gatherers in the rain forests of Central America and the South American interior. The nature of the interaction between Spanish settlers and these very diverse native communities influenced the character and identity of the particular Hispanic American societies that eventually emerged.

Spanish settlement was therefore limited, scattered and heterogeneous. Even so, these Hispanic areas were all connected to the old, central zones. At the heart of the northern network lay Mexico City; at the heart of the southern, Lima. And through these two major centres Spain communicated with her American dominions. Trade, information and government business came and went through Seville (and later Cadiz) in the Peninsula to Mexico City or Lima, whence the traffic fanned out to the different outposts of the empire along set routes.

In the early phase of settlement, the Spanish towns were situated inland, away from the low-lying coastal areas, which tended to be disease-ridden and vulnerable to attack from the sea. Each of the two capital cities therefore had an ancillary port: for Mexico, it was Veracruz on the Gulf; for Lima, it was nearby Callao on the Pacific and then, by way of access to the Caribbean,

Nombre de Dios (replaced later by Portobelo) on the isthmus of Panama (these Panamanian ports being not much more than collections of modest buildings augmented by encampments of traders which sprang up whenever the transatlantic fleets were expected). Given the enormously long Pacific coastline of South America and the natural barriers to overland trade, secondary cities in South America followed this arrangement: for instance, Santiago de Chile relied on the nearby port of Valparaíso to link it with Lima, while Quito had the port of Guayaquil, which also acted as one of several maritime staging posts between Lima and the isthmus. Other routes fed into this network, such as the New Granadan complex formed by Bogotá and Tunja, and their Caribbean outlet at Cartagena de Indias, a port which also acted as a station for transatlantic fleets bound ultimately for Peru. As silver-mining got under way, each of the networks was extended to their respective mining areas: Mexico City north to Zacatecas, while Lima was linked via provincial cities like Cuzco and La Paz to the great silver-mines of Potosí in what is now modern Bolivia. And so, the imperial system of trade and administration was articulated along two arterial routes – silver was drawn from the interior via the centres of Lima and Mexico City respectively and thence exported to the mother country, while European goods came via Seville along these same routes for eventual distribution to the Spanish settlements in the two viceroyalties of the New World.

This pattern of communications allowed an overstretched monarchy, with commitments throughout Europe, to employ its resources economically over vast distances. The basic structure was established early on in the sixteenth century, but was constantly ramifying at its extremities into such peripheral areas as were coming under Spanish influence. The pattern illustrates a fundamental characteristic of Spanish imperialism in America: it was a blend of private initiative and government control – new areas were continually being explored and conquered by Spanish warrior bands acting without direct government supervision, but once settlement began, a newly conquered area would be drawn into the existing network of communications, through which the Crown was able to relay its authority to the most distant corners. This interplay of local initiative and central authority would continue throughout the colonial period, and it accounts in large measure for the adaptability and resilience of the imperial state in the Indies.

Royal authority was transmitted in the very act of settlement. The principles which determined the sharing out of the fruits of conquest were understood to conform to the king's justice as dispensed by the *adelantado*, the chieftain of a band of conquistadors. For when the roaming band wanted to take possession of a territory, it would follow a procedure which had

governed all the previous Spanish settlements in the New World and in the
Canary Islands, and which, in fact, had been used for generations in the
Reconquest of the Peninsula itself. The *adelantado* would assume the functions
of a governor or captain-general of the conquered territory and take responsibility both for its military defence and its civil administration. He was
authorized by the terms of his *capitulación* from the Crown – the royal licence
for the initial *entrada* (enterprise of conquest) – to distribute the rewards of
conquest among the men in his company. Land and booty were divided up
according to the military or financial contribution each member of the
company had made to the success of the enterprise. Grants of land were
made in units termed either *peonías* (about 100 acres), which were allocated
to foot soldiers, or *caballerías* (about 500 acres), allocated to horsemen.

Access to Indian labour and tribute was a quite different matter from the
distribution of titles to land. Rights to receive labour and tribute from the
Indian communities were special privileges apportioned by the device of
encomienda, which fixed the amount of Indian labour and the quantity of
tribute due to the most worthy conquistadors. Those Spaniards who received
encomiendas formed the élite of Conquest society. However, they did not
become feudal overlords, for the *encomienda* did not confer feudal jurisdiction
over the tribute-paying Indians, who otherwise remained free subjects of the
Crown.

Social and economic aspirations, as much as a spirit of adventure, provided
the incentive for constant Spanish expansion in the New World. After the
distribution of rewards, some members of the expedition might prefer to
return to Spain with their newly acquired wealth; others would be content
to stay on and put down roots; yet others might not feel entirely happy with
their share and decide at a later stage either to invest or participate in another
entrada into alien territory, hoping thereby to rise further in the elementary
hierarchies that the Conquest threw up.

The Spanish conquest of America went hand in hand with the effort to
establish the elements of civilized life in a community. The *adelantado* was
also required by his *capitulación* to found a town and municipality. The ritual
act of foundation itself invoked the two essential sources of authority in the
Spanish state – the Crown and the Church: a tree or stake would be struck
with a sword to symbolize the implantation of royal justice in the territory;
the town's name would be proclaimed to the cries of '¡*Viva el Rey!*' by the
assembled company; and then Mass would be celebrated to sanctify the place
and impress the natives.

The conquistadors who chose to settle in the new town would constitute
themselves as the *vecinos* (citizens) of a Spanish municipality, electing their

military commander as its civic head and placing themselves under the vassalage of the king of Spain. From among the more important *vecinos* – the ones with the largest *encomiendas* – the *adelantado* would appoint a municipal council, the *cabildo*; the royal notary and the priest, who invariably accompanied an expedition of conquest, would become the magistrate and the ecclesiastical authority respectively of the new Spanish town. The essential organs of Hispanic society would thus be present from the start in the frontier colonies.

Indeed, a particularly striking feature of Spanish colonization was the way in which political and social relationships were expressed in the layout of new towns. Urban settlements in the Indies conformed to a standard plan, a *traza*, which *adelantados* carried with them on their expeditions. At the centre of the town a rectangular area was traced, around which were built the residence of the governor, the *cabildo*, the church, the prison and the houses of the principal *encomenderos*. Leading out from the sides of this plaza, eight parallel streets would divide the town into a grid composed of regular blocks of houses. The further away a Spaniard lived from the central plaza the lower was his position on the social scale. On the perimeters of the grid there would eventually live families of mixed-bloods and free blacks.

The work of building these towns was done by Indians organized for tribute service by their chieftains and supervised by the Spaniards. These Indians were not members of the Spanish municipality; they lived in their own villages under the authority of their traditional ethnic lords. Yet, in time, there might appear outside the grid of the Spanish town an unofficial Indian service-population housed in humble dwellings forming an untidy fringe, which would alter according to circumstances without affecting the Spanish centre. Such fringes developed into the Indian barrios that would eventually grow on the outskirts of every sizeable Spanish town. The urbanized Indians who lived there were fugitives from their traditional communities and, like the mixed-bloods and blacks, occupied an anomalous, ill-defined position at the lowest levels of Spanish society.

The Spanish town in America was, therefore, the nucleus of colonization. In the sixteenth century it provided a familiar cultural haven and a military refuge for the still small numbers of Spanish settlers, who were surrounded by a sea of potentially hostile Indian communities. The Spanish town also acted as an instrument of appropriation and control over the resources of a particular territory and its native population. Much of the land would be allocated to Spaniards for their private use, but it was worked by drafts of Indian labourers. In the early stages of Spanish settlement in America the greater part of a region's produce would have been grown by Indians on their own land and then either offered to *encomenderos* in tribute or else bartered in the weekly markets that the Indians were often allowed to hold in the squares of the Spanish towns. From the outset there was a constant economic and even cultural interaction between the Spanish town and the Indian communities, though there was to be no political or juridical integration of the two, for reasons which will be discussed below.

On the whole, the economy of the settlers was agrarian and geared to local needs. Their preference was for European crops and cattle, although Indian crops were consumed selectively. However, as the population of the Spanish towns grew, agriculture and ranching developed for commercial purposes, based on the original land grants and on additional holdings acquired through a variety of means – purchase, further royal grants, occupation of vacant land or the usurpation of Indian commons. Thus the most powerful settlers, usually but not always *encomenderos*, would begin to put together a complex of landholdings. This was the origin of the hacienda – the most enduring and most coveted of the rural institutions in Spanish America.

No Spanish town could remain a wholly self-sufficient unit; it had to establish commercial and administrative links with larger towns, through them with the provincial capital, and ultimately with the Peninsula. The fastest-growing towns were those in a favourable position to supply goods to the transatlantic economy; but enterprising settlers in some areas might specialize in the production of goods, such as sugar, tobacco, hides or dyestuffs, that were important in interregional trade. The largest landowners formed an élite controlling the *cabildo* and the major municipal offices. Yet no matter how thoroughly the leading families in each locality might dominate the municipal government, they had to deal with royal officials appointed to each province, as well as with higher courts of justice in the provincial capitals.

But, for all the attempts by the Crown to provide for the transmission of law and order, the early life of these Spanish settlements was turbulent and unstable. The Conquest remained a matter of individual enterprise and adventure, in which men participated not because they wished to fulfil a civilizing mission, but because they wanted to better their lot in life. The conquest of America, therefore, tended to attract commoners and men of the lower orders. No aristocrats came to the Indies, and few hidalgos to start with – not much more than about 4 per cent of Spanish arrivals until the late 1570s. Most conquistadors and emigrants to the Indies in the sixteenth century were labourers, artisans, traders, soldiers and sailors; in most expeditions there were also a few black slaves or mulattos from the Peninsula.

Having risked life and limb in the conquest of the New World, such men were set on material advancement, and, given the huge distances that often separated them from the Spanish authorities, the opportunities for misconduct, insubordination and, especially, for the exploitation of a racially alien and subjugated people were clearly enormous. Moreover, in addition to these first settlers, there were constant influxes of subsequent Spanish migrants seeking work, land and social betterment. These newcomers might settle or move on after a while to more promising areas, but at any rate they would begin to compete for the available resources, and this in itself contributed to the unruliness and social fluidity of life in the early settlements.

A very important factor in the formation of this Conquest society was the dearth of Spanish women. Until the 1540s, only about 6 per cent of Spanish emigrants to the Indies were female. This meant that Spanish males depended mostly on native women for sexual relations. Spaniards found them attractive, and the native women gained in status by consorting with the conquerors; so the rate of miscegenation was rapid. The Crown and the Church encouraged the legitimation of these unions through Christian marriage, and many settlers did in fact wed their native mistresses, but it was far more common for such liaisons to remain irregular. In the early phases of the Conquest, and in remoter parts of the Indies, individual Spaniards collected veritable harems, fathering large numbers of illegitimate offspring. Paraguay came to be referred to as 'the paradise of Muhammad', for Spaniards there lived openly with large numbers of women. A cleric reported, presumably in horror, that the Spaniards of Paraguay often had up to seventy native concubines, and rarely fewer than five or six. Black men also lacked for women of their own race in the early period and they too formed liaisons with Amerindian women. This was a particular source of concern to the Spanish authorities because of the strong prejudices that existed against Africans, and the resultant stigma which attached to the offspring of their unions with Indian females.

Once Spanish women began to arrive in larger numbers, they became the settlers' favoured marriage partners, though few men actually gave up their predilection for illicit partners of Indian or other non-white races. Whiteness was the ethnic ideal, and men in search of social improvement felt a strong urge to conform to the norms of their society of origin. European racial prejudices, reinforced by medieval Spanish concepts of blood purity, were translated to the New World and preserved as a legitimizing device in the emerging Spanish American societies – white children tended to be legitimate; those of mixed blood were almost invariably not.

Urban settlement was, then, the means by which the Spanish monarchy sought to control and consolidate the wayward process of conquest in what was, after all, a wholly unknown continent. But the urban nucleus, though it served to transmit the forms of civil order, was just as much a point of intersection for the many tensions and cross-currents – between Spaniard and Indian, white and non-white, men and women, personal ambitions and interests of state – which troubled the new hybrid societies that were gradually being formed.

The Impact of Conquest on the Indian World

The Indian world was characterized by its extreme diversity. Even in the areas of Aztec or Inca imperial influence there were an immense number of ethnic kingdoms and tribal groupings; some had been incorporated into the larger imperial structures, but there were also many others which remained outside these empires and were often openly hostile to the pre-Hispanic imperialists or engaged in constant struggles for territory and power against neighbouring kingdoms or tribes.

It would, therefore, be mistaken to assume that political or cultural unity existed in the Indian world. The term 'Indian' is useful to distinguish these American peoples from the Europeans, but it should not be taken to denote some uniform, seamless culture. All of these Indian societies, however, were affected by the Spanish Conquest, though not all in the same manner: some were utterly destroyed; some chose to ally themselves with the conquerors; some found the 'conquest' a welcome liberation from Aztec or Inca oppression. In most cases, traditional ways survived unchanged well into the period of Spanish domination.

The whole subject of the Indian societies under Spanish rule is fraught with difficulties. In the first place, the heterogeneity of the Indian world has not been taken into account by historians until comparatively recently, and the sheer variety of ethnic groupings and cultures makes it hazardous to generalize about the overall Indian response to so multi-faceted a phenomenon as the Spanish Conquest. Secondly, the question of the effects of Spanish rule upon the Indians has always been controversial. There remains a very strong predisposition to interpret historical change in the New World as a tragic loss of cohesion and authenticity in native cultures. Here the problem is aggravated by the mutually reinforcing influences of the 'black legend' of Spanish greed and cruelty, and the contrasting myth of the American Indian as 'noble savage'. To add to the difficulties, there is the unquestionable fact of the demographic collapse of the Indian population during the sixteenth and seventeenth centuries. The extent of this collapse was not appreciated until our own time, and Indian depopulation was formerly attributed solely to Spanish cruelty. But now it is known to have been overwhelmingly due to pandemics caused by European viruses to which the Amerindians had no immunities, although, certainly, Spanish treatment aggravated the effects of these viruses. This catastrophic decline in population is, understandably, a factor which influences the interpretation of change in the Indian world exclusively in terms of loss.

However, if the Spanish Conquest is regarded as an irreversible historical accident − one not necessarily more cruel in its purely military aspect than other less controversial experiences of conquest, say, the Norman Conquest of England − then the issue of change in the post-Conquest world can be discussed not as a uniquely savage despoliation of innocent peoples, but rather as a long-term process of adaptation − certainly very painful in many instances − made by innumerable Amerindian societies obliged by historical circumstances to come to terms with a different set of imperial masters.

Clearly, the Spaniards, like any other conquerors, did systematically, and often cruelly, intervene in native societies to extract resources for their own profit; but, equally, there was, as we shall see, a very powerful countervailing tendency within the Spanish state itself to protect and preserve Indian cultures. What can be affirmed with certainty is that the Conquest did not result in the wholesale ruin of native societies. At least in the areas that have been most closely studied, namely the territories of Middle America and, increasingly, Peru, there is evidence of a high degree of cultural continuity with pre-Conquest times. Indeed, the social historians James Lockhart and Stuart Schwartz have gone so far as to affirm that 'in general, Indian towns and provinces survived the Conquest essentially intact'.*

In the course of the Spanish Conquest and the decades immediately following it, the imperial structures of the Aztecs and the Incas were destroyed, their royal families and imperial nobility deprived of their power. It was this native ruling aristocracy which had most reason to lament the passing of the old order, and the expressions of their nostalgia and sorrow have come down to us in writings which have all too often been taken as representative of the generality of Indians.

Once the Spaniards had got the upper hand, the Indian aristocracy faced the choice of either collaborating with their conquerors or organizing rebellions in order to recover their former power. As we have seen, the young prince Manco Inca in Peru at first chose collaboration in the hope of

* *Early Latin America*, p. 113.

outmanœuvring dynastic rivals for the imperial title, but later decided to
rebel against the Spaniards once he realized that the conquistadors had no
intention of quitting the country. Even in later generations it was possible
for aristocratic collaborators to change their minds and attempt to rebel
against Spanish power. This type of resistance was élitist and dynastic, having
little to do with the defence of the mass of Indians. But dispossession was
not, in fact, the fate of the Aztec and Inca nobles; so long as they accepted
Spanish sovereignty, they were allowed to retain their aristocratic status in
post-Conquest society: they were awarded lands and *encomiendas* by the
Spanish monarch, and their children were educated in schools for nobles,
such as the college at Tlatelolco in Mexico and those of Huancayo and Cuzco
in Peru.

There were Indian kingdoms which actually formed alliances with the
Spanish invaders against their historic enemies. In Mexico the most famous
example is that of the Tlaxcalans, who attacked Tenochtitlán and helped
Cortés raze the city to the ground; in Peru the support of the Huanca people
was crucial to Pizarro's defeat of the Incas. 'Such alliances expressed the
internal contradictions and discontents that plagued Aztec and Inca rule, and
the failure of these empires to eradicate the independent military potential
of resentful ethnic kingdoms.'* Even after the Spanish Conquest had been
completed, numerous ethnic kingdoms and tribes decided to collaborate
with the new masters in order to seek advantage against rivals, regain lost
territory or rid themselves of domination by hated enemies. The crumbling
of the pre-Hispanic empires had the effect, therefore, of devolving identity
and autonomy to subjugated ethnic kingdoms, and of revitalizing the authority of ethnic chieftains. It was this class of chiefs, called *pipiltin* in Mexico
and *curacas* in Peru, that dealt with the Spaniards and organized their own
people to offer tribute and labour services to the Spanish *encomenderos*.

Within these Indian kingdoms and communities, traditional life went on
much as before, and, having accepted the new masters, it made sense also to
accept their religion. Even so, relations with the Spaniards were unstable in
the aftermath of the Conquest. If a kingdom or tribe came to believe that
its interests were no longer being served by alliance with the Spaniards, it
might attempt to resist them or even rebel. In Peru during the 1560s the
most radical of these rebellions was that of the millenarian movement called
Taki Onqoy in the region of Huamanga, where many tribes previously loyal
to the Spaniards turned against them in reaction to excessive labour demands,

* Steve J. Stern, 'The Rise and Fall of Indian–White Alliances: A Regional View of "Conquest"
History', *Hispanic American Historical Review*, 61, 3 (1981), pp. 461–91 (p. 461).

and called for the outright rejection of Spanish law and religion, appealing to their gods to help them expel the invaders.

Yet even though the basic structures of Indian life at the communal and tribal levels remained largely unchanged by the Conquest, none the less many villages, crops and individual lives were destroyed in the course of the wars (in Peru, it must be remembered, a bitter civil war had been raging for several years before the Spaniards arrived). There is no doubt that large numbers of Indians suffered torture and rape at the hands of the conquistadors. Labour for the *encomenderos* must often, though not always, have been harsh and exploitative, since many Spaniards were not interested in settling down but simply wanted to extract as much wealth as possible from the Indies before returning to Spain. The Conquest also disrupted communities; many Indians took to wandering the countryside as vagabonds or fled the Spaniards to hide in the wilderness. This kind of dislocation was particularly common in Peru, where the *mitmaq* system, based on 'vertical archipelagos' or outlying colonies, partially broke down, leaving many colonists cut off from their tribal homelands. One option for such displaced individuals was to enter the service of Spaniards as part of that class of commoner called *naborías* in Mexico and *yanaconas* in Peru – detribalized Indians who used to serve as personal retainers to the Aztec and Inca aristocracies and whom the Spaniards also employed.

The worst effects of the Conquest were felt over the longer term. Most destructive by far were the ravages of the pandemics which swept the continent within a few years of the arrival of the Spaniards. These were plagues of smallpox, measles, typhus and other as yet unidentified diseases. The Indian peoples of low-lying or coastal areas were the worst affected by these viruses: the population of the Caribbean islands was all but wiped out. In the highlands of the mainland, which were far more heavily populated any-way, the toll was not so great, but the loss of life was still disastrous. It has been estimated that over the century following the Conquest the population in central Mexico fell by about 90 per cent. The decline in Peru was slower and less drastic, but the fall was still roughly 40 per cent. These terrible epidem-ics came in waves every ten years or so until the end of the sixteenth century, and continued to ravage the population periodically after that – in Peru the demographic decline was not halted until the early eighteenth century.

The contribution of these epidemics to the victory of the Spaniards is incalculable, not just because they claimed so many lives, but also because they disrupted native power structures and demoralized the Indians, who were at a loss to explain what was happening to them. In Mexico, smallpox carried away several important Aztec leaders, not least the emperor

Cuitlahuac, thus weakening the natives' ability to counter-attack. Even before Pizarro had arrived, the Incas were plunged into a disastrous war of succession after the deaths of the emperor Huayna Capac and his chosen heir, Ninan Cuyoche, both from smallpox.

Another long-term effect of the conquest was the excessive burden placed on the resources of the Indian communities by the Spanish settlers' dependence on them for food and labour. It is difficult to know whether the Spaniards' tribute demands were heavier than those formerly made by the Aztecs and the Incas on the tribes they had subjugated, but many Indian communities protested or rebelled, and several individuals felt so oppressed by tribute obligations that they fled their villages to work for wages in Spanish towns. It is likely, however, that the tribute was often considered excessive not because the system as such was felt to be unfamiliar or inhumane by the Indians, but because the trends of demography in the Indies worked against it. In brief, as the Indian population fell through disease, the Spanish population rose steadily through immigration and reproduction. By the latter half of the sixteenth century, Spanish demand for tribute and labour was increasing precisely at a time when the human resources of the Indian world were being most rapidly depleted. The resultant pressures on Indian communities bred resentment and violence against the Spaniards. The suffering caused by the implantation of a new Spanish imperial regime is thus likely to have been enormously intensified and prolonged by the ravages of these mysterious epidemics.

Evidence points to extensive social demoralization – reports of suicides, apathy, abortions, loss of the will to procreate, as well as a certain weakening of traditional authority, manifesting itself in growing delinquency and drunkenness in the villages. Such phenomena have been taken to denote 'destructuration', the term used by Nathan Wachtel to describe the disorganization of the economic, social and ideological structures which formerly gave the Indian cultures their coherence and meaning. In Peru, for instance, Wachtel has argued that tribute-payment in the pre-Conquest period had been 'balanced' by rituals of reciprocity between the lord and his commoners and by rituals of redistribution in the form of a return by the lord of gifts – real and symbolic – to the tribute-payers. Under the Spaniards, tribute-payment resulted in a one-way transfer of goods to the new lords without any reciprocity. Similarly, for several decades after the Conquest, the Indians tried to assimilate the religion of the conquerors to their own understanding of the universe. The structures of their religious mentality survived their conversion to Christianity, and often resulted in an unbalanced syncretism of old and new. This phenomenon was more marked in Peru than in Mexico, and varied widely between different native peoples.* It is, nevertheless, extremely difficult to assess the process of 'destructuration', and more so to evaluate it in terms of actual suffering – must it be taken as purely negative, or is it simply the sign of an inevitable transition to new conditions, perhaps rendered far more disruptive than it need have been by demographic disaster?

What is remarkable is the cultural resilience of the Indians; their capacity to resist the multiple pressures, direct and indirect, exerted upon them by Spaniards; their willingness to pick and choose those elements of European culture that best suited them. The active conservatism of the Indian masses is evident in the continuance of social and religious rituals, the respect for tribal authority and the adaptation of Spanish novelties in dress, crops and tools to ancient methods. The basic social units, the kinship groups called *ayllu* in Peru and *calpulli* in Mexico, continued to function; the Spanish economy based on money and private property was not allowed to intrude into the Indian communities as such; internally, these continued to operate, as always, on the basis of subsistence production and the exchange of goods through barter.

The Spanish authorities did certainly intervene to transform Indian ways and to assert their authority. The most immediate and flagrant intervention was the sustained campaign to convert the Indians to Christianity – a consequence of imperial dominion understood and accepted by both conquerors and conquered, but which none the less involved significant changes to Indian society and behaviour, as will be seen below. Evangelization also involved the introduction of Hispanic forms of organization. Yet it must be recognized that Indian traditions owe their survival to the explicit policy of the Spanish Church and Crown, throughout the sixteenth century, to preserve as many of those traditions as were compatible with the Christian religion and the vital interests of the state.

Some effort was made to marry innovations with Indian customs. For instance, Indian communal government was traditionally centred on a head town, called a *cabecera* by the Spanish, which exercised jurisdiction over a number of subject districts or villages called *sujetos*. The *cabecera–sujeto* pattern was preserved in the late sixteenth century despite the introduction of Spanish municipal structures into the Indian communities – even in places where extensive Indian resettlement had been undertaken. This respect for Indian ways can be observed too in the larger Indian cities where Spaniards settled. In Mexico City, for instance, the exclusively Indian municipality of Tenochtitlán still existed, functioning alongside equivalent institutions for the

* Nathan Wachtel, *Cambridge History of Latin America*, vol. 1, pp. 212–30.

Spanish settlers; and Indian lords there still exercised considerable authority over their vassals.

In the latter half of the sixteenth century the Spanish state attempted to reshape the Indian world in order to bring it more fully under control. Once again, this intrusion was partly dictated by the scale of Indian depopulation. By the early 1570s the Spaniards found that in some regions they could no longer rely entirely on the traditional ethnic chieftains to deliver the tribute of labour and goods in the quantities required by the expanding Hispanic sector; Indian tribes were living in tiny villages dispersed too widely over a countryside that was moreover being emptied by famine and disease. Spanish officials therefore devised a programme of Indian resettlement: the scattered Indian population was concentrated in towns and villages modelled on the Hispanic gridiron pattern; each family received a plot of land and the community as a whole acquired the title to common lands for pasture, as well as for both subsistence and commercial cultivation, proceeds from the latter going towards the funding of communal enterprises.

This programme was applied at different times in various regions. It was first implemented in Peru during the early 1570s as part of a more general effort by the viceroy Francisco de Toledo to impose the authority of the Crown on a part of the empire which had been in a constant state of turmoil since the Conquest. The economic rationale for this was the discovery of new silver, gold and mercury mines in the previous decade, which led to a demand for a regular and plentiful supply of labour. Viceroy Toledo therefore instituted his programme of resettlement so as to facilitate the collection of tribute and the supervision of labour drafts for the mines by Crown officials. The labour system was modelled on the Inca practice of the *mita*, a form of labour tribute in which Indian villages would contribute a quota of able-bodied men to work for the Inca state. Under the Spaniards the *mita* system for the mines became a very cruel burden on a declining Indian population. In Mexico and Guatemala, programmes of Indian resettlement (called *congregación civil*) were carried out in some regions over the last decades of the century, though no more than 16 per cent of the Indian population appears to have been affected. In New Granada, resettlement was begun in the 1580s and was accompanied by the creation of *resguardos*, communal lands reserved by the Crown for the Indians and assigned to the new townships.

The Spanish authorities were sometimes divided over the extent to which Indian culture should be preserved. Spanish missionaries, for instance, wanted to prevent the Indians from learning Castilian, because they feared that this would expose them to the evil moral influence of the Spanish settlers. But the Crown feared that such monolingualism would give the missionary orders too much power over the Indians. It therefore became obligatory, at least in theory, to teach Castilian to an indigenous population on whose loyalty the Crown could not yet fully depend. The result was that in the central areas, where Hispanic influence was greatest, many Indian communities became bilingual; in more remote areas, the mass of Indians retained their own languages.

The cultural transformation of the Indian world after the Conquest was a slow, patchy, irregular process. The terrible destruction wreaked by the epidemics of new diseases, the disasters of war, and the escalating demands for tribute on a shrinking population by often greedy Spanish *encomenderos*, drove a steady stream of Indians out of their villages towards the Hispanic towns and cities, where they were more rapidly acculturated. Those who remained in the communities – which were in theory protected by the Crown – were also subjected to Spanish influences, but their resistance to acculturation and their capacity for adjustment were very strong. In the middle of the seventeenth century, once the population decline was arrested, the Indian communities began to flourish under new bicultural conditions, though the trend in the long term was for individuals to move into the Hispanic world to mix and be absorbed into the more intensively hybrid, mestizo culture that was forming there too.

The Institutions of State

The monarch of Castile was deemed to exercise 'natural lordship' over all the territories of the Spanish Indies. The land and its fruits might be granted to individuals by the grace of the sovereign, but his subjects had no ultimate rights over these properties. The state that came into existence in the New World was therefore a patrimonial state, for all power and authority issued from the person of the monarch, and the institutions of that state existed for the purpose of implementing the royal will.

The foundation of royal government in the Indies was a gradual process, which began in the 1490s and was finally consolidated in the 1570s. In the early Caribbean phase of the Spanish Conquest, the affairs of the Indies had been handled by a subcommittee of the Council of Castile, to whom the governors of the various islands were responsible. As the government of the New World territories became more complex after the conquest of Mexico, a separate Council of the Indies was created in 1524. But persistent disorder, first in Mexico and later in Peru, led to the establishment of a viceregal system designed to assert the king's authority over his overseas realms.

The Indies, however, were juridically distinct from the kingdom of Castile. Just as Castile itself was composed of a variety of realms – León, Navarre and Granada, in addition to the realm of Castile proper – so too were the Indies considered to be a plurality of realms under the one sovereign. Indeed, the Habsburg conception of empire embraced a diversity of kingdoms united only by the Crown and the Church. The Indies were conceived as forming part of this mosaic of imperial dominions, although as new states they were far more closely bound to the will of the sovereign than the European possessions, where the king's subjects had evolved complex rights and institutions which restrained royal power. Through his viceroys and the royal bureaucracy, the monarch could exercise absolute power in the Indies – at least in theory.

For the purpose of administration, the Indies were divided into two viceroyalties. The whole of the territory to the north of the isthmus of Panama became the viceroyalty of New Spain, governed from Mexico City. The Spanish possessions in South America came under the jurisdiction of Lima, capital of the viceroyalty of Peru. But these territories were so vast that they were subdivided into smaller administrative units, whose limits were determined by a number of factors – geographical, historical, military and economic. The actual structure of Spanish administration in the Indies thus formed a hierarchy, in which each territory occupied a position in relation to Mexico City or Lima that reflected its importance within the viceroyalty.

The basic administrative unit was the province, which was ruled by a governor. In the initial phase of the conquest of a particular territory, the governor was an important conquistador who would be responsible for several new Spanish settlements and the region they controlled, including the Indian communities which lived there. Once the territory had been secured for the Crown, the governor tended to be a member of the royal bureaucracy, who also acted as a magistrate and supervised the collection of taxes. Provinces would come under the jurisdiction of an *audiencia*, a court of law, with certain administrative and executive powers, situated in the capital cities of the larger provinces. In the sixteenth century, *audiencias* were established at Santo Domingo (1511), Mexico City (1529), Panama (1538), Lima (1542), Guatemala (1544), Guadalajara (1549), Santa Fe de Bogotá (1549), Charcas (1559), Quito (1563) and Santiago de Chile (1565). The territories administered by an *audiencia* constituted distinct realms within each of the viceroyalties. For instance, Central America was known as the Kingdom of Guatemala, comprising the provinces of Guatemala, Chiapas,

Nicaragua, El Salvador, Honduras and Costa Rica, with its *audiencia* at Santiago de Guatemala.

All the *audiencias* came under the jurisdiction of one or other of the two viceroys. These viceroys presided over the two most important *audiencias*, those of Mexico City and Lima. At first, the viceroys also served as presidents of the lesser *audiencias*, but eventually these acquired presidents of their own, and the realms they administered were called *presidencias*, although the viceroy would retain the functions of military governor and the ultimate responsibility for matters of policy.

Alongside this structure of the viceregal *audiencia* and its satellite *audiencias*, there were territories whose economic, military or demographic importance accorded them a more autonomous status. Though nominally within the sphere of a viceroyalty, such territories were the responsibility of a captain-general who, in practice, dealt directly with the Council of the Indies in Spain. There were four captaincies-general – Guatemala, Santo Domingo, New Granada and Chile; each enjoyed a status intermediate between a presidency and a viceroyalty.

Royal administration in the Indies was thoroughly absolutist in inspiration and design. All government posts were appointive. Officials had some execu-tive and administrative powers, but matters of policy had to be referred upwards through the bureaucratic hierarchy until they reached the Council of the Indies. The Council would deliberate and consult with the monarch and then relay his decision back through the established channels, until it reached, if necessary, the lowliest official in the remotest corner of the empire. With the partial exception of the *cabildos* (municipal councils), there were no elective bodies accorded the constitutional right to represent the interests of the king's subjects in America; nor was there any machinery for controlling or supervising the finances of the state. The only way in which the king's sub-jects could express their views was either by directing 'supplications' to the monarch or by appealing against a judicial decision to a higher authority. The Crown therefore held a monopoly over the official political life of its realms.

No Spanish sovereign ever visited the Indies. The authority of the Crown was embodied in the person of the viceroy, who in consequence possessed something of the mystique of the monarch himself. The viceroy was charged with the execution of royal decrees, the administration of justice, the super-vision of royal finances, and with safeguarding the spiritual and material welfare of the Indians.

After the viceroy, the most important officials in the Indies were the judges of the *audiencias*, called *oidores*. The *audiencia* was the supreme court of law for the territories under its jurisdiction. It heard criminal and civil cases, and was the final court of appeal for cases from the lower courts, from ecclesiastical tribunals and from the various special courts dealing with the affairs of corporate institutions. The viceroy could not intervene in the purely judicial decisions of the *audiencia*, though he could supervise its proceedings to ensure propriety.

Unlike their counterparts in Castile, the American *audiencias* had certain administrative and executive functions which they fulfilled in consultation with the viceroy. Even though authority rested with the latter, the *oidores* of the *audiencia* were in a position to influence a viceroy's decisions and thereby participate in the government of the colonies. In this respect, the *audiencias* acted as councils of state and acquired a political complexion. Furthermore, as the supreme guardians of the law, the *oidores* could watch over the conduct of the viceroy and might report irregularities directly to the Council of the Indies. Since their tenure was longer than that of a viceroy, the *oidores* provided continuity in the government of the territory, and for this reason they were very likely to become identified with local interests. In the late sixteenth century, when the Crown had recourse to the sale of public offices, the *audiencias* were increasingly filled by American-born Spaniards, though rarely in the parts of the Indies of which they were native. Still, this trend further Americanized a very important organ of imperial government and provided the élites of the Indies with considerable sway over the royal administration.

Officials of the treasury formed another important branch of government. Each expedition of conquest was accompanied by a treasury official to ensure that the Crown received its share of booty. Once an area had been settled, the Crown imposed taxes and duties on the inhabitants, and their collection was organized by royal agents appointed to each important town. The viceroy was ultimately responsible for the collection of the king's revenues, and the accounts were scrutinized by the *audiencias* before being sent to the Council of the Indies. The main sources of revenue were the *quinto*, a one-fifth share of the value of all precious metals produced in the Indies; the *almojarifazgo* (import duty); the *alcabala* (sales tax); the Indian tribute; income from rents, Crown monopolies and enterprises; tithes; and a special tax raised to finance wars against infidels. In times of hardship, the Crown might raise additional revenue by resorting to extraordinary taxes, the sale of government posts, requests for special donations or forced loans.

The Crown also had the right to appoint all bishops and clergy in the Indies under the *Patronato Real* granted to the Catholic Monarchs by the Pope in 1508. Given the power and influence of the Church in Hispanic society, royal control of the ecclesiastical hierarchy provided the Crown with another arm of government, running parallel to the civil administration. Bishops were capable of intervening in the affairs of state, even to the extent at times of contesting the actions of the viceroy. But within the Church, as within the civil administration, there were competing jurisdictions between different institutions and organizations, which made for friction, and even conflict, between the secular clergy and the religious orders, between the religious orders themselves, and between the episcopate and quasi-autonomous institutions such as the Inquisition.

Tribunals of the Inquisition were established in Lima in 1570 and Mexico in 1571 (a further tribunal for New Granada was set up in 1620 in Cartagena), but the Holy Office did not play as central a role in the Indies as it did in Spain; it had no jurisdiction over the Indians, the danger of Protestant influence in America was remote, and Judaizing practices were not so likely to occur (except for a period in the 1630s and 1640s when anti-Portuguese sentiment led to prosecutions of crypto-Jews, of which there were a considerable number in the Portuguese merchant communities of the Spanish Indies). Its business, rather, was largely devoted to the punishment of blasphemers, adulterers, errant clerics and other deviants, and to the often ineffectual censorship of books. In this respect, it did still play some role as an ideological watchdog for the Catholic monarchy, though it was far from inspiring terror in the population; if anything, men who became lay familiars of the Inquisition enjoyed social esteem in their communities.

This multiplicity of competing offices and institutions acted as a system of checks and balances against the rise of any challenge to the Catholic monarchy's monopoly of legitimacy in its far-flung empire. In fact, the Crown employed a number of safeguards against the concentration of too much power in its overseas realms. High officials were restricted in their dealings with local interest-groups – they were forbidden to marry into local families, engage in trade or buy land in the territory under their jurisdiction. The Crown tended to appoint peninsular Spaniards to the highest posts – viceroys were invariably sent out from Spain; and even when American Spaniards were appointed to *audiencias*, they were likely to have come from a different realm within the Indies. The performance of an official was subjected to a review called a *residencia* and, from time to time, independent judges would be sent out from Spain or from another part of the Indies on a *visita* to investigate the activities of particular institutions or officials.

Such safeguards and procedures were intended to maintain the autonomy of the state in relation to civil society, to uphold the neutrality of the law in the face of vested interests; for the monarch had to adjudicate a host of claims, petitions and supplications from his subjects, and could not be seen to be partial to any one interest or to prejudice the rights of any group. There was also a degree of latitude given to officials in the application of royal decrees to local conditions. Discretion could be exercised as to whether rigid compliance with a royal command might not be impracticable or inadvisable in particular circumstances. An official would then reply to a directive from the Crown with the formula *'Obedezco pero no cumplo'* – 'I obey but do not comply.'

Absolute though it was, the imperial state was not monolithic; it employed a variety of formal and practical devices to achieve impartiality, even-handedness and flexibility. Yet over time, and in the vastness of America, the dispersion of power through so many competing agencies robbed the king's authority of much effectiveness. Royal edicts were whittled down or quietly neglected as they filtered through the maze of bureaucracy in the Indies. What is more, the opportunities for corruption were too great: public office was regarded as a personal patrimony for a limited tenure, and, with generally poor salaries, officials were tempted to use their position for private gain. Graft flourished whenever a financially straitened monarch put up govern-ment posts for sale – for a consideration, laws might be bent, judgements bought and public tenders secured. Viceroys were mostly upright and con-scientious, and the men occupying the higher echelons of the administration were on the whole honourable servants of the Crown, and yet the regulations forbidding involvement with local interests were generally disregarded; in practice, royal officials established close links with the ruling families and clans of the regions they administered. It was at the lower levels of government that abuse of office was most widespread, and here precisely where its effects were most pernicious. For it was in the provinces and in the countryside that conflicts of interest between the conquerors and the conquered were at their sharpest, and where the copious legislation protecting Indian rights – a cause to which the Crown was sincerely committed – was least likely, in consequence, to be observed.

The structure of local government reflected the juridical segregation of Indian from Spaniard, which the Crown had devised in order to ensure the protection of the natives from exploitation by settlers. Each race was allocated its own municipalities, offices and courts, and each jurisdiction was separately supervised by royal administrators. In the Hispanic sector, provinces were divided into *corregimientos* (administrative units) under a *corregidor* (also known as an *alcalde mayor* in New Spain), who resided in the chief town of the district and who was supposed to have come from outside the region. The *corregidor* had limited judicial and executive powers, beyond which he depended on the authority of the provincial governor and the *audiencia* above him. In each town of the *corregimiento*, there was a *cabildo* (municipal council), whose membership was drawn from the local inhabitants. For the most part, town councillors were appointed by the *corregidor*, and even where elections were held, only the most prominent *vecinos* of the town were eligible to stand. The result was that municipal government was more oligarchic than democratic – seats on the *cabildo* were monopolized by prominent families, who would pass them on to relatives or political clients, thereby reinforcing the relations of patronage that were endemic in the Indies. The *cabildo* could impose local taxes, allocate municipal land, supervise local markets and maintain order; such powers clearly served the interests of the ruling families. Wider representation was afforded by the 'open' *cabildo*, held in times of crisis – and so very infrequently – when a range of other local voices could make themselves heard.

Indian local government retained its traditional form of hereditary rule by chieftains until the middle of the century. From the 1560s the Crown began to introduce institutions based on the Hispanic model. In the *cabeceras* (head towns) *cabildos* were set up with similar powers as their counterparts in the Spanish sector. These councils were also oligarchic, which in the Indian context meant the continuation under a new guise of hereditary rule by tribal chieftains and elders. Nevertheless, the elective or appointive nature of municipal office tended to erode the hereditary principles of Indian tribal government. This erosion was hastened in some regions by *congregación* and *reducción*, the programmes of Indian resettlement undertaken by both missionaries and Crown officials which resulted in the weakening of tribal loyalties. Indian commoners, non-tribal residents and even mestizos eventually came to hold office in many *cabildos* in the Indian sector. Spanish-style municipalities thus contributed to the levelling down of Indian hierarchies and to a degree of acculturation in the long term.

However, the administrative reform that was to have the greatest impact on native life was the division of the Indian sector into *corregimientos*. The *corregidor de indios* was not a native but a Spaniard, and often an American Spaniard, in league with Hispanic landowners of the region. As the royal official most closely in contact with the Indian world, he was the man upon whom the entire Indian policy of the Crown most depended for its success. He was responsible for the spiritual and material well-being of the Indians and for the administration of justice, yet he was also required to collect the native tribute and organize drafts of Indian labour for use by the Spanish sector; it was these latter activities which invited the most appalling abuse. For the *corregidor de indios* was appointed for two or three years only, his salary was meagre and had to be drawn anyway from the Indian tribute he collected, and he was allowed to engage in trade. It was little wonder then that he generally regarded his brief tenure of office as a licence to extort as much wealth from the Indians as he could manage.

The institutions of state created by the Catholic monarchy in the Indies were modelled on those that worked well in Castile. Much was done to adapt them to the particular conditions of America, and the legitimacy of the Crown was unquestionably preserved. Yet, in reality, the efficacy of these institutions was badly undermined. Distance, diversity and the racial antagonisms of the Indies all played their part, but it was the financial weakness of the Crown in the last decades of the sixteenth century that did most to frustrate the ends of royal government in the New World. Ironically, the period in which the Crown was exerting itself to institutionalize its authority in America was also the time in which its financial resources were entering into rapid decline. In 1557, the year before Philip II succeeded his father, Charles V, the royal treasury had been unable to pay its debts. In 1575, and again in 1596, the Crown was in default. Philip looked for ways to increase his revenues from the Indies: he raised new taxes and duties, and even auctioned certain minor government posts to the highest bidder. But the fact was that there was simply not enough money to pay for effective administration overseas. Worse still, the empire itself came to depend on the flow of bullion across the Atlantic in order to meet its multiplying commitments on the battlefields of Europe. In the final analysis, the Spanish monarchy's imperial ambitions contradicted its genuine concern for justice and good government in America.

The Evangelization of the Indians

One of the principal justifications for the Spanish conquest of America was the conversion of pagan peoples to Christianity. The Catholic monarchy pursued this aim with the greatest seriousness. However, the Caribbean experience had been disastrous; the rapacity of the Spanish settlers, compounded by virulent epidemics, had decimated the Indian population. Some missionaries had begun to denounce the enterprise of conquest and even to question Spain's fitness to undertake it. So when Hernán Cortés conquered the densely populated kingdoms of Mexico, the Crown resolved not to dishonour Spain's divine obligation to bring the Word of God to the natives of the New World. In 1524 twelve Franciscan friars landed in Veracruz to begin the work of conversion. This number, chosen to commemorate the twelve apostles of Christ, reflected the idealism which inspired the undertaking: the Spanish missionaries set out in the hope of recovering the purity and simplicity of the primitive Church in their evangelization of the American Indians.

The outlook of the Franciscans was influenced by a mystical understanding of their enterprise as ushering in the last great wave of conversion of mankind before the beginning of Christ's thousand-year reign on earth. The millennialism of the Franciscans gave them an apocalyptic sense of urgency; it also contributed powerfully to the idealization of the Indians and to the impulse to shield them from the corruption of the Old World by segregating them as far as possible from the Spaniards. The natives were regarded as simple souls whose existence had latterly been revealed by God so that Christianity might renew itself in the New World.

The Franciscans were shortly followed by a group of twelve Dominicans in 1526, and then by Augustinians in 1533. The work of evangelization was begun in the Valley of Mexico, and, as friars arrived in growing numbers, the mendicant orders expanded to other areas, the Franciscans concentrating on the north-west regions of Michoacán and New Galicia, the Augustinians on the north-east, and the Dominicans on the south around Oaxaca. Other orders were sent out in subsequent years, the most influential being the Jesuits, who first came in 1568 and began to establish successful missions in northern Mexico and Paraguay. The Jesuits and the Franciscans were to pursue the missionary drive in frontier zones until well into the eighteenth century.

The task these very small groups of missionaries had to face was truly daunting: there were millions of Indians, speaking a multitude of unknown languages and living in a huge uncharted continent. Few precedents existed for carrying out such a mission of conversion. Initially, the friars' policy was to eradicate the natives' religion and teach the neophytes the rudiments of the Christian faith before baptizing them *en masse*. Idols, temples and native codices – regarded by the missionaries as instruments of Satan – were destroyed, and churches built by Indian labour on the site of the natives' holy places. These first, apostolic missionaries claimed great success in baptizing thousands of converts; they saw signs of God's favour in numerous supernatural occurrences and miracles.

Later missionaries, however, were less convinced of the Indians' enthusiasm for the new religion; they believed that Christianity would be properly received only if it were incorporated into the native cultures. They therefore began to learn Indian languages, producing lexicons and grammars of native tongues; they also studied the history of the indigenous peoples, as well as the customs and traditions of their societies. This unprecedented attempt to understand the alien cultures of the New World laid the foundations for the development of ethnology; indeed, the works of the missionaries remain valuable sources for modern research into pre-Columbian civilizations.

An enduring problem was that there were too few missionaries for the immense numbers of Indians who had to be evangelized and subsequently sustained in the faith. To alleviate this problem, the friars would travel from town to town celebrating Mass and administering the sacraments. They also established *doctrinas*, regular assemblies of Indians for instruction and worship at the mission stations. But in some regions the Indians were too dispersed or else their villages had been destroyed by the wars of the Conquest or emptied by epidemics. In such cases, the missionaries adopted a policy of resettling the Indians in *congregaciones*, specially designed villages where the natives could be taught the civilized ways of the Europeans and nurtured in well-ordered Christian communities.

The prototypes for these settlements were the two Pueblos-Hospitales de la Santa Fe – established by the humanist cleric Vasco de Quiroga near Mexico City (1532) and at Pátzcuaro, Michoacán (1538), of which he became bishop. These model towns were inspired by the ideal society described in the *Utopia* of Sir Thomas More: the natives followed a regime of communal labour on common lands, elected representatives to a *cabildo*, founded a hospital and schools, and observed the cycle of the Christian year with processions, rites and festivals. Quiroga was one of a number of Spanish Erasmian humanists who provided the intellectual impetus for the evangelization of the New World. The Franciscan Juan de Zumárraga, who was created the first bishop in Mexico in 1527, wrote a catechism for Indian neophytes and a brief manual of Christian doctrine for use in the missions. He also founded the Colegio de Santa Cruz in Tlatelolco where the sons of the Indian nobility were taught Latin, philosophy, rhetoric and logic. Under his direction, the Bible was translated into a number of native languages.

The missionaries also imparted a technical education to their Indian charges, teaching them new agricultural methods and the use of new tools, introducing different crop varieties, building aqueducts and irrigation systems to bring arid land under cultivation. However, the authority of the missionaries over their Indians caused annoyance to Spanish landowners, who required Indian labour on their estates and resented clerical criticism of their exploitation of the natives. The suspicion of the Crown was also aroused by the autonomy the missionaries sought for their Indian settlements; they refused, for instance, to have their charges pay tithes to the secular Church and resisted the transfer of responsibility for Indian parishes to the secular clergy. The missionary orders at times came close to formulating a policy towards the Indians at odds with the interests of the Crown, and which threatened to call into question the nature of Spain's presence in America.

Outside the central areas of Mexico the enterprise of evangelization proved even more difficult. In the far north the nomadic tribes were almost wholly resistant to Christianity, and the work of the missions proceeded at the same faltering pace as military pacification; Franciscan and Jesuit mission stations resembled the defensive Spanish forts (*presidios*) that dotted these wild frontier territories more than they did the Utopian *congregaciones* of the central areas. Indeed, the success of evangelization was in proportion to the thoroughness of conquest and political control. In Yucatán and Central America, where the conquests had been particularly disruptive, Indian receptivity to the new religion was lower than in the areas of Mexico pacified by Hernán Cortés, but a determined programme of *congregación* during the 1540s resettled most of the scattered Indians of the Central American highlands, though progress in Yucatán was much slower.

Missionaries arrived in Peru in the 1530s, shortly after Pizarro, but what with civil wars between rival conquistadors, the upheavals of the earlier wars over the Inca succession, Manco Inca's rebellion and other Indian revolts, evangelization outside the main towns did not prosper until the 1560s, when the viceroy Francisco de Toledo began his extensive campaign of pacification. In fact, it was the royal authorities in Peru who initiated the programme of Indian concentration in *reducciones*. By the 1570s the missionary impetus had begun to slacken – at broadly the same time as the drive to explore and conquer was losing its momentum. Even so, the arrival of the Jesuits after 1568 revived the missionary spirit in very remote frontier zones like the far north of Mexico and south-eastern regions of Paraguay, and in fact sustained it into the eighteenth century, as did other orders like the Capuchins, who came in the late seventeenth century and evangelized the backlands of Venezuela.

In summary, the Christianization of the American Indians was highly uneven. Difficult though it is to gauge the depth and quality of religious experience, the overall result of the heroic endeavours of these quite small bands of Spanish missionaries was a syncretism of Catholicism and Indian beliefs for large numbers of natives: beneath the externals of Catholic practice there often persisted an attachment to pagan rites and beliefs. Nevertheless, the balance between paganism and Christianity varied widely from one region to the next, and even between individuals no doubt. Sometimes pagan survivals might endure as little more than popular superstitions or dabblings in magic and sorcery, much as they did in remote parts of rural Spain or Ireland. In the Andes, on the other hand, the residue of pagan beliefs was far more evident and, in many secluded regions of America, pagan cultures survived virtually intact.

Still, there is no doubt that Catholic rites and devotions were observed in the vast majority of Indian settlements throughout the principal areas of Spanish rule. What is more, the sacramental character of Catholic belief, the cult of the Virgin and of the saints, the ritual of the Catholic liturgy, the opulence and splendour of religious architecture, art and music, undoubtedly appealed to the Indians and served to transmute pagan religious feeling into new Christian forms. A remarkable example of this is the cult of the Virgin of Guadalupe among the Indians of Mexico. The church that commemorates the appearance of the Virgin to the Indian peasant Juan Diego in 1531 stands on the site of an Aztec shrine to the goddess Tonantzin, Mother of the Earth. Similarly, the practice of penitential self-flagellation among some Andean peoples may derive from kindred acts of expiation in their ancient religions.

The missionaries themselves evidently had reservations about the effectiveness of their campaign of evangelization. In Mexico, there were early attempts to train a native clergy, but these were abandoned by the 1560s, and, thereafter, Indians were deemed unfit for the priesthood. Despite some efforts by the authorities in Rome in the early seventeenth century to encourage the recruitment of Indians, the clergy of the Indies remained white until well into the eighteenth century. Mestizos were also excluded from holy orders, ostensibly because of their illegitimacy – though there was clearly an element of racial prejudice, for the situation did not improve even after a papal dispensation for illegitimate mestizos was granted in 1576.

The result was that the Church remained a Hispanic and colonial institution and, for all their dedication to the Indians and their defence of native rights against the settlers, the missionary orders never relinquished a tutelary and paternalistic attitude towards the native peoples. They showed extreme reluctance, for instance, to handing over the Indian ministry to secular clergy, as had been envisaged in papal bulls of the 1520s, claiming that secular priests did not share their commitment to Indian welfare and would collude with Hispanic landowners in exploiting the natives. In this there was some truth, for the secular priests who began to minister to Indian parishes in the last two decades of the century were all too often negligent, extracting exploitative fees and dues from their parishioners.

The Catholic Church, in the last resort, could not escape the ambivalence towards the Indians that characterized the entire Spanish colonial enterprise in America. Embracing as it did the societies of the conquerors and the conquered, it subsumed within itself the tensions between the two races. Still, fundamentally colonialist though it may have been, it did as an institution adopt a consistent stance in favour of the humane treatment of the American Indians: it worked to relieve their suffering, and promoted a life of dignity for them where it could. Moreover, being so closely interwoven with the Spanish monarchy, the Church was to have a decisive influence on the shape of the state and society that were finally to emerge in the Indies once the period of conquest and consolidation was over.

The Transatlantic Link

Spain's commercial links with her growing overseas empire had been established in the 1490s as a monopoly trade between Seville and Santo Domingo on Hispaniola. From the Peninsula would come the people, animals and provisions required for colonization, and in return the settlers would send gold from the Antilles. After the conquest of Mexico and Peru, the transatlantic connection underwent some modifications, but its essential character remained unchanged: it continued as a monopoly trade between authorized ports in the Peninsula and the New World, conducted under the supervision of the state at the Casa de Contratación in Seville.

The Casa de Contratación was the supreme regulatory body for the Indies trade. Founded in 1503, it was responsible for licensing ships, organizing the transatlantic fleets, inspecting and registering cargoes, collecting taxes and duties, and receiving the royal *quinto* of gold and silver from America. So central was it to the transatlantic connection that it became a quasi-autonomous body advising the Crown on all questions relating to imperial trade, and acting as a court of law on commercial matters. The Casa de Contratación was charged, in effect, with ensuring Spain's monopoly of the Indies trade, and this monopoly was maintained by channelling all commerce across the Atlantic through a small number of ports, thus facilitating control from Seville.

In the Peninsula, a few ports were allowed to participate in the trade with America in the early sixteenth century, but none displaced Seville; only Cadiz was later to assume importance, especially in the eighteenth century. At the American end, Santo Domingo was eventually superseded by Mexico City and then Lima, each capital acting as the commercial and distribution centre for all the trade of its viceroyalty. Three American ports were authorized as points of entry and exit for fleets: Veracruz for Mexico and Central America; Nombre de Dios (replaced by Portobelo by the seventeenth century) on the isthmus of Panama, mainly serving Peru and Chile; and Cartagena de Indias for the hinterland of New Granada. Cartagena was also used as a refuelling stop by vessels from Spain, as was Havana in Cuba for the return traffic.

The transatlantic sailings were known as the *carrera de Indias*, and they followed set routes and schedules still distantly related to Columbus's original voyage. From the early spring convoys would leave Seville, restock at the Canary Islands and sail across the Atlantic, taking a southerly route which brought them through the islands of the Lesser Antilles into the southern Caribbean; this journey took roughly one month. From the outer Caribbean ships heading for Panama would sail on to Cartagena de Indias, where they would be resupplied, and then to Portobelo on the isthmus to unload cargoes bound for Lima and South America; other convoys sailed to Veracruz with goods for New Spain; both of these journeys taking another month and a half. For the return journey, convoys would pick up cargoes bound for the Peninsula at either Portobelo or Veracruz and would make for Havana, where they wintered before embarking in the early spring on the Atlantic crossing back to Seville, which took about sixty-five days.

After the early 1560s, when the export of American silver increased enormously, the Crown took further measures to control and defend the transatlantic commerce by introducing a fleet system under armed guard. All shipping had to join one of only two annual fleets authorized to sail for the Indies. The fleet for New Spain, known simply as the *flota*, left Seville in the spring for Veracruz, taking with it also some vessels bound for silver-rich Honduras and a number of Caribbean islands. The second fleet, including ships bound for ports along the northern coast of Venezuela, left in August for Nombre de Dios with South American cargoes; since this fleet was to bring home the invaluable silver of Potosí, it was escorted by some half-dozen galleons and consequently became known as the *galeones* fleet. Both fleets would winter together in Havana and return to Spain in the spring.

Other sea links were established with Africa and Asia. The African slave-trade was conducted largely by Portuguese and foreigners under licence from the Casa de Contratación. No set routes were followed, but slaves taken in West Africa were brought to different ports in the Spanish colonies, particularly to Cartagena de Indias, which developed a huge slaving market. After the conquest of the Philippines by Miguel López de Legazpi in the 1560s, a transpacific trade was established between Manila and Acapulco on the west coast of Mexico. Manila became a great entrepôt for trade with the Orient: spices, silks and chinaware were exchanged for American silver. The Casa de Contratación tried to control this trade by licensing only two galleons a year for the Acapulco–Manila run. Direct links with Peru were allowed for a while but discontinued after protests by the merchants of Seville, jealous as always of their commercial monopoly.

Until the middle of the sixteenth century trade between Spain and her American colonies was reasonably complementary. The Caribbean islands to start with, and later Mexico and Peru, received an influx of immigrants, seeds, animals, grain, oil and wine from the Peninsula and sent back gold primarily, some silver, and, on a smaller scale, sugar, hides and dyestuffs. After the great silver strikes of the late 1540s and 1550s in northern Mexico and Upper Peru, silver became the principal export of the Indies, and so it was to remain for the entire colonial period. Yet even here a broad interdependence was maintained for the rest of the sixteenth century, since the extraction process for silver required mercury, which was mined at Almadén in Spain and in the Crown's Austrian dominions (though from the late 1570s some mercury was obtained from deposits at Huancavelica in Peru). The need to import mercury from Europe, and the fact that this product was reserved as a monopoly of the Crown, contributed to the complementarity of the transatlantic economy.

However, there existed trends that would serve to unbalance the colonial trade in the longer term. The development of silver-mining was a powerful stimulus to the economy of many American regions, for the mining towns had to be supplied with food, clothes, building materials, tools and animals, especially pack mules. As this internal American economy expanded in the second half of the sixteenth century, it began to displace supplies from the Peninsula. The result was that Spain, unable to substitute its agrarian exports to the Indies with the manufactures and luxury products required by the American colonists, was progressively reduced to act as a mere entrepôt for exports to the Indies from other European countries.

The transatlantic trade was in the hands of merchant houses in Seville, Mexico City and Lima. This monopoly was confirmed by the Crown when in 1543 it granted exclusive rights to trade with the Indies to a guild of merchants in Seville known as the *consulado*. For the greater part of the century, the Seville merchants had branches in the viceregal capitals, but as the economy of the Indies boomed, these colonial offshoots began to operate in their own right; the merchants of Mexico City were granted their *consulado* status in 1592 and those of Lima in 1613. These monopolists at either end of the transatlantic trade contrived to keep prices high in the captive markets of the Indies by manipulating the flow of goods, thus guaranteeing massive profits (of up to 100-per-cent gross on many export items). American prices were also raised by the range of duties and imposts levied by the Casa de Contratación, whose officials worked closely with the merchants of the *consulados*. It is little wonder, then, that this restrictive official trade with the Indies was bypassed through extensive smuggling of European goods at lower prices.

Spain's inability to supply the manufactures for which there was increasing demand in the Indies, together with the artificially high prices created by its monopoly of trade, encouraged the participation of European merchants in the transatlantic economy. The Europeans tapped the Spanish colonial markets either by working through licensed Sevillian merchant houses to cream off the lucrative profits of the official trade, or else by supplying goods direct to the Indies through contraband. Spain's transatlantic link, moreover, had always been vulnerable to piracy, the old scourge of European and Mediterranean maritime trade. As the Spanish possessions in America grew in size, the attention of corsairs and privateers was drawn to the new opportunities for plunder offered by the Indies run, especially so after the 1550s, when there was a sharp increase in the quantities of American silver being carried across the ocean. In the last decades of the century European trading interests would converge with the military designs of Spain's enemies, and the commercial assault on the Spanish monopoly acquired overtly political ends.

It was Spain's growing involvement in the struggles of central and northern Europe that turned traditional commercial hazards such as piracy and smuggling into resources of international politics. For, as Charles V embroiled Spain in the affairs of the Holy Roman Empire, the religious and dynastic wars of the European powers were carried into the waters of the north Atlantic. Those countries which had cause to fight Catholic Spain on the battlefields of Europe sought to weaken her by striking at the true source of her wealth; and this, as everyone knew, was not her domestic economy but the silver she received from the Indies.

Even though it never accounted for more than 20 per cent of imperial revenues, silver was the fuel that drove the Spanish war machine. In the latter half of the sixteenth century, as the Catholic monarchy's finances lurched from one crisis to the next, the regular injections of bullion from the Indies allowed it to stagger on by using the promise of American silver as security for war loans raised with Genoese and German bankers. The Spanish Crown's chronic debt-financing of its military commitments thus became another channel by which the wealth of the Indies drained away through the Peninsula into the wider European economy. And Spain's enemies realized that if the supply of silver could be interrupted or cut off, then the Spanish military effort in northern Europe would quickly collapse.

For this reason the exploits of the privateers received the backing of states hostile to Spain. French and English pirates harried the Spanish treasure ships and took to sacking Spanish American ports. For the English, particularly under Elizabeth I, the attacks on Spanish trade and shipping became an extension of a more general struggle for religious and national freedom against the threat of absorption by Catholic Spain. In the 1560s Sir John Hawkins began supplying the Indies with African slaves in violation of Spain's trade monopoly; in 1568, however, he suffered a crushing defeat by a Spanish squadron off Veracruz. A raid on Nombre de Dios in 1572 marked the beginning of Sir Francis Drake's long career of seizing Spanish treasure and plundering the ports of the Indies. Drake's daring feats in the 1580s convinced Philip II of the need to improve coastal defences in the Caribbean. In 1586 the Italian engineer Juan Bautista Antoneli was commissioned to design fortifications for the main ports of the *carrera de Indias* – Cartagena, Portobelo, the island of San Juan de Ulúa off Veracruz, Havana and San Juan in Puerto Rico. These defences, though costly, proved sound against the pirates, but from the last years of the sixteenth century, the Protestant Dutch, who had been in rebellion against Spain since the early 1570s, took their struggle to the coasts of America, adding a massive burden to the woefully stretched budget of the Catholic monarchy.

By the end of the century the strains of empire were beginning to tell: Spain received a stream of silver from the Indies but could no longer supply the Spanish American markets entirely from her own resources. Instead, the Indies trade was being taken over by foreign merchants, either through the re-export of goods via Seville or through contraband, leaving Spain as little more than a middleman in the economic exchange between America and Europe. Yet, as the Spanish American economy grew less dependent on the mother country, one might ask why the settlers remained attached to a system that prevented them from trading directly with the world at large, kept prices artificially high, imposed heavy taxes to pay for remote dynastic wars and generally interfered with everyday business in countless small and pettifogging ways.

Though Spain was to become, strictly speaking, superfluous to the commercial exchange between Europe and America, the Spanish Crown organized the transatlantic economy in such a manner as to afford the state a central role in its operation. Since commerce was funnelled through strategic bottlenecks, the Crown was able to supervise every major transaction in the system. More important still, the silver-mining industry, which was the driving force of the American economy, was critically dependent on the Spanish state. At the point of production, Spain held important levers of control: the state organized the major supplies of Indian labour to the mines;

it enjoyed a monopoly of the mercury that was needed to process the silver ore; its rights to the wealth of the subsoil entitled it to impose taxes on production, which were varied to exert influence on output.

The entire trading system was, therefore, predicated on the authority of the Crown, and however much the Spanish-American settlers might have wanted economic freedom, rebellion against the king was barely conceivable; the subtle, and indeed critical, strength of Spain in America was the settlers' overwhelming desire to remain loyal to the Catholic monarchy. Even so, the foundations of the Spanish state in the Indies were not entirely solid; there were flaws arising from the circumstances of the Conquest – none so grave as to bring it down, but still deep enough to weaken it and prevent it from achieving full coherence.

The Foundations of the State in the Indies

From the outset Spaniards asked themselves by what right the Catholic monarch ruled in America. There were three main reasons why the Crown needed to establish a clear and just title to its dominion in the Indies. First, it had to ensure that its authority in the New World was perceived by conquistadors and settlers to be as legitimate as its authority in the Old. Secondly, after the conquest of Mexico and Peru, it was clear that the Indians of those regions were not 'savages' like those of the Antilles, but lived rather in civilized polities under legitimate natural rulers. It therefore became a matter of the highest moral and juridical consequence to prove that the overthrow of such native rulers was not an act of tyranny by the Spanish king but a justified and necessary act. Thirdly, just title to the possession of all the territories of the New World was required in order to deter other European princes from establishing rival colonies in America or from trying to conquer lands already settled by Spain.

There were two main arguments to support the rule of Spain in America. The first was based on the traditional right of discovery and conquest of new territory. The second was more complex and arose from the unique historical character of the New World. Here were territories peopled by natives who had never been exposed to the truths of the Christian revelation; the discovery of such innocent races was therefore taken to be the work of divine providence, signifying that the Catholic majesties of Spain had been chosen by God to fulfil the sacred task of bringing the faith to the Indians.

The Spanish Crown wanted these two arguments to complement and reinforce each other, but the immoderate behaviour of the Spanish settlers in the Caribbean islands soon revealed a potential conflict – the reality of conquest threatened to give the lie to the mission of Christianization. For the best part of the sixteenth century Spain tried to reconcile these two claims, but it never in fact succeeded in clarifying the issue of just title to the Indies.

The appalling abuse of the Indians in the early days of colonization in the Caribbean had become a matter of grave concern to the Crown. Conquistadors would share out natives among themselves and put them to work panning for gold in rivers or cutting sugar on plantations in conditions little better than slavery. As the natives expired, the settlers would organize slaving raids to neighbouring islands to replenish their labour force. To the alarm of many Spaniards, and of religious missionaries in particular, the native population appeared to be vanishing from disease and overwork. The Spaniards did not realize that the rapid depopulation was being caused primarily by the Indians' lack of immunity against disease, and moral disquiet among the clergy led to open condemnations of the behaviour of the Spanish settlers. Such denunciations could not go unheeded by the Crown. For if indeed the Indians were being ruthlessly exploited instead of being educated in Christianity, Spain's right to rule in the Indies would be seriously compromised.

It had become clear early on that the Indians needed to be protected from abuse by the Spanish settlers. Queen Isabella expressly forbade the enslavement of Indians and declared them to be free and equal subjects of the Crown; although they could be compelled to work, their labour must be remunerated by a just wage. However, the fundamental problem in America was that the Indians (both of the islands and, as the Spaniards would later discover, of the mainland) were not used to working for money wages, and if not coerced in some way simply reverted to the traditional subsistence economy of their communities. Some form of forced labour seemed unavoidable, and the *encomienda* system, which had been introduced by Nicolás de Ovando, the first royal governor of Hispaniola, appeared to be a fairly humane solution to the problem. Nevertheless, in 1512, Ferdinand of Aragon issued the Laws of Burgos which sought to regulate the *encomienda* and eradicate its abuse by unscrupulous *encomenderos*, though its provisions for fair wages and conditions of work for the Indians had scant effect.

What complicated the issue of Indian rights even further was the fact that the Crown had obligations to the conquistadors as well as to the Indians. Spaniards who had been involved in a successful expedition of conquest fully expected to be rewarded for their efforts with grants of privileges, lands and the labour of the conquered. Failure to recompense them would have constituted an injustice, and by ancient custom the conquistadors could have invoked what Mario Góngora has called a 'right of resistance' to the authority of the Crown.* This implicitly contractual notion of justice was of long standing in the Peninsula and had underscored the development of the Spanish state during eight centuries of the Reconquest. It remained deeply ingrained in the attitudes and expectations of the conquistadors of America and their descendants. However, to the irritation of the conquistadors, the Crown, supported by the meddling friars of the missionary orders, appeared to regard the conquest of America in a quite different light from the reconquest of Spain itself: the conquered Indians were to be treated not in a manner comparable to infidel Moors or enslaved Africans, but rather as vulnerable innocents requiring special care and protection. The Spanish monarchy's defence of the Indians thus courted the danger of provoking disobedience or even revolt by resentful settlers.

The nub of the question was the status of the Indian. If he was a free subject, how could he be coerced into labouring for Spaniards against his inclinations? On the other hand, it was obvious that the whole colonial enterprise could be sustained only by the labour of the native population. The Spanish state never resolved this dilemma. A solution was sought in the juridical separation of the rights and obligations of the two races, constituting Spanish America as a dual society divided into a 'republic' of the Spaniards and a 'republic' of the Indians. The necessary economic transactions between the two republics would be mediated by the Crown through the institution of *encomienda*: the Indians had an obligation to offer tribute in the first instance to the king as their *señor natural*, but then the king would grant limited subsidiary rights to receive Indian tribute to deserving Spaniards, who would be required in return to protect their Indians and pay for their Christianization by the clergy.

And yet, despite its efforts, the Crown could not make the *encomienda* work justly in practice. Denunciations of the system continued. According to Las Casas and his followers, it had become a mere pretext for powerful Spaniards to appropriate Indian labour and goods, extracting maximum profits by overworking the natives – even to the extent of renting them out to work for other Spaniards – while neglecting altogether their spiritual and physical well-being. For their part, the powerful *encomenderos*, led by the highly influential Hernán Cortés, Marquis of the Valley of Oaxaca and by now all but a grandee of New Spain, pressed their suit at the royal court, urging an extension of the privileges of *encomienda* to include perpetual tenure and feudal rights of jurisdiction over the Indians, for it was argued that only

* *Studies in the Colonial History of Spanish America*, pp. 74–9.

when the Indians became true vassals of Spanish lords would the *encomenderos* have a direct interest in promoting their welfare. The Crown, however, was chary of such arguments, fearing that the creation of a powerful feudal class of *encomenderos* in America might lead eventually to direct challenges to royal authority and a consequent slippage into the sort of baronial politics that had afflicted Spain before the advent of the Catholic Monarchs. It was, therefore, not in the Crown's political interest to strengthen the *encomienda*.

Nevertheless, caught as he was between conflicting pressures from the *encomendero* lobby on the one hand, and the Indianist clergy on the other, Charles V decided to refer the whole question to a special council in 1541. The council came to the view that the *encomienda* was inherently unjust and open to great abuse, and that the system should therefore be abolished. Accordingly, the New Laws of the Indies that were promulgated in 1542 included provisions designed to phase out the system of *encomienda*; no new *encomiendas* would be granted and, more drastically, the rights of inheritance associated with the privileges of *encomienda* were withdrawn: on the death of an *encomendero*, the tribute of the Indians allotted to him could no longer be passed on to a relative but would be paid directly to the Crown. The *encomienda* would therefore survive as an institution only for as long as the longest-lived *encomendero*.

The New Laws provoked an extremely violent reaction in the Indies. In Peru, as in Nicaragua, they led to open rebellion by Spanish settlers; in Mexico, violence was avoided only by the suspension of the provisions that affected the *encomienda*. Though it did not repeal the New Laws, the Crown allowed them to lapse, temporarily yielding to the *encomendero* interest. But it continued to undermine the institution: in 1549 tribute in the form of personal labour services by Indians for Spaniards was abolished; tribute was to be paid in kind not money. Some time later, *encomienda* tribute was required to be delivered directly to the Crown, which would then distribute it in monetary form to the *encomenderos*, the system thereby coming to resemble a form of royal pension with little direct contact between the *encomendero* and the Indians. Above all, the Crown saw to it that the rights of succession to an *encomienda* were strictly limited; it would allow inheritance for two or three 'lives' but rarely for longer. By the 1570s the *encomienda* as an institution had been 'tamed';* the Crown had not conceded the crucial right of inheritance, and this prevented the *encomendero* class from evolving into a genuine aristocracy.

* Lesley Byrd Simpson, *The Encomienda in New Spain: The Beginning of New Mexico* (University of California Press: Berkeley, 1950), p. 145.

At the end of the 1540s the controversy over the *encomienda* became caught up in the wider issues of Indian rights and Spain's title to the Indies. A treatise written by Juan Ginés de Sepúlveda, one of the most eminent humanist scholars in Spain, argued that the Indians of America were a barbarous race, possessing inferior rational capacities to the Europeans, and as such they could be legitimately subordinated to the Spaniards. This was a theoretical justification both of the Spanish title to the Indies and of the *encomenderos*' right to acquire Indian vassals. According to J. H. Elliott, 'Sepúlveda was arguing not for the enslavement of the Indians, but for a form of strict paternalistic control in their own best interests. This was an argument for tutelage, exercised, however, by the *encomenderos* and not by the Crown'.★

In August 1550 a great debate was held at Valladolid between Sepúlveda and Las Casas over the Spanish title and the status of the Indians. The former marshalled classical arguments, based upon the authority of Aristotle, for the right of Spain to conquer and impose Christianity upon the Indians, as well as to exercise rights of lordship over them. Las Casas, on the other hand, argued that the Indians could not be classed as barbarians by Aristotelian criteria, and could therefore not be legitimately subordinated to Spaniards. He did not, however, call into question Spain's right to bring Christianity to the peoples of America; in effect, he too was advocating a form of tutelage over the Indians, but a spiritual tutelage, based on persuasion and not on force, and exercised by the Church in conjunction with the Crown.

This complex debate ultimately concerned the issue of responsibility for the Indians. Who was to have the right to protect and civilize them – a neo-feudal aristocracy of conquistadors and settlers, as was implied in Sepúlveda's case for the *encomienda*, or the Spanish missionary orders supported by the Crown, as Las Casas favoured? The question was never settled: the *encomienda* continued to exist, though in a controlled and truncated form. Sepúlveda was denied permission to publish his treatise, and Las Casas could draw some satisfaction from the fact that the Crown continued to assume ultimate responsibility for the welfare of the natives, expanding its role in the colonies as the supreme mediating institution between the republic of the Spaniards and that of the Indians.

From about 1550 until the end of the century, the Crown exerted itself mightily to stamp its authority upon the Indies. Only in the last decades of the eighteenth century would there be a comparable effort to intervene so con-scientiously in the affairs of the colonies. Viceroys of the highest competence were sent out to bring order to the turbulent Indies, especially in Peru,

★ *Cambridge History of Latin America*, vol. 1, p. 308.

with its murderous factions of white settlers and its restive Indian peoples.

Everywhere in America royal government was extended and fortified: new *audiencias* were created, and *corregimientos* drawn up with separate jurisdictions for the Spanish and Indian republics. When labour service was excluded from the privileges of *encomienda*, the Crown took direct responsibility for rationing Indian workers among Spaniards through the device of *repartimiento*, a system of rotary labour drafts organized by royal officials. The policy of concentrating scattered Indian communities into rationally planned settlements, which had been pioneered in Mexico by early missionaries like Vasco de Quiroga, was generally adopted by the state; from the 1560s, royal officials transformed Indian community life by a sweeping programme of resettlement accompanied by the creation of Spanish-style municipalities in the Indian towns. At the same time the Crown took steps to curtail the power of the missionary orders, ruling that once native converts had received elementary instruction in the faith from the regular orders, they should come under the responsibility of the secular clergy, over whom the Crown could exercise greater control through its right of ecclesiastical patronage.

This comprehensive royal intervention in the second half of the sixteenth century was an attempt by Philip II to build a just state that would stand above special interests and serve all sectors of the complex society that was coming into being in the Indies. A noble and humane aspiration of the Catholic monarchy, it soon proved, however, to be all in vain. For this strenuous interventionism required human and material resources which Spain at that time simply did not possess. On the contrary, Philip's military commitments in Europe forced him to rely increasingly on the silver of America. But in the Indies economic power was steadily being concentrated in the hands of élites of *encomenderos* and rich settlers acting in collusion with corrupt royal officials, and the Crown could not afford to upset their interests if it wanted to collect the revenues with which to pursue its religious wars in Europe. It was, then, Spain's economic and financial weakness that finally betrayed the ideal of a just society comprising two republics held in balance by a wise king. After the death of Philip II in 1598 it would become impossible to curtail the entrenched power of the Spanish American élites.

And yet, if these New World oligarchies grew to be so powerful, did they ever constitute a threat to the king of Spain, as Charles V had feared the *encomenderos* might have become? In 1566 a conspiracy had been uncovered in Mexico City to reject Spanish sovereignty and place Hernán Cortés's son Martín on the throne of an independent Mexican kingdom. The plot, hatched by the young Avila brothers, had the sympathy of many *encomenderos* who were still resentful of the New Laws of 1542. However, the proposed *coup d'état* did not command much active support, not even apparently from Martín Cortés himself; it was destroyed without trouble with the public execution of the Avilas. A year later Philip II sent out a judge who organized an exemplary show of state terror, in the course of which other presumed ringleaders were tortured and hundreds of suspects gaoled. Afterwards the Spanish American élites would not countenance any overt disloyalty to the Crown.

On the other hand, they would continue to resist attempts by royal officials to curtail their very considerable *de facto* power. In the 1620s an intrusive viceroy, the Marquis of Gelves, antagonized vested interests in New Spain when he tried to break up a monopoly which controlled the supply of grain to Mexico City and kept prices of staples artificially high. The Mexican establishment, including the judges of the *audiencia*, closed ranks against this royal meddler and had him removed, after inciting a mob to attack his palace on 15 January 1624. Limits to the interventionist power of the Crown had clearly been drawn by the compass of oligarchic interests, even though the legitimacy of the Crown's authority was not called in question. This paradox was encapsulated in the traditional cry of protestors, both Hispanic and Indian, throughout the colonial period: '*¡Viva el Rey, y muera el mal gobierno!*' – 'Long live the king, and death to bad government!' It was a sentiment that nicely distinguished the king's right to rule from the competence of his servants to enact the royal will.

How, then, to characterize the true nature of the imperial state in the Indies? It was a legitimate state with imperfect authority; for it had been captured by special interests, whose actual power it nevertheless refused to recognize. The Spanish American oligarchies, after all, had failed to evolve into a legitimate aristocracy: they had not succeeded in turning the Indians into their vassals; they were allowed no representative political institutions; access to high government posts in their native regions was on the whole denied to them; no special privileges and few titles distinguished them from the common run of Hispanics in the Indies. As a thwarted ruling class, these élites had to exercise much of their power in discreet defiance of royal authority – indeed, by corrupting royal officials. This can be regarded as political liberty of a kind, but as Mario Góngora has observed,

> it was a form of liberty existing outside the framework of the State, in contrast to the liberty within the State existing in the European Middle Ages. Liberty in the Americas was not based on any well-defined notion nor on any new concept of the State: it was rooted in laxity: it was, in other words, essentially 'colonial'.*

* *Studies in the Colonial History of Spanish America*, p. 126.

Even so, why should such powerful oligarchies have paid lip-service to this colonial charade? Because it was surely in their deepest interests to do so. Not only was the Crown invaluable as a mediator of disputes among the Spanish American élites themselves, but it was precisely the massive legitimacy of the Catholic monarchy, supported as it was by the arm of the Church, that could best evoke loyalty to the established order from the Indian communities and the lower classes of Hispanics, blacks and mixed-bloods in the colonies. In the final analysis, the white oligarchies accepted their formal colonial status as the price that had to be paid for the maintenance of that other, very real internal colonialism of which they were the main beneficiaries.

In summary, the Catholic monarchy in the Indies presided over a two-tier colonialism – of peninsular Spaniard over American Spaniard in the first instance, and then of white over non-white. The sixteenth-century ideal of a dual society based on the republic of the Spaniards and a parallel republic of the Indians in fact degenerated into a form of unequal racial segregation. Mediated with difficulty by an enfeebled Crown, the system of the two republics came to have the unintended effect of keeping open the racial wounds of the Conquest. For the gulf that divided the conquerors from the conquered was never bridged; no integrated society emerged, no sense of common identity came to be shared by masters and servants. Instead, the facts of conquest ran like a fault across the foundations of the state Spain had constructed in the Indies. As contrary forces rumbled on below, large parts of that edifice subsided and even collapsed altogether, leaving here and there nothing more solid than a beautiful façade. Still, the essential supports – the Crown and the Church – remained in place, preserving the Catholic monarchy's monopoly of legitimacy intact. As a result, peace and stability reigned in the Indies for another two centuries. It was when this royal legitimacy was itself undermined in the early nineteenth century that the entire edifice of state came tumbling down, and the Indies were finally plunged into the kind of bloody anarchy and turmoil to which they would appear to have been fated by the intrusion of Spanish adventurers into America.

4. The Spanish Indies

==

Spanish Decline and Imperial Development

The seventeenth century saw the emergence of a distinctive society in the Indies. Far from being an offshoot of the mother country, what resulted was a hybrid growth – a Hispanic society still, but one whose roots were nourished by a different soil and on to whose parent stock had been grafted cuttings from other races and cultures.

The coming to maturity of this society was facilitated by the decline of the mother country. Spain's economic and military weakness led to a loosening of its hold over the dominions in the New World, allowing colonial society to develop according to its own internal dynamics. The most significant factor here was the expansion of the hybrid Hispanic sector at the expense of the Indian world. The process of Indian depopulation continued spasmodically until the middle decades of the century, but native communities were further debilitated by a quickening rate of Hispanicization of individual Indians. Another important factor was the arrival – beginning in the last years of the previous century – of large numbers of African slaves. This influx contributed enormously to the racial mixture, which was one of the most visible distinguishing features of Spanish American society. Above all, the relative impotence of Spain permitted the formation of powerful local oligarchies, which became the effective ruling classes in the many and diverse regions that made up the Spanish Indies. This was the age of the creole (*criollo*) – the Spaniard native to America. Even though the term 'creole' was not current at the time, it is widely used by modern historians because it serves to indicate the growing sense of separateness from their peninsular cousins felt by these American Spaniards in the course of the century.

Spain went into decline because of proliferating military commitments for which it could not pay. Mounting debts led to rapid inflation, compounded by the repeated devaluation of the currency by a financially desperate state. After 1621, when a twelve-year truce with the Dutch rebels expired, the continuing tribulations of war brought the Spanish monarchy close to disintegration. By 1640, attempts at economic and political reform had foundered, and separatist rebellions sapped Spain's strength from within: the Catalans were in revolt, while the Portuguese, who had been united dynastically with the throne of Castile since 1580, declared the Duke of Braganza sovereign of an independent kingdom.

To meet these challenges Spain needed the silver of the Indies more than ever. But rising fiscal pressure on the colonies in the form of imposts, forced loans and confiscations of bullion precipitated a crisis of confidence in the transatlantic trade: less silver was being sent to Spain by American merchants, and therefore fewer goods could be shipped back to the Indies via Seville. Confidence was further eroded by the vulnerability of the Spanish treasure fleets to foreign marauders. The Dutch had now joined the English and the French in their attacks on Spanish maritime trade, adding another massive burden to the defence budget.

In 1615 a Dutch fleet penetrated for the first time into the Pacific Ocean – thought of until then as a 'Spanish lake' – with the result that large amounts of silver had to be retained in the Indies to finance the construction of coastal defences along the newly exposed western seaboard of Spanish America. From the 1620s the Dutch began to seize territory claimed by either Spain or Portugal, both kingdoms being at the time united under the same sovereign. In 1624, and then again in 1630, they took rich sugar-growing areas in the north-east of Brazil and forced Spain to mount costly expeditions to try and dislodge them. In 1634 the Dutch occupied Curaçao and other Caribbean islands; English and French privateers did likewise, until the seas of the Antilles were dotted with bases used by foreigners to pounce on Spanish treasure ships or to run contraband goods into the Indies. The greatest single blow to the *carrera de Indias* was delivered in 1628, when an entire treasure fleet was seized in the Bay of Matanzas off the coast of Cuba by the Dutchman Piet Heyn. Business confidence in the transatlantic link collapsed entirely towards the end of the 1630s; in 1640 no treasure arrived in Seville.

The problems of the *carrera* were compounded by a steady fall in overall output from the American silver-mines. Peru was most seriously affected, after about 1603, but Mexican silver production also suffered a sharp downturn from about 1635. This decline was caused by shortages of mercury from Huancavelica and technical problems in the production process. Starved of precious metals, Spain slumped into an economic crisis much more severe and protracted than the general depression which overcame Europe in the middle of the seventeenth century. But did the Indies as a whole also undergo a depression? It was once thought that the difficulties in the silver-mining industry, the drop in the supply of labour, high prices and the collapse of the *carrera* were all signs of a deep economic crisis in America. The evidence is still not conclusive, but it now appears that no disaster occurred: while economic activity did slow down in the seventeenth century, particularly in mining, other sectors such as agriculture, industry and trade, both inter-regional and transpacific, did flourish, at least in many parts of the Indies. What is more, the fall in cargoes registered as arriving in Seville suggests that greater amounts of silver were being kept back in the Indies, not just to pay for defence but for investment in local enterprises. This was, after all, the great age of public construction and architectural embellishment in Spanish America – ports, fortifications, roads, churches, palaces and mansions were built in the main centres of Spanish settlement.

The slow-down in the official transatlantic trade, moreover, disguises the extent of contraband activity, impossible by its nature to quantify, but likely to have grown considerably as Spanish American capitalists and European traders tried to circumvent the heavily taxed and cumbersome Sevillian monopoly through the newly established foreign entrepôts in the Caribbean. As John Lynch observed, 'The crisis in the *carrera de Indias* occurred not because the American economies were collapsing but because they were developing and disengaging themselves from their primitive dependence on the mother country. This was the first emancipation of Spanish America.'*

The relative economic autonomy of the Indies was accompanied by the growth of the *de facto* power of numerous creole élites. The financial diffi-culties of the imperial state afforded countless opportunities for leading creole families to infiltrate the institutions of the colonial government and Church, or else bend the law to their own interests by showering favours on royal officials. During this period the landholdings of the most powerful creole families expanded to form vast *latifundia*. Great creole clans bought seats in their local *cabildos* and kept them in the family. The interlocking interests of government officials and local patricians produced monopolies in the regional economies: the best lands, the water supplies and irrigation systems, access to dwindling Indian manpower, licensed monopolies to provision towns with basic necessities – all fell into the hands of closed oligarchies.

The seventeenth century thus saw the efflorescence of a Spanish American ruling class, exercising its power in partial or tactical disregard of the law and with little sense of responsibility for other sectors of society. As for the Indians, and those living in tribal communities in particular, they were treated as *gente sin razón*, persons of deficient reason, uncouth and shiftless.

* *Spain under the Habsburgs* (2 vols., Blackwell: Oxford, 1969), vol. 2, p. 193.

Even the Spanish state now abandoned the pretence of raising the Indians to civil equality with the Hispanic sector; officially, they were still to be protected, but only because their wretched condition was perceived to be irremediable:

> First rhetorically and later (in the 1640s) juridically, they became identified as *miserables*, people recognized in the Old Testament and defined by the Emperor Constantine's jurists as disadvantaged – widows, orphans, and the like – who deserved public compassion and protection.*

It was a far cry from the vision of Indian destiny under Spanish tutelage entertained by Las Casas, Vasco de Quiroga, or, indeed, Philip II himself.

The Economy

Land and Labour

The seventeenth century is conventionally associated with the development of the hacienda, the great landed estate, which was the most powerful economic unit in the countryside and the pre-eminent source of social status. The hacienda was a peculiarly Spanish American phenomenon, not because it differed qualitatively from Iberian land holdings but because it represented the attempt to embody an Iberian ideal of land tenure within the legal constraints imposed by the Crown in the Indies after the Conquest. This ideal, as defined by James Lockhart, 'would have combined jurisdiction over vassals with vast possessions of land and stock'.† Moreover, 'aside from his mansion and numerous servants, guests, and vassals, he [i.e., the great nobleman] must have land, cattle, and horses, and various agricultural enterprises from wheat farms to vegetable gardens'.‡ But since the Crown had prevented the *encomenderos* from turning Indians into their vassals, Spanish American landowners had to try and realize that Iberian ideal of lordly self-sufficiency with the opportunities available to them in the New World.

The roots of the hacienda went back to the land grants of the Conquest. These holdings, known usually as *estancias*, varied in size, and in the immediate post-Conquest period they were mostly cultivated for subsistence, not

---

* Lyle N. McAlister, *Spain and Portugal in the New World, 1492–1700* (Oxford University Press: Oxford, 1984), p. 395.

† 'Encomienda and Hacienda: the Evolution of the Great Estate in the Spanish Indies', *Hispanic American Historical Review*, 49, 3 (1969), pp. 411–29 (p. 427).

‡ ibid., p. 424.

for commercial purposes. The larger the *estancia* the more substantial its labour requirements, but since the main sources of labour were the Indian communities, the landowner had to find ways of procuring drafts of temporary labourers to work his estates. Thus a pattern emerged whereby the estate would employ a small permanent staff of workers – known as *naborías* or *gañanes* in Mexico and *yanaconas* in Peru – and would then by a variety of means recruit temporary labourers, usually from surrounding Indian villages. This pattern did not alter in the course of the colonial period. What did change was the size of the estates and the methods of recruiting temporary labour.

The evolution of the *estancia* into the hacienda was a continuous process, responding both to social values and economic rationale. Large estates were associated with nobility, and the acquisition of noble status was a prime motive of the conquistadors and early settlers. Thus the trend to form ever larger estates was inherent in the social dynamics of post-Conquest society. In economic terms the growth of the estate was linked to the expansion of the Hispanic population in the Indies. As demand grew for agricultural products, landowners steadily increased cultivation of special crops or products to meet specific market demands, without giving up their drive for self-sufficiency and diversification of activities. The coexistence in the one enterprise of both subsistence and commercial agriculture promoted the formation of large estates. Another factor making for growth was the urge to corner markets by driving out competition. This monopolistic tendency meant that the larger landowners were constantly seeking to absorb lands of smaller farmers.

Enrique Florescano has described the economic rationale of the large estates.* Agriculture was a risky enterprise subject to unpredictable climatic fluctuations which could ruin a farmer's harvest. It made sense therefore to diversify the range of products produced on an estate. Unpredictable climates also led to varying prices, and so the temptation was to minimize the risks by reducing competition and achieving a monopoly position in the market. A great, self-sufficient estate was therefore the best insurance against an otherwise volatile rural economy. The best land on the estate would be used to raise cash crops. Of the remainder, some would be used to grow staples for home consumption, some to be pasture for herds of cattle or other livestock; certain lands would lie fallow, and yet others might be rented out to tenants in exchange for labour or a share of their crops. The very large estates, as occurred with the big mining complexes, manufactured many of

* *Cambridge History of Latin America*, vol. 2, pp. 171–82.

their basic necessities, such as farm tools, carts, soap, candles, leather and textiles, in order to shield themselves further from the market.

The evolution of the sixteenth-century *estancia* into the seventeenth-century hacienda was achieved through various forms of land acquisition. Royal grants of land after the Conquest were made on vacant plots, but landowners enlarged their holdings either by purchase or by encroachment into common lands, the royal domain or Indian territory. By the end of the sixteenth century the question of boundaries and titles had become so confused that the Crown tried to regularize the status quo by a device known as *composición de tierras*, which allowed landowners to acquire legal title to land in their possession by payment of a fee to the royal treasury. *Composiciones de tierras* were permitted on several other occasions, partly as a means of increasing royal revenues.

Since the acquisition of land was a piecemeal process, the hacienda that eventually emerged was rarely a vast, continuous tract of territory. Rather, it comprised a number of scattered holdings of varying size, interlocking with the lands of other proprietors or of Indian communities. This was particularly the case in areas close to towns, where land concentration was greater and haciendas could expand only by absorbing smaller farms or Indian commons. In such areas there would be constant litigation over land titles and boundaries; Indian communities tended to be very jealous of property rights and were often extremely litigious, as might be expected given the pressures on their communities from Hispanic landowners. So it was not the case that the hacienda invariably swallowed up Indian land. In regions like Oaxaca, Yucatán, Chiapas and Guatemala, the Indian communities were almost entirely successful in resisting the usurpation of their lands throughout the colonial period.

Haciendas were not easy to hold on to beyond one or two generations. *Hacendados* were frequently in financial trouble, burdened as they were with the obligation to keep their numerous progeny and entourage in the high style expected of the *gran señor* – for that was the point of owning a hacienda in the first place. Social prestige also demanded that large sums of money be donated to the Church – a widespread practice among *hacendados*. With profit margins generally low, great landowners were often mortgaged to the hilt, and a poor harvest or a long drought could well spell financial disaster for them. Moreover, Hispanic laws of inheritance, which required the division of an estate among all legitimate offspring, often led to the breakup of a hacienda into properties that were too small to be financially viable, and these in turn might have to be sold off to other, rising landowners. Only a minority of the very grandest *hacendados* managed to obtain from the king the privilege of a *mayorazgo*, a legal entail which allowed them to pass on their estates undivided to the first-born son in the family. Families with *mayorazgos* constituted the most select élite in the Indies.

Prey to such financial insecurities, *hacendados* took to politicking in the hope of consolidating their position: they curried favour with royal officials, bought seats on *cabildos*, placed relatives in government posts, and formed cartels with other producers to corner a market or drive up prices. Such were the internal pressures that created the oligarchic regimes which dominated much of the countryside. Still, the hacienda was not the sole form of landholding; in virtually all regions there existed many smaller *estancias* and ranches owned by Hispanics, mestizos and mulattos; a few of these might in due course expand into larger estates, or else they might be the residues of a dispersed hacienda. Land tenure in the Indies was in a constant state of flux – fragmenting or consolidating as some landowners rose in the world and others came down.

The basic pattern of rural holding in the Indies, then, was an estate employing a small contingent of permanent workers but relying otherwise on temporary labour drawn from the Indian villages. The methods by which temporary labour was procured from the Indian pueblos changed over time. Until the 1560s the *encomienda* was the principal means of getting Indians to work Spanish estates. The Crown granted the right to an *encomendero* to receive labour services as a form of tribute from a fixed number of Indians for specified periods of time. However, when labour service as an element of *encomienda* tribute was abolished, it was replaced by the system of *repartimiento*, whereby Crown officials were responsible for rationing and distributing Indian labour among Hispanic landowners for limited periods. Wage scales and working conditions were stipulated by the authorities but rarely adhered to in practice. The *repartimiento* system, however, started to break down in the early seventeenth century, when continuing Indian depopulation made labour so scarce in some areas that it became increasingly difficult for the state to identify the real labour needs of the economy. Landowners took to bypassing state-directed labour drafts by hiring temporary Indian workers on their own account for slightly better wages than would be offered under the *repartimiento*.

Haciendas tended to increase the proportion of permanent to temporary workers. In some cases these workers were attached to an estate through debt-peonage – the extension of credit to a worker by a landowner on the understanding that it would be paid off through labour. However, debt-peonage appears not to have been as widespread as was once believed. The more common situation was for a *hacendado* to attract peasants from nearby Indian villages to work on his estates on a temporary basis; gradually, some of these Indians would choose to reside on the hacienda as permanent employees, enjoying higher wages and more material security than the temporary workers; the *hacendado* would then seek to retain his workers by establishing paternalistic relations of patronage and loyalty, through devices such as *padrinaje* (godparenthood) and *compadrazgo* (shared godparenthood). These informal labour arrangements were more prevalent in regions where there was a high density of Spaniards, such as central and north-central Mexico.

In parts of Central America and in the highlands of Peru and Upper Peru, the *repartimiento* survived until the late colonial period and even beyond, for there were many fewer Spaniards to Indians, and the competition for labour among landowners was therefore not so intense. Another reason for the survival of the *repartimiento* in Peru, where it was known by its Quechua name *mita*, was that it formed the basis on which labour was recruited for the silver-mines. A state-directed rotary system of labour drafts for the mines and public works had existed in Inca times and was also well-rooted in Andean tribal traditions. In Mexico a form of rotary labour draft called the *coatequitl* had existed in the pre-Conquest period, but because the silver-mines of northern Mexico were outside the areas of traditional Indian settlement, free wage labour appeared in the mines by the end of the sixteenth century. By the 1630s Mexican haciendas in the central regions were also abandoning the *repartimiento* system.

Agriculture and Stock-raising

In the sixteenth century agricultural production was overwhelmingly an Indian activity, and the crops grown were still indigenous – maize, beans, potatoes and manioc – as were the techniques employed to cultivate them. This produce would find its way into the still small Hispanic world of conquistadors and first settlers through the tribute offered by the Indians to *encomenderos*. As immigration increased and settlements grew bigger, the Hispanic market expanded, and so did the demand for European foodstuffs – wheat, meat, sugar and wine. Those settlers who had received land grants thus had an incentive to produce for markets in Spanish towns, as well as for their own subsistence. In the Indian countryside a European agrarian economy was slowly forming in which the principal medium of exchange was money, while Indian produce still circulated through tribute or barter. Over time many Indian communities close to areas of Hispanic settlement would develop a commercial sector directed at the Hispanic towns and would thereby partly enter the money economy, though they always retained a substantial agriculture in traditional produce for internal consumption and still used barter within the communities. The relative proportions of Hispanic agriculture to Indian varied enormously between regions, but throughout the colonial period there remained many areas where Indian agriculture predominated, or at least existed in parallel with the Hispanic sector.

Still, it was the Hispanic sector which in global terms expanded physically and developed commercially. Naturally enough, it tended to be most concentrated around major towns and cities. The growth of great centres of Hispanic population exerted a strong market pull over a very wide radius, extending eventually well beyond the surrounding districts and into other provinces. Cities like Mexico and Lima attracted diverse supplies from distant provinces in their viceroyalties, as did the great mining towns like Potosí or Zacatecas. This rising trend towards larger markets made for product specialization in various regions and for a thriving trade between different realms of the Spanish Indies, which often competed with and undercut similar produce imported from Spain, as was the case with olive oil and wine. By the early seventeenth century the Indies as a whole were self-sufficient in grain and meat. Some agricultural regions also entered the international export-economy by specializing in crops or commodities for which there was a demand in Europe.

Product specialization allowed parts of the Indies with no mining industries to rise above subsistence economies and accumulate capital to support substantial urban societies. For instance, central Chile and southern Peru specialized in supplying wheat and wine to Lima and the major cities of Peru. Potosí received supplies of these products from the haciendas of what is now north-western Argentina around Tucumán. Tucumán also specialized in raising mules as draught animals for the mines of Upper Peru. Sugar cane was grown on the Caribbean islands of Hispaniola and Puerto Rico, in the coastal areas of central Peru and in tropical zones of southern Mexico. Hides were produced by the ranching economies of the River Plate, the central plains of Venezuela and northern Mexico. In the Peruvian Andes coca was grown, often by Spanish planters, to supply Indian workers in the mines, who chewed it to quell hunger and improve stamina. Paraguay specialized in *yerba mate*, a plant whose leaves were used to brew a form of tea consumed very widely in the central Andes and the regions of the southern cone. Cacao was cultivated along the coast of Venezuela for export to Mexico, and around Guayaquil, which supplied Peru.

The late sixteenth century saw the development of a significant export-economy in a number of commodities, although the range of exportable agricultural products was limited by the problem of perishability. Dyestuffs, for instance, were in demand because of the growth of the European textile industries; cochineal and indigo were the main Spanish American exports. However, in general, the volume and value of agricultural exports were well below that of precious metals. In the eighteenth century improved maritime communications made certain products, such as cacao and coffee, viable for export to Europe.

Manufacturing

Like agriculture, manufacturing arose to supply the growing Hispanic and mixed-blood population. But the potential for expansion was severely limited by the direct competition of better-equipped producers in Spain. Perishable agricultural products could not be imported from Europe, but textiles, tools, furniture and suchlike could, and so manufacturers in the Indies tended to supply the lower end of the market with cheaper goods. In textiles, for instance, which represented the most important sector in manufacturing, there were two sorts of product on the market – the imported cloth of good quality, known as *ropa de Castilla*, and the inferior material produced locally to clothe the mass of the people, the *ropa de la tierra*.

Textile manufacturing in the Indies did not develop until the end of the sixteenth century. Before that time there was not a sufficiently large market, for the Indian communities wove their own cloth using traditional materials and techniques. It was when the Hispanic areas became populated with large numbers of lower-class Spaniards, creoles, mixed-bloods and blacks, who wore European-style clothes, that a textile industry as such emerged. By that time too the flocks of sheep imported from Europe had grown large enough to supply the workshops. The crisis in the *carrera de Indias* in the mid-seventeenth century also helped to boost the industry.

Cloth was produced in workshops called *obrajes*, at their largest employing no more than about 100 workers. Because of the technical nature of the work, these *obrajes* required a skilled, permanent workforce, but the low profit margins in the trade and the scarcity of labour made recruitment difficult, as wages could not compete with those in mining or agriculture. This led to primitive forms of coercion, such as the use of slaves, convicts or Indians who were trapped into working off debts incurred through the advancement of wages or who were simply locked up in the factories. Though there were *obrajes* in most parts of the Indies, some regions specialized in textile production. In New Spain the major centres were Puebla and Tlaxcala, supplying the metropolitan areas around Mexico City; the town of Querétaro supplied the northern mining regions. In South America the major centre was Quito, where flocks of sheep and Indian labour were plentiful; its markets were in central Peru to the south and the gold-mining regions of New Granada to the north. A significant textile industry also arose in Tucumán, whose economy as a whole was geared towards the silver-mining towns of Upper Peru.

Another major industry was shipbuilding. It reached its full development in the seventeenth century, when competition from Spanish shipyards was reduced and new opportunities were created on the Pacific coast. On the Atlantic side, Havana and Cartagena, both large ports serving the *carrera de Indias*, were the main centres. But as the sea-borne cacao trade between Venezuela and Mexico prospered, Maracaibo became a secondary centre. The major shipyards on the Pacific coast were at Guayaquil, which supplied the ships for the sea link between Panama and Callao, and later for the growing trade between Peru and Mexico. Realejo in Nicaragua supplied vessels for the transpacific trade with the Philippines. The industry as a whole went into decline in the eighteenth century, overtaken by technical advances in European shipbuilding and by the increasing importance of European merchant shipping in Spanish America's international commerce.

Other forms of manufacturing were carried out by artisans and craftsmen in the Hispanic towns and cities. (The Indian communities produced their own traditional crafts.) With abundant local sources of timber, leather and precious metals, artisanship reached very high standards. Craftsmen were usually Hispanics and worked from small shops, employing non-white assistants and apprentices. These trades therefore gave an opportunity to urbanized Indians, free blacks and mixed-bloods to achieve economic independence by setting up on their own after serving their apprenticeship. However, the guild system which developed in the seventeenth century to monitor standards and control admission tended to exclude the non-white elements, though it was never entirely successful, so that many artisans were men of colour.

Mining

Silver

The silver-mining industry constituted the largest and most complex of all enterprises in the Indies. It was the engine that drove both transatlantic trade and the interregional economy in America. It was concentrated in two areas – north-central Mexico around Zacatecas and Guanajuato, and the highlands of Upper Peru (modern Bolivia) – though there were significant secondary areas in Honduras and the Peruvian Andes. Silver-mining required massive, long-term capital investment, a large labour force, technical expertise and a high degree of social and economic organization to sustain the infrastructure of an industry situated in difficult territory, such as the freezing altitudes of the Andes or, in the case of Mexico, in remote underpopulated regions exposed to harassment by hostile Indian tribes. The Spaniards were able, none the less, to make a success of the industry through a combination of private initiative and state action.

The silver-mines of Mexico were discovered in the early 1540s in areas which had not formed part of the Aztec empire and where there were few sedentary Indians. The resulting shortage of labour posed a problem which was resolved by resettling *naborías* (Indians unattached to a community) from the central areas and by importing small numbers of black slaves – who were expensive – for skilled activities. Mexican mineworkers became rapidly Hispanicized, intermingled with other races and quickly evolved into a racially mixed, free-wage and specialized proletariat.

The situation in Upper Peru was very different. Here the mines were situated in densely populated areas of the Andes which had formerly been part of the Inca empire and where there was a long tradition of silver-mining. For instance, the Spaniards adapted the indigenous *huayra* method of harnessing the high winds of the Andes to ventilate the ovens used in the smelting process. There was also the *mita* labour system, which the Spaniards retained and expanded after the discovery in 1545 of the Cerro Rico at Potosí, the richest minefield in the Indies.

The bulk of Peruvian mineworkers, unlike the Mexicans, were, in fact, Indian peasants from the communities, recruited for temporary labour service every few years. They were therefore still closely bound to their ethnic roots, spoke little Spanish, if any, and their work in the mines formed part of their tribute obligation to the Crown. Indeed, the *mita* for the silver-mines was an awesome operation of state-directed labour. Over 13,000 Indian peasants from villages all over the central Andes – an area extending about 800 miles from north to south and about 250 miles from east to west – were annually assembled by their *caciques* under the supervision of Hispanic *corregidores de indios* and marched off in procession with families and belongings to pluck the precious ore from the great silver-mountain at Potosí.

Ownership of mines was invariably in private hands. Initially mine-owners were wealthy *encomenderos*, who had the capital to invest in production. But

as the surface deposits became exhausted within a few years and greater
technical expertise was required to work deeper veins, mine-owners tended
to be men who had risen within the industry. Running a mine was an
operation that called upon extensive resources. A mining camp, comprising
the shaft itself and a refinery, was a largely self-sufficient economic unit
employing both permanent and temporary labour – much like an agricultural
hacienda in this respect. It provided for many of its ancillary needs – growing
crops, raising animals, gathering its own fuel and manufacturing some of its
equipment. The permanent staff was trained in skilled work such as maintaining shafts, drainage and ventilation systems; temporary workers extracted
the ore from the pits. Human labour was supplemented by other sources of
power: at Potosí a system of reservoirs was constructed to provide water-
power; otherwise, mules and horses were used, particularly in the Mexican
mines, where water was scarce. A vital part of the operation was the refining
process, which used a technique of amalgamation with mercury invented by
a Spaniard; this permitted the mining of less pure ores, thus enormously
expanding output potential.

The Crown played a key role in the mining industry. Possessing the rights
to the wealth of the subsoil, it imposed a tax of a one-fifth share of all
silver produced, but this proportion was varied according to economic
circumstances, and could sometimes be reduced to one-tenth in order to
stimulate production. Tax collection in the silver industry was relatively
efficient, because the supply of mercury – essential to the refining process –
was a Crown monopoly mined only in Almadén in Spain and Huancavelica
in Peru; the true output of silver could therefore be estimated fairly accurately
by correlating the volume of mercury supplied to the mines with the amount
of silver actually declared by mine-owners for tax assessment. In Peru, of
course, the Crown's involvement in the industry extended to the supply of
labour through the *mita* service, which was organized by royal officials.

The output of silver rose sharply in the late 1570s, following the introduction of the mercury amalgamation process, and reached its peak in the
years between 1610 and 1645, after which it entered into a decline until the
end of the century. This downturn was not directly related to the decline in
the Indian population, as was once believed. The supply of labour to the
mines held up well, thanks to the *mita* in Peru and the specialist, Hispanicized
workforce in Mexico. The fall was due, rather, to technical gearing problems – the need for deeper shafts, better drainage, the opening of new seams –
which resulted in a time-lag between the mobilization of the huge capital
resources required for these purposes and the eventual return on the investment in improved output. The Mexican mines also suffered a shortage of

mercury when imports from Almadén were diverted to Potosí to compensate for declining productivity at Huancavelica.

The industry recovered in the early 1700s, with output rising steadily until it reached a peak in the last decades of the century. The Mexican mines now outstripped Peru's in production: they had a more modern, specialist workforce, they received supplies of mercury from Almadén which were cheaper and more plentiful than those from Huancavelica, and they enjoyed better access to the Atlantic coast and therefore to the European market. Moreover, Mexico City had developed a sophisticated financial system capable of delivering the enormous capital resources required to invest in the technical development of the mines. Some Mexican mines had grown to massive dimensions: the great Valenciana mine at Guanajuato employed about 3,000 workers, and had shafts approximately 2,000 feet deep and 100 feet in circumference.

By contrast, the Peruvian industry suffered severe disruption when Potosí and the other important mines in Upper Peru were reassigned in 1776 to the newly created viceroyalty of Río de la Plata, specifically to improve access for Andean silver to the Atlantic via Buenos Aires. But the result was that established economic and financial ties with Lima were broken and the readjustment to new conditions affected output. Another disadvantage was the archaic system of labour recruitment; roughly a quarter of mine-workers were still pressed into forced labour under the *mita* system. South American production never caught up with Mexico's, but it did, nevertheless, recover gradually from its recession of the latter half of the seventeenth century. By the end of the colonial period the silver-mining industry as a whole was enjoying a boom, and this stimulated the other sectors of the Spanish American economy.

Gold

Until the middle of the sixteenth century gold had been the most sought-after commodity in the Indies. The incentive to organize *entradas* into unexplored regions was largely provided by the prospect of finding new sources of the yellow metal. But the deposits actually discovered, whether in the islands of the Caribbean, Mexico or Peru, were never substantial enough to create a mining industry over a long period. Most deposits were found in riverbeds and had to be extracted by the somewhat haphazard method of panning sand and gravel.

However, a gold-mining industry that lasted throughout the colonial period was developed in the north-western region of New Granada, in the districts of Antioquia, Popayán and El Chocó. As in the Caribbean, these gold deposits were first exploited using Indian labour, but their numbers declined swiftly through a combination of disease and overwork. Towards the end of the sixteenth century they were replaced by African slaves imported through Cartagena.

Compared to silver-mining, the industry was volatile and speculative; it mostly took the form of placer-mining along riverbeds by gangs of black slaves under Hispanic overseers. The life of these slaves was harsh, and the mortality rate was high; but some were able to retain a share of the gold they had found, and so buy their freedom and set up on their own as prospectors. Hispanic owners of large slave-gangs were able to lead lives of considerable luxury in the major towns, where their social standing was comparable to that of landowners, merchants and royal officials. However, the yield from gold-mining never approached that of silver, and the importance of the industry within the imperial economy was further reduced by the difficulty of assessing production for tax purposes.

Still, the wealth from gold-mining afforded New Granada a greater degree of economic autonomy from both Mexico and Peru than any other region of the Indies. This was a major factor in its eventual elevation in status from captaincy-general to full viceroyalty in 1739. But gold, though it gave New Granada independent economic weight, never became central to the economy of what was in reality a huge territory whose geographical features made for extreme regional diversity and economic fragmentation.

Other gold-mining regions were to be found in Chile's north-central region, the Norte Chico; in New Spain around Guadalajara and in some northern areas like San Luis Potosí, Guanajuato, Durango and Chihuahua; and in districts of Peru and Upper Peru, where, as in Mexico, gold deposits were sometimes found together with silver. Gold production went into a depression everywhere in the middle of the seventeenth century, but like silver-mining, recovered in the following century.

Merchants and Commerce

For most of the sixteenth century, the major commercial route of the Indies was the transatlantic link with Seville, but the expansion of Spanish settlement created secondary routes of commercial distribution and exchange. Then, as the *carrera de Indias* passed through its crisis in the middle and late seventeenth century, commercial links between the different regions of the New World were strengthened. By this time a new oceanic link between Acapulco in

New Spain and Manila in the Philippines had also been established. The Crown authorized twice-yearly sailings of the Manila galleons, which exchanged silver from Mexico for silks, porcelain, spices and other luxuries imported into Manila from the Far East. Peru entered this Pacific nexus indirectly, by trading for Oriental goods in Mexico, thereby reinforcing the commercial ties between the capitals of the two viceroyalties.

Another commercial activity of growing importance in the seventeenth century and thereafter was contraband with European nationals in contravention of the Spanish trade monopoly. This was concentrated in two regions: the Caribbean basin, as we have seen, and the River Plate area, where Buenos Aires, in addition to receiving African slaves from Portuguese traders for the mines and plantations of Peru, became a centre for the illegal export of silver from Potosí through the Portuguese contraband entrepôt of Colônia do Sacramento on the opposite shore of the River Plate estuary.

The trade monopoly that Spain endeavoured so strenuously to maintain placed merchants engaged in transatlantic commerce in a uniquely powerful position within the colonial economy. They were the main beneficiaries of the restricted imperial trade, and so great were their profits thanks to inflated monopoly prices that they were eventually to acquire a high patrician status in a seigneurial society that otherwise despised commercial dealings.

Transatlantic commerce was at first dominated by the merchant houses of Seville, which sent out agents to the licensed American ports to deal with the other end of the trade. These agents would sell European products wholesale either to other merchants in the viceregal capitals or at the great trade fairs held at Veracruz and Jalapa in Mexico, and at Nombre de Dios and Portobelo on the isthmus of Panama. Sometimes they would be involved in supplying the larger regional cities and mining towns. Essentially, therefore, these transatlantic merchant houses would be involved in only the highest spheres of commerce, buying and selling European goods in exchange for the silver and gold of the Indies, and later participating in the luxury transpacific trade with Manila, or in the direct commerce between Mexico City and Lima, financed as it was by large amounts of Peruvian silver.

By the early seventeenth century the merchant houses of the colonial capitals had become independent of those in Seville. Some of the great merchants in the Indies were creoles, but the majority were *peninsulares*. These latter acted as effective intermediaries between Spain and the colonies. Although they tended to marry into creole families, they retained strong family connections in the Peninsula. In fact, there existed a curious practice of inviting young relatives to come over from Spain and work in the business; these younger *peninsulares* would then marry their creole cousins and take over the running of the firm; eventually, they, in turn, would send for a young relative from the mother country. Because their creole sons would move into other activities – such as running a hacienda or a mining operation – the peninsular merchants were closely connected to the creole élites, even while maintaining direct ties with Spain.

Another reason for the economic power of the transatlantic merchants was their possession of liquid capital, which made them important sources of credit in an economy where the major producers – mine-owners and *hacendados* – were in constant need of cash. The merchants, for instance, would loan mining entrepreneurs the capital required for investment in plant on the promise of being repaid in silver. Gearing problems and technical improvements during the seventeenth century required large infusions of capital, and so merchants became closely involved in the financing of silver-mining, often obtaining monopoly rights to provision mining towns or to purchase silver for minting.

By the eighteenth century the great merchant houses were acting as bankers to the creole élites. They provided investment funds for the mining industry, some of the merchants actually owning large mining complexes themselves. The lordly *hacendados* came to them to be tided over depressions in the rural economy. Even royal administrators were indebted to them for sums borrowed to purchase their offices, sums which they hoped to pay back by taking full advantage of their position. The international import–export merchants thus came to form closed circles, jealous of their considerable privileges. Following their counterparts in Seville, the merchants of Mexico City (in 1592) and Lima (in 1613) were granted royal licences to create *consulados*. Other such *consulados* were formed in the eighteenth century in secondary cities such as Caracas, Buenos Aires and Havana, where important long-range commerce was conducted.

Enjoying less social prestige than the transatlantic merchants, although they too were often peninsular Spaniards, were those merchants who were involved in interregional and regional trade. Their function was to supply the regions with the merchandise bought from the transatlantic houses in Mexico City and Lima, or to distribute goods from regional capitals to provincial towns. Petty merchants, or *tratantes*, operated at a very local level, provisioning Indian barrios in the towns and mining settlements and also buying up the products of Indian villages or of very small producers and distributing these in a wider provincial market.

The Church

In the Indies, as in Spain, the Church participated in the economy as the major corporate owner of land, real estate and capital after the Crown, and as the chief provider of educational and welfare services. Its enormous revenues consisted of tithes paid by the entire population, white and non-white, rents from its considerable properties, and voluntary donations from the faithful. These donations were usually bequests of money or property by a lay person, endowments from rich benefactors and dowries for daughters entering a religious order. Each diocese and religious house received such gifts from its parishioners or supporters, and degrees of wealth would vary widely between them. Naturally, these enormous capital assets were put to use in the economy; they were not 'unproductive', even though they were not invested with a view to maximum profitability; huge sums were lavished on the construction of churches and convents, and on the *ornato del culto*, religious art and ornamentation, which were often sumptuous.

Church capital entered the secular economy through two principal channels. Like the merchant community, the Church acted as a major financial institution, providing laymen with credit and investment capital. Loans mostly took the form of mortgages on property over a long term and at low rates of interest. Alternatively, a diocese or religious house might receive bequests of haciendas, mines or plantations, and these could be leased out or managed directly by the clergy. Religious orders, which were often in charge of Indian communities, might employ these Indians to work their properties; in other cases ecclesiastical estates would receive their share of *repartimiento* workers or employ wage labour. Such enterprises tended to be managed very efficiently and were perhaps among the most vigorous and profitable in the colonies. The accumulation of Church land was considerable because it was held in mortmain and, unlike secular holdings, could not be alienated by individuals.

The other major economic function of the Church was as a provider of education, health care and poor relief to the general population. A great part of its income and manpower was employed in these activities. Religious orders such as the Jesuits and the Dominicans would use profits from their haciendas to finance their schools, seminaries and colleges. A large number of orders, male and female, worked on this basis, running educational and training establishments which were fee-paying for the wealthy but free for the poor. Others operated hospitals, hospices for the mentally ill and the dying, poor houses, orphanages, shelters for homeless girls, and suchlike. The Church therefore played an important economic role as a circulator of

capital, as a profit-making concern in some areas of the economy, and as a
supplier of social services.

Society

The division of the Indies into two juridically distinct 'republics' of Spaniards
and Indians remained a basic feature of social organization throughout the
colonial period. However, this bipartite social pattern became progressively
more complicated as a result of two factors. First, there was a constant
and even accelerating drift by Indians towards Spanish urban areas, and,
conversely, growing Hispanic influence in the Indian communities. Secondly,
there occurred an increasing intermixture of the races, to which the influx
of large numbers of African slaves to many parts of the empire contributed.
Even so, the institutional division remained between a Hispanic society and
a clearly separate Indian sector comprising many and diverse communities –
a distinction which has in practice persisted to this day.

The Republic of the Spaniards

The Hispanic society that emerged in the Indies was shaped by the circumstances of the Conquest. The distribution of rewards after an expedition
of conquest created a rudimentary social hierarchy, which was expressed in
the physical layout of the towns that the conquistadors were required to
found. The result was the creation of a seigneurial society led by a natural
aristocracy composed of those Spaniards who had received the biggest
land grants and the greatest *encomiendas*. Throughout the colonial period,
possession of land was to be the single most important criterion of social
eminence: the larger the estate the higher the social status. The evolution of
the hacienda in the seventeenth century and beyond owed its fundamental
stimulus to this aspiration of all Hispanics in the Indies to achieve the noble
status implicit in being a large landowner.

  Nevertheless, the concept of nobility was inherently unstable because
there were very few fixed symbols of status, other than wealth, that could
differentiate the aristocrat from the commoner. The Crown, which was the
true source of nobility, had refused to concede the traditional privileges of
an aristocracy to the natural ruling class of the Indies. This accounted for the
undercurrents of resentment and grievance against the mother country that
existed among the creoles and which surfaced from time to time throughout

the colonial period. The *encomenderos* had failed in their bid to convert the vanquished Indians into their vassals and lost the right to receive Indian tribute in the form of labour; they were not even permitted to keep as a hereditary privilege the limited rights to Indian tribute that were conceded in *encomienda*. They were also denied both a voice in the governing of the state and right of access to the higher echelons of Crown service. Unlike the gentry in the Peninsula they could not distinguish themselves from the lower orders by their exemption from direct taxation. In Spain commoners paid a head tax called the *pecho*, while noblemen from hidalgos upwards were exempt from it. In America there was no such distinction, for all Spaniards and creoles were free of any head tax; it was the Indians alone who paid direct tribute to the Crown. Finally, the Crown accorded American notables very few titular honours. Other than the earliest discoverers and conquerors, such as Columbus, Cortés and Pizarro, few creoles were awarded titles. In the seventeenth century some of the most eminent creole families were ennobled, others were admitted into one of the four military orders of chivalry, but such honours were granted very sparingly by the Crown. By the very nature of its foundation, Spanish American society was seigneurial and status-ridden, yet it lacked the means effectively to institutionalize differences in social status.

The creole élites had to fall back on less well-defined symbols of status – landed wealth, racial purity and reputation. The standing conferred by landownership can be appreciated by the fact that merchants and mine-owners, once they became sufficiently wealthy, would invariably purchase a hacienda in order to acquire social prestige. This applied also to officials in Crown service. Yet, as we have seen, haciendas were not financially secure enterprises, and so whatever nobility a landed estate conferred could be lost through financial ruin.

A white skin was an indispensable qualification for nobility, for any taint of Indian or African blood would just as surely diminish a creole's status as suspicion of Jewish ancestry compromised the nobility of a peninsular Spaniard's lineage. Medieval Spanish concepts of 'purity of blood' were thus transferred to the Indies, but given new meaning in a markedly different racial environment: whiteness distinguished those who belonged to the race of the conquerors from the conquered or the enslaved. Hence the obsessive interest shown by American Spaniards in classifying and ranking the various permutations of race (see below). But even racial purity was an unreliable guide to social eminence, for by the late seventeenth century miscegenation had become so widespread that very few families of *hacendados* were totally free of mixed blood. Since whiteness was no longer a sufficient criterion of

superiority, it had to be supplemented, or the lack of it compensated for, by
other symbols of social quality – the most powerful of which was the
pedigree or reputation of a family.

The surest source of reputation was *mando*, the power to command
subordinates and bestow favours on clients: it was the closest a socially
eminent creole could come to the condition of the European aristocrat who
had rights of jurisdiction over vassals. *Mando* was necessarily more diffuse
and could be exercised in different spheres. Thus, the higher clergy, the great
mine-owners and the very wealthy transatlantic merchants possessed *mando*
and could belong to the upper class. The hacienda, in a sense, was an accessory
of *mando*, not its source; it was the theatre in which a man of authority,
whatever the origins of his wealth, could represent to others the extent of
this authority in the number of his dependants, clients, retainers, servants and
workers. Because it lacked the true stamp of royal approval, nobility in the
Indies was highly gestural and charismatic – a matter of striking the right
attitudes through lavish acts of generosity, disinterested hospitality, con-
spicuous consumption or displays of gallantry and honour. Thus the 'non-
economic' behaviour of the creole upper class – taking out a large mortgage
for no other purpose than to endow a chapel, say – was no arbitrary
indulgence, but a social performance whose object was to advertise social
rank.

The quest for nobility had to be undertaken also in the field of politics,
and was yet another incentive for oligarchic practices: the unlicensed grandees
of colonial society sought to maintain their reputation by forging alliances
through marriage with other distinguished families; they would also secure
for their kinsmen positions of prominence in society by purchasing a seat in
the *cabildo*, endowing a chaplaincy for them, obtaining a position in the royal
bureaucracy, and so on. Once established, a great family or clan was a social
entity which was capable in itself of conferring high status on its individual
members, but the family as a whole had to maintain its standing from one
generation to the next. Pedigree came to play a part in defining aristocratic
status, though its quality was always more evanescent in America than in
Europe.

At the apex of the social pyramid in any Hispanic region were clusters of
interrelated creole families enjoying undisputed patrician status. Immediately
below them was a varied class of families which had not attained the same
prominence either because they lacked pedigree or sufficient wealth, or
because they were simply not engaged in the right sort of trade. The
professions, particularly the law and the Church (medicine was not held in
high regard), were fitting occupations for the younger sons of noble families

and had high status in so far as they were practised by patricians and were associated with patrician interests. Important positions in the royal bureaucracy also conferred status, and the top administrators, judges and treasury officials, many of whom were *peninsulares*, would be members of the upper class.

In the towns the middle classes of white society comprised self-employed artisans, craftsmen, petty officials, clerks and shopkeepers; these people would be quite as anxious as the upper classes to preserve their status in society – artisans, for instance, would seek to exclude rivals from below, who were often non-whites, by forming guilds and corporations. In the countryside, the middle classes comprised the major-domos of large haciendas and the owners of middle-sized estates and ranches.

At the bottom of the social pyramid were to be found the common run of Hispanics without trade or property, poor whites whose only distinction within the lower orders was the colour of their skin, for around them swarmed the masses of urbanized Indians, free blacks and mixed-bloods who lived in the republic of the Spaniards without being juridically members of it.

The Republic of the Indians

The republic of the Indians came into being as a separate polity within the realms of the Spanish Crown, and it possessed its own laws and institutions. The intention of the Crown was to protect the Indians from exploitation by the Spanish settlers, and to allow them to retain their culture in so far as this did not conflict with Catholicism. Thus Spaniards and creoles were forbidden to reside within the Indian communities, and Indians equally were confined to their lands. But the 'protection' of the Indians through segregation was undermined by the fact that they had to offer tribute in kind to Hispanics and work periodically in the Hispanic sector, where they tended to be harshly treated and exposed to European cultural influences. As epidemics ravaged the Indian villages in the sixteenth century, the burdens of the tribute and labour service forced many individual Indians to flee their tribal lands and seek work in the Hispanic settlements or on Hispanic estates. They joined, in effect, that class of detribalized Indian known as *naborías* in Mexico and *yanaconas* in Peru; these Indians were not members of either republic, but formed part of a mixed population of undefined status.

Conquest, disease and tribute put such stress on the Indian villages in many regions that by the 1560s the Crown decided on a policy of resettlement and

concentration in new rationally planned communities. The programmes of
congregación and *reducción* were disruptive in themselves, and many Indians
had to be resettled by force. However, by the turn of the century, the
new settlements were providing the basis for the reintegration of Indian
community life. These communities had been remodelled by the Spanish
state – and to this extent they were culturally hybrid – but they none the
less retained much of the traditional structure of Indian society. Many
communities were reorganized within the boundaries of tribal lands. Where
resettlement took place outside tribal territory, new community lands were
designated by the Crown. The traditional Hispanic pattern of provincial
jurisdiction, consisting of *cabecera* (head town) and *sujetos* (subordinate
villages), was reproduced, but the authority of dynastic ethnic chieftains
continued to be exercised in the Indian *cabildo*, which became a sort of council
of tribal elders. Thus the Indian world was constantly assimilating and
adapting Hispanic influences for its own ends:

> Elements which were originally introduced from the outside became integrated
> inside Indian patterns of thought and behaviour to form stable associations of
> traits, all of which the Indian community identified with, not questioning
> which was indigenous, which Spanish, which a combination. On examination,
> nearly everything usually turns out to be the latter: Indian at the root and
> altered in some way at the surface, like the provincial units themselves.*

The Indian corporate world was still rooted in the kinship group called the
calpulli in Mexico and the *ayllu* in Peru. Land tenure remained predominantly
communal; agricultural work was performed on a reciprocal basis between
groups of kin; and rotary labour systems were employed for the larger
enterprises undertaken by the community. These were the abiding strengths
of Indian life; yet elements of Spanish culture – clothing, artefacts, tools,
farming methods, crops and animals – might filter through into the communities and be duly absorbed to suit Indian needs. This was particularly the
case with the reception of the new religion and its practices.

Once it had been imposed, Catholicism performed a central role in
strengthening and maintaining communal bonds. Church services, processions and festivals became focal events in the life of the native pueblos.
Communities adopted particular saints or aspects of the Virgin as their
patron, and used this very Catholic practice to reinforce their tribal identity
and territoriality. Ritual dances and pageants, originating in pagan cults,
acquired a Christian gloss while continuing to articulate tribal myths. The
Hispanic medieval tradition of forming *cofradías* (religious brotherhoods)

*James Lockhart and Stuart B. Schwartz, *Early Latin America*, p. 175.

under the special protection of a saint was adopted enthusiastically by the Indians and became a prime means of expressing social solidarity. Church and municipality were closely knit together through the *cajas de comunidad* (community funds), which were used to finance religious festivals and to pay for the decoration of the community's church, a source of enormous pride. The Hispanic practice of *compadrazgo* (social bonding through god-parenthood) became widespread among the Indians in the seventeenth century.

Indian communities, therefore, were profoundly conservative, demonstrating an extraordinary ability to incorporate alien influences and to make them underscore collective identities. But also they turned these influences to positive advantage in their relations with the outside world, using them to assert their independence. In the seventeenth century they actively defended their interests against Hispanics or rival Indian tribes, and learned to use techniques of lobbying and petitioning the Crown which were fundamental to the political life of the Hispanic world. They were, moreover, notorious for their relentless litigation over property rights; in the 1600s special courts, *juzgados de indios*, were created to hear civil and criminal cases involving disputes between Indians or between Indians and non-Indians. When such methods failed, the communities would often riot to wring a particular concession from the Crown or overturn a ruling or have an official removed; this was a familiar political technique in the Hispanic world, which was also employed by other ethnic communities – creole, mestizo and black – and to which the authorities would respond according to circumstances, but as often as not by appeasing rather than repressing such collective displays of outrage.

Indeed, in parts of the Indies, such as in the *zona indígena* of southern Mexico, in Yucatán, and in Guatemala Indian communities and Spanish settlements existed as parallel structures largely independent of one another. In the region of Oaxaca, as William B. Taylor has shown, the Indian corporate presence was dominant and assertive.* Indian communities and individuals controlled about two-thirds of the agricultural land during the last century of Spanish rule, and the Indians chose to grow traditional crops – maize, beans and maguey – even though they were quite capable of producing an abundant variety of European foodstuffs.

In the long term, however, the overall trend was towards a more fundamental Hispanicization. Within the communities themselves, traditional features underwent change. For instance, the reciprocal bonds which tied ethnic lords to their commoners came under strain. The *caciques* were allowed

* *Landlord and Peasant in Colonial Oaxaca* (Stanford University Press: Stanford, 1972).

privileges by the Spaniards, such as bearing arms, owning horses and wearing Spanish dress. They also collaborated with the Spaniards in organizing the tribute labour of the common Indians, and some used this as an opportunity to exploit Indian labour for their personal gain, amassing private land and property beyond that which was customary in traditional communities. Yet, at the same time, the hereditary *caciques* began to lose their hold over the *cabildos*, which were gradually filled by Indian commoners and even by non-tribal outsiders, including mestizos who happened to have settled within the territory of a community. Hereditary and dynastic authority was being superseded by a more elective kind of municipal government. Further social levelling occurred when, as a result of widespread depopulation, *caciques* were required to pay tribute themselves in order to make up the community's quota.

Interaction between the Indian world and the Hispanic increased in the seventeenth century. Indians were constantly being drawn into the Hispanic economy by the settlers' demand for labour and goods. There were natives who hired themselves out as temporary labourers in Spanish towns or estates. Others migrated from villages to settle permanently or for long periods in Spanish areas, where they were free from tribute and exploitation by *caciques* and *corregidores*. Communities located near Hispanic towns raised crops for sale in their markets. Entry into the market economy, with the consequent use of money, very slowly wrought changes in native attitudes to land tenure and production, with a shift occurring from reciprocal and communal arrangements to a more individualistic conception of property. Conversely, there was a movement from the Hispanic areas into the Indian corporate world. Creoles and mestizos from the lower classes took up residence illegally in Indian territory and brought alien values into the communities when they employed Indian workers or established social ties with *caciques* through marriage or *compadrazgo*.

These informal contacts accelerated the rate of cultural change within Indian communities. However, James Lockhart and Stuart Schwartz have identified a pattern of acculturation which occurred at different rates in the various parts of the Indies. In the central areas of Mexico, there was a period of some fifty to eighty years, from about 1570 until roughly 1650, which they call a 'plateau of consolidation', when the communities had adjusted to the new Hispanic structures and flourished in a hybrid cultural situation, with their traditional social mechanisms operating effectively through Hispanic institutions.* This was a time when Indians from the pueblos built churches

* *Early Latin America*, pp. 165–7.

and decorated them with frescoes and carvings; they also participated in the Catholic liturgy in their communities, performing, and even at times composing, the rich sacred music introduced by Spanish priests. By the middle of the seventeenth century, the underlying rate of Hispanicization had reached a critical point, after which a majority of Indians could, as individuals, satisfy their aspirations more effectively in the Spanish sector proper than within their communities. From that point, the Indian communities of central Mexico can be said to have been steadily relegated to the margins of Indian life.

Lockhart and Schwartz trace this phenomenon in the interaction of Nahuatl with Spanish. Until the 1650s or thereabouts the native language borrowed only nouns from Spanish, but then verbs, prepositions, conjunctions and idioms were used, suggesting a rapid increase in bilingualism as more and more Indians learned to deal with the Hispanic sector in a whole range of areas. In other regions where the interaction was not so intense or where it had not started so early, the process of acculturation would have occurred later.*

Africans

A third major ethnic group, blacks from the continent of Africa, came to form part of Spanish American society. This group at first consisted entirely of slaves. Slavery had been common in Mediterranean societies – both Christian and Muslim – since the Middle Ages, and black slaves were included in the earliest expeditions to the New World. But for most of the sixteenth century their numbers were not significant, because labour was provided by the Indians. When labour became scarce as a result of the decline of the Indian population, the demand for slaves rose, until by the end of the century the Spanish Crown was forced to permit the systematic importation of Africans.

Spain relied on the Portuguese to import slaves, for the Treaty of Tordesillas had granted the west coast of Africa to Portugal and a trade in African slaves had long been established by the Portuguese. When in 1595 the Spanish Crown began to award contracts, called *asientos*, to Portuguese slave traders, the number of slaves transported to the Spanish Indies rose sharply. The total number of Africans imported into the Indies between 1595 and 1640 has been estimated at 132,600, whereas the total for the period between 1521

* *Early Latin America*, pp. 167–8.

and 1595 had been little more than 50,000. Much as the Crown tried to control the trade by setting import quotas, it could not stop the extensive contraband that sprang up to meet the demand for labour in the Spanish colonies.

For the rest of the colonial period the traffic showed little sign of diminishing, because the black slave population in America did not reproduce at a natural rate; as deaths exceeded births, constant imports of slaves were required to meet labour needs. The Portuguese were soon joined by Dutch, English and French slavers; initially they brought Africans illegally into the Spanish Indies, but, by a provision of the Treaty of Utrecht of 1713, Spain was obliged to grant an *asiento* to the English South Sea Company to supply slaves to her colonies. The eighteenth century, in fact, saw a surge in the slave traffic when Cuba and other Spanish islands set up a sugar-plantation economy relying exclusively on black slave labour, as the English and French had done so successfully on their Caribbean possessions.

Before the Spanish created a sugar industry in Cuba and the Caribbean, black slaves went to most parts of the Indies. They were concentrated in lowland or coastal regions, for these were the areas where the Indian population had fallen beyond recovery, at least in Mexico and Peru. In New Granada, Africans were the mainstay of the gold industry, while in Venezuela they worked the cacao plantations along the coast. In the north-west of present-day Argentina, black slaves were to be found in cattle-ranching, wine-growing and wheat production, having been imported through Buenos Aires by Portuguese smugglers from Brazil. In the towns, blacks were often used in the textile *obrajes*, but they were also highly prized for their status value as domestic servants in wealthy Hispanic households. More modest creoles could afford to own a few slaves; artisans and craftsmen, for instance, quite often employed black slaves as assistants in their workshops. By the middle decades of the seventeenth century, blacks had become a major presence in the Indies; the main cities had substantial black populations, and it is even possible that almost half the population of Lima was black or mulatto.

The sheer volume of the slave-trade caused moral unease in the Church and the royal government. Slavery in itself, however, had never been considered morally objectionable in Europe. Aristotle had sanctioned the enslavement of people belonging to an inferior civilization, and Africans had long been regarded as such by Europeans. The Church condoned slavery as the unfortunate lot of certain races, though it professed to believe that slaves could win salvation and should be converted – indeed, it saw merit in the enslavement of savages as a means of bringing them to knowledge of the true faith. It stipulated only that they be treated humanely.

But it became clear that the Indies slave-trade was far from humane: horrendous manhunts took place on the coasts of West Africa; the wretched captives were packed tight in the filthy holds of slave ships and later unloaded like animals to be sold off at huge markets in American ports. Missionaries tried to Christianize the blacks who were flooding into Spanish America, yet never with the zeal they had shown in converting the Indians. The slaves were scarcely in a frame of mind to absorb Christian doctrine, and the scale of the influx made anything more than perfunctory instruction and baptism impracticable. Still, some priests, particularly the Jesuits, did persevere in their attempts to convert the Africans effectively and to win humane treatment for them. But on the whole, black slaves arriving from Africa acquired an imperfect grasp of Christianity and retained a good deal of the animistic beliefs and rituals brought over from their native land. Fused at times with elements of Catholicism, animism was passed on to subsequent generations, and a number of Afro-American cults are practised widely to this day in those parts of Spanish America that have large black populations.

As occurred with the Indians who had left their communities to work in the Spanish sector, the black slaves of the second generation became Hispanicized. The word *criollo* (which passed into English as 'creole' by way of French) was originally used to distinguish acculturated blacks, born and bred in Spanish America, from newly imported Africans with no knowledge of Spanish, who were called *negros bozales*, by analogy with savage, unbroken animals requiring a muzzle (*bozal*). Such terminology betrays the anxiety that existed among white owners concerning the potentially violent nature of their slaves. But, in fact, slave rebellions were rare; it was far more common for individuals or groups of slaves to escape from bondage and take refuge in the wild. The runaway might survive there and unite with others in a settlement called a *palenque* or *cumbe*. These precarious neo-African communities, refashioned in America, were capable of surviving for quite long periods before succumbing to punitive attacks by white forces or, more likely, to malnutrition or disease. But even in captivity, the Africans and their descendants kept alive some memory of their former tribal identities by associating with other slaves from their nations of origin in Spanish-style religious brotherhoods, invoking their ancestral deities and practising secret tribal rites. This cultural fragmentation appears to have been encouraged by the Spaniards as a means of preventing any wider solidarity among the blacks, which could have led to large-scale rebellion.

Conditions under which slaves lived varied considerably. A slave family living in a wealthy household under a compassionate master might enjoy a degree of dignity and security denied to those labouring in sugar plantations, where they were exposed to harsh physical punishments by overseers and had little opportunity to establish personal relationships with the master's family which might mitigate the inhumanity of their condition. Women slaves suffered from the additional hazard of being forced into sexual relations by their masters, a phenomenon which, given the growth of the mulatto population, must have been common. The quality of life for most slaves was extremely low – they were badly housed, clothed and fed, and their health was usually of little concern to the master. However, it is unlikely that the actual material circumstances of many slaves, especially in the towns, would have been much worse than those endured by the bulk of the free poor.

The Spanish state paid lip-service to the ideal that slaves should be capable of winning their freedom. As the general population increased in the latter half of the seventeenth century, and the supply of labour improved, the rate of manumission accelerated, masters absolving their slaves from bondage as a reward for loyal service, or at least allowing them to purchase their freedom. By the late eighteenth century the majority of blacks in Spanish America were free and were to be found working as wage-labourers, self-employed artisans or humble peasants.

Being a free person, the black was accepted as an integral, though distinctive, member of a corporate society: he was a subject of the Crown and a rightful son of the Church; he could own property, enter into legal transactions and strive for prosperity and social dignity; and some limited educational opportunities were available to him. But, even so, in a society where whiteness was a mark of social distinction, he was inescapably the victim of endemic colour prejudice and therefore occupied a lowly position on the social scale. The descendants of the slaves brought in such huge numbers from Africa thus came to be assimilated at the lower levels of the white-dominated society transplanted from Spain, and together with the Indians, they contributed to its ethnic diversity, particularly as a result of the miscegenation that occurred between the three races.

Race Mixture

Although the Indies were legally constituted as a dual society of Spaniards and Indians, Spanish American social reality was far more mixed as a result of the presence of Africans, and even more so as a result of the growth of a population of intermediate ethnicity, collectively known as *castas*. People of mixed blood lived in the republic of the Spaniards, but their status was never clearly defined; they were free yet had to pay a special poll tax imposed on the *castas*, and they were also subject to legal restrictions which impeded their social advancement; they were forbidden to hold public office, enter the priesthood or study at university. And yet, even though non-white blood was regarded as a taint which prevented full acceptance into the society of the Spaniards, the actual social circumstances of mixed-bloods were dependent on a number of variables such as legitimacy, degree of colour, occupation, extent of Hispanicization and the closeness of the relationship to the father, if he were white. In any case, the process of miscegenation was so intense over such a very long period that full assimilation became possible for large numbers, especially in the eighteenth century when most Hispanic families had been affected.

In the sixteenth century, miscegenation occurred predominantly between Spaniards and Indians, and their offspring were known as mestizos. These unions were mostly irregular, since the dominant position of Spanish males in the period after the Conquest enabled them to take indigenous women as partners outside wedlock. The arrival of African women slaves in the latter part of the century multiplied the opportunities for such liaisons, and the issue of these unions were known as *mulatos*.

Crown and Church encouraged the immigration of Spanish women in order to foster legitimate family bonds in the Indies. Yet if Spanish settlers preferred to marry white women for social and economic reasons, circumstances still allowed them to conduct extramarital liaisons with women of other races, who invariably worked as servants or slaves. Illegitimate children were in many cases tolerated within the extensive households of the wealthier Spaniards, where they occupied an undefined position – somewhere between family retainers and blood relations; they were offered some education and were included in their father's will. These were the fortunate few who could find shelter in the patriarchal structure of Hispanic family life, but the majority had to endure a strong social stigma. This was particularly the case with the children of mixed Indian and black parentage, who were initially known as mulattos but were later called *zambos*. Ironically, illegitimacy was less common in such mixtures because of the relative lack of social prejudice against intermarriage among non-white groups.

The correlations between social and racial status were fairly complex. Unquestionably, pure Spaniards were regarded as socially and ethnically supreme, and provided the standard by which the status of the other groups was evaluated. Indians were at the bottom of the social scale, and yet their colour and physical characteristics were deemed to be closer to those of Spaniards, and so mestizos enjoyed the highest status of the mixed-bloods. Black creoles were socially more familiar to Spaniards than Indians, but racially more alien, and so mulattos ranked below mestizos. By this logic, the *zambos* – black–Indian mixtures – were both socially and racially inferior to the other groups.

In a society where the colour of a person's skin determined juridical as well as social status (since fiscal obligations and legal privileges ultimately depended on it), ethnic gradations were of consuming interest, and the permutations between them subjected to refined genealogical analysis. For instance, if the mestizo daughter of a Spaniard married a white, her children would be considered *castizo* and could revert to juridical whiteness. However, if the daughter of a white–mestizo union – that is, a *castiza* – married an Indian, her children would belong to the republic of the Indians; and if she married a mestizo, the offspring would become mestizo. The children of the latter combinations, and others, were eventually identified by distinctive names, though these had no bearing on legal status.

Towards the end of the colonial period the sheer complexity of assigning a separate category to each degree of ethnic mixture became too great. Since the vast majority of the population was of mixed blood, ethnic status was determined more by appearance and social behaviour than by genealogical or strictly ethnic analysis. The growing population of mestizos and mulattos cut across the division between the Hispanic and Indian republics. At one extreme, people of mixed blood spilled over into the white sector, entering the university, the professions and the guilds legally reserved for whites, while, at the other, they seeped into the Indian communities, sitting on *cabildos* and occupying other offices assigned to Indians. After independence, this broad middle range of *castas* would acquire full civil rights, but social standing would still be very largely influenced by perceptions of ethnic features.

The Patriarchal Order of Society

The social world of the Spanish Indies was patriarchal and hierarchical. The ideal was to live like a lord, owning vast estates and holding sway over other men. Such an ideal took its pattern from the Iberian family unit, in which the paterfamilias exercised a benevolent but unquestioned authority over his wife, children, dependants, servants, slaves and an extensive clan of relatives and clients. The rule of the patriarch was exercised through patronage rather than outright force: favours were extended in exchange for respect and loyalty; special protection in a harsh world was the reward for obedience from social inferiors; who were often bound to the family by ties of *padrinaje* and *compadrazgo*.

These values permeated political and economic behaviour. In politics, they led inevitably to oligarchy, for patriarchal clans sought to maintain their influence by infiltrating powerful institutions and conducting public affairs with the methods that ruled family business – namely, the exchange of favours between patrons and clients. Economic practice, too, was oligarchic, tending to the exclusion of equal competition as favours were used to dominate markets, to create cartels of producers which kept prices high, to win monopoly rights from the state, and so on. In short, the great clans tried to capture and control markets in order to turn ordinary consumers into passive clients who would have to pay high prices for goods as a sort of tribute to the patriarchal power of the producer. On the other hand, high profits and rents were spent by the great families in economically 'unproductive' ways – in acts of public generosity through donations to the Church, Crown and community, and in sustaining a luxurious style of life which would enhance the prestige and power of the patriarch and his kin.

Monarchy set the seal on this patriarchal order of society. The king was the father of the people, the personal source of justice and law, ruling also by virtue of his ability to grant favours in return for loyalty and obedience. His subjects had no inherent rights; instead, they directed petitions to the monarch for the concession of some grace or reward. Above the king stood only God, the Supreme Father, and indeed, the social world was nothing but the material reflection of the spiritual hierarchy instituted by the Creator Himself. Because religion provided the ultimate rationale for political authority, the Catholic monarchy was a powerful force for unity: it acted as an overarching structure which held together the myriad, interlocking networks of reciprocal ties radiating outwards and upwards from the authority of the father in the humblest family unit.

Culture

The Foundations in the Sixteenth Century

The discovery, conquest and evangelization of the New World brought forth a substantial body of writing which still forms the basis of our knowledge of this momentous enterprise. These books and documents were written mostly by men who were actively involved in the Spanish colonization of America, and they are either chronicles of the European invasions or historical studies of the Indian civilizations that preceded them.

Some of the major discoverers and conquistadors left records of their experiences. Columbus wrote a diary of his four voyages to the Indies, later edited by Bartolomé de las Casas. Hernán Cortés's account of the conquest of Mexico can be construed from the letters he sent to Charles V. A history of the Conquest which exalted Cortés's role was published by Francisco López de Gómara in 1532, even though the author never set foot in the Indies. Partly in reply to this book a *True History of the Conquest of New Spain* was written in the middle years of the sixteenth century (but not published until 1632) by Bernal Díaz del Castillo, a soldier in Cortés's army, who resented Gómara's excessive glorification of Cortés and who gave a version which stressed the collective and indeed providential nature of the foundation of the Spanish colony. The conquest of Peru and its turbulent aftermath were chronicled by participants like Pedro Cieza de León and Pedro Pizarro, a cousin of Francisco, and by a royal servant, Agustín de Zárate.

Many Spaniards were curious about the Amerindian empires they had subdued. In the absence of native written sources, knowledge of the pre-Hispanic civilizations came from oral accounts by Indians which were transcribed into Spanish. In this task of cultural transmission priests and mestizos were prominent. The Franciscan friar Bernardino de Sahagún wrote *Historia general de las cosas de la Nueva España* ('A General History of the Things of New Spain', 1570–82), which gave a native version of the Conquest and discussed Aztec mythology and culture. The Franciscan missionary Toribio de Benavente, known as Motolinia after the Nahuatl word meaning poor (he had worked for decades with the Indians as an indigent friar), brought out an important history of the Indians of New Spain in 1541. Both histories remain outstanding sources of knowledge about the Aztecs. The mestizos Fernando de Alva Ixtlilxochitl, a descendant of the lords of Texcoco, and Alvarado Tezozomoc wrote chronicles in Spanish about their forebears; Father Diego Durán, a mestizo priest, compiled a history of the Indians of New Spain based on hieroglyphic codices and oral accounts. In Peru, Atahuallpa's nephew, Titu Cusi Yupanqui, dictated a history of his family; the priest Martín de Murúa, who was a friend of members of the royal family, recounted the story of the Conquest from the Inca point of view. Peruvian mestizos, such as the Inca Garcilaso de la Vega, Felipe Guaman Poma de Ayala and Juan de Betanzos, produced chronicles of Indian society before and after the Conquest. The Jesuit José de Acosta gave an account of the history and geography of Mexico and Peru in his influential and scientifically objective *Historia natural y moral de las Indias* ('Natural and Moral History of the Indies', 1590), amongst other works.

This great wealth of chronicles and *relaciones* on the Conquest and the native empires was produced not simply to obtain an objective record of events, but as often as not to provide support for one side or the other in the great sixteenth-century debate over the rights of the Indian peoples. Bartolomé de las Casas wrote a history of the Indies between 1552 and 1561 to help his defence of Indian rights. By contrast, the great Spanish viceroy in Peru, Francisco de Toledo, commissioned Pedro Sarmiento de Gamboa to write a history of the Incas which would justify Spanish sovereignty; it was completed in 1572, the year of the final campaign against the neo-Inca state of Vilcabamba. Juan de Matienzo, a jurist who had been involved in Spanish diplomacy with the Incas of Vilcabamba, also wrote a treatise on the government of Peru, which supported the Spanish right to supplant the Incas. Yet, as John Hemming points out, 'it is an extraordinary fact that the authors who made the most powerful arguments in favour of Spanish rule – Sepúlveda, Matienzo and Sarmiento de Gamboa – never had their works published in Spain in the sixteenth century; whereas everything Las Casas wrote was published'.*

Indeed, the cultural life of the Indies was conditioned by the overriding belief of Crown and Church that the best justification of Spanish rule lay in the Christianization of the Indians. As a result, the earliest expressions of Hispanic culture in the New World had a markedly religious and didactic character. As in Spain, there was a strict censorship of all books in order to guard against heresy and immorality, but official concern for the impressionable minds of Indian neophytes also led to a ban on imports of works of fiction to America (a ban which soon proved to be unenforceable in practice). Printing-presses were established early on in the major cities: Mexico City had one in 1535, Lima in 1583. These first presses published works of devotion and manuals for preachers.

By the middle of the sixteenth century the full apparatus of an educational system had been set up: missionaries were responsible for schooling the Indians in Christianity and the Castilian language, as well as in other practical skills; colleges were instituted in New Spain and Peru to provide a sound humanist education for Indian and mestizo aristocrats; seminaries were founded to train clergy; and universities, modelled on Salamanca, were chartered in Santo Domingo (1538), Mexico City (1553) and Lima (1551).

* *The Conquest of the Incas* (Macmillan: London, 1970), p. 415.

These institutions were run by the Church and, as in all seats of learning in contemporary Europe, theology and Latin played a central role in the curriculum.

For most of the sixteenth century secular culture was limited by the size of the European population and its scattered nature: Spanish settlers, most of whom were not highly educated anyway, tended to live in small, isolated townships surrounded by Indians. However, by the middle of the century the main cities, and particularly Mexico, Lima and Cuzco, were able to sustain some degree of cultural life outside the Church. The creation of viceregal courts and *audiencias*, where well-educated royal officials, clerics and noblemen were concentrated, provided a focus for high culture and social display, which attracted rich *encomenderos* and transatlantic merchants.

In these refined circles the culture of the European Renaissance – the secular counterpart of the missionaries' religious humanism – was applied with some discrimination to the experience of America. For instance, by the 1550s Francisco Cervantes de Salazar, professor of rhetoric at the University of Mexico, official chronicler of the Conquest, and a distinguished Erasmian humanist, who knew Hernán Cortés personally, was able to write poetic eulogies and Latin dialogues about life in the 'great city of Mexico'. An American-born Spaniard, Francisco de Terrazas, was an accomplished poet in the manner of Petrarch and the Castilian Garcilaso de la Vega (he was to receive praise from Miguel de Cervantes). Bernardo de Balbuena, who studied at the University of Mexico in the late 1580s and later served as Abbot of Jamaica and Bishop of Puerto Rico, wrote a celebrated poetic eulogy of New Spain, *Grandeza Mexicana* ('The Grandeur of Mexico', 1604), in accordance with Italian models, as well as a long pastoral poem, *Siglo de Oro* ('The Golden Age', 1608), after Sannazaro's *Arcadia*, and a verse epic, *El Bernardo, o Victoria de Roncesvalles* ('El Bernardo, or the Victory of Roncesvalles', 1624), on the legendary medieval hero of the Reconquest of Spain, Bernardo del Carpio – this last influenced by the *Orlando* epics of Boiardo and Ariosto.

Men like Cervantes de Salazar, Terrazas and Balbuena were outstanding writers in the as yet small cultural élite which was to be found in the capital of New Spain towards the end of the sixteenth century. What is more, through this milieu there passed figures of the first rank who had made their literary reputation in the Peninsula or who would eventually do so, but whose talents and interests must have exerted some influence on the quality of intellectual culture in colonial Mexico. Juan de la Cueva, who would become a precursor of the new Spanish drama of the seventeenth century, lived for several years after 1574 in Mexico. Gutierre de Cetina, a major poet, was also resident in New Spain for some years. The most illustrious figure was Mateo Alemán, author of one of the most popular and influential works in all Spanish literature, *Guzmán de Alfarache* (1599; 1602), the founding novel of the picaresque genre; he came to Mexico in 1608 and lived there until his death in 1615. Juan Ruiz de Alarcón was a creole born in Mexico City in 1580, who went to Spain and became a major playwright in the Golden Age of the Spanish theatre; his most celebrated play, *La verdad sospechosa* ('The Suspect Truth', 1634), inspired Pierre Corneille's *Le menteur* and Goldoni's *Il bugiardo*.

In the second half of the century the historical impulse to record the great feats of the Conquest became more consciously literary, as if refined by the poetic sensibility cultivated by the élite. The result was the rise of the heroic epic written in verse as well as in prose. The supreme exemplar of the genre was Alonso de Ercilla's *La Araucana* (1569; 1578; 1589), the best Renaissance epic in the Spanish language, which took for its subject the frontier wars in Chile against the Araucanian Indians. Of Ercilla's imitators, Pedro de Oña produced a competent epic in *Primera parte de Arauca domada* ('First Part of the Araucan Conquest', 1596), and Francisco de Terrazas produced fragments of an epic poem, *El Nuevo Mundo y su conquista* ('The New World and its Conquest', 1580). The other literary master of Spanish American culture in the century of the Conquest, and a figure whose works were destined to become classics of Spanish literature, was a Peruvian mestizo, Garcilaso de la Vega, the illegitimate son of a descendant of the great Castilian poet of the same name, and of an Inca princess. His first major work was a prose epic on the conquest of Florida by Hernando de Soto (1605). He had already translated into Castilian (1590) the seminal book of Renaissance Neoplatonism in Spain, the *Dialogues of Love* by Leo Hebraeus. His masterpiece, however, was his *Comentarios Reales que tratan del origen de los Yncas* ('Royal Commentaries of the Incas', 1609), a chronicle written in a prose style of the highest quality, which presents the civilization of his ancestors as a providential prelude to the coming of Christianity to the New World, much as the Renaissance had characterized Graeco-Roman antiquity as preparing the ground for the eventual triumph of the true faith in the Old. This was followed by *Historia general del Peru* ('General History of Peru', 1617).

The spread of Hispanic culture to the Indies was not confined to the viceregal capitals. The Iberian Peninsula was rich in popular literary traditions – ballads, songs, folk-tales, ditties, proverbs and satirical verses. These were brought over to America by the numerous humble Spaniards who settled in that alien environment, and they took root there, as did their music and dances. In fact, the divide between the high and low culture of Spain was not very clear-cut, and there were several crossing-points, which increased in importance towards the end of the sixteenth century. A 'national' dramatic tradition developed which was capable of attracting noblemen as well as commoners; cultivated poets such as Lope de Vega, Luis de Góngora, and even the aristocratic reactionary Francisco de Quevedo, wrote songs and poems in popular modes, which circulated freely among the *vulgo*. The theatre itself was one of several places where Spaniards of high and low birth could share cultural activities. Others were the church and the public square – religious ceremonies, processions and civic pageants were regular features in the calendar of any town, and formed part of the tradition of the fiesta, which had long held a central place in Hispanic culture.

Religious ritual and the public fiesta provided links with the other ethnic cultures – Indian and African. The initial contact was primarily through the missionaries, who introduced into the Indian communities medieval Catholic practices such as public processions and festivals on saints' days. A favourite method of instruction was the morality play, which represented visually the mysteries of the faith. The Indians were encouraged to stage other plays and pageants – often using masks and costumes derived from their indigenous lore – to commemorate Spanish historical legends such as battles between Moors and Christians during the Reconquest, the feats of Charlemagne and Roland, or even the exploits of the conquistadors of America. But there was considerable influence in the other direction too, particularly when the rate of migration from the Indian communities to the Hispanic settlements accelerated towards the end of the century. These detribalized Indians mixed with lower-class Hispanics, blacks and half-castes and brought to bear their own customs on the Spanish music, dances, songs, cuisine, manners and expressions that were to become the patrimony of the popular classes of America.

In Hispanic towns all over the Indies there took place a vital cultural intermingling, a *mestizaje* of traditions. The character of this interaction would depend on the ethnic and cultural composition of the different regions, and might even vary significantly between towns in the same province: this largely accounts for the extremely rich and diverse regional traditions of Spanish America. But all such variations occurred round a Spanish core: Spain provided the paradigm, while the free Indians and the African slaves modified it with their ancestral influences. It would be an error, however, to suggest that the colonial culture of Spanish America formed a harmonious whole. There were deep divisions between races and classes: the exploitation of Indians and African slaves called forth numerous rebellions. Unquestionably, these subjugated ethnic groups bitterly resented their oppression, and often used their native lore – Afro-American voodoo or the various forms of Amerindian animistic magic – to subvert and resist the culture of their masters.

The mentality of the mestizo, in particular, was a cauldron of contradictions. Evidence of these tensions can be found in a curious document, called *El primer nueva Corónica y Buen Gobierno* ('The New Chronicle and Good Government'), written some time between 1567 and 1615 by a Peruvian mestizo, Felipe Guaman Poma de Ayala. This chronicle was intended both as a denunciation of the abuse of the Indians by the Spaniards and a treatise on the need for just government in Peru. Guaman Poma was clearly distressed by a sense of illegitimacy and dispossession. His chronicle disparages the Incas, for he claimed descent on his father's side from the lords of Huánuco, who had been defeated by the lords of Cuzco and whose lands had been incorporated into the Inca empire. Guaman Poma's chronicle thus reveals divisions between Indians as much as between natives and Spaniards. The author had worked as an interpreter for several officials of the Spanish Crown, touring the countryside in a campaign to destroy pagan idols. On the death of his father in 1580 he became embroiled in litigation over his right of inheritance to lands bequeathed to him. In later life he clashed repeatedly with Spanish officials over his allegations of abuse of native rights. He suffered imprisonment and banishment, dying in poverty at an advanced age, probably in 1616.

Yet, for all that, the *Nueva Corónica* was addressed to Philip III, and it was accompanied by letters requesting favours in recognition of the services rendered to Spain by Guaman Poma's father. The other famous mestizo chronicler of Peru, Garcilaso de la Vega, also petitioned the Spanish king repeatedly for favours, as a reward for the services rendered by his Spanish father to the Crown during the conquest of Peru. He met with no success, and on the death of his Indian mother he appended the unofficial title 'the Inca' to his name as if to reclaim his Amerindian identity, even though he had lived in Spain since he was twenty-one.

The colonial culture of the Spanish Indies was not a seamless whole, but, even so, these multifarious and racially divided post-Conquest societies all revolved about the political and cultural axis of the Catholic monarchy. The Crown was their central point of reference, and as such acted as a force for unity and order, drawing the disparate ethnic groups, tribes and classes into its patriarchal system of values, much as it linked together politically the numerous realms that made up the global empire. For this reason *mestizaje* was no threat at all to the Spanish order of things. The imperial state did not impose cultural uniformity, although it insisted formally on a broad religious loyalty from its subjects. The high degree of cultural and ethnic pluralism that existed in the Indies could be tolerated under the Catholic monarchy because the political unity of the empire was so secure.

The Culture of the Creoles in the Seventeenth Century

The seventeenth century saw the emergence of distinctive creole societies in the various regions of the Indies, as towns and cities expanded and the Spanish American economy grew away from the economy of the Peninsula. As more silver was kept back in America instead of being exported to Spain, creole notables could spend more of their wealth on patronage of the arts. The main American cities were thus able to develop an aristocratic culture of considerable luxury.

An important feature of culture in this period was the creoles' growing desire to assert their own identity as *españoles americanos* in opposition to the Spaniards who had immigrated from the Peninsula. A certain resentment against *peninsulares* is evident in the writings of the Americans, and, in a Church-dominated society, this was often filtered through the expression of an indigenous religious sensibility alleged to be purer than that of Spain itself. Creole preachers strove to prove that the New World had been specially favoured by God. Manifestations of the Virgin in America served to canalize creole patriotism – the Virgin of Guadalupe was the object of fervent devotion in Mexico among creoles and Indians alike, and she was preferred to her peninsular counterparts, including the Virgen de los Remedios, who had been venerated by the conquistadors. The same held true of other *vírgenes criollas*: the Virgin of Copacabana in Peru, the Virgin of Guápulo in Ecuador.

The creoles would in time even lay claim to aspects of the pre-Hispanic past in order to distinguish themselves from the *peninsulares*. Jacques Lafaye has shown how by the eighteenth century the Mexican clergy attempted to Christianize the Nahuatl god Quetzalcoatl by arguing that he was in reality the apostle St Thomas, who had come to the New World before the conquistadors in order to bring the word of God to the Indians: thus Christianity was presumed to have roots in America which were independent of the Peninsula. It was a way of rejecting the cultural dominance of Spain and of compensating for the colonial sense of inferiority.

If these are clear examples of creole patriotism, it is perhaps anachronistic to see in them signs of an emerging 'national consciousness', much less a nationalism that might have constituted any kind of political threat to the empire, or which could have sown the seeds of a spirit of independence that

Spain might have had to repress. The Crown could accommodate a very high degree of cultural diversity within its realms. What is more, creole patriotism was a defensive response to the wounding arrogance of peninsular immigrants and officials; it was not in any way directed against the Catholic monarchy itself, an institution which the creoles well understood to be vital to the interests of their society.

Above all, creole patriotism must be set in the context of wider cultural developments in the Hispanic world towards the end of the sixteenth century which served to propagate and reinforce the ideological attractions of the Catholic monarchy. The most seductive of these developments was the flowering of a strong dramatic tradition, particularly so after the emergence of Lope de Vega's *comedia nueva* at the turn of the sixteenth century. Lope discovered a dramatic formula which remained dominant until well into the eighteenth century. It was remarkably effective in representing the motive forces in Hispanic society and in examining its central values, both political and religious. And at the heart of the formula lay the patriarchal idea of the king as healer and guarantor of the social order. This idea informs the plays of Lope himself, of Tirso de Molina, Calderón de la Barca and all the major dramatists of the Golden Age of the Spanish theatre. The *comedia nueva* thus displayed the value-system of the Hispanic world in artistic forms that were hugely popular, appealing as they did to the *vulgo* as much as to the aristocracy.

Creole society loved the theatre and public spectacles. As in Spain, plays were performed in *corrales* (courtyards) before enthusiastic crowds. Most plays were imported from the Peninsula, but an indication of the depth of creole interest in the theatre is the fact that one of the greatest dramatists of the Golden Age was the Mexican hunchback Juan Ruiz de Alarcón, though his career unfolded largely in Spain. A theatrical genre that flourished in the seventeenth century was the *auto sacramental*, a complex allegorical drama on the subject of the Eucharist performed in the open air with lavish properties on the feast-day of Corpus Christi; it was brought to a high art by Calderón de la Barca in Spain. These *autos sacramentales*, so popular with the creoles, grew out of the same tradition of medieval mysteries which the early missionaries had used to help evangelize the Indian masses.

In the former Inca capital of Cuzco, where traditional Andean culture was very strong and where there still lived a significant Inca nobility, albeit Hispanicized, the Spanish theatre underwent a curious *mestizaje* – religious and even secular *comedias* were sometimes written in the Quechua language; the well-known play *Ollantay*, of unknown authorship but presumed to have been written in the late seventeenth or early eighteenth century, evinces the themes and structure of the contemporary Spanish drama. The most accomplished of the Cuzco playwrights was Juan de Espinosa Medrano, known as El Lunarejo who wrote in both Spanish and Quechua and was celebrated for his *autos sacramentales* and biblical plays (he composed *The Prodigal Son* in Quechua and set it in Peru, using Indian characters).

This fondness for theatrical spectacle ran to the staging of elaborate pageants and public ceremonies on the occasion, say, of the arrival of a new viceroy, the enthronement of a bishop, or the anniversary of some historic event or personage. Allegorical tableaux portraying scenes from classical mythology might be staged even in provincial backwaters, and by Indians as well as creoles. 'The town of Chiapas,' observed the English Dominican friar, Thomas Gage,

> lieth upon a great river, whereunto belong many boats and canoes, wherein those Indians have been taught to act sea fights with great dexterity, and to represent the nymphs of Parnassus, Neptune, Aeolus, and the rest of the heathenish gods and goddesses, so that they are a wonder of their whole nation.*

Public spectacle was an intrinsic feature of this hierarchical society. Quite apart from festive *máscaras* (processions in thematic fancy dress) and pageants with great parades of floats, the culture required frequent displays of social standing, such as the daily ritual of the late-afternoon *paseo*, when the creole upper classes would step out in their finery to grace the avenues of their towns. Even poetry was very much a public art, written to celebrate a grand civic occasion or to be read at a contest. Its elaborate formality precluded too much introspection; rather, it tended to cultivate language in the spirit of a game in which wit and ingenuity were highly prized. In short, the style of literature in the heyday of creole culture was baroque – with ornate metaphor, technically intricate and decked out with conceits. This style continued to dominate creole letters until the late eighteenth century and was perhaps a crucial element in the emergence of a distinctive Spanish American sensibility. At least, so it was believed by major Spanish American artists of the twentieth century, and certainly much modern poetry and fiction displays a conscious affinity with baroque art.

However, unlike the modern writer, the baroque artist was not an individualist; the very medium in which he expressed himself formed part of the ceremonial fabric of his society, as can be appreciated from the description given by Mariano Picón-Salas of a carnival procession held in Lima in 1627:

* Quoted in Irving I. Leonard, *Baroque Times in Old Mexico*, (University of Michigan Press: Ann Arbor, 1959), p. 122.

Among its features were crocodiles drawn by mules draped with pelts of mythical unicorns, whales, astrologers, Polyphemus with an enormous eye, Ganymede and Aeneas, Jason in pursuit of the Fleece, Saturn carrying an hour-glass, and Mars. Apollo's chariot also appeared bearing an effigy of the poet, Luis de Góngora.*

Indeed it was Góngora, more than any other writer, who was the personification of baroque aesthetics in the Hispanic world, and it is significant that just a few months after his death in the Spanish city of Córdoba, his memory was being publicly honoured in distant Lima, along with the gods of antiquity.

Pleasure-loving, gregarious and sexually lax though it may have been, creole society was not shallow. Despite its recent foundation, it produced artistic figures of great distinction, some of them approaching the first rank of contemporary Hispanic culture, as we shall see. And if secular literature was so extrovert and ritualized, it was because the most intimate expressions of the human conscience were largely reserved for pious and religious works. In fact, it was the Church which was the greatest patron of art in the Indies. Its immense influence on contemporary drama has already been noted, and its role in promoting architecture, the plastic arts and music was greater still.

Church architecture in the sixteenth century was fairly rudimentary, in keeping with the pioneering, missionary spirit of the period following the Conquest. The friaries, churches and mission stations built by the religious orders were functional structures, though with decorative features around doorways and windows following a long Hispanic tradition. The basic designs tended to be Gothic – employing arches, arcades and pillars, and particularly cross-vaulting, which was very resistant to earth tremors. Indeed, practical considerations may account in part for the stylistic eclecticism of architecture in the Spanish Indies. A balance had to be struck between functionalism and aesthetics – the cathedral at Santo Domingo, for instance, combines a sturdy Gothic structure with Italian Renaissance ornamentation. Indeed, the destruction caused by earthquakes all over the continent accounts for the mixture of styles, for many churches and convents had to be periodically repaired or partially rebuilt after seismic damage. The cathedral in Mexico City was added to repeatedly throughout the colonial period: having been started in 1563 in the Spanish classical style, it had acquired many baroque features by the time it was consecrated in 1667; finally, it was given towers and neo-classical saucer-domes by a Spanish architect in the last decade of the eighteenth century.

* *A Cultural History of Latin America: From Conquest to Independence* (University of California Press: Berkeley, 1964), p. 91.

This eclecticism, then, is the overriding feature of Spanish American architecture, a *mestizaje* born of function, geography, climate and, of course, taste. For the many stylistic combinations, varying according to region and available materials, often possess an inherent integrity and serve to establish a rich visual aesthetic, deriving from Spain and Europe, but creatively transformed by the circumstances of the New World. A good number of the major cathedrals, churches and convents of the Indies were initiated in the last decades of the sixteenth century and were designed in the monumental and very sober classical style perfected in Spain by Juan de Herrera, the architect of the Escorial and the cathedral of Valladolid. A disciple of Herrera, the Extremaduran Francisco Becerra, drew up the plans for the cathedral of Puebla in Mexico, and for the cathedrals of Lima and Cuzco, as well as for convents in Quito. But if structures were fairly standard, decorative features, as we have seen, varied widely: they might include Italianate motifs, wood-block ceilings in the Arab-influenced *mudéjar* style and façades in the plateresque mode, which fused Gothic, Arab and Italian elements. With the development of the essentially dramatic baroque style during the seventeenth century, the dynamic nature of this *mestizaje* was intensified through the use of spiral columns, tapering *estípite* pillars, ornate altar pieces and retable-façades with expressive statuary.

The creative mixing of local materials gave indigenous tonalities to the fabric of buildings. The dark-red rock called *tezontle* found in the volcanic regions of central Mexico was used extensively there and produced a uniquely sombre aspect. It was sometimes combined with other kinds of stone, such as the sand-coloured *chiluca*. In the Andean areas of Peru and Upper Peru, hard stone, usually granite, was used for major buildings, but in the coastal cities the materials were mostly adobe, brick or *quinche* (reeds and clay covered in plaster). As in the Peninsula, *azulejos* (coloured glazed tiles) were widely used to ornament façades as well as interiors, allowing for much variation according to local traditions.

Craftsmen, often mestizos or Indians, gave an indigenous character to the enormous output of wood carvings, furniture, sculpture and silverware that was required by churches all over the Indies. Starting inevitably from a Spanish pattern, a profusion of hybrid regional styles developed. A very distinctive mestizo style can be found in cities such as Arequipa, Potosí and La Paz, where native flora and fauna are incorporated in sculpture and carved ornaments.

Painting was very largely religious in subject-matter. In the first century after the Conquest Italian and Spanish painters were employed in various regions of the Indies, but native talent reached a peak of achievement under the influence of the great Spanish painter Francisco Zurbarán in the late seventeenth and early eighteenth centuries. In Mexico, two notable figures were Cristóbal de Villalpando and Juan Correa. At about the same time in Peru there appeared the celebrated Cuzco school of painters, of whom the Indian Diego Quispe Tito was the founder. The works of these Cuzco painters, with their use of gold leaf for decorative effect, resemble icons in their simplicity. The outstanding painter of the period in the Andean region is judged to be Melchor Pérez de Holguín.

As with the other arts, music thrived under the patronage of the Church – above all in the great cathedrals. Chapel masters, a number of whom were Indian or mestizo, traditionally composed and performed sacred music, and several first-rate musical talents emerged. Here again the late seventeenth century saw the culmination of artistic endeavour. Mexico produced Francisco López Capillas, a composer of great erudition, whose prowess extended to composing four distinct Masses to be sung in perfect harmony by as many choirs at the simultaneous consecration of four bishops in Mexico City in 1656. The greatest of the Mexican musicians was Manuel de Zumaya, active until the middle of the eighteenth century, whose liturgical music, psalms and hymns, according to Robert Stevenson, 'count among the most profound and beautiful monuments of native-born colonial genius in any of the arts'.* In South America, the outstanding genius was Juan de Araujo who served first in Lima cathedral and later in La Paz during the last three decades of the century and until his death in 1712.

Yet ecclesiastical music, for all the high skill and learning it required, did not stand aloof from the common people or the ethnic communities. Performed regularly before large congregations, it too was a supremely public art. The musical culture of the Spanish Indies shared the twin characteristics we have observed with regard to literature during the colonial period: it could assimilate non-European styles and interact with popular modes. From the earliest, the Church began to absorb Indian musical traditions. In mission stations throughout the Indies friars mixed European with indigenous musical styles and instruments at the Mass and other services. Even in the towns the Indians continued to play their own styles of music on traditional instruments, and these in time were selectively absorbed into the ecclesiastical repertoire. Robert Stevenson describes how a precedent was set at Corpus Christi in 1551 by Juan de Fuentes, the chapel master of Cuzco cathedral:

* *Cambridge History of Latin America*, vol. 2, p. 793.

Dressing up eight mestizo boys in Inca costume (not six, as was the conventional number of choirboys in a Spanish cathedral, but eight in deference to Inca numerology), Fuentes had them sing an Inca *haylli*. At refrains, the Spanish-born adult choristers sang part-music, to Garcilaso de la Vega's delight ... So great was the success of Fuentes's mixing of Inca and Spanish music that the Cuzco cathedral chapter decided ... to hire henceforth a full complement of choirboys.*

The vigorous musical traditions of the African slaves also made an impact on Spanish American culture. In the seventeenth century it became customary for white, cultured composers and poets to write songs in hybrid styles, called variously *negros*, *negrillas* or *guineas*, which employed African rhythms, black Spanish dialect and emphatic African refrains such as *gulungú gulungú* or *he he he cambulé*. This was a creole variant of the long Spanish tradition of writing *villancicos* and *canciones* – songs and ballads in the popular verse-forms and metres, a tradition which, needless to say, flourished equally in the Indies. Its most gifted exponent in New Spain was the creole nun Sor Juana Inés de la Cruz, whose spirited *villancicos*, many of them set to music by successive chapel masters of Mexico City cathedral, sometimes incorporated snatches of Nahuatl or Afro-Spanish dialect.

Sor Juana represents the creole culture and society of New Spain at its zenith towards the end of the seventeenth century. Hailed as the Tenth Muse during her lifetime, she became the greatest literary figure of the Hispanic world after the death of the Spanish playwright Pedro Calderón de la Barca in 1681. She was born in 1648, the illegitimate daughter of a creole woman and a Spaniard of whom nothing is known. Brought up by her mother on a hacienda outside Mexico City, she made a great impression as a young woman at the viceregal court for her intellectual and musical gifts. She took the veil because the convent afforded her the best conditions to cultivate her love of poetry and scholarship. San Jerónimo was a liberal convent, where well-to-do women could withdraw from the world and take their maid-servants and slaves with them to live in a cell which in reality was more like a suite of rooms. There Sor Juana flourished as a grand literary hostess, visited by friends from the highest social circles, including the viceroy and his consort. The relative leisure of religious life accounts for the significant number of women among the poets and devotional writers in the Spanish Indies. Sor Juana herself excelled in all the genres, including verse drama and the *auto sacramental*.

The experience of Sor Juana illustrates both the freedom and rigidity

---

* *Cambridge History of Latin America*, vol. 2, p. 774.

of Hispanic creole culture. There was a remarkable tolerance of personal aberrations so long as the basic principles of society were not called in question. Juana's bastardy was no impediment in her career. Her mother had six children by two men, neither of whom was her husband, but was still able to make respectable marriages for her daughters, who themselves were to have children out of wedlock and live openly with their lovers. Yet Sor Juana eventually fell foul of the Church authorities when she allowed herself to become caught up in a power struggle between her protector, the viceroy, and the Archbishop of Mexico. She eventually renounced her books, submitting to her Jesuit confessor in a document signed in her own blood. Juana's writing had offended powerful interests in the Church and she was finally persuaded that, as a woman, the pursuit of learning would jeopardize her soul.

The fate of Sor Juana remains an enigma. Does it simply reveal the repressiveness of a patriarchal society, or is it also an index of cultural colonialism, proof that Spain stifled the creative spirit of the creoles? Such explanations have been offered by modern scholars, but Sor Juana's act of renunciation must be seen against the wider background of Catholic baroque culture. Juana was indeed one of a very talented creole generation, which enjoyed a lively intellectual culture centred on the universities, convents, aristocratic salons and courts of the viceregal capitals. A regular intellectual companion of Sor Juana was the polymath Carlos Sigüenza y Góngora. He was mathematician, astronomer, archaeologist and historian, but a man whose religious orthodoxy and scholastic training placed constraints on his wide-ranging curiosity. Much the same can be said of the other prominent intellectual figure of the colonial period, the Peruvian Pedro Peralta Barnuevo, a professor of mathematics in Lima. He was a man of encyclopedic interests, yet one who, like Sor Juana, repudiated secular learning towards the end of his life in an ascetic work entitled *Pasión y triunfo de Cristo* ('The Passion and Triumph of Christ', 1738). This spirit of final renunciation was a characteristic movement of the Hispanic baroque mind, and it is evident also in the acidly satirical verse of the most remarkable of the poets of colonial Peru, Juan del Valle Caviedes. Such forms of spiritual disillusionment with the attractions of the human world, and a consequent dedication to matters of the soul, are as much in evidence in contemporary Spain itself as in the Indies.

The Eighteenth Century

If such creole figures as Sor Juana, Sigüenza y Góngora and Peralta Barnuevo displayed a degree of scientific interest and a passion for secular learning, there is little sign that they were in advance of intellectual currents in Spain itself. They lived in a period when the culture of the Counter-Reformation had begun to lose its vitality, but when the new critical ideas had yet to break through the shell of traditional ideology which enclosed the entire Hispanic world. It was the change of dynasty in Spain from Habsburg to French Bourbon after 1700 that would eventually allow the thought of the Enlightenment to filter slowly to a small minority of the intellectual élite of the Peninsula. Even then an accommodation was sought between authority and reason in a cautious ideology which has been termed the Catholic Enlightenment.

Its earliest and most famous proponent was the Spanish priest Benito Feijóo, who from the 1720s initiated a critique of traditional Spanish culture and education. By the middle of the eighteenth century, enlightened thinkers close to the Bourbon monarchy, like the influential Gaspar Melchor de Jovellanos, had conceived a comprehensive project of reform to be undertaken throughout the Hispanic world. (The impact of these reforms on the Spanish Indies is discussed in Chapter 6.) The old view that illicit French books smuggled modern ideas into the Spanish colonies is no longer valid. According to Mario Góngora, 'the Enlightenment was brought to Spanish America by Spanish officials and ecclesiastics, with whom the creoles associated themselves'.* Its first effects were evident in reforms of the university curriculum designed to break the hold of uncritical scholasticism and to promote a more open, inquiring attitude to the natural world.

For most of the eighteenth century the clergy – the Jesuits in particular – and a small technocratic élite fostered the ideas of the Enlightenment. But, after the expulsion of the Jesuits from the Spanish dominions in 1767, there occurred an important break in the culture of Spanish America. Most of the Jesuits banished from the Indies were creoles and they settled in Europe, especially in Italy. There it was that the 'process of negation of Spain' by the Spanish Americans was begun.† For many of these Jesuits, resentful of the Bourbon's 'enlightened despotism' that had led to their expulsion, contributed by their writings to the long-standing 'black legend' that had been propagated against Spain by her European enemies since the sixteenth

* *Studies in the Colonial History of Spanish America*, p. 191.
† Góngora, *Studies in the Colonial History of Spanish America*, p. 183.

century. And so, if before the 1770s the creoles had identified with the conquistadors and had taken pride in their affiliation with Spain, now dissident Jesuit voices denounced the exploits of the conquerors as atrocities and attacked the 'tyranny' exercised by the imperial monarchy over the creoles. By contrast, they praised the splendours of the natural environment in the New World and wrote eulogies of the pre-Columbian civilizations. These were the origins of the anti-Spanish *americanismo* which was to play such a prominent role in the history of the independent republics.

Within the Indies themselves the ideological separation from Spain was more gradual, but from the 1770s, too, elements in the creole intelligentsia began to lose their inherited respect for the motherland as the standard-bearer of a universal Christian order. France increasingly became the beacon of civilization, since the Enlightenment in the Iberian world was but an extension of French ideas. In the arts, the latter decades of the century saw Hispanic baroque styles give way to a neo-classicism of French inspiration associated with modernity and progress.

An index of this development is the increasing recourse to foreign-born artists and musicians for major works in the main cities. In the late eighteenth century commissions for public buildings and new churches went to Italians, Frenchmen and peninsular Spaniards. The cathedral of Buenos Aires was designed by an Italian, as was Santiago de Chile's fine neo-classical Moneda Palace. In Mexico City, an Academy of Fine Art was founded by Charles III in 1785, and one of its most influential masters was a Catalan, Manuel Tolsá, who designed the excellent School of Mining and gave the baroque cathedral its neo-classical towers and dome; his equestrian statue of Charles IV in Mexico City is regarded as a masterpiece of its kind. A creole pupil of Tolsá, Eduardo Tresguerras, was responsible for many neo-classical buildings in the city of Celaya. In painting, the late eighteenth century saw a rise in portraiture and secular themes as opposed to the religious subjects that had been dominant since the sixteenth. Music continued to be centred in the churches, but after the middle of the eighteenth century the great cathedrals tended to employ Italians and peninsular Spaniards as chapel masters.

The intellectual counterparts of neo-classical academies for the arts were the 'Economic Societies', or 'Societies of Friends of the Region', formed in the 1780s and 1790s in many parts of the Indies to foster the useful sciences and technical education. These circles of educated creole gentlemen provided the background for the intellectual 'precursors' of the independence movements. But progressive creoles constituted a mere fraction of the white élites of the Indies. What is more, their ideology was anything but uniform – there were Jacobins, Freemasons and republicans among them, but there were also constitutional monarchists and devout Catholics. Indeed, an important current in the movement for independence emanated from the clergy, who resented the centralizing reforms of the Bourbons and invoked the Virgin of Guadalupe in their struggle to achieve a purer form of Christianity in the New World. It was, for instance, this current that provided the impetus for the largely Indian insurrection launched against the Crown by Father Miguel Hidalgo in Mexico in 1810.

The Enlightenment brought new and grave divisions to Spanish American society. In the first place, it split a minority of modernizing creoles from the bulk of the traditionalist white oligarchies. Even more seriously, it created a very deep gulf between, on the one hand, an intellectual élite of creoles committed to liberalism, and, on the other, the overwhelming mass of people of all ethnic groups, who were wedded to the patriarchal order of the Catholic monarchy. When in 1808 Napoleon's forces invaded the Iberian peninsula, the Catholic monarchy was effectively destroyed, and these divisions immediately opened up in the Indies, with consequences that are evident to this day.

Perhaps the most important consequence of the break with Spain was the dilemma of cultural identity faced by the new republics. The culture of the Catholic monarchy possessed enduring strengths: it pervaded all strata of society, linking high culture and low; it could accommodate *mestizaje* in all spheres, from sexual relations to architecture; and, finally, it was capable of reconciling great ethnic and regional diversity with a sense of underlying unity. The Catholic monarchy, in short, provided a bedrock of cultural identity for the Spanish Indies.

Independence from Spain, then, would divorce the greater part of the creole intellectual élite from the common people, and, as a result, the question of cultural identity would become a central concern of writers and intellectuals in the new nations. The irony was that liberal modernizers would denigrate the Church and attack its privileges, yet it was the Church that had always nourished a genuinely popular culture throughout the Indies, a culture that could provide the kind of social solidarity required by the builders of the independent states. In time, the great Liberator Simón Bolívar would be cruelly disappointed by the disunity that afflicted the territories he had helped to free, and his project of a pan-American federation based on a common Hispanic heritage would come to nothing. As far as the intellectual vanguard of the white élites was concerned, independence may have heralded progress towards modernity and enlightenment, but for the mass of Indians and Spanish Americans it represented rather a leap in the dark.

The Patriarchal Colonialism of the Catholic Monarchy

The Spanish Indies, as we have seen, were heterogeneous and conflict-ridden; they were fragmented into numerous, largely isolated regions, and split in various ways between Hispanics and Indians, whites and non-whites, creoles and peninsulars. Moreover, the creole oligarchies constituted a frustrated ruling class. Had the Spanish monarchy not been so impotent and lax in the seventeenth century, would these élites have tolerated imperial rule? There is evidence to suggest that the creoles were often seething with resentment against Spain. And yet their discontent did not boil over into serious rebellion. At several points in the course of the seventeenth century, and in the latter part of the eighteenth, there were conspiracies and tumults directed at alleged abuses of particular viceroys, but there were no overt bids for independence, no direct challenges to the authority of the Crown as such.

Even in the 1640s, when the imperial monarchy was tottering as a result of multiple internal and external attacks, the creole élites failed to act. Most of the other realms of the empire rose against the Spanish monarchy. The Dutch, of course, had been in rebellion against Spain for some seventy years. The Catalans, the Portuguese, the Sicilians and the Neapolitans rebelled in the middle decades of the century. Even the Duke of Medina-Sidonia in Andalusia openly defied the Spanish king. Yet the creoles remained outwardly loyal. True, in 1642 Don Guillén de Lampart, an Irishman established in Mexico City, upon learning of the revolts of the Portuguese and Catalans, conceived a plan for the independence of New Spain, hoping to capitalize on the creoles' simmering resentment of the Crown's fiscal impositions. The conspiracy, however, came to nothing, and it is doubtful whether it would have attracted much support had it been put to the test. For the typical creole reaction to unpopular policies was to criticize, and perhaps even to conspire against, the viceroy, but never to move openly against the king himself.

The relative submissiveness of the American élites perhaps demonstrates the truly colonial character of the Indies. The European realms of the Catholic monarchy possessed a separate identity, which predated the imposition of Spanish authority; the Dutch, the Portuguese, the Catalans and others had alternative traditions and sources of legitimacy that could be invoked against Spain to justify their rebellions. But the imperial state in America was the unique creation of the Catholic monarchy, and the creoles, no matter what their frustrations, had no source of legitimate authority other than the Spanish king. To act against him would have required them to take a step into a constitutional void. Few creoles, if any, were prepared to carry their griev-

ances that far. For, in the last resort, the Indies suffered from a double
colonialism: the inequality of creole in relation to Spaniard was as nothing
compared to the subordination of Indians and non-whites to the creoles
themselves. Any direct attack on the monarchy ran the risk of bringing
down the complex ideological edifice which kept the double colonialism of
the Indies from collapsing in bloody chaos.

The creoles clearly accepted the colonial pact for some three centuries.
And the peculiar strength of this pact was that it cast the colonial relationship
in a familiar patriarchal mould: the creoles loyally offered their tribute of
silver to the Spanish king in return for the unifying authority he graciously
bestowed as a form of patronage on his otherwise fragmented and racially
divided American realms. It was only in the first decade of the nineteenth
century, when external forces unforeseeably destroyed that royal authority
in the Peninsula itself, that this patriarchal colonialism was unable to function
as of old, and the hapless American clients of the Catholic monarch were at
last propelled into the void they had resisted entering for so long.

5. Colonial Brazil

Discovery and Settlement

In the course of the fifteenth century, Portugal had far surpassed Castile in her expansion overseas. While the latter was settling Hispaniola and exploring other islands of the Caribbean, the Portuguese had sailed round Cape Horn and were establishing trading stations along the eastern coast of Africa. In 1498 Vasco da Gama reached India, and from there the Portuguese would extend their commercial empire to Ceylon, Malacca and the colony of Macao on the Chinese mainland.

This lucrative network of colonial enclaves on two continents would absorb the interest of the Portuguese for the next century or so, but in 1500 an expedition led by Pedro Álvares Cabral, which was on its way to India to follow up Vasco da Gama's epoch-making voyage, strayed too far off course and on 22 April made a chance landfall on an unknown coast lying well to the west of Africa. This discovery gave the Portuguese a foothold in the New World, though at the time it was impossible for them to know that they had arrived in the same continent as the Spaniards. Indeed, for another two or three decades neither of the Iberian nations had reason to perceive the connection between their discoveries in the Western Hemisphere: the Spaniards, as far as anyone knew, had come across a few islands in the western Atlantic some years earlier, and now the Portuguese believed they had landed on an island much further to the south, their first name for this territory being 'The Island of the True Cross'. Over time, further maritime explorations would reveal that these territories in reality formed part of a huge new continent.

Further expeditions were sent out in 1501 and 1503/4 to explore and to assess the commercial potential of the new discovery. The only commodity of interest that was found was a species of dyewood known as 'brazil', and a number of small trading stations like those on the African coast were set up to collect and export the wood. For the next thirty years Portugal concentrated on India and the Far East, paying little attention to her modest colony in the west, which was settled by petty merchants, castaways and common delinquents known as *degredados*, who had been banished from Portugal to remote parts of the empire. Relatively free from political authority in the early years of the Brazilian settlement, many of these *degredados* managed to win acceptance by Indian tribes: they learned the native languages, took chiefs' daughters as wives and concubines, and fathered a large progeny of half-caste children; of these 'squaw-men', João Ramalho in São Vicente and Caramurú of Bahia have since become legendary, being romanticized as forerunners of a new hybrid cultural type – the first Brazilians.

The brazil-wood trade, however, attracted the attention of the French, who began seizing Portuguese ships and trading directly with Indian tribes along the coast. There was a danger that the French might establish trading posts along the coast to rival the Portuguese. When France proclaimed its right to trade in any part of Brazil not actually occupied by Portugal, the Crown was forced to take the threat seriously and the nature of the Portuguese presence had to change from small African-style factories to the kind of extensive colonization that had been promoted on the Azores and Madeira. In 1530 Martim Afonso de Sousa was sent out with about 400 men to found a royal colony at São Vicente near present-day Santos.

However, the occupation of the entire known coastline of Brazil was beyond the resources of the Crown. It therefore tried to mobilize private interests to secure its claims in the New World. Brazil was divided into twelve territories and placed under the lordship of 'donatary-captains', who were chosen for their loyalty to the Crown. These captains received great powers: hereditary rights to the territory; the authority to make grants of land known as *sesmarias* to settlers; civil and criminal jurisdiction over the inhabitants; the privilege of raising certain taxes and licensing trade and industry. The Crown nevertheless retained its prerogative of natural lordship over Brazil as a whole, setting out the constitutional rights of settlers in relation to the donatary-captain and reserving for itself the right to raise fiscal revenues from major commercial activities.

With the exception of Pernambuco, the donatary-captaincies failed as enterprises of colonization. They faced hostility from Indian tribes, they did not deter the French, and commercial ventures did not prosper. Once more the Crown had to intervene in order to secure control of Brazil, creating the post of governor-general to oversee all the captaincies. In 1549 Tomé de Sousa was sent out as governor-general to the vacant captaincy of Bahia and established his seat at Salvador, which in effect became the first capital of

Brazil. With him came six Jesuit priests as an advance party for the very powerful missionary and educational presence that this order would develop throughout Brazil.

A prime reason for the failure of the donatary-captaincies was their lack of success in recruiting Indian labour for the nascent sugar industry. Since growing sugar was far more profitable than trading in brazil-wood, it was thought likely to entrench further the Portuguese presence in Brazil by attracting larger numbers of settlers. What is more, the Portuguese knew the business of sugar cultivation well from their plantations on the Azores, Madeira and the Cape Verde islands. But the difficulty was that the Indians, who had previously been happy to barter brazil-wood with settlers and even to co-operate with them in felling and transporting trees, could not, as hunter-gatherers, adapt to the exhausting work-schedules of a plantation economy.

As far as the Portuguese settlers were concerned, Indian reluctance to work was due to laziness, and in order to prevent the collapse of the sugar industry they took to seizing Indians as slaves. Enslavement was already common practice among the Indians, who would raid rival tribes and capture individuals for ritual sacrifice and cannibalism. But Portuguese slave-taking was commercially motivated and unrestrained; it resulted in the breakdown of relations with the native tribes, whose attacks on white settlements began to threaten the economic development of the Portuguese colonies.

The arrival of the Jesuits marked the determination of the Portuguese Crown to institute a coherent polity in Brazil. The Jesuits were sent to stabilize and regulate the relations between Indians and Europeans. Their aim was to convert the Indians to Christianity and European ways by educating them in specially designed villages or *aldeias*, which were modelled on the *congregaciones* of the missionaries in Spanish America. But the Jesuits soon encountered opposition from the settlers who did not want to see their access to Indian slave labour impeded by missionaries. The conflict between Jesuits and settlers was to become a permanent and very disruptive feature of colonial life in Brazil.

The Jesuits also encountered opposition from the secular clergy, who tended to take the view that the Indians were savages and could therefore be legitimately held in bondage. Friction between the Jesuits and the first bishop of Brazil, Fernandes Sardanha, forced them to move in 1554 from Bahia to the captaincy of São Vicente, where they set up an *aldeia* at Piratininga, the site of what was eventually to become the city of São Paulo. Fuller development of the *aldeia* system had to wait Sardanha's replacement and the appointment in 1557 of a new governor, Mem de Sá, who was more in sympathy with the aims of the missionaries.

For ten years or so after the arrival of the first governor-general and the first missionaries, the situation in Brazil remained volatile. In addition, the 1550s saw a further threat from the French to the Portuguese Crown's position in the New World. An expedition of some 600 mainly Protestant Frenchmen set up a colony, which they called France Antarctique, at Guanabara Bay in an area not settled by the Portuguese. This grave threat to Portuguese interests called forth a determined response and several expeditions were sent down from Bahia until the French were finally ousted from Brazil in 1567. On the site of their colony a new settlement of Rio de Janeiro was founded and a royal captaincy was created to secure the area from further incursions.

The Portuguese were thenceforth masters of Brazil, but the threat from European rivals did not entirely disappear. Portugal's union with Spain in 1580 under the sovereignty of Philip II would lead its imperial possessions to suffer the attentions of the Dutch. In 1630 the Dutch seized Pernambuco – one of the richest sugar-growing areas of the Brazilian north-east – and very nearly took over Portugal's entire Atlantic trade when they conquered Portuguese Angola in 1641. But the Portuguese fought back, regaining Angola in 1648/9 and, after offering stiff resistance in Brazil for many years, finally expelled the Dutch in 1654. The Dutch, however, took with them the expertise they had acquired in running sugar mills and plantations, and set up a rival industry in the Caribbean to the eventual detriment of Brazil.

Sovereignty and the Question of Slavery

The attempts of rival European powers to occupy Brazil had to be countered in part by establishing a clear title to the land. The Crown was content to base its claim on prior discovery and effective occupation. The Portuguese did not face the same juridical and moral difficulties with regard to Indian sovereignty as had the Spaniards in Mexico or Peru. The Indians of Brazil did not belong to advanced sedentary societies with forms of government that sixteenth-century Europeans might regard as 'civilized'. Nomadic and cannibalistic, the hunter-gatherers of Brazil were classed as savages, who could not therefore be deemed to exercise true natural lordship over the land. The correct analogy was not with Mexico or Peru, but with the experience of the Spaniards among the Arawaks and Caribs of the Caribbean islands.

Nevertheless, from a combination of principle and expediency, the Crown came to favour a missionary policy of evangelization. Evangelization would reinforce its title to Brazil in much the same way as it had strengthened Spain's claim to Mexico and Peru – in any case, it was an established practice in Iberian enterprises of expansion overseas to proselytize among the natives. A policy of concentrating the Indians in villages and teaching them sedentary habits would also greatly assist the pacification of the colonies. Finally, it was important for the good government of colonial society – particularly as regards relations between settlers and natives – that the Indians' rights be defined; and the question, as in Spanish America, turned upon the matter of slavery.

Here the analogy with the Spanish experience in Hispaniola is the most relevant. Like the Indians of the Caribbean islands, the Brazilian tribes had no tradition of offering labour services to overlords or of working at routine tasks. Iberian settlers could therefore satisfy their labour requirement only through enslavement. In the four or five decades of 'neglect' of Brazil by the Crown, the settlers had had plenty of time to develop the skills and lore of slave-hunting in the bush – able-bodied Indians were a precious commodity that fetched good prices in the labour market for the plantation economy.

Thus when the Crown sent the Jesuits to convert the Indians in the 1550s, conflict with the settlers was inevitable. The Jesuit model of relations with the Indians was tutelary and paternalist – on humanitarian grounds, if on no other, the natives had to be protected from exploitation. But the missionary enterprise, based on the *aldeia* system, was also a form of intrusion into, and reorganization of, Indian society, albeit well-intentioned. The Indians were converted into childlike charges of the Jesuit fathers and were transformed into a submissive, industrious workforce on the missions' highly profitable fields and plantations. It is little wonder that the settlers envied the wealth of the Jesuit *aldeias*, and resented what they saw as the Jesuits' obstruction of their efforts to procure an adequate supply of labour for their own plantations.

Enslavement was, then, a necessity in Brazil, given the nature of the settlers' economy. But since the enslavement of barbarians was not regarded as a sin in itself, Indian slavery did not become so controversial an issue as it did in the Spanish Indies, where the question of the Indians' barbarism was much more difficult to decide. Still, the sheer cruelty of the slave-hunts gave rise to moral qualms among the clergy and the missionaries, and the Crown would eventually be forced to intervene.

What brought the slavery question to a head in Brazil was the arrival of European diseases. The first epidemic hit Bahia in 1562 and was followed by a more general outbreak in the following year. The toll of death was appalling: it is estimated to have been between a third and a half of the Indian population of the coastal areas under Portuguese control. Having no immunities against European diseases, the natives succumbed to measles, smallpox, tuberculosis and other viral infections. Famine quickly followed and the terrified Indians, their societies in disarray, began to sell themselves to settlers in return for food and shelter.

The crisis demanded some legal regulation of natives' relations with whites. Royal officials, jurists, bishops and missionaries debated the question, and the king finally issued a decree in 1570, declaring that the Indians were born free and could be enslaved only if they practised cannibalism or were taken captive in a 'just war'. The widespread practice of *resgate* – whereby wild Indians captured by rival tribes were 'ransomed' by slave-hunters and brought to serve on plantations – was outlawed, but this provoked such an outcry from the settlers that the decree had to be revoked in 1574.

In practice, the royal legislation concerning the enslavement of Indians was ignored virtually in its entirety by the Portuguese in Brazil. The hunting of Indian slaves was to continue throughout the colonial period. However, the nature of slave-holding in Brazil underwent a slow but eventually decisive change after about the middle of the sixteenth century. Indians along the coast were becoming scarce: as hostilities between settlers and natives grew fiercer, tribes withdrew into the hinterland; at the same time diseases started to thin their ranks. The available labour force was drastically depleted, intensifying the competition between missionaries and planters for Indian manpower.

An obvious solution lay in the importation of African slaves to work on the Brazilian plantations. The Portuguese had been operating a slave-trade along the African coast for nearly a century, and they were splendid mariners, so there was therefore no impediment to extending the trade to the New World. Even though African slaves were more expensive than Indian, there were two distinct advantages to the owners: the Africans had the same immunities to viral infections as the Europeans, and they were reputed to be better suited to the kind of hard labour required on the plantations. The demand for labour in the burgeoning sugar industry of Brazil was to lead to an enormous expansion of the African slave-trade (and demand would grow a few decades later in the 1580s when planters in the islands and coastal areas of the Spanish Indies began to seek a replacement for vanishing Indian manpower).

How many slaves were imported into Brazil is not reliably known, and what figures there are remain in dispute, but it is clear that the numbers were very high. By the end of the sixteenth century there may well have been between 13,000 and 15,000 black slaves in Brazil, constituting some 70 per cent of the labour force on the plantations. The white population of Brazil in around 1585 has been estimated at 29,000. During the first half of the seventeenth century about 4,000 slaves a year were imported into Brazil; from about 1650 to 1680 this figure rose to about 8,000, after which it began to tail off. In the eighteenth century the volume of imports began to increase once more when the gold-mining industry pushed up overall demand – Bahia alone received some 5,000 to 8,000 slaves a year. In the north-east as a whole slaves made up about half the population – over two-thirds in the sugar-growing areas. So many were imported partly because the mortality rate of the black slave population was so high and because its rate of procreation fell consistently below the level of replacement – an index of the tremendous demoralization and physical strain that afflicted the slaves. Philip Curtin estimates that in the course of the seventeenth century Brazil took a 41.8 per cent share of the total number of slaves transported to America.*

The arrival of Africans in such huge numbers was to add a new demographic dimension to the Portuguese colonies in the New World. Since such a great part of the population was non-white, race mixture soon produced, as in the Spanish Indies, very many people of intermediate ethnicity – mulattos or *pardos* (white-black), *mamelucos* or *caboclos* (white-Indian) and *cafusos* (Indian-black). Brazil would become an extremely colour-conscious society, and racial features were an important element in social ranking and cultural identification. The inescapable reality was that the sugar economy, as created in the middle of the sixteenth century, made slavery a founding fact of Brazilian society.

The importation of African slaves did not do away with the enslavement of Indians. Brazil had been a slave society from its origins; the sugar industry only magnified the scale of enslavement and introduced a new population from another continent. The importation of Africans simply accentuated the displacement of Indians towards the margins of settlement, where the pressures of disease and persecution had been forcing them anyway. We find therefore a divergence in the development of Brazil, leading to two very different kinds of society. First, 'Brazil' proper, where the sovereignty of the king of Portugal was fully acknowledged and where there existed an appar-

* *The Atlantic Slave Trade: A Census* (University of Wisconsin Press: Madison, 1969), table 34, p. 119.

atus of state and Church governing a settled society of towns and plantations comprising whites, blacks and people of mixed race. In the late sixteenth century and for most of the seventeenth, this 'civilized' society was concentrated in the sugar-growing enclaves of the north-eastern coasts and in some secondary regions around the still fairly primitive colonies of São Paulo and Rio de Janeiro, where some sugar was grown as well as other commodities.

The other society was located on the edges of the wilderness – on marginal, ill-defined stretches of territory, where settlement was sparse and the writ of law scarcely ran. Indeed, these frontier zones survived economically largely by plundering the hinterland for whatever commodities it might yield. It was on this frontier that the interaction between the Portuguese and the nomadic Indian tribes continued in all its barbarous ferocity.

The Indians gradually began to disappear from the society of 'civilized' Brazil. Although some were still to be found as slaves on the plantations until about the 1730s, the demographic presence of the Indian became less and less noticeable. By the middle of the eighteenth century, when the notion of the 'noble savage' had been made fashionable by the European Enlightenment, the Indian had become an exotic figure to most Brazilians. Ironically, this allowed him to be idealized as a cultural prototype, to the point where, after independence, romantic nationalists would urge the urban middle classes to learn indigenous tongues so as to become more fully 'Brazilian'.

The Moving Frontier: Sertão *and* Selva

The frontier was to play a far more important role in the development of Brazil than it would in the Spanish Indies. Middle America and Peru, with their precious metals and sedentary Indian manpower, would act as the twin poles of attraction for Spanish settlers. The bold and wide-ranging Spanish explorations of the sixteenth century were motivated by the desire to find new Mexicos and Perus. In South America it was the Spaniards who discovered the great river-systems in the hinterland of the River Plate, and they too who first ventured into the rain forests of the interior to explore the Amazon and its basin. However, when these quests for Eldorado came to nothing, the Spaniards, by and large, lost interest in their frontier zones, concentrating on developing their two major areas of colonization, and a few other regions that had reserves of settled Indian manpower.

Brazil was very different. In the sixteenth century the Portuguese found nothing that could remotely compare with Peru, and, after setting up sugar plantations in a handful of enclaves along the Atlantic coast, they had nowhere to turn but towards the vast and mysterious interior. It was this *sertão* which offered a wide horizon of possibility to those Portuguese and half-castes who were unable to establish themselves adequately on the coast. The interior would always beckon, for it was full of Indians to enslave and there remained the promise of precious metals to be discovered.

Until the eighteenth century, slaves were to be the chief commodity of Brazilian frontier society. Hunting for slaves became something of a speciality of the São Paulo region. It developed into a highly organized enterprise often involving expeditions of several thousand men equipped with ammunition, shackles and provisions, including livestock, to provide sustenance on the march. These companies of slavers were known as *bandeiras*, and they would set off into the bush or the jungle for several years at a time with the aim of rounding up Indians for eventual sale to sugar planters and *fazendeiros* in the captaincies of São Paulo and Rio de Janeiro, and possibly further afield. The *bandeirantes* were particularly active in the early seventeenth century, when the Portuguese lost Angola to the Dutch and the Brazilian plantations were cut off from the African slave-trade.

After Portugal recovered Angola in 1648, demand for Indian slaves tailed off and *bandeirantes* had to look for other sources of wealth, setting off into the interior in search of minerals or possible trade routes to the silver-mines of Spanish-held Potosí. In 1648–51 the infamous Rapôso Tavares led a *bandeira* from São Paulo across the Chaco of Paraguay to the foothills of the Andes, after which he veered north and stumbled into the Amazon basin, from where he followed the course of the great river down to the sea. The men of São Paulo became so renowned for their skills as trackers and Indian-fighters that governors of captaincies in the north-east repeatedly enlisted their services to make war on the aggressive Indian tribes of the *sertão* and so clear these backlands for cattle-ranching. It was the *bandeirantes* of São Paulo who would make the first gold strikes in Minas Gerais in the 1690s, following these up with new strikes in Goiás and the Mato Grosso. Such excursions into the wilderness served to extend the radius of Portuguese control deep into the hinterland of South America. As the *bandeirantes* penetrated into the *sertão* and came upon resources worth exploiting, rudimentary settlements would spring up and the Brazilian frontier would move further towards the heart of the continent.

For their part, the Jesuits also went in search of wild Indians to convert and reduce to 'civilized' life in their missions. As disease decimated the tribes of the coast, the priests ranged inland and founded new mission stations in the outback. In the region of São Paulo, where they had set up their first base at Piratininga, the Jesuits established various mission villages, but they found themselves in competition with the settlers of São Paulo, who claimed a right to a share of Indian labour. Constant friction between Paulistas and Jesuits resulted twice in the expulsion of the missionaries from the São Paulo region in the seventeenth century.

However, the most serious confrontations with missionaries occurred in the basin of the Paraguay and Paraná rivers. This region became one of the most turbulent of the frontier zones because of frequent boundary disputes between Portugal and Spain. What aggravated the geopolitical tensions were the missions founded by Spanish Jesuits among the Guaraní Indians in an area midway between São Paulo in Brazil and Asunción in Paraguay. The Guaraní proved to be willing converts and very docile labourers, so the Jesuits were able to create large and highly productive plantations of sugar, *mate* tea and other crops. The *bandeirantes* of São Paulo could not resist preying upon the large pool of Guaraní manpower that the Spanish Jesuits had so conveniently 'civilized' on their plantations. Paulista *bandeiras* took to raiding the Jesuit missions, carrying off converted Indians as slaves. Although the Spanish Jesuits moved their missions to the south and west, and even armed their Indians to fight off the Paulistas (which they did successfully after a full-scale war in 1641), the *bandeirantes* kept up their raids and, in doing so, helped eventually to define the southern and south-western boundaries of Brazil.

The other great frontier territory of colonial Brazil was the northern equatorial region comprising Maranhão and Pará. The slave-hunters roamed the *sertão* of Maranhão and, from the settlement of Belém do Pará at the mouth of the Amazon, they penetrated up-river in search of Indians. These excursions were known as *tropas de resgate* and they were carried out with fleets of canoes paddled by Indians under the command of *caboclo* slavers. *Tropas* would probe the Amazon and its tributaries, bringing back produce of the forests as well as their human cargoes. The many populous tribes of the rain forests suffered terrible depredations at the hands of these half-caste slave-hunters: an ecclesiastic reported that within thirty years of entering the regions of Maranhão and Pará in 1616, a few hundred settlers may have caused the deaths of up to 2 million Amazon Indians. In 1637, a notorious exploiter of Indians, Bento Maciel, was granted the captaincy of huge territories (modern Amapá), which he used as a personal hunting-ground for native labour.

The frontier territories of Maranhão and Pará became important mission fields for the Jesuits. They arrived in 1653 under the leadership of the Brazilian

Jesuit António Vieira, who had achieved great fame throughout the Luso-
Hispanic world as a preacher, diplomat and confessor to the king of Portugal.
Vieira immediately denounced slave-hunting and proceeded to institute a
regime of Jesuit-run *aldeias* along the lines of those in Paraguay. At Vieira's
request, the king issued a decree in 1655 forbidding the enslavement of
Indians. But even though the Jesuits were successful in persuading many
Indian tribes to convert and settle voluntarily in the mission villages, their
promises of humane treatment were undermined by epidemics of European
diseases – which carried off large numbers of natives – and by the harassment
of the Indians by Brazilian settlers anxious for manpower.

The last decades of the seventeenth century saw many clashes between
settlers and Jesuits over the supply of Indian labour. In 1661 and 1684 the
Jesuits were expelled from their mission fields by angry settlers. Finally, a
compromise was reached by which the mission Indians were allowed to
work for Brazilian settlers for specified periods and fixed wages (which were,
in fact, paltry). Despite various royal decrees to regulate slavery, expeditions
into the Amazon basin by *tropas de resgate* would continue throughout the
colonial period.

As the *bandeirantes* of São Paulo had done in the south, the slave-hunters
of the north pushed the Brazilian frontier well beyond the line established
by the Treaty of Tordesillas as the demarcation between the territories of
the two Iberian monarchies. In 1637 an expedition led by Pedro Teixeira set
off up the Amazon and drew the north-west boundary of Brazil some 1,500
miles west of the line of Tordesillas, roughly where it is today. The king of
Spain was advised by one of his agents that the Amazon basin should be
settled rapidly to prevent the Portuguese taking over vast areas that had been
allocated to Spain. However, the king (who at the time was also sovereign
of Portugal) failed to act, and Brazilian frontier society was allowed to extend
deeper into the jungle. When the borders of Brazil were agreed by the Treaty
of Madrid in 1750, the existence of Jesuit mission villages along the far western
tributaries of the Amazon influenced the decision to confirm Portugal's claim
to most of the territories at the centre of South America.

The division between frontier and civilized society was to remain deeply
ingrained in the mentality of Brazilians. The frontier was enormous and ill-
defined, a place from where the wilderness could be plundered with virtual
impunity. There, European culture became permeated by indigenous
customs: white and mixed-blood settlers around São Paulo and the equatorial
north adopted Indian habits and mores – they slept in hammocks, ate manioc,
kept concubines and spoke a *lingua franca* based on Tupi. Beyond the full
reach of the state, the frontier provided a free-ranging environment for

Indian-fighters, bandits, runaway slaves and thousands of desperadoes; what order it knew came from the arbitrary personal rule of rough captains and *poderosos do sertão*, the powerful ranchers who controlled the great herds of cattle on the plains of the outback. The state had an effective existence only in the other, civilized Brazil, but once frontier zones successfully established a stable economy they tended to evolve towards the norms of this latter society.

State, Government and Church

The history of Brazil in the sixteenth century shows the determination of the Portuguese Crown to hold on to a territory that had come into its possession by chance. Royal authority was imposed piecemeal, and in response to multiple threats from foreign powers, from Indian hostility and from the turbulent internal affairs of the developing colony. The state that resulted was in many respects similar to that of the Spanish Indies, but there were significant differences arising from the circumstances of the Brazilian experience itself.

As in the Spanish Indies, the Crown claimed natural lordship and patrimonial rights over the land, and its authority was based upon a monopoly of legitimacy underwritten by the Catholic Church. Thus, even though it had donated extensive rights of colonization and jurisdiction to individuals in the 1530s, it retained ultimate sovereignty over the donatary-captaincies and would intervene in their government if necessary. There was to be no attempt to remove the original captaincies from private hands, but a more centralized state was gradually created by sending out Crown officials to occupy vacant captaincies and to govern newly conquered territories, and by investing the governor-general in the royal captaincy at Bahia with the right to oversee the government of all the captaincies of Brazil. Still, a tension would persist between the private authority of the donatary-captains and the theoretically overarching authority of the royal governor-general.

Considered as a whole, the Portuguese imperial state was far more unitary than the Spanish. This was largely accidental, arising from the fact that, as nomadic hunter-gatherers, the Indians of Brazil were plainly savages by contemporary European criteria. There were a number of juridical and political advantages that flowed from this state of affairs. The Portuguese monarchs were not faced with the thorny problem of having to justify the violent overthrow of native rulers of civilized kingdoms. Since the Portuguese Crown could claim a right to Brazil without reference to prior native lordship, it did not have to constitute the colonies in Brazil as realms distinct from Portugal in the way that the Spanish Indies were theoretically kingdoms separate from Spain itself. As a result, Brazil was regarded as a simple extension of Portuguese territory and its inhabitants felt themselves to be Portuguese subjects on the same basis as those in the Peninsula. The various colonial enclaves along the Atlantic coast were able to communicate more directly with Portugal than with each other, and the fact that the bulk of the labour force was not indigenous but made up of black slaves imported from Africa further reinforced the sense that Portugal had an intrinsic right to Brazil. There did not arise, therefore, the same degree of friction between settlers and Crown as existed in the Spanish American realms.

The Portuguese Crown, furthermore, was less interventionist than the Spanish. Because the status of the Indian population was easier to define by traditional Aristotelian criteria of barbarism, the Crown did not have to struggle to implement an unworkable policy of protecting Indian lands and communities by administering an indigenous 'republic' separate from that of the whites, a policy that might have caused resentment among the Brazilians as it did among the Spanish American creoles. Then there was the absence of silver. In a mercantilist age which considered the possession of bullion to be a sufficient index of economic power, the discovery of silver in Brazil might have led the Crown to attempt to impose strict controls over crucial sectors of the export-economy, with all the associated military and bureaucratic costs. The relative lack of state interference served to smooth the relationship between the Brazilian planter élites and metropolitan Portugal.

Because sugar was Brazil's prime commodity until the end of the seventeenth century, Portugal was able to adopt a flexible colonial regime more in keeping with the resources of a small country already fairly stretched by its activities in Africa, India and the Far East. Still, the hand of the state did make itself felt in the economy of Brazil. The Crown operated a commercial monopoly based on the licensing of merchant ships for the sugar and slave trades; but licences were eventually granted to vessels of friendly powers and were given to individual slave-traders, which reduced the expense of organizing and protecting the scheduled voyages by convoy from Lisbon which operated until the middle of the eighteenth century. The Crown also collected a range of import and export duties.

Brazil, in fact, was administered as if it were a projection of Portugal overseas; colonial affairs were not, in principle, given separate treatment from those of the metropolis. Matters of general policy were decided by the king in consultation with the Council of State. A number of other councils had jurisdiction over more specialized areas: finance, justice, ecclesiastical and religious affairs. In 1642 John IV created the Conselho Ultramarino (Overseas Council) to discuss colonial business, but its agenda often overlapped with those of the other councils.

Lisbon remained the administrative focus of the various transatlantic colonies, and further attempts were made during the seventeenth century to consolidate the royal administration's control over the various captaincies by regrouping territories into larger administrative units. In 1621 Portugal's American colonies were divided into two states: the state of Maranhão, with a governor-general at São Luís, comprising some newly established captaincies in the underpopulated northern regions, and the state of Brazil, with its capital at Salvador in Bahia, extending southwards to São Vicente and including all the old captaincies. However, there were continual conflicts of jurisdiction between the governor-general at Bahia and the captains of important centres like Pernambuco, São Paulo and Rio de Janeiro. In the early eighteenth century the status of these three captaincies was enhanced and neighbouring territories were subordinated to their authority.

This concession signalled the growing economic importance of the south-central captaincies in relation to the much older sugar-growing areas of the north-east. By the middle of the century the centre of gravity had shifted decisively to the south, owing to the discovery of gold and to the persistent frontier disputes with Spain along the south and south-western flanks of Brazil. The seat of royal government was transferred from Salvador to Rio de Janeiro in 1763. Finally, in 1774, the distinction between the states of Maranhão and Brazil was abolished and the whole territory was administered from Rio de Janeiro.

For most of the sixteenth century, the administration of justice was entrusted to a Crown judge (*ouvidor*) appointed to each captaincy and responsible directly to Lisbon, but in 1549 the judges were brought under the authority of an *ouvidor geral* in Bahia, and in 1588 they were further subordinated to the judges of a high court, the Relação da Bahia, which in turn came under the jurisdiction of the supreme court in Lisbon. Like the Spanish American *audiencias*, the Relação was authorized to deal with certain administrative and political questions in consultation with the governor-general. Fiscal matters were handled by treasury officials in each captaincy.

The conditions of service of high-ranking royal officials were similar to those of their counterparts in Spanish America. There were regulations designed to prevent them from establishing ties with local society: they could not serve in their native regions, engage in business locally or marry local women. These rules, however, were not generally observed, for it was in the interests of the local oligarchies to form connections with royal officials in order to obtain favours or special treatment. Graft and corruption became endemic in the imperial bureaucracy in spite of the Crown's use of the *visita* and the *residencia* to scrutinize the conduct of royal officers. Nevertheless, as occurred in Spanish America, the collusion between royal administrators and local élites had the effect of adjusting laws to particular circumstances, albeit to the advantage of established interests. Similarly, the impact of absolute royal power was diffused through the various overlapping jurisdictions which made up the imperial government, and it was softened too by the political tensions that existed between the authority of the donatary-captains and that of the governor-general.

The centralizing powers of the state bore down less heavily upon local affairs in Brazil than in the Spanish Indies. This is evident from the degree of self-regulation enjoyed by the municipal councils, the *senados da câmara*, which, like the Spanish American *cabildos*, were to be found in every town of importance. The *câmara* comprised up to six councillors (*vereadores*), one or two magistrates (*juizes ordinarios*) and a *procurador* responsible for fiscal matters. They were elected by a suffrage limited to *homens bons*, men of property and of certified pure blood. This elective principle was maintained until the very end of the seventeenth century, when the rotating chairmanship of the council was superseded by the appointment of a Crown judge 'from outside' (*juiz de fora*) and by the selection of the other members of the council from among local notables. Even so, membership of the municipal councils changed regularly and never became hereditary as in the Spanish Indies. Since they had jurisdiction over a wide range of affairs relating to taxation, public works, municipal contracts and law and order, the *câmaras* served as a useful forum for local political interests.

The Church as an institution can be regarded as an arm of the imperial government. The monarchs of Portugal enjoyed rights of patronage in Church affairs thanks to the *Padroado Real*, a concession from the Pope granted in 1551 allowing them to nominate candidates for ecclesiastical posts in Brazil. All matters pertaining to the organization of the Church were decided in Lisbon, not in Rome, and this clearly extended the political authority of the Crown. The *Padroado Real* was conceded by the papacy in recognition of the special responsibility of the Portuguese monarchy for the propagation of the faith in the New World. The Church in Brazil was thus conceived as a missionary enterprise in its origins, and the religious orders – mainly the Jesuits, but also Franciscans, Benedictines, Carmelites and Capuchins – tended to dominate religious life for most of the colonial period, their activities being geared principally to the conversion and instruction of the Indians. The secular clergy was introduced at a later stage, since its purpose was to serve those areas in which a settled Portuguese society had been established. However, it was some time before diocesan structures took root – until 1676 the diocese of Salvador in Bahia served the whole of Brazil; additional dioceses were created after that date and in the course of the eighteenth century. This very patchy presence of the secular clergy meant that religious discipline was fairly weak in Brazilian towns and settlements, especially in frontier zones.

The Church, however, still possessed considerable influence throughout society. In major towns, religious orders ran hospitals, schools, orphanages and hospices for the sick and poor. Revenues from tithes and donations financed the acquisition of land and property, which provided employment and also yielded capital that was loaned to merchants and planters at a low fixed interest rate of $6\frac{1}{4}$ per cent. In a more indirect way, the Church exercised its influence through *irmandades*, religious brotherhoods for lay people, which were widely popular among all classes and races. These self-regulating associations provided social services to their members. The most famous was the Santa Casa da Misericórdia, which had branches in Portugal and all over the empire. Membership conferred social status – no one with the taint of Jewish or coloured ancestry was admitted, and even within the organization itself a distinction was observed between wealthy members and others of lower rank, such as artisans and petty merchants. The brotherhoods for blacks and people of mixed blood functioned as an important source of corporate solidarity for these oppressed groups. In addition to offering social welfare, *irmandades* organized religious festivals, where the various ethnic groups found an outlet for cultural expression. (The practice survives today in the quite profane context of the Carnival at Rio de Janeiro, for which elaborate floats and parades are prepared by 'samba schools' formed largely by blacks and mulattos from different poor neighbourhoods.)

It was thus not just the *Padroado Real*, but the traditional, if diffuse, presence of the Church itself in Portuguese society that afforded very considerable benefits to the Portuguese monarchy in the maintenance of the imperial state. The Church acted as a cohesive force in scattered territories whose political allegiance would otherwise have had to be secured by the commitment of resources that were quite beyond the financial means of the Crown. In fact, large areas of Brazil escaped effective control by royal officials, but the pervasive influence of religion in Portuguese culture fostered at least a nominal acceptance of the king's sovereignty. In the turbulent gold-mining region of Minas Gerais, where it proved exceedingly difficult for royal officials to prevent massive tax evasion, a good proportion of private wealth was donated to the clergy in order to finance the building of extravagantly decorated churches. The success of the missionary orders in instilling loyalty to the monarchy and attachment to Portuguese culture can be judged by the contrasting experience of the Dutch. Charles Boxer has observed that 'during the twenty-four years in which the Dutch held all or part of north-east Brazil the subjugated population obstinately refused to learn the language of their heretic overlords, and it is believed that only two Dutch words have survived in the popular language of Pernambuco'. Indeed, many of the Dutch in Pernambuco were won over to the Church of Rome, 'whereas converts from Catholicism to Calvinism were as rare as hens' teeth'.*

The Economy

Brazil was the first European colony in the Americas to found its economy on the export of a dominant commodity to Europe, and this basic pattern would prevail until the middle of the twentieth century. In the colonial period the growth of the Brazilian economy can be divided into three phases. For most of the sixteenth century the principal export was brazil-wood. In the 1580s it was superseded by sugar, and the steady expansion of the sugar industry transformed Brazil over the next century from a marginal colony into the most important overseas possession of the Portuguese Crown.

By the 1690s competition from plantations in the Caribbean contributed to a profound crisis in the sugar industry, which caused it to decline in the early part of the century. However, the Brazilian economy as a whole revived after the discovery of gold in 1695 in the south-central region of Minas Gerais. Although sugar remained the principal export, the economy of Brazil in the eighteenth century would be driven by gold until about the 1760s, when revenues from exports started to fall once again and the gold cycle lost its impetus. Reforms were then undertaken by the state in order to raise general productivity, but they met with little success in the long term. By the end of the century, a revival of world demand for sugar helped economic recovery, as did the diversification into new export crops such as cacao, rice, cotton and, increasingly, coffee. After independence, coffee would become the major export until the 1940s.

Colonial Brazil was far more part of the world economy than Spanish America. Agriculture there produced sugar mainly for export, whereas in

* C. R. Boxer, *The Portuguese Seaborne Empire* (Penguin Books: Harmondsworth, 1973), pp. 126, 128.

the Spanish Indies it concentrated on supplying domestic markets. Brazil, as a result, had to import most of its requirements in exchange for sugar, and since the economy of Portugal was too small and unproductive to supply Brazil, the bulk of these imports, especially manufactures, came from various countries in Europe. Officially, all trade had to be licensed by Lisbon, but in practice much of it was conducted through contraband.

However, to talk of a Brazilian economy is to misrepresent the true state of affairs. Until the eighteenth century the Brazilian economy amounted to little more than a few coastal colonies growing sugar for export to Europe, concentrated mainly in the north-eastern tip of the territory. Further south, the marginal captaincies of Rio de Janeiro and São Paulo supplied a number of commodities to the north-east and grew a little sugar too. São Paulo was mainly a base for slavers who raided the *sertão*, but the gold strikes of the 1690s in neighbouring Minas Gerais would provide a stimulus for this part of Brazil and also for the southern plains of Rio Grande do Sul, where stock-raising and wheat-growing would predominate. The economic geography of Brazil thus tended towards regional specialization; internal trade would always be less important than the commercial links which each area had separately with Europe.

Sugar

The heart of the sugar industry was the plantation. The Portuguese used the word *engenho* (literally, an engine) to denote not just the mill where the sugar cane was refined but also the whole complex of fields, workhouses, slave-quarters and buildings that were required for the production of sugar. Unlike the Spanish American hacienda, the *engenho* was not meant to be a self-sufficient economic unit; its purpose was to produce for export, but it incorporated most of the ancillary activities required for sugar production in order to cut costs and minimize risk. But the financial situation of an *engenho* appears to have been fairly precarious, for the growing of sugar involved a large labour force – up to 200 slaves in the bigger *engenhos* – while refining, which was a complicated, semi-industrial process, required heavy investments in machinery and maintenance, and the employment of highly skilled technicians and managers. Overextended credit, debt and bankruptcy were recurrent hazards. In consequence, membership of the planter class was liable to change as some families went out of business, while others set up a new operation or bought into an established one.

Besides the large plantations, there were several small sugar planters, the *lavradores da cana*, who grew their own cane but had to contract with the *senhor de engenho* to process the cane at his mill. The humblest *lavradores da cana* were little more than sharecroppers, leasing land from an *engenho* and paying rent in the form of a proportion of their produce. Most *lavradores da cana*, however, owned their own cane-fields and kept slaves to work them. The more substantial members of this class might eventually accumulate enough capital to buy a bankrupt *engenho* or to build a new one. Cane-growing was, then, a recognized route to becoming one of the grand *senhores de engenho*.

The sugar industry prospered for most of the seventeenth century though there was some dislocation in the 1640s and 1650s as a result of the Dutch occupation of Pernambuco. Rising prices for sugar brought wealth to the planters and cushioned Brazil from the general economic depression which affected Europe and, to a lesser extent, the Spanish Indies in that period. But even after the Dutch were expelled, there was to be no return to the peak years of the first four decades of the century. A crisis of overproduction was building up as new sugar economies on islands in the Caribbean began to compete with Brazil – for Brazilian plantations were relatively inefficient compared to those in the French colony of Saint Domingue or the British and Dutch islands. The world price of sugar started to decline: by the mid-1680s it stood at about a third of its price thirty years earlier. During the 1680s drought, disease and recession threatened to destroy the Brazilian sugar economy altogether. There was some recovery of growth in the 1690s, and sugar would remain an important export crop in the following century, but the long-term trend for prices was downwards. The economy of Brazil would have been in acute crisis by the end of the seventeenth century had it not been for the timely discovery of gold.

Gold

The explorations of the *bandeirantes* had brought reports of the existence of gold deposits in the *sertão* of Bahia as early as the sixteenth century, but it was not until the 1690s that substantial gold strikes were made in Brazil. The first significant deposits were found in the region of São Paulo. Shortly afterwards, other strikes were made in the captaincies of Bahia and Espírito Santo. However, the richest deposits were found in the area to the north of São Paulo that became known as Minas Gerais, the 'general mines', where the gold industry was to be largely concentrated. From Minas, further exploration westwards towards the interior would reveal in the course of the 1720s and 1730s other major deposits in the Mato Grosso and Goiás.

The discoveries caused a rush to the gold-fields by prospectors from the north-east and from Portugal itself. These newcomers were resented by the Paulistas, who wished to establish exclusive rights to exploit the deposits. Friction led to armed hostilities in 1708–9 in what has become known as the War of the *Emboabas* (outsiders). The struggle curtailed the ambitions of the Paulistas and allowed outsiders to participate in the exploitation of the mineral wealth of the interior. Disgruntled Paulistas, however, set off to explore other regions of the *sertão* and made the additional strikes in the Mato Grosso and Goiás, as well as discovering rich deposits of diamonds in the Serro do Frio region north of Minas Gerais, which later became known as the district of Diamantina.

Since gold was mainly found along riverbeds, prospectors used pans to sift for particles. Mining in veins was rarer, and the method was scarcely used in Minas Gerais. Technology was primitive, and consisted chiefly of hydraulic machinery to wash the ore-bearing soils and to clear water from quarries. Black slaves did the sifting and panning – punishing work that broke the health of slaves and led to a high rate of mortality; the working life of a slave in the gold-fields seldom exceeded twelve years.

Minas Gerais was by far the most productive region in the eighteenth century, reaching its peak in the decade after 1735, when its annual output was over ten times that recorded in the first five years of the century. The mines of the Mato Grosso and Goiás peaked at about the same time but at much lower levels – Goiás's peak annual output was approximately two-thirds of Minas Gerais's, and Mato Grosso's about one-seventh. In the second half of the century production fell steadily for various reasons – lack of capital investment and technical innovation, exhaustion of deposits and bureaucratic restrictions.

The Crown was forever trying to bring the highly speculative mining industry under control, largely in order to tax it more effectively. Miners had to pay a duty of a fifth of all gold produced, and royal officials constantly sought to certify claims and to estimate the value of finds for fiscal purposes. But the irregularity of placer-mining made government supervision very difficult and tax evasion was common. Efforts were made to regulate the industry by imposing a head tax on the number of slaves employed by a miner. Alternatively, royal foundries were set up to which miners were obliged to bring their gold, and these were used as collection-points for the royal fifth. None of these measures, however, was sufficient to put a stop to the extensive tax evasion and contraband.

The fact was that the mining regions were lawless places. A measure of stability was secured by setting up institutions of local government in the larger mining settlements, including the appointment of Crown judges to administer the law and the creation of militia companies to enforce it. However, the size and remoteness of these territories and the temptations that the traffic in gold and diamonds offered to most people contributed to widespread corruption of officials. Royal government was further consolidated by raising the three major mining regions of the interior to the status of captaincies: Minas Gerais (1720), Goiás (1744) and Mato Grosso (1748). Finally, the importance of the gold industry to the economy of Brazil, and indeed Portugal, was recognized by the transfer in 1763 of the seat of imperial government from Salvador in the north-east to Rio de Janeiro, a port city which afforded more direct communication with the captaincies of the interior.

Gold was to rescue the economy of Portugal from a debilitating imbalance of trade with Great Britain, its closest commercial ally. But it also vastly increased demand in Brazil for manufactured goods from Europe and luxuries from the Orient. Through gold Brazil would become far richer than the mother country, which she would effectively reduce to the position of intermediary in her trade with foreign nations, especially Great Britain.

Other Sectors

Brazil's major export commodities, sugar and gold, provided the stimulus for the development of subsidiary products and for economic expansion into new areas. Tobacco became an important crop, even though it constituted only a fraction of agricultural output; like rum it was used by the Portuguese as a commodity with which to barter for slaves on the coasts of Africa. In some areas of Brazil stock-raising developed as a major concern in order to supply the *engenhos* with draught-animals, meat, hides and tallow. The need for pasture took the cattlemen deeper into the *sertão* of the north-east around the São Francisco River, and even as far north as Piauí and the Maranhão. Before the discovery of gold, the captaincy of São Paulo was largely an area of subsidiary economic activities, supplying foodstuffs and slaves to the north-east. The *fazendas* (farms) on the plateau upon which the town was built produced wheat, flour, cotton, wine and cattle.

Just as the sugar industry of the north-east had indirectly created a cattle-ranching economy in the north, so too did the need to supply the mining towns of the centre-south lead to the development of agriculture and stock-raising in the pampas of the extreme south near the Spanish-held territories of the River Plate. This area was to become known as Rio Grande do Sul and its economy was based on the rounding-up and slaughtering of cattle from the great wild herds roaming the plains, and on *fazendas* producing wheat for Minas Gerais. Ranching, though, was the principal activity and Rio Grande do Sul's *gaúcho* way of life was virtually indistinguishable from that of the Spanish provinces that were to become Uruguay and Argentina.

The far north was a very poor frontier society, whose population consisted mainly of squaw-men, half-caste *caboclos* and Indian slaves. Attempts to grow cash crops such as sugar, cotton and coffee had limited success until the late eighteenth-century administrative reforms. By the end of the seventeenth century only cacao had become a major export commodity. It was collected from the Amazonian jungles, where it grew wild, by Indian slave labour. Other products of the jungle, such as vanilla and sarsaparilla, were also collected and exported, but in much smaller quantities.

Society

The society that emerged in the major settlements of Brazil took its basic shape from Portugal. Portuguese society closely resembled that of its Iberian neighbour, Castile: there was a similar preoccupation with nobility and purity of blood; the extended patriarchal family formed the basic social unit; and the influence of Catholicism was pervasive.

Moreover, the early settlers of Brazil tended to regard themselves as 'conquerors' of the land and exhibited the same aspirations to lordship over a servile native labour force as the conquistadors of the Spanish Indies. The earliest forays into the outback in search of Indian slaves were styled *entradas*, as were the expeditions of conquest undertaken in Spanish America, and the founding of settlements also followed the practice in the Spanish Indies: the commander of an expedition would select a suitable site and establish a town in the name of the king by implanting a symbol of the royal power and allocating plots of land to his followers according to rank. The offices of the *senado da câmara* would be filled by the principal settlers (*moradores*).

As in the Spanish colonies, an elementary social hierarchy was created in the very act of settlement. Initially, there was some differentiation on the basis of nobility – what members of the gentry (*fidalgos*) there were among the first settlers retained their hereditary privileges – but aristocratic prerogatives were not accorded by the Crown to the upper classes of Brazil and the effective social divisions were determined by wealth and the manner in which it was made: ownership of sugar mills and plantations conferred the highest status, while commerce and, of course, manual labour were regarded as demeaning.

The *senhores de engenho*, therefore, constituted the élite of Brazilian society. Their status derived from their possessing an economic weight equivalent to that of mine-owners in the Spanish Indies, while enjoying the aristocratic prestige traditionally accorded in Iberian societies to great landowners with authority over subordinates. And so, a *senhor de engenho* was at once a profit-making capitalist, with economic interests that were closely bound up with those of the import–export merchants, and a slave-owning patriarch who was the social equal of the highest-ranking royal administrators and clergy.

Below these great lords of the sugar industry, in status if not in wealth, came the transatlantic merchants, who provided credit to the *senhores de engenho* and often owned land and mills themselves; the wealthiest could aspire to marry into planter families. A peculiarity of this class, however, was the presence of a significant minority of New Christians. These were men descended from forcibly converted Jews; they carried the stigma of impure blood and their membership gave the class of merchants as a whole rather a bad name – especially in Spanish America, where the community of Portuguese and Brazilian merchants who did business in Peru, for instance, was associated with crypto-Judaism.

The wealthiest of the *lavradores da cana* can be placed in this second group. Next in status was a class that consisted of smaller growers, and retailers and traders involved in the internal markets. Then came artisans and craftsmen, who had a more humble position not only because they worked with their hands, but also because there were many free persons of colour engaged in these trades. And at the bottom of the social ladder were large numbers of white delinquents and vagrants – their existence can be accounted for in part by the general disdain of the Portuguese for manual occupations shared by non-whites.

The division between free man and slave was the most basic of all in Brazilian society. And since slaves, moreover, were not of European extraction, colour in itself was a powerful determinant of status, for the darker one's skin, the closer one was associated with the slave class. Whiteness, in consequence, was treasured as a sign of social worth, and, in the case of mulatto or mestizo individuals who had achieved a measure of prominence, it became a polite fiction to regard them as white. This pretence was fairly common in marginal captaincies such as São Paulo and Maranhão, where there were relatively few Portuguese settlers in the first two centuries of the colony.

The existence of this huge class of non-white slaves was the most salient difference between Brazilian and Portuguese society. There were few free peasants in Brazil: the lower classes in the countryside were slaves on the *engenhos* and the *fazendas*, many of whom were allowed to cultivate small plots on their master's land for their own subsistence. The authority of the master was beyond question and conditions for the slaves tended to be harsh – the picture of a benevolent patriarchy on the plantations is greatly exaggerated. But domestic slaves could enjoy some degree of affection and loyalty from the master's family – manumission, by which an owner granted freedom to a slave in recognition of loyal service, was a fairly common practice and accounts for the growth during the seventeenth century of a free coloured population.

However, manumission has to be set against the widespread phenomenon of flight from plantations and gold-mines by slaves worked to the limit of their endurance. Out in the *sertão* these runaways formed settlements known as *quilombos* or *mocambos*. The most famous was the colony of Palmares, where several thousand fugitive slaves established a number of towns and villages that endured for virtually the whole of the seventeenth century in the backlands of Pernambuco until their destruction by punitive military force in 1695.

Even though the society of colonial Brazil was deeply divided by class and race, there were also powerful integrative factors, and, as in all traditional Iberian societies, it was religion that played a critical role. The Catholic Church underwrote patriarchal hierarchies in numerous ways. For instance, the brotherhoods for laymen, which were dedicated to the Virgin or a saint, affirmed particular social identities, from *senhores de engenho* to black slaves, while giving them all an organic cohesion under the authority of God and king. Social bonds were also cemented through *compadrio* (godfatherhood shared by a patron and his subordinate) which gave a sacramental quality to the fabric of patronage in which differences of class and race were enveloped.

The overall effect of Church influence was to entrench a social pyramid at whose apex were installed the lords of the sugar plantations. But although there are evident similarities with Spanish America, colonial Brazilian society was more rudimentary; the capital, Salvador, was no Lima or Mexico City: there was not the same opulence of architecture or sumptuousness of social display, and this comparative poverty was reflected in its cultural life.

Culture

The earliest writing about Brazil followed the establishment of royal government and the arrival of the first Jesuits in 1549. A number of chronicles
describing the climate, environment and native peoples were written in the
second half of the sixteenth century, notably by the Jesuit Fernão Cardim in
1584 and by Gabriel Soares de Sousa in 1587.

Throughout the entire colonial period no university was founded and no
printing-press was set up in Brazil – the sons of the élite were sent to the
ancient university of Coimbra in Portugal. The Jesuits established seminaries
and colleges, and provided the schooling for the settlers. Literary output was
slight: the most distinguished writer in the seventeenth century was the Jesuit
António Vieira, who defended the Indians in letters and sermons. An Italian
Jesuit, using the *nom de plume* Andre João Antonil, wrote an account of
Brazil's natural and economic resources between 1693 and 1711. There were
few native-born Brazilian writers of note before the end of the eighteenth
century: Gregório de Matos of Bahia wrote satirical verse which is remembered today; Vicente do Salvador produced a history of Brazil in 1627 and
this provided a basis for Sebastião da Rocha Pitta's *História da América
portuguesa* 'History of Portuguese America', which was published in 1730.

In architecture, both ecclesiastic and domestic, Brazil followed the styles
of Portugal very closely. Indeed, it has been observed that, in this respect,
Brazil must be regarded 'as being as much a part of Portugal as, say, the
Minho'.* Not surprisingly, the most notable churches and convents are
concentrated in the capitals of the wealthiest sugar- and gold-producing
areas, namely, the coastal cities of Olinda in Pernambuco, Salvador, Rio de
Janeiro, and the region surrounding the inland city of Ouro Preto in Minas
Gerais. A particular feature is the high number of baroque and rococo
churches in Minas Gerais built with the extraordinary wealth of the gold-
mines. At the end of the eighteenth century Minas produced a sculptor of
genius in the mulatto Antônio Francisco Lisboa, o Aleijadinho ('the Cripple'),
whose masterpieces include the series of statues before the church of pilgrimage at Cogonhas do Campo, and the wooden figures for the stations of
the cross leading up to it. He established an individual style, a form of rococo
known as the *estilo aleijadinho*, which was employed in the decoration of
church interiors, including altars, pulpits and reredos.

The wealth of Minas Gerais, combined with its distance both from the
seat of royal government and from the old aristocratic centres of the north-

* J. B. Bury, *Cambridge History of Latin America*, vol. 2, p. 769.

eastern sugar areas, made it particularly receptive to the ideas of the Enlightenment, and in the 1780s the city of Ouro Preto produced the most talented of the poets and writers of the colonial period. Men such as José de Santa Rita Durão, Claudio Manuel da Costa, José Basílio da Gama, José Inácio de Alvarengo Peixoto, helped to inaugurate a republican tradition and played a part in the conspiracy known as *Inconfidência mineira* of 1788–9, the first attempt in Brazil to challenge the colonial authority of the Portuguese monarchy.

However, the plot failed: Minas Gerais was only briefly an exception to the rule in Brazil. There were too many cultural, economic and even personal ties binding the Brazilian élites to Portugal, and few major discriminations against the colony. What is more, the lack of a strong, autonomous cultural life – there being no university or printing-press – delayed the emergence of a separate identity. Such factors reinforced the unitary conception of the Portuguese empire, so that when Napoleon threatened the Iberian monarchies in 1807–8, Brazil and Portugal would arrive at a markedly different solution to the crisis from that of Spain and her American colonies.

PART TWO

THE CHALLENGE
OF THE MODERN WORLD

6. Reform, Crisis and Independence

====

A Change of Dynasty in Spain: from Habsburg to Bourbon

Towards the end of the seventeenth century the balance of economic power in the Hispanic world had shifted across the Atlantic to the Indies. New Spain and Peru had burgeoned as prosperous, well-ordered societies with a flourishing aristocratic culture; they were effectively the metropolises of the Americas, engaging in extensive commerce with each other and with other regions, and even operating a lucrative trade with the Far East through the Philippines, the major Spanish colony in Asia. By this time the restrictions on trade with countries other than Spain had been largely undermined by widespread contraband. Colonial administration was lax and corrupt, the creole élites having absorbed high officials from the Peninsula into their circles. In any case, the highest positions in the colonial government, other than that of viceroy, were effectively open to creoles. In other words, the Habsburg imperial state had settled into a comfortable inertia which gave the creole oligarchies in practice what was denied to them in theory: access to the North Atlantic trading system and power to shape their societies largely to their own advantage.

The mother country, in contrast, languished in misery: she had suffered a long economic depression and severe depopulation; her military power had been sapped by repeated defeats in Europe and separatist rebellions at home; the transatlantic trading system had all but broken down on several occasions, thinning perilously the flow of bullion on which she depended to keep up her imperial pretensions. As a colonial power Spain now presented the curious spectacle of a metropolis that needed her colonies more than they did her; and in the league of world powers, she had clearly slipped to the second rank.

The state of Spain was embodied in the weak and imbecilic Charles II, the last of the Habsburg line and a monarch incapable of male issue. Upon his death in 1700 there followed a war among the European powers to decide the Spanish succession. Philip of Anjou, the grandson of Louis XIV of France, eventually acceded to the throne of Spain, but his right to it was recognized by his enemies at the price of important concessions set out in the Treaty of Utrecht of 1713. Flanders and the Italian dominions were lost to Austria and Savoy; Great Britain kept Gibraltar and Minorca, and was allowed the exclusive right to supply African slaves to the Spanish Indies, and to an annual shipload of merchandise for trade with the American colonies; Portugal retained her smuggling centre of Colônia do Sacramento on the east bank of the River Plate. These concessions to Britain and Portugal underscored Spain's imperial debility, since they infringed, at least for a time, the monopoly of trade with the Indies, which she had done so much to defend. Spain's sovereignty was now reduced to the Peninsula and her realms in America and the Philippines.

This curtailment of power, though humiliating, at least unburdened Spain of dynastic possessions in Italy and the Low Countries which had drained her over the past two centuries. The Treaty of Utrecht, in fact, forced Spain to relinquish the Habsburg concept of empire, based as it had been on an essentially medieval vision of a supranational constellation of kingdoms under a single sovereign pledged to the defence of Catholic integrity in Europe. The new dynasty of French Bourbons would rule Spain as a European nation state among others, and her still very substantial dominions overseas would be regarded as resources to be exploited economically so as to strengthen her position in the theatre of European power politics. Over the course of the new century, therefore, the Bourbons were to recast the aims and methods of Spanish imperial government.

The spirit of reform significantly altered the ideological basis of the Catholic monarchy, which the Habsburgs, having taken it over from Ferdinand and Isabella, had developed as the guiding principle of their imperial statecraft. The peculiarly Spanish symbiosis of Crown and Church, which endowed the Catholic monarchy with its monopoly of legitimacy, gave way under successive Bourbon kings to a more stringent absolutism of French regalist inspiration. According to this new doctrine of the divine right of kings, the monarch was invested with the authority to rule by God Himself; his power, therefore, was not limited in principle by religious and ethical sanctions upheld by the Church, and much less so by the more ancient, medieval sense of contract with or obligation to his subjects which was still latent in Spain and which had always been much closer to the surface among the conquistadors and their successors in the Indies.

The new regalism permitted the monarch to do what the Habsburgs had been restrained from doing by the force of religious counsel: it allowed the

Crown to frame policies on pragmatic grounds of national self-interest. Impracticable chimeras upon which Catholic Spain had spent so much blood and treasure – the defence of orthodoxy against Dutch rebels and English schismatics, the crusade against the Turk, the protection of Indian rights in the New World – no longer needed to be pursued beyond reasonable limits, for the light of reason had to be allowed to filter through the blinds that kept Spain in her neo-medieval 'darkness'. And yet, those blinds could not be removed altogether; the Catholic Church was too well entrenched in the state and society and, in any case, the Bourbons realized the value of the Church as both a pillar of the social order and a unifying factor in a far-flung empire.

The ideology of the Bourbon reformers has been aptly called the Catholic Enlightenment, for it was a cautious attempt to adjust to the scientific and rationalist spirit of the eighteenth century without disturbing the fundamentals of the Catholic faith. The reformers introduced into the administration of Spain and her empire principles of reason and utility which had been carefully extracted from their wider philosophical framework for fear of promoting ideas subversive of religion. But this derivative and lukewarm ideology at once went too far and not far enough: it precluded the radicalism that might bring enduring economic success, yet weakened the political foundations of the Catholic monarchy.

In Spain itself the Bourbons created a more centralized and executive form of government. The array of advisory councils of the realm, which reflected the consultative nature of the Habsburg monarchy, was superseded by a bureaucratic machine consisting of secretariats of state run by an administrative élite whose overriding aim was the modernization of the country. The landed aristocracy was excluded from the administration, and its privileges curtailed; the traditional rights of the kingdom of Aragon (which included Catalonia) were abolished; a standing army staffed by career officers was established and the navy was strengthened through a programme of shipbuilding.

These changes were facilitated by an economic recovery which appears to have begun as early as the 1680s, especially along the Mediterranean littoral. Yet, despite the Bourbon attempts to stimulate further growth in the Spanish economy, there was little lasting success: although there was an increase in the volume of transatlantic trade, agriculture and industry did not improve sufficiently to enable Spain to regain a dominant role in the economic life of her American colonies. Indeed, the impact of reform in the New World served to unsettle the status quo – connived at by the later Habsburgs – which had allowed the creole élites to prosper. The result was that the authority of the Crown in the Indies was grievously weakened by measures that, ironically, had been designed to strengthen it.

Bourbon Reforms in Spanish America

The reforming hand of the Bourbons was not generally felt in the Indies until the reign of Charles III (1759–88). During the Seven Years War the loss of Havana and Manila to the British in 1762–3 brought home to Spain the need to rebuild its imperial power. In 1765 an able and dynamic administrator, José de Gálvez, was sent to the Indies on a number of *visitas generales* to review the state of the colonies. His reports to the Crown formed the basis for a programme of comprehensive change. The fundamental purpose of the reforms was to raise revenues for the Crown. This involved administrative reorganization to improve the tax yield from America, and the restructuring of imperial commerce so as to stimulate the Spanish economy. It was not clear what benefits these reforms were designed to bring the colonies, and both the creoles and the Indians were to react against them.

Gálvez recommended the creation of a new viceroyalty and several new *audiencias* in order to reinforce administrative controls and develop the economies of regions on the Atlantic seaboard. In 1776 the viceroyalty of Río de la Plata was founded with its seat in the small port of Buenos Aires. This new viceroyalty comprised all those vast underpopulated territories to the east of the Andean chain which had previously come under the jurisdiction of Lima, but it also included the province of Upper Peru (modern Bolivia) where the bulk of the silver-mining industry was concentrated. The creation of the new viceroyalty entailed a massive shift in economic orientation away from Lima and the Pacific towards the Atlantic, for the silver of Potosí would now be transported to Buenos Aires and shipped from there to Spain, cutting the time and cost of transatlantic commerce. But reorganization would dislocate many local economies in the Andean region, which had for centuries been geared towards Lima.

In fact, a viceroyalty had already been created in 1739 by merging the captaincy-general of New Granada with the territory of Venezuela. The latter had been part of the captaincy-general of Santo Domingo, coming ultimately under the jurisdiction of Mexico City. Although Bogotá was the viceregal capital, the growing commercial importance of Venezuela as a producer of cacao was recognized by the creation of an *audiencia* at Caracas. The viceroyalty of New Granada would experience geographical and economic tensions – mainly between traditionalist, land-locked Bogotá to the west of the Andes and, to the east, the thriving port of Caracas, which faced towards the multinational Caribbean islands, North America and Europe.

This redrawing of territorial boundaries was accompanied by measures to enhance the authority of Madrid. Most of the posts in the old Habsburg bureaucracy had come to be occupied by creoles, but Bourbon reformers now began to replace them with Spanish-born officials; the courts of the *audiencia*, for instance, were gradually filled by peninsular judges. The new executive bureaucracy reached out into the regions with the replacement of provincial governors by French-style intendants sent out from Spain. These officials were backed by servants of the royal exchequer charged with the collection of taxes from the creoles. In the Indian communities, Spanish *subdelegados*, directly responsible to the intendants, took over from corrupt creole *corregidores de indios* and attempted to increase the yield from the tribute by bringing more categories of Indian into the tax net, and by abolishing the *repartimiento de comercio* and other forms of bureaucratic private enterprise which diverted fiscal resources due to the Crown.

The Bourbon attempts to reshape colonial commerce to Spain's advantage were faced with the problem that Spain's products, with the exception of precious metals, were broadly similar to those of the colonies. Bourbon reformers, therefore, tried to create a meaningful market for Spanish exports by prohibiting the production of certain commodities such as wheat, wine and olive oil in the colonies. The textile industry of Catalonia was protected from competition by the forced closure of *obrajes* in Peru and New Spain. Thus the economic autonomy allowed the Indies under the Habsburgs was threatened by an artificial economic exchange with the mother country imposed by an interventionist state.

At the same time some more liberal measures were taken to stimulate the colonial economy. Tariffs and tax incentives were adjusted to encourage production, especially of silver. Indians were induced to enter the labour force for wages. Colonial exporters were allowed wider access to markets in the Peninsula and other regions of the Indies. And even though the official Spanish monopoly of transatlantic trade remained in force, goods were no longer channelled exclusively through Mexico City or Lima to Seville or Cadiz. Other colonial centres, such as Buenos Aires, Caracas, Cartagena and Havana, could trade directly with a number of ports in Spain. The term employed to describe the new colonial exchange was *un comercio libre y protegido* – free trade under the protection of the state.

Despite this restructuring of imperial commerce, the Spanish economy proved incapable of satisfying demand in America. A large proportion of the trade from Spain continued to take the form of the re-export of goods from other parts of Europe to the Indies. And so, even though the new policy of *comercio libre* did much to stimulate the colonial economy, American expansion was limited by restrictions of a political nature obviously serving the interests of Spain. Moreover, the fact that the Spanish trade monopoly was still dominated by peninsular import–export merchants exacerbated anti-Spanish resentment among creoles.

Indeed, all sectors of society in the Indies had reason to complain about the Bourbon reforms. Increases in the sales tax hit the general population. Wealthy creoles were continually being pressured by the servants of the Crown for donations to the royal treasury to pay for remote dynastic wars in Europe. The forced sale of Church lands deprived the clergy of rents, and hit the livelihood of poor parish priests in particular. Indian communities were harassed for greater yields of tribute. Resistance to these exactions led in places to riots and open revolt. Significantly, the regions which saw the greatest unrest were those where administrative reorganization had caused the greatest dislocation: Peru, Upper Peru and New Granada.

The most serious uprising had its origins in southern Peru, where an Indian *cacique*, José Gabriel Condorcanqui, began to agitate against the abuses the Indians had to bear at the hands of Spanish officials. By 1780 the discontent had reached the point where Condorcanqui, who claimed descent from the Inca royal line, assumed the name of Tupac Amaru II and raised a rebellion against the royal authorities. The rebellion spread to other areas and in Upper Peru there occurred large risings in 1781 which led to the siege by Indians of the provincial capital of La Paz. Tupac Amaru called for an end to the *mita*, forced loans and other exactions from the Indian pueblos by the hated Spanish officials. His declared aim was to get rid of the Spaniards, and he invited creoles to join him. But though at first there was some sympathy for his cause among the creoles, it soon subsided when the Indians started to slaughter whites indiscriminately, raising the terrifying spectre of a race war.

Whether or not Tupac Amaru meant to put an end to Spanish rule altogether remains unclear. Certainly the scale of his revolution revealed the extent of Indian anger against a centuries-old system of exploitation. But Tupac Amaru failed to unite all the Indian tribes against the whites; some chieftains even opted to side with the Crown against the rebels. After wholesale carnage, which claimed the lives of thousands of mostly Indian victims, Tupac Amaru fell into the hands of the Spanish authorities, who had him spectacularly torn limb from limb by horses in the great square at Cuzco. The Indian revolt continued for several months and was finally put down in early 1782.

Another great rebellion took place in 1781 in the region of Socorro in

New Granada (modern Colombia), though it had no connection with Tupac Amaru. Once again, it was sparked by the excesses of Spanish officials, who were pressing tax demands too hard and trying to rationalize private tobacco-growing to suit the requirements of the government tobacco monopoly. The rebels were an assortment of modest planters, mestizos and Indians. Yet their grievances found sympathy among the clergy, provincial creole officials and even the élite of Bogotá, who had no liking for the Bourbon administrators. A force of several thousand rebels which had marched on the viceregal capital was dissuaded from attacking the city by an agreement negotiated between the archbishop and their leaders. This compromise failed to satisfy some of the insurgents, who continued their struggle together with Indian communities demanding the return of usurped lands. The *comunero* revolt, as it became known, acquired the characteristics of a social and ethnic war, a half-caste, José Antonio Galán, emerging as its leader. The creole élites sided with the royal authorities and the insurrection was eventually crushed, along with a similar *comunero* revolt in neighbouring Venezuela.

Neither the Peruvian Indian risings nor the *comunero* rebellions of New Granada signified any coherent bid for independence. They were intense but ultimately limited reactions to the interventionism of the Bourbon monarchy. Yet rebellions of such scope and ferocity had not been seen in the Indies since the middle of the sixteenth century when the Habsburg state was being consolidated in the decades after the Conquest. The outbreak of these large revolts in the late eighteenth century may perhaps be taken as an outward sign that the imperial relationship between Spain and the Indies was undergoing a further change.

The Bourbon reforms threatened, in effect, to precipitate a crisis of political legitimacy. Under the Habsburgs, the Crown had enjoyed a monopoly of legitimacy due principally to its compact with the Church. This had been reinforced in America by the award of land and favours to the conquistadors and their descendants in return for their conquests, and, as regards the Indians, by virtue of the Crown's professed intent to protect their ancestral rights in the name of the true God, to whose religion they were required to convert. But, in addition to the monopoly of legitimacy, the loyalty of the creole aristocracy had endured in the seventeenth century (even at a time in the 1640s when other élites of the empire, such as the Portuguese, the Catalans and the Sicilians, had rebelled), because the economic enfeeblement of Spain had allowed the creole élites to satisfy in practice their two crucial aspirations: the exercise of power within their own societies and their participation in international trade through smuggling. The Bourbons' vigorous reassertion of metropolitan power now threatened to frustrate these two creole aspirations.

What is more, at a time when Crown policies were disturbing the customary life of the Indies, Bourbon reformers were also attacking the power of the Church, which was a prime source of the Habsburgs' political legitimacy and a binding-force in colonial societies that were deeply divided by region and ethnic identity. Bourbon reformers regarded the wealth of the Church as unproductive, and so they tried to transfer its property and lands to private hands wherever possible. French-inspired regalists, moreover, considered the Hispanic Church to be a potential obstacle to the unfettered exercise of the royal will; and their particular ideological enemies were the Jesuits, who were immensely powerful in America and owed explicit allegiance to the Pope. Friction with the Church culminated in the expulsion of the Jesuit order from all the Spanish realms in 1767. The forcible exile of Jesuit priests, the majority of whom were creoles, caused deep bitterness among the American clergy and laity.

The Bourbon regalists were, then, revising the historic basis upon which the Spanish Crown justified its power. And it was perhaps no coincidence that their opponents should invoke rights and claims which had formed the traditional conditions for legitimate royal authority. The Church resisted the doctrine of the divine right of kings because it left little place for religious counsel to the monarch. The *comuneros* of New Granada (their name brought to mind the *comunero* revolt in Spain of 1520–21 when the Castilian towns had rebelled against the abolition of their liberties by Charles V) acted to reassert the medieval 'right of resistance' to unjust royal policies. Tupac Amaru's claim to the Inca succession recalled the fact that the Spanish title to the Indies rested crucially on the obligation to treat the Indian communities in accordance with Christian principles of justice.

All three currents of American resistance to Bourbon regalism pointed to the absence of religious and traditional restraints on royal power that it implied. In terms of scholastic thought (which had been revitalized partly as a result of the Spanish conquest of America and still flourished in Spanish American universities and seminaries), there were grounds for arguing that the Bourbons were acting as tyrants in pressing their reforms. Some clerics, like the exiled Peruvian Jesuit Juan Pablo Viscardo or the Mexican friar Servando Teresa de Mier, were among the first Spanish Americans to protest against the 'tyranny' of the Spanish Crown, and they would eventually call for independence in order to preserve the integrity of the Catholic faith in the New World. A good number of the leaders of uprisings during the independence wars would emerge from the lower clergy, especially those who ministered to Indian communities; as heirs to the early missionaries, they would lead revolts against the modernizing Spanish state, invoking the protection of the Virgin of Guadalupe in their efforts to establish a Utopian order of Christian simplicity in America.

Clerical criticism of the Bourbon monarchy was essentially conservative, looking back to the sixteenth-century debates about the limits of royal power generated by Bartolomé de las Casas and other scholastics. But these religious critiques of tyranny ran parallel with more modern attacks on despotism, formulated by liberals concerned with the rights of the individual against the state and the notion of the sovereignty of the people. These ideas of the secular European Enlightenment – ironically, the very ideas that American clerics wanted to exclude from the Indies – began to circulate from the 1780s among educated creoles. Their influence, however, was limited to small circles often gathered in Economic Societies which promoted the scientific study of the characteristics of their regions for 'patriotic' ends.

Such milieux produced more radical individuals, inspired by the North American and French revolutions, who advocated republicanism and total independence from Spain. In retrospect, these men can be seen as the intellectual and political 'precursors' of independence, men like Francisco de Miranda in Venezuela, Antonio Nariño in Bogotá, Manuel Belgrano and Mariano Moreno in Buenos Aires, all of whom were well read in the literature of the Enlightenment and were admirers of the French and American revolutions; some fell foul of the Inquisition and were imprisoned, others fled into exile or went abroad to conspire against Spain in England, France or the United States.

But support for revolutionary republicanism was negligible among the creole aristocracy. Plans to start insurrections failed: in 1806 Miranda landed a party of volunteers at Coro on the Venezuelan coast, but was unable to interest his compatriots in revolution against Spain; a further attempt in 1811 received support in Caracas but it too was easily crushed within a year. The reality was that the majority of the creole élite were Catholic and conservative. If anything, the French Revolution caused them intense alarm. It was feared that disobedience to the monarchy might unleash a race war. There were awful precedents: the Negro risings in Haiti against the French planters in 1793, the Indian rebellions in Peru under Tupac Amaru and the revolt of the *comuneros* had already given whites a foretaste of what might happen if royal authority were to collapse in the Indies. For the colonial pact was not purely economic; the creole élites had been prepared to accept Spanish restrictions on commerce in return for the effective maintenance of the internal colonialism of white over non-white which the Catholic monarchy had been able to provide. But in the changing circumstances of the late eighteenth century how much longer could this colonial order be maintained?

By the 1790s the massive inertia of creole America appeared to have triumphed over regalist innovation and modern ideas: the Bourbon reforms had run out of steam and royal officials had once again been co-opted by the colonial oligarchies. The determining factor was not so much the disaffection of the creoles as Spain's inability to exercise colonial authority and protect her colonies. The degenerate and venal government of Charles IV, dominated by the queen's lover, Manuel Godoy, pursued an erratic foreign policy which led the country into a disastrous alliance with revolutionary France. The ensuing wars with Great Britain would devastate Spanish naval power and cut Spain off from her colonies, destroying her monopoly of trade with the Indies. Nelson's defeat of the Spanish fleet at Cape St Vincent in 1797 was followed by a blockade of Cadiz and Spanish American ports. Spain, as a result, had little option but to open transatlantic trade to neutral shipping. When peace came in 1802 she regained a measure of control, but it was wrested from her when war with Britain broke out once more in 1805 and Nelson put paid to Spanish sea power in the Atlantic at the Battle of Trafalgar. After Trafalgar, the Spanish trade monopoly with the Indies was gone for good; by 1807 no treasure ships arrived at Cadiz, and Spain sank into a severe economic depression as her American markets were closed to her and the flow of bullion dried up. In the colonies the impotence of the mother country and the shortage of supplies caused by the British blockade resulted in a shift to direct trade with neutral countries such as the United States, and even with Spain's great enemy, Britain herself.

With the breaking of the economic link with Spain the creoles had effectively achieved one of their historic aspirations: unrestricted trade within the Atlantic system. But what of the political link? The great value of the Catholic monarchy to the creole élites was that it provided a source of law and order for their societies, and kept the non-whites in their place. Yet that colonial arrangement was now open to question in ways which had been previously inconceivable: the Bourbon reforms had eroded the legitimacy of royal authority in the eyes of sections of the Church (much of the lower clergy, the Jesuits and even some bishops), the Indians and the common people; with the great political upheavals that had occurred in the Americas and in Europe, ideas of liberty and equality were in the air; and Spain's current prostration made creoles doubt her capacity to defend or keep order in the Indies.

This last problem was brought home to the Spanish Americans by the British invasions of Buenos Aires and Montevideo in 1806 and 1807, when a maverick British admiral tried to prise away a portion of the Spanish empire. It was the creole militias, not the forces of the viceroy, that fought off the British attacks. During the emergency the Spanish viceroy was overruled by the *audiencia*, and, though no disloyalty to the king was intended, this usurpation of legal authority gave the creoles of Buenos Aires a taste of direct power over their own affairs – a privilege denied by the Crown to the Spanish American élites since the Conquest.

The collapse of transatlantic commerce with Spain and the abject condition of the mother country made it unlikely that the creole élites would be content to return to their former political subservience to the Peninsula. Imperial relations at the turn of the century clearly needed to be revised in order to give the creoles a recognized role in their own governance, but what institutional form might creole power take? Would it be possible to remodel the absolute monarchy so as to give the élites of the Indies a measure of autonomy? Was a constitutional monarchy the way forward? Or might a republic, after all, prove to be the only solution? Nothing could yet be clear given the confusion created by the continuing hostilities between the European powers. And yet, within barely a year of the British invasions of the River Plate, those remote conflicts in the Old World would take an unexpected turn, and the political fortunes of Spanish America would be thrown open to all the hazards and opportunities that seethed in the wake of Napoleon's triumphant progress through the kingdoms of Europe.

Reform in Brazil

Though Portugal in the seventeenth century did not experience Spain's severe decline, her position in relation to the major European powers was one of weakness and dependence. She owed her political emancipation from Spain in 1668 to the special protection of Great Britain, who became the major supplier of goods to the Portuguese empire. Portugal was to remain in constant deficit in her trade with Britain; she imported British manufactures and wheat in exchange for oil and wine, and made up the shortfall by the export of Brazilian gold. Brazilian gold, in fact, allowed the extravagant John V to put off reform. But when gold production ran into difficulties in the 1750s, the new king, Joseph I, approved a far-reaching programme of economic and political change.

The overhaul of Portugal and her empire was conceived and directed by the Marquis of Pombal, whose despotic rule as first minister lasted from 1750 to 1777. Pombal's programme resembled that of the Bourbon ministerial élite in Spain. He realized that economic efficiency required the modernization of society and the state. Like his Bourbon counterparts, he espoused the doctrine of regalism or enlightened despotism, which he tried to promote by reforming the curriculum of the University of Coimbra, and by appointing sympathetic clergy to powerful positions in the hierarchy. The privileges of the nobility were curtailed and its ranks opened to men of wealth and talent. Restrictions on New Christians – men of Jewish descent who tended to be successful in commerce – were lifted. In the colonies there were attempts to incorporate Indians and free people of colour into Portuguese society. The overall aim was to release new energies so that the economy of the Portuguese empire might free itself from its dependence on Britain.

As would occur in Spain, the new doctrine of the divine right of kings espoused by Pombal and his circle would arouse hostility from sections of the Church. And, as in the Spanish dominions, the most resolute opponents of enlightened despotism were the Jesuits. In the Portuguese case, however, the clash between the Crown and the Jesuits took on a bitter and even violent character. This was due partly to Pombal's own extraordinary animus towards the order, and also because the Jesuit missions in and around the areas of the Paraguay and Paraná rivers spanned the long-disputed frontiers between Brazil and the territories of the Spanish Crown.

Friction with the Jesuits over the doctrine of regalism became caught up in the geopolitics of territorial claims against Spain in South America. The Treaty of Madrid (1750) promised to put an end to these costly border conflicts: Spain agreed to surrender her claim to territories in the Amazon and east of the Uruguay river in return for Portugal's withdrawal from Sacramento, its centre of contraband in silver on the River Plate opposite Buenos Aires. But the treaty could not become effective so long as Spanish Jesuits and their Guaraní charges in the Paraguayan missions continued to resist the jurisdiction of the Portuguese authorities. Their refusal to evacuate their missions led to open warfare in 1754–6. In Amazonia, Portuguese Jesuits were thwarting Pombal's attempts to recruit Indians into the labour force.

This Jesuit recalcitrance led Pombal to regard the order as a supranational force conspiring against the Crown. He accused the Jesuits of creating a state within a state in Paraguay, thereby usurping the rights of the monarchs of Portugal and Spain. The dispute with the Jesuits rumbled on through the 1750s until finally in 1758 Pombal managed to implicate them in an attempt to assassinate the king. The order was expelled from all the territories of the empire in 1759 and had its lands and properties confiscated. Pombal went on to expropriate much of the wealth of other religious orders and to restrict entry into convents and monasteries, for as a modernizer he regarded the economic weight of the Church as an obstacle to regeneration.

The strengthening of royal power resulted in more centralized control of the administration in Brazil. In 1763 the viceregal capital was transferred from Salvador in the north-east to Rio de Janeiro, and the two states into which Brazil had been divided were merged in 1774 under one viceroy. The powers of royal officials throughout the imperial bureaucracy were increased in relation to the elected local councils. An office of the treasury was established in each captaincy-general to ensure efficient collection of taxes and renewed efforts were made to control the contraband trade in gold and diamonds. Pombal himself took charge of treasury affairs in Lisbon, conscious of the need to co-ordinate the fiscal policy of the Crown in order to maximize revenues.

Pombal and his successors knew that the key to the revival of Portugal lay in the growth of the economy of Brazil. Pombal wanted to increase and diversify exports from the empire in order to end the deficit with Britain, reserving the projected growth in trade for subjects of the Portuguese Crown. He also wanted to rationalize the commercial exchange between Portugal and Brazil by reviving manufacturing in the mother country while restricting the colony to the export of gold, sugar and other primary goods. A sign of the desire to stimulate trade was the abolition in 1766 of the slow and unreliable fleet system, which channelled trade exclusively by convoys of ships on scheduled voyages between Lisbon and the Brazilian ports of Salvador and Rio de Janeiro. Instead, individually licensed ships were allowed to cross the Atlantic freely to various ports in Brazil and Portugal.

Pombal's favoured instrument of economic revitalization was the mono-poly company. A company would be given exclusive control of trade in a given area and would provide credit, capital and slave labour to local producers so as to stimulate production and encourage the cultivation of new commodities. Investment in the company was open to foreigners, but executive posts were reserved for Portuguese subjects. In Brazil the company of Grão Pará e Maranhão was founded in 1755 with the object of developing the vast regions of the Amazon and northern Brazil. New crops like cacao, cotton and rice were introduced and an extensive plantation economy, based on an African slave-trade organized by the company, was built in Maranhão. The exploitation of the Amazon regions in Pará was much less successful, chiefly because of difficulties in recruiting Indian labour. The Indian tribes resisted assimilation and there was determined opposition to the company from the Jesuits. A similar company for Paraíba and Pernambuco was formed in 1759 with a view to reactivating the sugar economy of the north-east, which had suffered as a result of competition from the sugar islands of the Caribbean. Exports did increase, but the highest profits went to the foreign merchants, who dominated the trade with Portugal. The monopoly also made for high prices, which acted as a brake on production.

Although the death of Joseph I in 1777 brought about the resignation of Pombal, his followers remained in office and pursued his policies until well into the next century. A significant departure was the closure of the Brazilian monopoly companies in 1778–9. But this was part of a wider policy of reducing monopolistic activities in order to stimulate trade, a Pombaline seal in any case. During Pombal's period of office, the economy of the Portuguese empire had not been able to emerge from recession and dependence on Britain – the sugar industry in the north-east of Brazil was in decline and production of gold and diamonds in Minas Gerais was falling. However, in the 1780s the situation improved steadily until by the mid 1790s the balance of trade with Britain showed a large surplus, which continued until 1807. After the revolt of her American colonies in 1776 Britain was continually at war, and Portugal found herself in a good position to supply British demand. Pombal's policy of diversification into new crops and stimulation of production began to pay off as Brazil's economy shifted from mining to agrarian produce (coffee, in particular, would grow in importance until it became the dominant export crop in the nineteenth century).

It was generally recognized in Portugal that Brazil was the engine of the imperial economy. Though Portugal might have reversed her trade deficit with Britain, it was only because she was herself in chronic deficit with her largest colony. The imbalance, however, did not lead to political frustration in Brazil. The Portuguese had been conspicuously successful in creating a unitary sense of empire in which the colonial élites could strongly identify with the mother country. In contrast to Spanish America, there was no great resentment against peninsular Portuguese: there existed little by way of a separate Brazilian culture for the élite; the involvement of sugar planters in the export-economy made for a common interest with Portuguese merchants, slave-traders and royal officials; finally, the massive presence of Africans and mulattos reinforced the identification of white Brazilians with their European cousins (family ties were, indeed, close).

The political value of this unitary sense of empire was well understood by Portuguese statesmen. Pombal, for instance, was careful not to alienate the Brazilian élites by his reforms. Posts in the bureaucracy and in the newly founded militias were open to Brazilians; local oligarchies were allowed to invest in the monopoly companies; the introduction of new crops into hitherto unsettled areas and the general expansion and liberalization of trade were designed to favour American as much as European Portuguese. Even the expulsion of the Jesuits, who had always opposed the white settlers' Indian slaving and occupation of native lands, met with Brazilian approval – the large, well-managed estates of the Jesuits, as well as the Indian labour released by the destruction of the missions, provided excellent economic opportunities for wealthy merchants and planters. Brazil was considered to be fully a part of Portugal, even though it happened to be situated on the other side of the Atlantic Ocean; so much so, that the possibility of transferring the imperial court to Brazil in a time of peril had been mooted in Lisbon as early as the middle of the seventeenth century.

The American and French revolutions were to plunge all of Europe, Portugal included, into ideological and military turmoil. The ripples reached Brazil, mingling with provincial grievances against taxes and high-handed officialdom to produce occasional conspiracies in which the notion of a republic was entertained. The most substantial of these plots was the *Inconfidência mineira* of 1788–9, uncovered at Ouro Preto, the centre of the depressed gold-mining industry of Minas Gerais: many members of the local élite, including army officers, landowners, mine-owners, lawyers and priests planned to overthrow the authorities and declare an independent republic. The rebels were punished, and one of their most charismatic leaders, known as Tiradentes ('the Teeth-puller'), was hanged to set an example. Another republican conspiracy was foiled in Bahia in 1798. Here there was a racial dimension – many of the conspirators were mulattos or black slaves; their rhetoric was influenced by French revolutionary ideas of equality and fraternity. These disturbing echoes of the Haitian revolts elicited a severe reaction from the authorities – the leaders were hanged and their bodies put on public display. Further plots came to light and were swiftly repressed at Rio de Janeiro in 1794 and Pernambuco in 1801; and a conspiracy to provoke an uprising of African slaves in Bahia was discovered in 1807.

These were all local, isolated episodes, and the danger to the Crown lay not in the degree of republican dissent but in the fact that it had showed itself at all. Treason and rebellion were nothing new to the monarchy; the difference now was that some of its subjects were able to conceive of a society in which monarchs were superfluous. That the thought might be put into practice was still a remote possibility in Brazil, but events in Europe were so unpredictable that within a few years the Portuguese Crown would be facing a mortal threat from French armies. How would Brazil react then?

Napoleon and the Crisis of Legitimacy in the Iberian World (1808–10)

As the eighteenth century drew to a close, the relationship between the Iberian monarchies and their respective colonies had become strained by modernizing reforms, rebellion and the vicissitudes of war in Europe. The American élites had cause to feel frustrated with their subordination to the metropolis: the liberalization of the trade monopoly had created prosperity in most regions, but this largely served to expose the self-serving, colonial nature of the limits still placed upon direct commerce with other countries, especially Britain. On the other hand, the French Revolution and the example of Haiti brought home to the white élites of the colonies the value of the Crown as a guarantor of law and order within their own racially divided societies. And yet the anti-clerical regalism of reformers in both Portugal and Spain had eroded the traditional basis of the legitimacy of the Iberian Catholic monarchies, while in the ideas of the Enlightenment potential alternatives to royal sovereignty could be found, as the revolutionaries in English America had demonstrated. In short, imperial relations in the 1800s were exposed to criticism in ways that had not been possible since the formative period of the American empires; but, once again, the American élites had to weigh the benefits of political freedom against the risks of internal disorder and race war.

Still, there was no compelling force from within the colonies that could have led to a breakdown of imperial authority. It was a series of external events in Europe that precipitated a crisis of royal legitimacy in the Iberian world that was wholly unpredictable in its depth and suddenness. In August 1807 Napoleon put pressure on Portugal to close its ports to British ships. For its part, Britain sent a fleet and threatened to bombard Lisbon and attack Brazil if the Portuguese complied with French demands. When a French army invaded the country in November, the prince regent decided to save the throne of Portugal by evacuating it to Brazil. Under British escort the entire court removed to Rio de Janeiro, which suddenly found it had become the capital of the Portuguese empire at a time when royal authority had been destroyed in the mother country.

This extraordinary train of events thus preserved, and indeed reinforced, the legitimacy of imperial authority in Brazil. The colonial élites benefited both politically and economically. With the court in Rio, a new sense of unity was given to a vast colony whose regions had hitherto been extremely isolated from one another. Moreover, with Portugal under French occupation, the trade monopoly became inoperative, and so freedom to trade with all other nations was declared by the prince regent. (Britain demanded and got a preferential tariff and soon dominated trade with Brazil.) Yet there were strains: the Crown brought with it several thousand Portuguese courtiers and the full apparatus of absolute rule. Tighter central control from Rio over the captaincies, combined with political jealousies at court between the local oligarchs and peninsular nobles, fuelled resentments. Ironically, it was while the monarchy was based in Rio that the rivalry between its peninsular and American subjects became most marked. Even so, from 1807 until 1822, Brazil was to know stability, order and continuity under the Crown. It was to be a very different story in the Spanish Indies.

Napoleon's intervention in Spain led to the collapse of royal authority in the Peninsula and in the colonies. Having occupied Portugal, Napoleon sent a French army into Spain in March 1808. The Spanish court was thrown into confusion: Charles IV was persuaded to abdicate in favour of his son Ferdinand, but Napoleon enticed them both to Bayonne, where he extracted a renunciation of the throne from father and son in turn. He then contrived to have them both detained indefinitely in France, and delivered the crown of Spain to his own brother Joseph. Napoleon, however, failed to reckon with the Spanish people: on 2 May 1808 the inhabitants of Madrid rose in rebellion against the French troops, and this uprising sparked revolts throughout the country in favour of the legitimate monarch, Ferdinand VII, *el deseado* ('the desired one'). The Frenchman had imposed a new dynasty on Spain, but in doing so he had broken the tacit compact between the Spanish king and his people which alone could justify the absolute rule of a sovereign. As a result, juntas sprang up in various towns, and in the absence of the desired monarch, these councils assumed provisional sovereignty, eventually placing themselves under the authority of a Supreme Junta at Seville.

The installation of Joseph Bonaparte as king of Spain produced an acute constitutional crisis in the Spanish Indies, for it brought to a head their contradictory situation. Unlike Brazil, they were, strictly speaking, kingdoms in their own right, constitutionally distinct from Spain as such but sharing a common monarch. The abrupt disappearance of the dynastic sovereign now posed the question as to where legitimate authority lay: did it belong to Joseph Bonaparte, the American viceroys, or the Supreme Junta in Seville? Did it perhaps lie with the creoles themselves, who might set up juntas following the Spanish example and assume provisional sovereignty in the absence of Ferdinand? This last course had revolutionary implications, since it meant that for the first time in their history the creoles could legitimately exercise power in America without either deferring to a viceroy or being disloyal to the king. Naturally, this was the option favoured by those creoles who wanted to see the Indies move eventually towards some form of autonomy from the Peninsula.

The issue of sovereignty divided creole from creole, and creole from Spaniard, and responses varied from one region to another. In Mexico the matter was soon settled: a faction of Spanish merchants pulled off a *coup d'état* against the viceroy Iturrigaray, who had shown sympathy for the idea of an autonomous Mexican junta, and put in his place a new viceroy pledged to Seville. In other regions the advocates of creole juntas were defeated and the royal bureaucracy under the authority of Seville retained central control. Only the creole juntas of Quito and La Paz held out for a while, but they too were forced to submit.

This preliminary skirmish showed two things: first, the strength of Spanish authority in the Indies among the creoles themselves; secondly, the scattered and divided character of the opposition to peninsular rule. But the vacillation on the part of some Spanish officials – Iturrigaray in Mexico, for instance – was evidence of the political confusion that underlay the apparent restoration of order. For authority in the Indies depended on what might happen in the war against Napoleon currently raging in the Peninsula, and this uncertainty meant that all the interest-groups in Spanish America were caught up in a fluid situation, where political gains could suddenly be reversed and failing causes just as soon quicken with renewed vigour.

The fall of Andalusia to the French in the spring of 1810 turned the situation round in Spanish America. The Supreme Junta at Seville took refuge in Cadiz, where it precariously survived under siege from the enemy. There it reconstituted itself as a 'Regency Council' and, falling under the influence of 'liberals' – it was the first time the word had been used in European politics – summoned Cortes to include representatives from the whole empire in order to draft a constitution, the first in the history of Spain. This development left the creole élites with two main options: they could send delegates to Cadiz to negotiate a new relationship with the mother country, or they could take the revolutionary step of rejecting the authority of the Regency Council and set up juntas of their own in Ferdinand's name. The fact was that with the fall of Andalusia it looked as if Napoleon would soon clinch total victory in the Peninsula. Many otherwise conservative creoles were therefore persuaded that it was futile to submit to Cadiz.

Once again, however, the Indies were divided in their response to events in Spain. In New Spain, the pro-Spanish *coup d'état* of 1808 precluded the creation of a revolutionary junta in Mexico City by members of the creole élite. Instead, the call to reject the Cadiz liberals and pledge allegiance directly to Ferdinand VII came from below; it was uttered in the town of Dolores in the central region of the Bajío by a priest, Miguel Hidalgo, who soon found himself at the head of a violent movement of mostly Indian and mestizo insurgents.

The situation in South America was very confused. Peru, the old heartland of the Spanish empire, obeyed its viceroy and followed Cadiz. In the viceroyalty of New Granada, revolutionary juntas were proclaimed in various provincial cities, the most radical to emerge being the junta of Caracas in Venezuela, which fell under the sway of republicans like Francisco de Miranda and Simón Bolívar. In Chile, after some uncertainty, a revolutionary junta took power in Santiago. The viceroyalty of Río de la Plata fell apart. Its capital, Buenos Aires, established a junta ostensibly pledging loyalty to Ferdinand, but which was in fact riven by conflicts between moderates and those who actually favoured secession, such as Mariano Moreno, Manuel Belgrano and Bernardino Rivadavia. On the other hand, provincial cities like Montevideo, Córdoba, La Paz and Asunción in Paraguay opted to accept the authority of Cadiz. The junta in Buenos Aires therefore sent military expeditions to reduce the provinces to its authority. As well as these disturbances among the creole élites, there were also the masses of Indians and *castas* – the mestizos, mulattos and blacks – whose reactions to the crumbling of Spanish rule no one could as yet predict – though in Mexico the Indians who responded to the call of Father Hidalgo had taken to killing their white oppressors, regardless of whether they were Spaniards or creoles.

The contrast with Brazil could not have been greater. The Portuguese Crown had eluded Napoleon and had preserved legitimate authority in its empire. Brazil, in consequence, remained united and at peace. That outcome had been denied to the Spanish Indies, for, once Napoleon had usurped the Spanish throne, all the old certainties upon which the imperial chains of command had depended for their effective operation began to dissolve. The simple cry of loyalty to Ferdinand concealed a range of different and often conflicting motives among the creoles. There were some who genuinely wished to keep faith with the absolute monarchy, others who hoped to use the crisis to wring constitutional rights from the Crown, yet others who conceived of a Spanish American monarchy independent of the Peninsula. And there were a few – perhaps as yet only a very few – who saw in the profession of loyalty to the captive Ferdinand little more than a pretext for complete secession and the declaration of a republic.

By 1810 the three centuries of the *Pax Hispanica* in America were over. Cut off from the Catholic monarchy, the creoles found themselves adrift on the open sea of politics, borne away by currents which no one was quite able to navigate. Political options barely conceivable a few years back now appeared dimly over the horizon as possible destinations. A number of radicals seized the chance to steer the Indies towards such ends, but they too would be blown off course by the continuing storm of events in the Peninsula. The crisis of royal legitimacy hopelessly divided the creoles, and political disagreements would soon lead to fratricidal struggles and then to a series of bloody civil wars.

Spanish America: The Road to Independence

The First Phase (1810–14)

In the period 1810–14 the winning of some form of autonomy for the Indies within an imperial framework under a restored Bourbon monarchy seemed feasible, and it was a political solution that commanded the support of the majority of creole opinion. The beleaguered Regency Council at Cadiz had declared the equality of all the realms of the empire and summoned delegates to a constituent assembly. In 1812 a liberal constitution was proclaimed; it effectively provided for the establishment in Spain of a limited monarchy in which royal power would be accountable to elected Cortes and individual rights would be guaranteed. The 1812 constitution of Cadiz thus became the rallying symbol of Spanish American as much as peninsular liberals, for it promised the creoles what they had always aspired to – a greater voice in their own government, while retaining the monarchy as a source of legitimate authority.

However, the liberalism of the Cadiz government had its limits when it came to dealing with the empire. The government at Cadiz rejected a proposal from American delegates for a kind of commonwealth of autonomous constitutional kingdoms under one monarch – a liberal reincarnation, as it were, of the Habsburg theory of empire. The creoles wanted the right to trade with foreigners, proportional representation at the Cortes, and equal access to all government posts. However, the liberal Cortes in Cadiz was not prepared to concede any of this, for even the Spanish liberals could not contemplate surrendering political control over the Indies. Such control, after all, afforded the Spanish state huge revenues from taxes, duties, forced loans and Indian tribute, as well as guaranteed profits from the transatlantic trade monopoly for Spanish exporters and the merchants of Cadiz (many of whom were, not surprisingly, supporters of the liberals in the Cortes). The reality was that the economic dependence of Spain on its American colonies made stubborn imperialists out of political liberals.

Still, the Cadiz constitution enshrined rights to free elections and to a free press, which in principle gave the creoles the chance to express their grievances openly and to participate more directly in the political life of their regions. In the Indies, however, the viceroys, who were used to the ways of an absolute monarchy, tried to ignore the freedoms conceded by Cadiz, or, where that proved impossible, they sought to manipulate elections to the American *cabildos*. By 1814 the imperialism of the Cadiz Cortes, no less than the intransigence of royal officials, seemed to impede a negotiated solution to the imperial crisis, and this alienated many creoles. But so long as metropolitan authority was divided between liberal parliamentarians in Cadiz and conservative administrators in the colonies, the political situation would remain fluid.

While the search for a political solution had been going on, groups of creole radicals throughout the Indies had since 1810 taken to arms in order to win full independence from Spain. Though still small in numbers, they could only stand to benefit from the frustration of the majority with the inflexibility of the imperial government. The rebellions they led differed in character and extent from one region to another, and their effect on the creole majorities in their respective areas was likewise varied.

The Rebellion in Mexico

The rebellion in favour of independence in Mexico differed from all the other risings in that it came from outside the creole élite. It was sparked off by a creole priest, Miguel Hidalgo, who had been the rector of the prestigious college of San Nicolás in Valladolid (now Morelia), but had fallen foul of the royal authorities because of his interest in the ideas of the Enlightenment and his personal life (he lived openly with the mother of his two daughters). Hidalgo had been removed by his bishop to the small parish of Dolores near Querétaro, where he worked among Indians and mestizos. In 1810 he joined a conspiracy of wealthy creoles to set up a revolutionary junta. When the plot was uncovered, Hidalgo hurriedly called for a general uprising against the Spanish. This was the famous *Grito de Dolores* of 16 September (now celebrated as Independence Day in Mexico). The *Grito* was a cry for independence in the name of Ferdinand VII and the Virgin of Guadalupe. Hidalgo's aims were sweeping but unfocused: abolition of the Indian tribute, the return of Indian lands and death to all Spaniards.

The reaction of the peasantry was explosive, for the rich agricultural region of the Bajío had been suffering from drought and famine for the last two years, and the peasants were desperate. A mass of Indians and mestizos rose up and began looting and killing the whites. Within a week the rebels had captured two towns and entered the provincial capital, Guanajuato, where they besieged the Alhóndiga – the fortified municipal granary in which terrified creoles and Spaniards had taken refuge. A bloody massacre occurred, followed by the pillage of the city. Three weeks later Valladolid, the provincial capital of Michoacán, had fallen, and the insurgents, their numbers having swelled to over 80,000, moved on Mexico City itself. Their advance, however, was checked by a costly encounter with royalist forces. The rebels decided to retreat, but on their way back to Querétaro they were engaged by another royalist army and suffered a devastating blow. They divided into two dwindling forces, one withdrawing to Valladolid and thence to Guadalajara under Hidalgo, the other to Guanajuato under Ignacio Allende. Though Hidalgo was able to recruit more peasants at Guadalajara, his forces were crushed by royalists in January 1811. He fled north, but was captured in March and shot, along with most of his commanders; their heads were displayed at the infamous Alhóndiga in Guanajuato for the next ten years.

Resistance was patchy for about a year, after which the rebels recovered some of their former strength under the leadership of José María Morelos, a mestizo priest from Michoacán, whose military skill and political intelligence gave the independence movement greater coherence than under Hidalgo. Morelos cast aside the profession of loyalty to Ferdinand VII and outlined a radical programme, which included land redistribution and the full integration of Indians and mestizos into society. Capturing the city of Oaxaca in the south-west, he proceeded to organize a congress at Chipalcingo in 1813, where independence was declared on 6 November. This alternative republican government and its small army was continually harried by royalist troops – Oaxaca was recaptured early in 1814 – and failed to attract wide support among the creoles. Nevertheless, despite internal disputes which led to the removal of Morelos from the leadership, the insurgency persisted doggedly against heavy odds. The republican congress issued a constitution at Apatzingan in October 1814, but by this time Ferdinand had been released and the absolute monarchy was restored in Spain and its dominions. Morelos was captured in 1815 and executed.

The Rebellion in New Granada

Of the several revolutionary juntas that appeared in 1810 in the viceroyalty of New Granada, the one at Caracas moved soonest towards republicanism and the inevitable armed struggle. The creole élites acted with dispatch to safeguard their privileges once it appeared that Spain had fallen to Napoleon. For the whites of Venezuela were in a minority, surrounded by a mass of blacks, Indians and half-caste *pardos*, whose advancement under the Spaniards they regarded as a threat to their social authority. A congress was duly elected in March 1811 on a franchise which excluded non-whites.

However, a more radical group, calling itself the Patriotic Society of Caracas, urged the declaration of an independent republic. The Patriotic Society was led by men such as Francisco de Miranda, who had returned to Venezuela in 1810, and Simón Bolívar, a member of one of the richest and most powerful families of the Venezuelan oligarchy of cacao planters. It was this social group that had most to gain from severing ties with Spain, seizing political power over the non-whites and opening up trade with Britain and the USA. On 5 July 1811 the congress declared independence and founded the first republic of Venezuela. Miranda was nominated supreme commander of the republican army. The constitution provided for a federal structure, the legal equality of citizens of all races and the abolition of clerical and military privileges. Yet, in reality, it did little for the non-whites: the *pardos* were mostly excluded from voting by a property qualification, slavery was retained, and the *llaneros*, the free-ranging horsemen of the plains, were alienated by policies designed to bring the *llanos* (plains) under private ownership. When a small Spanish force arrived from Puerto Rico in March 1812 under the command of Domingo de Monteverde, the non-whites threw in their lot with the royalists and within a few months the republican army had surrendered to Monteverde. Its chief, Miranda, was deported to Spain and died in prison some years later.

Simón Bolívar, however, escaped to New Granada, where the provincial juntas were quarrelling amongst themselves over the terms of their association. A precarious federation – the United Provinces of New Granada – had been achieved under the leadership of Camilo Torres late in 1811; but the junta of the viceregal capital, Bogotá, rejected the federal constitution and set itself up instead as the independent state of Cundinamarca, under the leadership of Antonio Nariño, a noted liberal dissident under the Bourbons. Other cities and provinces, such as Panama, Santa Marta and Pasto, remained loyal to the Regency Council in Cadiz. The extreme political fragmentation of the viceroyalty resulted in bouts of armed conflict between revolutionary creole factions.

Despite this disorder, Bolívar managed to enlist the help of the United Provinces of New Granada for a renewed campaign against the royalists of Venezuela. His political objective on this occasion was to exploit the refusal of the Cadiz liberals to make concessions on autonomy for the Indies. In 1813 Bolívar entered Venezuela and declared a 'war to the death' against the authority of Spain with the aim of forcing wavering creoles to choose between independence or submission to an unyielding colonialism. Fighting a *campaña admirable* he reached Caracas in August and declared a second republic, assuming the functions of a military dictator, since he had become disenchanted with democratic assemblies after observing the chaotic situation in New Granada. The Second Republic nevertheless collapsed within a few months: Bolívar had failed to win over the *pardos*, many of whom were recruited by a Spaniard, José Tomás Boves, into a guerrilla movement loyal to the king. At the battle of La Puerta on 15 June 1814 Bolívar's army was defeated by Boves's royalist guerrillas.

Returning to New Granada, Bolívar joined in the perennial squabbling between centralists and federalists until he became disillusioned with the unruliness of the revolutionaries and left for Jamaica in 1815. The independence movements in New Granada would, in any case, soon fall to a royalist counter-strike organized from Venezuela by Pablo Morillo, an extremely able Spanish general who had been sent out from Spain in the spring of 1815 to pacify the Indies with an army of 10,000 men. By 1816 both Venezuela and New Granada were back under royalist control.

The Rebellion in Río de la Plata

The other theatre of military conflict in South America was Río de la Plata, a territory which, like New Granada, had been raised to the status of a viceroyalty only in recent decades, and where political authority had not become firmly rooted in the new capital, Buenos Aires. On 25 May 1810 a junta proclaiming direct loyalty to Ferdinand VII seized power in Buenos Aires and very soon fell under the rhetorical sway of Jacobin radicals such as Mariano Moreno, a liberal journalist and the translator of Rousseau's *Social Contract*. The liberal junta opened the port of Buenos Aires to trade with all nations and proclaimed the equality of all citizens regardless of race. But, in fact, the junta expressed the interests of the *porteños* – the Buenos Aires élite – whose measures were directed against the Spanish import–export merchants and who were careful to exclude non-white sectors from government.

The radical hue of the Buenos Aires junta did little to recommend it to the oligarchies of the interior provinces, and a loyalist reaction in the old city of Córdoba, seat of an *audiencia* and a university, was suppressed by the *porteño* liberals and its leaders executed; they included Santiago Liniers, who had commanded the militia forces which had expelled the British from the River Plate in 1806–7. Provincial hostility was, however, mollified when delegates from the interior were at last included in the Buenos Aires junta; their conservatism moderated the Jacobin fervour of the *porteño* politicians, but creole government in the capital continued to be riven by factionalism in the absence of any one strong leader. In 1813 the junta called a national assembly of what it now designated as the United Provinces of Río de la Plata, although independence from Spain had not yet been declared.

There were, nevertheless, important provinces of the viceroyalty which refused to accept the authority of the revolutionaries in Buenos Aires, namely Paraguay, the Banda Oriental (modern Uruguay) and Upper Peru (now Bolivia) – the Andean province where the great silver-mines of Potosí were located and whose economy until 1776 had been oriented towards Lima. Buenos Aires sought to reduce these provinces by force of arms. An army led by Juan José Castelli took Potosí and combined with local rebels to wrest Upper Peru from the royalists, but within months had been defeated by an army from Peru. Another expedition led by Manuel Belgrano reconquered Potosí, but was again expelled by royalists. A third attempt to take Upper Peru was repulsed in 1815, and the silver-rich province had finally to be abandoned by Buenos Aires.

Paraguay too was lost to Buenos Aires. A *porteño* army led by Manuel Belgrano was beaten back by loyalist militias in 1811. Shortly afterwards, a junta was set up in Asunción which eventually gave way to the dictatorship of José Gaspar Rodríguez de Francia, under whose eccentric, unwavering rule this province thenceforward pursued an independent course. The Banda Oriental across the River Paraná was to give Buenos Aires constant trouble both during the independence wars and long afterwards. José Gervasio Artigas, a local cattle-rancher, initiated the revolt against the royalists of Montevideo and called on Buenos Aires for assistance. Yet Artigas proved reluctant to submit to the authority of the *porteños*, and relations between the allies fluctuated during the war to liberate Montevideo. With the fall of the city in 1814, Artigas won control of the province and proceeded with a radical land policy of breaking up the large haciendas and distributing land to Indians, half-castes and small farmers. However, in 1816 he was overwhelmed by an invading army from Brazil.

Already by 1815 the leadership of Buenos Aires over the United Provinces of Río de la Plata was decidedly shaky. Large areas of the viceroyalty had eluded its authority altogether, while other inland provinces were proving fractious; the *porteño* élite itself remained divided, and the conservative majority was becoming increasingly irritated with the political radicalism of lawyers turned professional politicians. As the movement for independence began to falter, it was Buenos Aires's great distance from the metropolis that saved the liberal revolutionaries from immediate military punishment by Spain after the restoration of Ferdinand VII to the throne.

The Return of the King (1814–19)

With the defeat of Napoleon in the Iberian Peninsula in 1814, Ferdinand VII, newly restored to his throne, sought to rebuild the authority that had so suddenly collapsed six years earlier. His return to Spain had been celebrated by the common people as a national victory and, taking advantage of this immense popular devotion, Ferdinand reverted to absolute rule: the Cortes of Cadiz were dissolved, the 1812 constitution abrogated and the breach with the Church repaired, even to the extent of reinstating the Inquisition and the Jesuit order. Conventionally portrayed by liberal historians as a mulish autocrat blind to his own self-interest, Ferdinand, though a Bourbon, was attempting to recover the traditional monopoly of legitimacy enjoyed by the Habsburg monarchs, a legitimacy which had served to secure over two centuries of obedience from the Crown's subjects in the Indies. After all, the modernizing reforms of his immediate Bourbon forebears had done little but weaken the authority of the throne and damage its compact with the Church; the liberals of Cadiz had gone even further, recasting the whole basis of royal sovereignty by deriving it from the will of the people. And the result of these innovations had only been rebellion in America and the risk of losing the empire to some foreign power such as Great Britain.

The prospects of Spain's regaining the ground lost in the Indies were very good: Mexico was all but pacified; New Granada had been won back by 1816 and was in the capable hands of General Morillo; the hunta of Buenos Aires had proved unable to extend its authority to the interior provinces, and a well-equipped Spanish army would make short work of the revolutionary forces, composed as they largely were of the creoles' reluctant peons and black slaves. Indeed, Spain would come very close to crushing altogether the creole bid for independence, and her rule could conceivably have lasted for the whole of the nineteenth century, if not longer. (Cuba, Puerto Rico and the Philippines did not become independent until 1898.) The tide had turned against the advocates of independence, and it would run strongly in favour of the Catholic monarchy until 1820.

After 1814 the creoles faced a very different political situation from when Napoleon had seized the Spanish Crown and had apparently conquered the entire Iberian Peninsula. With the legitimate king back on his throne, opposition to the colonial administration could no longer be construed other than as treason. It seemed possible, therefore, that the traditional colonial pact might be restored, whereby the creoles forsook formal self-government in exchange for the unity and stability which the Catholic monarchy afforded the diverse and racially fragmented societies of the New World. As in the period 1808–10, the majority of creoles had to choose between embracing the devil of absolutism, which they at least knew, and taking a stride into the unknown behind a small number of squabbling radicals.

The leaders of this radical minority were aware of the change in the political circumstances and of the need, in consequence, to make their programmes for independence palatable to the mass of conservative creoles. Even in Buenos Aires – once a hotbed of republicanism – creole leaders were actively seeking a monarchical solution to the independence struggle. Although an accommodation with Ferdinand VII seemed out of the question, given his aversion to constitutionalism, envoys of the Buenos Aires junta had been sent to Europe to look for a prince willing to sit on the throne of an independent kingdom in the River Plate. Influential figures such as Manuel Belgrano, formerly a Jacobin republican and a supporter of Mariano Moreno, now argued for a monarchy under a descendant of the Inca. José de San Martín, a professional soldier who had served in Spain and who was shortly to take command of an army of liberation, also favoured the creation of an independent Spanish American monarchy.

Even that unwavering republican, Simón Bolívar, saw fit to give his programme a very marked conservative slant. Dismayed by the anarchy he had witnessed in New Granada, he concluded that republicanism in South America could not follow the North American model, much less that of the French Revolution. He became more and more convinced that unqualified electoral democracy would lead to catastrophe in societies which he believed had been kept in a condition of political immaturity by what he saw as the 'Spanish tyranny'. Instead, the way forward must be a compromise between authority and democracy. In his Jamaica Letter of 6 September 1815 he revealed a pragmatism born of disillusion, observing that Spanish America should 'not adopt the best system of government, but the one that is most likely to succeed'.* Without abandoning his commitment to republicanism, Bolívar now found a model for Spanish American constitutions in the British monarchy, and he envisaged that Great Britain would be invited to become tutor and protector of the nations freed from the Spanish yoke.

These ideological readjustments were accompanied by changes in political and military strategies. Both Bolívar and San Martín saw the futility of direct confrontations with royalist armies. Instead, they would seek the advantage of surprise by seizing vulnerable territory and setting up an independent government, thus offering the creoles an alternative political destiny to the Catholic monarchy. By 1817 San Martín and Bolívar were each ready to undertake new campaigns in their respective theatres of war.

The Wars of Independence in South America

In the River Plate, San Martín put together an 'Army of the Andes', but instead of advancing on Upper Peru, where three previous campaigns had come to grief, he chose to cross into Chile and, having liberated it, to proceed by sea towards Lima, the centre of royalist power in South America. Traversing the Andes in February 1817, he engaged a royalist force at Chacabuco and went on to the capital, Santiago. There he installed a government under Bernardo O'Higgins, a Chilean commander in his army, and in February 1818 independence was formally declared. After the victory at Maipú in April the liberation of Chile was virtually complete, though loyalist troops would continue to resist for a good while longer.

The next task was to prepare for the assault on Peru. For this he received material and financial support from the O'Higgins regime; many Chileans volunteered to serve in the army of liberation and San Martín's small fleet of warships, under the command of the Scottish adventurer Lord Cochrane, was manned mostly by Chilean sailors. Yet San Martín's underlying position was weak. A crucial element in his strategy was the logistical support O'Higgins would provide from liberated Chile. But even before San Martín had set sail for Peru, O'Higgins had run into difficulties: he had assumed dictatorial powers to impose liberal reforms which alienated important sectors of the Chilean élite. He had also failed to destroy the remaining strongholds of loyalist resistance. With O'Higgins's political base visibly deteriorating (he would be driven from office in 1823), the outlook for San

---

* *Escritos del Libertador* (Caracas, 1964–), vol. 8, p. 241. Quoted in translation by John Lynch, *Simón Bolívar and the Age of Revolution* (University of London, Institute of Latin American Studies' Working Papers, no. 10: London, 1983), p. 15.

Martín, as he set out in August 1820 to take on the might of the Spanish empire, was highly uncertain.

In 1817 Simón Bolívar had returned to Venezuela, where he initiated a campaign in the west, taking the strategic town of Angostura which, being situated on the Orinoco, allowed him to receive assistance by sea as well as providing him with a route upriver into the central plains. By the end of the year he had made contact with José Antonio Páez, the redoubtable leader of the half-caste *llaneros* (plainsmen), who had been conducting a guerrilla war against the royalists. This time Bolívar was careful not to repeat the mistake that had cost his Second Republic so dear: he provided certain limited political incentives for the *pardos* and black slaves to fight on his side. The alliance with Páez was to prove vital for the campaign, for not only did it widen the ethnic base of the revolution, but it also gave Bolívar access to the central plains, enabling him to circumvent the northern coastal areas and especially Caracas, where General Morillo and the bulk of the royalist forces were concentrated.

At Angostura, Bolívar called a national congress in February 1819 and outlined a constitution for the future republic. He proposed a strong executive president, who would be financially accountable to a legislature consisting, like the British parliament, of two chambers, one elected, the other a hereditary senate. Bolívar also recommended an independent judiciary, and, as a further check on the evils of unlimited democracy, a 'moral power' formed by an unelected body of notable citizens charged with the promotion of virtue in the conduct of public affairs. The congress, however, rejected both the hereditary senate and the moral power.

From the central plains of Venezuela, Bolívar went east towards New Granada, avoiding the royalists in the north, and planning to join with republicans under the command of Francisco de Paula Santander on the other side of the Andes. His objective was to spring an attack on Bogotá, the seat of the viceroyalty. After suffering terrible hardships during the march across the plains and the even more arduous ascent over the freezing heights of the Andes, Bolívar's men linked up with Santander's and the republican army inflicted a decisive defeat on royalist forces at Boyacá in August 1819. When Bolívar entered Bogotá a few days later, New Granada had to all intents and purposes fallen to the revolutionaries. In December the independence of all the provinces of the viceroyalty was declared and the Republic of Colombia was founded. The rebels had created the framework of an alternative state: they had taken the viceregal capital, and large areas of both New Granada and Venezuela had come under their control. But there remained Quito, Panama and the most populated regions of Venezuela, including Caracas; and the main royalist forces under Morillo had yet to be engaged.

For five years after the restoration of Ferdinand (1814–19) the balance of power in the struggle for independence was with the royalists. Nevertheless, the two main secessionist armies in South America had made important strategic gains – they had still to confront the full force of the imperial state, but before this confrontation there would occur another wholly unexpected change in the political situation which would shift the balance of advantage decisively in their favour.

The Cadiz Mutiny of 1820

The next critical turning-point in the zigzag process of independence came not in the Indies but, once again, in the Peninsula. On 1 January 1820 an army of some 14,000 men, which had been assembled at Cadiz for the express purpose of reconquering the rebel territories of the River Plate, suddenly mutinied. Most garrisons in Spain joined the *pronunciamiento* (revolt) and Ferdinand VII, his army having turned against him, was forced to renounce absolutism and accept the Cadiz constitution of 1812.

Why did the army revolt? The immediate cause had less to do with liberal convictions than with discontent over pay and with plans to reduce the size of the armed forces. But the consequences were so momentous because the Cortes of Cadiz had provided in the 1812 constitution an alternative source of political legitimacy which opponents of the royal will could invoke regardless of whether or not they were actually liberal in ideology. In earlier times this alternative had simply not been available to rebels against the Crown. The truth was that after Napoleon's intervention in the Peninsula it had become impossible for the Spanish Crown to reconstruct its monopoly of legitimacy; the Catholic monarchy itself had been set adrift on the sea of politics, and this latest storm in Cadiz would lead to the end of its authority in America.

The Cadiz mutiny undermined the position of Spanish viceroys and field commanders in the Indies. The new liberal government in Spain ordered the colonial authorities to seek a truce with the insurgents as a preliminary to the negotiation of a settlement of the protracted colonial crisis. As the Spanish American revolutionaries realized, this amounted to capitulation by Spain; for it showed that the Catholic monarchy could not hope fully to regain its authority either in Spain or in America, and, with royal legitimacy so contested and curtailed, what benefits could Spanish liberals offer the colonies that the creoles could not achieve for themselves? There was certainly no reason to submit to a trade monopoly and a political administration run by liberal imperialists in the Peninsula.

In effect, the Cadiz revolt put paid to the one outstanding benefit for which the creoles had been willing to accept colonial restrictions, namely, the unifying, stabilizing authority of the absolute monarchy. Once that had gone, the colonial pact was a dead letter. After 1820 the majority of creoles would move away from their inveterate loyalty to the Crown towards acceptance of the inevitability of independence. There remained, of course, the daunting task of defeating the royalist armies on the field of battle, but the political and psychological war had already been won by the secessionists.

The Independence of Mexico

Nowhere did the sudden shift of political and psychological advantage brought about by the Cadiz mutiny have a more dramatic effect than in Mexico. From 1815 until 1820 the cause of independence still flickered in the resistance offered by a harried force of rebels in the south, led after the death of Morelos by a mestizo, Vicente Guerrero. In November 1820 the viceroy Apodaca sent Agustín de Iturbide, a trusted creole veteran of the campaigns against Hidalgo and Morelos, to deliver the final blow to the secessionists. But news of the Cadiz mutiny had changed Iturbide's attitude to the question of Mexico's ties with Spain: he made contact with the rebel leader Guerrero and forged an alliance with him against the Spanish government. Together they issued the Plan of Iguala on 24 February 1821, and this became the document which steered Mexico through a virtually bloodless transition to independence.

According to the Plan of Iguala, Mexico would become an independent monarchy, limited by the 1812 constitution of Cadiz, with either Ferdinand VII or one of his brothers as emperor; Catholicism would remain the only legitimate religion and the Church would retain its property and privileges; all subjects, including Indians, mestizos and the many Spaniards living in Mexico, would enjoy equality before the law. These were to be the three pillars of the new order – Independence, Religion and Union – and they would be defended by an *Ejército Trigarante*, an Army of the Three Guarantees, formed by a fusion of Iturbide's royalist troops with Guerrero's rebel forces. The Plan offered something – though not everything – to every major interest in Mexico, from Catholic traditionalist to liberal reformer; it even honoured Spain as the mother country, a sentiment that was still shared by most Mexicans. Iguala, in short, was a creative compromise which very soon gelled into a national consensus. Within six months it had received the support of all the principal garrisons in Mexico, and the new viceroy sent out from the Peninsula had to recognize that the country had effectively won its independence, a fact that was ratified by treaty on 24 August 1821. A month later, Iturbide entered Mexico City in triumph and was installed as president of the Regency of the Mexican Empire.

The Plan of Iguala succeeded because it reconciled two historic interests of the creole élites which had never before coincided in the one political settlement: it allowed for legitimate creole self-government, while providing for social authority based on a monarchical and religious framework. It is little wonder, then, that it attracted other regional élites. The new Mexican empire invited the captaincy-general of the Yucatán, as well as the Central American provinces which comprised the Kingdom of Guatemala (namely, Chiapas, Honduras, El Salvador, Nicaragua, Costa Rica and Guatemala itself), to join it under the terms of Iguala. All agreed, except for El Salvador, which was promptly compelled to do so by a Mexican army.

But Spain would seek to destroy the settlement of Iguala by its unwillingness to come to terms with political facts. The liberal government in the Peninsula refused to recognize Mexican independence. Worse still, neither Ferdinand nor any Spanish prince could be induced to accept the Mexican Crown. This repudiation of a Mexican monarchy by the Bourbons removed the lynchpin of the Iguala Plan, for with a break in dynastic continuity the legitimacy of the Mexican Crown would be compromised beyond repair.

Iturbide, nevertheless, tried to save the institution of monarchy in Mexico. On the evening of 18 May 1822 a public demonstration led by soldiers from his own regiment proclaimed him Agustín I of Mexico; succumbing to popular pressure, congress accepted him as emperor. But Iturbide would prove unable to conjure up the sacred aura of royalty, which alone could command the allegiance of all his subjects. The creole aristocracy would not forgive him for being the son of a merchant, his brother officers regarded him as a political schemer, and Spaniards resident in Mexico still wanted a real prince of the blood. Finally, calls for a republic, which until then had mostly fallen on deaf ears, began to find a response in Mexico. As the consensus which had sustained the Plan of Iguala crumbled, the new creole emperor took arbitrary measures to shore up his authority, and in doing so stirred up even more hostility. In December 1822 an ambitious young colonel, Antonio López de Santa Anna, opportunistically proclaimed a republic and swiftly won the backing of several dissatisfied generals. The bulk of the army came out in support of the rebels and on 19 March 1823

Agustín I abdicated. He would be shot a year later when he returned to Mexico from his European exile on the mistaken assumption that he could regain his throne.

Thus, only two years after the declaration of independence on the basis of the Plan of Iguala, the principle of monarchy had been destroyed by a military *coup d'état*, the first of many in independent Mexico. A federal republic was declared with General Guadalupe Victoria as its first president. The Central American provinces, except Chiapas, seceded, and after a prolonged civil war, their federation broke up into five separate republics. For the next fifty years Mexico itself would be repeatedly torn apart by civil wars, and not the least of the many complicating factors in the labyrinthine affairs of the young Mexican republic was the stubborn survival of conservative hopes for the restoration of a Mexican monarchy, hopes that would not die until well past the middle of the century.

The Independence of South America

In South America, where the insurgencies had been far more substantial than in Mexico, the immediate effect of the Cadiz revolt was to cut the ground from under the feet of the commanders of royalist forces. Ordered by the new liberal government in Spain to offer the rebels a truce, the colonial authorities found that the morale of their troops began to disintegrate; many creole officers and soldiers in the royalist armies started to defect to the insurgents, and even peninsular officers were divided between liberals and absolutists.

The events of 1820 in Spain influenced the tactics employed by San Martín in his campaign to take Peru. Establishing a base north of the capital, he did not attack Lima straight away, calculating correctly that if he waited long enough, the political confusion in the royalist camp would deliver a substantial portion of Peruvian creole opinion to him. San Martín therefore entered into discussions with the colonial administration in order to reach a negotiated settlement. He argued for a solution similar to Iturbide's Plan of Iguala: he wanted to establish a wholly independent constitutional monarchy with a Spanish prince of the blood on the throne. These discussions did not get very far because the royalists were too divided; a military *coup d'état* deposed the viceroy, replacing him with the intransigent José de la Serna, who decided in July 1821 to withdraw from Lima and take to the highlands, where stronger defences could be organized against the secessionists.

In July, therefore, San Martín entered Lima and declared the independence of Peru. But soon he was in trouble: the deeply conservative Lima aristocracy disliked the discriminatory measures he took against peninsular Spaniards, as well as the levies he imposed on creoles to finance his army; and logistical support from Chile was becoming unreliable as the O'Higgins regime ran into difficulties. By 1822, after a year of tactical delay, a delay which was beginning to look like a lack of resolve in the face of the royalist armies entrenched in the sierra, San Martín left for Guayaquil to confer with Simón Bolívar.

For his part, Bolívar had played to the full the advantage given him by the Cadiz mutiny. The Spanish general Morillo, having received orders to seek a truce with the rebels, resigned his post soon after it was declared. Hostilities broke out again within a few months, and in June 1821 Bolívar defeated Morillo's successor at the battle of Carabobo. When Caracas fell some days later, the whole of Venezuela was finally liberated. At the Congress of Cúcuta, Bolívar was acclaimed president of Gran Colombia, a state comprising Venezuela, New Granada and Quito (still to be liberated), and with its capital at Bogotá. A constitution was approved which incorporated many of the Liberator's authoritarian and centralist prescriptions for a republic. Bolívar next turned south and accomplished the conquest of the province of Quito (modern Ecuador) jointly with his lieutenant Antonio José de Sucre.

Thus, when Bolívar arrived to confer with San Martín at Guayaquil on 27 July 1822, he came in triumph as the great Liberator, with a series of resounding military victories to his credit and as head of the vast new independent state of Colombia. By contrast, San Martín's campaign had been bogged down for the past two years in Peru, and his control of Chile was uncertain. Bolívar was clearly in a far superior position, and so, after their famous secret discussions, San Martín chose to withdraw from the fray and leave for Europe, never to return. Bolívar's political victory over San Martín at Guayaquil signified the demise of monarchism as an option for a post-independence settlement; the new states of South America would be given republican constitutions.

Arriving in Peru in September 1823, Bolívar began to prepare for the final offensive against the royalists. By the middle of 1824 he launched his campaign, winning an important battle at Junín, which opened to him the road to Lima, the ultimate prize. In December, while Bolívar was in Lima, Marshal Sucre defeated Viceroy De la Serna's army at the battle of Ayacucho. Spanish power in America had been decisively broken and the Indies were at last free.

The Emancipation of Brazil

While the Spanish viceroyalties of South America were in the grip of civil war, Brazil retained its unity and stability under the absolute monarchy of John VI, based as it had been in Rio de Janeiro since 1808. There had been no comparable crisis of legitimacy, no political drift such as had allowed the Spanish American republicans to seize the initiative at critical moments during the prolonged Napoleonic intervention in the Peninsula.

But the presence of the Portuguese court in Rio had brought its tensions to Brazil, not least in the case of the regional oligarchies, who resented the centralism of the royal government. The most serious expression of this resentment was the republican revolt in Recife of March 1817, when all the elements of the Pernambucan oligarchy – sugar planters, cattle barons, merchants, the clergy and government officials – rose against the Crown and declared a republic. The rebellion, however, failed to gain ground outside the captaincy of Pernambuco, and within two months had been put down by royalist forces from Bahia and Rio. Still, the readiness of the Pernambucan élites to defend their power against central authority by declaring a republic suggests that Brazil, had it not been for the transfer of the monarchy to Rio, might have suffered the regional disintegration and chronic violence which befell the Spanish Indies.

Brazil's passage to independence, however, was not without its risks of political catastrophe. Though the attachment to monarchy was very strong, there had emerged here and there a considerable feeling for republicanism, as attested by the *Inconfidência mineira* of 1788–9 and intermittent republican revolts since. In the event of a sufficiently grave crisis of royal authority, these republican sympathies could have cohered to challenge the Catholic monarchy of Portugal.

Such a possibility arose in 1820, when events in the Peninsula again placed the Crown in difficulties. After the defeat of Napoleon in 1814 Portugal had been ruled by a Regency Council in the absence of the king, but in late 1820 a series of revolts by liberals led to the establishment of a government committed to a constitutional monarchy. A Cortes was called in Lisbon to draw up a constitution modelled on the 1812 constitution of Cadiz, and the king was summoned to Portugal by the liberal government.

In Brazil there was extensive sympathy for the liberal revolution and John VI came to accept the principle of a constitutional monarchy, but he was torn as to whether or not he should return to Lisbon, fearing that he might lose Brazil if he did, or else Portugal if he did not. Finally, he decided to go back, but he left behind his son Dom Pedro as prince regent in Brazil. Thus the Portuguese monarchy put out an offshoot in its most important overseas colony in an attempt to span the political rift that was opening up between Brazil and the mother country.

That rift was to widen into an unbridgeable gulf once it became evident to the Brazilian delegates at the Lisbon Cortes that the peninsular liberals were determined to return Brazil to its colonial status prior to 1808. The liberal government proposed to cancel the political equality of Brazil with Portugal and the freedom of trade which the king had decreed for Brazil when he had first arrived in Rio. This the Brazilians would not countenance and, when the Lisbon government recalled the prince regent in October 1821, the Brazilians urged him to ignore the order. Perversely, Lisbon was pushing the mostly reluctant Brazilians towards some kind of separation, but it was still unclear what form this separation would take and how it might come about. At this juncture, in the final months of 1821, a political crisis arose which could have led to one of a number of outcomes – even to a republic, for which there was considerable support among radical liberals.

It was Dom Pedro's chief minister, José Bonifácio de Andrada e Silva, a conservative monarchist who had spent over thirty years in the service of the Crown in Portugal, who steered Brazil towards independence. On 9 January Dom Pedro had declared that he would stay in Brazil, thereby asserting his autonomy from Lisbon. After his appointment a week later, José Bonifácio edged the country along an independent path, allowing indirect elections for a constituent assembly and disregarding orders from Lisbon. The final break with Portugal came when the Lisbon government tried once again to assert its authority over Brazil by recalling the prince regent. On 7 September 1822, on the banks of the River Ipiranga near São Paulo, Dom Pedro finally rejected Portugal and proclaimed the independence of Brazil.

After his famous *Grito de Ipiranga* the prince regent was crowned emperor and the former colony became a constitutional monarchy in its own right. Portuguese troops in various captaincies in the north and north-east put up violent resistance to independence, but by 1824 the whole territory had been won for Dom Pedro's regime. In the following year Portugal, under pressure from Britain, recognized the independent state of Brazil; Britain also extended recognition, in return for a promise from Brazil to abolish the slave-trade and a commercial treaty which accorded imports from Britain a preferential tariff.

Legitimacy and Ungovernability

In its transition to independence Brazil had achieved, by a combination of good fortune and wise statecraft, a constitutional monarchy under a prince of the ruling dynasty. This formula allowed for self-government while preserving legitimate royal authority. It was a triumph of conservative pragmatism, for the Brazilian élites had seen to it that the necessary political adjustments were made so that everything might continue to be the same as, if not better than, before.

The Brazilian formula had been sought by the majority of creoles in the Spanish Indies in the years following Napoleon's invasion of Spain in 1808; yet circumstances, and the inflexibility of both the Bourbons and the peninsular liberals, had precluded that outcome. As a result, there had been no alternative to republicanism as the guiding ideology of the nascent states. In deeply traditional, aristocratic societies, however, a republican constitution could not command the same loyalty as a monarch; the Spanish American creoles soon found that even though they had won the right to self-rule, their new states would be constantly undermined by the lack of a legitimate and generally accepted political authority.

Simón Bolívar, though unwavering in his republican convictions, became aware early on of the problem of authority in the new nations, and he was to move towards ever more authoritarian constitutions for the territories he liberated. In the constitution he devised for Bolivia in 1826 he developed further the recipe for strong government that he had set out at the 1819 congress in Angostura: the notion of a 'moral power' was revived in provisions for a body of 'censors' who would safeguard civil rights and the principles of the constitution; as for the president, he would serve for life and would appoint his own successor. Bolívar's aim was to avoid elections, 'which are the greatest scourge of republics and produce only anarchy'; his Bolivian constitution, he declared with pride, would have 'all the strength of centralized government, all the stability of monarchical regimes'.*

Yet stability, save for a few relative exceptions, was to remain a mirage in Spanish America. Unity also proved impossible to achieve. Bolívar's great dream of a pan-American union came to nothing. A congress he called in Panama in 1826 to discuss an alliance of the Spanish American nations met with little response. The idea of an Andean confederation comprising Gran

* *Circular Letter to Colombia*, 3 August 1826. Quoted in John Lynch, *Simón Bolívar and the Age of Revolution*, p. 17.

Colombia, Peru and Bolivia never got off the ground. Even his own state of Gran Colombia started to disintegrate, with Venezuela and Ecuador cutting loose from the authority of Bogotá. On 17 December 1830 Bolívar died of tuberculosis while on his way to self-imposed exile in Europe. He had become a disillusioned man; shortly before he died he made his most famous observation on the colonies he had helped to emancipate: 'America is ungovernable. Those who have served the revolution have ploughed the sea.'*

What had gone wrong? Colonial America had certainly not been ungovernable; the constitutional empire of Brazil had not fallen apart. It was the Spanish American republics which were cursed with chronic turmoil after independence. For when the monopoly of legitimacy of the Catholic monarchy finally dissolved during the prolonged crisis that was triggered by Napoleon's invasion of the Peninsula, the Spanish imperial state crumbled into the myriad regions and localities which in reality made up the Indies, and there remained no unifying myth, no rule of law, which could assist the leaders of the new states in their efforts to navigate that great, shifting sea of particular interests. Only in retrospect was it possible to perceive that the colonial pact which had kept the creoles loyal to the Crown for centuries had involved the exchange of precious metals for the intangible but no less precious benefits of legitimate royal authority.

---

* Letter to General Juan José Flores, 9 November 1830, in *Simón Bolívar: Obras Completas*, ed. Vicente Lecuna, 2nd edn, 3 vols. (Editorial Lex: Havana, 1950), vol. 3, p. 501.

7. *The Quest for Order: Conservatives and Liberals in the Nineteenth Century*

═══

THE AFTERMATH OF INDEPENDENCE

The Demise of Royal Authority

The emancipation of Latin America in the second decade of the nineteenth century amounted to a political revolution: the Catholic monarchy had been destroyed and replaced by the liberal principle of the sovereignty of the people. In Brazil the monarchy was limited by constitutional restraints, and representative government accepted as the norm; in Spanish America the very principle of monarchy had been rejected and liberal republicanism in various forms had been officially adopted everywhere.

This transformation had come about without a comparable revolution in the economy or in society: no new classes had risen to power and the oligarchic structures of the colonial period remained unchanged. Latin America was still composed of aristocratic societies of whites employing a mass of variously coerced non-white labour in agrarian or mining economies which exported primary products in return for manufactures or luxury goods. In this important respect the *ancien régime* had not disappeared, rather the monarchical state that had allowed it to function effectively had broken down.

Independence is therefore best understood as the realization of the age-old aspiration of the colonial élites to become the legitimate ruling classes in their own territories. But, having achieved the freedom to rule in their own right, and to participate directly in international trade, the élites now had to find an alternative apparatus of state to regulate their societies. Here a contradiction appeared: the only coherent political ideology available to them was liberalism, but democratic values such as liberty and equality – not to mention fraternity – tended to undermine state authority in regionally dispersed societies which were still seigneurial, hierarchical, racially divided and often based on slavery.

The subsequent political history of Latin America can be characterized as a struggle to reshape society in the light of the liberal values handed down by the intellectual founding fathers of the independent nations. In the immediate aftermath of independence, disintegration and conflict hindered the economic recovery of the new nations. An exception was Brazil, where the survival of the monarchy in its limited form delayed and moderated the impact of liberalism, so that territorial integrity at least was preserved. There was, then, an irony about independence – it brought the creoles the freedom they wanted, but at the price of a perennial instability that frustrated their efforts to achieve power and prosperity comparable to that of the advanced European countries.

After about 1850, however, overseas demand began to pull a few Latin American economies out of stagnation. This led to a degree of political consolidation and, in some republics, to a period of constitutional politics and the rule of law. By the 1880s many of the larger nations were trading very profitably with the outside world and were able to modernize rapidly in some areas. At the turn of the century the creole élites appeared to be well on their way to achieving the economic progress they had hoped for from independence. They had also found in scientific positivism an ideology which partially reconciled liberalism with oligarchic rule. But economic progress brought social change which in time would result in new political challenges to the authority of the creole élites. The nineteenth century would not see a solution to the deep-seated crisis of political legitimacy unleashed by independence, only its abatement in some nations for several decades.

A Divided Ruling Class: Liberals, Conservatives and Caudillos

What caused the crisis of political legitimacy was that the terms on which independence had been won irreparably divided the creole ruling classes and prevented the emergence of a consensus on the basic rules of politics. The division was not one of economic interest, but of political values. After the end of colonial rule, the creole oligarchies faced two options: either to rebuild as much of the old order as possible so as to secure their authority over the lower classes, or to create a modern liberal state without prejudice to vital creole interests. The oligarchies therefore split into factions of conservatives and liberals, each with different and mutually incompatible views on how to achieve the same ends – the power and prosperity of their own class and race.

Conservatives in Spanish America regretted the passing of the Catholic monarchy and found positive value in shoring up the institutions that had survived the fall of empire: they wanted to preserve the wealth and social influence of the Church, the special legal privileges of the clergy and the army, the separate 'republic' of the Indians, the legal and social restrictions on the *castas* – in short, all the trappings of a hierarchical society. Conservatives also identified with the Hispanic past and felt themselves to be the heirs of the conquistadors. The problem with the conservative position was that aristocratic, hierarchical values required a monarchy for their rationale, but monarchy was no longer an available option, at least in Spanish America.

Not all creole conservatives were averse to international trade or economic development; the most enlightened favoured foreign investment and the development of industry. Such men were the natural heirs of the Bourbon reformers; they wanted a strong state to sift the purely technical benefits of modern life from those modern ideas and values which might disturb traditional culture. In Mexico, for instance, the outstanding advocates of industrialization were conservatives such as Lucas Alamán and Estevan de Antuñano. Alamán founded a state bank designed to redirect revenues from protectionist tariffs towards investment in mining and the mechanization of the textile industry. Antuñano was a tireless champion of manufacturing, who believed that free trade would ruin the artisans and thereby threaten to turn Mexico into an economic dependency of foreign powers. The involvement of such men in the issues of economic development made them view with dismay the ignorance of the masses, the absence of enterprise among the élite, the lack of a profit-seeking work-ethic in society. They had to confront the basic conservative dilemma of wanting to preserve traditional society for political reasons while appreciating how traditional values stood in the way of economic prosperity. Antuñano, in fact, turned to liberalism in later years, arguing for social regeneration by limiting the influence of the Church in education and by reducing its wealth. Alamán became more of a traditionalist and saw in the power of the Church a bulwark against the civil disorder that plagued Mexico.

Liberals believed in the sovereignty of the people and in individual rights to property, to personal security and to the freedoms of speech, thought, association and religion. The powers of the state therefore had to be restrained and government made accountable to its citizens through periodic elections to representative institutions. Further safeguards against tyranny would be provided by the separation of powers – the executive arm of the state being checked and counterbalanced by the legislature and an independent judiciary.

No hereditary or legal privileges would be accorded to any groups or corporations such as the aristocracy, the army or the clergy – all citizens would be equal before the law and subject to the same legal code. In the economic sphere, liberals disliked state intervention, believing that the free market would best allocate resources and underwrite the political freedoms of the individual.

Latin American liberals, however, were not without their problems when it came to implementing these beliefs. Like Bolívar, most soon observed that the character of their societies was such that the application of liberal principles on the French or North American models was doomed to failure. The Mexican liberal and ex-friar, Servando Teresa de Mier, wrote in 1823:

> They [the North Americans] were a new people, homogeneous, industrious, hard-working, enlightened, with all the social virtues, and educated by a free nation. We are an old people, heterogeneous, without industry, enemies of work, wanting to live from public employment like the Spaniards, as ignorant in the mass as our fathers, and impaired by the vices of three centuries of slavery.*

Such pessimism led many liberals to retreat from egalitarianism, *laissez-faire* and the doctrine of the minimal state. Instead, they emulated the Bourbon reformers and advocated change from above through state action in promoting secular education, abolishing corporate privileges and encouraging economic growth through subsidies, tariffs and fiscal incentives. Thus it was precisely their overriding concern to modernize traditional society that led many liberals to embrace a republican form of enlightened despotism, which often resulted in full-blooded dictatorships where democratic freedoms were suspended for the sake of progress. Like the more enlightened conservatives, therefore, moderate liberals faced a dilemma of their own, for, in order to prepare their societies for liberty and equality, political freedoms might have to be suspended indefinitely. Both reforming conservatives and liberals thus ended up following the progressive ministers of the Bourbons in their belief that a strong state should be the vehicle of change.

Given their tendency towards authoritarian reform, liberals were easily absorbed by the pervasive influences of custom and tradition. They were mostly drawn to the same methods as their conservative rivals. For these ostensibly liberal republics were, in fact, decapitated kingdoms, ruled by the same oligarchies as in the past. It was small wonder that the old political values

* Quoted in Charles Hale, *Mexican Liberalism in the Age of Mora, 1821–1853* (Yale University Press: New Haven, 1968), p. 197.

were still dominant. The disappearance of the king had simply removed the ultimate justification for a personalist and patriarchal society, but personalism and patriarchy remained vigorously alive in what were still overwhelmingly landowning societies. The actual business of politics was conducted through networks of alliances between clans and factions led by charismatic individuals who would reward their clients with favours in return for personal loyalty and services rendered.

Liberalism failed to make significant inroads into this traditional culture of patronage and clientship. Not surprisingly, adoption of a political ideology was often a matter of family or regional loyalty. In general, individuals and families formerly occupying positions of influence in the major power-structures of colonial society, especially in the viceregal capitals and cities where an *audiencia* had been established in the sixteenth century, tended towards conservatism. Other no less wealthy or powerful creoles who happened to come from more peripheral regions, or who were engaged in the newer export-economies of the eighteenth century (for example, cacao in Venezuela; cattle-raising in Buenos Aires), or who saw themselves for whatever reason as marginally disadvantaged in relation to a conservative establishment, usually opted for liberalism. Thus liberal ideals, no less than, say, conservative support for religion, could be used as a camouflage for patriarchal interests or as a flag of convenience for political buccaneers.

In the conditions prevailing after the wars of independence there were plenty of opportunities for political buccaneering. Economic depression, the breakdown of law and order, the militarization of society, all contributed to the phenomenon of the *caudillo* – a charismatic leader who advanced his interests through a combination of military and political skills, and was able to build up a network of clients by dispensing favours and patronage. *Caudillos* were the major power-brokers and power-seekers in the political world; in fact, they treated politics as a form of economic enterprise, adopting liberalism or conservatism as best suited their strategy for winning control of public funds in order to enhance their capacity to offer patronage and so build up their networks of power.

Based as it was on personal charisma and military skill, *caudillismo* was one of the few careers actually open to talent in the seigneurial republics of Latin America, and in the post-independence period it represented a way up for ambitious men of mixed blood. Some made it to the top, as did the *pardo* José Antonio Páez, who became president of Venezuela. But *caudillismo* existed at all levels of national life, in the marginal provinces as much as in the central areas. There were *caudillos* from the upper classes, as well as from humble backgrounds. As wielders of power, *caudillos* were men to be reckoned with, and patrician creole families had to come to terms with them, regardless of their social or ethnic origins. In many cases, the *caudillos* entered into a mutually dependent relationship with aristocratic clans: they offered creole property-holders protection against the dangers of social anarchy and lawlessness (the great Argentine *caudillo* Juan Manuel de Rosas liked to be known as 'the restorer of the laws') in return for political power and the spoils of government office.

Caudillismo, however, was not a new phenomenon as such, for *caudillos* simply embodied the political culture of patronage and clientship in its primitive state. The term itself originated during the Reconquest of the Iberian Peninsula from the Moors, when a *caudillo* was the chieftain of a warrior band who organized raids against the enemy and built up a power base for himself from which he could bargain with the king for the grant of titles and lands. This, in essence, was the mechanism by which America was conquered and settled by the Spanish and Portuguese. The emergence of *caudillos* in the nineteenth century suggests that there had occurred a reversion to political conditions analogous to those in the sixteenth. For, as in the decades following the Conquest, politics in Latin America after independence were violent and extremely fluid, and the reason for this was the same – the absence of a stable state with the authority to regulate disputes between interest-groups. Once the Catholic monarchy became institutionalized in America, *caudillismo* receded because the politics of patronage could be conducted through the royal bureaucracy. Yet, when the monarchy was overthrown, *caudillismo* emerged once more. In Brazil there occurred an upsurge of the equivalent phenomenon of *coronelismo* after the fall of the empire in 1889.

Still, even if the forces of traditional society were strong and insidious in Latin America after independence, liberalism was more than just a political label to be adopted and discarded at will by ambitious *caudillos*. It postulated a quite different vision of human destiny from that of the Catholic monarchy; it introduced new concepts and values into the political arena and, as a result, it was capable of transforming the structures of Latin American society, for when liberal *caudillos* and dictators took power, even if it was for cynical reasons of their own, they enacted legislation which eroded the position of traditional institutions, particularly the Church. In fact, one of the most dangerous attributes of liberalism from a conservative perspective was its unlimited potential for democratic change. After all, its ideals of equality and liberty could in principle be invoked against any restriction or privilege whatever, no matter how necessary these might appear for the maintenance of order. Thus, for instance, liberals could and would attack the institution of slavery, agitate for universal suffrage and concede freedom of religion.

Such a democratic slippage began to occur towards the middle of the century when a new generation of creoles, many of them urban professionals – lawyers, teachers, government employees – and some of them of mixed blood, young men who had not known life under the Catholic monarchy, and who were enthused by the European revolutions of 1848, embraced a more radical liberalism than that of their elders, and indeed, frightened many patrician liberals of the independence period into joining forces with conservatives. The generations of the 1840s and 1850s would produce the great builders of the liberal order in Latin America in the latter half of the century. It was the time of the Asociación de Mayo in Argentina, which included future statesmen and intellectuals such as Bartolomé Mitre, Domingo Sarmiento and Juan Bautista Alberdi; of Benito Juárez and the Lerdo de Tejada brothers, who were to become the architects of *La Reforma* in Mexico; of the anti-slavery and republican movements in Brazil, which provided the ideological impetus for the overthrow of the emperor. And so, even though the differences between liberals and conservatives were often very blurred by personal ambitions and by similarity of political methods, there remained substantive issues which divided them. The major consequence of independence was, then, the bitter ideological conflict that split the white ruling class – and with a ruling class divided against itself on the most fundamental questions of state, it was little wonder that no consensus was found either to hold Spanish America together or to legitimize stable institutions of government in the continent.

Matters of Conflict

Regionalism and Centralism

The breakup of the Spanish Indies into separate republics has often been attributed to the immense geographical barriers of the continent and to the weakness of interregional trade during the colonial period. However, the example of Brazil, where comparable natural obstacles and a similar lack of economic integration existed, suggests that the decisive factors in the fragmentation of Spanish America were political.

The problem of bringing different regions under a central authority has been at the heart of Hispanic statecraft since at least the reign of Ferdinand and Isabella. In fact, the historical importance of the Catholic Monarchs stems from their success in finding a political formula capable of unifying the Iberian Peninsula and of keeping a vast overseas empire together. The nature of the conquest and settlement of America had led to the development of widely dispersed and isolated centres of population, and, once the framework of the imperial state had been removed, the underlying diversity of the Indies was laid bare, and the regions started to pull away from the centre.

Yet these centrifugal tendencies were so powerful because conservatives and liberals could not agree about the ultimate source of legitimate authority in the state. Without such agreement, on what basic principle could the regions be organized into larger units of administration? The old Hispanic problem of regional separatism became caught up in the question of building new nation states and, within those states that did emerge, in the issue of federalism as opposed to centralism. For if sovereignty in a republic was vested in the will of the people, how much popular sovereignty would a particular region be prepared to cede to a national government? Given that the regions were effectively controlled by networks of influential families, the creation of a national authority was bedevilled by a host of provincial interests and oligarchic jealousies.

In the event, imperial custom outweighed republican design in the demarcation of national boundaries. The territories of the new Spanish American republics would broadly correspond to the areas of jurisdiction of the royal *audiencias* created in the sixteenth century, and the cities in which the *audiencias* had their seat would become the centres of national authority, for the established oligarchies of these cities could call upon the customary allegiance of lesser regional groups. Thus, there was little question but that cities like Lima, Mexico City, Santiago de Chile or Bogotá would emerge as the capitals of whatever nations might arise after independence.

The most bitter disputes over national boundaries after independence occurred precisely in those areas – such as the former viceroyalties of New Granada and Río de la Plata and the Kingdom of Guatemala – where sixteenth-century jurisdictions had been redrawn or superseded in the middle to late eighteenth century by the Bourbon reformers, creating conflicts of allegiance between the newer centres and older focuses of authority. Bogotá, the viceregal seat of New Granada, proved unable, as the capital of the republic of Gran Colombia, to retain the loyalty of areas under the jurisdiction of Quito or Caracas. Quito had been the seat of an *audiencia* since the sixteenth century, and until 1739 had formed part of the viceroyalty of Peru. Caracas had come under the jurisdiction of the *audiencia* at Santo Domingo, which was part of the viceroyalty of New Spain; in 1739 it had been raised to the status of a captaincy-general within the viceroyalty of New Granada. Soon after independence Caracas broke away from Bogotá to become the capital of the republic of Venezuela, and so did Quito, which became the capital of Ecuador. In Río de la Plata, the city of Buenos Aires, raised in 1776 to viceregal status, was quite unable to exercise authority over sixteenth-century *audiencia* seats like La Paz in Upper Peru, which seceded and became the capital of Bolivia, or Asunción, which became the capital of Paraguay. Several other regions made determined bids to separate, but only Montevideo eventually succeeded, becoming the capital of the republic of Uruguay in 1828. Central America also dissolved into separate republics. Santiago de Guatemala had been the seat of an *audiencia* since the sixteenth century, but in 1785 the Bourbon reformers carved up the provinces under its jurisdiction into a number of semi-autonomous intendancies, which became the nucleus of independent republics after Central America seceded from Mexico in 1823 and an experiment in federal union failed in 1838.

The disintegration of the Spanish empire into nation states thus occurred where colonial jurisdictions had been weakened by the Bourbon reforms. Even where nation states cohered easily around an agreed capital – as occurred in Peru, Mexico and Chile – the question of regional autonomy became a bone of contention between federalists and centralists. Regional élites sought in federalism to dress up as much of their traditional oligarchic power as they could in suitable republican form without actually seceding from the nation. Federalism could appeal to conservatives as much as to liberals, depending on the political complexion of the élites in the national capital against which the provinces were reacting. In the Argentine provinces, for instance, the *federales* were conservatives from the interior who resented the dominance of the liberal *unitarios* of the busy outward-looking port of Buenos Aires. But in Mexico federalists tended to be liberals, because the élites of the capital were deeply conservative and centralist, given that the Valley of Mexico had been the hub of state power since the time of the Aztecs. The association of federalism with either the conservative or the liberal cause was therefore determined by the configuration of oligarchic politics in a particular country.

Church and State

No other issue gave rise to greater disputes between liberals and conservatives than that of the role of the Church in the life of the independent nations. For liberals, the matter was clear-cut: the Church should be entirely separate from the state so that all citizens might enjoy equality before the law irrespective of race, status or creed. The enormous wealth of the Church in land, property and capital from tithes and donations was regarded by liberals as a massive obstacle to the formation of a modern free-market economy. Church control of schools and universities prevented the state from disseminating the rational, scientific and utilitarian education which liberals believed to be necessary for progress.

The position of conservatives, on the other hand, was well expressed by Lucas Alamán in a celebrated letter to General Santa Anna in March 1853, in which he urged him to assume dictatorial powers in Mexico in view of the recurrent civil wars and the recent loss of half the national territory to the United States:

> First and foremost is the need to preserve the Catholic religion, because we believe in it and because even if we did not hold it to be divine, we consider it to be the only common bond that links all Mexicans when all the others have been broken; it is the only thing capable of sustaining the Spanish-American race and of delivering it from the great dangers to which it is exposed. We also consider it necessary to maintain the ceremonial splendour of the Church, as well as its temporal properties, and to settle everything relating to ecclesiastical administration with the Pope.*

Apart from the intrinsic matter of faith, the value of the Church was that it ensured social cohesion – the basis upon which a stable political order could be built; the Church was, additionally, a fertile source of cultural identity for an otherwise heterogeneous people threatened with despoliation by the United States. The case for religion presented by Lucas Alamán was intelligent and pragmatic, but one vitiated by the fact that a union of Church and state appeared at the time to be irreconcilable with the ideology of republicanism. Paradoxically, then, the conservatives, inasmuch as they upheld the historic privileges and authority of the Church, became themselves the enemies of constitutional order. From being a central pillar of the Catholic monarchy, the Church was converted into one of the greatest factors behind the chronic instability of the republican system.

Indeed, the Vatican did not begin to recognize the new republics until after 1835. Even then, there was the unresolved matter of the *Patronato Real*, the historic right of the Spanish and Portuguese monarchs to make ecclesiastical appointments in America. The papal authorities refused to extend this right to those presidents of liberal republics who claimed it, so with independence many bishoprics remained unfilled, adding to the number of dioceses left

---

* Miguel León-Portilla *et al.* (eds.), *Historia documental de México* (Instituto de Investigaciones Históricas, Universidad Nacional Autónoma de México, 1964), vol. 2, p. 243; my translation.

vacant after the return of peninsular clergy to Spain. The leadership of the Church in Latin America was gravely weakened by this dispute – religious vocations declined; parishes languished unattended – and this was a further symptom of the tremendous dislocation that had been caused by independence, for the relaxing of traditional social controls exercised by the Church contributed to the general climate of lawlessness in the years following emancipation.

After the mid-century the Church made a determined effort to recover its strength by reforming the clergy and reactivating its pastoral work, especially in the countryside. But this ecclesiastical renewal coincided with the radicalization of liberalism as the new generation of creoles entered politics. Church–state conflict therefore intensified from the 1850s, and if republican governments ceased to claim the rights of the *Patronato*, it was only because they sought the complete expulsion of the Church from public affairs. In most Latin American countries, liberals engaged in long, complicated struggles – sometimes conducted in congress but more often than not through force of arms – to divest the clergy of its legal privileges, to wrest education from clerical control and to expropriate the wealth of the ecclesiastical establishment. In these struggles the Church hierarchy sided with the conservatives, thereby identifying itself with the forces of reaction and with the colonial past. For their part, conservative rulers, seeking to recover the enviable monopoly of legitimacy once enjoyed by the Catholic monarchy, would try from time to time to incorporate the Church into the state.

In the nineteenth century, then, the Church was on the defensive against liberal republicanism and did what it could to resist the attack on its wealth and its exclusion from affairs of state. Yet in opposing modern developments it was bound in the long term to find itself fighting a losing battle. By the last decades of the century it had lost its hold on the governing élites, who were intellectually won over to positivism, as we shall see. In the expanding cities the clergy could no longer count on the loyalty of a great number of the swelling masses of workers, who were being exposed to anarchist and socialist ideas brought over from Europe by the great influx of immigrants. In the 1890s the Latin American Church, responding to the encyclical *Rerum novarum* issued by Pope Leo XIII, which enshrined the rights of the worker in the new industrial age, began to rise to the challenge of the secularization of the urban proletariat by organizing clubs and associations for Catholic workers, and social Catholicism would grow in importance in the new century.

Still, the broad mass of the people, if not actually observant, nevertheless shared in a culture that was utterly permeated by Catholicism, and this was a sociological reality from which the Church drew enormous strength. This was particularly true of the countryside, where the peasants remained firmly loyal to the Church, having little understanding of the republican idea and even less sense of belonging to a nation state as such. In rural areas the ethos of the Catholic monarchy took a long time to disappear. When the emperor of Brazil was overthrown in 1889, it was the dispossessed Catholic peasants who rose up for God and Crown against the republic set up by the white liberal élites. The Indian communities in Spanish America were strongly attached to Catholic devotions and liturgy, and they often made common cause with the Church against liberal governments intent on depriving them of their lands.

These very deep roots in the countryside and in popular culture were to stand the Church in good stead after liberalism lost its intellectual hegemony in the 1920s and 1930s, when a strong resurgence of nationalism led to the search for indigenous values. By that time the liberal idea of a completely secular state, deriving its sovereignty from the will of the people, had been accepted virtually everywhere, but the very acute sense of vulnerability to foreign cultural influences would partly vindicate the belief of a conservative like Lucas Alamán that it was from Catholicism that Latin America derived an identity which linked white, Indian and black.

Non-white Peoples

Another major legacy of the Catholic monarchy which was contrary to liberal ideology was the difference in juridical status of the various racial groups. Large numbers of blacks were still enslaved in parts of the Americas. The *castas* (free persons of colour) suffered from legal and social restrictions in education and government employment, and paid a special tax. The Indian communities belonged to a separate 'republic' under their own body of law and local government, and paid tribute to the state – another form of ethnic taxation. All of these inequalities were abolished in law in most countries during the first half of the nineteenth century. There was not much conflict with conservatives over such issues; the problems, rather, were of a practical nature.

In the case of black slavery, proprietors feared economic ruin. Although the slave-trade had been abolished in Spanish American republics by 1825, and various countries passed laws of free birth (the special case of Brazil will be referred to below), slavery continued in republics with significant plantation economies such as Peru, Venezuela, Ecuador and Colombia.

Gradually the practice withered away because of the lack of supply from Africa after the ending of the trade. Freed slaves then came to form a wretched class of underemployed drifters in cities and day labourers in the rural areas. The laws affecting the *castas* were repealed in most countries without much difficulty, partly because they had little economic consequence, but also because many people of mixed blood had improved their social position in the course of the independence wars, particularly through service in the army. Although the creoles still valued 'purity of blood', it was impossible to reconcile that ideal with republican law.

The most difficult problems arose with regard to the Indians, a highly vexed issue also for the Catholic monarchy, which had tried, with only limited success, to respect Indian rights by governing the communities under a separate jurisdiction from the Hispanics. The chief difficulty until the middle of the seventeenth century had been economic – the creoles needed Indian labour, so the separate *república de los indios* had been undermined by the exploitation of Indian resources by the whites. In the later colonial period and until the 1850s the position of the Indian communities had stabilized because economic demands on them had receded. It was after the mid-century, when the Spanish American economies began to expand, that renewed economic pressure was exerted on the Indians, and legislation was passed by liberal governments in various countries to integrate them as equal citizens in a wholly new kind of republic of whites.

For liberals, the existence of a special body of law for Indians was a civic aberration similar to the privileges of the clergy. Liberal governments wanted to impose equality before the law, and so the Indian tribute, tithes and the *mita* were abolished. However, in republics with large Indian populations, some of these fiscal reforms were reversed because they depleted the revenues of an impoverished state or, where tribute was paid in kind, because shortages of certain agricultural products affected the creole economy. In countries like Bolivia, Peru and Colombia, the tribute was reimposed in the form of a 'contribution' from the Indian communities until late in the century, and labour services such as the *mita* were allowed to persist until the end of the century and beyond in certain Andean mining regions in order to maintain production.

The liberal reform that had the worst impact on the Indians was the legal conversion of community land into private property to be divided up among individual Indians. Unfamiliar with the operations of a market economy, many Indians lost their lands to the expanding haciendas, and from the 1860s Indian land generally came under intense pressure from creole landowners responding to the demands of the revitalized export-economies. Thus the prime effect of republican land policy was to dispossess many Indian communities and push their members into the rural proletariat, thereby strengthening the system of *latifundia* – the vast estates already held by creole magnates, who were themselves the main actors, whether as liberals or conservatives, on the political stage of the new republics.

Indian rebellions increased after independence as a result of growing pressure on community land. In Mexico, for instance, the massive Indian rebellions that occurred from time to time in the nineteenth and early twentieth centuries – such as the uncontrollable race war unleashed by Miguel Hidalgo in the Bajío in 1810, the bloody caste wars of 1847 in the Yucatán and the Sierra Gorda rebellion of the same year – can be regarded as violent reactions to the encroachments of a modern capitalist economy on traditional Indian society, as a continuation and indeed an intensification of the tradition of defensive revolts by Indians against white society which had been a recurrent feature of the colonial period.

The new nation states also had to come to terms with the *indios bárbaros*, the nomadic or 'unpacified' Indian tribes which had been more or less left to themselves during the colonial period because the territories they occupied were not then deemed to be of much economic value. Such Indian tribes existed in the vast, underpopulated spaces of the northern Mexican provinces (most of which were annexed by the USA in the mid-century and became the 'Wild West'); in the south of Chile beyond the Bío-bío River; in the pampas of Argentina, and in Patagonia; and, of course, there were scores of even more primitive tribes of hunter-gatherers in the rain forests of Amazonia and Central America. The Catholic monarchies of Spain and Portugal had permitted 'just war' against such Indians only if they had rejected the offer to convert to Christianity, but the result in practice was that creoles and mestizos of these frontier lands saw fit to hunt barbarous Indians for slavery.

After independence such tribes continued to be regarded as *indios bárbaros*, and, as the wheels of economic progress turned ever more rapidly after the mid-century, creole society pushed further into their lands, and began to make war on the 'barbarians' in the name of modern civilization. In northern Mexico the republican government encouraged settlement by creoles and mestizos in military colonies, which became the object of attacks by Apaches, Comanches, Navahos and other nomadic tribes. These raids led even liberal governments to experiment with early colonial policies of *congregación* – the forced resettlement of scattered Indians into concentrated units – and religious missions, where nomads would be compelled to settle down and learn 'civilized' ways. From the 1860s progressive liberal governments of Argentina sent armies into the pampas and Patagonia to win the frontiers for settlement and cultivation. In Chile the territories of the Araucanians were gradually taken over by creole and European settlers. As these Indian peoples fell back and their cultures disappeared, they made way for ranches, immigrants and railways, the bases for the subsequent prosperity of modern republics like Argentina and Chile. In Brazil, Peru, Colombia, Venezuela, Ecuador and the Central American republics the penetration or economic exploitation of wilderness and forest through clearance and settlement damaged, where it did not destroy, the culture of the Indian tribes – a process which continues to this day in many places.

The independent nations of Latin America thus inherited from the colonial authorities the fearsome cultural and political difficulties of reconciling the rights of the great diversity of Indian peoples with the norms of the dominant society. Conservatives did not object to the continuation of colonial legal differentiation, but liberals believed that the best solution was the integration of the Indians as equal citizens of the republic. In the twentieth century there was a revival of the attempt to preserve Indian communities by promoting their right to traditional culture: after the Mexican Revolution a version of communal landholding was introduced as an element in land reform; in Peru during the 1970s Quechua was made an official language of the state as well as Spanish. And yet, traditional Indian societies continued to retreat as the populations and economies of modern Latin America grew and consumed ever greater resources.

THE STRUGGLE TO BUILD A STATE

Not all the nations of Latin America suffered from political instability as independent states. There was a very small number which managed to contain the divisions in their ruling classes within a constitutional system of government. Brazil, as we have seen, was unique in that it was able to negotiate the transition to independence without losing the dynastic continuity of the legitimate royal house, and this provided a powerful focus of allegiance for all classes. Costa Rica, after breaking away from the Central American Federation in the 1840s, founded a constitutional system which was able after 1889 to evolve into a wider democracy with free elections and genuine political freedoms. This was largely due to its geographical isolation and its small, homogeneous population of coffee planters, among whom there were few conflicts of interest. Chile was the one large republic where constitutional government put down deep roots. Its élites too were relatively united and therefore able to arrive at a political consensus early on.

Brazil

It took Brazil nearly three decades to function as a settled constitutional monarchy. The immediate problem was the suspicion that Pedro I harboured absolutist designs and had not entirely severed his links with the Portuguese court. These anxieties arose because the relationship between the emperor and the Brazilian élites had not yet been properly worked out – the general desire for strong government had to be balanced against the interest of the regional oligarchies in retaining some form of local autonomy.

In the year since Pedro had uttered his cry of independence at Ipiranga opposition to him had become highly vocal and had even resulted in the resignation of his first minister, José Bonifácio de Andrada e Silva, the architect of the political emancipation, who feared that Pedro was being unduly influenced by a faction at court comprising Portuguese administrators and merchants. When the emperor dissolved the constituent assembly in 1823, such fears seemed well-founded. However, the constitution which Dom Pedro's royal commission eventually drafted for Brazil proved to be a sound one; it lasted until the fall of the monarchy in 1889. The 1824 constitution established a parliamentary government consisting of two chambers: a senate whose members were chosen by the monarch and served for life, and a chamber of deputies elected indirectly on a limited male suffrage. The emperor had a role as the 'moderating power' in the parliamentary system: he had the right to appoint and dismiss cabinet ministers, he had a veto on legislation, and he could dissolve parliament and call for elections. A Council of State advised the monarch on these matters and was also charged with the responsibility for ensuring the separation of the executive from the legislature and the judiciary, and for the observance of civil liberties.

The empire of Brazil, like all monarchies of the period, including the British, combined constitutional rights with traditional privileges. In public affairs the award of titles, the appointment to administrative posts and offices were in the gift of the Crown. Since Catholicism remained the established religion, the Crown retained its rights of patronage in ecclesiastical appointments under the *Padroado Real*. Indeed, patronage was crucial to the whole system, even to the winning of elections, for most voters tended to return the candidate supported by their local patron to the electoral colleges which selected deputies for the national and provincial assemblies, and these deputies in turn would try to reward their backers with favours and government jobs. These extensive networks of patronage meant that incumbent governments tended to be re-elected, and so the emperor's 'moderating power' was employed to shuffle and recompose cabinets so as to allow the various oligarchic factions a fair share of the fruits of office.

The benefits of such a system for a new state like Brazil were enormous. It made for stability by satisfying the important interest-groups in a vast nation that was extremely fragmented both geographically and economically. It balanced national authority with local ambition by having the central government appoint the presidents of the provincial assemblies and oversee the allocation of posts in the regional bureaucracies. Moreover, in a country where over two-thirds of the population consisted of poor blacks and mulattos, and where over a quarter of these were slaves, the institution of monarchy drew upon very deep reserves of loyalty from the common people by virtue of its immense mystique, buttressed as this was by the support of the Church.

Still, in the early years Dom Pedro himself, if not the monarchy as an institution, failed to overcome mistrust and suspicion. In 1824 a rebellion broke out in Pernambuco, a region where federalism and republicanism repeatedly attracted a planter élite which was suffering from the long-term decline of the sugar industry. The revolt was suppressed by imperial troops, but resentment was again stirred up by the Anglo–Brazilian Treaty of 1826, which granted commercial privileges to British traders in return for recognition of Brazilian independence and, worse still, stipulated an end to the slave-trade within three years. This last provision was regarded by the planters, to whom there appeared to be no substitute for slave labour, as evidence of the Crown's readiness to sacrifice a vital Brazilian interest to a foreign power.

The dispute over the Banda Oriental, the territory on the left bank of the River Plate – a bone of contention between Spain and Portugal for over a century – flared up into a costly and unpopular war against the Argentine provinces in 1825. Brazilians bitterly resented military conscription, and public opinion reacted badly to defeats at the hands of the Argentines. The conflict was finally settled in 1828 with the creation of the buffer state of Uruguay, but the prestige of the emperor had suffered a further blow as a result of this reverse, as it was perceived.

Finally, hostility towards Portuguese merchants, of whom there were many still domiciled in Brazil, grew in the late 1820s, when inflation pushed up the cost of living. There were calls for the expulsion of all Portuguese, and renewed suspicion of Dom Pedro's Portuguese sympathies and absolutist tendencies. In March 1831 street violence broke out in Rio de Janeiro between Brazilians and Portuguese: bottles were thrown, and in those nights of breaking glass – the *Noites das Garrafadas* – the compact between throne and people was shattered. The emperor tried to appease Brazilian anger by appointing an ostensibly pro-Brazilian cabinet, but in less than a month he suddenly decided to impose his authority, and on 5 April 1831 he announced a new cabinet, which was immediately alleged to be pro-Portuguese. The next morning restive crowds gathered in Rio, and the army itself urged Dom Pedro to reinstate the former cabinet. He refused, and on 7 April chose to abdicate the throne in favour of his son, a boy of five. A week later, Pedro departed Brazil aboard a British warship.

A regency which lasted ten years followed. It was a confusing period of drift and rebellion, when the heterogeneity of Brazil threatened to overwhelm the institution of monarchy and fragment the empire, as had occurred in Spanish America. The Additional Act of 1834 abolished the Council of State as the 'moderating power' of the constitution and introduced a number of liberal reforms which devolved power to the provincial assemblies. It was the work of moderate liberals trying to steer a middle course between conservative restorationists and the republican demands of more radical liberals. Still, the Act weakened national authority – it coincided with, and itself provoked, serious uprisings in different regions.

In some rural areas of the north the abdication gave rise to politically unfocused but very bloody revolts by poor half-castes, blacks and Indians, ostensibly in support of the emperor and religion, but fuelled as much by racial and social hatred of the white élites. In Pernambuco, the War of the Cabanos, a guerrilla conflict lasting three years, broke out in 1832 and shook the slave-owning plantation society of the north-east to its foundations. A similar rebellion of free Indians and mestizos, known as the Cabanagem, swept through the frontier territory of Pará in 1835 after a liberal secessionist rebellion by local whites was taken over by lower-class elements. The rebels proclaimed their loyalty to monarch and Church while calling for regional autonomy. Their young leader was finally arrested late in 1836 and the rebellion petered out, though fighting continued until 1840. The neighbouring province of Maranhão erupted in 1838, once more as a superficially traditionalist but chaotic revolt of the oppressed against the whites after a liberal federalist rebellion failed to control its supporters.

Liberalism was largely the cause of the white middle and upper classes, who agitated for greater local power in the guise of federalism, or even for republicanism, where this might bring increased oligarchic control over provincial politics. In Bahia a federalist rebellion led by urban professionals broke out in November 1837 and quickly won the support of the rank and file in the army and police; but it acquired a secessionist and even republican temper, scaring the slave-owning sugar barons, who came down in favour of the troops of the Regency, which eventually suppressed the rebels some six months later. But at the other extreme of the country, in the southern gaucho province of Rio Grande do Sul, whose *caudillos* shared economic interests with Uruguay and adjacent gaucho provinces of Argentina, cattle-ranchers rose against the Regency in 1835 and proclaimed a republic, which remained independent for the best part of a decade (its revolutionary republicanism was influenced by the presence of Giuseppe Garibaldi, who led forces into neighbouring Santa Catarina, which also declared a republic).

Decentralization in the absence of a reigning monarch put Brazil in danger of being dismembered like Spanish America. By 1840, fear of such an outcome, and of the social chaos that might ensue in a country with such a high proportion of non-whites and slaves, persuaded liberal as well as conservative elements in the élites – especially those of the central provinces of Rio de Janeiro, São Paulo and Minas Gerais – that the fourteen-year-old prince Pedro should ascend the throne as soon as possible, even though he would not legally come of age for another four years. Once the young Pedro had been crowned, the Additional Act of 1834 was repealed and the administration of the country recentralized – the powers of the provincial assemblies were curtailed, a national police force established and the Council of State restored.

The consensus that had favoured the enthronement of Pedro was destroyed in 1842 by liberal anxieties about the extent of recentralization. Rebellions broke out in São Paulo and Minas Gerais, where the wealthiest planters wanted to avoid losing too much power to conservative cabinets based in Rio de Janeiro. These rebellions were soon suppressed, and by 1844 a new consensus was established after liberals were allowed to form a government. During the next twenty years the constitutional monarchy worked smoothly, for a balance had been struck between the conservative governing élites of Rio de Janeiro – the traditional seat of royal administration in Brazil – and the liberal élites of the two central provinces with the most dynamic economies, namely São Paulo and Minas Gerais, both now concentrating on the production of coffee, a commodity which from the 1830s had superseded sugar and cotton – grown in the north-eastern coastal provinces – as Brazil's major export.

The exceptional stability of the second empire rested on the coincidence of interests of the élites of the three key provinces of São Paulo, Minas Gerais and Rio de Janeiro. But the overlap of interests was not total: the first two provinces were economically powerful, and formed a liberal bloc against Rio de Janeiro, around which tended to coalesce a more conservative bloc of economically weaker provinces. Stability depended on ensuring that the

São Paulo and Minas Gerais coffee élites remained amenable to being governed from Rio. This meant giving them a share of the spoils of office, and so the 'moderating power' of the emperor was skilfully employed to that end. As the coffee boom got under way in the 1850s and 1860s, parliamentary politics, if anything, became too stable; the emperor made use of his constitutional powers to fine-tune the system of *conciliação*: ministries were shuffled and then shuffled again to satisfy the Liberal and Conservative parties, each of which was composed of white, seigneurial planters, with little of substance to divide them beyond personal jealousies and regional affiliations – so long, that is, as nothing were to arise which might induce the coffee barons to believe that their economic interests would be better served by arrangements other than the emperor's politics of 'conciliation'.

The hothouse atmosphere of parliamentary politics under Pedro II bred a fretfulness and unease even within the ranks of the white ruling classes who so richly profited from it. In the 1860s a younger generation of patrician liberals began agitating to open up the system; they attacked the royal moderating power and the Council of State, and advocated a series of reforms such as a wider suffrage, more power to the provincial assemblies and the abolition of slavery. Once more, the spectre of regionalism had appeared under the mantle of federalism, but it was the slavery question which ventilated the frustration of the younger generation with the inertia of the parliamentary *conciliação*.

The importation of slaves from Africa had continued despite the provisions of the Anglo-Brazilian Treaty of 1826. But after indifferent success in curbing the trade, Britain's Royal Navy stepped up its pressure on Brazilian slavers in 1850 and within a few years the trade had been halted. In effect, this meant that slavery would in time dwindle and disappear, because the slave population in Brazil did not reproduce at a natural rate and numbers rapidly declined unless replenished from Africa. Once the Atlantic slave-trade had been stopped, the question turned on the outright abolition of slavery itself within Brazil. Anti-slavery agitation increased to the point where in 1871 the Conservative government of Viscount Rio Branco passed measures such as a 'law of the free womb' – by which the new-born children of slaves would be allowed their freedom – and a system of compensation for owners who chose to free their slaves. The real concern was over the labour supply to the coffee plantations, since the bulk of the slave population was based in São Paulo, Minas Gerais and Rio de Janeiro; without a labour force to replace the slaves, the pillars of the Brazilian economy would tumble. During the 1870s planters looked increasingly to free rural peasants and Italian and Portuguese immigrants for an alternative source of labour. Large numbers of European immigrants came to São Paulo; new technology and better transport systems were gradually making free wage labour more advantageous to the planters than slaves.

The anti-slavery campaign gathered strength in many parts of Brazil, especially in the cities. In 1884 a Liberal bill offering freedom to slaves over the age of sixty without compensation to their owners provoked a political crisis that unsettled Conservative as well as Liberal cabinets. The politics of *conciliação* was breaking down, and the slavery question was straining the patience of the São Paulo coffee élite with the parliamentary system. In 1885, a Conservative government won approval in parliament for a modified version of the 1884 bill; the political momentum of the anti-slavery movement was becoming unstoppable, and over the next three years it became clear even to the Paulista coffee barons that slavery was doomed. On 13 May 1888 a law abolishing slavery without compensation was passed by parliament with only nine dissenting votes. As it turned out, the economic consequences of abolition were far from disastrous: some planters went bankrupt, but the great majority survived on immigrant labour and freed slaves who remained to work the plantations for miserable wages. Other ex-slaves moved to the cities to live in abject poverty as an exploited service class.

The anti-slavery question was only one, but perhaps the most important, of several factors which contributed to the discrediting of the constitutional monarchy in Brazil during the 1870s and 1880s. Economic recession, financial difficulties, tensions between Church and state and, more ominously, the battered morale of the officer class in the army after the Paraguayan War stoked up frustration with an arthritic parliamentary regime articulated by the 'moderating power' of the emperor, whose care to reconcile established interests and observe constitutional punctilio appeared to stifle the forces of progress and reform.

In the early 1870s republicanism emerged as an intellectual force among the younger political generation. It was promoted through small political clubs in cities all over Brazil, but grew fastest in São Paulo. Though it did not in itself pose a serious challenge to the monarchy, republicanism was a potential vehicle for the resentments of the planters of São Paulo, despite the fact that this élite remained in favour of slavery until the late 1880s. For São Paulo, as the richest province, had reason to feel that the empire was no longer serving its interests: it was under-represented in parliament and in other national institutions; it contributed more to the royal treasury than it got in return; it disliked the appointment of non-Paulistas to its provincial administration; and the nationwide anti-slavery campaign only served to sharpen the political frustration of the slave-owning Paulista élite. In short, as the interests of the São Paulo planters diverged from those of Rio de Janeiro and its more conservative allies, the republican federalism of the young intellectuals began to appeal to them as a means of redressing the balance of national power in their favour. By 1887 the republicans had also attracted malcontents in the army, who felt that the military were not being adequately represented in governing circles. The support of the São Paulo oligarchs and of frustrated generals for the republican cause was to seal the fate of the monarchy: on 15 November 1889 a military *coup d'état* deposed the emperor. It was a bloodless take-over, which elicited no active opposition from within the Brazilian ruling classes.

With the fall of the empire the structure of the monarchical system was swept away. The liberal constitution abolished the Council of State, the 'moderating power' and the appointment of senators for life; it separated Church from state, introduced universal suffrage for literate adults and established a federal system, with each province now governing itself as a state in its own right. Federalism suited the strong provinces best, and São Paulo most of all. The republic, in fact, marked a transition to a more oligarchic form of politics because the old nationwide parties under the empire lost their influence when the new federal structure allowed power to devolve to regional élites.

The republican regime would be deeply marked by the circumstances of its birth, for it owed its existence to military intervention in politics: the first two presidents of the republic were military men – marshals Deodoro da Fonseca (1889–91) and Floriano Peixoto (1891–4). This started a tradition of periodic involvement by the army in modern Brazilian politics, for in the absence of a monarchy the army was the one national institution that could effectively cut across the boundaries of oligarchic federalism. But even though the army replaced the Crown as the major centralizing force in politics, there was a qualitative difference in its effect upon the Brazilian state: military interventions would be unconstitutional, and would therefore contribute in themselves to the political instability of the republic.

The constitutional monarchy in Brazil had been the most powerful, if not the crucial, factor in preserving the political unity of the new nation. The constitutional monarchy had also gone a long way – but not far enough, as it turned out – towards creating a nation state capable of transcending special interests. Brazil's experience in the nineteenth century was, after all, analogous to that of Spanish America: it too had to cope with regional separatism, with conflicts between conservatives and liberals, with democratic pressures from the liberal radicals of the mid-century to democratize its hierarchical and racially stratified society, with the influx of foreign capital and the great surge of the export-economy; but the survival of the monarchy ensured that these problems would be contained within a broad framework of constitutional order. In the end, however, it was the disruptive influence of the export-economy that delivered the *coup de grâce* to the empire of Brazil. It fed the oligarchic ambitions of the coffee planters of São Paulo, who chose to uproot the legitimate authority of the Crown rather than induce it to respond more fully to their interests.

Chile

Of the major Spanish American republics only Chile achieved a stability that would rival Brazil's. The constitution of 1833 proved to be the most enduring of modern times in the Hispanic world, and certainly more durable than many European constitutions of the period. It lasted (with only a brief interruption in 1891) until 1925, and the weight it gave to the rule of law influenced democratic practice in Chile until 1973.

Chile's democracy was founded by conservative oligarchs reacting to the instability of the various liberal dictatorships that had followed the overthrow of Bernardo O'Higgins in 1823. A powerful faction of landowners and merchants, with the support of a section of the army, staged a *coup d'état* in 1830, after a number of constitutions incorporating the usual repertoire of liberal measures – federalism, the abolition of corporate privileges, the alienation of Church property – had failed to bring order to the new state. The presiding genius of this conservative reaction was Diego Portales, a merchant from Valparaíso, who never assumed the presidency but was acknowledged to be the supreme power-holder until he was assassinated in 1837. Although deeply sympathetic to monarchy, Portales saw clearly that any attempt to restore a monarchical system after independence was bound to fail. His 1833 constitution was therefore designed as the kind of constitutional monarchy in republican dress that had come to appeal to Simón Bolívar. It was strongly presidentialist and centralized; the president was given extensive powers over the judiciary and the legislature, though the congress retained the right to sanction the budgetary and fiscal policies of the executive. The right to vote was restricted to males who fulfilled certain literacy and property requirements, and the federal structure was replaced by a system of centrally appointed provincial intendants to supervise regional affairs – a legacy of Bourbon reformism.

Indeed, authoritarianism characterized the practice of politics. Elections were habitually manipulated by government officials to ensure victory for the ruling party. Troublemakers were liable to be dealt with by arbitrary arrest and exile. The army was held in check by purging liberal officers who had shown a penchant for political involvement, and by a conservative national guard of reservists, who could be used to counteract a military rebellion. Finally, the Church was allowed to retain its great social and economic influence in society.

But the stability of the Portalian system must ultimately be ascribed to the peculiarity of Chile. The central valley around Santiago constituted the demographic and agricultural heartland of this strangely elongated country hemmed in between the Andes and the Pacific. Its agrarian economy was dominated by a close-knit oligarchy of creole landowners and merchants. Ethnic divisions were not as deep as in most other countries of Latin America: the lower classes comprised large numbers of whites and mestizos, the small black slave population declined fairly quickly after independence, and few separate Indian communities survived, though a large population of Araucanian Indians (about 200,000) lived an independent existence outside the republic in their ancestral homelands south of the Bío-bío River. Chile, therefore, was a very integrated country by comparison with her fellow Spanish American republics, and Portales was able to find a constitutional formula which created a consensus among its élite. The anarchic politics of *caudillismo* were thus avoided by containing the quarrels between conservatives and liberals within an accepted institutional framework.

The rewards of Portales's pragmatic conservatism were considerable: Chile went on to become a formidable military and economic power in the region, after having been one of the least prized territories of the Spanish Indies. Between 1836 and 1839 it fought a short war to thwart the attempt of Peru and Bolivia to unite in a confederation which might have tipped the regional balance against it. Military victory served as a tonic for Chilean national pride, and brought substantial economic benefits too. Valparaíso took over from Callao in Peru as the leading port on the Pacific coastline of South America. Foreign investment poured into the northern territories and by 1840 had transformed Chile into the chief producer of copper in the world and a leading exporter of other minerals – silver, gold and coal were successfully mined after the introduction of new technology. The export-economy was given a further boost in the early 1850s by the building of railways linking the centres of production to the main ports. From the late 1840s military campaigns against the Indians south of the Bío-bío River were undertaken, together with a policy of settlement, so that by the early 1880s the territory of the Araucanians had been taken over and the Indians converted into peons on wheat-growing haciendas.

Economic development, however, brought a new regional diversity: the emerging élites in the northern mining areas and the southern provinces exerted pressure on the central oligarchy in the 1850s, and the political system broke down briefly on two occasions. Portales's constitution was to come under strain too from a shift towards a more radical liberalism by the 'Generation of 1842'. Much of this cultural ferment was stimulated by innovations in education. A system of secular schooling had been introduced by the progressive conservative Manuel Montt in the 1840s, and in 1843 the modern University of Chile was founded, with the great Venezuelan savant Andrés Bello as its first rector. Foreign liberals in Chile, of whom the most notable was the Argentine Domingo Sarmiento, a future president of his country, contributed to the upsurge of liberal ideas, and joined with the Chileans Francisco Bilbao and José Victorino Lastarria in attacking Hispanic traditions and the authoritarianism of politics.

The decade of the 1850s, then, was a period of trial for the Portalian constitution, which allowed two five-year terms as the maximum tenure of a president. Manuel Montt was elected in 1851 as the third president under this decennial system. His election was contested by a coalition of Liberals and southern oligarchs, and a three-month civil war ensued, which Montt won. During the second term of his decennium Montt became involved in a dispute with the Church hierarchy over a minor issue of jurisdiction, and this lost him crucial support among the Conservatives. The vexed question of the relations between Church and state was to occupy Chilean politics for the rest of the century, but it was kept largely within the bounds of constitutional practice. However, in the late 1850s it occasioned a complex realignment of party politics which weakened the president, even though Montt went on to defeat a rebel army in the brief civil war of 1859.

The weakening of presidential power was evident in Montt's inability to impose his chosen successor in 1861. The new president, José Joaquín Pérez, called on Montt's opponents in the Liberal–Conservative Fusion to form a government. Pérez's decennial term was marked by liberal advances against the Church (a measure of religious freedom was allowed in 1865), and by an important amendment to the 1833 constitution prohibiting the immediate re-election of the president. Both tendencies – towards the separation of Church and state, and the curtailment of presidentialism – became more pronounced in the 1870s and 1880s, decades which saw the Liberals split from the Conservatives (over the issue of the Church's control of education) to become the dominant party in an increasingly parliamentary system based on a suffrage enlarged by the abolition of the literacy qualification.

The growing unruliness of politics was exacerbated by the recession of the

1870s, caused by a sharp decline in the production of copper. This was offset later in the decade by an increase in the output of nitrates from fields controlled by Chileans in territory belonging to Peru and Bolivia. A rise in world demand for nitrates for use as fertilizers provoked a dispute over rights to the nitrate fields, and eventually led to the War of the Pacific (1879–83), in which Chile inflicted a crushing military defeat on Peru and Bolivia. The annexation of the nitrate-producing regions gave a tremendous boost to the Chilean economy (though the nitrate companies had by now come largely under the control of the British, notably that of John Thomas North, the 'Nitrate King'), and taxes on exports brought large revenues to the government.

However, civil war would erupt again in 1891. The then president, José Manuel Balmaceda, wanted to tax the nitrate industry in order to finance an ambitious programme of state expenditure on infrastructure, building, public education and social welfare. His plans met with huge resistance in parliament. It was a complex political crisis, touching upon issues of economic development that were to become widely debated throughout Latin America in the next century, issues such as the influence of foreign investors in the economy and the real capacity of Chilean capital to finance economic modernization on its own. At bottom, the 1891 crisis called into question the nature of the Chilean state: was it still the creature of oligarchic interests, or had it achieved sufficient autonomy to act in the name of the nation as a whole?

The bloody eight-month war saw the defeat of Balmaceda, who committed suicide shortly afterwards. Politics was now controlled by parliament, and factionalism prevailed as parties splintered into unstable, self-serving groups. Although Portales's constitution was not formally rewritten, the power of the presidency was severely limited – the president could no longer dissolve parliament or manipulate elections. The 'parliamentary republic' that followed was a triumph of oligarchy (an 'aristocratic Fronde', as it was called), but within two decades it would have to face quite new challenges from the social classes of the expanding urban and industrial areas. It remained to be seen in the coming century whether the Chilean state could transcend the economic interests of its ruling élites.

Mexico

The struggle to transform the Catholic monarchy into a constitutional republic was nowhere more chaotic and violent than in Mexico. The Plan of Iguala, which had steered New Spain towards a largely bloodless declaration of independence in 1821, had been a compromise between the royalist creole Agustín de Iturbide and Vicente Guerrero, the mestizo rebel and heir to Miguel Hidalgo's secessionist revolt of 1810. But the Plan proved to be no more than a device which temporarily bridged the divisions that the crisis of independence had opened in Mexican society. Its three guarantees of Independence, Union and Religion were not sufficient to withstand the pressures of ideological conflict within the ruling classes. For the next fifty years the quarrels between liberals and conservatives would repeatedly plunge the country into civil war, and order would not return to Mexico until its historic centralism could be reflected in a new political settlement among the creole élites; only this would create a national authority capable of bringing stability, and therefore prosperity, to the country as a whole.

The trouble was that Mexican liberals were dogmatically federalist, seeing in the US Constitution the ideal model for their own heterogeneous country; they were also intensely anti-clerical, in reaction to the wealth and historic influence of the Mexican Church. For their part, the Mexican conservatives were extremely powerful and strongly centralist; not only were they attached to the Church, but they could not let go of their nostalgia for the Crown – and the greater the disorder they observed, all the more were they tempted to restore a monarchy. This irreconcilable split within the white ruling classes gravely weakened Mexico, rendering it vulnerable to Indian rebellion, economic disarray and the aggressive designs of an expansionist USA. Various attempts were made to put together coalitions of conservative centralists and liberal federalists, but these could not overcome their internal contradictions. In such circumstances, the army became the chief power-broker; but even the generals were prone to compete for power against each other and against regional *caudillos*; the result was a bewildering succession of *pronunciamientos* (revolts) that in the mid-century brought the republic to the brink of collapse.

The Plan of Iguala had begun to unravel when no Spanish prince could be persuaded to accept the Mexican Crown. For the Plan's guarantee of 'Independence' had been taken to mean that Mexico would be ruled under a constitutional monarch linked to the legitimate royal house of Spain. The Plan was further weakened by the fall of the substitute creole 'emperor' Agustín I. Inevitably, when a federal republic was proclaimed in 1823, conservative royalists and the Church felt betrayed and were thenceforward to remain ambivalent about the new state.

Within four years, the second guarantee of Iguala – the 'Union' or equal status between creoles and Spaniards living in Mexico – began to dissolve. Peninsular Spaniards were suspected of hatching a plot to restore Spanish rule, and this inflamed tensions between the federalists, who dominated congress, and the conservative centralists, who were accused of sympathizing with Spain. A rebellion by conservatives was defeated, and elections over-ruled by a liberal putsch in 1828, which delivered the presidency to the former guerrilla leader of the war of independence, Vicente Guerrero, who promptly decreed the expulsion of all Spaniards resident in the republic. A few months later, in July 1829, a Spanish expeditionary force landed at Tampico with the aim of reconquering Mexico, but it was rapidly ravaged by malaria and then defeated by republican troops under General Antonio López de Santa Anna. As the hero of the hour, Santa Anna won for himself seemingly inexhaustible reserves of honour as a patriot, reserves which he would repeatedly draw upon in the course of a long and chequered political career.

'Religion' was left as the third, and last, guarantee of the Plan of Iguala, and that too would come under attack from liberals. But it would be some thirty years before the Church could be written out of the constitution altogether and have its wealth expropriated by the state. For without this guarantee of 'Religion' there was nothing that could command the allegiance to the new republican state of the very substantial numbers of conservatives in Catholic Mexico (numbers which included much of the peasantry and the Indian communities as well as the old aristocracy). More than any other issue, religion would divide Mexico into two warring camps, and even after Church and state had been formally separated in the late 1860s, Catholic creoles would not be entirely reconciled to the state until the 1940s. Until then, the liberal republic in Mexico would remain an unstable, partisan construct, lacking political consent and requiring the iron grip of a dictator to keep it from falling apart.

The liberal victory over Spain did not prevent the overthrow of Vicente Guerrero by the conservatives in 1830. The new president, Anastasio Busta-mante, tried to impose a centralized government on the federal republic and, when Guerrero revolted, he was captured and executed, an action that was to rankle with the liberals and poison the political atmosphere for the next decade. The moving force behind the conservative government was the able and intelligent patrician Lucas Alamán, who launched several projects to revive the stagnant, war-ravaged economy. An attempt to revitalize silver-mining, the mainstay of the colonial economy, did not prosper; investment through a state bank in the textile industry succeeded in substituting imports with the help of protectionist measures; but agriculture, the key sector, riddled as it was with fiscal restrictions and antiquated practices, resisted productive change. The conservatives proved unable to regenerate the economy, for their political commitment to tradition stood in the way of meaningful economic reform.

The liberals, for their part, found an intellectual champion in the disaffected priest José María Luis Mora, an advocate of the free market who argued that only the disentailment of Church property and Indian community lands, together with the abolition of tithes, tariffs and other duties, would create a dynamic economy for Mexico. Mora's economic liberalism found favour with many creole landowners, who were impressed with the emphasis he placed on the sanctity of private property, and with the further prospect of privatizing corporate lands. In time, however, Mora came to accept a degree of state intervention and protectionism, while the conservative Alamán would see the virtue of free trade in certain spheres. Indeed, this political argument among the creole élites would focus increasingly on the issue of Church wealth and Indian lands, and on the *fueros* (legal immunities) enjoyed by the clergy and the army.

The conservative government of Bustamante fell in 1832 after a *pronunciamiento* led by General Santa Anna with the support of the liberals, who were still bitter about the execution of Guerrero. The following year, Santa Anna, a man of no fixed political convictions, was elected president and Valentín Gómez Farías, a disciple of the liberal theorist Mora, became vice-president. The latter now launched a determined assault on the Church's wealth and *fueros*, and also tried to reduce the size of the army. Sensing trouble, Santa Anna, who preferred the peace of his hacienda in Jalapa to the everyday travails of office, responded to the protests of the clergy and the army by sacking Gómez Farías. The president now decided to bolster national authority by giving the country a more centralist constitution, but his plan annoyed liberal federalists and discontent in several states would boil over into revolt.

When Zacatecas rose against the national government in 1835, Santa Anna had to lead a punitive expedition to pacify the region; no sooner had this been achieved than the state of Texas (already settled by over 20,000 Anglo-American ranchers, despite the warnings of conservative patriots such as Alamán) rebelled against the centralist constitution and, by the time Santa Anna's army had reached Texas, the rebels had already declared independence. Arriving in San Antonio in February 1836, Santa Anna overwhelmed the determined resistance of a small band of Anglo-American settlers defending the mission station of El Álamo. Outraged by this defeat and by the subsequent massacre of prisoners, the Texans rallied to the cry of 'Remember the Alamo', and finally defeated Santa Anna's ragged army of Indian peons at San Jacinto on 21 April. While in captivity, Santa Anna recognized the independence of Texas and won his release, but by the time he got back to Mexico City in disgrace, the new centralist constitution had come into effect and an elected conservative government under Bustamante refused to accept the independence of Texas.

The question of federalism now plunged Mexico into political chaos. To make matters worse, French troops occupied Veracruz in 1838, seeking to wring compensation for damages to the property of French nationals in Mexico. The disgraced Santa Anna took the opportunity of redeeming himself by expelling the French. A hero once again (his right leg was blown off by a French cannon), Santa Anna regained the presidency for a short period while Bustamante tried unsuccessfully to suppress federalist revolts. In the ebb and flow of events a federal republic under Gómez Farías surfaced in July 1840, but was put down after a few days. Then the Yucatán decided to declare its independence after the example of Texas. Bustamante failed to turn the federalist tide and he was deposed. Santa Anna was nominated provisional president, but elections returned a federalist majority to congress. However, a military *coup d'état* overcame that setback, and a conservative, centralist constitution was imposed, with Santa Anna as president. By now, the old warhorse had begun to appreciate the virtues of monarchy, and he proceeded to rule in a quasi-regal fashion. Indeed, his attempts to recapture the mystique of royalty would reach the extreme of having his severed leg exhumed and translated to the capital for a ceremonial interment in the cathedral. But the dictator's financial extravagance shortly provoked yet another military revolt and in 1844 he was deposed and went into exile in Cuba. It was by no means the end of his career.

While Mexico was tearing itself apart, the Texas problem dragged on, with the USA threatening periodically to annex the territory, which it finally did in 1845. Given the dire straits in which Mexico found itself, the president, General José Joaquín Herrera, tried to negotiate a settlement. Mexican public opinion was outraged at this prospect. The army staged a *coup d'état* and its leader, General Mariano Paredes, encouraged the idea, which had been mooted from time to time by Lucas Alamán and other conservatives, of establishing a monarchy under a European prince. It was a last-ditch attempt to put together a national consensus in the spirit of the Plan of Iguala; the Plan had resolved the crisis of independence and now something like it was sorely needed to overcome the equally grave crisis provoked by insistent US pressure on the beleaguered country. But it was too late: in April 1846 a US army crossed into Mexico and war was declared.

The occupation of Mexican territory by US troops under General Zachary Taylor brought down the conservative General Paredes. His replacement was none other than Santa Anna, now allied with his former enemy Gómez Farías and the liberals. Gómez Farías proposed confiscating Church property in order to finance the war effort, but the clergy reacted by provoking yet another military uprising. Meanwhile, a second US army, under General Winfield Scott, invaded Mexico, took Veracruz and marched on the capital, where it encountered a desperate, heroic resistance by the civilian population. With the fall of Mexico City in September 1847, the war was as good as over: Santa Anna went into exile and a peace treaty was signed in February 1848 which made over to the USA fully a half of Mexican sovereign territory. North American aggression on a hopelessly divided Mexico had paid off handsomely: 'manifest destiny' yielded up lands that were to become the future US states of Texas, New Mexico, Arizona, Nevada, Colorado and California.

Why was this catastrophe allowed to happen? Bad as US aggression was, it was not the only disaster that befell the creole ruling classes in the late 1840s. A series of massive Indian revolts threatened to overturn the internal colonialism that prevailed in Mexico. The Yucatán, whose bid for independence in 1840 had not quite been checked by the central government, was convulsed in 1847 by a huge uprising of the Maya Indians against the small white élite of henequen planters. Unable to call on the embattled Mexican army, the panic-stricken planters offered their state for annexation to any foreign power capable of putting down the Indians. Simultaneously, a revolt known as the Sierra Gorda Rebellion broke out in the vital mining states of Guanajuato, Querétaro and San Luis Potosí among rural Indians and mestizos, who called for the redistribution of the haciendas to the landless peasants. Meanwhile, estates in the central areas of the country were being ravaged by marauding groups of bandits, and, in the north, waves of fierce nomadic tribes pillaged settlements and haciendas with impunity. It looked as if the whole country would disintegrate, and since the Mexican army was being cut to pieces by superior US forces, there was nothing for it but to capitulate.

The disasters of the mid-century made the creole élites – from the liberal Mora to the royalist Alamán – close ranks in defence of their common Hispanic heritage, at least in the immediate post-war years. The financial indemnity paid to Mexico by the USA for the loss of her territory helped the national government rebuild the army, and the Indian rebellions were thus brought under control. Divisions, however, were quick to reappear, and with them fresh military *pronunciamientos*.

With politics spinning into chaos once again, both liberals and conservatives came to believe that the smack of firm government was the only solution to the nation's woes. Yet who would administer it? There was no one at hand – except, of course, that obliging veteran of disasters, General Santa Anna, who was duly recalled from exile to assume the presidency in March 1853. Contradictory counsels were now offered to this somewhat battered political messiah. Lucas Alamán proposed his usual recipe – an end to federalism and the strengthening of the Church and the army, the traditional pillars of order; but liberals feared that this would just be the first step towards the restoration of a monarchy. Santa Anna opted for a government of national unity, and made a coalition which included conservatives like Alamán and young radical liberals such as Miguel Lerdo de Tejada, who would rise to prominence in the course of the next few years.

Despite the very mixed political character of the governing coalition, and even though the royalist Alamán died within a couple of months of taking office, Santa Anna once again warmed to the idea of a monarchy – but it would be a creole monarchy *à la* Iturbide, with himself at its centre. Assuming the title of Most Serene Highness, Santa Anna revived Iturbide's Order of Guadalupe and presided over a showy, pseudo-imperial court in which the elements of traditional Hispanic absolutism – the alliance of throne and altar – made their appearance: the clergy had some of their legal privileges restored and the Jesuits were recalled, among other pro-clerical measures. However, this ramshackle and increasingly tyrannical parody of the Catholic monarchy was scarcely a recipe for stability, let alone legitimacy. Within a year, a group of army officers had pronounced against Santa Anna, issuing the Plan of Ayutla (1854), which called for a new constitution and a return to republican principles.

This was the start of a wayward process, known as *La Reforma*, which over the next twenty years would finally establish a secular state enshrining liberal principles of popular sovereignty and equality before the law. But the political death-throes of royalist, Catholic Mexico were to prove extraordinarily violent and agonizing, for the great liberal reform would not be achieved without one last effort by conservatives to set up a constitutional monarchy along the lines of the Plan of Iguala.

Santa Anna was finally overthrown in August 1855, and the liberal government that succeeded him contained young radicals who were to become the great names of *La Reforma* – the Zapotec Indian lawyer and future president, Benito Juárez, Melchor Ocampo, the brothers Lerdo de Tejada, Guillermo Prieto, Santos Degollado and Ignacio Ramírez. Although in coalition with moderate liberals, these radicals were appointed to key ministries and quickly passed laws curtailing the immunities of the clergy and the army. The *Ley Juárez* of 1855 abolished clerical privileges and restricted military *fueros*. It provoked a conservative uprising, responding to the cry of *religión y fueros*, which led to the fall of the city of Puebla. Accusing the Church of using its wealth to finance the rebels, the liberal government passed another law, the *Ley Lerdo*, aimed at the disentailment of all corporate land, ecclesiastical and Indian. This legal onslaught on the Church, the army and the Indian communities struck at the foundations of the traditional order and called forth the expected response from conservatives. But the configuration of Mexican politics was changing to the long-term advantage of the liberals. For the privatization of Church and Indian corporate property released new land on to the market, which was acquired by large landowners and financial speculators. Thus, a good number of creole *hacendados* were won over to the liberal cause by reforms promoted for ideological reasons by progressive, urban intellectuals. By contrast, the conservative bloc was enlarged by expropriated Indians, impoverished parish priests and disgruntled army officers.

In 1857 a new liberal constitution was passed, incorporating the Juárez and Lerdo laws and omitting to declare Mexico a Catholic nation; it was to become a rallying symbol for Mexican liberals in much the same way as the Cadiz constitution of 1812 had been for the Spanish. A civil war broke out which at first went badly for the liberals. Benito Juárez, who had become the constitutional president of the republic, was, in fact, little better than a fugitive in a black carriage, trying to evade the conservative armies under the rival presidency of a general installed in Mexico City. Gradually, the tide turned in the liberals' favour and victory finally came in December 1860, when the capital was won from the conservative president, General Miguel Miramón.

In 1861 Benito Juárez was elected the first civilian president in the country's history. He inherited a bankrupt treasury and, when harried by foreign creditors, had little option but to default on debt payments. At this, France, Spain and Britain joined forces to send a punitive expedition to Mexico. However, when it became clear that this expedition was little more than a cover for the colonialist designs of Napoleon III, Britain and Spain withdrew their forces. The French pressed on, were checked at Puebla, but with further reinforcements took Mexico City and occupied the central areas of the country. Juárez escaped to San Luis Potosí, where he established his government.

Napoleon III's plan was to create for France an American client state by realizing the Mexican conservative dream of a constitutional monarchy under a European prince. The prince chosen to fulfil this role was the Archduke

Maximilian of Austria; he was a young man who belonged to the royal house of Habsburg and therefore possessed impeccable credentials for a monarch. After being persuaded by a contrived plebiscite that the Mexican people would welcome him wholeheartedly, Maximilian and his Belgian wife, Carlota, ascended the throne of Mexico in 1864.

Maximilian turned out to be a good-natured and well-intentioned sovereign, but he was a man of liberal views, which came as a disappointment to his mainly conservative and clerical supporters in Mexico. Setting out to behave as a good constitutional monarch, he forbore to repeal the anti-clerical legislation of *La Reforma*; indeed, his first cabinet was composed of Mexican liberals prepared to collaborate with him. Moreover, he showed a genuine concern to represent the Mexican people as a whole: he saw to it that debt-peonage was abolished on the haciendas, that working hours were reduced and peasants free to leave their employers without retribution; he also restored common lands to Indian communities which had lost them by the 1857 constitution. But Maximilian owed his throne to a French army of occupation, and this he could not live down. Juárez's republican forces prosecuted a guerrilla war against the French and, when Napoleon III was compelled to withdraw his troops from Mexico to meet a growing threat from Prussia in Europe, the balance of power turned sharply against Maximilian – without French support he was no match for Juárez. Deserted by his liberal followers, Maximilian turned instead to the conservatives, but Juárez's soldiers inflicted several defeats on the royalists and then laid siege to the emperor's camp at Querétaro. Maximilian was finally betrayed by one of his own commanders and met his death by firing squad on a hill above Querétaro on 19 June 1867. With him was laid to rest at last the chimera of a Mexican monarchy.

The restoration of the republic under the presidency of Benito Juárez represented the triumph of the liberal *Reforma*: Mexico now had a secular state in which the privileges of the Church were abolished and the power of conservative landowners was decisively weakened. The greatest supporters of Juárez were middle-class urban professionals and merchants, and those *hacendados* who expected enrichment from the implementation of the provisions of the 1857 constitution regarding the expropriation of Church and Indian community lands. The largely Indian peasantry got very little out of *La Reforma*: many communities lost land to the haciendas; debt-peonage increased accordingly, and the burden of taxation fell most heavily on them, the class which was least able to shoulder it. Partly for this reason, political unrest bedevilled Juárez's government: peasant rebellions, revolts of regional *caudillos* and wars against the Apaches on the northern frontier prevented the consolidation of national authority. Even so, Juárez, who could count on a large reserve of political support after his expulsion of the French, was able to serve his full term and was re-elected in 1871.

La Reforma, then, may have given Mexico the legal structure of a modern state, but it had not gone very far towards ridding the country of *caudillismo*. Disgruntled regional *caudillos* were continually attempting to overthrow Juárez; some were conservatives, but the real danger came from within the ranks of the liberals, and the most ambitious of the liberal *caudillos* was the young hero of the wars against the French, Porfirio Díaz. Díaz had already fought and lost the 1867 election against Juárez, and when he lost again in 1871 he called for a national uprising in support of his declaration that presidents should not be re-elected. Díaz was defeated, but within a few years he would make another bid for power.

After Juárez's death in office he was succeeded in 1872 by another important figure of *La Reforma*, the lawyer Sebastián Lerdo de Tejada. A more uncompromising liberal than Juárez, he pursued the expropriation of Church and Indian lands, and gave an impetus to economic development by approving the building of the first railway in Mexico, which linked the port of Veracruz to the capital. As the election of 1876 approached, Porfirio Díaz again proclaimed the principle of no re-election and called for an uprising. This time it succeeded and Díaz duly assumed supreme office.

Porfirio Díaz had reached power by the classic route of the *caudillo* and, despite his principle of no re-election, was to hold on to it for over thirty years, although he had to rely upon the token presidency of a corrupt stooge between 1880 and 1884. Over the period 1876–1910 Mexico would make more economic progress than at any time since independence. The economy grew at an astonishing rate – an average of 8 per cent a year. The population increased by about 50 per cent to 15 million, even though European immigration remained very low. The modernization of the export-economy, by extending railway links and introducing new technology into mining and agriculture, transformed Mexico. As the railway replaced mule transport, mining production increased sharply: in addition to the traditional silver and gold, it became feasible to mine copper, zinc and lead, while the output of silver rose by some 150 per cent. In agriculture, cash crops for export such as sisal, rubber, cochineal, sugar and coffee stimulated the rural economy of many regions and led to the consolidation of the hacienda and to more rapid expropriation of Church and Indian lands. In the 1880s and 1890s there occurred significant industrial development in textiles and light industrial goods and the processing of mineral ores. In 1902 the first steel plant opened in Monterrey, but on the whole heavy industry did not grow very rapidly:

the government, wedded to *laissez-faire*, granted it no special protection and did little to train an industrial workforce.

The economic liberalism of the Díaz regime was most obvious in its open attitude to foreign investment. Indeed, the capital needed to transform the infrastructure and the productive base of the country was overwhelmingly foreign; throughout the period most of the dynamic sectors of the Mexican economy were controlled by foreign companies. Díaz welcomed capital from the USA, but also made efforts to offset this by encouraging investment from European sources, mostly from Britain but also from France and Germany.

This long period of economic progress and political stability, known as the Porfiriato, was made possible by the consolidation of the central authority of the state. In fact, modernization and stability were mutually reinforcing: the *Pax Porfiriana* attracted foreign investors, while increased economic resources strengthened the power of the central government against regional *caudillos*. And yet stability was not achieved by constitutional means: no centralizing consensus existed among the Mexican regional élites which could have produced the semblance of a constitutional regime, as occurred in republics like Chile or Argentina. Porfirio Díaz was a *caudillo*, and he kept himself in power through the well-tried personalist methods of *caudillismo*.

Military repression was an important means of pacifying a country as turbulent as Mexico. A well-funded army and an even better-paid paramilitary force, the much-feared *Rurales*, brought a measure of order to the countryside: the Apache menace was contained, banditry suppressed and rebellious provincial *caudillos* put in their place. Repression of strikes and peasant revolts, and control of the press, saw to the political opposition. The democratic institutions of the republic were soon manipulated by *caudillo* practices: rigged elections effectively banished opponents from the congress and by 1888 that body had agreed to amend the constitution so as to enable Don Porfirio (who had twice sought power with the cry of 'no re-election') to yield to the wishes of the people and accept election to the presidency every six years.

Still, it did not all boil down to the use of force: Díaz maintained himself in power for so long because he was able to co-opt all the major forces in the country into a nationwide system of patronage. Military officers were kept happy with arms purchases, lucrative state sinecures and land grants. Regional bosses retained their local influence, but were encouraged to see the advantage of allying themselves with governors nominated by Díaz, who could facilitate interesting business deals with foreign investors. Growing state and provincial bureaucracies provided employment for the urban middle classes, from among whom there nevertheless emerged an intellectual opposition, which remained active despite government harassment.

The Porfiriato therefore rested on the personal authority and patronage of one man: it was a supreme form of *caudillismo*, albeit liberal and progressive, but not a modern nation state. And yet economic development was producing complex social changes, to which the personal regime of Don Porfirio would have to adapt in order to survive. The growth of export agriculture had thrown large numbers of Indian peasants off their communal lands and reduced them to debt-peonage; many parts of the countryside were seething with discontent. Drought or recession might set off a wider social conflagration than the peasant rebellions that erupted from time to time. The expansion of mining and manufacturing had created a substantial urban working class, which by the last years of the century had started to organize into labour unions and to absorb radical political ideologies. If a severe economic crisis occurred or some accident should befall Don Porfirio, the country might once again be plunged into disorder. Economic modernization, in short, called for a corresponding modernization of the apparatus of state.

This problem was acknowledged by some of the dictator's leading ministers. They formed a clique of progressive technocrats who were known as *científicos* because they advocated a 'scientific' politics which would allow for the suspension of democratic rights while economic progress transformed a country otherwise vitiated by unenlightened values and racial deficiencies. The *científicos* wanted to create a national party that would institutionalize the regime and provide for a peaceful succession once Don Porfirio gave up the reins of power. But the *científicos* were opposed by another clique within the Díaz élite, consisting of army officers and regional bosses, who were loath to give up the personal basis of traditional *caudillo* power. Porfirio Díaz, as a *caudillo* himself, resisted the *científicos'* proposals, but in the first decade of the new century, as he approached the age of seventy and a new round of elections loomed in 1910, he too appeared to appreciate the risks of building a modern economy on the political foundations of one-man rule. When those elections came, a combination of economic recession, political errors and divisions within the governing circles allowed a groundswell of political discontent to surge up and sweep the Porfiriato away.

The ruling classes of Mexico were so deeply divided for most of the nineteenth century because the terms of the Plan of Iguala had kept alive for fifty years the hopes of a monarchy – of a Brazilian solution, as it were, to the crisis of independence. This made it virtually impossible for conservatives and liberals to arrive at the kind of pragmatic consensus over a republican constitution that was achieved in Chile. Even after liberalism had got the upper hand in the 1870s, traditional *caudillismo* continued to fragment the ruling classes, and it was only the overmastering authority of Porfirio Díaz that was able to provide stability long enough for economic modernization to get under way. But Díaz failed to solve the key problem of nation-building, and the price that was paid came in the form of a chaotic revolution that plunged the country into an orgy of violence lasting some twenty years. The Mexican Revolution was to reveal the intrinsic fragility of a state whose authority was based on personal power rather than on representative institutions enjoying wide political consent.

In contrast to Mexico, the restoration of a monarchy was out of the question in the other countries of Spanish America. (Except, for a time, in Ecuador, where the strongman, Juan José Flores, who had been one of Bolívar's aides, organized a major conspiracy in the 1840s which included General Andrés Santa Cruz, another former lieutenant of Bolívar and first president of the republic of Bolivia. Its aim was to set up monarchies in Ecuador, Bolivia and Peru. Flores again contacted the Spanish Bourbons in the 1860s in the hope of restoring a monarchy that might stabilize a country that was constantly at the mercy of feuding *caudillos*.) Yet, even so, the conservatism of the creole élites was so profound that repeated attempts were made to curtail liberalism in order to fashion a republican equivalent of the status quo before the demise of the Catholic monarchy. The conflicts between conservatives and liberals thus took on the intensity of religious wars in republics like Peru, Colombia, Ecuador and Bolivia, countries with deeply traditional élites that had exercised de facto power for centuries, and where there existed also large *repúblicas de indios* that were staunchly Catholic and set in their ways. In these countries liberal abstractions such as the 'sovereignty of the people' or the 'equality of all citizens before the law' were hard to reconcile with existing realities. It was simpler to cling to the wreckage of the past or to try to salvage as much of it as possible in the building of the new states.

Throughout the century and beyond, conservative *caudillos* would employ great ingenuity in their attempts to recapture the ethos of the *ancien régime*. It was in the regions surrounding the River Plate that the conservative reaction took on the most original and inventive forms. For the traditionalists of the interior were reacting to the ideology emanating from the former viceregal capital, Buenos Aires, which had been the seat of the most revolutionary version of liberal republicanism in Latin America during the period of independence. *Caudillos* such as Dr Gaspar Rodríguez de Francia of Paraguay and his successors, or Juan Manuel de Rosas of the rural province of Buenos Aires, reacted against liberalism by trying to erect traditional structures on a republican base. In doing so, they contributed in their way to the political culture of the modern world, since they discovered techniques of state organization and mass mobilization which foreshadowed many aspects of populist authoritarianism in Latin America and elsewhere. Their rule, in turn, called forth a reaction from a new generation of liberals, who would go on to build in Argentina the most successful of all the liberal republics in Spanish America.

Paraguay

Paraguay effectively began its life as an independent nation in 1814, when a revolutionary junta broke away from the control of Buenos Aires, to which it had been subordinate under the viceroyalty of Río de la Plata. The liberals of Buenos Aires tried several times to reduce Paraguay to their authority by force of arms, and successive Argentine governments would refuse to recognize Paraguayan independence. This hostility bred a defensive, isolationist mentality in the new nation. Soon after independence, power was seized by the redoubtable Dr Francia, who built an idiosyncratic neo-traditionalist state which outlived him by three decades. In liberal eyes, Francia was a blood-stained tyrant who stayed in power through a reign of terror. But in the peculiar circumstances of Paraguay, his political system was by no means irrational nor even entirely inhumane.

During the colonial period, Paraguay had been a remote backwater, sparsely settled by Spaniards and yielding no commodities of great value to the wider imperial economy. The relatively small number of conquistadors who put down roots there often married into the ruling Indian families and adapted to the society of the native Guaraní. The isolation of this outpost of empire was reinforced by its lack of access to the sea other than through the long descent of the Paraná River to the South Atlantic. As a result, Paraguay had always moved at its own tempo: lying so far from the major centres, it responded very late, if at all, to imperial decrees. For instance, the abolition of *encomienda* in the late sixteenth century had little effect in Paraguay, where traditions of labour services and tribute predated the arrival of the Spaniards; the enslavement of Indians from the tribes in the jungle continued regardless of royal prohibitions; the Bourbon reforms virtually passed it by, except to redesignate it as a province under the jurisdiction of Buenos Aires. And so, with the survival of the *encomienda* and Indian slavery, labour relations remained deeply servile, while the economy did not receive sufficient external stimulus to lift it much beyond subsistence. The object of Dr Francia's rule was to preserve the basic structures of this peculiar society against the multiple crises unleashed by independence. He perceived that in a country in which the population was overwhelmingly Indian and living mostly in agrarian communities outside the money economy, the nostrums of democratic liberalism would be very destructive of the traditional life of the native peasantry (as indeed they proved to be all over Latin America). Accordingly, Francia resolved to nip modern ideas in the bud by breaking the power of the small oligarchy of creole landowners and Spanish merchants. When this liberal élite rose against him in 1820, Francia responded with a campaign of terror which earned him his grisly reputation as the worst kind of Latin American tyrant.

Francia's state, though officially secular and separate from the Church, drew its inspiration from pre-European forms of political and economic organization, as well as from the Jesuit missions, which themselves harked back to the sixteenth-century Utopian settlements created for Indian converts by Spanish friars in Mexico. Indeed, Francia's Paraguay may be regarded as an eccentric experiment in creating an enlightened, republican version of the New Jerusalem which the Spanish missionaries had wanted to build in the New World. The austere and incorruptible Dr Francia, whose doctorate was in theology, was, in fact, an admirer of Rousseau, Robespierre and Napoleon, but he made few concessions to the principles of liberal democracy.

After ridding the country of its Europeanizing élite, Francia installed the machinery of a paternalist, all-embracing state, placing himself at its head as a kind of lay philosopher-king to the equable Guaraní. Its informing principle was that the state should order and control the lives of the people. Much of the land was already in public ownership, having formerly belonged to the Crown or the Church; to this were added the estates confiscated from the banished élite. Public land was either leased out to small farmers or else developed into state farms to be worked collectively by peasants and, in some cases, by slaves under the direction of state officials. Some of the produce from these state farms was used for export, but most of it was destined for home consumption, either to feed the army or to store up food reserves for the poor when times were bad. Private farmers had to fulfil quotas stipulated by the state in exchange for imported goods. The principal commodities of this simple economy were *yerba mate*, timber, tobacco, sugar and hides. The export trade was rigorously controlled through two authorized outlets, a practice which recalled the colonial trade monopoly. Money and market forces played little part in the economy; rather, the aim was autarky in the face of the permanent political threat from Buenos Aires and the difficulties placed upon Paraguayan commerce by the *caudillos* of the riparian provinces of the Paraná.

Even though Francia's regime was vestigially republican, and his power was derived theoretically from the will of the people, the highly personalist state he created survived his death, and his successor, a mestizo lawyer, Carlos Antonio López, was to govern in the same manner for a further twenty-two years. López it was who took the next logical step in securing the stability of the state by establishing a family dynasty: he was succeeded in 1862 by his son, Francisco Solano López, who ruled until 1870. The absolute rule established by Dr Francia thus provided Paraguay with a stability unmatched even by successful constitutional republics like Chile and Costa Rica. Despite its secular, republican foundation, it came very close to achieving the dynastic continuity of a monarchy. And yet, in the final analysis, there was an underlying contradiction between personalist absolutism and republicanism – Paraguay could not seal itself off for ever from the modern world.

The elder López continued the policy of state control, but he initiated material development by importing technology and expertise to build up the armed forces and modernize the infrastructure; a railway, shipyard, arsenal and factories were built. When the navigation of the Paraná became freer after the fall of the Argentine dictator Rosas in 1852, external trade was allowed to expand and foreign imports of cotton and wood began to undercut domestic products, unsettling the rudimentary economy.

The new openness also brought with it increased dangers from Paraguay's neighbours – Brazil still had territorial ambitions in the region, and after 1862, when the liberals had consolidated their power in Buenos Aires, the new republic of Argentina too would turn against the Paraguayan 'tyranny'. On his succession in 1862, the younger López built up the country's defences: the army was equipped and reinforced and it became the most powerful in South America. Military superiority tempted López to play a more aggressive role in the complex geopolitics of the River Plate. He sought actively to support the government of the traditionalist Blanco Party in Uruguay, an unstable buffer state currently being harassed by both Argentina and Brazil.

By 1864 López's manœuvring had embroiled Paraguay in a war against Brazil, Argentina and the liberal Colorado Party of Uruguay. This War of the Triple Alliance was as much an ideological war as a struggle for power; a conflict between modernity and tradition, between 'civilization' and 'barbarism', according to the propaganda of Argentina and Brazil. When it ended in 1870, after López had been killed in battle, Paraguay had been all but destroyed as a nation: the population had been halved by the ravages of warfare and disease, leaving mostly women, children and old people; large tracts of territory were annexed by Argentina and Brazil, who had agreed secret protocols to that end in their treaty of alliance.

The neo-traditionalist state founded by Dr Francia was pulled down never to be restored. When the Paraguayan liberals returned from exile, they tried to apply the political programmes of their mentors in Buenos Aires, but this archaic, mutilated republic sank into a morass of endless *caudillismo* and dictatorships, condemned to be the economic pawn of Argentina and Brazil. War had ruined Paraguay, and war would ruin it yet again in the 1930s, when it fought neighbouring Bolivia to a standstill, losing over 50,000 lives in a wholly fruitless contest over erroneously charted oilfields in the wastelands of the Chaco.

Argentina

The early years of independence brought chaotic struggles between liberals and conservatives to the former viceroyalty of Río de la Plata; the centralist *unitarios* of the port city of Buenos Aires clashed with provincial *caudillos* intent on carving out separate fiefdoms for themselves with their irregular gaucho cavalry, known as *montoneros*. The representative of the liberal position was the intellectual Bernardino Rivadavia, who served in governments of the 1820s, becoming president of the United Provinces in 1826 until he was overthrown by conservative interests the following year.

Rivadavia believed in a unitary liberal state which should rapidly modernize by encouraging foreign investment, European immigration and free trade. But liberals from the city of Buenos Aires possessed little economic power; this lay with the big cattle ranchers, who ran a primitive export-economy based on hides and salted beef. These *estancieros* were traditionalist and xenophobic: they disliked the anti-clericalism of the liberal *unitarios*, and were strong supporters of the Church; the *estancieros* of the up-river provinces of Santa Fe, Entre Ríos and Corrientes were unhappy with Buenos Aires' exclusive control of the customs revenues from foreign trade, and wanted trading rights for their own river ports; constitutionally, they supported the idea of a loose federation of provinces which would allow them to retain power in their own regions. Not surprisingly, the Argentine provinces were a fertile breeding-ground for *caudillos*, and among these Juan Manuel de Rosas, the owner of great estates in the province – as opposed to the city – of Buenos Aires, swiftly achieved pre-eminence.

Elected to the governorship of Buenos Aires province two years after

Rivadavia had fallen, Rosas was voted full powers as dictator by the Federal Party and proceeded to restore order after his fashion. In the view of his liberal enemies he ran the province like one vast *estancia*, where he was the boss and the citizens were little more than peons. His power was built up in the traditional manner of conquering kings – through grants of land to his clients; these grants were made possible by the Desert Campaign of 1833, which won huge tracts from the nomadic Indians of the pampas south-west of Buenos Aires. Viscerally opposed to liberalism and all its works, Rosas manipulated the law as he saw fit and presented himself as the champion of the lower orders against the sophisticated liberals of the city of Buenos Aires.

Rosas was an inventive despot who knew the value of mystique and propaganda. When his term as governor expired in 1833, he departed Buenos Aires on a military campaign against the Indians, leaving his wife behind to organize a mass movement in favour of his 'restoration' to power; it became known as *La Mazorca*, because its symbol was an ear of wheat, which was taken to represent the unity of the people in much the same way as the Roman fasces or the yoke-and-arrows were adopted for similar purposes in Italy and Spain, respectively, a century later. A personality cult was created in order to identify the cause of federalism with the person of its leader – red, the colour of the Federal Party, became the sign of loyalty to Rosas. Ritual denunciations of the liberal *unitarios* were encouraged: the slogan 'Long live the Federation! Death to the filthy, savage *unitarios*!' rang out in schools, churches and meeting halls. Indeed, the language of religion infilt-rated the cult of Rosas: during his absence the Federal Party split into supporters of Rosas, calling themselves the *apostólicos*, and the moderates, who were branded *cismáticos*. The clergy, moreover, preached loyalty to Rosas, allowing his portrait to be displayed in their churches. When at last Rosas returned to Buenos Aires in 1835, the grateful citizens offered him total power to rule the province, which he did for another seventeen years. Rosas forced the liberal opposition into exile and his *Mazorca* became an organ of state terror, employing spies and death squads to keep the dictator in power.

Yet behind the populist trappings of his regime, Rosas had little to offer the dispossessed groups he had enlisted in his movement. The gauchos and blacks, upon whom he relied so heavily for his military campaigns and public rallies, remained impoverished servants of the *estancieros* or lowly workers in the towns. The slave-trade actually revived under Rosas, partly because of the labour shortage on the expanding frontier. In reality, Rosas was a representative of the landed interest, and his aim was to exploit the pampas for a cattle-raising export-economy which would benefit a narrow élite, who would also control the lucrative customs house of the port of Buenos Aires.

The great irony of the period, as the liberal Domingo Sarmiento pointed out, was that Rosas, though a federalist, did more than anyone to ensure the economic and political dominance of Buenos Aires over the other provinces, and therefore unwittingly preparing the ground for the eventual unification of Argentina. Still, Rosas did little to develop the United Provinces into a nation state as such. He was the most influential of the *caudillos*, but preferred a system of pacts with chieftains like Estanislao López of Santa Fe or Facundo Quiroga of La Rioja to any formal constitutional arrangements.

Nevertheless, he did act for the United Provinces against foreign enemies: he fought Bolivia to prevent it from merging with Peru; he kept intervening in the *caudillo* politics of Uruguay in order to thwart its bids for independence; he attempted to force Paraguay through blockade to join the United Provinces. These actions brought him into conflict with Brazil, and also with France and Britain, all of whom had a stake in opening up the River Plate and its tributaries to international trade. Rosas, however, became caught up in too many wars against too many internal and external foes, and the very turbulence of his regime contributed to his undoing. From the 1840s the economy of the Buenos Aires pampas, based on exports of hides and jerked beef, was being superseded by the rearing of sheep for wool in response to the demands of the textile industries of Europe; the *estancieros*, Rosas's main constituency, needed stability for investment and restructuring, and the belligerent dictator gradually outlived his usefulness to them. In the end, his enemies combined to defeat him. The *caudillo* of the riparian province of Entre Ríos, Justo José de Urquiza, with the support of Brazil, Uruguay and the liberal *unitarios* in exile, marched against Rosas and defeated him in February 1852 at the battle of Monte Caseros. Rosas fled Argentina and ended his days in England.

The fall of Rosas did not bring an end to the provincial conflicts which had raged since independence. However, Urquiza was more concerned than Rosas to create a coherent national structure for the United Provinces, and in the constitution of 1853 he provided for a federal republic under a strong presidentialist regime. But the *unitarios* of Buenos Aires refused to accept federalism until compelled to do so by Urquiza, who defeated their forces in 1859. Two years later the province of Buenos Aires again revolted against the federation, and this time its leader Bartolomé Mitre succeeded in imposing his will on the *federales*. From 1862 Buenos Aires won acceptance of its position as capital of a united Argentine republic under the presidency of the liberal Mitre. Even though some *caudillos* of the internal provinces resisted the new unitarian order, their rebellions were put down by Mitre and his successor, Domingo Sarmiento.

With Buenos Aires at its head, the new Argentina was set upon the road to stability and modernization. In the course of the 1860s and 1870s, the liberal presidents Mitre, Sarmiento and Nicolás Avellaneda created the institutions of a centralized nation state: a professional army, an integrated judicial system, a national bank, a system of public schooling, public libraries, an academy of science and other technical institutions. The railway and telegraphic communications began to link the hitherto fractious conservative provinces to Buenos Aires and, through it, to the world outside. The 1870s were also a time of expanding frontiers and absorption of massive new territories. Victory in the Paraguayan War (1865–70) yielded territory in the north and north-west. Then, in the south, General Julio Roca led another Desert Campaign (1879–80), which exterminated or reduced the nomadic Indians of the pampas, releasing vast acres for settlement and cultivation.

From 1880, the year in which Buenos Aires was constitutionally recognized as the federal capital of the nation, Argentina embarked on an astonishing rate of growth – sustaining an annual average of at least 5 per cent until 1914 – to become one of the richest nations in the world. The territorial acquisitions of the 1870s invigorated the economy, based as it was on cattle, sheep and, increasingly, cereals. As always in Argentina, there was a pressing need for labour, and now more so than ever – labour to work the land, to fence in and convert the barren pampas into wheatfields, and to lay the railway that would link up the provinces and turn the disparate regions into an integrated, modern nation. European immigration was therefore encouraged, and workers – mostly from Italy and Spain – flooded into this vast, empty country. In 1870 the population was less than 2 million; in the next fifty years approximately 3.5 million immigrants would come to Argentina.

The capital investment and technical expertise required for such a massive economic transformation were beyond the resources of a country that had been continually drained by military upheavals and whose economy had been based on rudimentary cattle-raising. Such resources were provided overwhelmingly by the British, who became the major customers for Argentine wheat and meat, the latter now available for export to Europe thanks to faster steamships and the introduction of *frigoríficos* (meat-chilling plants). A bilateral pattern of trade emerged: Argentina imported manufactured goods from Britain in exchange for her exports of foodstuffs for the British industrial working classes. However, British business also established a commanding position in the internal structure of the Argentine economy: British companies owned the railways, the telegraph, the new meat-processing plants and many of the banks and merchant houses operating in Buenos Aires; this made Argentina potentially vulnerable to external economic pressures, though it was not perceived to be a problem by any political force in the country at the time. A significant Anglo-Argentine community came into being, its upper echelons setting the social tone for the new plutocratic *estanciero* élite.

There were other structural imbalances. The opening up of the new territories after the 'Conquest of the Desert' did not lead to the emergence of a rural middle class of medium-sized farmers, as had occurred in the Midwest of the USA and as Argentine social reformers had advocated. The sheer volume of land was too great for the number of available purchasers; over-supply kept prices low until the end of the century and this cheap new land was snapped up by established landowners and merchants, who were able to expand their existing holdings. Impoverished European immigrants, on the other hand, could not initially afford substantial holdings; they started off as tenant farmers or sharecroppers in the hope of eventually purchasing their plots and extending their property, as in fact many of them did. Yet the pull of world demand for Argentine foodstuffs was such that agrarian export development encouraged ever greater concentration of resources, so that the pattern of distribution of new land in the end came to resemble the classic *latifundia*, the huge estates characteristic of the Hispanic seigneurial regimes established in America since the sixteenth century.

The immigrants filled jobs in industry and public works, and worked as seasonal labourers in the countryside, returning to live in the cities out of season. Wages in the country were generally good – good enough to attract the *golondrinas*, the 'swallows' who arrived from Italy and Spain for the harvest and then returned home. But most immigrants stayed and settled in the cities, especially Buenos Aires, where they suffered the vicissitudes of inflation and recession. Towards the end of the century, the market became over-supplied with labour and wages began to fall, exacerbating social tensions. Argentina's transformation in the last quarter of the century thus resulted in a strangely skewed economic structure: the rural economy was in the hands of a relatively small creole élite of *estancieros*, the cities were inhabited by a large and growing proletariat, many of foreign extraction, while the booming export-economy was dominated by British financial and commercial interests.

The wealth and power of the *estancieros* of Buenos Aires permitted a country racked for so long by *caudillo* factionalism to acquire a Chilean-style constitutional system, based on the rule of law, elections and respect for the classic liberal freedoms. Yet the liberals of the 'Generation of 1880' were so apprehensive that the country might slip back into its earlier chaos that in practice they operated a one-party monopoly, rigging elections in order to exclude the opposition. Julio Roca, the man who had completed the Conquest of the Desert, formed the PAN (National Autonomist Party), which monopolized power for three decades after Roca's election as president in 1880. *Caudillismo* had not disappeared entirely, rather it had been domesticated by a political system that relied on party bosses to dispense patronage to regional clienteles in exchange for their votes.

The opposition, however, also wanted an opportunity to share out government patronage to its clients, so in 1890 the excluded politicians formed the Unión Cívica and took to arms in July, bringing down the president Miguel Juárez Celman. But Carlos Pellegrini, the new president, succeeded in splitting the Unión Cívica by including some of their leaders in the distribution of the spoils of office. Those political *caudillos* who still remained on the outside then went on to found what was to become the Radical Party, which included new interest-groups such as the urban middle classes. The Radicals, led by Leandro Alem and his nephews, Hipólito and Bernardo Yrigoyen, staged a number of armed revolts in order to break open the electoral system, but they failed (Alem committed suicide in 1896). In 1912, however, the franchise was widened and the Radical Party was at last able to enter the game of oligarchic democracy.

By the end of the century Argentina had achieved a high degree of national integration; its economy had grown to a level where it rivalled those of the advanced European countries; politics, which had once been so anarchic, appeared to have been contained broadly within constitutional norms. The Argentine liberals, in short, had routed the forces of Hispanic traditionalism. It was, to employ the terms used by the great liberal state-builder Domingo Sarmiento, a triumph of modern European 'civilization' over the 'barbarism' of the *caudillo* politics represented by Rosas. And yet, how solid was the political consensus that underpinned prosperity? Had Argentina become a modern nation state? The urban classes had yet to be fully incorporated into the political system. The economy was wide open to fluctuations in world markets, and in a time of crisis would British interests take due account of Argentine needs? These questions were as yet unresolved, but in the 1920s and 1930s they would come to the forefront of Argentine public life.

THE TRIUMPH OF LIBERALISM

The wars of independence had been the result of a complex constitutional crisis caused by Napoleon's invasion of the Iberian Peninsula in 1808. But in so far as the creole élites had any coherent aims in seeking independence, these had been twofold: to become a legitimate ruling class, and to gain direct access to international trade. It took some fifty or sixty years for these aims to be realized, and then only in a few countries. For in many republics nostalgia for the Catholic monarchy was still very strong, and the creole élites quarrelled over the nature of the states they wanted to build. Even though liberalism was the official ideology of most republics, its roots were too shallow in societies that were steeped in the values of traditional Iberian and Indian cultures: personal authority, patronage and clientship were the means by which power was actually won and distributed – the outward forms of political culture had changed, but the substance remained the same and had even been strengthened by the collapse of law and order. Finally, chronic warfare brought financial ruin, which itself retarded the political stability of the new states. What, then, had allowed some of the independent nations eventually to rise from the morass into which they had been plunged by the crisis of the Catholic monarchies of Spain and Portugal and to make economic progress?

As the examples of Brazil, Chile, Costa Rica and Argentina show, it was consensus over basic constitutional principles that consolidated the authority of the state and facilitated rapid economic progress. Most republics failed to find such a consensus, but in the second half of the century liberalism gained ground when a younger generation of creoles attacked conservative regimes with greater determination, and measures to sell off Church land directly benefited many creoles and gave them a stake in the success of liberalism. Additionally, these internal developments were accelerated from the 1860s by the rising demand in Europe for minerals and foodstuffs, both of which the Latin American countries were in a good position to supply.

Political consolidation was therefore hastened by the prospect of economic progress through international trade. As Latin American countries were pulled into the world economy by rising demand for their commodities, the basic norms of the liberal state won the general acceptance, in theory, of the creole élites. Yet, in most countries, regionalism and *caudillo* factionalism proved exceedingly difficult to overcome; stability, other than through periods of dictatorship, was rarely achieved. In some republics conflicts between liberal and conservative *caudillos* would continue well into the next century – Colombia, for instance, was still fighting civil wars of this kind until the 1960s.

The second half of the nineteenth century saw the formation of the modern Latin American export-economies. Strictly speaking, this was merely a resumption of a structure of international trade that had been established by the Spaniards and Portuguese after the Conquest, and which had been curtailed during the half-century of political disorder following independence. But there were two new elements: first, trade no longer had to pass through a colonial intermediary such as Spain or Portugal; and secondly, many features of the trade had changed – precious metals and sugar had been replaced by other minerals and commodities as major exports, and formerly marginal regions such as Chile, the River Plate countries, northern Mexico, Venezuela and the São Paulo region of Brazil had become the most dynamic export areas.

The crucial feature of an export-economy is that the major productive resources of a country are geared to supply external markets. Because the range of exports is very limited, and usually confined to primary goods and raw materials, such economies are extremely vulnerable to changes in world prices and follow unpredictable boom-and-bust cycles. Other features of the Latin American export-economies have led some historians to call them 'neo-colonial'. These countries depend heavily on a wide variety of imports, especially of manufactured goods. When export prices are low, necessary imports can be bought only by contracting foreign loans or by printing money; export-economies are therefore prone to external debt and high inflation. Moreover, the ownership and control of the basic resources for export are largely in the hands of foreign business interests; in some countries, the export-economy has been described as a kind of 'enclave' run by foreigners. For most of the nineteenth century the British replaced the Spanish and Portuguese merchant houses as the commercial middlemen in the transactions of international trade. By the turn of the century North American interests had begun to displace the British in some areas, particularly in Mexico and Central America.

The effects of Latin American export-economies were the subject of controversy for several decades after the 1950s. It was argued that the export-economies depended excessively on the more developed nations of Europe and North America. This dependence condemned Latin America to economic 'backwardness' or 'underdevelopment' because foreigners controlled all the crucial economic levers, thereby preventing national governments from implementing policies that would benefit the nation as a whole. Latin American countries were unable to initiate industrialization because foreign interests drained away potential investment capital through profit remittances to Europe. The massive social inequalities and regional imbalances that accompanied Latin American development were caused by the modern sector of the economy exploiting the resources of the traditional rural sector, while preventing it from developing.

These views, however, have been contested, and probably a majority of economic historians would not now subscribe to them. For it is unrealistic to expect Latin America to have taken any other path to economic modernization. None of the republics possessed the capital, the educational system or the social structure required to compete with British, German or French industry. Nor could Latin America have developed its natural resources without foreign assistance, for it needed to create an infrastructure of railways, roads and docks and to acquire the technical know-how for mining and food-processing. There is little evidence that foreign capitalists imposed an export structure on a reluctant Latin America; the external orientation of the economy was generally perceived to be beneficial – in Argentina, for instance, even non-élite parties such as the Radicals and the Socialists did not question the fact that the export-economy was highly desirable.

It is now also appreciated that a considerable degree of industrial development occurred 'spontaneously' in the private sector during the latter part of the nineteenth century as an indirect result of the new prosperity generated by the long boom in exports. Furthermore, it seems that industrial development was positively stimulated by links with the international economy, since buoyant export earnings increased incomes, raising demand for home-produced manufactures and providing the capital to import essential machinery for domestic industry. (Some dependency theorists had argued that external links hindered industrial development and that only breaks in the linkages with the international economy – as in times of war or world recession – allowed Latin American industry to grow because it could supply the domestic market without unfair competition from stronger foreign rivals.) It is doubtful too whether there was a net loss of wealth from the area through deterioration in the terms of trade. The imbalances produced by the export-economies, their vulnerability to external pressures, and their domination by foreign business interests were the inevitable results of rapid and profound socio-economic changes, and were offset by the huge strides in material progress achieved in Latin America from the 1870s.

These great material and technical advances were regarded at the time as triumphs of modern liberal civilization and an index of the much-desired Europeanization of Latin America. The expansion of the railway, the building of great steel bridges, the steamships that linked previously isolated regions or permitted travel abroad, the mechanization of so many everyday activities, the coming of gas-lighting to the cities – all these marvels were received with the same wonderment and pride as in Europe or North America.

This was an age of optimism, fired by a belief in progress and in the limitless benefits of science. Academies of art and literature, opera houses, scientific institutes, zoological and botanical gardens were founded in the various capital cities. The appearance of these cities changed: Buenos Aires, Rio de Janeiro, São Paulo, Lima, Mexico City, Caracas – all were endowed with their Hausmann-inspired Parisian boulevards and avenues, their *fin de siècle* villas and apartment buildings for the prospering middle and upper classes. Newspapers carried reports of the latest scientific inventions or the fashions in Paris, London and New York. The very rich could dream of being received by European high society – Paris came to be acquainted with the figure of the *rastaqouère*, the Latin American plutocrat who splashed his money about in the fleshpots of Europe. For the less rich, it was a matter of importing the *belle époque* – inviting theatre companies, singers, music-hall performers and French *cocottes* to add style and spice to their impressively transformed cities.

In the 1880s and 1890s the educated classes were absorbing a truly secular, materialist culture; in other words, liberalism had become more than a set of slogans to throw at the conservatives. The dominant intellectual influence was positivism, which held that only scientifically demonstrable propositions could be accepted as true. But positivism in Latin America was more than a doctrine; it reflected the determination of the governing liberal élites to pursue progress regardless of obstacles such as religion, superstitions and other 'primitive' cultural manifestations. Positivists advocated a form of technocracy: strong government, even dictatorship, was necessary to contain the forces of regression while material conditions could be transformed to pave the way for genuine liberal democracy; the watchword of positivist nation-builders was 'order and progress'. In Mexico, the positivists were known as *científicos* and they exerted a growing influence at the highest levels of the dictatorship of Porfirio Díaz; in Argentina the 'Generation of 1880' rationalized electoral fraud as necessary to prevent a relapse into the disorder of *caudillismo*; the positivists of Brazil provided much of the intellectual justification for the overthrow of the monarchy, condemning it as an out-dated institution which stifled development.

Latin American positivism also absorbed the ideas of Social Darwinism, which posited a racial hierarchy in which whites were deemed superior to other races. In Latin America such doctrines relegated the majority of the population to an inferior status, and they were partly responsible for the attempts to encourage European immigration in many countries so as to whiten the population and improve the chances of progress. Scientific positivism thus provided a modern rationale for the great historic goal of the white creole élites – the right to become a genuine ruling class.

At the end of the century Latin American liberalism had acquired a self-serving, complacent quality. Though conscious of the fragility of the nation state, it actually contributed to its inherent weakness by accepting racial divisions as insuperable and by failing to generate a truly inclusive sense of nationhood. Moreover, by justifying the leadership of the white minorities over other classes and races, it glossed over critical shortcomings of those same élites.

The fact was that the traditional seigneurial mentality of the creole élites was not dispelled by the export-economies. For the creole magnates were not forced to act as risk-taking capitalists; they could afford to retain the economic outlook of mercantilists or *rentiers* because they were merely exploiting commodities in which they possessed a near monopoly in world markets, and which could be produced relatively easily because of an abundance of land, minerals and servile labour. And so, for all the enormous material progress of the last quarter of the nineteenth century, Latin American capitalism remained essentially weak: 'The imminent necessity to revolutionize continually the forces of production, possibly the major driving force in metropolitan capitalism, tended therefore to be rather deficient in Latin America'.* It was little wonder, then, that the comparatively inert structures of the economy and society of Latin America were unable to withstand the strain when in the early decades of the twentieth century new social forces articulated political demands and economic crises disturbed world markets.

---

* Bill Albert, *South America and the World Economy from Independence to 1930*, Studies in Economic and Social History (Macmillan: London, 1983), p. 40.

8. 'Civilization and Barbarism':
Literary and Cultural Developments I

The unrest which afflicted Spanish American societies well after the wars of independence were over was to leave its mark on the culture of the new republics. There was a general awareness among educated creoles that lawlessness threatened to become endemic and might frustrate the creation of the free and prosperous nations envisaged by the Liberators. It was fear of this 'barbarism', this appalling breakdown of social and political order, that informed much of the literature that would be produced in the nineteenth century and beyond.

It was clear that barbarism would have to be tamed by 'civilization', but the question was: what form of civilization was best able to achieve this? Traditionalists looked to the Catholic heritage of Spain, suitably modified to take account of the fact of independence. Liberals turned to the modern values of the Enlightenment – the primacy of reason, sovereignty of the people and equality before the law. This lack of consensus among the ideological leaders of the new nations was itself a powerful factor in the perpetuation of 'barbarism'. Neither camp, in fact, enjoyed a cogent position. The political recipe of the traditionalists was flawed by the absence of a monarchy, an indispensable ingredient. Liberals, on the other hand, might have won the broad constitutional argument for a republic, but so long as they failed to change the customs of the people they would remain a largely urban minority in overwhelmingly rural societies dominated by tradition.

As a result, both conservatives and liberals had difficulty in defining a cultural identity for the new nations. If conservatives extolled the virtues of Hispanic tradition, how could they justify the break with Spain? Liberals, on the other hand, were fond of asserting a distinctive American identity in opposition to Spain, but their ideas were obviously derived from the European Enlightenment and were quite alien to the common people of all ethnic groups; this made liberals vulnerable to the charge of acting as the agents of foreign influences that went against the true spirit of the people. The two great themes of modern Latin American literature thus originated in the experience of independence: first, the aspiration to found a just social order, whether on conservative or liberal principles; and secondly, the quest for an authentic American identity. Both themes remain as vital today as they were in the early 1800s, though political circumstances would, of course, change the terms in which they were presented at different periods and in different countries.

A prime example of this variation is the divergence that is evident in the cultural development of Brazil and Spanish America. What set Brazil apart was its comparatively smooth transition to independence under a constitutional monarchy. Because links with the colonial past were not so brutally severed and a broad consensus among the ruling classes was preserved, Brazilian culture was able to evolve without experiencing the convulsions of its neighbours. Continuity and stability allowed artists to produce their work without the pressures of constant ideological strife. Brazil's artistic achievement in the nineteenth century was therefore considerably greater than Spanish America's: by the end of the century Brazil could boast two major novelists and at least one of the best poets it has yet produced.

In Spanish America, on the other hand, cultural life was weakened by political turbulence and economic uncertainty. Polemics tended to overwhelm invention and, in the circumstances, no great writer emerged, certainly no writer capable of producing a substantial body of work at a consistently high level. Some powerful literary works were created, but they were isolated phenomena that managed to condense the confusions of their age in memorable forms. Towards the end of the century, when the major republics had become integrated into the world economy and their ruling classes had begun to cohere and prosper, literary creation was better able to flourish – the last three decades or so saw the appearance of a few literary masterpieces. At the turn of the century a new receptivity to modern European culture, especially in poetry, paved the way for the great literary efflorescence that was to come in the 1920s.

Neo-classicism and the Romantic Revolt

By the end of the eighteenth century France had largely replaced Spain as the cultural lodestar of Latin America, and French-inspired neo-classical styles and tastes had succeeded the Iberian baroque traditions that had held sway since the early seventeenth century. Bolstered by the political triumph of liberal republicanism, neo-classicism dominated the arts during the period of the independence wars and until the 1840s. For the men who first seized the Napoleonic crisis of 1808 as an opportunity to make a clean break with the Spanish monarchy were animated by secular, radical attitudes inspired by the French and American revolutions: Antonio Nariño, Francisco de Miranda, Simón Rodríguez and Simón Bolívar in New Granada, and the Argentines Mariano Moreno, Manuel Belgrano and Bernardino Rivadavia, all dreamed of building modern, rational liberal republics on the ruins of the Hispanic 'tyranny'.

The critical thrust of this neo-classical Enlightenment culture is evident in the first major novel to appear in Spanish America, El periquillo sarniento ('The Itchy Parrot', 1816) by the reforming Mexican journalist Fernández de Lizardi. Written in order to circumvent the censorship of the viceregal government, it was an attack on the corruption and injustice of colonial society and advocated liberal values – freedom of thought and speech in particular. And if Lizardi's novel anticipated the theme of founding a just society, the matter of cultural identity would be raised by the Ecuadorian poet José Joaquín de Olmedo even at the moment of celebrating the heroic emancipation of the colonies in his paean to Bolívar, La victoria de Junín ('The Victory of Junín', 1825). Into his sonorous neo-classical verse praising the creole heroes of the war Olmedo introduces a consciously indigenous element, as the spirit of the Inca Huayna Capac predicts the final victory over the Spaniards at Ayacucho. Thus we find liberal creoles essaying a new americanismo – disclaiming the heritage of Spain by evoking an ideal vision of the Indian past.

Yet in the years following independence most republics experienced a conservative reaction in the face of political disintegration. Even liberals tempered their revolutionary fervour with an awareness of the need for stability and for some continuing link with Iberian traditions. Indeed, post-independence liberalism came to have more in common with the cautious reformism of colonial Bourbon and Pombaline officials than with the radicalism of the Liberators and their 'precursors'. The exemplary figure in this respect was the architect of the Brazilian transition to independence, José Bonifácio de Andrada e Silva, a man of encyclopedic learning – lawyer, statesman, essayist and neo-classical poet. His closest equivalent in Spanish America was the Venezuelan Andrés Bello, once tutor to Bolívar but later an exile in Chile, possibly because of his belief in a monarchical solution to the crisis of independence.

Bello's major works were in the fields of philology, law, philosophy and education – he was in effect the founder of the modern University of Chile – but he was also an accomplished poet, and it is in his poetry that one observes the true direction of his thought: he was an advocate of a cultural reconciliation with Spain and of building bridges to the European past in order to civilize the barbarism of America. His neo-classical aesthetics, in striving for harmony and measure, were well suited to his conservative liberalism. Yet he did not renounce *americanismo*, rather he produced the first important work on an Americanist theme. In his *Alocución a la poesía* ('Allocution to Poetry', 1823) he exhorts the spirit of poetry to leave Europe, old and exhausted as it is, and to come to find new vigour in the virginal lands of America. The complementary *Silva a la agricultura de la zona tórrida* ('Agriculture in the Torrid Zone', 1826) was conceived as a *Georgics* of the New World, counselling the gentle husbandry of the soil and its copious fruits as a means to founding a rationally ordered society. For Bello, then, independence did not entail a denial of the civilization of the Old World; his aim was to bring the new-born republics within the embrace of the classical traditions of Greece and Rome.

By the 1830s and 1840s, however, Bello's Virgilian ideal of a fruitful partnership of man and Nature, of past and present, was no longer convincing to a younger generation of intellectuals, who were appalled by the rule of bloodthirsty *caudillos*. As liberalism acquired a radical political thrust once more, the restraints of neo-classicism gave way to an impassioned romanticism, which made its first appearance in Argentina in the 1830s in the course of the long struggle against the tyrant Juan Manuel de Rosas, who embodied for liberals the worst vices of the Spanish heritage.

The man conventionally credited with bringing romanticism to Spanish America was Esteban Echeverría, who spent five years in Paris before returning to Buenos Aires in 1830, where he was to combine a career as a man of letters and as a political agitator against Rosas. As a poet, Echeverría was popular though not particularly skilled: he is chiefly remembered for his narrative ballad *La cautiva* ('The Captive', 1837), the story of a white girl's escape from enslavement by nomadic Indians. Echeverría inaugurated the theme of the pampas as an archetypal landscape – a place of barbarism, but also the crucible of national identity for Argentina. He also wrote *El matadero* ('The Slaughterhouse', 1838), a short satirical prose piece in which a slaughterhouse becomes a powerful symbol of Rosas's oppression of liberals in Buenos Aires. In 1839 Echeverría helped to found the Asociación de Mayo, a group of young anti-Rosas activists, many of whom were to become important writers and future liberal leaders of Argentina. His *Dogma socialista* (1837) was regarded as the manifesto of this group and, despite its title, set out the principles of classical liberalism; the term *socialismo* referred to a consensus of values that would provide the basis of a cohesive social order. Another notable liberal writer belonging to the Asociación de Mayo was the poet José Mármol, whose period of incarceration under Rosas provided the creative impetus for poetry and plays, as well as *Amalia* (1851), his celebrated romantic novel with its marked anti-Rosas theme.

Bartolomé Mitre, the general who finally broke the power of the conservative *caudillos* and assumed the presidency of the republic in 1862, founded the newspaper *La Nación* in 1870, which developed into one of the great organs of the Argentine press, and wrote a romantic novel *Soledad* ('Solitude', 1847). Mitre shared the ambivalence of the Argentine romantics towards the common people: they were portrayed at times as agents of barbarism (as in Echeverría's *El matadero* or Mármol's *Amalia*) and yet idealized on other occasions because of their folk culture, the basis of an authentic American identity. Though a patrician and a Europeanizing liberal, Mitre was the first to compose a poem about the legendary gaucho *Santos Vega* (1838), a favourite subject with later gauchesque poets.

The gauchesque genre had its origins during the wars of independence in the River Plate area. It was influenced by the Spanish tradition of the *cuadro de costumbres*, a witty sketch of popular customs whose literary pedigree went back to the fifteenth century at least. Gaucho *costumbrismo* appealed to the romantics because it seemed to them to reflect a truly American way of life. In fact the genre, as Jorge Luis Borges was fond of pointing out, was favoured by educated city men who wrote impersonations of the manners and idioms of the gaucho. The most skilful poems were the *cielitos* and *diálogos* of the Uruguayan Bartolomé Hidalgo, which were used to comment on public issues at the time of the independence struggles. The liberals of the Asociación de Mayo adopted this tradition of popular satire as a vehicle of propaganda against Rosas and the conservative *federales*. Hilario Ascasubi won great acclaim between 1850 and 1872 for mordant sketches written in the name of the gaucho Santos Vega. Estanislao del Campo is remembered for his classic *Fausto* (1866), which transposed the old gauchesque topic of a duel with the devil to the city of Buenos Aires in the odd tale of a simple gaucho who recounts his experience of seeing a performance of Gounod's *Faust* in the fashionable Teatro Colón. It was a double-edged subject, for the rude country ways of the gaucho provided amusement for the elegant classes of Buenos Aires; but, at the same time, did not the gaucho's puzzlement at an imported French opera on the Faust theme betray a general anxiety that Argentina might lose its soul to the devil of European commerce?

This romantic ambivalence towards the gaucho underlies what may be regarded as the single most influential literary work of modern Spanish American culture – the long polemical essay by Domingo Sarmiento, *Facundo o la civilización y la barbarie* ('Facundo: Civilization and Barbarism', 1845), where the liberal project for Latin America is most fully and passionately expressed. It takes the form of a biography of the federalist *caudillo* Facundo Quiroga, who rose to power in the interior province of San Juan and pursued a violent career in the blood-soaked national politics of the period following independence until he was treacherously assassinated, probably on the orders of his rival Rosas. Sarmiento's *Facundo* is important because it squarely addresses the question of nation-building at a time when Latin American liberalism had been in retreat after the cruel disillusionment which had overcome the generation of Bolívar and San Martín in the aftermath of independence.

A crude and tendentious view of Sarmiento's essay has it that the author associated America with barbarism and civilization with Europe. But this is to misunderstand the issue. Barbarism for Sarmiento simply meant the lack of good government based on legitimate authority, a ruinous anarchy resulting from the lawless power struggles of regional tyrants. Sarmiento well understood the inherent weakness of the Latin American state after independence, and the resultant vulnerability of society to abuses of civil rights. His essay provided a prophetic insight into the features of populist dictatorship that were to become endemic all over Latin America. He shows how Rosas maintained himself in power through a hysterical personality cult – by manipulating lower-class fears and superstitions, by mindless sloganizing and neighbourhood spying, by control of the press, and even by the use of death squads. It was this kind of political barbarism which needed to be civilized by just laws and democratic institutions. Barbarism was not a Latin American problem as such, but a perennial risk run by all human societies.

For Sarmiento, the young republics of Spanish America would have to overcome the perils of barbarism by drawing on the political theory and institutions developed in Europe since the Enlightenment, as the USA had managed to do so successfully. He made a distinction between two forms of civilization available to rulers of Spanish America: there was the clerical civilization of Catholic Spain and the modern liberal civilization of the Enlightenment. The former, in his view, was incapable of turning back the tide of barbarism which had surged up from the outback and had all but engulfed the cities. Sarmiento portrays the inland city of Córdoba as a somnolent relic of Hispanic traditionalism, its venerable buildings reflected on the stagnant waters of an ornamental lake. By way of contrast he describes the vitality of Buenos Aires, standing at the mouth of the great river-system of the Plata and open to the currents of the Atlantic, a thriving port equipped to trade in goods and ideas with the world at large.

Sarmiento's seminal essay became embroiled in endless controversy (still very much alive today) because he allowed his hatred of Rosas to distort his analysis of the condition of post-independence Argentina. The great flaw in his argument is his identification of the pampas as the source of barbarism and of the gaucho as its agent. In this he was influenced more by his friend Echeverría and the stereotypes of gauchesque literature than by direct observation – Sarmiento was a city man with minimal experience of life on the pampas when he wrote *Facundo*. The fact was that neither Facundo Quiroga nor Rosas were gauchos; they simply used them and other lower-class groups to further their own ambitions. Sarmiento could well have argued that these reactionary *caudillos* had exploited the gauchos and perverted their values. In this way he would have avoided the controversial association of the gaucho with the 'barbarism' which had to be overcome. As would occur with the cowboy in the USA or the *bandeirante* of São Paulo in Brazil, the gaucho could have been converted by the Argentine liberals into a mythical figure of progress, an authentic son of the Argentine soil whose rugged individualism and love of freedom foreshadowed the entrepreneurial culture that would carry the young republic towards greatness and prosperity. Instead, he was portrayed in *Facundo* as the embodiment of barbarism and cultural backwardness.

This missed ideological opportunity haunts the pages of *Facundo* in the ambivalence with which Sarmiento depicts the life and customs of the gauchos. As a romantic, he cannot fail to admire the strength of their autochthonous culture – their intimate knowledge of the pampas, their rustic skills, their prowess with knife and guitar; and yet the manner in which he has framed the argument demands that he reject their way of life as a pattern for modern Argentina. After *Facundo* the idea of progress in Argentina would forever seem to be at odds with the country's very fragile sense of identity.

This self-defeating conflict would be given a mythical resonance by José Hernández's highly influential narrative poem, *El gaucho Martín Fierro* (part I, 1872; part II, 1879), written well after the fall of the *caudillo* Rosas in 1852, when Sarmiento himself had become president of the republic and the free-wheeling life of the pampas was rapidly giving way to a modern economy based on well-defined property rights, wheat-growing *estancias*, settlements of foreign immigrants and a network of railways.

José Hernández realized in a single work of art the enormous mythic potential of the gaucho when his traditional way of life was on the point of disappearing. The first part of *Martín Fierro* tells the story of an innocent gaucho's forced conscription into the army to serve in a frontier garrison against the Indians of the pampas. After constant abuse and exploitation by the authorities he deserts and is forced to take refuge with the Indians. This first part is a moving lament for a doomed way of life, in which the gaucho enjoyed the freedom of the pampas as well as a sense of camaraderie with his fellows under the patriarchal authority of a benevolent *patrón*. It reads as the protest of a Hispanic conservative against a modernizing government that had broken faith with the gauchos, the authentic representatives of the Argentine people.

The sequel, however, is confused; it was written seven years later, when the author was famous and had become a supporter of a new liberal president Avellaneda. Still, the unevenness itself reveals the ideological problems of nation-building in Argentina. *Martín Fierro* is repelled by the barbarism of the Indians, but when he returns to 'civilization' he finds that nothing has changed: all that society can offer him is work as a hired hand on an *estancia*. Since Hernández could do nothing with his persecuted gaucho that would not humiliate him, the central narrative breaks up into a number of rambling stories by different characters until it draws to an inconclusive end with Fierro offering his sons the counsels of an errant father before they all ride off once more into the unknown.

Taken as a whole, the poem's imaginative power derives from the fact that it traces the fall of a traditional patriarchal order, whose members are uprooted from their native soil and finally forced to live as nameless fugitives at the mercy of chance. The poet Leopoldo Lugones called *Martín Fierro* the national epic of Argentina, but it is a strange epic indeed, for instead of celebrating the exploits of a mythical hero of the nation it enshrines a sense of betrayal at the heart of the Argentine self-image: the modern liberal state is implicitly personified as a dishonourable *patrón* willing to break old bonds and loyalties for the sake of material progress.

By transforming the gaucho into an ambivalent national symbol, Hernandéz crystallized the problem of national identity which all the Latin American republics would experience. And yet this occurred in Argentina because the problem was perceived there earlier, and more starkly, than in other parts of the Indies. Of all the republics, Argentina had the strongest liberal culture, largely based in the port city of Buenos Aires; and its liberalism was so strong precisely because the region had very weak links with colonial institutions, including the Church, having been a fairly empty and neglected outpost of empire until the last decades of the previous century. What is more, because there were no ancient communities of sedentary Indians in its territory, it could write off the nomadic tribes of the pampas as 'barbarians'. As a result, even the conservative classes of Argentina did not appreciate the political virtues of the Catholic monarchy as deeply as their counterparts in, say, Mexico or Peru. Liberalism was the only intelligent response to the anarchy of the *caudillos*, but liberalism threatened also to rob the young nation of a specific identity. Elsewhere the ideological contest between liberalism and conservatism was more evenly matched, and the problem of identity therefore less acute, because the intellectual case for Catholic traditionalism was so much more persuasive.

The powerful clashes between conservatives and liberals, and the resultant instability in most republics of Spanish America, explain to a degree the absence of a substantial literary culture such as developed in Brazil and among liberals in Argentina. The fierce quarrels within the creole ruling classes and the rapid turnover of political regimes prevented artistic life from evolving at its own pace and on its own terms. In these troubled times the public went for uncontroversial subjects. A highly social art such as the theatre failed to produce any dramatist of note. Audiences knew what they liked, and this tended to be Spanish *zarzuelas*, Italian opera, song recitals and the odd comedy of manners or historical melodrama. In painting, architecture and music the academies clung to outdated or derivative styles, and in most cases a pallid neo-classicism prevailed. Economic stagnation also accounts for the general mediocrity of artistic production; the market for art and literature was limited and usually restricted to the larger cities, where cultural institutions such as universities, academies, publishing houses and newspapers were able to provide a public for the artist or the man of letters. The patronage of the Church, which was such an important stimulus to art in colonial times, was on the decline, due as much to the fiscal assaults on ecclesiastical wealth by liberal governments as to the increasing secularization of national culture.

In literature, romanticism held sway until roughly the last decade of the century. There was little development towards realism in the novel as would occur in Europe, including Spain. The reasons for this are not clear. It is possible that there was not enough of an urban middle-class readership for the kind of capacious novels of character and social analysis that were to become so popular in the Old World. Social criticism there indeed was but, as we have seen in Argentina, it took the traditional Hispanic form of the *cuadro de costumbres*, the witty snapshot of social types written either as a prose sketch or as a short theatrical piece. Another minor Hispanic genre that found favour in America was the *leyenda*, a brief prose poem on a historical subject created by Spanish romantics such as the Duke of Rivas and Gustavo Adolfo

Bécquer. In Peru the *leyenda* and the *cuadro de costumbres* would blend into the *tradición*, a genre created by Ricardo Palma in the 1850s, and which appeared as a regular series of prose pieces between 1870 and 1915.

The Peruvian upper classes had remained attached to things Spanish. Thanks to the improbable wealth derived from the *guano* bonanza, Lima was able in the mid-century to recover the odd glimmer of the social brilliance she had enjoyed in her colonial heyday. Peruvian men of letters were prone to sing 'a serenade under the balconies of the viceroyalty'.* Skilful playwrights like Felipe Pardo and Manuel Ascensio Segura used *costumbrismo* to satirize the vulgarities of the republican regime; some writers like José Antonio Lavalle openly displayed their admiration for the colonial period. Ricardo Palma's achievement was to have taken this colonialist nostalgia and infused it with the sardonic wit of the *limeños*. His *tradiciones* strike an ironic balance between past and present. Under the pretence of having found his material in the archives, Palma elaborated piquant fantasies which allowed him to poke fun at perennial Hispanic vices and to dress up criticism of his own society in period costume. Somewhat neglected nowadays, Ricardo Palma is none the less an important figure, whose work, according to a modern critic, 'laid the basis of a national literature'.†

Of the major genres of narrative fiction, historical and sentimental romances predominated. The historical romance, modelled on the works of Sir Walter Scott, Victor Hugo and Chateaubriand, was especially popular in new nations searching for a historical identity. But since the past was such a controversial subject in Spanish America, historical romances tended to reproduce the stark divisions of politics: liberals generally denounced Spain and somewhat improbably idealized the ancient Indian civilizations, while conservatives harked back to the colonial period. In Mexico the more notable writers of historical fiction were associated with the mid-century liberal movement of *La Reforma*. Manuel Payno produced the first serial novels to appear in Mexico; Vicente Riva Palacio, a friend of Benito Juárez, wrote novels attacking the Spanish Inquisition, as well as melodramas and short stories; Eligio Ancona took themes from the Conquest, presenting the Aztecs in a heroic light.

The sentimental romances, too, reflected political allegiances. As a literary mode, romance describes a quest for personal fulfilment in an ideally integrated order. The fact that these Spanish American love stories have unhappy endings reveals both an intense longing for a unified society and a fateful

---

* José Carlos Mariátegui, 'El proceso de la literatura', *Siete ensayos de interpretación de la realidad peruana* (Biblioteca Amauta: Lima, 1975 [1928]), p. 245.

† Gerald Martin, *Cambridge History of Latin America*, vol. 3, p. 832.

awareness of its elusiveness. Love across racial or social boundaries was the quintessential theme of these romances, whose plots usually involved a girl of mixed race or unorthodox background falling in love with a white creole. Liberal writers portrayed the obstacles to happiness as deriving from the unjust legacy of the colonial power. The liberal Argentine romances *Amalia* and *Soledad* have already been mentioned. Cirilo Villaverde, a Cuban patriot who narrowly missed being garrotted by the Spanish, produced a classic anti-slavery novel in *Cecilia Valdés* (part I, 1839; part II, 1882), in which a mulatto girl loves a white man without realizing that he is the legitimate son of her own natural father. A history of racial exploitation thus leads to personal and social frustration.

Even more interesting as cultural documents are the romances written by conservative Catholics. Invariably they invoke traditional Hispanic patriarchy (often associated with the society of the hacienda) as a social order uniquely capable of integrating the races and classes under a just and benevolent authority. Implicitly, at least, there is a yearning for the Catholic traditions of Spain. *Cumandá* (1879), by Juan León Mera, a fervent supporter of the ultra-Catholic dictator of Ecuador, Gabriel García Moreno, tells of a young girl raised in a community of Indians who cannot realize her love for the son of a white landowner. Though the races remain unreconciled, Mera portrays Christian love as the only force capable of bringing them together. Manuel Galván's *Enriquillo* (1882), set in Santo Domingo during the early days of the colony, tells of the love of an Indian youth for a half-Spanish girl, and introduces Bartolomé de las Casas, the friar who famously championed Indian rights, as a character in the story in order to suggest that Christian tutelage alone can provide for just relations between the races.

By far the most successful romance of the nineteenth century was *María* (1867) by the Colombian Jorge Isaacs. It remains one of the best-loved works of fiction ever produced in Latin America. The narrative is subtly paced to produce an intense emotional response from the reader, its prose style admirably evokes a fresh, idyllic picture of the natural world, and the characters are portrayed with exceptional psychological delicacy. Although *María* affords an idealized picture of social and ethnic relations in a hacienda society under the authority of a benign patriarch, it alludes to a mysterious crisis that prevents the love of the *hacendado*'s son for his fragile cousin from being fulfilled and duly socialized in marriage. And so *María* allows its readers to dream of a traditional Spanish American order untouched by historical change, while its gentle fatalism points to the imminent dissolution of that exquisite reverie and to the darkness and violence that lie beyond.

Brazil: Romanticism and the Indian

A sense of cultural independence from Portugal was fairly slow to appear in Brazil, the separation of the two Crowns having been so gradual. Only after 1838, when the Historical and Geographical Institute of Brazil was founded, did the search for a distinctive national identity acquire general significance. It was at this time that intellectuals first began to consider the Indian – long ago wiped out from the major areas of European and African settlement – as the indigenous prototype of the new Brazilian. The historian Francisco Adolfo de Varnhagen urged the establishment of schools of native languages so as to foster a national literature as the basic foundation of cultural independence and unity. The other great stimulus to the development of an Indianist movement was romanticism, whose origins in Brazil can be traced to the publication in 1836 of a collection of verse, *Suspiros Poéticos e Saudades* ('Poetic Sighs') by Domingos José Gonçalves de Magalhães. Aristocratic and conservative, Brazilian romanticism tried to knit an idealized native prehistory with sentimental reflections on colonial life. Until the 1870s romantic Indianism dominated Brazilian letters and inspired a flood of novels, plays, lyrics and narrative poetry.

The greatest romantic poet, and one who achieved an authentic Brazilian accent in his work, was Antônio Gonçalves Dias, the illegitimate son of a Portuguese immigrant and an Afro-Indian mother, who rose to prominence as public servant, ethnographer and a friend of the emperor Pedro II. His poems endure as elegies for bygone ages of heroism and idyllic happiness; the famous 'Canção do Exílio' ('Song of Exile') is one of the most cherished pieces of all Brazilian literature. Gonçalves Dias depicted the Tupi Indian in numerous poems as a worthy symbol of the national spirit, and in 1857 published four cantos of an Indianist epic – *Os Tambiras* ('The Tambiras') – which remained unfinished. Yet, at the same time, he worked towards accommodating the Portuguese and the despised African within his idealized account of Brazilian origins. For instance, his idiosyncratic *Sextilhas de Frei Antão* ('Sextets of Brother Anthony', 1848) is a heroic poem written in medieval Portuguese about Portugal's crusades in North Africa. It shows how the realities of racial mixture in Brazil were, in fact, too laden with guilt to be treated other than at a safe distance through historical fantasy.

The romantic agony of the *poète maudit* made its appearance much earlier in Brazil than in Spanish America, where it would not make any real impact until the 1880s. The death-haunted Alvares de Azevedo, the 'poet of doubt', expired in 1852 at the age of twenty-one. The sweet love lyrics of Casimiro de Abreu, who died at the same age in 1860, can still appeal to the young. Antônio de Castro Alves, though he too died at a premature age after a debauched life, possessed a more powerful imagination – it was compared to the flight of a condor – and he achieved a great reputation for his spellbinding recitals in the cause of the abolition of slavery. His poem 'O Navio Negreiro' ('The Slave Ship') is a classic. Castro Alves drew attention to the plight of the contemporary black, whose widespread presence in Brazilian society had been virtually ignored in the romantics' account of the origins of the nation.

The optimistic view of Brazil's origins was powerfully expressed by the romantic novelist José de Alencar, who was born in 1829 into a distinguished family of Pernambuco. Alencar took to heart the problem of founding a national literature, and in 1856 made his name by attacking, for being too European in style and form, the attempts by Gonçalves de Magalhães, the founder of Brazilian romanticism, to write an epic on an Indianist theme. But a truly American verse epic eluded Alencar too: his attempt at one, *Os Filhos de Tupan* ('The Children of the God Tupa', 1867), remained unfinished. Nevertheless, he continued to write novels, whose subject-matter ranged from Indianism and colonial history to contemporary urban and rural life. These novels, he came to realize later, would serve as the foundation of the national literature he wanted to see established.

Certainly, no novelist before Alencar had produced work of such quality and breadth. The first romantic novelist, Manoel de Macedo, wrote cloyingly sentimental stories, of which *A Moreninha* ('The Little Dark Girl', 1844) is still remembered. Other romances in a similar vein were *A Escrava Isaura* ('Isaura the Slave', 1875) by Bernardo Guimarães, Escragnolle de Taunay's *Inocência* ('Innocence', 1872), and the historical fiction of Antônio Gonçalves Teixeira e Sousa. These works are similar to the Spanish American romances about star-crossed lovers of different social or racial backgrounds. An exception was the novel *Memórias de um Sargento de Milícias* ('Memories of a Militia Sergeant', 1853) by Manuel Antônio de Almeida, which evoked life in Rio de Janeiro during the period following the Portuguese king's arrival in Brazil. Its focus on social types and its plain, ironic style anticipate the realist novels of the late nineteenth century.

José de Alencar was the outstanding talent because of the fertility of his imagination, the power of his prose style and his great talents as a myth-maker. Encompassing most aspects of Brazilian life and history, his fiction catered, in the words of Antônio Cándido, to the 'profound Brazilian desire to perpetuate a convention that gives a nation of half-breeds the alibi of a heroic racial past and which provides a young nation with the resonance of a legendary history'.* The fundamental theme of Alencar's mythologizing is the fusion of Indian innocence and purity with Portuguese bravery, resulting in the birth of Brazil. His most famous novels such as *O Guaraní* ('The Guarani Indian', 1857) and *Iracema* (1865) describe love affairs between Indians and whites in which Alencar invariably sacrifices the Indian world to the Portuguese, though it is a process which, like childbirth, is depicted as painful but life-giving – for instance, Moacir, the son of the Indian girl Iracema by the conquistador Martim, bears the qualities of both races: he is the first true Brazilian.

What is remarkable about Alencar is his desire to incorporate the colonial experience in the historical self-image of the new nation. By contrast, in Spanish America, the colonial period became an ideological battleground between liberals and conservatives, with writers stressing division and rupture by exalting the achievements of one race to the exclusion of the other. And yet, as the mythologist of the white Brazilian élites, Alencar was unable or unwilling to find a place for the enslaved African in his version of national origins, for this was a problem which threatened to disrupt the comforting dream-world he had so brilliantly concocted. Alencar's work reflects the great optimism of Brazil's ruling classes, their interest in preserving national unity and their appetite for progress. This attitude would be a constant feature of Brazil's independent history and one which would distinguish it from most of the republics of Spanish America, where the creole élites were prone to recurrent bouts of historical pessimism.

The Rule of Positivism

From the 1870s the white élites of both Spanish America and Brazil were able to enjoy the mounting benefits of trade with Europe. As the export-economies flourished in the major countries, ideological conflicts subsided and, on the whole, liberals took control of the state either by constitutional means or by establishing progressive dictatorships. The romantic liberalism which had inspired the struggles for liberty and political rights during the middle decades of the century was superseded by a more hard-headed doctrine which appealed to science in order to justify the political leadership of the white élites in the multiracial nations of Latin America.

This new version of liberal ideology was derived from the positivism of

* Quoted in David Haberly, *Three Sad Races: Racial Identity and National Consciousness in Brazilian Literature* (Cambridge University Press: Cambridge, 1983), p. 17.

the French philosopher Auguste Comte. It regarded scientific method as the only means to truth: by observation and experiment it was possible to arrive at a knowledge of facts and the basic laws of nature and society. Because only an enlightened minority was capable of acquiring this scientific outlook, the business of government should be conducted by an élite prepared to undertake the measures necessary to modernize backward countries where 'the people' had been vitiated by superstition and unproductive habits.

In republics with large non-white populations, this kind of 'scientific politics' came very close to an officially sanctioned racism – Indians, mestizos and blacks tended to be regarded as irredeemably unskilled, indeed as obstacles to the nation's progress. Under such conditions, as the Mexican positivist Justo Sierra famously observed, it might be necessary to 'try a little tyranny' for the sake of development. Mexican *científicos* like Sierra, in fact, provided a modernizing rationale for the forty-year dictatorship of the liberal *caudillo* Porfirio Díaz. In Brazil, positivists were in the van of the attack on the monarchy, and it was their influence on the high command that encouraged the army to interfere in politics: the *coup d'état* that ushered in the republic in 1889 inaugurated a long tradition of technocracy underwritten by military governments.

The attitude of Latin American positivists towards the question of racial difference was conditioned by Herbert Spencer's evolutionary theories of social development and racial determinism. These were oversimplified into a crude Social Darwinism, which held that certain races were better adapted to the struggle for survival than others. The nordic races were the fittest; Latins were less capable; further down the scale came coloured peoples such as the Amerindians; last of all came the blacks. People of mixed blood, of which there were huge numbers in Latin America, were woefully degenerate. Social Darwinism thus provided a 'scientific' underpinning for white rule. In many countries it led to a policy of encouraging the mass immigration of whites with the object of improving the genetic stock of the population, thereby enhancing the prospects of modern development. Unfortunately, most of these immigrants were not of the highest quality by the criteria of the Social Darwinists: there were too many southern Italians, Spaniards, Portuguese and East European Jews instead of the blond nordic farmers who might conceivably have performed the trick of turning Latin America into another Midwest of the USA.

Positivism strongly reinforced a tendency to admire modern trends in Europe and the USA. As the export trade enriched the big cities, their centres were patterned on the urban planning of Haussmann's Paris – straight thoroughfares and wide boulevards flanked by imposing blocks of flats and other grand public buildings. By the beginning of the twentieth century the appetite for modern living had become insatiable in the cities: bicycles, trams and motorcars made their appearance, as would electricity, the telephone and other technical inventions. An urban popular culture emerged based on cheap newspapers, the music hall, variety theatres and circuses. These were the early forms of mass entertainment in Latin America, and the public they catered for would in due course be won over by the cinema and radio.

All of this was not so different from what was happening in Europe or North America at the time. In fact, a great gulf was opening up between the life of the big cities in Latin America and the traditional ways of the country. To a city-dweller, whether rich or proletarian, urban Europe would have been less alien than the Latin American countryside, where a largely coloured mass of peasants toiled in semi-feudal haciendas or in the Indian communities. So much so that in the early decades of the twentieth century city-bred writers would go out into the rural areas and appraise the natural world with a mixture of wonderment and dread. These attempts to bridge the gulf between the country and the city would give rise to a 'regionalist' movement in literature and the arts.

Positivism encouraged a reaction against romantic passion in literature. Parnassianism in poetry and naturalism in fiction aimed at a kind of scientific objectivity, tempering emotion by impeccable formalism or by detached social analysis. Brazil was to absorb these French influences earlier and more fully than Spanish America.

Brazil: Parnassianism, Symbolism and Naturalism

Parnassianism began to make its mark in the 1870s in the poetry of Luís Guimarães and Joaquim Maria Machado de Assis (the latter is now more celebrated as a novelist, as we shall see below). After the coming of the republic, Parnassians took over the literary establishment and in 1897 they founded the Brazilian Academy of Letters, with Machado de Assis as its first president. For poets such as Raimundo Correia, Alberto de Oliveira and Olavo Bilac, art was an autonomous domain capable of distilling experience into controlled and immutable forms.

Yet, when Parnassianism was at its height in Brazil, it had been superseded by symbolism in Paris. Symbolism, which entailed a measured return to romantic subjectivism, made little headway in Brazil, but it did produce one poet of exceptional quality, João da Cruz e Sousa, a pure black born to slaves and educated by his father's owners, but treated as a literary outcast throughout his short life. Cruz e Sousa's bitterness at his condition burst through Parnassian formalism and issued in powerful, blasphemous poems which explored the painful contradictions between white culture and his African roots. Known as the 'black swan of symbolism', he gave the lie both to romantic myths of Brazil's Indo-Portuguese origins and to positivist fantasies of white supremacy. Refused entry to Parnassus, he died in wretched circumstances, his work neglected until the 1940s.

In narrative fiction, Parnassian objectivity found expression through naturalism, which in Brazil tended to reflect the scientific determinism of positivist thought. The first naturalist novel, *O Mulato* ('The Mulatto', 1881) by Aluízio de Azevedo, shocked the public by its exposure of the obstacles facing a man of colour in society. Azevedo portrayed deprived urban milieux in his other novels, and in *O Homen* ('The Man', 1887) he won notoriety with his analysis of the character of a hysterical woman. Júlio Ribeiro also created a scandal with his frank treatment of sex in *A Carne* ('The Flesh', 1888). Perhaps the most sensational of these naturalist novels was *Bom Crioulo* ('Good Nigger', 1895) by Adolfo Caminha, which described the love of a Negro mariner for an angelic cabin-boy. Arguably the finest of the naturalist novels was Raul Pompéia's *O Ateneu* ('The School', 1888), which gave a psychologically convincing picture of boarding-school life. These followers of Zola dispelled any romantic illusions about social realities, but their works tended to reinforce pessimism about a country which appeared to be so vitiated by race mixture. The result was that social observation often degenerated into mere prurience.

Joaquim Maria Machado de Assis, a mulatto born to parents in the service of wealthy landowners, transcended naturalism altogether and developed into one of the greatest and most original novelists in Latin America. A short-sighted, stammering epileptic, he started his working life in lowly clerical jobs, but rose eventually to become a pillar of the cultural establishment, married to a white woman of good family. His novels and stories, however, are far from complacent: they reveal a profoundly disenchanted vision of the world, a vision which is none the less expressed in a prose style that sparkles with ironic humour. In his three greatest novels *Memórias póstumas de Brás Cubas* ('Epitaph of a Small Winner', 1881), *Quincas Borba* (1891) and *Dom Casmurro* (1899), the travails of individual consciousness are held in balance with the demands of social order, but literary realism is playfully called into question by a probing of narrative illusions (Machado greatly admired Laurence Sterne's *Tristram Shandy*).

Machado's novels have been seen by some critics as anticipating the self-conscious experimental fiction of twentieth-century Latin American writers.

His work, like theirs, is a reaction against the scientific rationalism of the positivists. But Machado, of course, was responding to an ideology which was in the ascendant, while the reaction of later writers came when positivism was on the decline. This in itself is a measure of Machado's importance and originality. Machado, however, was more of a conservative sceptic than a progressive: though a low-born mulatto, he regarded the monarchy as a necessary fiction for unifying a nation whose inherent divisions he knew all too well from his own experience. His aesthetic position is therefore complex: a Parnassian coolness liberated him from romantic agonizing, even though he could see through the specious modernity of the positivists. It was a complexity that befitted the chronicler of a society in transition from monarchy to republic.

Spanish American Modernismo, Realism and Naturalism

Parnassianism and symbolism exerted an influence in Spanish America through the peculiarly Hispanic literary movement called *modernismo*, inaugurated with the publication of the collection *Azul* ('Azure', 1888) by the Nicaraguan poet Rubén Darío. (*Modernismo* must not be confused with European or North American modernism, which appeared in the first decades of the following century and would not make an impact in Latin America until the 1920s.) The movement was felt to be 'modern' because of its Frenchness, its *galicismo mental*, as a Spanish critic put it. This referred to the unheard-of notion of 'art for art's sake' and to the decadent, *fin de siècle* pose of the *poète maudit* affected by *modernistas*.

Modernismo was actually an eclectic movement. It was in some respects a development from romanticism, stressing the darker, more perverse elements, which had tended to be overlooked by the public-spirited romantic liberals of the mid-century. But even though Darío and his disciples discovered the romantic agony, they also took from Parnassianism an aestheticist concern with formal perfection, experimenting with prosody, verse forms and diction. The theory of symbolism was not fully assimilated: it was the Verlaine of the *Fêtes galantes*, rather than Mallarmé, who had the greatest influence. Verlaine was admired for his musicality and the poetic ambience of aristocratic refinement, which Darío successfully captured in his *Prosas profanas* ('Profane Proses', 1896). Darío believed the artist was a spiritual aristocrat, ennobled by his painful search for *lo ideal* through the creation of poetry itself and through a sacralization of sexual love. Indeed, the rapid spread of *modernismo* indicates that Catholicism was losing its central place in the culture of educated creoles.

This might explain why political radicals were attracted to a movement which was essentially élitist – its anti-traditionalism was coupled with a disdain for bourgeois materialism and positivist science. José Martí, the great leader of Cuba's struggle for independence, was also a poet of the first rank, whose work foreshadows and overlaps with Darío's. The Peruvian Manuel González Prada was another important political activist who wrote in a *modernista* vein. More exclusively drawn to literature were Manuel Gutiérrez Nájera (Mexico), Julián del Casal (Cuba) and José Asunción Silva (Colombia). Rubén Darío's residence in Buenos Aires in the late 1890s stimulated the growth of *modernismo* in the River Plate republics. Outstanding poets there were Julio Herrera y Reissig (Uruguay), who cultivated a precious, highly metaphorical style, and Leopoldo Lugones (Argentina), for some a poet equal to Darío himself, who experimented in a variety of genres and who was to remain a dominant figure in Argentine letters for some three decades.

The stylistic effects of *modernismo* are also evident in prose and fiction. Most *modernistas* turned their hand to the prose poem, the short story and the essay; some wrote poetic novels. Otherwise, fiction at the turn of the century came under the influence of French naturalism, though to a much lesser degree than in Brazil. There was a tendency to emphasize heredity and environment as determinants of social behaviour, but novelists were prone to lapse into Hispanic traditions of moralizing and *costumbrismo*. Alberto Blest Gana wrote novels about contemporary Chilean society, and is sometimes likened to Balzac in the breadth of his social observation, but Santiago society was still too small to provide material for a true *comédie humaine*. The influence of Zola can be seen in Baldomero Lillo's stories about the sufferings of Chilean miners in the collections *Sub terra* (1904) and *Sub sole* (1907).

In Buenos Aires, which was growing into a veritable metropolis as the liberal export-economy boomed, novelists turned to social realism and at times to naturalism in order to capture the bewildering social transformations. Lucio Vicente López's *La gran aldea* ('The Big Village', 1884), one of the most celebrated works of realism in Argentina, condemns the loss of traditional values as commercialism pervades the city. The novels of Eugenio Cambaceres, which appeared in the 1880s, were more consistently naturalist and dwelt on topics that were meant to shock – not the least of which was the tide of immigrants, portrayed as bringing corruption to Argentina. Roberto Payró wrote in a vein that mixed the traditions of the picaresque with contemporary realism. A series of novels published between 1906 and 1910 attacked political corruption in the provinces and in the capital. The prolific Manuel Gálvez, influenced by Galdós, Flaubert and Zola, even though he was deeply Catholic himself, chronicled the life of Buenos Aires and the Argentine provinces in a series of skilful novels; his most important work appeared in the 1910s.

More than ever, France was the dominant influence on Spanish American culture. Like the prodigal *rastaquouères* – those Latin American millionaires who flaunted their wealth in Paris in the hope of gaining entry into the *beau monde* – writers and intellectuals loved to put on cosmopolitan airs after visiting the French capital – they had left their Hispanic backwaters and could now swim with the tide of modern life. Indeed, the genre which best reveals the historical significance of *modernismo* is the *crónica*, a journalistic essay on topics that could range from current affairs to the latest marvel of technology. It became a minor art form, at which *modernistas* like Darío and Martí excelled. The master of the *crónica* was the Guatemalan, Enrique Gómez Carrillo, who for some thirty years wrote pieces from Paris that were syndicated in newspapers throughout the continent. Through the *crónica* the middle classes in the cities of Latin America received news of the styles and inventions of the great cultural metropolises of Europe. And despite the *modernista* writers' professed contempt for the beastly bourgeois, the literary ideas of *modernismo* were also a product of that great opening of Spanish America to the modern world which occurred towards the end of the century after the political triumph of liberalism.

Early Reactions against Positivism

During the first decade of the twentieth century a reaction began to set in against positivist ideas, a reaction that would lead to the discrediting of liberalism in the late 1920s. Three historic events served to stimulate this reaction. First, there was the defeat of Spain by the USA in the war over Cuban independence in 1898. Spain's humiliation aroused fears of an 'Anglo-Saxon' threat to the Spanish-speaking world in general, and prompted a revaluation of Hispanic 'spiritual' traditions to counter the materialism of modern civilization. Secondly, in 1896 there occurred at Canudos in the north-east of Brazil a rebellion of Catholic peasants against the liberal republic. This revolt was to reveal the inequalities of progress: there existed a terrible divide between regions like São Paulo, which were rapidly modernizing, and stagnant areas, where traditional society was deeply entrenched. Finally, in 1910 an electoral challenge to the dictator Porfirio Díaz and his positivist *científicos* resulted in the cataclysm of the Mexican Revolution. All three events would call into question the modernizing aims of the liberal élites, and associated with each of them is a key literary text that reflects the new misgivings of intellectuals about the value of modern civilization.

The Spanish defeat of 1898 in Cuba was a demonstration of the power and imperialistic vocation of the USA. It prompted the publication in 1900 of *Ariel*, an essay by the Uruguayan journalist José Enrique Rodó. *Ariel* is a meditation on the nature of civilization, in which Rodó contrasts two forms of society symbolized by Ariel and Caliban. The latter is associated with the USA and represents a state where utilitarian ethics combined with the unguided appetites of the masses produce a new barbarism in which society is no longer ruled by moral values and spiritual ideals. By contrast, Ariel represents civilization, which is characterized by the leadership of an élite capable of subordinating material urges to reason and to spiritual concerns. While stating his admiration for the dynamism of the USA and recognizing the need to modernize, Rodó believed that Latin America should preserve the exalted spirit of Ariel, bequeathed to it by ancient Greece and Rome, and approach mass democracy and modern capitalism with caution.

The impact of *Ariel* was enormous throughout Spanish America in the 1910s and 1920s. It awakened a general desire for cultural affirmation, although this would take diverse forms – a defence of 'Latinity', a search for national 'essences', a renewed preoccupation with *americanismo*. More specifically, it stimulated resentment against US cultural influence. But it made its deepest mark on the young; for instance, the University Reform Movement in Argentina in 1918 invoked the spirit of Ariel in its attack on positivism and entrenched privilege in the universities. *Ariel* also inspired young intellectuals in Mexico to found the 'Athenaeum of Youth' in 1907, a forum for anti-positivist writers which nurtured several prominent supporters of the first phase of the revolution. *Arielismo* even persuaded some positivists to revise their outlook: Justo Sierra, one of the grandest of the *científico* mandarins in Mexico and a minister of education under Porfirio Díaz, delivered a famous lecture on 22 March 1908 in which he exhorted the positivist intelligentsia to dare 'to doubt' the truths of science.

The revolt at Canudos has become a cultural landmark, because it led to the writing of one of the classics of Brazilian literature *Os Sertões* ('Rebellion in the Backlands', 1902) by Euclides da Cunha, a journalist of positivist convictions, who was sent to cover the story for a Rio de Janeiro newspaper. As he witnessed the heroic resistance of the royalist peasants against the increasingly brutal assaults of republican troops, Da Cunha felt torn between his intellectual adherence to liberalism and a compassionate respect for wretched people who would have been dismissed by positivists as degenerate fanatics. This ambivalence of the author gives *Os Sertões* its tremendous emotional force. For the certainties of racial determinism break down before the humanity of the rebels, laying bare the complex realities of Brazil. Da Cunha does not renounce progress, but he begins to see that its fruits cannot be monopolized by an élite. Still, he finds himself at a loss as to how to incorporate the people of the *sertão* (backlands) in the life of a modern nation without destroying their integrity. The dilemmas raised by the book are still unresolved in Latin America today.

The revolution of 1910 shattered the self-confidence of positivists in Mexico: a violent social whirlwind rose up and did away with the progressive dictatorship of Porfirio Díaz. And yet the whirlwind did not subside after the holding of elections; it swept on, leaving a trail of chaos and barbarism over most of the country. This alarming phenomenon is the subject of *Los de abajo* ('The Underdogs', 1916), the classic novel of the Mexican Revolution by Mariano Azuela, a liberal doctor who joined Pancho Villa's forces. Azuela shows how the revolution fails to deliver its promise of reform and justice. Instead, the peasant rebels are caught in a spiral of violent lawlessness that brings no good to anyone (other than to a cynical intellectual who is prepared to exploit the confusion for material gain). The other major chronicler of the Mexican Revolution, Martín Luis Guzmán, author of the excellent novels *El águila y la serpiente* ('The Eagle and the Serpent', 1926) and *La sombra del caudillo* ('The Shadow of the Caudillo', 1929), also gave a disillusioned account of his experience. But *Los de abajo* is the work which most sharply questions the notion of progress, and it is the first novel to present the actual social reality of Latin America as an enigma.

'Civilization and Barbarism' Revisited

If in the first decade of the new century the reality of Latin America presented itself as an enigma, it was because misgivings about positivism raised more general doubts about the established liberal scheme for understanding the historical goals of the independent republics. This scheme can be traced back to the 'precursors' of the independence movement, but, as we have seen, it was most clearly articulated by the Argentine romantic liberal Domingo Sarmiento in his *Facundo* (1845) – the 'barbarism' of lawlessness and violence could be brought under control only by modern 'civilization' based on the rule of law and a system of education informed by the rationalist humanism of the European Enlightenment. However, the three texts discussed above forced a revision of Sarmiento's key terms: *Ariel* warned of a new barbarism lurking within modern societies like the USA; *Os Sertões* cast doubt on the benevolence of the forces of liberal civilization; and *Los de abajo* posed the question whether civilization was possible at all given an endemic tendency to violence in Latin America and the corruptibility of men of liberal education.

Dealing as it did with the newly perceived enigma of Latin American social reality, the bulk of the literature of the 1910s and 1920s inevitably engaged with Sarmiento's nineteenth-century dichotomy between civilization and barbarism. For the most part, this literature was pessimistic, in Brazil as in Spanish America: it was the literature of educated, largely city-raised writers observing life in the outback or in traditional rural areas and despairing of ever creating a modern civilized society. The great new literary theme was the merciless power of nature in America, against which man's puny efforts were doomed to fail. This was a far cry from the classical faith in nature's bounty expressed by Andrés Bello in the 1820s; and the difference indicates how far the morale of liberal intellectuals had declined by the turn of the century.

The success of *Os Sertões* led to a strong regionalist trend in Brazilian literature. In reality, one can observe a bifurcation in the course of Brazilian culture from the 1900s: one strand would persevere with the project of modernization and would remain receptive to international influences; the other would dwell on the backward areas, either on the declining sugar-growing region of the north-east, with its huge black population, or on the *sertões*, the vast backlands of savannah and jungle, the locus of barbarism *par excellence*. The decline of positivism thus engendered a rich literary dialectic of city and *sertão*, the drive for modernity in São Paulo and Rio de Janeiro being accompanied by a running critique of the bases of modern society itself.

The harsh life of the *sertão* was to sap the confidence in the nation's future of the earliest Brazilian regionalists. One of the best regionalist novels, *Chanaan* ('Canaan', 1902) by José Pereira de Graça Aranha, described the bewilderment of two German immigrants experiencing the multiracial ferment of Brazil. José Bento Monteiro Lobato invented in his stories a comic rustic, Jeca Tatu, who embodied the recalcitrant attitude of the inhabitants of the interior to the prospect of development. City life was likewise treated pessimistically by the mulatto author Afonso Henriques de Lima Barreto, who is remembered for a fine novel set in Rio, *Triste Fim de Policarpo Quaresma* ('The Sad End of Policarpo Quaresma', 1915).

In Spanish America there was a similar preoccupation with the inhabitants of the rural areas and the outback. The idealizing Indianism of the nineteenth-century romances was to give way to a preoccupation with the actual condition of contemporary Indian communities. This concern was fore-shadowed in a remarkable novel by the Peruvian Clorinda Matto de Turner, *Aves sin nido* ('Birds without a Nest', 1889), which describes the degradation of the Indians and yet sees no way of restoring their dignity and well-being. In Bolivia, Alcides Arguedas, a positivist historian who had written a disillusioned essay on Bolivian society, *Pueblo enfermo* ('A Sick People', 1909), wrote a novel about the Indian tribes of Lake Titicaca, *Raza de bronce* ('The Bronze Race', 1919), which evinces compassion for their state of social degeneration, but regards them as an obstacle to the progress of the nation as a whole.

The Uruguayan Horacio Quiroga is an important figure, both as a pioneer of the short story and as one of the most powerful exponents of the theme of man's weakness before natural forces. A city man and initially a *modernista* poet, he lived for long periods in the Chaco and the tropical region of Misiones. Quiroga's fiction, which was influenced by Poe and Kipling, shows 'civilized' characters meeting horrible ends in the jungle and the outback. The stories began to appear in 1904 and continued until his suicide in 1937.

Underpinning Quiroga's short stories is the familiar dichotomy between civilization and barbarism, which extends also into the 1920s with a category of novel which critics have called *la novela de la tierra*. Although it encompasses very different works, this is a useful label inasmuch as it highlights the overriding theme of nature as a force hostile to man. One of the masterpieces of this genre is *La vorágine* ('The Vortex', 1924) by the Colombian José Eustasio Rivera, a remarkable work of fiction, whose literary qualities have only recently come to be appreciated. It is a novel about the failure of an attempt to realize the pastoral idyll – such as Andrés Bello, for instance, conceived it – in the plains and jungles of Colombia. A *modernista* poet flees the city with a pregnant girl he has dishonoured in the hope of establishing a new household away from the hateful prejudices of traditional society. He finds himself sucked instead into a vortex of brutality and enslavement, in which the viciousness of life in the rubber plantations of the Amazon is exceeded only by the cruelty of the natural world itself, which finally causes his own destruction. The crazily uneven narrative can veer abruptly from self-pitying bitterness to flights of poetic rhetoric couched in an exalted *modernista* style that often spills over into the ridiculous. Once regarded as a defect, this brilliant instability of tone is designed to capture the unhinged mentality of the hysterical narrator, and is in fact a superbly eloquent vehicle for conveying the failure of the nineteenth-century liberal dream of civilizing the barbarism of America.

By way of contrast, another famous *novela de la tierra* invokes Domingo

Sarmiento's 'civilization'/'barbarism' dichotomy and opts explicitly for the classical liberal aim of civilizing the outback. *Doña Bárbara* (1929), by Rómulo Gallegos, is set in the plains of Venezuela in an environment similar to that of *La vorágine*. It narrates the struggle of a young city-educated lawyer to make good his claim to a hacienda against the eponymous female *caudillo*, a violent half-caste who bewitches and corrupts men. In this novel of thesis, Gallegos tries to show how the hero is able to overcome the sinister power of Doña Bárbara and introduce the rule of law, clear property rights and efficient production into the backlands of Venezuela.

Once exiled for his opposition to the dictator Juan Vicente Gómez, Gallegos was active in politics as a liberal, and in 1947, like his great Argentine mentor Sarmiento in 1868, he was elected president of the republic, but was forced into exile once more by a military coup after only nine months in office. As a writer, Gallegos was always sensitive to the natural beauty of his country and expressed sympathy for the Indians and *pardos* of the outback in fine novels like *Cantaclaro* (1934) and *Canaima* (1935), the latter relating a situation similar to that of *La vorágine*, but in this case the city man survives his struggle against the jungle and can look forward to a time when nature and society may be harmonized in America.

Another classic of the *novela de la tierra*, *Don Segundo Sombra* (1926) by Ricardo Güiraldes, also attempts to strike a balance between civilization and barbarism. It tells the story of a young, illegitimate boy who is taken under the wing of an experienced gaucho and taught the skills of the cowboy. After a series of trials in the wilderness of the pampas the boy discovers his true identity when he inherits an estate left to him by his natural father. Now he can live no longer as a gaucho, but must acquire a modern education and shoulder new responsibilities.

At a time when Latin Americans were becoming concerned that foreign influences might threaten their sense of national identity, Güiraldes takes up the rich traditions of gauchesque literature and, placing his novel in the context of the argument between Sarmiento's *Facundo* and Hernández's *Martín Fierro*, produces a skilful fictional reconciliation of civilization with barbarism. He adopts the narrative pattern of the *Bildungsroman* in order to suggest an analogy between the process of a boy's growing up and the nation's evolution from elementary contact with the native soil to a more complex engagement with the wider world. However, Güiraldes's master-stroke was to have converted the traditional gaucho into a moral teacher, and the pampas into a spiritual proving-ground: the confrontation with the barbarism of nature, in which the gaucho is expert, is thus portrayed as a necessary preparation for the challenges of modern society.

At the heart of Güiraldes's preoccupations is the question of national identity. In *Don Segundo Sombra* he returns to the old opposition of civilization and barbarism in order to frame a solution to the problem. He does so by avoiding the error which caused Sarmiento so much trouble – the gaucho is given positive qualities and presented as a prototype of the modern Argentine. But Güiraldes's elegant solution came too late: the delicate balance suggested by *Don Segundo Sombra* could not withstand the general discrediting of liberal ideas that followed US expansionism and economic crisis. Already in the 1920s the dialectic between civilization and barbarism that had shaped the debate over nation-building in the nineteenth century was being replaced by a new one that set the quest for an authentic cultural identity against the lure of modernity.

PART THREE

THE TWENTIETH CENTURY

9. Nationalism and Development: An Overview

Tradition and Change

By the beginning of the twentieth century the goals of the liberal champions of independence had largely been fulfilled: the white creole élites were masters in their own house and they participated directly and profitably in the world economy. Yet Latin American societies remained essentially traditional; no bourgeois capitalist revolution had occurred. The white creoles operated within their countries much as their forebears had done since the Conquest: politics were based on patronage and informal bargaining between power-holders and their clients. For the hacienda, with its vast landholdings and tied labour force, dominated the economy more fully than ever and continued to be the prime source of status. Society, as a result, remained rigidly patriarchal, stratified along racial and economic lines.

Exposure to the world economy had not significantly modified the economic behaviour of the élites. As always, they looked to make a profit by selling to a market, and to this extent they were capitalist, but because of their enormous privileges and their power to monopolize markets through political deals, they lacked the incentive to compete and innovate. They prospered in the world economy whenever it was possible to exploit a situation in which they were virtually the sole suppliers of commodities that happened to be in great demand abroad. Moreover, the wealth that accrued from international trade was spent in the traditional manner of landowning aristocracies: on the consumption of luxuries to enhance social prestige. Investment in public works or in technical and industrial enterprises was left to foreign capitalists, immigrant entrepreneurs or the state, which financed them from import duties. The material rewards of progress, then, remained highly concentrated, and did not substantially alter the values and customs of the creole magnates and their clients.

Economic growth had not produced the liberal democratic states that liberators like Bolívar had envisaged. Only a handful of republics, such as

Argentina, Brazil, Uruguay, Chile and Costa Rica, had secured constitutions which allowed an orderly transfer of power, but, on the whole, rivalry between regional *caudillos* continued to plunge states into periodic turmoil. Whether constitutional or despotic, politics were entirely oligarchic: power was acquired and upheld through elaborate networks of patronage and trade-offs between vested interest-groups.

Even though the export-economies had not altered the basic pattern of society, some features had undergone changes. As a consequence of steady export growth since the 1870s, cities had expanded, roads and railways had been built, and a secondary economy in light manufactures had sprung up. Wealth from trade had strengthened central governments, which led to enlarged bureaucracies, to improved standards of education, health and housing, and, in most countries, to the immigration of European workers. Thus, openness to the world economy had infused some modern elements into the body of traditional society: there emerged sizeable urban populations, comprising middle-class professionals, white-collar employees and a growing industrial working class. During the coming century there would be a constant tension between city and country, and within the city itself there would emerge a quite new kind of friction between the classes.

Overseas trade also brought with it exposure to the vagaries of international markets. The new century was to see major disruptions, which would force important changes on all Latin American countries. Until the First World War the export-economies continued to function profitably. After 1918, however, structural readjustments in world markets unsettled Latin American trade and loosened the hold of the white élites on their societies. The Wall Street Crash of October 1929 and the depression that followed in the 1930s brought new social forces, particularly the urban classes, into national politics.

Wherever they won power, these social forces tried to replace oligarchic liberalism with some form of corporate state, whose leaders proceeded to initiate programmes of state-led industrial development. By the 1960s these industrial revolutions had changed the face of countries like Mexico, Brazil, Chile and Argentina. Industrialization, however, was accompanied by acute political instability as the displaced landed oligarchs clashed with the new *caudillos* of the urban middle classes. After 1945, and despite the inducements of the USA, which now wielded enormous economic influence in Latin America, it proved impossible to secure a new consensus for constitutional democracy: the stresses of rapid industrialization were too great. From the mid-1960s virtually all the advanced Latin American states underwent periods of internal war and military despotism. By the 1980s their economies – still not fully industrialized – had been crippled by a massive burden of foreign debt, which forced a revaluation of the principles on which their programmes of economic modernization had been based.

These general developments affected the various Latin American republics at different rates and in different ways, depending on their internal characteristics and on the degree of their interaction with the world economy. Until the 1970s small agrarian republics like Ecuador, Paraguay or the Central American states were ruled in the traditional way by landed oligarchies or despotic *caudillos*. In other largely agrarian countries with big non-white populations but with a substantial export trade and some light industry – countries such as Peru, Bolivia, Colombia or Venezuela – the challenges to the traditional order came sooner, with the appearance of new kinds of urban-based *caudillos*, who attacked the rural barons as early, in some instances, as the 1920s; but unresolvable conflicts between landed and urban interests delayed state-led industrialization in these countries until the 1950s – and in Peru until 1968. The peculiar circumstances of Cuba were to produce in 1959 the most profound political revolution in Latin America since the early nineteenth century; yet this did not lead to the dismantling of its export-economy in sugar.

The earliest changes came in republics such as Chile, Argentina, Uruguay, Brazil and Mexico, which had the most open and dynamic economies and highly Europeanized liberal élites. Here oligarchic democracies had been working well for decades (the Porfiriato in Mexico is the exception). Yet from the 1920s there started to occur military *coups d'état* and drastic revisions of nominally democratic constitutions, and by the early 1940s manufacturing industry was subsidized by an authoritarian state in Brazil, Argentina and Mexico.

Such variations make it very difficult to generalize about Latin American development in the twentieth century, but the historical course of the largest and most economically advanced countries evinces certain economic, political and social trends which the more traditional republics have followed or are likely to follow at later stages. The turning-point in the modern history of Latin America is therefore identified by historians as the decade of the 1930s, when the World Depression stimulated the leading countries to undertake a fundamental transformation from traditional to modern structures of economy and society.

The Social and Political Impact of Progress (1900–1930)

The historic strength of the creole oligarchies lay in their dominance of rural society through their paternalist authority over the peasants employed to labour on their haciendas. So long as the economy remained overwhelmingly agrarian, the old ways of doing things would prevail. But the export trade that so enriched the creole élites brought changes that would progressively undermine traditional patriarchal authority over other social classes.

A flourishing export trade stimulated the growth of towns and cities. In the urban areas small-scale industrial enterprises supplied clothes, shoes, furniture, processed food and other light consumer goods to the growing population. The nature of the labour force changed accordingly: there emerged an urban proletariat employed in the docks, railways, factories and processing plants, in addition to the traditional urban working classes which comprised artisans, craftsmen and small traders. White-collar employees also multiplied, as the activities of the state became more complex and commercial firms expanded.

Though indirectly linked to the export-economy, these new urban classes did not form part of the traditional nexus of authority and subservience which had ensured the age-old passivity of the peasantry. In the cities workers newly arrived from the countryside had effectively broken the ties of allegiance which had bound them to the rural hierarchies. Another factor in the alienation of the urban classes from traditional authority was the mass immigration from Europe, which affected precisely those cities that were expanding at the fastest rates – in the 1920s very large numbers of industrial workers in Buenos Aires or São Paulo retained Spanish, Portuguese or Italian nationality. The urban classes, moreover, were more vulnerable than the peasants to the cycles of international trade, since they could not withdraw into subsistence agriculture – growing maize on a small plot of land and raising a few chickens or pigs – to feed themselves and their families when times were bad. Urban populations were therefore more volatile and aggressive than rural communities.

By the turn of the century new parties representing the middle and working classes of the cities had begun to agitate for political rights and social benefits. Newly formed labour syndicates struggled to achieve improved working conditions – a shorter day, greater safety in the workplace, social insurance arrangements and health provision. Socialist and anarcho-syndicalist ideas, often brought over from Europe by Italians and Spaniards, circulated in the working-class organizations. Anarchism was initially the more influential, but with its emphasis on direct action and the revolutionary general strike, it tended to be an expression of working-class frustration rather than a serious threat to the established order. Until the late 1930s the urban working class, even in countries like Brazil, Argentina and Mexico, was too small to have a direct effect on national politics.

But the rising incidence of strike action in the cities in the 1910s and 1920s alarmed traditional politicians. Their initial response was repression: strikes were broken through police violence and widespread arrests, union leaders were imprisoned, and foreign workers deported. In 1917–20 there was a remarkable upsurge of labour unrest throughout Latin America in a delayed reaction to the inflation and low wages that had hit the urban classes during the First World War. As international hostilities drew to a close, industry revived and rising demand for labour put unions in a strong position: workers pressed for better wages and conditions, inspired to a degree by the examples of the Russian and Mexican revolutions.

The bitterness of these strikes called forth a more sophisticated response to labour conflict from the bosses than simple repression. As urban workers began to be perceived as a potential danger to the social order, sections of the traditional oligarchies saw the need to co-opt labour into the political system. In the 1920s social legislation to improve working conditions was passed in the more highly industrialized countries in order to pre-empt labour unrest. A significant factor in the political 'revolutions' of the 1930s and 1940s was the desire to incorporate organized labour into the apparatus of the state. Mexico had led the way: its constitution of 1917 enshrined certain rights for workers and laid the basis for the inclusion of the trade unions in the machinery of the revolutionary government. Similar attempts at labour co-option would occur in other countries during the rest of the century, though none was capable of repeating the enduring success of the Mexican state.

The greatest political challenge to the creole oligarchies, however, was to come from the middle-class parties whose demands were framed in the language of radical liberalism: a wider suffrage, clean elections, respect for civil rights and an end to privileges and monopolies. Although none of these radical parties questioned the free-trade philosophy that underpinned the export economies, they did advocate greater state intervention to direct resources such as housing, social welfare, public works and more government jobs towards the population of the cities.

Another strain in the rhetoric of the middle-class urban parties was xeno-phobia – resentment against the tide of proletarian immigrants, foreign merchants, Protestant capitalists and, in places like Buenos Aires or São

Paulo, East European Jews. These were the roots of the nationalism which was to grow so strongly from the mid-1920s and was to shape the self-perception of Latin America for the rest of the century. The University Reform Movement, which in 1918 spread from Córdoba in Argentina to most universities of Spanish America, called for democratic reforms and for the cultivation of the 'indigenous spirit' as opposed to the 'materialist' attitudes fostered by the export-economy operated by the liberal élites. It was a *cri de coeur* of middle-class urban youth, distressed as much by wartime inflation as by working-class unrest. From this movement were to emerge the anti-oligarchic nationalist politicians of the 1930s and 1940s.

The demands of the middle-class radicals were difficult for the oligarchs to resist because, unlike those of the working-class militants, they did not challenge the foundations of the liberal state; they involved no more than the extension of the democratic principles on which republican constitutions were based. Still, there was resistance, for the oligarchic parties were able to rig elections so as to exclude the radicals from government. Persistent electoral fraud led to growing political frustration in the 1920s and 1930s, which was reflected in street violence and student agitation.

By themselves the urban radicals were not strong enough to reform the system. Only when disaffected elements within the creole élites found an opportunity to win power through a tactical alliance with the middle classes did the radical parties enter the political arena to any effect. Such was the case in Mexico in 1910, when Francisco Madero and his aristocratic clan called for a limited democratic reform (their chief demand was that there should be no re-election to the presidency), and saw fit to mobilize middle-class, and even some working-class, support for their attack on the ageing strongman Porfirio Díaz. The result was the cataclysm of the Mexican Revolution, whose outcome the urban classes did little to affect, though the post-revolutionary settlement eventually incorporated some of their economic and nationalist aspirations.

The cause of the middle classes first bore fruit in Uruguay when the leadership of the old Colorado Party fell to José Batlle y Ordóñez; he sought to widen his power-base by extending the electoral franchise, expanding state employment and introducing social legislation during his two periods of government (1903–7 and 1911–15). It was the wealth from the Uruguayan export-economy which permitted this first experiment with a form of social democracy in Latin America. Much the same occurred in Argentina, where strong export growth persuaded the creole oligarchs to respond to middle-class agitation with the liberalization of the electoral law in 1912. As a result, the Radical Party won the election of 1916, and the *caudillo* of the Radicals,

Hipólito Yrigoyen, proceeded to carve out a permanent place for urban interests in the politics of Argentina.

In some countries the army had to intervene to break open the oligarchic system. In Chile it required a military coup in 1925 to allow the former Liberal, Arturo Alessandri, to rewrite the constitution so as to let in the middle classes. In Brazil, agitation by intellectuals and members of the urban-based Democratic Party, and even a number of revolts by junior army officers in the early 1920s, proved insufficient to dislodge the oligarchs until a military rebellion ushered in the 'revolution' of 1930.

The entry of the middle-class parties into national politics between 1900 and 1930 did little to alter the structure of the export-economies; the aim of these parties was to devote part of the national income to higher wages and to increased state spending on social services and public works. Clearly, the success of such policies depended on the health of external trade. Should export revenues fall, then conflict would ensue between the urban classes and the agricultural and mining interests over the distribution of a smaller national product. After 1918 the pattern of world trade began to change to the disadvantage of Latin American exports, and clashes between the city and the country became correspondingly sharper. Yet trade in the 1920s was sufficiently good to prevent any questioning of the export model. It was the collapse of the world economy in the early 1930s that provoked a critique of Latin America's relationship with the industrial countries. This led to the first attempts at planned industrialization in a bid to assert national control over economic resources.

External Changes (1914–30)

The extraordinary growth of the Latin American economies from the 1870s was due to the rising demand in Europe for raw materials to supply manufacturing industry and for food for the expanding populations of the cities. Thanks to their tied labour force and plentiful land, Latin American landowners could undersell the peasant farmers of Europe, whose standard of living suffered very badly in this period. From this perspective the Latin American hacienda can be regarded as one of the various scourges that afflicted European agriculture in the late nineteenth century and contributed to the Great Depression that hit most of the rural areas of Western Europe in the 1890s, causing severe political instability as governments struggled to reconcile the demand of European farmers for protection against imports of cheap food with the insistence of industrialists on a policy of free trade, which would keep food prices low for the factory workers in the cities.

For fifty years or so the balance of world trade strongly favoured Latin America. All significant political groups in the region therefore supported free trade, which was given a rationale by the doctrine of 'comparative advantage': a country's economy would prosper if it exported the goods it was best suited to produce. It was a view that commended itself to the creole élites, because circumstances had placed them in a near monopoly position on the world market without their having to alter fundamentally the traditional techniques of producing primary commodities. But comparative advantage is not static: it can be reduced by changing circumstances. This had begun to happen even before the First World War.

The progressive loss of Latin America's comparative advantage can be attributed to two main causes. First, there was a long-term decline in European demand for food, as the size of urban families became smaller and higher industrial wages left more money to spend on factory goods, whose prices accordingly rose. Secondly, European demand for primary goods fell just as the world supply was rising. Oversupply in the world economy meant sharper competition between producers: prices of minerals and agricultural goods began to fall, while the price of industrial manufactures climbed steadily. The terms of trade were gradually turning against the Latin American export-economies: the real value of their traditional products was falling even as their imports of industrial goods were becoming more expensive.

Comparative advantage was further eroded when Great Britain lost her international hegemony to the USA after the First World War. Until 1914 Britain had been Latin America's biggest trading partner: Latin American commodities were exchanged for British industrial goods and financial loans. However, once the USA had displaced Britain as the foremost industrial power in the world, Latin America could purchase manufactures on better terms from North America. The bilateral trade with Britain was replaced by a more complicated three-way trading pattern: Latin American countries increasingly relied on high-value industrial imports from the USA, but had to pay for these by selling low-value exports to declining markets in Britain and Europe.

This pattern put Latin American trade under new constraints: agricultural exports could not be switched from the British to the US market, because many of these goods – cereals, cotton, sugar and meat – were already produced in the USA and were protected by high import tariffs. At the same time, colonial producers within the British empire, faced with the more competitive international environment, were pressing the British government to give preferential treatment to imports from the imperial dominions so as to squeeze out rivals from places like Latin America. The abandonment of the gold standard in the early 1930s caused a general instability of international currencies that made trade between Latin America, Britain and the USA far more difficult to manage than before the war. As world currencies fluctuated in relation to each other and to the mighty dollar, the value of the foreign exchange Latin American countries earned in European markets could rise or fall unpredictably when it came to paying for US industrial imports in dollars.

The nature of US economic ascendancy itself increased dissatisfaction in Latin America with the export model of growth. In the 1920s US capital and business enterprises began to displace established British concerns. But US participation in the Latin American export-economies was different from the British, which had largely been concentrated in utilities, infrastructure and finance capital. US companies invested more directly in the process of production, especially in minerals and oil, so that large parts of the export sector of Latin American countries came under the control of US interests. A precedent for this type of investment had been set by the take-over of sugar mills and plantations by US companies in Cuba from the 1880s, a process which had accelerated in the early decades of the twentieth century. In Central America, too, the United Fruit Company had by 1899 converted small states like Honduras and Nicaragua into single-export 'banana republics'. After 1918 this kind of absorption of large productive sectors by US corporations began to occur more systematically. By the early 1920s the Chilean copper-mining industry was dominated by subsidiaries of the Anaconda and Kennecott corporations. US companies acquired large stakes in Bolivian tin-mining, the mainstay of the economy, which had been monopolized anyway by only three tin barons, Patiño, Hochschild and Aramayo; Standard Oil took over several local oil companies in 1922. In Peru the mining of copper was dominated by US companies, and a subsidiary of Standard Oil controlled the petroleum fields. The Mexican oil industry was also owned largely by US companies, which had displaced the British after the revolution.

Investment in Latin America was excellent business for US companies. In return for providing the technical and capital assets that Latin America lacked, US businessmen could get national governments with little power on the international scene to concede generous tax privileges and very high profit margins. The result was that in the course of the 1920s the foreign presence in the Latin American export-economies was more visible than before the war, and the remittance by these foreign companies of large profits to their home countries slowed down the rate of growth in Latin America itself at a time when traditional export markets were in any case becoming harder to maintain.

Changes in the world economy had therefore begun to cut into the profitability of the Latin American export-economies well before the Depression in the 1930s. Increasing world competition called for improved efficiency and new production techniques; falling European demand and difficult access to overseas markets should have stimulated a search for new outlets and new products; the adverse effects of currency instability could have been reduced through less exposure to external trade. Yet these trends were not clear to Latin American governments at the time. Even if they had been, it is unlikely that the creole élites, being monopoly producers, would have possessed the dynamism and the flexibility to adapt to the changing conditions. But as conflict sharpened over the distribution of a diminishing national product, the urban classes began to call into question the economic liberalism that underpinned the export trade.

The growing presence of US business in the export-economies heightened nationalist consciousness. Anti-US feeling was not new, although before the 1930s it had been largely political and cultural. The Depression, however, precipitated economic nationalism, and the USA came to be perceived as a neo-imperialist power bent on the exploitation of Latin America.

The Rise of US Imperialism

For most of the nineteenth century the North American republic had been held up as a shining example of enlightened modernity by Latin American progressive élites. There was, too, a degree of common interest between the young republics of North and South inasmuch as they were all former colonies of European monarchies – they feared renewed interference from Europe to curtail their sovereignty as free nations. Such fears were to be aggravated in the course of the century by the growing economic power wielded by Great Britain throughout Latin America. During the colonial period Britain had shown her readiness to seize bits of territory here and there, such as Belize and the Mosquito Coast of Nicaragua, although she now professed to have no grand territorial ambitions in Latin America. Latin American fears were also aroused by Russia's expansionist designs in Alaska and other north-western areas of the hemisphere, by Spain's somewhat feeble attempts to invade Mexico and Peru, as well as her brief reoccupation of Santo Domingo in the 1860s (she was still in possession of Cuba and Puerto

Rico), and, of course, by Napoleon III's ambition to turn Mexico into a client state of France by imposing a Habsburg princeling on a restored Mexican throne. As early as 1823, President Monroe of the USA had warned that 'the American continents, by the free and independent condition which they have assumed and maintained, are henceforth not to be considered as subjects for colonization by any European powers', and he pledged US assistance to any American country whose sovereignty was threatened by nations from outside the hemisphere.

The Monroe Doctrine, as it became known, was to some extent a piece of bravado by a young country which was still very weak in military and economic terms. It did, however, articulate the notion of collective security and co-operation between American countries against external threats. This notion would remain influential in the formulation of US policy towards its Latin American neighbours throughout the nineteenth and twentieth centuries. It became the conceptual cornerstone of various US-backed initiatives – mutual defence treaties, regional economic aid programmes and pan-American conferences; it was eventually institutionalized in the Organization of American States founded in 1948.

Nevertheless, in the course of the nineteenth century, as the USA grew in strength and extended its borders at the expense of Spanish America or began to exercise economic influence abroad, the Latin American republics were able to appreciate how easily the Monroe Doctrine could be used to justify US meddling in the internal affairs of other, weaker countries in order to advance its own interests. The self-serving notion of 'manifest destiny', which had underwritten the settlement of the great plains and the opening of the 'Wild West', would be used to justify the military conquest of half Mexico's territory in the war of 1845. The existence of huge US sugar interests in Cuba prompted Washington to send in its forces to 'liberate' the island from Spanish rule in 1898, whereupon both Cuba and Puerto Rico became US protectorates after direct negotiations with Spain. The province of Panama would break away from Colombia in 1903 thanks to the critical intervention of US gunboats – the USA had for some years nursed the ambition to construct a canal across the isthmus so as to provide a shorter naval passage from its Atlantic seaboard to California, itself acquired by force from Mexico some decades earlier. After the canal opened in 1914, the economy of the republic of Panama would come to depend entirely on the USA.

Having drawn an arc of vital strategic interest round the Caribbean and Central America, the USA then felt obliged to apply the big stick from time to time to keep order in its client states. It was Theodore Roosevelt who embodied the self-righteous attitude of the USA towards its Latin American neighbours at the turn of the century. The imperialistic potential of the Monroe Doctrine was made plain when he added the famous Roosevelt Corollary in 1904 arrogating to the USA the right to act as an 'international police power' wherever 'chronic wrong-doing, or an impotence which results in a general loosening of the ties of civilized society' required intervention 'by some civilized nation'. This attitude led to intervention by US troops in several Central American and Caribbean countries, the overthrow of governments deemed hostile to US interests, and the installation of puppet dictators likely to be friendly to US investors.

From 1912 to 1933, for instance, Nicaragua suffered repeated occupations by US marines sent to quell the series of civil wars that followed the downfall of the corrupt Liberal strongman José Santos Zelaya. Zelaya's looting of the country delivered its chaotic finances into the hands of a US collector of customs, charged with settling the Nicaraguan foreign debt, and a consortium of New York bankers, who made a series of loans on the security of the country's railway system and control of its national bank. The vacuum left by Zelaya's downfall was such that violent contests for power between Liberal and Conservative *caudillos* resumed whenever the marines were withdrawn. The USA therefore became increasingly anxious to provide political stability for the expanding operations of the United Fruit Company in Nicaragua. When in 1928 a national accord secured by the USA allowed the election of a malleable Liberal president, one Liberal *caudillo*, César Augusto Sandino, refused to accept the deal and pursued a guerrilla campaign against the central government and the US troops. In the nationalist climate of the late 1920s Sandino became a hero of the resistance to US imperialism. The marines finally departed in 1933, but in the following year Sandino was treacherously murdered by members of the Nicaraguan National Guard, which had been set up and trained by the USA. The commander of the Guard, Anastasio Somoza, took over the government in 1937 and turned Nicaragua into a personal fiefdom under the aegis of the USA. A presidential dynasty of *caudillos* from the Somoza family was to run the country until 1979, when it was overthrown by a guerrilla movement, the Sandinista National Liberation Front, named in memory of Sandino.

The example of US action in places like Cuba, Panama and Nicaragua stood as an awful warning of what might befall other republics that displeased the 'Colossus of the North'. But, in fact, US relations with Latin America were not always as aggressive as Theodore Roosevelt's 'big-stick' diplomacy might suggest: there were periods in which genuine goodwill was promoted. In 1933 Franklin D. Roosevelt proclaimed the United States' desire to act as a 'good neighbour' towards Latin America, and this Good Neighbour policy resulted notably in Washington's decision not to intervene in Mexico when Lázaro Cárdenas nationalized the US-controlled oil industry in 1938; it also laid the basis for US–Latin American co-operation during the Second World War and in the years that followed.

Nevertheless, as the cold war between the USA and the Soviet Union dominated the world scene in the late 1940s and the 1950s, there occurred strategic lapses in the Good Neighbour policy: the big stick would be used in Central America and the Caribbean whenever Washington suspected that Soviet agents were trying to use local communists or radicals to install unfriendly regimes. The most notorious example was the overthrow of the reformist government of Jacobo Arbenz in Guatemala by a US-financed proxy army in 1954. A few years later, when Fidel Castro defeated the dictator Fulgencio Batista in Cuba, the USA at first showed caution but later turned extremely hostile after Castro tried to implement a radically nationalist economic policy in Cuba. In 1961, when Castro proclaimed himself a Marxist and an ally of the Soviet Union, the USA's global antagonist, he caused profound alarm in Washington, and an economic blockade was imposed with the intention of strangling the Cuban economy. For the rest of the 1960s the Central Intelligence Agency (CIA) did what it could to get rid of Castro, backing the disastrous Bay of Pigs invasion by Cuban exiles and carrying out a number of sometimes farcical attempts to assassinate him (these included a plan to blow him up with a doctored cigar).

The USA's anxiety to forestall 'another Cuba' dominated its policy towards Latin America for three decades. It adopted a carrot-and-stick approach, wooing friendly governments with loans and aid – as in President Kennedy's Alliance for Progress in the 1960s (see below, p. 349) – while punishing where it could those countries that showed any signs of sympathy towards its great communist enemy. For their part, the Cubans derived no little satisfaction from goading the 'Colossus of the North': for instance, in 1967, when the USA was embroiled in a bloody war against communists in Vietnam, Che Guevara, who was in hiding in Bolivia, declared his hopes of 'creating a Second or a Third Vietnam' on the American continent by starting a guerrilla war. He was shortly hunted down and killed by US-trained Bolivian troops, and thenceforward the USA would increase its military aid and training programmes to anti-communist governments in Latin America in order to help suppress or contain the many guerrilla movements – most of them inspired by the example of Che and the Cuban Revolution – that sprang up all over the continent in the late 1960s and 1970s.

This great fear of 'another Cuba' lay behind the direct or indirect interventions of the USA in the internal affairs of countries within its Caribbean and Central American 'backyard': it sent the marines to the Dominican Republic in 1965 to suppress a rebellion by reformist officers (which it feared had communist backing) against the corrupt political heirs of the strongman Rafael Trujillo, who had presided over a grotesque thirty-year tyranny until his assassination in 1961; in the 1970s it propped up a number of unsavoury dictators and military juntas in Central America so as to contain guerrilla wars in Nicaragua, El Salvador and Guatemala; the tradition of big-stick diplomacy shaped the policy of President Reagan towards the Sandinistas of Nicaragua in the 1980s, when he persisted in financing a proxy army to carry out a war of attrition against the Marxist Nicaraguan government from bases in Honduras and Costa Rica, despite frequent opposition to this policy in the US Congress.

Against such examples of imperialistic behaviour one must set instances of more positive and constructive attitudes towards Latin America. The USA, after all, saw itself as the standard-bearer of freedom and democracy in the world, and it is understandable that it should have wanted to uphold these values when it perceived them to be threatened by an openly hostile ideological enemy such as the Soviet Union – particularly so in the Western Hemisphere, where it had claimed since 1823 a commitment to resist external threats and where it had substantial security interests in the Caribbean basin and the isthmus of Central America. President Kennedy's Alliance for Progress was far more than a cynical exercise in imperialist self-interest; it represented an attempt to foster in Latin America, through a process of peaceful reform, the democratic values that the USA itself professed to live by. And in the late 1970s, when most Latin American republics were ruled by military juntas bent on suppressing guerrilla insurgencies, President Carter pursued a policy of making aid to Latin American governments conditional on a good record of human rights. It was his withdrawal of financial and military aid to the Somoza regime in Nicaragua that was crucial to the Sandinistas' success in overthrowing the dictator and creating a revolutionary government, which Carter then supported with an aid package of over $80 million.

The imperialistic behaviour of the USA towards Latin America was basically motivated by two factors. First, a readiness to defend its growing investments in the region and to safeguard sea passages for its shipping in the Caribbean and through the Panama Canal; this was pre-eminently Theodore Roosevelt's concern in the early years of the century. Secondly, a fear of communist penetration of the Americas; this was essentially a product of the cold war, but it was aggravated by the Cuban Revolution and the guerrilla insurgencies it subsequently inspired on the mainland.

However, by the late 1980s both of these factors had lost much of their substance. In the 1950s Latin America had been a prime area of investment for US capital abroad; by the 1980s overall US investment in Latin America was well below that in Canada and less than half that in Western Europe. Besides, the main target areas for US investors in the 1990s were likely to be the new democracies of Eastern Europe, not to speak of the Soviet Union itself, which was actively wooing US capital and technology under its reformist president Mikhail Gorbachev. With the collapse of communism throughout Eastern Europe in 1989 and the travails of the Soviet Union as it struggled to dismantle its centrally planned economy, the international communist threat swiftly melted away and the coming decade seemed to promise an end to the global rivalry between the USA and the Soviet Union. Two principal motives for US 'imperialism' had been removed, or at least reduced, and it was possible to conceive of a new era of mutual goodwill between the USA and the Latin American countries.

Still, in the early years of the twentieth century Theodore Roosevelt's big-stick diplomacy would contribute to the demise of liberalism as a political and economic ideology in Latin America. After the US–Spanish war over Cuba in 1898, even the creole élites had begun to regard the USA more as a threat to their cultural heritage than as a model to emulate. This was a pan-Hispanic phenomenon, which had its parallel in Spain in the '1898 Generation' of intellectuals and writers, whose soul-searching with regard to the challenge of modernity gave rise to a ferment of ideas, both revolutionary and reactionary, that made early-twentieth-century Spanish politics extraordinarily volatile and led indirectly to the civil war of 1936.

The cultural anxieties of the Latin Americans were articulated in 1900 by the Uruguayan political essayist José Enrique Rodó in *Ariel*, a book that was to acquire considerable influence throughout the Hispanic world (see p. 305). Rodó, in effect, was mounting a last-ditch defence of the seigneurial creole spirit in the face of the rise of the USA, a nation portrayed as a vigorous yet barbaric power whose extreme individualistic liberalism had eroded social hierarchies and produced valueless mass democracy and an amoral industrial capitalism. (In 1929 the Spaniard José Ortega y Gasset would voice similar feelings of disquiet about the impact of the common man on the conduct of politics in his famous essay *La rebelión de las masas* ('The Revolt of the Masses').

Nationalist Reactions against Liberalism

Such misgivings about the vulgarity of US society marked the onset of self-doubt among the governing liberal élites. However, to doubt the value of liberalism was to call into question the historic path taken by modernizers in Latin America since independence. For the ideals of liberalism and democracy, deriving from the thought of the European Enlightenment, had inspired the leaders of the wars of independence against Spain. It had then taken another forty or fifty years for liberalism finally to replace Hispanic Catholic conservatism as the guiding ideology of the new republics; but, despite all of this, the élite consensus on liberal principles started to break down from the early 1900s. By the 1930s liberalism had become intellectually discredited, even though there was no single ideology which could effectively take its place. Latin American republics, in short, became ideologically rudderless and the result would be chronic political instability, for there ceased to exist the basis for a consensus on which the state could build its authority.

The plethora of ideologies that competed to occupy the vacuum left by the strange death of Latin American liberalism converged on a number of themes: the replacement of individualism by a socially integrated community under the guidance of the state; the need to reclaim the natural resources of Latin America from foreigners; a rejection of the materialistic and utilitarian outlook fostered by capitalism in favour of an authentic national culture based on human and spiritual values.

Among the urban classes nationalism and anti-US feeling were forged into political weapons against the traditional oligarchies of landowners and import–export merchants. For in the landed élites and the foreign capitalists the urban middle-class politicians had highly visible enemies, whom they could blame for the unemployment and inflation which were widespread in the unsettled world economy after the First World War. Accordingly, ideologues of both right and left advocated the breakup of the vast landed estates as well as the nationalization of mining and petroleum companies. The emotive charge of *vendepatria* tended to be used by nationalist politicians against compatriots deemed to have sold their heritage for a mess of foreign potage.

Some of these urban-based ideologies had, like liberalism itself, been imported from Europe. On the left, socialism and, increasingly, communism, attracted middle-class intellectuals. With the eclipse of anarcho-syndicalism after the defeat of the great strikes of 1917–20, these ideologies began to make headway in the organized working class – in many republics communist parties were founded in the late 1920s. But the small size of the industrial workforce and the amorphousness of the lower classes in the cities meant that ideologies of the left would not make much impact until after the 1940s, when industry had developed further and fascism had been discredited by the defeat of the Axis powers in the Second World War. On the whole, the lower middle classes, the rootless migrants to the city from the rural areas and the numerous European immigrants whom fortune had failed in the New World were drawn to the quasi-fascist movements that from the 1920s to the 1940s appeared under different guises in every Latin American country; their basically authoritarian, corporatist ideology often overlapped – as in Spain and Portugal in this period – with social Catholicism.

In countries with large Indian and mestizo populations anti-liberal ideologies would acquire a more original character, in so far as they urged the recovery of the traditional culture of the indigenous communities. *Indigenismo* could take left- or right-wing forms, and was itself imbued with corporatist and authoritarian ideas. The Mexican Revolution, and particularly the struggles of Emiliano Zapata's Indian peasants to win back their ancestral community lands, gave an impetus to the vindication of Indian rights throughout Latin America. The first minister of culture after the revolution, José Vasconcelos, a man deeply influenced by Rodó's *Ariel*, brought *indigenismo* to the forefront of politics in the 1920s when he instigated a government campaign to integrate the Indian and the mestizo into the national culture. But the victors of the Mexican Revolution vacillated between socialist rhetoric and fascist-style political mobilization. Under President Calles, squads of political thugs were used to intimidate opponents of the regime, and the foundations of a one-party corporate state were laid. In the late 1930s Calles's successor, Lázaro Cárdenas, further institutionalized the corporate state, but gave a more socialist temper to his nationalism and modelled his land reform on traditional Indian modes of tenure.

Peru produced several gifted ideologists of *indigenismo*, such as Manuel González Prada, Luis Valcárcel, José Carlos Mariátegui and Víctor Raúl Haya de la Torre, who shared a vision of Indian culture as the source of true national values. Mariátegui and Haya de la Torre were able to translate their ideas into durable political movements. In 1929 Mariátegui founded a socialist party, which later affiliated with the Communist International. But his Marxism was permeated with *arielista* concerns about cultural integrity. He found inspiration in the communal character of the Inca state and believed in the revitalization of the Indian communities through the redistribution of land. Haya de la Torre's *indigenismo* was embodied in the APRA (Alianza Popular Revolucionaria Americana), conceived originally as a continentwide alliance of 'Indo-America' against US imperialism, but which in fact took root only in Peru as an essentially middle-class party advocating national regeneration through the expropriation of large estates and foreign companies, and the socialization of the economy.

Nationalist Revolutions

Nationalist politicians were nowhere strong enough to win power through the ballot-box, for the electoral process was firmly in the control of the oligarchic parties, which could manipulate the vote through extensive networks of political clients, especially in the rural areas. It was, therefore, the armed forces that became the determinant of the rise to power of nationalist movements from the mid-1920s.

The Latin American armed forces maintained a large degree of autonomy from civil society. Military officers, although predominantly of middle-class background, were possessed of a caste mentality which kept them apart from other social groups. Nevertheless, the armed forces saw themselves as the guardians of the nation's honour. To this extent they were receptive to nationalist ideas, but they were also concerned with 'order and progress', the watchword of the liberal élites. In effect, the ideological divisions of civil society were reflected in the armed forces, and the nature of military intervention in government was determined as much by the interplay of political beliefs among the officer caste itself as by external pressures. Whether the army backed the city-based nationalists or supported the export élites depended on their perception of which of the two broad interest-groups could best secure orderly progress.

In countries like Brazil, Chile and Argentina, where urban populations were relatively large and politically active, nationalism began to influence junior officers in the 1920s, although senior figures remained wedded to the liberal order. But as the export-economies started to falter in the 1920s, and especially after the Wall Street Crash of 1929, the armed forces began to intervene in politics. In some cases their aim was to shore up the export-economy, but more commonly it was to repudiate liberalism and bring about a nationalist revolution.

Chile was the first major country to experience a nationalist revolution led by the army. In 1924 a *coup d'état* put an end to the stale politicking of the oligarchic parliamentary republic and ushered in a fascist-style dictatorship under Carlos Ibáñez. However, in 1931, the dictator fell victim to the economic disorders caused by the Depression. A period of instability followed, during which another nationalist revolution was attempted after a further military coup by Marmaduke Grove, who briefly instituted a socialist republic.

Electoral politics in Argentina succumbed to a *coup d'état* in 1930, but the military junta was divided over policy and the nationalist revolution had to wait until 1943, when another military revolt paved the way for a full-blown corporate state under Juan Domingo Perón. In 1930 the Brazilian armed forces delivered the presidency to Getúlio Vargas, who proceeded to construct a 'New State' bearing the corporate trappings of fascism. Even Cuba, which had one of the most comprehensive export-economies, saw an abortive nationalist revolution by non-commissioned officers in 1933. In Peru, by contrast, a succession of military *caudillos* resorted to force and fraud to exclude Haya de la Torre's nationalist APRA from power during the 1930s and 1940s, and periodic recourse to military strongmen enabled Peru's liberal élites to retain an open export-economy until 1968, when the armed forces themselves unexpectedly opted to create a radical nationalist revolution.

Economic Nationalism

The shock of the Depression led to the conviction among nationalists that Latin America was at a permanent economic disadvantage in relation to the industrialized countries. Export prices were too dependent on the state of overseas demand and in any case the value of Latin American exports was in long-term decline. This made Latin America extremely vulnerable to downturns in world trade when export earnings dropped sharply and industrial goods became very costly to import. Moreover, difficulty of access to European and US markets brought home to nationalists the extent to which Latin American economies were subject to political decisions taken abroad.

Until the late 1930s nationalism had been largely cultural and political. Hostility to foreign business had become another tactical weapon in the inveterate struggles of political factions for state power, and it was largely wounded national pride that lay behind calls for the expropriation of the mineral and agrarian resources controlled by foreign capital. But after the experience of the Depression, nationalists in countries like Brazil and Argentina began to argue that it was the agrarian structure of the economy which in itself caused subservience to foreign interests. The build-up of manufacturing industry came to be regarded as a way out of these difficulties, for the domestic economies would become less dependent on imports and would therefore be more self-sustaining in times of world recession.

Although the major countries already had a sizeable industrial sector, its growth had not been planned and it was ancillary to the export-economy, being mostly confined to light manufactures such as textiles, leatherware and household equipment. The nationalists, however, now proposed to launch a programme of industrialization planned by the state and designed to develop eventually the capacity to manufacture at home the full range of industrial products which had to be imported from abroad. This was economic nationalism, and its goal was true national sovereignty through industrial self-sufficiency.

The Second World War turned out to be a watershed for Latin American industrialization. The worsening international situation had exacerbated the historic rivalry between the armed forces of Brazil and Argentina. Sensing the drift to war in Europe, the military establishments in both countries wanted to develop their own armaments industries instead of relying on imports. But the manufacture of arms required the setting-up of steel and electrical industries, and so from the 1940s the armed forces of Brazil and Argentina pressed their governments to develop an industrial base. Furthermore, as the outbreak of war created strong international demand for raw materials and foodstuffs, the Latin American export-economies boomed, and as wartime conditions abroad reduced the flow of imports, especially luxury goods, Latin American countries were able to build up large surpluses in their balance of payments: this enabled national debts to be paid off and led to the accumulation of domestic capital for investment in industrial projects.

The USA played a decisive part in fostering industrial development during these years. Needing Latin American raw materials for its war effort, it offered loans, technical expertise and equipment to assist the Latin American countries in their programmes of industrialization. During the early 1940s numerous US missions went to Latin America and signed trade agreements. The major republics duly declared war on the Axis powers and supplied the Allies with minerals and commodities. The notable exception was Argentina, where sympathy for Italy and Germany within the military junta caused it to adopt an awkward neutrality, for which it forfeited the kind of technical and financial assistance from the USA that Getúlio Vargas was getting for Brazil. The lack of US aid was an important cause of the economic difficulties which General Perón had to face in the post-war years and which contributed to his downfall in 1955. Still, even though the USA helped Latin American countries to initiate industrial development, the policy of industrialization as such was the late product of the nationalism that had evolved since the turn of the century, intensifying in the 1920s and 1930s.

This evolution continued after the Second World War, when industrialization was incorporated into a comprehensive nationalist theory of Latin America's relations with the external world. The theory was formulated by the economists of the Economic Commission for Latin America (ECLA), founded in Santiago de Chile by the United Nations in 1948. The most distinguished of these ECLA theorists was the Argentine Raúl Prebisch, who had been the director-general of the Central Bank of Argentina after its foundation in 1934.

The Prebisch–ECLA theory divided the world into a 'centre' or 'metropolis' of developed industrialized nations and a 'periphery' comprising those countries that only produced raw materials and agricultural goods. Because of the higher value of industrial products in relation to commodities, the peripheral countries were structurally dependent on the industrialized centre, where the crucial decisions affecting international trade were taken. For this reason the peripheral countries were incapable of breaking their economic dependency and achieving balanced growth on their own. The solution lay in reforming the structure of the world economy through international agreements designed to uphold commodity prices, while stimulating industrial development in the peripheral countries by grants of aid and long-term credit from the centre. Within the peripheral countries themselves the state should undertake structural reforms to create the right economic conditions for industrial development: the internal market should be enlarged through agrarian reform, and income redistributed in order to raise the purchasing power of the majority of the population.

The structuralist dependency theory would change Latin Americans' understanding of their position in the world, for it challenged the classic liberal doctrine of comparative advantage, which had for so long provided a rationale for the export-economies. Complacently supported by agro-mercantile élites who richly benefited from it, the doctrine of comparative advantage appeared to discount the possibility of actively changing the economic destiny of a country. But the ECLA theorists, who were attuned to the Keynesianism that was so influential in the post-war years in Europe, believed that the state should play a guiding role in the transformation of the economy, both internally and through international co-operation. (The ECLA was, after all, an agency of the United Nations.)

The ECLA's statism was evident, for instance, in its belief that inflows of capital from abroad should come from foreign governments in the form of loans and aid rather than from private sources. However, this statism was in conflict with the views of the USA, which disliked state controls and wanted a larger role for private enterprise. Since the USA was to be the dominant economic influence in Latin America after the war, the divergence between its views and those of the ECLA had an unsettling effect on the conduct of policy and economic management, for Latin American governments had to contend with ECLA-influenced nationalist opinion in their own constituencies while having to deal with the free-market demands of US private investors and corporations.

Import-Substituting Industrialization (ISI)

After the Second World War many governments, following the lead of Brazil, Argentina and Mexico, and with the assistance of the USA, chose to industrialize their economies through the substitution of imports. Import-substituting industrialization (ISI) required the intervention of the state in the economy on many fronts. To begin with, the state placed high import tariffs on those foreign manufactures it planned to replace by local products. The protected home industries were then boosted with credits from state banks and by guaranteed prices. Demand for these expensively produced industrial goods was stimulated by controlling wage and price levels and by manipulating tax and exchange rates. The state also had to invest heavily in setting up an infrastructure in transport and energy. ISI meant, therefore, an enormous expansion of the state's commitments, and a corresponding increase in its spending.

Although the ultimate aim of ISI was to achieve economic self-sufficiency, the process itself necessarily involved multiple contacts with world markets. Technology and expertise had to be imported from abroad to equip factories and set up plant; and the massive capital investments required to finance ISI could come from only two sources – foreign earnings from the export-economy and foreign loans. Indeed, the tendency of ISI development was for imports to exceed exports because of domestic industry's dependence on foreign technology. Governments tried to ease the burden on domestic industrialists by keeping the exchange rate artificially high so as to hold down the price of imports, but this policy produced recurrent deficits in the balance of payments, for the high exchange rate pushed up the price of Latin American exports in world markets and so reduced foreign earnings. These balance-of-payments deficits had to be covered either by borrowing abroad or by printing money. The results were mounting foreign debts and chronic inflation – the twin scourges of all industrializing countries in Latin America, no matter what the political complexion of the regime.

During the 1940s and 1950s economic policy was dominated by the drive to industrialize. In several Latin American countries manufacturing industry grew at a much faster rate than agriculture. Between 1945 and 1960 the annual industrial rate of growth in Brazil was on average 9.4 per cent, while the agricultural rate of growth was 4 per cent. The respective figures in Venezuela were 8.5 per cent and 4.7 per cent; in Colombia, 7.2 per cent and 2.1 per cent; in Peru, 6.6 per cent and 3 per cent. Even in the coffee and banana republics of Central America manufacturing outpaced agriculture: in Nicaragua the figures were 7.8 per cent and 5.5 per cent; in El Salvador, 7.3 per cent and 2.5 per cent; in Honduras, 8.5 per cent and 1.7 per cent.

Industrial development brought numerous advantages. Wages in industry were up to 4 or 5 per cent higher than those on the land. The standard of living of an industrial worker was therefore superior to a peasant's: he had a better diet, benefited from easier access to education, housing and health care, enjoyed more leisure time and personal freedom, and had a wider choice of consumer goods. The pull of the city – where manufacturing was invariably concentrated – thus increased enormously as a result of industrial development. Latin American cities could offer a range of social amenities and technical services – hospitals, schools, shops, electricity, running water and sewerage – which were largely lacking in the rural areas.

During the 1950s the population in Latin America grew at an annual rate of 4.5 per cent in the cities, and only 1.5 per cent in the countryside. In 1950, 61 per cent of the population of Latin America lived in the countryside; by 1960 this figure had dropped to 53.8 per cent. In Venezuela and Mexico the 1950s saw the population of the cities surpass that of the country. In Argentina, Uruguay and Chile, where the urban population was already higher than the rural, cities continued to grow, while the rural population fell to well below 40 per cent (in Uruguay it was only 29.1 per cent in 1960).★

During and after the Second World War the major Latin American countries were undergoing a profound industrial revolution. Like all industrial revolutions, this one brought severe dislocations and great social stress. There were, however, historical and political factors which made ISI exceptionally traumatic. Latin American countries had to industrialize in an international economy where there were already fully-fledged and extraordinarily powerful industrial competitors. In order to create an industrial base, the Latin American countries had to accumulate capital for investment, build an infrastructure and acquire technology and expertise. This they could not do on their own; they were forced to depend on foreign resources to a very large degree.

★ For additional data on urbanization, see Statistical Appendix, table 2.

There was, moreover, no alternative but for the state to take the leading role in industrial development. The traditional economic élites were engaged in trade and agriculture, and there was no incentive for them to behave like risk-taking industrial entrepreneurs. Yet the foreign exchange earned by these élites through the export trade constituted the main source of domestic capital for the state's programme of investment in industry. In short, Latin American development necessarily involved a very delicate interrelationship between the state, foreign capital, the export élites and, of course, the emerging industrial sector.

Although these relations were economic, the fact that they were so crucially mediated by the state meant that ISI was peculiarly vulnerable to political pressures. As we have seen, the extreme dependence on imports of technology created trade deficits and rising prices; this led to labour unrest, which forced governments to find ways of satisfying wage demands without fuelling inflation. The nationalist legacy of the interwar years also introduced distortions into the process of ISI. Aiming at self-sufficiency, governments tended to be overprotective towards domestic industry, inadvertently reducing its productive efficiency through lack of any real competitive stimulus. Excessive protectionism made domestic manufactures very expensive and kept consumer goods out of reach of the mass of the population; ironically, this self-imposed limit on the growth of the internal market put a ceiling on the expansion of domestic industry itself.

Industrial efficiency suffered badly too from the very close links that were established between the state and domestic industry. Traditional relations of patronage and clientship were reinforced in situations where public servants were responsible for awarding contracts, subsidies and licences to businessmen; the opportunities for graft and corruption were obviously very great. Perhaps the most important political factor was the bias against exports, which tended to characterize nationalist governments. Since ISI had been embraced by military juntas and urban interest-groups as an alternative to the oligarchic export-economy, government planners discriminated against exports by imposing heavy duties and pouring resources into manufacturing industry in preference to agriculture. This anti-export bias resulted in development programmes which suffered from a deadly combination of sluggish industrial output and declining export sectors.

The Rural Crisis

The most damaging effect of ISI, as it was applied in the decades after the Second World War, was the acute crisis it caused in the rural areas. Agriculture was of critical importance to Latin America, because, in addition to providing cheap food for the growing urban masses, it was by far the greatest source of foreign exchange. But the problem with the agrarian economy was that it was both inefficient and socially unjust. It was dominated by the hacienda, where too much available acreage went uncultivated, farming methods were antiquated, and landowners did not invest enough. Historically, the hacienda had expanded by encroaching on the land of smaller farmers and of Indian communities, and this age-old trend had greatly accelerated after the dissolution of Church estates and Indian communal lands by liberal governments in the late nineteenth century. There was, in consequence, an entrenched problem of landlessness and unequal land tenure in the countryside.

Modernizers had long understood the need for agrarian reform, as much for the sake of efficiency as for social justice. But reformers were caught in the dilemma of how to reorganize agriculture without causing a disastrous fall in production: how could the haciendas be broken up when the life-blood of the economy depended upon them? The economic nationalists of the twentieth century espoused land reform as a prerequisite of a just society, but whenever land was redistributed, production dropped and exports slumped, causing acute difficulties throughout the economy, not least among the urban masses. In Mexico, for instance, land reform after the revolution was mostly confined to the areas with large Indian communities, and even so, it was wound down in the early 1940s to become a mere symbol in the gestural politics of the ruling party. In countries like Bolivia and Guatemala in the 1950s, or Chile and Peru in the 1960s and 1970s, land redistribution caused severe political conflict and economic disruption, resulting in perilous drops in food production and agricultural exports. Brazil tried to circumvent the opposition of the landowners to land reform by encouraging peasants to clear the rain forests of its vast interior in order to release new land for settlement. However, from the 1980s this policy met with mounting international criticism because it threatened the last nomadic Indian tribes with extinction and seriously endangered the ecological balance upon which the climate of the earth depends. Similarly, in Panama the hunger for land caused the progressive destruction of tropical forest by settlers, but the consequent reduction in rainfall threatened to silt up the canal – the country's economic lifeline. Only in Cuba in the early 1960s and Nicaragua in the early 1980s were large private estates broken up into co-operatives or state farms, but this redistribution was made possible because of the prior conquest of state power by revolutionary forces. Here too, though, land reform was accompanied by massive drops in productivity. With the exception of these two countries, no nationalist government was able to persevere with land reform.

What occurred instead was the transfer of capital from agriculture to industry by means of government-imposed high duties and low prices on agricultural produce. This had the doubly negative effect of eroding agricultural productivity while leaving the structural inequities of land tenure intact. The result was to convert the flight from the land into a veritable haemorrhage of human resources. For bad prices and poor returns hit small farmers and Indian villagers much harder than the *hacendados*; they also depressed rural wages, making the life of the peons even harsher. As people were driven off the land to look for a better life in the city, the hacienda expanded and consolidated. Mechanization to improve profitability reduced the size of the rural labour force, adding to the flow of migrants to the cities. More land was turned over to cash crops for export, progressively reducing the acreage given over to staples such as maize or potatoes, which traditionally fed the broad mass of the people. By the 1960s countries like Mexico had reached a point where they could no longer produce enough food to supply adequately their own rapidly growing populations. From being self-sufficient in, or even net exporters of, food, many Latin American countries became importers, diverting a portion of their precious and diminishing export earnings to this end.*

The General Crisis of Development

The rural crisis had the effect of swelling the cities with impoverished peasants seeking work. In any normal process of industrial development, such former country-dwellers would supply the factories with labour. However, in the late 1950s – and possibly earlier in Brazil and Argentina – the crisis in the countryside began to interact with a crisis of industrial production. The consequence was that the human influx from the rural areas could not be absorbed into the industrial labour force, and appalling problems of unemployment and underemployment in the cities occurred.

* For illustrative data on food imports, see Statistical Appendix, table 8.

What was causing the simultaneous crisis in industrial production? By the end of the 1950s the more advanced countries had reached the limit of their internal market in what is generally known as the 'easy' phase of import-substitution: the production of non-durable consumer goods such as textiles and leatherware. Since such manufactures are labour-intensive and low-technology, factories were able to absorb the migrants from the countryside fairly easily while the internal market was still expanding. Once this phase of internal market expansion had come to an end, governments could have avoided unemployment in two ways. First, the internal market could have been extended further by putting more resources into agriculture in order to raise purchasing power in the rural areas and stem the flow of rural migrants to the cities. Secondly, industrial production could have been increased by selling light manufactures abroad and establishing a competitive position for Latin American products in world markets – a development strategy that the industrializing countries of the Far East, such as Taiwan, Hong Kong, Singapore and South Korea, followed in this period. Such a strategy, however, would have required the pragmatic revision of some aspects of the economic nationalist outlook inherited from the 1930s and 1940s.

These adjustments to ISI were not made at the time because they went against the grain of current thinking on Latin American development: investing more resources in the countryside would have been regarded as aggravating the national economy's dependence on exports, and a policy of selling manufactures abroad would have appeared to extend this export dependency to industrial products. In any case, it could not have been done without a selective reduction in import tariffs to improve the efficiency of overprotected home industries so that they might be competitive in international markets. Such adjustments to ISI would have been opposed politically by industrialists, for whom import-substitution meant a captive home market, government subsidies and guaranteed high profits. Instead, the Latin American countries decided to intensify the process of import-substitution by moving from light manufactures directly into the production of durable consumer goods such as motor cars, aircraft, electrical appliances and machinery.

This process, known as the 'deepening' of import-substitution, which took place in Latin America from the late 1950s to the early 1970s, aggravated all the social and economic problems so far described. For deepening involved a qualitative change in production from the 'easy' phase of ISI, involving labour-intensive, low-skilled, low-technology manufacturing to the 'hard' phase of capital-intensive, high-skilled, high-technology industries. The result was that the rising tide of fugitives from the crisis in the countryside could not be absorbed by industry in the cities, so that during the 1960s urban unemployment began to soar. Also, the new industries required far higher imports of machine tools and investment capital. Import-substitution became increasingly self-defeating, as dependency on certain foreign consumer goods was broken only by establishing an even greater dependency, in some cases, on imports of the machine tools and capital required to manufacture those consumer goods at home.* As Stephany Griffith-Jones and Oswaldo Sunkel observed, the 'central failing' of the import-substitution policy was that 'the importation of capital and intermediary goods necessary to produce consumer goods was substituted for the importation of the consumer goods themselves'. This was one reason why the development process became in structural terms 'increasingly dependent, vulnerable and unstable'.†

Indeed, by 1960 ISI, as it had been pursued from the 1940s, had not solved the underlying structural problems that the Latin American economies had been facing since the 1920s. Their exports were still largely confined to raw materials and foodstuffs, and their share of world trade had been in constant decline. Between 1948 and 1960 the total volume of world trade had doubled, but Latin America's share of this trade (excluding Venezuela's oil windfall) had fallen from 10.3 per cent to 4.8 per cent. Moreover, the composition of this fast-declining share of international trade was overwhelmingly traditional – cotton, sugar, coffee, petroleum and minerals‡ – despite the fact that overall international demand for these commodities was weakening, and that competition was increasing from African, Asian and Middle Eastern countries (which in many cases had been accorded preferential status for their exports by the European Economic Community).

The military and city-based nationalists who had been taking over governments since the 1930s and 1940s had not, therefore, succeeded in eliminating the structural deficiencies which the country-based liberal oligarchs had failed to address. Latin America's position in the world economy was, if anything, worse in the 1960s than it had been in the 1920s. The terms of trade were still unfavourable: exports were continuing to decline in value as the value of imports rose sharply, particularly after the deepening of ISI. While the export-economies lost their earning capacity, the growth of domestic industry remained too sluggish to absorb the huge labour surplus arriving from

* For illustrative data on technological imports, see Statistical Appendix, table 8.

† *Debt and Development Crises in Latin America: The End of an Illusion* (Oxford University Press: Oxford, 1986), p. 24.

‡ For illustrative data, see Statistical Appendix, table 8.

the countryside. And so, Latin American countries were finding, broadly speaking, that their national cake was shrinking at a time when the population was expanding faster than ever before: per capita the value of exports was actually lower in 1960 than in 1948, and the balance of payments with foreign countries was continually in deficit.

The juggernaut of industrial development, however, pushed forward uncontrollably, consuming scarce resources and leaving a trail of conflicts as it pursued the ever-receding goal of economic self-sufficiency. Strong world growth in the 1960s allowed exports to do relatively well, and this kept ISI going, despite its defects. By the early 1970s the 'hard' phase of ISI had itself been exhausted in the advanced economies of Argentina, Brazil and Mexico: the domestic manufacture of durable consumer goods had reached the limits of expansion within the existing structure of the home market. Once again, a new strategy for industrial development was required: a move into competitive exporting of manufactures together with investment in the rural areas to raise purchasing power in the internal market.

Indeed, the deep world recession after 1973 might have provided the external shock required to force a structural adjustment to ISI, but Latin American governments were able to continue on the same pattern through the 1970s by covering their ever larger deficits with foreign loans, until international interest rates started to rise in the late 1970s and a new world recession made the burden of foreign debt too heavy to bear.

The State and the Politics of the Industrial Revolution

The Latin American industrial revolutions had come about as a result of the transfer of state power from the landed and mercantile élites to national coalitions of dissident landowners, the middle classes and the organized industrial workforce. This transfer involved the use of unconstitutional force, which in most cases took the form of a *coup d'état* by the army. The shift was as much one of ideology and economic interest as of power: from liberalism to economic nationalism, from an agrarian and mining export-economy to city-based, inwardly directed industrial development.

As we have seen, the programme of import-substituting industrialization required a delicate interaction between the export sector, foreign capital and the rising urban interest-groups. In this interaction it was indispensable that the state perform the role of mediator between the different sectors. This called for political authority, which could be achieved only through perceived legitimacy based on widespread consent for the institutions of state. And yet it was precisely legitimacy and consent which Latin American states had been unable to find since independence, except for a period of about sixty years from the 1870s to the 1930s, when some of the larger republics had found a degree of constitutional order through a consensus between liberal and conservative élites.

It was the challenge to this kind of oligarchic consensus that had ushered in the nationalist revolutions of the 1930s and 1940s in the advanced countries. Therefore, the outcome of these nationalist revolutions – and it must be remembered that such revolutions were to continue to occur in other countries in subsequent decades – was the fragmentation of power in the state. Although they still ran the export-economies, the traditional élites were forced to give up their exclusive control of political institutions, and there resulted a fundamental cleavage in the state between political power and economic influence. No new consensus would be possible so long as politics and vital economic interests conflicted with each other.

A further reason for the fragmentation of power was that the nationalist coalitions were themselves composed of rival interest-groups: landowners and merchants, whose fundamental interests remained tied to the export-economy; the urban middle classes, who were particularly miscellaneous, comprising industrialists, entrepreneurs and professionals, but also shop-keepers, clerks and artisans; the organized industrial workers, and a large mass of employees in the service sector and the state bureaucracy. Moreover, as industrialization advanced, there appeared a further cleavage of interests between the new industrial capitalists and the labour unions. The social appeal of nationalism was therefore too heterogeneous to provide for a cohesive political ideology: it attracted different classes for different reasons and at different times, and not even a Getúlio Vargas in Brazil or a Juan Perón in Argentina – both of whom flirted with fascism – was able to turn that loose bundle of conflicting interests into an enduring revolutionary reality.

Instead nationalism brought a further structural weakening of the historically fragile Latin American state. Politically, it created a situation analogous to that of the early and middle nineteenth century, when after the collapse of the Catholic monarchy the independent republics found themselves bereft of legitimate authority to regulate the disputes between conservative and liberal regional élites. In the advanced countries such as Argentina, Brazil, Uruguay and Chile, which had known long periods of settled constitutional government, nationalism and the associated traumas of ISI development brought a return to uncentred, conflict-ridden politics with new urban *caudillos* leading their client-groups into battle against the old rural oligarchs.

What makes the politics of the majority of Latin American republics so extraordinarily complex after the middle decades of the twentieth century is that the traditional nineteenth-century conflicts between conservative and liberal oligarchs had not even settled into a semblance of constitutional order (as they had done in places like Argentina or Chile) before nationalism and the problems of industrialization and urbanization were superimposed upon them. In Peru, for instance, the historic contest between the conservative landowners of the inland sierra and the liberal export élites of the coast – complicated enough by the presence of large numbers of traditional Indian communities – was further aggravated by conflicts with middle-class nationalists, and these in turn by disputes between industrial capitalists and the urban working classes. Such a fragmented polity could be held together only by recurrent dictatorships. Military strongmen managed to exclude the nationalists from power until 1968; the army then imposed a nationalist revolution that lasted seven years before a further *coup d'état* in 1975 paved the way for a return to civilian rule under a democratic system which by the 1980s had shown itself incapable of containing the country's explosive social tensions.

Colombia was another large but deeply divided country. Here too constitutional government had failed to take root; only the periodic rule of a strongman offered some relief from the bitter quarrels between Catholic conservatives and anti-clerical liberals over the issues of regional autonomy and the role of the Church. These troubles continued well into the twentieth century. In 1899–1903 the 'War of the Thousand Days' between Conservatives and Liberals cost some 100,000 lives. In the 1930s and 1940s nationalism began to permeate both the Conservative and Liberal parties, and tended to polarize at the extreme wing of each camp: in the Conservative Party there emerged a fascistic religious conservatism – its leader Laureano Gómez was an ardent admirer of General Franco in Spain – while in the Liberal Party Jorge Eliécer Gaitán's demagogic leftism won huge support. The political feuding reached a bloody nadir on 9 April 1948 when rioting engulfed the city of Bogotá after Gaitán was assassinated. The *bogotazo*, as these riots have come to be called, unleashed a civil war between Conservatives and Liberals – known simply as *La Violencia* – which persisted, especially in the rural areas, until the 1960s. It claimed between 200,000 and 300,000 lives and fostered a tradition of rural warfare and banditry, which was prolonged by the mounting social problems of the 1970s and 1980s, when several Marxist guerrilla movements sprang up and made war on the state. This chronic lawlessness of the Colombian outback contributed also to the emergence of an illicit industry based on the growing, processing and exporting of cocaine. International contraband produced the notorious cartels of vastly rich drug barons in Medellín and Cali, who exercised power through mafia-style organizations. By the late 1980s these *narcotraficantes* posed a grave threat to the authority of the state; they indulged in terror campaigns of bombings and assassinations in order to intimidate the government into legalizing cocaine and rejecting US demands for the extradition of drug traffickers.

Yet, ironically, the turbulence of Colombian politics may account for the pragmatism which characterized the country's economic development, for no single interest-group could hold power for too long without arriving at some rough compromise with rivals. Despite the lack of law and order, the endemic split between Liberals and Conservatives served to contain the new economic interests spawned by nationalism within the historic two-party pattern. Whenever the leadership of the two parties arrived at a practical accord for carrying on the business of government – as they did in the 1930s and early 1940s and again from the late 1950s to the 1980s – the broad thrust of economic development could be maintained in spite of the superficial turmoil of everyday life. ISI was, therefore, pursued undogmatically, without discriminating against the export-economy and without unduly penalizing the rural areas. By the 1960s Colombia had become the fourth largest industrial nation in Latin America, and in the following decade its economic growth was one of the highest in the region.* A long history of bipartisan feuding thus led indirectly to a kind of rough consensus between the old landed oligarchies and the new business élites which prevented too radical a cleavage between economic and political power once industrial development had got under way. In Colombia industry was able to develop successfully despite the acute weakness of the state, for in this case circumstances made for a flexibility that was precluded elsewhere by dogmatic economic nationalism.

Mexico, whose history had been so chaotic in the nineteenth century, was, however, the country which produced the most resilient and authoritative state. The peculiarity of Mexico was that, as a result of its revolution, it was able to consolidate an unprecedented national consensus in the 1930s – just before it embarked upon industrialization. Since the landed élites who created that consensus were also responsible for initiating industrial development, no cleavage occurred between economic and political power. On the

* See Statistical Appendix, table 3.

contrary, the Mexican Revolution led to a corporate state in which capital, labour, the middle classes and even the armed forces were given a function in the machinery of government. The social tensions produced by rapid industrial development were thus subsumed in the state apparatus: after the 1930s Mexico experienced no *coups d'état*, no serious civil conflict and no violent changes of government. Such stability allowed it to become the second most dynamic economy in the region, overtaking Argentina by the 1950s.*

Why did the corporate state prosper in Mexico and not in Argentina or Brazil, where corporatism was also tried between the 1930s and 1950s? Essentially, it was because the corporate state in these countries did not include the holders of the most substantial economic power, namely the agrarian export-élites. The states created by Getúlio Vargas and Juan Perón were largely vehicles for the middle classes and the trade unions, and failed to incorporate the élites who earned the foreign exchange needed to finance industrialization. Therefore, instead of resting upon a consensus, as in Mexico, the corporatism of Vargas and Perón simply institutionalized the split between political authority and economic power, a split that rapid industrialization only made worse. On the other hand, neither Perón nor Vargas was strong enough to destroy the traditional élites and take control of the export sector. The results were acute social conflict, hyperinflation, indebtedness and military take-overs. With the exception of Mexico, then, the rise of nationalism combined with import-substitution to destroy the liberal consensus where it existed, as in Brazil and Argentina, or to deepen political divisions in countries where oligarchic consensus had not yet been achieved, such as in Peru and Colombia. Social conflict became progressively more acute, making genuine democratic government and the rule of law impossible to establish.

The armed forces would remain the decisive power-brokers throughout the twentieth century. The military, after all, had opened the door to government for the urban nationalists in the 1920s and 1930s, and it was the military in Brazil and Argentina which had first linked nationalist ideology to a programme of state-led industrialization. Rapid industrial development was to impose great strains on the authority of the state; and lacking the general political consent that would give them enduring legitimacy, Latin American states tended to be sustained, if not replaced, in times of crisis by the institutionalized violence of the armed forces.

* See Statistical Appendix, table 3.

The Post-war Years: The Developmental State, Natural Corporatism and Electoral Politics

Latin American nationalism underwent a transformation after the Second World War, when the USA finally replaced Great Britain as the supreme global power. Having defeated the fascist Axis countries, and finding itself in a cold war with the Soviet Union, the USA was concerned to consolidate its spheres of influence and spread its liberal–democratic values abroad. In Latin America it disapproved of dictatorships, but it also, as elsewhere, feared communist influence (membership of Latin American communist parties had increased fivefold overall during the war). In 1948, therefore, the USA was instrumental in founding the Organization of American States with the aim of promoting regional co-operation and protecting member countries against external aggression. In the early 1950s the USA concluded mutual defence pacts with several Latin American governments (as it had done with West European states) in order to bring Latin America into the structure of worldwide strategic defence against the growing international power of the Soviet Union. These pacts were an extension into the cold war of the military alliances established during the recent world conflict; US armaments, military training and economic aid for Latin American industrialization were exchanged for raw materials and geopolitical loyalty.

For their part, Latin American governments in the post-war years were anxious to show democratic credentials in order to maintain the flow of US loans and investments which they needed to finance import-substituting industrialization. Communist parties were banned or excluded from power; dictators put away their fascistic trappings and held elections. In Chile the Radical government suddenly outlawed the Communist Party, its recent partner in a Popular Front which had held power throughout the 1940s. Getúlio Vargas in Brazil, Fulgencio Batista in Cuba, and Juan Perón in Argentina all turned to the ballot-box. Despite the fact that nationalism had emerged as a reaction to the classic liberalism of the creole élites, nationalist governments now tried to reach an accommodation with the more egalitarian democratic liberalism championed by the USA.

Although a nationalist policy of state-led industrialization continued to be pursued after the war, the USA still offered financial and technical assistance, despite its professed disapproval of state intervention in the economy. But as the 'easy' phase of ISI drew to an end in the late 1950s, the social conflicts it generated were becoming too explosive to control: the cleavages between protected industrialists and traditional exporters, and between industrialists and workers, undermined the authority of elected governments. Faced with such conflicts, liberal democracy displayed a tendency to crumble away.

How did Latin American democracies compensate for the lack of a real political consensus to support them? Governments had recourse to the practices of traditional societies: patronage and clientship, though adapted as necessary to the conditions of developing economies. Political scientists have called this phenomenon 'natural corporatism', because even though revolutionary attempts in the 1930s and 1940s to create a corporate state had largely failed, the nominally democratic post-war states continued to try to reconcile rival interest-groups by co-opting their leaders into a system of mutual bargaining for privileges and benefits.

The extension of the state's activities through ISI facilitated this process. Where once the Catholic monarchy had been the supreme source of favours, now the developmental state could act as the central dispenser of patronage, offering concessions, licences and subsidies in return for political co-operation. State intervention in the economy brought forth new webs of *intereses* – businessmen, industrialists, professional associations, trade unions – whose welfare often depended on decisions taken by bureaucrats and politicians. The object of these interest-groups, therefore, was to influence public policy so as to extract the best deal for themselves in the distribution of the national income. The government, in turn, would seek to appease as many *intereses* as it could so as to weave them into a fabric of favours and rewards that might keep the social order from breaking down.

Elections were just one of the means by which aspiring clienteles tried to assert their claim to patronage from the state. Others might include various forms of threatening behaviour such as strikes, demonstrations and even riots. In the case of aggrieved élites it might involve conspiring with other excluded *intereses* to provoke a *coup d'état*. Whenever an interest-group had demonstrated sufficient disruptive capacity, the government would attempt to secure its own position by trying to co-opt the leaders of the group into the informal network of patronage. For instance, after the serious student rioting that shook Mexico City in 1968, state spending on the universities rose sharply and the government adopted a markedly left-wing rhetoric so as to defuse the threat of further trouble from that quarter.

Natural corporatism tended to encourage populism, the phenomenon whereby a politician tries to win power by courting mass popularity with sweeping promises of benefits and concessions to large interest-groups, usually drawn from the lower classes. Populist leaders lack a coherent programme for social change or economic reform, but try to manipulate the existing system in order to lavish favours on underprivileged sectors in return for their support. One of the most successful populist leaders in Latin America was Eva Perón, who won idolatrous devotion from the urban masses of Argentina in the late 1940s and early 1950s, particularly after she established a semi-state charitable foundation, to which businessmen and other interest-groups were invited to contribute funds.

Natural corporatism was, then, the means by which historically weak states tried to buy off disorder and maintain a tolerable degree of stability in order to conduct their industrial revolutions. But from the late 1950s, as ISI moved into the 'hard' phase of capital-intensive heavy industry in the advanced countries, the soaring rates of inflation and unemployment made social conflicts between *intereses* increasingly hard to remedy through patron-age or co-option. The Peronist unions in Argentina proved impossible to woo back into an electoral system run by Radical governments. Getúlio Vargas's democratic government in Brazil was destroyed by irresolvable conflicts between demands for higher wages from the labour unions and the anti-inflationary measures advocated by industrialists and exporters. And in the 1960s Chilean democracy showed dangerous cracks, as parties of the right, centre and left sought to pull the economy in different directions.

The great political problem for Latin American governments from the 1950s through to the 1980s was how to control inflation without sacrificing social welfare. Since political authority tended not to coincide with economic power, the corporatist largesse of the state had its limits: democratic govern-ments proved unable to take effective control of the export-economy and were too weak to remove the inefficiencies and injustices of the vast haciendas by redistributing land. In these circumstances the effect of natural corporatism was to increase the strong inflationary pressures which industrialization itself generated.* And so democratic governments were torn between the high spending required to improve living standards and the anti-inflation pro-grammes needed to stop the rise in prices which fuelled wage demands and undermined the earning power of exports.

Despite the extensive influence of the USA in the post-war years, political debate was still dominated by nationalist themes. Until 1959 this nationalism was mostly reformist in outlook, seeking to extend the powers of the state over the economy without destroying democratic pluralism. But after the Cuban Revolution reformism was challenged by a revolutionary socialist nationalism that advocated the destruction of the capitalist economy as the only way of integrating political and economic power in a strong, legitimate state capable of pursuing balanced industrial development.

* For illustrative data for inflation over three decades, see Statistical Appendix, table 4.

The desire for a strong state was not confined to the revolutionary left. Traditional export élites, having lost control over the electoral process, and seeing their interests threatened as much by inflation as by economic nationalists, often looked to military intervention for a release from the turbulence of electoral politics. For, as in the inter-war years, it was still the armed forces which in the last resort held a veto on the conduct of government, regardless of the façade of liberal democracy that had been established in many countries in order to attract the Yankee dollar.

The Alliance for Progress (1961–70)

The weakness of liberal democracy in Latin America in the post-war years was illustrated by the fate of the Alliance for Progress, a US programme of aid and reform devised in 1961 by the administration of President Kennedy. Its aim was to forestall Cuban-style revolutions by promoting social reform and economic development in the continent. The essential instrument was the channelling of public and private capital to elected governments whose reform proposals met with US approval. A number of democratic reformers received US endorsement: Rómulo Betancourt in Venezuela (1959–64), Jânio Quadros in Brazil (1961), Arturo Frondizi in Argentina (1958–62), Fernando Belaúnde Terry in Peru (1963–8), Eduardo Frei in Chile (1964–70), Alberto Lleras Camargo (1958–62) and Carlos Lleras Restrepo (1966–70) in Colombia. In effect, the programme meant US support for moderate economic nationalism – state-led ISI combined with land reform and the reduction of income inequality.

The Alliance for Progress might have worked had centrist governments been able to command greater authority. But it suited both right and left to discredit the reformist option, and the effect of this hostility was to prevent the control of inflation and stall agrarian and other social reforms. By 1970 the Alliance for Progress had foundered: the democratic governments it favoured succumbed either to military regimes or to mounting social turmoil, accompanied by guerrilla warfare.

Nevertheless, the case of Colombia can be considered a partial success for the principles of the Alliance for Progress. In 1958 a national accord between the leadership of the Liberals and Conservatives, allowing for a strict alternation in government between the two parties, pulled the country some way out of its historic quagmire of political feuding and gave it a measure of consensus and stability, tempered by periodic elections. The government of Alberto Lleras Camargo embraced the Alliance for Progress with enthusiasm and received generous funds for development and reform. Although land redistribution was largely a disappointment – being opposed by both land-owners and rural guerrillas – Lleras Camargo laid the groundwork for prudent and undogmatic economic policy-making. As Rosemary Thorp and Laurence Whitehead observed, the 'amazing strength of Colombia's development' over three decades was made possible in part by the 'consociational nature of the system binding the two major parties to the democratic framework'; this 'helped to maintain a rather broad social consensus that ... assisted economic managers and ... kept their disagreements within pragmatic and prudential grounds'. Continual electoral tests contributed to the state's 'record of flexibility and relative responsiveness to social pressures'. Colombia, as a result, 'managed to mesh short-term adjustment with its long-term development strategy'. In this it resembled Brazil 'but without the inflation' (Colombian prices generally rose at an annual rate of no more than about 20–25 per cent), and it stood in marked contrast to 'such strife-torn countries as Guatemala, El Salvador and Nicaragua'.* In the 1960s and 1970s Colombia showed the strongest economic growth of any republic other than Brazil and Mexico.†

Colombia, however, was an exception in Latin America, and its performance was little noticed, for in the course of the 1960s reformist nationalism was generally perceived to be an option that was bound to fail. Both left and right regarded the democratic state as being too weak either to bring about social change or to secure orderly progress. From the mid-1960s until the 1980s most countries experienced acute and prolonged crises of authority as the political centre crumbled and the revolutionary left joined battle with the modernizing right for the opportunity to refashion both the state and the economy.

As in the 1920s and 1930s, it was the armed forces which felt called to determine the course of the nation. Brazil experienced a *coup d'état* in 1964 that opened the way to continuous rule by military juntas until 1985. Argentina underwent a coup in 1966 and, after a brief neo-Peronist interlude in the early 1970s, endured military juntas until 1984. Peru was governed by the armed forces from 1968 until 1980. Uruguay, which had a record of uninterrupted electoral politics since 1903, succumbed to military intervention in 1973 and did not return to civilian government for over a decade. Chile, which had been another 'model' Latin American democracy, suffered

---

* *Latin American Debt and the Adjustment Crisis*, Macmillan Press Series (Macmillan: London, 1987), pp. 330–3.
† See Statistical Appendix, tables 3 and 4.

a very bloody coup in 1973 and was ruled by a military strongman until 1989.

Military Dictatorships and the State

The appearance of military regimes in some of the most advanced countries within the space of a decade signified the breakdown of the state under the stress of industrial development. The cleavages between the export sector and protected domestic industry, and between capital and labour, had deepened to the point where any possibility of consent and legitimacy had all but evaporated, leaving military force as the residue of fruitless statecraft.

There was, of course, nothing new about military intervention in politics; it had occurred countless times in Latin America, but these frequent intrusions had been largely instrumental – a matter of replacing one government or *caudillo* by another. In the 1960s and 1970s however, the armed forces entered politics as an institutional bloc determined to fill the void left by the demise of the democratic state. The object was to proceed with modernization by suspending politics altogether and installing technocrats to reorganize the economy while the armed forces imposed law and order. In fact, these 'bureaucratic-authoritarian regimes', as they were termed, attempted to create a strong state in very different ways, and their policies, moreover, often underwent radical changes as they too tried to contend with crises of development.

In Brazil and Argentina the military juntas of the 1960s opted to continue with state-led ISI by arbitrating between the export élites and the new élites of protected industrialists, while using force to repress the wage demands of the trade unions. By the early 1970s both countries were in a state of internal war between soldiers and Marxist guerrillas. Three-figure inflation fuelled by intensive ISI and uncheckable public spending led to tight financial policies in the latter half of the decade; but the social cost was so high that policies of monetary restraint had to be modified, if not abandoned, and inflation spun out of control once again.

By contrast, the army in Peru launched a coup and chose, uniquely, to adopt the radical nationalist policies of the revolutionary left, for in the early 1960s the armed forces had been called upon to put down a guerrilla insurrection in the Andes and many officers had been appalled by the poverty of the Indian peasantry. In 1968 the Peruvian generals nationalized the commanding heights of the export-economy: large estates and plantations were expropriated and turned into co-operatives so as to break the economic power of the agrarian élites. The military government then mobilized workers, peasants and shantytown dwellers under an umbrella organization directed by the regime. This strategy represented a partial return to the corporatism of the 1940s, as in Cárdenas's Mexico or Perón's Argentina, but the land reform and the socialization of production was carried much further, and modelled on the communist Cuba of the 1960s.

The strategy failed: inflation soared as export prices fell and production stagnated. Despite the corporate structures, industrial action for higher wages intensified when world recession after 1973 drove down living standards. In 1975 a new chief of the military junta began to dismantle this experiment in radical economic nationalism in order to prepare for a return to electoral politics in 1980. The elected civilian president, Fernando Belaúnde Terry, introduced a policy of free enterprise and privatization, but was faced with massive labour protests and renewed guerrilla violence. The conflicts that had torn apart the Peruvian state in the late 1960s were no closer to being resolved after twelve years of military rule.

In Chile the armed forces chose a course diametrically opposed to the Peruvians. After an attempt by the elected Marxist government of Salvador Allende (1970–73) to achieve the socialist transformation of the economy, the military under General Pinochet set out to destroy the left and restore the free market. This was the first systematic departure in Latin America from the orthodoxies of economic nationalism and state-led ISI, which had ruled policy on development since the 1930s. The cleavage between capital and labour, having already deepened disastrously as a result of Allende's policies, would become a gulf under Pinochet with the savage repression of trade unions and the very high levels of unemployment caused by Draconian anti-inflation measures. However, the rival demands of protected home industry and the export sector were dealt with, not by some form of corporatism in the usual way, but by removing tariff barriers and letting the free market allocate resources between the two sectors. Pinochet's harsh dictatorial rule endured through to the end of the 1980s, and though economic productivity eventually improved and hyperinflation was curbed, the social costs were unprecedented in their severity.* Until the departure of Pinochet it would not become clear whether such drastic military surgery had actually done anything to solve the fundamental problem of authority in the state.

* For comparative figures on inflation, see Statistical Appendix, table 4.

The Marxist Challenge

Until the 1960s Marxism played only a marginal role in Latin American politics. Before the development of import-substituting industrialization, the working class was small. Communist parties had been founded in the latter half of the 1920s, but they remained insignificant until the late 1940s. In Cuba, however, where there existed large industrialized sugar plantations run by US companies, and in Chile, where copper-mining produced a sizeable proletariat, the Communist Party sank deep roots in the working class.

Another reason for the limited success of the communist parties was their subordination to Stalin's Communist International. In the Comintern's scheme of things Latin America did not count for much because it was overwhelmingly agrarian. According to orthodox Marxist theory, socialism was possible only after a bourgeois industrial revolution had taken place. Therefore, the role assigned to the Latin American parties by Moscow was that of building up support in the emerging industrial workforce and joining with economic nationalists in pressing for protectionism and state-led industrialization. The most successful example of this policy was the coalition of Communists and Radicals in a popular front in Chile, which was responsible in the early 1940s for the setting-up of state corporations to encourage industrial development.

The Cold War anti-communism of the USA was reflected in Latin America by the exclusion of communists from government, and even from political life in some countries. Yet the communist threat was more a figure of political rhetoric than a reality, and tended to be invoked by the USA whenever it saw fit to practise 'big-stick' diplomacy. In Guatemala the radical nationalist government of Jacobo Arbenz was accused of being a stalking-horse for the Communist Party by the US government, which had been upset by proposals for land reform affecting the immense holdings of the United Fruit Company. Arbenz was duly overthrown in 1954 by an invasion force financed by the CIA. These events were witnessed by a young Argentine doctor, Ernesto 'Che' Guevara, who was to become the embodiment of the US government's worst fears of Marxist penetration of the Americas after he joined the nationalist rebel Fidel Castro in 1956 in a bid to topple the US-backed dictatorship in Cuba.

The success of the Cuban Revolution in 1959 transformed the prospects of Marxism in Latin America. After Fidel Castro declared himself a Marxist in 1961, an entire generation of Latin American socialists looked to Havana rather than to Moscow for revolutionary inspiration. For the Cuban Revolution discredited the cautious reformism of the communist parties, identifying socialism with long-standing Latin American traditions of armed rebellion. It also held out the hope of realizing the highest aspirations of nationalism: the forging of an authentic cultural identity once foreign imperialists and their agents had been driven out of the country. The Cuban guerrilla struggle was to provide a pattern for other wars of liberation in the continent, as well as in Africa and Asia. More generally, the revolution, having taken place in an agrarian country and without the aid of the Soviet Union, renewed interest in Marxist theory and played a significant part in the rise of an intellectual 'New Left' in Latin America, as well as in Europe and the USA.

New Left theorists took the reformist notions of economic dependency, which had been elaborated by ECLA economists in the 1950s, and used them to recast the Leninist theory of imperialism. In the New Left view, international trade was intrinsically imperialistic, for the European powers had been able to accumulate the capital required for their own development by exploiting the human and material resources of Latin America ever since the Conquest. After political independence, this pattern of imperialism did not change; it was reinforced by an international division of labour which integrated the Latin American countries of the 'periphery' into the world economy by gearing their agricultural and mining resources for export to the 'metropolis' in return for higher-value industrial goods. In addition to making the entire economy of the peripheral countries excessively vulnerable to fluctuations in world prices, this unequal trade allowed capital to build up in the industrial countries for further investment in technological development. It followed that when the peripheral countries tried to industrialize, they would find themselves dependent upon financial and technical assistance from the metropolis. Therefore, their industrial development would lag behind and remain subservient to neo-colonialist powers, in whose interest it was to maintain the division of labour which condemned the periphery to produce low-value commodities or, at best, less sophisticated industrial manufactures.

The economic imperialism of the industrial powers was, however, sustained ultimately by a system of class relations in both the metropolis and the periphery. Metropolitan capitalists dominated Latin American countries because the local élites collaborated with them in operating cheap-labour export-economies in return for luxury imports and the finished goods of industry. Thus the old and the new in Latin America were inextricably connected: the paternalistic labour relations of the traditional hacienda were as much a part of the international capitalist order as the assembly line of a factory. Given this complicity of the Latin American élites in economic imperialism, it was only by mobilizing the working class and the peasants to seize power in the state that the complex ties of dependency could be broken. Socialist revolution was the prerequisite of true national sovereignty and balanced development.

The Cuban Revolution made such an impact on the international socialist movement because it stimulated fresh thinking to explain 'under-development' and furnished a practice by which to end it. The Revolution coincided with the 'deepening' of import-substitution in the more indus-trialized nations of the region. It therefore occurred against a general back-ground in Latin America of acute rural misery, the growth of vast, inhuman shantytowns around the main cities, gross disparities of income, desperate unemployment and uncheckable inflation. At the same time university edu-cation had expanded, so that a new and larger generation of students – the majority from middle-class backgrounds – looked to the Cuban guerrilla war as a model for ending the terrible social inequalities of the continent.

The upsurge of revolutionary socialism during the 1960s occurred outside the communist parties. It amounted to the release of new political energies which communist organizers and trade-union leaders were unable to harness. The new revolutionaries, on the other hand, lacked a broad social base among the industrial proletariat, and were to have even less success with the peasantry, who were mostly Indians working on haciendas or living as ever from subsistence agriculture and sometimes outside the money economy altogether.

The Marxist guerrillas of the 1960s and 1970s remained largely cut off from the masses. The role they chose for themselves was that of a revolutionary vanguard, their task being to induce a terminal crisis of the capitalist state through direct violence. Often this brought them into conflict with the established organizations of the working class. In Argentina, for instance, young Peronist guerrillas engaged in a protracted bloody struggle against the official Peronist machine for control of the trade unions. The strategy of armed struggle at times led to sporadic terrorist violence against 'bourgeois' targets such as businessmen, foreign diplomats, and soldiers, and even against peasants or workers who were deemed to merit 'revolutionary justice'. Guerrilla action thus contributed to the weakening of the rule of law in states that were already extremely fragile, and it provided the armed forces with a pretext to ride roughshod over political and human rights in order to root out 'subversives'. The 1970s saw a grave breakdown of law and order in the more economically advanced countries of the continent such as Brazil,

Argentina, Uruguay and Chile. In their determination to stamp out the guerrilla insurgencies, the armed forces resorted to imprisonment without trial, torture, abduction and the execution of suspects by death squads.

In highly urbanized countries such as Argentina and Uruguay there arose a new type of Latin American insurgent – the urban guerrilla, who chose the big city, with its sprawling anonymity, as the battlefield against the ruling classes. Very much the product of the New Left in the universities, these guerrillas nevertheless defined themselves within a native tradition of revolt against colonial oppressors. Hence their names: the Tupamaros of Uruguay invoked Tupac Amaru, the Indian chieftain who led a massive uprising of Andean communities against white creoles and Spaniards in the eighteenth century, while the Montoneros of Argentina, a Marxist offshoot of the Peronist movement, recalled the nineteenth-century phenomenon of the *montoneras*, rebellions of gaucho horsemen led by provincial *caudillos* against the forces of the cosmopolitan Buenos Aires liberals.

Urban guerrillas proved difficult to defeat. They operated through a network of small cells in which the identity of the members of any one cell remained unknown to the others. This structure was designed to prevent the police and the military from discovering the size and composition of the organization as a whole. Urban guerrillas, moreover, were able to melt into civilian life after their attacks, and they learned to manipulate the sensation-hungry news media through spectacular exploits against the authorities, creating for themselves a romantic mystique with the public. The urban guerrillas were finally crushed by the end of the 1970s, but at the cost of lawless 'dirty wars', which tore civil society apart and utterly discredited the armed forces' claim to be the guardians of the nation's honour.

The experience of Argentina and Uruguay suggests that the more industrialized countries had already developed societies too complex and diverse for a strategy of armed violence by a revolutionary vanguard to succeed. In Chile a different route to socialism was attempted after the election to the presidency in 1970 of the Marxist Salvador Allende at the head of a coalition of Socialists, Communists and Catholic radicals. Allende's government proposed to create a socialist society by constitutional means. It was a strategy similar to that advocated at this time by several West European communist parties, and this was one reason why the Chilean experiment in peaceful revolution attracted immense international interest. Allende's government, however, was eventually overthrown by the armed forces.

Marxist guerrilla insurgencies fared best in small agrarian countries where there was a legacy of frustrated nationalism and where government was exceptionally corrupt and tyrannical. Cuba is the paradigm, but in the

1970s and 1980s Central America saw the development of major guerrilla movements in Nicaragua, El Salvador and Guatemala. However, Fidel Castro's amazing victory of 1959 had become difficult to repeat some twenty years later. The USA feared the geopolitical consequences of a socialist revolution in its 'backyard', given the proximity of the Panama Canal and the precedent of the Cuban missile crisis of 1962. The US government acted to defeat, or at least contain, the guerrillas by equipping and training Central American armed forces, and by pouring in dollars to support non-Marxist governments in the region – preferably democratic ones, but also military juntas and personalist dictators.

In 1979 the Nicaraguan guerrillas succeeded in toppling the infamous Somoza dictatorship. The US president Jimmy Carter had withdrawn US support for Somoza because of his violations of human rights. After the victory of the Sandinista National Liberation Front, he offered economic assistance to encourage the foundation of a liberal democratic system in the country. But the Marxist parties within the Sandinista Front wanted to follow the Cuban example and build a revolutionary socialist state. This provoked a split in the Front, which led to non-Marxist Sandinistas taking up arms once more against the new regime. Eventually most of these now anti-Sandinista rebels joined forces with former members of Somoza's national guard to form a guerrilla army with bases in neighbouring Honduras and Costa Rica. The guerrillas were financed and trained by the USA, for Carter's successor, Ronald Reagan, saw these Contras (from *contra-revolucionarios*) as a proxy force that could undermine the Sandinista government without the USA having to commit its troops directly in Central America.

A feature that distinguished the Nicaraguan Revolution from the Cuban was the participation in the post-revolutionary government of progressive Catholic clergy. Nicaragua was a more deeply Catholic country than Cuba, and the Sandinistas were aware of the need to win over, rather than antagonize, the Church if the loyalty of the common people was to be assured. But the Catholic hierarchy and the Vatican were unsympathetic to the revolutionary government. In any case, the mounting problems – food shortages, hyperinflation, a US economic blockade, the ravages of the Contra war and government mismanagement – alienated large sectors of the population and drove huge numbers of Nicaraguans, including peasants, into exile. By 1988 the Sandinista regime seemed close to economic collapse, although scandals and congressional pressure in the USA forced the Reagan administration to suspend military (but not 'humanitarian') aid to the Contra guerrilla forces.

In reality, an impasse had been reached in the conflict between the Sandinistas and their enemies. The guerrilla war in neighbouring El Salvador was also in deadlock. This allowed the Central American governments to agree a peace plan in 1986–7 which was put forward by the Costa Rican president Oscar Arias (for which he won the Nobel Peace Prize) requiring the suspension of hostilities by all combatants in the region, the holding of clean elections, guarantees of political freedom for opposition parties, and progress towards the setting up of a Central American parliament. The principle of the Arias plan was that the Central Americans should solve their own problems by negotiation. The USA remained an interested party, although the election of George Bush to the presidency in 1989 heralded a change of emphasis from Reagan's policy of indirect military aggression to one of continued economic attrition. By early 1990 this policy of economic blockade and political isolation had paid off: when the Sandinistas held free elections to show their democratic good faith in the spirit of the Arias plan, they lost unexpectedly to their opponents, who had gathered in a fractious electoral coalition under the leadership of Violeta Chamorro. The Nicaraguan Revolution had failed to survive in its Marxist form.

In the 1980s the Marxist challenge to the traumatic process of capitalist industrialization appeared to have receded. Although Marxist nationalists saw the class struggle as the key to ending imperialism and dependency, it had become clear that there could be no blueprint for revolution in Latin America. The political violence of left and right, the experience of guerrilla terror and military counter-terror, had exhausted the population of one country after another. Even the massive debt problem of the 1980s – which caused a worse depression than in the 1930s – did not immediately revive the fortunes of the revolutionary left. One reason for this was that Cuba lost its political prestige during the 1970s as revelations about repression of dissent, institutional authoritarianism and economic stagnation cooled the enthusiasm of Latin American youth for Fidel Castro. In the 1980s the dominant feeling was that human rights and basic freedoms had to be respected, and that the state, which had all but collapsed in several major countries, must be strengthened not by force but by consent for the rule of law. There was a widespread and growing desire to return to the liberal democratic values that had inspired the makers of Latin American constitutions at the time of independence.

This is not to say that Marxism had ceased to be a potent ideology. Substantial guerrilla movements continued to operate in El Salvador, Guatemala and Colombia. In Chile, the Communist Party remained a powerful though clandestine force, and in the 1980s included guerrilla struggle in its overall strategy to overthrow the military regime. Most remarkable of all was the emergence in the early 1980s of an idiosyncratic guerrilla movement in the central Andean highlands of Peru, which went by the mystical name of *Sendero Luminoso* (Shining Path), and whose ideology was nebulous but seemed to consist of a synthesis of Maoism and the Indianism of José Carlos Mariátegui, the intellectual mentor of Peruvian Marxism.

Founded by Abimael Guzmán, a philosophy professor at the University of Ayacucho, the *Sendero Luminoso* remained a shadowy force. Shunning the news media, it preferred to communicate with the wider society through a variety of apocalyptic signals, such as causing power failures in the cities, blowing up trains and setting huge crosses ablaze on hilltops. The movement employed the guerrilla methods of the 1960s to put into practice the ideals of the *indigenismo* of the 1920s; it rejected European influence in order to forge a national identity from the cultural heritage of the Indian peoples. *Sendero Luminoso* was the most radical expression of Marxist nationalism yet seen in Latin America, and, as with other guerrilla movements, its chances of success appeared to depend on the depth and duration of the economic depression induced by the staggering foreign debt crisis of the 1980s.

The Catholic Church

Economic progress in the period of rapid capitalist growth from the 1870s to the 1920s had deeply affected the role of the Catholic Church in Latin America. For so long as society remained overwhelmingly rural, the Church's influence would be strong. But as the experience of Europe had shown, there were no greater solvents of religious belief than those twin indices of modernity – urbanization and industrialization. As increasing numbers of peasants left the villages to settle in the big cities, the bonds of obedience that tied them to their priests were loosened in the amorphous urban mass. Immigration also stretched the Church's resources and compounded its pastoral problems. And when governments from the late 1930s began to adopt a policy of rapid industrial development, the Church faced the gravest threat yet to its authority.

The Church, which had once been an integral element of the Catholic monarchy, had been losing intellectual ground since independence to the principles of liberalism. By the early decades of the twentieth century there were few republics that had not effectively separated the affairs of Church and state. Even so, the Church wielded enormous social and cultural influence. Although largely deprived of a constitutional role, Catholicism provided a defensive bulwark for the traditional communities against the incursions of modern life. For instance, the coming of the republic in Brazil at the end of the nineteenth century was accompanied by uprisings of Catholic peasants against the liberal state. During the Mexican Revolution, the insurgency led by Zapata was as much a defence of traditional communities imbued with Catholicism as a revolutionary attack on capitalism. Indeed, next to the seizure of their lands there was nothing more likely to move peasants to rebellion than an attempt to interfere with the practice of their religion, as was attested in Mexico by the Cristero wars against the revolutionary government in the 1920s. For despite, or perhaps because of, the triumphs of liberalism, the Church was by far the most effective guardian of the vital sources of cultural identity for the common people. Traditional Catholicism appealed most to the mestizos, caught as they had always been between white society and the Indians, and, even though often mixed with pre-Christian elements, the religious culture of the Indian communities themselves would scarcely survive the destruction of Catholic devotion in Latin America.

Thus, when liberalism came under attack in the early twentieth century, Catholicism attracted many nationalist intellectuals because of its historic resistance to alien liberal ideas and its deep roots in popular culture. But this brand of nationalism tended to be conservative, if not reactionary: it simply equated cultural authenticity with a rejection of the modern world. It was, in fact, the heir of the clerical traditionalism of the previous century, and indeed, in most countries – although the priests in the rural parishes often strongly identified with the interests of the people – the Church hierarchy remained associated with the conservative landed interest. Catholicism made little headway on the left, where it was identified as the ideology of the Spanish colonial oppressor. Left-wing nationalists tended to search for their cultural roots in the pre-Columbian Indian civilizations or in the culture of the African slaves.

The Catholic Church thus found itself threatened from two directions. First, there was the disruptive progress of liberal capitalism itself, whose reliance on the market and on individual enterprise undermined the hierarchical, paternalist ethos which the Church had done so much to preserve in the New World. Then there was secular nationalism, often allied to fascism or socialism, which challenged religious authority and was advancing in the cities, precisely where the Church was most rapidly losing ground among the mass of the people. For these reasons the Catholic Church sought a middle way for Latin American society between liberal capitalism and atheistic revolutionary ideologies.

This search had its origins in the Church's response to the problems of industrialization in Europe in the middle of the nineteenth century. The framework for Catholic social thinking about the rights of labour and the obligations of capital was eventually provided by the papal encyclical *Rerum novarum* of 1891. In Latin America, as in Europe, this papal exhortation to promote social justice led sectors of the Church to set up organizations for the working classes – trade unions, co-operatives, educational centres, peasant leagues and newspapers. Social Catholicism was reformist: it rejected the class struggle in favour of intervention by the state to foster the welfare of the most disadvantaged. It was therefore very sympathetic to corporatism and to the emerging economic nationalism of the 1930s. But it found enemies in the growing numbers of socialists and communists, who perceived in it a powerful rival in the field of social mobilization.

In a country like Chile where the Church was strong and had a tradition of social action, it competed with the burgeoning communist movement for the leadership of workers and peasants. The Church's policy was to step up the organization of workers into Catholic unions while training a political élite in its social principles at institutions like the Catholic University of Santiago. Chile produced a generation of young politicians, men like Eduardo Frei, Radomiro Tomic and Bernardo Leighton, who in the late 1930s formed a social-Catholic party which antagonized both the conservatives and the left. For what such progressive Catholic movements in Chile and elsewhere in Latin America were groping towards was a democratic, socially responsible form of capitalism guaranteeing workers' rights and promoting agrarian reform.

The political opportunity for this type of reformism came in the late 1950s, when industrialization was well advanced and the USA had made continued aid for development conditional upon democratic government. Progressive Catholicism found expression in Christian Democratic parties, notably in Chile, Venezuela, Peru and El Salvador, though in some countries social Catholicism shaped the attitudes of other parties, as in the case of the Conservatives in Colombia or the PAN in Mexico. In the 1960s Christian Democratic parties began to participate in government. Eduardo Frei was elected president of Chile in 1964, but his ambitious programme of reform foundered on the opposition of right and left. The Christian Democrat Rafael Caldera became president of Venezuela from 1969 until 1974. Christian Democrats in Peru gave tactical support to the reformist government of Belaúnde Terry between 1963 and 1968.

The fortunes of Christian Democratic reformism, however, were epitomized by the fate of the party in El Salvador. Founded in the early 1960s, its leader José Napoleón Duarte won the presidency in 1972, but was ousted and tortured by the highly conservative armed forces. From 1979 Duarte, following a coup by liberal junior officers, participated in a government which tried to introduce nationalist economic measures, including a thorough land reform in this small but badly overpopulated country. The reforms were blocked by the army which intensified its savage repression of labour leaders. The result was that El Salvador erupted in revolutionary guerrilla war. Though Duarte reasserted his ideal of democratic reformism (he was elected president in 1984), he was to become by the late 1980s the prisoner of intransigent military chieftains. The Christian Democratic government thus lost its cohesion by trying to hold to a centre ground in a conflict increasingly polarized by the activities of military death squads and Marxist guerrillas. (The radical wing of the Christian Democratic Party had opted for armed struggle alongside the forces of the left.)

The political radicalization of Catholicism was a phenomenon of the 1960s. In part this was a reflection of the enormous influence of the Cuban Revolution. But it was primarily a consequence of the Second Vatican Council (1962–5), which re-examined the Catholic Church's role in the modern world, encouraging theological innovation and sharpening awareness among the clergy of social and economic issues. In a continent undergoing the acute social stresses of industrialization, the most notable result of this *aggiornamento* or updating of Catholicism was a 'theology of liberation' which departed from orthodoxy by arguing that Christian charity must be interpreted as a commitment to work for the liberation of the oppressed and the poor, even if this involved the use of violence. Clearly, liberation theology was permeated by Marxist concepts of class struggle, exploitation and imperialism, and it split opinion in the Catholic Church. But the intellectual convergence with Marxist ideas allowed radical Catholics to make common cause with revolutionary socialists in the fight against capitalism.

In the 1960s and 1970s some clergy supported armed insurrection. A number of priests actually joined Marxist guerrillas in the countryside. The most celebrated of these was Camilo Torres, a Colombian from an upper-class family of Bogotá, who incurred the displeasure of the conservative hierarchy when he issued a radical political manifesto in 1965. Choosing to be laicized, he joined a Cuban-style guerrilla force and was killed in action in February 1966, earning a worldwide fame that was overshadowed only by the murder of Che Guevara in Bolivia the following year.

Less dramatically, many radical priests took jobs in factories in the industrial belts of the big cities, where they could live in the midst of the de-Christianized workers. Others organized religious and social activities in the shantytowns. Missionaries working in the Indian communities encouraged political action to win land reform. Liberation theology inspired a new form of pastoral organization, the *comunidad de base*, a grass-roots community of lay people who tried to set the liturgy and teaching of the Church in a context of action for better social conditions. This revitalization of the Church's missionary energies in the Western Hemisphere was signalled at the 1968 Conference of Latin American Bishops held at Medellín in Colombia (it was opened by Pope Paul VI, the first Roman pontiff to visit Latin America). It was declared that the Church had made an 'option for the poor', a phrase that seemed to endorse liberation theology. Such an impression was reinforced when a number of distinguished prelates, such as Dom Helder Câmara of Recife in Brazil, attracted worldwide attention by supporting striking workers and denouncing economic dependency.

Even though a section of the clergy had clearly adopted positions which implied acceptance of the need for revolutionary change, the vast majority of Latin American laity and clergy was not drawn to the theology of liberation. The Church's 'option for the poor' must be seen rather as a further development of social Catholicism in response to the painful industrial revolutions taking place in Latin America after the Second World War. The 1960s and 1970s, in particular, saw a general deepening of Catholic commitment to social justice (especially on the issues of landlessness and agrarian reform), and there was criticism of capitalist development, though no condemnation of capitalism as such.

In the course of the 1970s, as industrialization took its toll in political breakdown and internal war, another function was thrust upon the Catholic Church. It began to champion the human rights of the individual citizen against the abuses of power by authoritarian regimes, especially in countries where the armed forces were engaged in the repression of guerrillas. With the collapse of democratic institutions, and in the absence of the rule of law, the Church acted as a political sanctuary, a refuge of last resort for a defenceless citizenry in countries where legal order had given way to social war.

Such a role had already been adumbrated in the mid-1950s, when the Church in Argentina, during the last years of Perón's government, acted as the final institutional barrier against the wholesale 'Peronization' of civil society. In Chile, after the fall of Salvador Allende in 1973, the Church was one of the few autonomous institutions able to criticize the military dictatorship and provide relief to the mounting numbers left destitute by its economic policies. In Cuba, where religion was historically weak, the Church was unable to resist the tightening of the Communist Party's grip on civil society in the 1970s. However, in Nicaragua during the 1980s it became a focus of opposition to a similar monopolization of power by the Sandinista

Front, even though the revolutionary government there contained a number of prominent Jesuits and priests and enjoyed the support of clergy adhering to liberation theology. In neighbouring El Salvador, which suffered an inconclusive guerrilla war throughout the 1980s, the clergy consistently denounced the activities of right-wing death squads and the use of torture by the military. Such opposition led to the murder in March 1980 of the Archbishop of San Salvador, Oscar Romero, on the steps of his own cathedral as he was celebrating mass before a large congregation. As the crisis of the state in many Latin American countries became ever more acute, the Catholic Church detached itself from any direct association with either the right or the left, and maintained a position of critical independence from political interests. This stance was explicitly reinforced by Pope John Paul II, who, during a visit to Brazil in July 1980, forbade clergy from holding political office and condemned the use of violence as a means of social change.

In the course of the twentieth century the Latin American Church finally gave up its aspirations to enjoy an official position in the state. Nevertheless, it recovered two of its historic functions at a time when Latin America was undergoing its most profound social and economic transformation since the Conquest. Reviving the spirit of Bartolomé de las Casas, churchmen criticized the abuse of state power by despotic élites, while the energy with which many of the clergy pursued the 'option for the poor' recalled the commitment of the early missionaries to the creation of a just society in the New World. In many countries the Church acted as the conscience of an otherwise brutalized society, bearing witness to a sense of the common good as the vital seed of authentic nationhood.

The Debt Crisis of the 1980s

The mounting problems caused by the economic distortions of import-substituting industrialization and the associated weakening of the state came to a head in the 1980s. The crisis had been deferred in the 1960s by strong world growth, and in the 1970s, when international demand was slack, by foreign loans. But a sudden change in the world financial system effectively cut off the flow of capital to Latin America.

In August of 1982 the Mexican government announced that it was unable to pay the interest on its debt to foreign banks. Mexico was followed shortly by virtually all the Latin American countries, including Cuba. (Suspension of debt payments occurred also in African and Asian countries, but the sheer size of the Latin American debt focused international attention on the continent.) The total outstanding Latin American debt in 1982 was estimated at $315.3 billion, although over $270 billion was owed by just five countries – precisely those which had undergone the fastest ISI growth in the 1960s and 1970s. Brazil was the largest debtor, owing $87.5 billion; Mexico owed $85.5 billion, Argentina $43.6 billion, Venezuela $31 billion and Chile $17 billion.*

What had caused the crash? The immediate factor was the steep rise in US interest rates in 1979–82. This was a response to the high rates of inflation and the consequent weakness of the dollar caused by the producers' cartel, OPEC, sharply raising the price of oil in 1973 and again in 1979. A world recession followed, which had a disastrous effect on the economies of Latin America: commodity prices started to fall on world markets just when higher export earnings were needed to cope with sharply rising interest rates on the foreign debt.

The bonanza of lending and borrowing that Latin American governments and Western banks had indulged in throughout the 1970s had its origins in the very phenomenon that would cause it to come to an abrupt end a decade later: the OPEC cartel's oil-price rises of 1973 and 1979. High oil prices allowed producer countries, especially the Middle Eastern Arab states, to build up huge surpluses on their balance of payments. Profits from oil exports were too large to be fully absorbed by investment in their domestic economies, and so these OPEC countries deposited vast sums of money in European and North American banks. Western bankers then set about looking for ways of getting a good return on these windfall deposits, and their most willing clients were the developing countries of the Third World, who were hungry as always for development capital.

Latin America was especially susceptible to the blandishments of the Western banks, for in the early 1970s, as we have seen, the most advanced of the industrializing countries in the region had come to the limit of the 'hard' phase of import-substitution; the process of state-subsidized inward-looking development could be kept going only by borrowing abroad to cover the yawning deficits between national income and expenditure. There followed a mad spiral of irresponsible, profit-driven lending and unwise borrowing, in which Western bankers as much as Latin American officials appeared to overlook the implications of taking out huge loans on 'floating' instead of fixed interest rates. However, after the shock of the second oil-price rise in 1979, conservative administrations in the USA and other industrial countries like Britain decided to bring their domestic inflation under control by restricting the supply of money and credit; this economic policy choked

* See Statistical Appendix, table 5.

off demand in the West and produced a worldwide recession. International interest rates on foreign debt suddenly started to 'float' ever upwards until by the middle of 1982 most Third World countries found it impossible to meet their interest payments.

Indebtedness and high inflation were not, therefore, peculiar to Latin America. In fact, most governments in the industrial countries had been running up debts during the 1970s. The US budget deficit in 1982 was actually larger than that of the worst Latin American debtors, and throughout the 1980s the Reagan administration, for fear of electoral unpopularity, was unwilling to cut it by raising taxes or reducing imports. Yet it was the Latin American debt and not the US deficit which caused international alarm, because a country's economic health was judged according to its perceived ability to overcome its financial difficulties, a factor expressed in terms of the ratio of interest payments to export earnings. Latin American countries scored badly here, given their relative neglect of the export sector in the pursuit of import-substitution. In 1982 most had ratios in excess of 20 per cent of interest payments to exports; Brazil and Argentina came off worst with ratios of 57.1 per cent and 54.6 per cent respectively, while Mexico, despite being a major oil exporter, had a ratio of 39.9 per cent.* In other words, the economies that had grown fastest in the 1970s were the most deeply indebted in the 1980s.

What had gone wrong with ISI development? In essence, it had failed to cure the underlying malaise which had begun to show itself as early as the 1920s – lack of productivity. With the aim of achieving self-sufficiency, economic planners had concentrated on substituting industrial imports by setting up national industries and protecting them behind high tariff walls to the general detriment of agriculture and the export sector. (Brazil was a partial exception since from the mid-1970s it had begun to subsidize industrial exports – an expensive exercise that did not tackle the underlying problem of productive efficiency.) National industry had been overprotected for too long and had failed to become efficient and competitive: the price of its manufactures was often up to three times the world price. Latin American economies therefore ended up with not only an unproductive export sector, dominated still by low-value primary commodities, but also an unproductive industrial sector, which nevertheless consumed expensive imports of technology.† The chronic shortfall between exports and imports resulted in high inflation and mounting debts.

* See Statistical Appendix, table 6.
† For illustrative data on the structure of imports and exports, see Statistical Appendix, table 8.

To make matters worse, the debt problem had been badly aggravated by the financial instability caused by hyperinflation in the 1970s. As confidence in the economy evaporated in the late 1970s, there occurred massive capital flight. Instead of investing their money at home – where the currency was virtually worthless and industries regularly made losses – rich Latin Americans put it into real estate abroad or deposited it in the very banks that were issuing loans to their own governments and companies. Huge sums were taken out of these countries: the World Bank estimated that between 1979 and 1982, $27 billion left Mexico, nearly a third of its foreign debt in 1982, and $19 billion left Argentina, whose debt in 1982 was $43.6 billion. (Brazil and Colombia were relatively unaffected because of their sustained growth and high domestic interest rates.) US and European bankers colluded fully in this crazy financial cycle, pressing high-yield loans on Latin American governments while turning a blind eye to the lucrative deposits coming in from private Latin American sources (which were more often than not the indirect recipients of those very loans).

When the crash finally came, the wage-earners and the poor felt it most: inflation soared even higher in the 1980s than in the 1970s, real wages fell, and government spending on food subsidies, transport, health and education was slashed.* In 1980–84 overall growth in Latin America fell by nearly 9 per cent. Consumption per capita dropped by 17 per cent in Argentina and Chile, by 14 per cent in Peru, by 8 per cent in Mexico and Brazil. Urban unemployment doubled in Argentina, Uruguay and Venezuela between 1979 and 1984, reaching unprecedented proportions everywhere else. This enormous rise occurred, moreover, in countries where unemployment was already endemic, and where there existed few if any social security benefits for the jobless.

In order to avoid complete economic collapse, governments needed further loans to service their debts and resume investment. Additional finance from foreign banks was made conditional on the implementation of austerity packages designed to cut inflation and adjust the balance of payments. In order to balance the internal and external accounts, imports had to be drastically reduced and exports increased. But such a task placed a crushing and sometimes self-defeating burden on the people of Latin America: the slashing of imports meant that many everyday goods, including food items, became unavailable or else prohibitively expensive, while factories were unable to acquire the spare parts and machinery they needed to improve output and performance. The export of manufactures thus became more

* For inflation figures see Statistical Appendix, table 4.

difficult to achieve precisely at a time when an increase in traditional exports of minerals and agricultural products was limited by low world-commodity prices.

Throughout the 1980s economic growth remained sluggish or even negative.* With living standards so badly depressed, black markets and crime were the only boom sectors: in the Andean countries the growing of coca leaf and marijuana allowed peasant farmers to survive, but the smuggling of the processed drugs to the USA and Western Europe by vicious mafia rings left a trail of corruption and lawlessness in all countries through which the drug traffic passed. In general, the dire poverty of large sectors of the population made the risk of social conflagrations alarmingly high: in great cities like Buenos Aires, Rio de Janeiro and Caracas the poor from the shantytowns were reduced on occasion to looting supermarkets for food.

The conditions set by the foreign banks were understandably resented by Latin American countries, but all accepted the financial discipline, though with varying enthusiasm because of the tremendous social costs involved and the consequent political difficulties. For the rest of the decade Latin American governments entered into complex negotiations with creditor banks over terms for rescheduling their debts. As new loans were secured to meet interest payments on earlier loans, so the total burden of debt continued to accumulate at a rate of about 9 per cent a year. By 1987, according to some calculations, Latin America had become a net exporter of capital to the developed world, having already remitted to the banks a sum ($121.1 billion) which was larger than the total amount it had received in the period 1974–81 ($100.7 billion).

Some countries tried to break out of the spiral of ever-rising debt by trying to limit payments of interest. In Peru, the APRA government of Alan García, when elected in 1985, declared that it would limit repayments to 10 per cent of export earnings so that state spending on social welfare would not have to be cut so drastically. But what was gained from non-payment was lost through runaway inflation and lack of further lending from the banks, which refused to reschedule Peruvian debts. Desperate for credit, García proposed to nationalize the domestic banking sector, but this raised a storm of protest and deeply divided the nation. By the end of García's term of office, the country was on the verge of social and economic collapse, with hyperinflation running at an annual rate of 2,700 per cent. Brazil, too, was anxious about loss of sovereignty to external agencies, and under President José Sarney declared a moratorium on interest payments in Feb-

* See Statistical Appendix, table 3.

ruary 1987; but the outcome again was hyperinflation, a dearth of foreign credit and acute social unrest; so the moratorium was abandoned in early 1988. It was a fear of unleashing uncontrollable domestic crises that deterred debtor countries from coming together and forming a debtors' cartel against the banks or from repudiating the debt outright as Fidel Castro was urging at this time.

There appeared to be no way out of the debt crisis other than through some co-ordinated international effort to write off all or part of the debt and to relaunch the depressed economies of Latin America by providing new capital for productive investment rather than for the rescheduling of old debts. But the creditor nations were unable to agree on such a strategy, even though an economic relaunch in the Third World would have boosted world demand and restored the health of the international economy, which remained in recession until the late 1980s. Governments in the creditor countries were reluctant to take over the debt risk from the private banks, and these banks were not prepared to sustain any losses on the loans they had lavished on the Third World during the boom years of the 1970s. Some larger banks reduced their exposure to possible default by setting aside a proportion of their record profits in order to offset such a risk; this strategy put the banks in an even stronger position in negotiations with the Latin American debtors, since default no longer represented so great a threat to the financial system.

Other than profit-making by the banks, what stood in the way of relief or cancellation of the debts was a concern that new lending would simply encourage a return to the old inward-looking model of development based on import-substitution, and it was feared that this would surely lead to further debt crises in the future. However, in 1985 the US treasury secretary, James Baker, announced a plan which attempted to link a degree of debt relief with economic restructuring. According to the Baker Plan, debtor countries would receive new funding through the World Bank over the next three years if they agreed to accept a programme of economic reform drawn up by the International Monetary Fund (IMF), which entailed reducing government spending, privatizing the large state sector of the economy, removing barriers against foreign trade and investment, and stimulating exports. The debtor countries had little option but to negotiate such deals with the IMF, but the plan misfired because most of the new money it made available was at variable interest rates and this simply added to the overall burden of debt.

In March 1989, after the election of President George Bush, the new US treasury secretary, Nicholas Brady, introduced a plan which involved some write-down of debt by the banks, as well as swaps of old loans for long-term bonds bought at a discount or converted to a fixed rate of interest, and the provision of new loans over four years at more stable rates of interest. This was some recognition by the USA of the impossibility of Latin America ever being able to meet the accumulated volume of debts and interest payments in full, no less than an acceptance of the intolerable social and economic burdens that the debt problem represented for the population of the region. But the Brady Plan fell far short of the level of interest relief required to allow the debtor countries to resume significant growth, and it was thought unlikely to result in much new lending or even in reducing the overall volume of debt in the long run. As the *Wall Street Journal* observed of the Brady Plan: 'It primarily addressed the banks' desire to get out of Latin America and other big Third World borrowers, paying little heed to satisfying those nations' need for international finance.'* Western bankers were now more interested in the countries of Eastern Europe, where the demise of the communist regimes had opened up a potentially huge market for fresh credit.

Clearly, the debt crisis could be resolved only in an international context. But in the 1980s world conditions were extremely unfavourable to Latin America and prevented it from exporting its way out of debt despite enormous efforts: the prices of minerals and agricultural goods were very depressed on the world market, while exports of industrial manufactures were held back through lack of capital to import the necessary technology and because of a degree of protectionism against Third World manufacturers in the developed world. According to the Peruvian banker and former minister, Pedro-Pablo Kuczynski, the solution to the problem would arise through 'a mixture of policies and events – such as reform within the debtor countries, the renewal of capital inflows and a more buoyant international economy'.†

By the end of the 1980s there was a growing consensus among a new generation of Latin American politicians and planners on the need for internal structural reform of the economy. The central idea was that the state sector had grown far too large and domestic industries had been overprotected and for too long. The control of inflation, the cutting of budget deficits and a switch to realistic exchange rates were seen as priorities. Moreover, it was generally felt that industrialization had been too rapid, with too many planning mistakes and wasteful projects, while relative neglect of the rural

---

* 23 January 1990.

† *Latin American Debt: A Twentieth Century Fund Book* (The Johns Hopkins University Press: Baltimore and London, 1988), p. 176.

economy had resulted in terrible economic dislocations and political upheavals. The improvement of agricultural production, especially for home consumption, would help to stem the rural exodus and broaden the domestic market for industry.

And yet if such reforms were aimed at restoring the workings of a free market to allocate resources more efficiently, it was also generally acknowledged that the circumstances of developing countries required some regulation by the state to provide basic services. In most Latin American countries there was a huge population increase – about 32 million for the region as a whole in 1982–9, an amount about equivalent to the numbers of the unemployed.* The reform of agriculture also demanded state intervention: there remained the question of the overlarge, inefficient hacienda and the related problem of landlessness. Since large-scale redistribution of land was both politically explosive and economically unproductive – at least in the medium term – land reform would require a delicate balance between economic growth and social justice. In short, while the free market was necessary to correct the mistakes of the past, some mediation by the state would be indispensable in badly divided societies.

In the last years of the 1980s several new leaders were elected in major countries who were prepared to revise the dogmatic economic nationalism inherited from the 1930s, which had produced, in the view of the Argentine economist and Peronist politician Guido di Tella, a model of industrial development based on 'an economic strategy that ... emphasized the internal market, assuming the impossibility of industrial exports'.† The new Latin American presidents discarded this bias towards autarky and regulation, and accepted the basic principles of a market economy, proposing, with a degree of caution given the immense difficulties, to open their economies to foreign trade and investment. In 1988, Carlos Salinas de Gortari was elected president in Mexico; in 1989 the Peronist Carlos Menem won the presidency of Argentina, and the Christian Democrat Patricio Aylwin became the first freely elected president of Chile since 1970; in 1990 Brazil elected the forty-year-old Fernando Collor de Mello, the liberal Violeta Chamorro defeated the Sandinista Daniel Ortega in Nicaragua, the reform-minded Luis Lacalle was elected in Uruguay, and in Peru, Alberto Fujimori, an agronomist of Japanese descent who had no links with any of the established parties but who advocated change, won an election against the novelist Mario Vargas

---

* For size of population in selected countries and projected growth, see Statistical Appendix, table 1.

† Thorp and Whitehead, *Latin American Debt and the Adjustment Crisis*, p. 162.

Llosa, another independent, who campaigned on neo-liberal free-market policies.

As in the early 1960s, Latin America had produced a generation of political leaders committed to democracy and reform. Then the USA had embarked on the Alliance for Progress, a major programme of economic and political co-operation, but the times did not favour it. In the 1990s, however, circumstances were more propitious: economic and political attitudes in Latin America were far more attuned to those in the USA, and the likelihood of communist penetration had receded as the Soviet Union faced growing domestic difficulties. It was a matter too of self-interest, for Washington was deeply concerned by the international narcotics trade and had already offered the Andean countries some military and economic aid to combat the traffic. But the best long-term remedy was the economic development of the region, and the USA and other developed countries were in a position to offer assistance with the stabilization of the Latin American industrial revolutions and with the consolidation of the democratic state. This would be a task of historic significance, for in the 1990s Latin America had arrived at a juncture in its development where it had the best opportunity since independence to realize the democratic ideals of its great liberators.

Development and Nationhood in Historical Perspective

The 1980s were 'the decade of democracy' in Latin America in contrast to the 1960s and 1970s, which had been racked by guerrilla wars against the state and reactionary military dictatorships. In the mid-1970s only Colombia, Venezuela and Costa Rica had elected governments. Little over ten years later, democracy was the rule except in Cuba, the troubled nations of Central America, Chile and Paraguay, although even in these last two countries elections were held in the final years of the decade in preparation for a return to constitutional government. What significance could be ascribed to this phenomenon?

The debt problem had, in fact, exposed an underlying, long-term crisis of the state, as much as a crisis in the model of economic development. The revival of democracy in the 1980s evinced a general desire to return to the first principles upon which the Latin American republics had been constituted, principles which since the time of independence had been more honoured in the breach than in the observance. The experience of the 1970s had shown that a strong, enduring state could not be secured by military power or revolutionary violence alone. To this extent the democratic restorations of the 1980s can be regarded as an affirmation by the broad mass of the population of Latin America of the need for a legitimate state that could command the assent of the people as a whole: the return to democracy reflected, in short, a general aspiration to genuine nationhood.

The discredit of the armed forces as political actors indicated that the era of inward-looking nationalism, which had begun roughly in the 1920s and had consolidated during the Depression of the 1930s, was drawing to a close. This kind of autarkic nationalism had been ushered in and sustained in one form or another by the armed forces; the technocratic military dictatorships of the 1970s can be regarded as the political end result of this process of development. By the 1980s dogmatic nationalism was in terminal crisis: economic and social realities had grown too complex to yield to the imposed solutions of military officers. On the contrary, the 'strong state' after which army officers perennially hankered had proved elusive because military juntas were unable to create a legitimate authority based on popular consent.

During the 1980s it was the relative authority of the state that determined the ability of governments to cope with the consequences of the foreign debt. In the early years of the decade one military dictatorship after another was obliged to resign from power, having exhausted the possibilities of economic management by force and decree. On the other hand, elected civilian governments that were unable to assert themselves over sectional interests floundered in the disarray caused by hyperinflation. For instance, the Radical government of Raúl Alfonsín in Argentina was squeezed between rebellious military officers and intransigent Peronist unions as the rate of inflation climbed in the course of the decade to reach a rate of about 1,500 per cent a year in 1989. In 1985 the first nationalist APRA politician ever to be elected to the presidency of Peru found himself with four-figure inflation by the end of the decade, having incurred the hostility of the urban middle classes and the business sector by his attempt to take over the banks and persevere with expansionist policies regardless of the foreign debt.

The countries best able to restructure their economies were those with pragmatic and unified technocratic élites, governing with a degree of consent based on social responsibility: Mexico, Brazil, Colombia and Venezuela exercised some control over inflation, diversified and increased exports, and more or less kept up with their debt payments. General Pinochet's Chile did very well too; it had begun to liberalize its economy by force since the 1970s and, despite its horrifying record on human rights, managed to gain the tacit support of the middle classes until it ran into inescapable problems of political consent in the mid-1980s. In 1989 Chile, at last, held free presidential elections and returned a Christian Democrat who was pledged to control inflation and continue with free-market economics; the election was likely to strengthen the political legitimacy of the Chilean state and improve its chances of overcoming the debt crisis. For all that, the state remained fragile even in these countries because it was not built upon a sufficient depth of popular allegiance. (In Mexico the election of Carlos Salinas of the ruling PRI had been accompanied by vociferous protests against ballot-rigging.)

It is possible to argue that the factor that repeatedly vitiated the modernization of Latin America was the weakness of the state. It was a weakness that can be traced back, in the first instance, to the circumstances of independence, to that profound crisis of royal authority that had led by tortuous and dangerous byways to a political secession which few creoles had initially contemplated and whose ultimate constitutional form fewer still were content with. For the white creole oligarchies, whose power derived from the pattern of grants and bounties created at the time of the Conquest, found themselves constrained after independence by republican constitutions written to the alien prescription of Enlightenment liberalism. The builders of the new nations were therefore faced with the prospect of accommodating a stratified patriarchal order, fragmented into countless regional clusters of power, within the rationally conceived structures of a liberal republic. The result was the chronic squabbling of oligarchic factions with intervals of order under a strongman.

However, this weakness of the state had even more distant origins: it derived from the peculiar deficiencies of the state in the New World. The almost preternatural stability of the Iberian empires over three centuries should not mislead one to assume that the imperial states were particularly strong: they were resilient and adaptable, but the actual power of the Crown was circumscribed by the oligarchic interests of landowners and merchants in America. In the Spanish Indies, in particular, the Crown's determined efforts to consolidate the authority of the state had foundered by the early 1600s through royal indigence and Indian depopulation. What remained was the monopoly of legitimacy of the Catholic monarchy, a not inconsiderable asset which bound the colonies to the mother country more closely than the direct exercise of power might have done. That monopoly of legitimacy more than compensated for the fretful condition of the creoles as a thwarted ruling class: it provided a mediating institution for their oligarchic disputes, it brought the dispersed focuses of regional power under a loosely unified polity, and, above all, it kept the non-whites quiet. Indeed, the real 'colonial pact', as we have seen, was not economic but political: the creole élites acquiesced in the ostensible authority of the Crown in return for its priceless justification of the internal colonialism which served them so well.

What held the realms of the Indies together, then, was not force but the silver threads of royal legitimacy. However, when Napoleon invaded the Peninsula in 1808, these barely visible threads became tangled and then broke – and the inherent weakness of the imperial state caused the Indies to fall to pieces. The many divisions that had in reality always fragmented these American societies surfaced in the violent play of *caudillos*, a kind of latter-day baronial factionalism restrained from time to time by the debased absolutism of charismatic tyrants. Only a handful of republics succeeded in taming *caudillismo* by manipulating or abridging the electoral process so as to allow the interests of the creole élites to find satisfaction through political institutions.

Until roughly the 1920s the mass of the population – poor whites, mixed-bloods, Indians and blacks – were excluded from the political system. It was nationalism that acted as the vehicle of the enfranchisement of the masses; nationalism that extended the idea of civil rights and the common good beyond the confines of the white creole élites; and nationalism, finally, that acted as the force for the democratization of Latin American culture. Nationalist politicians, however, came to power through *caudillo* politicking and military intrigue. Moreover, most had been tainted by European fascism or Catholic authoritarianism, so that the *idea* itself of liberal democracy was mistrusted as much as its oligarchic perversion by the creole élites. Nationalism thus never broke free from *caudillismo* and the politics of patronage, since it tended to operate through sectional interest-groups, populist electoral machines and labour unions run by political bosses. And so the process of state-led industrialization that nationalists set in train in the 1940s was plagued also by *caudillo* factionalism and bitter social confrontations, not to mention the numerous mistakes and distortions that amplified the turbulence of these rapid industrial revolutions.

State-led development added hugely to the stresses suffered by an endemically weak state, straining it to the point where in the 1970s the armed forces stepped in to try and shore it up. But such intervention had the reverse effect: the state all but broke down as most countries were plunged into internal wars, and civil society found itself terrorized by guerrillas and death squads. Still, from that breakdown of the nominally democratic Latin American state there arose in the mid-1980s a new popular sentiment for genuine constitutional democracy; and the conditions for its fulfilment had never been so favourable.

By the 1980s the social interest-groups that had originally supported nationalism were already dominant in the major Latin American countries: the urban middle classes were large and influential; industrialists, entrepreneurs and technocrats constituted the most powerful economic élites; and the organized working classes had become crucial players on the political stage. Sociologically, so to speak, the advanced countries had arrived at a point in their development where a modern, comprehensive sense of nationhood was at last possible to achieve. Nationalist industrial development, and the rapid urban expansion that went with it, were in themselves conducive to a transformation of traditional values and practices. The major Latin American republics were no longer dominated by agrarian economies controlled by seigneurial oligarchs. Between the 1940s and 1980s they had evolved into socially varied, dynamic consumer societies with myriad interests operating in the market-place. Under these conditions, customary practices originating in rural aristocratic societies were increasingly ineffectual in satisfying the political and economic needs of large urban populations.

The traditional ways of patriarchy – patronage and clientship, the pursuit of personal status and the defence of honour, the weaving of clannish loyalties through favours and rewards – had pervaded society in the pre-Columbian era as in the colonial, and they had survived strongly in the political culture of nineteenth-century liberal and conservative *caudillos*. In the twentieth century these traditional values had been given a new lease of life by the 'natural corporatism' of bureaucratic states motivated by a dogmatic, inward-looking economic nationalism. However, just as rural *caudillos* had been replaced by urban *caudillos* when industries began to develop, so too the further growth of the industrial economy would in time surely render superfluous a complex of patriarchal values whose origins lay in oligarchic agrarian societies. The literature and arts of the 1980s betrayed signs that such a transformation was indeed taking place (see Chapter 15). Despite the terrible recession induced by the foreign debt, therefore, it was possible to conceive of a consensus emerging among key urban interest-groups in support of the principles of a modern pluralist state, a state based on representative and accountable institutions under the rule of law – a state such as Bolívar or San Martín might have wished for.

This qualified optimism was possible only on a very long view. The severity of the debt crisis made social unrest, popular insurrections and further military adventures highly likely, particularly in the smaller republics with large, traditional Indian communities, where industrialization and urbanization were still in the early stages. But in republics where economic modernization was well advanced and where there existed a certain tradition of electoral politics – republics such as Brazil, Mexico, Chile, Uruguay,

Colombia, Venezuela, perhaps Argentina and possibly Peru – the calamitous effects of the foreign debt, together with the memory of the terrible internal wars of the 1970s, might have served to engender an embryonic popular consensus to uphold the institutions of a legitimate democratic state.

Latin American leaders of the 1980s held up as a model for their own countries the transition from traditionalist dictatorship to pluralist democracy which had taken place in both Spain and Portugal in the mid-1970s. These democratic transitions in the Peninsula were indeed proof that the Iberian heritage, which had so often been cited by progressive Latin Americans as a cause of their countries' backwardness, had not eternally prevented the former colonial powers themselves from creating a modern economy and society.

10. Mexico: Revolution and Stability
===

The End of the Porfiriato

For the last quarter of the nineteenth century, Mexico, like Argentina and Chile, had enjoyed political stability and economic progress. Unlike those republics, however, it had failed to establish the conditions for constitutional democracy. Instead, it had been ruled throughout this period by a Liberal dictator, Porfirio Díaz, who paid no more than lip-service to the great liberal constitution of 1857.

The Porfiriato owed its success to the old dictator's mastery of the very difficult art of pleasing all the interest-groups that really mattered in Mexico. In a nominally federal and still highly diversified nation he had achieved just the degree of centralism required to permit rapid economic development without upsetting the many local apple-carts that had to be kept in place if the whole country was not to collapse once more into the kind of disorder it had experienced repeatedly since independence. A vast web of patronage linked all the institutions and groups which might otherwise clash with one another in the usual scramble for the spoils of office. In that web were caught the great regional oligarchies, the potentially fractious generals of the army, the Church, the merchants and the urban professional classes. But the flaw in this arrangement was that it had to rely for its continuity upon the survival of its great artificer, and in 1900 Don Porfirio had turned seventy – how long could he go on for?

Mexico had yet to solve its basic political problem: how to manage the transfer of power from one ruler to the next without risking a catastrophe. A clear solution lay in the creation of a national party. Such a party would maintain the central source of patronage, which was essential for the running of the state, but would depersonalize it by laying down agreed rules for the presidential succession. A system of this sort was to come into being in 1929, but not before Mexico had gone through two decades of civil war. For the real obstacle to the institutionalization of state patronage was the need for legitimacy, that life-prolonging elixir that had eluded all Mexican state-builders, including Don Porfirio himself, since independence.

As the question of the succession to Díaz became more pressing, tension increased between the two most powerful factions within the regime. On the one hand, there were the *científicos*, progressive liberal technocrats connected with the business establishment of Mexico City, though with contacts in the provinces. This group was in favour of creating a ruling party. On the other hand, there was a more traditional faction of *caudillos* with strong roots in the regions, who feared institutionalization because it threatened the personal basis of their power in their home territory. These men preferred the old style of power-broking between regional barons and their clans. They were led by General Bernardo Reyes, the minister of war, and this gave them great influence in the army. As ever, the underlying cause of political tension in Mexico was the conflict between regionalism and centralization.

In the first decade of the new century the old dictator's political touch appeared to be deserting him. He created resentment in the Reyes camp by showing signs of favour towards the *científicos*. In 1903 he nominated a *científico* as his vice-president, and shortly afterwards he dismissed Bernardo Reyes from the ministry of war. These moves were generally interpreted to mean that Díaz was preparing to form a national party, as the *científicos* wanted. This faction therefore set about extending and consolidating its political influence in the regions by placing its own men in key positions in provincial governments or by forging new alliances with rising local interest-groups. As a result, many established élites in the regions began to feel alienated from the central power, especially in the northern border states such as Sonora, Chihuahua and Coahuila, where Bernardo Reyes's influence was particularly strong. In Coahuila, for instance, the great landowner Venustiano Carranza was prevented by a manipulated election from becoming state governor despite the support he had from the leading local families. The state of Chihuahua was thrown into turmoil when the powerful Terrazas family formed an alliance with the *científicos* and assumed a monopoly of local power, expropriating peasants' land to make way for a new railway. Outside the north, the state most deeply affected by the *científico* drive for centralized control was Morelos, which lay to the south-west of Mexico City. Here particular alienation was felt by Indian communities whose lands were threatened by sugar barons seeking to capitalize on the replacement of the traditional *caudillo* by a *científico* sympathizer.

The *científico* challenge to the established regional élites was an attempt to carry out the centralization of political authority which successive modernizers since the time of the Bourbons had failed to achieve. It was the kind of centralization by a dominant élite that had allowed republics like Chile and Argentina to overcome the problem of regional separatism and move rapidly towards prosperity and stable constitutional government. But regionalism in Mexico proved too well-entrenched, and the *científicos* were not equipped with either the legitimacy or the military might to oust the local families from their traditional bastions of power. In the twilight years of the Porfiriato, then, the web of patronage the old dictator had spun was coming apart in places, but no one *caudillo* or political faction appeared capable of repairing the damage.

In addition to the developing struggle for power at the top, there was a ground swell of discontent in the general population. For in 1907 the worst economic crisis of the Porfiriato, triggered by recession in the USA, affected the living standards of all the social classes. The recession was compounded by a series of bad harvests, which dislocated food supplies and drove up the price of staples. Inflation, falling wages and unemployment spread unprecedented misery among the peasants and the industrial workers. Even before the crisis, workers had responded to rising inflation with major strikes – particularly in Veracruz, Chihuahua and Sonora – some of which had been put down with great brutality. This repression radicalized sections of the working class and gave new strength to the Mexican Liberal Party (PLM), led by the revolutionary Flores Magón brothers, which absorbed anarcho-syndicalist ideas and inspired a wave of strikes in response to the recession.

The middle classes, too, were affected by the inflation, and also by increased taxes and tougher credit from the largely foreign-owned banks. A young generation of educated middle-class Mexicans, who felt excluded from jobs in a bureaucracy controlled too rigidly by the Porfirista élite, gravitated towards the PLM and agitated for the opening-up of the political system through greater democracy and free discussion. Even upper-class *hacendados* who did not belong to the national élite felt the effects of the recession through the credit squeeze and the calling in of debts by the banks.

This general discontent assumed nationalist overtones. The new dominance of the technocratic *científico* élite, combined with a great influx of foreign investment from 1900, created a widespread impression that the *científicos* were prepared to sell the nation to foreigners, particularly the USA. In the northern border states, workers building the Chihuahua railway, as well as the miners of Sonora, protested at the far better wages and conditions reserved for US nationals working alongside them. Anxiety about the designs of the USA on Mexico were not dispelled by articles in the US press advocating a further annexation of Mexican territory.

It was the disaffection of the northern oligarchs, however, that represented the greatest danger to Don Porfirio. This disaffection might find expression either by way of a military *pronunciamiento* in support of the northerner Bernardo Reyes's struggle against the *científicos*, or as a challenge to the legitimacy of the regime itself by a northern *caudillo* taking advantage of the popular discontent caused by the economic recession.

As the presidential elections scheduled for 1910 approached, Bernardo Reyes began his manœuvering by forming the Democratic Party to contest the vice-presidency against the *científico* candidate picked by Díaz. His prospects looked favourable when Díaz declared in an interview with the US journalist James Creelman in 1908 that he would not be standing for president and that it was time for opposition groups to participate more fully in the democratic process. Díaz, however, soon changed his mind about democracy and sent Reyes off to Europe. Reyes – a member of the governing élite after all – drew back from open defiance and complied.

It was not so with another challenger to the regime, Francisco Madero. In 1908 he published *La sucesión presidencial en 1910* ('The Presidential Succession in 1910'), in which he invoked the democratic principles of the 1857 constitution to denounce the illegality of the regime, adding for good measure criticism of Díaz's land policy and the repression of workers' strikes. Madero was the scion of one of the most powerful families in the state of Coahuila, with huge interests in cereals, textiles, cattle-ranching and mining. Yet in his bid for power he managed to present himself as the 'apostle of democracy' to the lower and middle classes. Madero began touring the country and, in 1910, founded the Anti-Re-electionist Party, putting himself forward as its presidential candidate.

Although the challenge to Porfirio Díaz had come from outside the political establishment, the rival Porfirista cliques were still in the game for power. Given his influence in the army, the exiled Bernardo Reyes would in time try a *coup d'état*. But first the *científicos* would seek to co-opt the upstart Madero and his clan into a new anti-Reyes power structure.

The Mexican Revolution

The Liberal Revolution of Madero (1910–13)

Porfirio Díaz responded to Madero's challenge by putting the 'apostle of democracy' in prison for sedition. He then went on to win the election with the customary landslide. Once safely back at the helm, Díaz felt confident enough to release Madero on bail, but from now on it was not to be plain sailing: Madero fled to Texas and planned an insurrection. On 20 November 1910 he issued the Plan of San Luis Potosí, in which he denounced the recent elections as fraudulent and assumed for himself the title of provisional president, urging Mexicans to rebel against Díaz. Madero's revolt fizzled out and he returned to Texas, but his call to arms served to release the frustrations of the peasants and workers in several regions. In Chihuahua, farm labourers and agricultural colonists rose under the leadership of Pascual Orozco and the former bandit Francisco 'Pancho' Villa. Other revolutionary groups emerged in the northern border states and began attacking and taking towns. Further south, in the state of Morelos, the Indian pueblos rose to reclaim their ancestral lands under the leadership of Emiliano Zapata. In these regions, Madero's liberal–democratic revolution was assuming the alarming character of a peasant war for land. In February 1911 Madero crossed into Chihuahua and took over as leader of the insurgents; on 10 May the border city of Juárez was captured by Orozco, and Madero set up a provisional government there. For its part, the USA, which had decided to give tacit support to Madero, mobilized 20,000 troops along the border and sent warships to major ports.

Faced with the threat of an uncontrollable rising from below and the obvious displeasure of the USA, the *científicos* realized it was time to reorganize the affairs of state – Don Porfirio had to go, and the young Madero must be given his head. On 21 May 1911 a compromise was reached between the *científicos* and the Madero clan. Porfirio Díaz would leave the country and Francisco Madero would call free elections; in return Madero would cooperate with the provisional government in disarming the rebels. This plan succeeded, except in the state of Morelos, where Zapata and his Indians continued their fight against the white landowners in spite of Madero's attempts to mediate.

The new presidential elections of October 1911 were preceded by highly complicated manœuvres, in which old and new factions tried to gain the advantage in the construction of the post-Porfirio power structure. The *científicos* offered the Madero clan conditional support in order to foil their rivals in the Reyes clique. Francisco Madero was elected by a huge majority in a clean and free contest. His first cabinet included *científico* sympathizers, such as his uncle Ernesto Madero, who stayed on as finance minister after having served in the previous government. However, Madero's triumph at the polls did not put an end to armed insurrections. Victory at an election was not sufficient to confer legitimacy upon a government. There were too many claims outstanding against the central power, and Madero had not yet been able either to appease or to crush the various claimants.

As was to be expected, the excluded Bernardo Reyes tried to stage a *coup d'état*. But it was too late: politics had become too fluid and his influence in the army had waned; the military revolt collapsed and Reyes found himself in prison. Madero's chances of survival now depended on his being able to keep order. This he failed to do. In November, Zapata proclaimed the revolutionary Plan de Ayala urging the wholesale return of land to Indian pueblos; a fresh uprising occurred in Chihuahua; and there was unrest too among the industrial workers, who took advantage of democratic freedoms to organize trade unions and call strikes. Finally, Madero lost the sympathy of the USA when he introduced a tax on oil production, which sharpened the rivalry between British and US oil interests for concessions from the Mexican authorities.

In 1912 renewed struggles took place between the factions to dominate the state. The Maderos – Francisco, his brother Gustavo and his uncle Ernesto – tried to sever their ties with the *científicos*. The latter reacted by mounting a *coup d'état* in October led by Félix Díaz, Porfirio's nephew. When this was put down, a further coup was attempted by a *científico* general in February 1913, but this too failed, though much blood was shed in a ten-day episode which became known as *La Decena Trágica*. (Bernardo Reyes was killed in the fighting; Félix Díaz and other rebel leaders resisted in La Ciudadela, an arsenal in the heart of Mexico City, where they were bombarded by the army, causing many civilian casualties.)

The old factions had lost ground; none had been able to carry the army. But, as it turned out, neither could the Maderos. The one man who had shown that he could maintain order was Victoriano Huerta, the general who had suppressed the various revolts and *coups d'état*. He was clearly the new strongman of Mexico, and, on 18 February 1913, confident of the backing of the army and of the USA, he mounted his own coup against the Maderos. The brothers Francisco and Gustavo were arrested. Next day Gustavo was murdered; four days later Francisco, the constitutional president, and his vice-president, Pino Suárez, were assassinated while in custody. General Huerta had himself declared provisional president and formed a cabinet which included leading *científicos* and members of the Bernardo Reyes faction (his son Rodolfo Reyes was appointed minister of justice). The established cliques of the Porfiriato had regrouped to oust the Madero usurpers, and in Huerta they appeared to have found a worthy successor to Don Porfirio himself.

Huerta in Power (1913–14)

Although Madero's liberal challenge to the Porfiriato had been defeated, there was no going back to the stability of the past. Madero had cracked open the national structure of politics just wide enough to encourage other peripheral forces to compete for central power. What followed was, by and large, a civil war between the oligarchies of Mexico City and the central areas – the traditional ruling élites – and new factions from the northern border states. Except for the forces of Pancho Villa and Emiliano Zapata, which fought for socially radical ends, and particularly for land, there was little to choose between the aims of the northern *caudillos* and those of the traditional élites. Circumstances, nevertheless, provided the northerners with a number of pretexts for rebellion.

The most obvious pretext was that Huerta's coup against Madero was unconstitutional. In March 1913 Venustiano Carranza, the governor of Coahuila, who had once been a Porfirista and then turned to Madero in 1911 in reaction to the *científicos*, proclaimed the Plan of Guadalupe, which called for the overthrow of Huerta and a return to constitutional government. By October, the anti-Huerta forces in the north had been organized into a 'Constitutionalist Army', of which there were three main branches: the Army of the North-East, commanded by Carranza's cousin, Pablo González; the Army of the North-West, led by a young rancher from Sonora, Alvaro Obregón; and the Division of the North, covering the north-central states of Chihuahua, Durango and Zacatecas, whose leader was Pancho Villa. The first two armies were based on existing state militias supplemented by peons from the haciendas of the rebel *caudillos* and their cronies. But Pancho Villa, who had once been an outlaw, attracted more varied recruits: militiamen, unemployed labourers, landless peasants, delinquents and cowboys; he was thus potentially more refractory to Carranza's authority than the other commanders and his struggle had a more radical social thrust than Carranza's: in the areas he conquered Villa experimented with land distribution, public education and other measures of social welfare.

Indeed, the need for social reform was to provide the politically more acute northern *caudillos*, especially Alvaro Obregón, with another pretext for rebellion. He would in due course outmanœuvre Carranza by advocating a political programme that would attract workers and peasants, as much to undermine the old regime as to draw lower-class support away from Villa and Zapata – especially the latter, who acted quite independently of the Constitutionalists, and from whom the northern oligarchs had as much to fear as the oligarchs of the centre.

Huerta's increasing concessions to the Church furnished the rebels with yet another pretext: it gave the northerners the opportunity to portray their enemies as anti-liberal reactionaries, accusations that conjured up visions of an unchanging order of aristocratic and clerical privilege, harking back to the days of the Spanish colony. As it happened, the Church had far deeper roots in central and southern Mexico than in the north, where there had been little Indian settlement and where Spanish colonialism had therefore been very weak. By reasons of geography and history, therefore, the northern *caudillos* had fewer ties with the ecclesiastical hierarchy and were in consequence more easily drawn to anti-clericalism. Their military campaigns would be characterized by a venom against the Church which resulted at times in atrocities committed against priests and religious orders. This anti-clericalism would become an intrinsic element in the post-revolutionary state, leading to further civil conflict. It contrasted with the Catholicism of Zapata and his Indian followers, who came from central areas where the missionary Church had always been strong.

Among the forces ranged against Huerta and the survivors of the Porfiriato must also be counted the USA. Washington was to play a continuing role in the fluctuating course of the revolution. Its overriding interest throughout was to re-establish business as usual with a stable Mexican government, but the vicissitudes of the conflict led it to back different factions at different stages. The new US president, Woodrow Wilson, disliked Huerta because of his association with the *científicos*, who were thought to favour British oil interests rather than American. Wilson tried various means of unseating Huerta: he lifted an embargo of arms for Carranza; he persuaded the British government to withdraw its support for Huerta; and when Huerta refused to comply with an outrageous demand that he personally salute the Stars and Stripes in atonement for an incident in which Mexican officials had arrested US sailors in Tampico, Wilson sent a fleet to occupy the principal Mexican port of Veracruz.

On 21 April 1914 US troops gained control of the city and its customs house, which provided the major source of revenue for the Mexican government. In the event, all the warring Mexican factions united in condemning this violation of national sovereignty, but Wilson used the occupation of Veracruz as a lever in the war, first against Huerta, then against Carranza, until finally the US troops withdrew on 23 November 1914. After the Veracruz episode, Wilson resorted to the supply of arms and funds to chosen factions in order to influence the outcome of the labyrinthine conflict to the advantage of the USA. In the end, US interference was to prove a marginal factor in settling the conflict, which was decided on the field of battle. In any case, all the Mexican factions knew they would ultimately have to deal with Washington if they were to have any chance of establishing themselves in power. To that extent, the USA was an important, if secondary, participant in the war.

Victoriano Huerta succeeded in consolidating his power during 1913. He increased the strength of the Federal Army and the Rural Police, and was able to recover most of the ground he had lost in the north and north-east, though not in Sonora. In Morelos the government forces came close to smashing Zapata. Huerta also survived an economic crisis caused by low silver prices and poor harvests. By the autumn of 1913 he felt strong enough to rid himself of Félix Díaz and other *científico* notables. Huerta was striking out on his own, building a new power base for himself from the ruins of the old order.

However, by April 1914, the tide of war began to turn against him, and his capacity to respond was seriously impaired by the US occupation of Veracruz. Zapata overran the silver-mining state of Guerrero and had recaptured his home state of Morelos by May; he then invaded Mexico State and Puebla, thus drawing perilously close to the capital. In the north, important towns began to fall to the Constitutionalists. Villa took the crucial railway centre of Torreón, blocking the government forces' route to the north. Pablo González captured the industrial city of Monterrey, and Tampico, a major port for the oil industry. Obregón swept down the west coast and on 7 July defeated a large Federal army at Guadalajara. Huerta had lost control of the country; a week later he resigned and went into exile.

The Insurgents' Struggle for Power (1914–15)

The revolutionaries had foiled the attempts of the old élites to find a replacement for Porfirio Díaz. The *ancien régime* had been effectively destroyed, but the war was not over yet. A new power structure had to be put together, and the insurgent forces would fall out among themselves in their struggle to build it. Even as the Constitutionalist armies were closing in on Huerta's forces, their First Chief, Venustiano Carranza, had begun to manœuvre to prevent Pancho Villa, whose radical land policy he disliked, from getting to Mexico City first. For his part, Villa had devised the Torreón Pact, an arrangement between Constitutionalist chieftains which would eventually have led to Carranza's disqualification from supreme office. In the event, it was Carranza's lieutenant, Obregón, who was the first to enter the capital on 15 August after the official surrender of the Federal Army. Six days later Carranza installed himself in the National Palace as provisional president.

The preparations for a convention to arrive at a new political settlement involved considerable wheeling and dealing among the factions. Carranza wanted to exclude Villa and Zapata. Villa at this point happened to enjoy the favour of Washington, which strengthened his hand sufficiently to attract, in addition to his fellow radical Zapata, some of Carranza's own lieutenants, among them Obregón, to a convention in the town of Aguascalientes, near his base at Torreón. The convention approved in principle Zapata's radical Plan of Ayala, with its demands for a massive redistribution of land to the peasants. Carranza was removed as First Chief and a new provisional president elected.

Carranza, however, succeeded in winning back the loyalty of errant commanders like Obregón, and in November 1914, shortly after the US troops had left Veracruz, he set up a Constitutionalist government in that port, where he could control the customs house. Pancho Villa and Emiliano Zapata entered Mexico City. There followed a civil war between the supporters of the revolutionary Aguascalientes Convention and the northern Constitutionalist armies.

In the ebb and flow of a turbulent war prosecuted simultaneously in various theatres, the forces of the Aguascalientes Convention, led by Villa and Zapata, lost ground to Carranza. Mexico City changed hands several times. But the turning-point came when Obregón defeated Villa on 15 April 1915 at Celaya, a town close to the capital. Villa was pushed northwards in a long, hard-fought campaign until he was thrown back on to his home territory in Chihuahua, where he would keep his insurrection alive for several years more, even though his grip on national power was thenceforth irrevocably broken. In the central areas, Pablo González chased the Zapatistas out of Mexico City and occupied the capital in August 1915. By September, Zapata too had been forced back to his home territory in Morelos. With both Villa and Zapata in retreat, the truly revolutionary challenge from the lower orders receded; the danger of a peasant war, which might have resulted in a fundamental reallocation of land, had been contained. In October the USA recognized Carranza's government.

Carranza in Power (1916–20)

For the next year, until he was able to open a constitutional assembly at Querétaro in November 1916, Carranza had to weather one crisis after another in his efforts to consolidate national authority. Not only were Villa and Zapata causing trouble for him in the north and south-west respectively, but his own commanders began to jockey for power within the Constitutionalist camp. To add to his difficulties, Woodrow Wilson once again tried to influence events in Mexico by exerting diplomatic, financial and military pressure on Carranza. An expedition led by General John Pershing crossed into Mexico, ostensibly to punish Villa's guerrilla bands for their destructive raid on the town of Columbus, New Mexico. This obliged Carranza to embark on a series of negotiations with Wilson in defence of Mexican sovereignty. Wilson kept up pressure on Carranza by periodically threatening further military punishments.

When the Querétaro convention was finally assembled, the draft constitution presented by Carranza offered little social change other than a mild gesture towards land distribution and some nominal concessions on social welfare to the working class. Its only innovations with regard to the great liberal constitution of 1857 were strictly political: a stronger executive presidency (but no re-election), an independent judiciary and more centralized government combined with certain guarantees of municipal autonomy. But Alvaro Obregón – a largely self-made rancher who had amassed considerable influence in the course of the war – well understood the need to go beyond mere political tinkering if social rebels like Zapata and Villa were to be prevented from regaining lost ground. His followers at the convention succeeded in amending Carranza's proposals and the constitution that resulted was a model of radical liberalism, the legal foundation of the new state that was to emerge from the long anti-Porfirista upheaval.

The 1917 constitution provided for the complete separation of Church and state; article 3 abolished religious education, while article 130 set limits to religious worship and prohibited clerical interference in political matters. Workers were guaranteed important rights: an eight-hour working day, the right to organize trade unions and to call strikes, as well as compulsory arbitration in labour disputes. For peasants on haciendas it promised an end to debt-peonage and the company store. On the land question it authorized expropriation of *latifundia* where necessary and the return of usurped lands and commons to the Indian communities. Article 27 claimed for the Mexican state all ultimate rights to the subsoil and to the land, a claim which was to lead to repeated clashes with the US oil companies, although it was, in fact, a historic right which the Spanish Crown had asserted since the Middle Ages.

Had the constitution of 1917 been rigorously implemented, the wars that destroyed the Porfiriato could have ushered in a genuine social revolution. But 1917 did not lead to a transfer of power between classes; it marked instead the eventual accession to national government of new landowning élites from the north. During his term of office as president (1917–20), Carranza failed to evolve into a truly national leader. Despite returning land to old *hacendados* and granting haciendas to his own clients, he was unable to harness the traditional conflicts of interest between rival *caudillos*. Nor did he restore social order – a crucial failing for an aspiring strongman. Clearly, the state of politics in Mexico called for further remodelling.

The imminence of the 1920 presidential election, at which Carranza was prevented from standing by the constitutional rule of no re-election, produced a situation not unlike that of 1910. Carranza hoped to rig the poll in favour of his own chosen candidate, but this manœuvre split his north-eastern faction, for his cousin Pablo González broke with him to form a Democratic League and declared himself a candidate for the presidency. The *caudillos* from the north-west rallied behind Alvaro Obregón of Sonora, who decided to present a more radical candidature than his rivals' by founding a Labour Party, linked to the trade union confederation CROM. In this way he wooed the Zapatistas of Morelos (Zapata himself had been treacherously murdered by González's forces in an ambush on 10 April 1919), and eventually won the backing of his former enemy Pancho Villa.

Violence finally erupted when Carranza tried to arrest Obregón. The latter's home state of Sonora, whose forces were now led by Plutarco Elías Calles, declared independence. Calles and the governor of Sonora, Adolfo de la Huerta, issued the Plan of Agua Prieta, in which Carranza was denounced for having violated the 1917 constitution; they rallied the rebel forces into a Liberal Constitutionalist Army, broadly in support of Obregón. Faced with this military challenge to his authority, Carranza tried to patch up his quarrel with his cousin, but attempts to reach a settlement fell through and González mounted a *coup d'état*. Carranza was forced to flee Mexico City, and once again made for Veracruz where he hoped to regroup his forces, but he met a violent death *en route* in mysterious circumstances.

When Obregón's Liberal Constitutionalists had got the upper hand in the fighting, Pablo González withdrew from the contest for the presidency, and Alvaro Obregón was able to win the election by a landslide on 5 September 1920. The *caudillos* from the north-western state of Sonora had finally emerged as the true victors of the immensely complicated and horrendously violent struggle unleashed by Francisco Madero's call for clean elections in 1910.

The Construction of the Post-revolutionary State

In the wake of Porfirio Díaz's downfall in 1910, Madero, Huerta and Carranza had tried successively to set up a new system of power, and each in turn had failed. The chieftains from Sonora, despite their provincial origins, were to succeed, and brilliantly, in building nationwide authority. The state they created proved to be the most enduring and stable in the independent history of Latin America.

The reconstruction of the Mexican state was carried out by methods which were entirely traditional – it helped of course that the Sonorans had routed all other military rivals. The victors set about rewarding the various interest-groups that were prepared to support them, starting with their own commanders. The immediate instruments of patronage had been thrown up by the war itself. Emergency institutions such as the offices of requisitioned property and agencies for regulating commerce were used to reallocate land, wealth and privileges from the vanquished oligarchs to the victorious *caudillos* and their kinsmen, friends and political clients. In this way a 'revolutionary family' came into being, with few, if any, ties to the Porfirista élites they had supplanted.

Although these new men did not change the economic and social structures of Mexico, they none the less introduced novel arrangements which made for political longevity. In essence, they brought within the capacious umbrella of state patronage the leadership of new and hitherto neglected social forces – industrial labour and the peasants. Thus the settlement forged in the 1920s and 1930s did not usher in new 'bourgeois' values in politics; rather, it adapted ancient methods of patronage and clientship to the requirements of a modernizing state: oligarchic politics were extended to include new *caudillos* – the bosses of trade unions and agrarian leagues – who became the partners of political chieftains and revolutionary generals in the business of government. In brief, the radical liberal constitution of 1917 was infused with the spirit of corporatism.

But corporatism does not in itself explain the extraordinary endurance of the state in modern Mexico. The key to its stability lies in the Sonoran chieftains' success in legitimizing their power. Unlike any other ruling group before them – monarchists, liberal republicans, personalist *caudillos* or technocratic *científicos* – the Sonorans created an ideology persuasive enough to win the consent of most interest-groups in the country.

The new legitimizing ideology rested on an astute exploitation of the notion of Revolution. On 20 November 1920 the provisional president Adolfo de la Huerta inaugurated the first celebration of Francisco Madero's rebellion against Porfirio Díaz in 1910; that rebellion and the factional wars that followed it were now officially designated the 'Mexican Revolution'. It was a fruitful concept, fertilized as it was by association with other great progressive watersheds such as the French Revolution and the recent Bolshevik Revolution in Russia. The concept of Revolution implied an irrevocable break with a corrupt past and a consequent opening to a better future. Accordingly, the progressive technocracy which was the Porfiriato had to be caricatured as a reactionary *ancien régime* which had sold out the noble ideals of Benito Juárez and *La Reforma* to the greed of pro-foreign aristocrats and an obscurantist Church.

More positively, the idea of Revolution obliged an aspiring Mexican ruling class to address itself, for the first time since independence, to creating an idea of the nation which would unite the people behind a common identity. The Revolution was to recover the heritage of the Aztecs and the Maya, which had been perverted for so long by Spain and her champions before and after independence. In this respect, the new order was anti-Spanish and anti-clerical. Now the true Mexican identity would be forged from the fusion of Indian and Spanish traditions. The day of the mestizo and the Indian had arrived: they too must be found a dignified place as full citizens in the new Mexico.

The Revolution was converted into the ultimate source of the government's authority. In effect, appeals to the spirit of the Revolution could function as a transcendent sanction for political power, a modern equivalent of the divine will which had theoretically underwritten the decrees of the Catholic monarchy. The state thereby acquired a mystique which the illiterate multitudes found easier to sympathize with than such bloodless liberal abstractions as the 'sovereignty of the people'. But to achieve a monopoly of legitimacy that would rival that of the Catholic monarchy, the new rulers had to convert the Revolution into a permanent reality. Authority could not be vested for too long in any one person, for this would dissipate the mystique that legitimized the state. The Revolution had to be a self-perpetuating and impersonal process.

In practice, this meant that the problem of legitimate succession had to be solved – a problem that had eluded all previous Mexican rulers. It had brought down Porfirio Díaz after thirty years because he had failed to find a means of transferring the reins of power to a successor. The solution to the problem, as Díaz's *científicos* had seen, lay in a one-party state in which power would pass from one ruler to the next according to accepted conventions. But the *científicos* had become a discredited and contested clique in the early 1900s; they lacked the means to create a popular, unifying political vision, and this was precisely what the idea of Revolution gave to the *caudillos* from Sonora. Even so, a self-perpetuating one-party state legitimized by a transcendent Revolution was to take a further decade of bloody struggle to create.

The Presidency of Obregón (1920–24)

During Alvaro Obregón's term of office, some of the foundations of the new system were laid. Placemen were assigned positions in the federal and state administrations. The control of the labour movement was undertaken by the trade-union confederation, CROM, and its political arm, the Labour Party. Peasants were organized into Agrarian Leagues, which were represented politically by the National Agrarian Party, led by one of Zapata's former colleagues. The bosses of these organizations were induced to remain loyal to the state by being allowed access to public office and to state funds, with all the opportunities for patronage that this brought with it. These leaders of labour thus had an interest in preventing the workers and peasants from pressing their demands too hard. The social provisions of the 1917 constitution had to be implemented, but not so vigorously as to upset the balance of forces in the country. Land reform was hesitant: it went nowhere near breaking up the *latifundia*, and the 10 per cent of the peasantry who did receive land were not provided with the credit and technical support required to make agrarian reform economically productive. As regards industrial workers, the CROM, under its boss Luis Morones, opted for a policy of co-operation with employers, which was successful in raising workers' living standards but also pre-empted disruptive militancy from non-recognized unions.

In effect, what Obregón and his 'revolutionary family' were setting up was a capitalist system under the corporate direction of the state. Such a system rested on a fundamental ambiguity, which the Mexican state has had to wrestle with ever since. The official rhetoric and ideology were nationalist and socialistic, as was dictated by the notion of the liberating Revolution, but economic realities were not qualitatively different from those of the Porfiriato: capitalist development financed by the export of raw materials and foreign capital investment. Obregón and his successors therefore found themselves having to satisfy the nationalist aspirations of their domestic constituency without alienating foreign companies and investors.

Education and culture were promoted intensively in order to disseminate the new revolutionary vision of Mexico. The great instigator of cultural nationalism was José Vasconcelos, Obregón's minister of education, who believed that the future lay in the formation of a 'cosmic race' created from the eventual fusion of all the ethnic groups in America. It was this belief that provided the inspiration for the tremendous effort in the early 1920s to rehabilitate the Indian and the mestizo in the cultural self-image of Mexico. This campaign was undoubtedly one of the triumphs of the Revolution; it represented the earliest and most enduring attempt to overcome the racial divisions which had been the worst legacy of the Spanish Conquest, and to forge a coherent sense of national identity. Mexico's political stability in the twentieth century is due in no small degree to the success of this policy of incorporating the Indian heritage in the idea of the nation.

Vasconcelos started a great drive to promote literacy among the rural masses. Schools were built, libraries were founded and cadres of young volunteers sent out to teach in the villages and pueblos. This campaign was accompanied by extensive official patronage of indigenous arts and crafts, as a means of fostering pride in the achievements of the people. In this period too was born the muralist movement under the auspices of the state. Vasconcelos, the '*caudillo* of culture', became the patron of painters such as Diego Rivera, David Alfaro Siqueiros and José Clemente Orozco, commissioning them to paint frescoes on the walls of ministries and public buildings depicting revolutionary and indigenous subjects. It was of no great concern to the Mexican government that some of these muralists were Marxists; so long as their themes were appropriately 'revolutionary', the actual nuances of ideology could be left for the painters themselves to fight over. (Their disagreements were to climax on 24 May 1940 when Siqueiros, a Stalinist, machine-gunned the villa in Coyoacán of his fellow muralist Diego Rivera, narrowly failing to assassinate Leon Trotsky, who was staying there at the time.)

The outpouring of images and pictorial themes which came from the muralist movement disseminated the notion of the legitimizing Revolution among the illiterate masses, and served to consolidate a state ideology of common citizenship and progressive nationalism. After the resignation of Vasconcelos in 1924, the cultural and educational policies of the state focused on the more narrowly political aim of wresting the peasantry from the grip of the Church, and this secularization was to lead to a renewal of violence in the deeply religious Mexican countryside.

By contrast, economic policy was designed to restore Mexico's financial health and to develop a vigorous capitalist agriculture. Booming oil exports from 1920–26, a programme of cut-backs in public spending (including wage reductions in the public sector and the privatization of the railways), together with the imposition of an income tax, increased government revenues and allowed it to renew payments on the massive public debt incurred as a result of the war. These fiscal measures restored business confidence in the country and attracted new loans and investment from abroad. The creation of the Banco de México and national credit institutions encouraged domestic investment in irrigation, infrastructure and agriculture, especially in the north-west, the home territory of the revolutionary caudillos.

The obstacle to harmonious relations with foreign business was article 27 of the 1917 constitution, which gave the state rights over all mineral deposits. The US oil companies persuaded Washington to withhold recognition of Obregón's government until he agreed to exempt from the law any oil concessions granted prior to 1917. Obregón who, as we shall see, had to cope with political challenges at home, granted these concessions in 1923 in return for recognition and the arms that went with it. Nevertheless, this was just the first round in a protracted dispute over mineral rights, which was brought to an end only in 1938 with the nationalization of the oil industry.

As the presidential election of 1924 approached, tension rose within the revolutionary family. Obregón's choice of his fellow Sonoran Plutarco Elías Calles as his successor alienated important generals, who rose in rebellion and persuaded the third member of the Sonoran triumvirate, Adolfo de la Cuesta, to join them. With two-thirds of the revolutionary army supporting the dissidents, Obregón needed the recognition of the USA to bolster his domestic authority. He therefore signed the Treaty of Bucareli, agreeing oil concessions to the American companies in order to obtain the arms he required to meet the emergency. In the ensuing civil war, Obregón managed to defeat the rebels. There followed a thorough purge, which claimed the lives of many former revolutionaries (Pancho Villa had been pre-emptively murdered in August 1923 even before hostilities had broken out). In 1924 a victorious Obregón placed his crony Calles in the presidency thanks to a rigged poll. The principle of no re-election, the battle-cry of the revolution against Porfirio Díaz, had been observed in the letter, though scarcely in the spirit.

Calles and the Maximato (1924–34)

Over the next ten years, Obregón's protégé, Plutarco Elías Calles, would make a fair bid to become the new strongman of Mexico. There were two obstacles in his way: the provisions of the 1917 constitution and the ideological authority of the Catholic Church. Because both proved insuperable, Calles was forced to institutionalize the power of the new revolutionary élite in a national party, formulating rules for the presidential succession which would preserve oligarchic government behind a democratic façade. The result has been called the Maximato (a word modelled on Porfiriato), which describes the continuing rule through presidential stooges of the *jefe máximo*, as Calles was known, after his official term of office had been completed in 1928.

Calles's presidency was overshadowed by the massive insurrection of the Catholic peasantry known as the War of the Cristeros, from their battle-cry *'¡Viva Cristo Rey!'* ('Long Live Christ the King!'). Rural Mexico – especially central and western regions – was overwhelmingly Catholic, and the attempts by the anti-clerical *caudillos* from the north to replace church education with secular schooling created serious disaffection among the peasants. The immediate cause of the war was a dispute between Calles and the bishops over a law passed in 1926 which enforced and extended the religious restrictions of the 1917 constitution. The Catholic hierarchy responded by suspending all church services throughout the country. Coming on top of virulent anti-religious propaganda, which included the setting up of a rival Church by the CROM, this threat to the very existence of religious life outraged Catholic layfolk. In the west-central states of Jalisco, Michoacán, Guanajuato, Colima and Zacatecas, there were large risings of peasants.

Calles's hard line towards the Church had been intended partly to strengthen his authority at home while he was involved in a nationalist confrontation with the USA over oil rights (Calles had refused to implement Obregón's Bucareli Treaty of 1923.) But his policy backfired: by January 1927 he was faced with an insurrection of peasants, which in a few months would spread to thirteen states. Severe repressive measures – such as the gunning-down of unarmed *campesinos*, scorched-earth tactics against their lands and the forcible relocation of Indian communities – failed to subdue the Catholic peasant guerrillas. A year later their numbers had risen to some 35,000, with thousands more sympathizers, and by 1929 there were about 50,000. The armed forces appeared unable to crush the rebels.

While the Cristero war raged, the issue of the presidential succession surfaced once again, and became yet another threat to the survival of the new state. Alvaro Obregón, who was still at this time the most influential man in Mexico, disapproved of both Calles's handling of relations with the Church and the oil dispute with the USA; he therefore compelled Calles to agree to a constitutional reform permitting him to stand for re-election for an extended six-year term. Obregón's was a highly risky manœuvre which smacked of Porfirista personalism. A conspiracy in the army was uncovered and further purges of discontented officers took place in 1927. Obregón was eventually elected on 16 July 1928, but was assassinated by a Catholic militant the following day. (Calles was suspected of having had a hand in the elimination of the man who had now become his rival.)

At this juncture Calles made the historic decision to institutionalize the Revolution and enshrine the principle of no re-election as the cornerstone of the political system. He founded the National Revolutionary Party and resisted the temptation to stand for president himself, choosing instead a colourless diplomat as the official candidate. However, the election would have to be rigged because Obregón's former minister of education – the highly respected José Vasconcelos, who was now in opposition – had come forward as an Anti-Re-electionist candidate and was touring the country openly invoking the memory of Francisco Madero and winning mass support.

There was a real danger that Cristero sympathizers and followers of Vasconcelos might combine at the polls and defeat the candidate of the 'institutionalized' Revolution. Were that to occur, the Cristero rebels might well overthrow the revolutionary family. To avoid such an outcome Calles decided to sue for peace with the Church. The American ambassador acted as a mediator (the USA, as ever, wanted a stable government in Mexico), and a compromise was reached by which the anti-clerical laws of 1926 were allowed to lapse in return for the resumption of church services. In the manipulated elections of November 1929, Calles's candidate won by a landslide. Vasconcelos chose to flee the country.

For the next five years – the Maximato proper – Calles remained the strongman of Mexico, ruling through token presidents. As the World Depression began to affect the Mexican economy and production fell, the rule of the shadowy *jefe máximo* became more repressive. Anti-clericalism flourished once more, and fascist-style Goldshirts terrorized Catholics and other opponents of the regime. The governor of the state of Tabasco contrived to rekindle the Cristero revolt when he passed extreme anti-Catholic laws that were brutally enforced by church-burning *pistoleros*. (The troubles in Tabasco provided the setting for Graham Greene's novel *The Power and the Glory*.)

Calles believed that agrarian reform had been a failure, and had neglected it in favour of investment in irrigation and export agriculture on large private estates, especially in the north, but the unrest caused by the economic crisis forced him to resume the programme of land redistribution. This took place mainly in the central and south-western states, where historically land hunger was most intense, but the irregular implementation of the reforms led to corruption and to murderous disputes in the countryside. Agrarian reform was of great symbolic importance for the moral prestige of the Revolution, and yet the turmoil its implementation provoked among the peasants threatened to bring the Revolution into disrepute.

Calles and his circle had become an incestuous clique of millionaires enriched by graft and plunder, but the party of the Revolution, ironically, proved stronger than the personalism of its founder. There were rumblings of discontent within the rank and file, and Calles, in the hope of co-opting his internal critics, designated one of their number, Lázaro Cárdenas, as the official candidate for the presidential elections in 1934. Cárdenas, however, chose not to treat his candidacy as a sinecure, and began touring the country building up a political base among the common people.

Lázaro Cárdenas and the Renewal of the Revolution (1934–40)

After Cárdenas won the election, he refused to perpetuate the Maximato by becoming yet another political stooge. The new president moved cautiously, and over the next two years purged Calles's placemen from government. Eventually, in order to forestall a *coup d'état*, he forced the *jefe máximo* and his cronies into exile in 1936.

Having taken the reins of power, Cárdenas worked to regain the revolutionary credibility that Calles had all but destroyed. The centre-piece of his domestic policy was the renewal of agrarian reform. During his six-year term, a total of 44 million hectares of land passed into the hands of the peasants, twice the amount that had been distributed under previous governments. Land was redistributed as private small-holdings, co-operative profit-sharing farms or in the form of the *ejido*, a modern version of the traditional Indian communal holding, whereby the title to the land was held by the community, which then leased plots out to individual heads of family. Credit, machinery and technical support were provided by a state bank and agrarian agencies. Despite Cárdenas's good intentions, the results were mixed: the peasants resented their dependence on state officials and tended to revert to traditional subsistence farming. There were flaws too in the application of the policy. Distributed land was often of poor quality; many plots were too small; the supply of credit and machinery was inadequate, partly because of petty corruption among government officials. Overall, agricultural production fell. Yet Cárdenas went a long way towards appeasing the dreadful land hunger of the Mexican peasantry in the depressed 1930s, and this earned the Revolution a fund of popular goodwill.

In the first years of his administration Cárdenas faced labour unrest over wages and rising unemployment, but under his labour minister, Vicente Lombardo Toledano, industrial relations tended to favour the trade unions and the workers' living standards rose. This pro-labour orientation led to a confrontation with the foreign oil companies, which refused in 1937 to meet a wage claim by the unions, even though the arbitration tribunal had ruled in the workers' favour. After the Supreme Court had upheld the decision of the tribunal and the companies still would not comply, Cárdenas nationalized the industry on 18 March 1938. Despite pressure from the oil lobby, Franklin D. Roosevelt decided to adhere to his Good Neighbour policy towards Latin America and refused to intervene in Mexican affairs. The oil companies organized a boycott of Mexican oil for the next three decades, which finally collapsed when world demand for oil rose sharply in the early 1970s. Cárdenas's nationalization of the oil industry made him a hero of the Revolution. Like the land redistribution and the *ejido* system, the nationalization of Mexico's oil was taken as proof that the Revolution had not come to an end; it was a continuous process capable of transcending the deviations of individuals such as Calles and his cronies.

Cárdenas also left his mark as a state-builder: he gave definitive shape to the self-perpetuating, one-party state. The National Revolutionary Party founded by Calles was reorganized into four main branches: agrarian, labour, military and 'popular', this last embracing organizations of state employees. Conflicts of interest would be subsumed in the state apparatus and managed by the leaders of the party and the government. It was a form of corporatist structure analogous to those created in Spain, Portugal and Italy during this period. But the difference was that the founding document of the state, the constitution of 1917, was democratic and liberal, with socialist elements, and this prevented Mexican corporatism from becoming totalitarian. A degree of pluralism had to be tolerated; there could exist a free press, with little overt censorship, freedom of speech and association, and rival political parties. Furthermore, the official rhetoric under Cárdenas became tinged with revolutionary socialism and Cárdenas liked to make gestures to the international left: Trotsky was granted political asylum in 1937 (he was finally assassinated in Coyoacán in 1940 by Ramón Mercader, a Spanish agent of Stalin), and in 1939, at the end of the Spanish Civil War, thousands of Spanish republicans were allowed to settle in Mexico.

On the other hand, an important objective of the government was to heal and bind the wounds of the traumatized nation. A pragmatic reconciliation with the Church was begun under Cárdenas and reaffirmed by his successor Ávila Camacho, himself a practising Catholic. But the anti-clerical laws of Calles were not repealed; they remained as an insurance against any interference by the Church in matters pertaining to the state. For the tolerance of the system had its limits; differences of opinion were allowed only so long as the interests of the Revolutionary Party were not seriously threatened. The party must remain in power at all costs, and this meant that elections at every level had to be routinely manipulated to ensure large majorities for its candidates. Any real threat to it would have to be neutralized through the patronage and jobbery machine, or else repressed by force.

The system operated on the basis of an alternation between social responsiveness and control from above. Its epitome was the presidency. Cárdenas finally perfected the mechanism for transferring power at the apex of the state by institutionalizing the indispensable function of strongman: the Mexican president would be all-powerful – but only for six years. Cárdenas understood that the principle of no re-election had to remain inviolate if the legitimacy of the Revolution was to be preserved. Not even proxy rule through stooges – the temptation, successively, of Carranza, Obregón and Calles – could be tolerated. Once his *sexenio* had been completed the president would have to step down for good. Still, the outgoing president would be allowed to pick his successor, though his choice would have to be made in consultation with the bosses of the various branches of the party so as to arrive at an internal consensus, and, just as important, to gauge the mood of the grass roots and of the country as a whole.

By 1940 a political order stable enough to replace the Porfiriato had been found; it had taken thirty years and countless deaths. It consisted of a one-party state run by a strictly temporary autocrat, pledged to an ideology of revolutionary nationalism yet committed to a path of intensive capitalist development. The system was to last for over fifty years. Obregón and Calles had laid the political and economic foundations. They believed in state-led development based on modern agricultural production and financed by a combination of public and foreign private investment. This outlook remained unchanged under their successors, except that after Cárdenas the motor of development would be manufacturing industry rather than agriculture. From 1940 the revolutionary élite, operating through the Institutional Revolutionary Party (PRI), as it was finally designated in 1946, embarked on a policy of state-led industrialization through import-substitution and protection for domestic enterprises. This was the pattern of development followed by all the major Latin American countries since the 1940s. But it is a measure of the political achievement of the PRI that, whereas other Latin American countries were racked by violence and brutal repression, the acute stresses engendered by industrialization in Mexico were assuaged, where they were not stifled, by the embrace of the corporate state.

Stability and Growth (1940–82)

Over the next four decades the growth of the Mexican economy was prodigious. Mexico was transformed from an agricultural country into a predominantly urban and industrial society. In the 1960s and 1970s it achieved an average growth rate of over 6 per cent a year. The growth of manufacturing industry was even higher at an average annual rate of 9 per cent. In 1960 just over half the population lived in urban areas; by 1980 the urban population had climbed to 69 per cent. By the 1970s Mexico had become the second largest economy in Latin America after Brazil. The social responsiveness of the Mexican political system ensured high public expenditure on welfare, health and education, while its comprehensive apparatus of control prevented discontent from exploding into violence, as it did elsewhere.

The stimulus to industrialization came with the Second World War, when the USA offered technical and financial assistance for the industrial exploitation of the country's mineral wealth to help in the war effort against Germany and Japan. Manufacturing industry was also developed to substitute for the decline in imports. Mexico declared war on the Axis powers in 1942 and later sent an air squadron to the Philippines in 1945 to fight with the US Air Force. The new era of friendship was marked by the meeting in 1943 on the US–Mexico border of the two presidents, Ávila Camacho and Franklin D. Roosevelt.

The pattern of intensive economic development that characterized the post-war decades was set under the ambitious and entrepreneurial administration of Miguel Alemán (1946–52). Its key element was rapid import-substituting industrialization. Alemán knew that capital needed to be accumulated for investment in infrastructure, technology and education. Accordingly, he created fiscal incentives for private investors, both domestic and foreign, to put money into the Mexican economy. He also developed tourism as a means of earning foreign exchange; the Pacific port of Acapulco was converted into a modern luxury resort for the North American market (similar projects in places like Cancún and Cozumel were initiated in subsequent years). Agricultural exports were also promoted to earn foreign exchange. There was substantial state investment in irrigation schemes in the north-western states and an 'agribusiness' in cotton and winter vegetables came into being with the participation of US companies.

The strategy, in industry as in agriculture, was to promote development by creating a partnership of private business and the state. The state provided the infrastructure and the basic utilities through its corporations, while the private sector followed the broad lines of development indicated by government planners in a business environment protected from external competition by high tariff barriers and stimulated by easy credit from state banks. Foreign and particularly US transnational companies were allowed to set up subsidiaries in Mexico, despite earlier legislation requiring 49 per cent representation of Mexican nationals in any company. The PRI's control of the trade unions assured private business a co-operative labour force remunerated through state-approved wage settlements.

Alemán therefore carried forward the economic pragmatism of the founding fathers of the Revolution and adapted it to the development model that generally prevailed in Latin America after the war. Power in the PRI passed from *caudillos* and military men to an élite of civilian technocrats, recruited through the National University and the Colegio de México and often trained in economics and business at top US institutions. The higher echelons of the bureaucracy had family and social connections with business and industry. For instance, the Alemán family owned extensive real estate in the new tourist resort of Acapulco, and they were prominent in the setting-up of a powerful network of communications media, which, in conjunction with the media empire of Emilio Azcárraga, virtually monopolized the cinema, radio, TV and press in Mexico, giving the PRI an informal yet very strong ideological sway over the mass urban society that was taking shape in the decades after the war.

The PRI, then, successfully transformed the corporatist structures of the 1920s and 1930s into a paternalist government machine capable of spearheading intensive development precisely because its comprehensive control from above was largely indirect and always tempered by an openness to influences from below. It was hardly liberal democracy – elections continued to be manipulated – but it was far from being a dictatorship. For the next two decades or so successive presidents steered a middle course of development between the free-market capitalism of the USA and the socialistic nationalism still enshrined in the official ideology of the party. According to the prevailing wind, they steered to the right or to the left, but ensuring always that the ship of state would remain firmly under the direction of the PRI.

Alemán's successor, Adolfo Ruiz Cortines (1952–8) instituted a regime of sound money and cautious public spending. In 1954 the peso was devalued, which boosted exports, and the exchange rate was fixed against the dollar, which attracted foreign investment. This fiscal conservatism was broadly maintained for the next fifteen years, and it kept Mexican inflation exceptionally low by regional standards until the 1970s.* However, the next president, López Mateos (1958–64), veered towards the left – partly to defuse labour militancy (in 1959 he broke a railway strike which threatened the PRI's control over the trade unions), but also to reclaim the PRI's revolutionary heritage in view of the triumph of Fidel Castro in Cuba. The programme of land reform was relaunched and some 30 million hectares redistributed, only about a quarter less than Cárdenas had achieved; North American companies in the motion-picture and electricity industries were nationalized; a large number of rural schools were built; diplomatic relations were maintained with revolutionary Cuba against the wishes of the USA.

Gustavo Díaz Ordaz (1964–70) moved to the right again to reassert the PRI's control over the electoral system after the right-wing PAN party had made some gains thanks to a limited opening conceded in 1964 by López Mateos. But Díaz Ordaz is remembered chiefly for his repression of the student left in 1968. As in many other countries, 1968 was a year of violent protests against established authority; it was also the year in which Mexico was due to host the Olympic Games. The PRI was anxious to present a flattering picture of the country to the world at large. The radical student movement, however, saw the presence of the international news media as an opportunity to denounce the government. A series of confrontations between students and troops culminated in a blood bath on 2 October at the Plaza de las Tres Culturas in Tlatelolco, a district of Mexico City.

The Tlatelolco massacre seriously tarnished the PRI's revolutionary credibility, exposing the depth of frustration in the country, as well as the determination of the PRI to hold on to state power. In 1971 revolutionary socialism surfaced in the form of guerrilla movements similar to those that had emerged in Argentina, Uruguay and Brazil roughly at this time. In these latter countries, civilian governments were overthrown by military juntas in the course of the guerrilla insurgencies. But in Mexico there was no need for *coups d'état*, for military chiefs had been an integral part of the corporate state since its foundation in the 1920s, along with the leaders of the organized

* See Statistical Appendix, table 4.

working class. The Mexican army contained and destroyed the guerrillas before they could pose any credible threat to the state.

What lay behind these challenges to the PRI's monopoly of power from the left and, to a lesser extent, from the right? By the end of the 1960s the high rates of industrialization and urbanization had produced social tensions which even the PRI machine found hard to manage. The root of the problem was that industrial import-substitution had saturated internal demand, so that Mexican industry could not continue to grow without finding new markets abroad or enlarging the market at home. The industrial sector, therefore, could not absorb much more labour. On the other hand, the expansion of capital-intensive agriculture for export increased the migration of peasants to the cities, and this rising labour surplus was aggravated by a demographic explosion due to a combination of lower mortality rates and traditionally high birth rates. The result was, on the one hand, a rural society in obvious decline and, on the other, swelling populations in cities disfigured by vast shantytowns, to which the benefits of the Mexican economic miracle had not filtered down. The distribution of wealth was grossly uneven, the top 10 per cent of the population receiving about 40 per cent of the national income.

The condition of Mexico in the late 1960s contradicted the revolutionary ideology of socialist nationalism that the PRI claimed to defend; what had become of agrarian justice, social equality and economic sovereignty? The student left in Mexico now drew revolutionary inspiration from Marxist Cuba; intellectuals began to write about the 'betrayal' of the Mexican Revolution. On the right, the rival party PAN attracted businessmen and industrialists – especially from the more dynamic northern states – by advocating the virtues of a freer market to stimulate production. There began to occur too a renaissance of the democratic liberal principles which had died with Madero, but which nevertheless had an honoured place in the Mexican intellectual tradition. Liberals criticized the PRI's unaccountability to the people and the arrogance of its power. Octavio Paz, the greatest Mexican poet of the century, resigned his post as ambassador to India after the Tlatelolco massacre. On his return to Mexico, he elaborated a critique of the self-perpetuating one-party state run by the PRI, which he described as a 'philanthropic ogre'.

Populist philanthropy was indeed the tactic employed by the PRI to maintain its overbearing presence in public life. The new president, Luis Echeverría (1970–76) – minister of the interior at the time of the Tlatelolco massacre – attempted to cope with social tensions and the critical state of the economy by employing the usual PRI formula of combining social welfare and socialist rhetoric with rapid economic growth. To mitigate the effects of the population explosion and rural misery, he greatly extended state spending on food subsidies, education, house-building and health, touring country villages and dispensing favours with patriarchal largesse. He proposed to pay for the increase in spending through higher taxes and by raising industrial productivity – tariff barriers would be reduced to encourage competition in the excessively protected Mexican market, and new markets abroad would be found through the promotion of industrial exports.

But by 1973 the Mexican middle classes and the business lobby had pressured him into dropping these proposals; instead he resorted to borrowing money to cover the growing deficits in state budgets and in the balance of payments, which got worse in 1974 after the sharp rise in world oil prices. The result was a jump in the rate of inflation, which rose from a yearly average during the 1960s of 3.5 per cent to 20 per cent in 1974 and 27 per cent in 1976. Under Echeverría the Mexican policy of sound money as the cornerstone of development fell to pieces; the peso began to drop in value in real terms, but because the 1954 exchange rate of 12.5 pesos to the dollar was maintained, Mexican exports became overpriced – world commodity prices were depressed anyway – while imports poured into the country; the balance of payments was thus aggravated further, creating a cycle of rising foreign debt feeding even higher inflation, which further undermined the peso and led to massive capital flight by investors.

Echeverría found himself in a cleft stick: he had to do something about the economy without losing too much popular support to the left. As his sexenio drew to a close, he made a bungling attempt at a devaluation of the currency to help exports – 60 per cent in September 1976, which turned out not to be sufficient, followed by a further 40 per cent a month later. Then in November he tried to compensate for this smack of fiscal discipline with a 'revolutionary' gesture, redistributing private land to peasants in Sonora – a move that failed to satisfy the left and yet outraged the right. In the 1970s the Mexican miracle of rapid expansion slowed down somewhat to an average of 5.4 per cent a year, and this expansion, moreover, was being fuelled increasingly by foreign loans.

When Echeverría's finance minister, José López Portillo (1976–82), acceded to the presidency, it seemed that he would be condemned to struggle to retain the PRI's monopoly of power. An IMF austerity programme stabilized the peso, but at the cost of a drop in real wages and rising unemployment. Like his predecessor, López Portillo hoped to stimulate Mexican industrial production by reducing protectionism and fostering non-traditional exports. Once again, however, this restructuring was put off; not because of political pressure this time, but because of a huge economic windfall – the discovery of oil reserves of up to 70 billion barrels (and potential reserves of about 200 billion, which would last for about sixty-five years), enough to place Mexico among the top producers in the world, and this at a time when the oil price was being kept high by the OPEC producers' cartel.

Mexico's sudden access to wealth afforded an opportunity to achieve genuine economic independence: the balance of payments could have been painlessly corrected, public debts paid off, and development, combined with social welfare, financed without borrowing abroad. However, the dynamics of the PRI's corporate state, with its overlapping networks of politicians, bureaucrats and businessmen, and its political culture of patronage and favours, were hugely stimulated by the oil money. The massive influx of capital led to often wasteful or misconceived development projects. Semi-autonomous state bodies incurred staggering loans: the oil corporation Pemex borrowed $10 billion in 1981 alone, when its previous total debt was only $5 billion. In any case the intense demographic pressure forced upon the government a very high level of public spending on social welfare, agricultural investment and food subsidies: in 1980 government spending rose by 61.5 per cent compared with 36 per cent the previous year.

Financed by oil revenues and escalating foreign loans, the Mexican economy resumed 'miraculous' annual growth rates of over 7 per cent. But the oil bonanza masked continuing structural problems. Export earnings in 1980 were well over double what they had been two years earlier, but oil now accounted for 67 per cent of total exports. Meanwhile the manufacturing sector languished: the rate of growth over the same period fell by 3 per cent and industrial exports grew by less than 4 per cent through lack of international competitiveness. The volume of imports, nevertheless, increased due to the need for industrial technology, the huge middle-class demand for consumer goods and the purchase of foodstuffs abroad to meet basic domestic requirements (this in a traditionally agrarian country).

The result of these structural defects was a persistent deficit in the balance of payments, which led to more foreign borrowing and accelerating inflation (up to 35 per cent in 1980); and when the price of oil dropped sharply in 1981, further recourse to external credit became inevitable. The situation might have remained manageable had not US interest rates suddenly risen, causing a deep world recession. Mexican inflation took off again, reaching 100 per cent in 1982. Finally, in August of that year Mexico became the first country in Latin America to announce a suspension of interest payments on its foreign debt of $85.5 billion (with a ratio of interest payments to export earnings of 40 per cent).

The Foreign Debt and the Erosion of the Corporate State (1982–90)

Once again it fell to a new president, Miguel de la Madrid (1982–8), to cope with the critical state of the economy. Rescheduling facilities for the foreign debt were available at the price of a severe austerity programme prescribed by the IMF. The government sought some popular understanding for the belt-tightening by blaming much of the problem upon the corruption of officials in López Portillo's administration. A campaign of 'public morality' was declared by the new government, and the publication of financial scandals concerning previous servants of the state turned into the officially sanctioned pastime of the newspapers. The former head of Pemex, Jorge Díaz Serrano, was prosecuted for corruption on a relatively minor matter, but he was the man who had engineered the oil boom and his downfall in the highly ritualized public life of Mexico served the purpose of providing a scapegoat for the general economic débâcle. The most notorious case was that of the former chief of police of Mexico City, who was indicted on charges of embezzlement. His splendid estate outside the capital, with its own race-course and a residence modelled on the Parthenon, became a favourite weekend attraction for ordinary citizens curious to see what perquisites might be obtained in the public service.

The burden of the austerity programme, needless to say, fell upon the shoulders of the poor and the working classes. Average wages rose by 40 per cent in 1983, when inflation was running at 100 per cent; reductions in subsidies of staples and transport drove up the cost of living for the broad mass of the people. Their plight was made worse by the devastation caused by a powerful earthquake that hit Mexico City and western parts of the country in 1985; the shantytowns and working-class barrios sustained the greatest loss of life. The government's inefficiency in dealing with the consequences of this disaster fuelled rising public anger. The middle classes too were affected by cuts in public spending and in imports of consumer goods. For the foreseeable future economic growth would be negligible, since the bulk of export earnings would have to go towards servicing the foreign debt rather than into investment.

This situation jeopardized the PRI's historic strategy of responsiveness and control. With IMF-imposed austerity, it was difficult to retain the loyalty of workers and peasants, but overt repression would play into the hands of an already combative opposition. Cracks began to appear in the monopoly of the ruling party. In 1986 impatience with the customary manipulation of the electoral process produced hunger strikes in Mexico City by candidates of the PAN who claimed to have been defeated by fraud in elections in the northern states of Chihuahua and Durango. But opposition parties could not make much headway so long as the PRI exercised indirect but effective control of all the institutions of state, the television and major radio stations, and even most of the press.

Yet so strong was public disaffection that it made itself felt within the PRI itself, threatening the very cornerstone of the Mexican revolutionary state – the unquestioned right of the outgoing president to pick his successor. The designated PRI candidate for the 1988 presidential election, Carlos Salinas de Gortari, a Harvard-educated technocrat who had been minister of the budget under De la Madrid, found his candidacy opposed by a self-styled 'democratic movement' within the party. What made this development particularly threatening to the party managers was that it was led by Cuauhtemoc Cárdenas, the son of Lázaro Cárdenas, one of the most revered heroes of the Revolution and the man who had stood up to Yankee imperialism by nationalizing the oil industry in 1938. At a time when Mexico was struggling in a vain effort to pay fabulous sums to the bankers of Wall Street and the City of London, the call to defy the foreign creditors gave Cárdenas a huge following. Cuauhtemoc presented himself as a rival candidate and concluded an electoral pact with the PAN and the socialist parties in order to denounce the alleged malpractices of the PRI machine. The PRI candidate eventually won the election, though not by the usual landslide. The opposition parties united in claiming that 'electoral alchemy' had given Salinas his victory and large street demonstrations took place to protest at his inauguration.

Salinas, nevertheless, took the reins of power and soon asserted the formidable authority commanded by a Mexican president. He proceeded with the orthodox strategy of monetary restraint and privatization of significant parts of the vast public sector. In January 1989 he even dared to take on and defeat – in a shoot-out between police and armed bodyguards – the fearsome trade-union boss Hernández Galicia, a man who ran the immensely wealthy petroleum workers' union like a personal fiefdom. His gaoling on charges of tax evasion was a powerful signal that the new president was preparing to assert financial control over the oil industry. Pemex, that most untouchable of the sacred cows of the revolutionary state – it had been the creation of Lázaro Cárdenas – would not be immune from the effort to relaunch the economy. It was a calculated gamble, for Salinas's power play could only succeed for a limited time: without a resumption of growth, the entire Mexican system, which had held good for sixty years, threatened to unravel.

Salinas, therefore, took a lead in calling upon the USA, the main creditor nation, to sanction relief of the debt burden for the Latin American countries. It was, in a sense, an appeal for the USA to perceive its own interest in the continuation of the extraordinary political stability of its southern neighbour. Mexico was the first Latin American nation to respond positively to the Brady Plan, and in January 1990 concluded a debt-relief arrangement, underwritten by the US Treasury, with the creditor banks. A few months later the Mexican government was proposing to negotiate a free-trade agreement with the USA and Canada which would abolish tariff barriers between the three countries.

These economic strategies became possible because Salinas had pursued an orthodox liberal policy at home: a 3 per cent growth rate was achieved in 1989 by cutting public spending and opening the economy to foreign trade. In February 1990 Salinas announced plans to privatize the main state-run steel companies; in May he authorized the privatization of the banks that López Portillo had suddenly nationalized in 1982. The overall strategy was to liberalize the economy in order to grow out of the debt problem.

The PRI's control from above depended ultimately on the party machine's capacity to respond to pressures from below. The government maintained its programme of basic subsidies to the poorest sectors, but the strict controls on wages threatened to fuel popular discontent with the PRI even further. This was reflected in the mounting criticism of the electoral fraud that routinely sustained the PRI machine. Opposition parties such as PAN and Cuauhtemoc Cárdenas's Party of the Democratic Revolution (PRD) continued to attract wide popular support, so that ballot-rigging no longer seemed a feasible option in future elections. By 1990 the PRI's corporatist machine was beginning to break down: the Confederation of Peasants had broken away to ally itself with Cárdenas's PRD, while the PRI-dominated Confederation of Labour Unions (CTM) found itself competing against other independent unions. The fact was that Salinas's policy of economic liberalization would sooner or later undermine the corporate state that the victors of the Revolution had created for Mexico in the 1930s. The question would then arise whether the stability that corporatism had afforded Mexico would crumble into chronic disorder or whether the genuine democratization of politics would strengthen the legitimacy of the Mexican state and make it better able to tackle the immense economic and social problems that faced the country.

The Mexican Revolution did not in itself change Mexican society. What it did was to throw up a dynamic nationalist élite, which managed eventually to centralize power in the form of a unique one-party system in which *caudillo* politics were adapted to the task of rapid economic modernization. The corporate state that was gradually built by the 'revolutionary family' provided the country with unparalleled stability. And thanks to its revolutionary emphasis on egalitarianism and the common citizenship of all ethnic groups, it committed itself to maintaining the basic welfare of the poor, especially during the profound industrial revolution which transformed the face of Mexico in a mere two or three decades.

However, the oil bonanza of the late 1970s and the debt crisis which followed revealed the weaknesses of corporatism. The monopoly of power enjoyed by the PRI neutralized opposition so effectively that the virtually omnipotent presidents became unaccountable to the electorate. In the closed environment of the ruling party the culture of patronage and favours flourished too well, debilitating the structure of the economy and fostering corruption in public life. The result was that the huge numbers of unemployed people in a fast-growing population could not be absorbed by an industrial sector whose excessive nurturing had drained vital resources from the rural areas. Towards the end of the twentieth century the Mexican state, crippled by its foreign debt, faced the difficult task of restoring economic growth without renouncing its historic commitment to social welfare.

11. Brazil: Order and Progress

The First Republic (1889–1930)

The republican state in Brazil was born with surprising ease on 16 November 1889. Its midwife was the army, and the army remained its tutelary spirit, fixing upon the nation the twin ideals inscribed in the republican flag – *ordem e progresso*. Inevitably, the task of balancing order with progress brought the military into politics as the final arbiter of the nation's will, but what characterized the will of the armed forces was an overriding determination to turn Brazil into a great power in the modern world. Because of this zest for progress, the armed forces retained their independence from any one class or political interest. Their wish for order often made them shore up conservative institutions but, equally, they did not refrain from imposing change whenever conservatism appeared to block modernization.

Tensions between the old and the new surfaced in the early days of the republic. The democratic constitution approved in 1891 was the work of Rui Barbosa, a lawyer from the state of Bahia in the north-east and a radical liberal republican who had been a leading advocate of the abolition of slavery. Largely modelled on that of the United States, the constitution gave Brazil a federal structure consisting of twenty self-governing states with a national government headed by a directly elected president answerable to a senate and a chamber of deputies.

Yet behind this model republican constitution there persisted the traditional politics of an oligarchic and unequal society. As ever, the real business of Brazilian politics at the national level derived from the rivalry between regional élites. In theory, federalism was meant to benefit the weaker states by allowing them greater autonomy from the centre. In fact, it suited the strong best. Rui Barbosa's home state of Bahia, like the other sugar-growing states of the north-east, was in economic decline. By the end of the nineteenth century it was coffee that drove the Brazilian economy, and the state of São Paulo was the power-house of the nation. São Paulo accounted for up to 40 per cent of GNP; its foreign debt was larger than that of the national government; its population would treble between 1890 and 1920 as immigrants from the other states and from Europe poured in to benefit from its coffee boom.

The coffee planters of São Paulo had clung to the empire in its last decades because slavery had seemed the only answer to their labour needs. But when the emperor approved the final act of abolition in May 1888, there was little reason, politically, for the Paulistas to defer any longer to the imperial government in Rio de Janeiro; for, in economic terms, São Paulo gave to the imperial government far more than it received. And so the empire had to die in order to prevent São Paulo, its richest province, from striking out on its own.

In effect, the federal republic could only hold Brazil together by giving São Paulo its head: the new federal structure allowed individual states to levy their own taxes, raise foreign loans, set their own tariffs on foreign imports and even impose duty on trade with other Brazilian states, and in the case of São Paulo such powers conferred upon it what amounted to economic independence. If it contributed heavily to the federal budget, it was because this gave it a preponderant influence over national politics.

The coming of the republic did not do away with oligarchy. To start with, only literate adult males could vote. The electorate was thus restricted to about 3 per cent of the population, of which the overwhelming majority was white. Federal elections, in any case, were formalities which set the seal on arrangements between regional oligarchies. Within states, politics remained a contest between clans, with each province having its own pyramid of power which reached down to the localities through a hierarchy of political bosses known as colonels or *coronéis* (the equivalent of local *caudillos* in Spanish America).

At the grass roots, republican democracy was to a large extent a matter of bargaining with the *coronéis* for access to state patronage – a promise of funds, jobs and commercial licences in return for delivering the vote. Between states, bargaining was necessary to secure support in federal elections from the political machines in the regions. Federal government was therefore determined by a 'politics of the governors' rather than by genuine tests of public opinion. The politics of the governors obviously favoured the wealthiest states, since they could afford the most effective patronage, and here of course São Paulo was pre-eminent.

In reality, the Brazilian republic owed its stability to an arrangement between the bosses of São Paulo and those of Minas Gerais (a less wealthy but populous state), according to which the presidency would alternate between them. Of the eleven presidents of the republic between 1889 and 1930, six came from São Paulo and three from Minas Gerais. The other states were unable to break this duopoly, except for Rio Grande do Sul, which after 1909 was capable of making a president in certain circumstances. This was partly due to the vigour of its cattle-raising *gaúcho* economy (similar to Argentina's and Uruguay's), but more to its connections with the army. Situated on the perennially troubled frontier with Spanish America, Rio Grande do Sul was of special importance to the armed forces and tended to produce top-ranking military men, a factor which gave Riograndense political bosses added weight in federal power-broking.

Thus, although the politics of the first Brazilian republic turned upon what became known as the *café com leite* (*café au lait*) alliance between the coffee élites of São Paulo and the cattle barons of Minas Gerais, the armed forces in the last instance presided over this deeply oligarchic arrangement. The capacity of other states to rebel against this system was limited. The army liked order, and order was best assured by centralized control, which effectively meant upholding the São Paulo–Minas Gerais axis.

But the republic was not created without bloodshed, nor did its politics survive without challenge. Violent opposition to the republic as such came from the rural poor in the backward provinces. The dispossessed peasantry of the declining sugar states resented the incursions of modern capitalism, particularly with the coming of the railway. Despite their harsh lives, they reacted by trying to cling to a familiar, traditional world, rising up to defend God and the empire. The most famous of the various millenarian rebellions against the republic took place at Canudos in the declining north-eastern state of Bahia, where in 1893 a Catholic visionary, Antônio the Counsellor, led a movement of up to 30,000 people in resistance to the authority of the secular republic. The Canudos rebels held out for four years and were put down only after a series of increasingly savage assaults by government troops. In 1911 a similar uprising in favour of the monarchy occurred among the poor in the southern states of Paraná and Santa Catarina. Led by another Catholic visionary, José Maria, who was revered as a saint after he was killed early on in the struggle, the Contestado movement lasted until 1915, when it was destroyed by the republican army.

Another form of rural violence was the phenomenon of banditry, which was widespread in the *sertão*, the bleak interior of the north-eastern states. This was not so much anti-republican in character – it had originated during the empire – as a sign of indifference to organized society. But the *cangaços*, groups of armed desperadoes who raided farms and pillaged towns, have been regarded as social rebels. Certainly the most famous *cangaceiro*, Lampião, active from the early 1920s until he was killed in 1938, acquired a reputation as a Robin Hood figure among the poor of the *sertão*.

The Crisis of the 1920s

A far greater threat to the republican order than social rebellion came from upsets in the *café com leite* alliance. One such occurred during the preparations for the 1910 election, when both the approved presidential candidate and the incumbent president died within months of each other. This opened a breach between the two main states which allowed Rio Grande do Sul to side with Minas Gerais in support of a military candidate, Marshal Hermes da Fonseca. São Paulo backed Rui Barbosa, the liberal champion of federalism, who campaigned against oligarchic practices and military intervention in politics. The marshal won and during his unsettled term of office the army proceeded to meddle in the affairs of various states in an attempt to increase central control.

In subsequent elections the São Paulo–Minas Gerais axis worked fairly well, but in 1922 a more serious crisis developed when the *café com leite* candidate, Arturo Bernardes, was opposed by a new coalition of lesser states led by Rio Grande do Sul and backed by the army. During Bernardes's term of office it became apparent that there were undercurrents of discontent with the republic. The power of the export-oriented coffee planters of São Paulo was resented by other states, especially Rio Grande do Sul. The urban middle classes were also unhappy with the export-economy; in 1926, a nationalist, anti-oligarchic Democratic Party was founded in São Paulo calling for an end to manipulated elections and promising to keep Brazil for the Brazilians at a time of high foreign investment and mass immigration from Europe.

Intellectuals and artists assumed a key role in the developing challenge to the coffee export-economy, contributing to the ferment of nationalism with their explorations of the problem of cultural identity. At the Week of Modern Art held in São Paulo in February 1922, young artists, musicians and writers exhibited their work in the new styles of the European avant-garde. This event is taken as representing the beginning of Brazilian modernism, a many-sided artistic phenomenon which exhibited in its often conflicting political manifestations a common revolutionary impatience with the established order (see Chapter 15). For instance, one of the leaders of modernism, the poet Oswald de Andrade, was drawn to Marxism, while another major figure in the modernist movement, the writer Plínio Salgado, founded a fascist party that acquired considerable strength in the 1930s and came close to pulling off a *coup d'état* in 1937.

Most disquieting of all was evidence of discontent in the army. In 1922, 1924 and 1926, junior officers in various garrisons staged revolts against Bernardes. These 'revolts of the *tenentes*' (lieutenants) were sparked by insults against the honour of the armed forces published in the press in 1921 under the forged name of Bernardes himself. Needless to say, wounded pride was the more keenly felt because of frustration over promotion and conditions of service. The *tenentes* did not adhere to any specific political ideology, but wanted to do away with the oligarchic 'politics of the governors' and put an end to the dominance of the coffee exporters of São Paulo. After the 1924 rising, however, many *tenentes* moved to the left; this was largely the result of their experience of tramping through the interior of the country for over two years as a guerrilla force, known as the Prestes Column after their commander Luís Carlos Prestes, who went on to become the leader of the Brazilian Communist Party over a period of three decades. In several respects, the atmosphere of the 1920s was reminiscent of the last years of the Brazilian empire when regional dissatisfaction, intellectual ferment and a malaise within the armed forces combined to undermine the dominant oligarchic arrangements.

Economic Crisis

As in the 1880s, a fundamental reason for the political turbulence was that the São Paulo coffee industry was in crisis. Since the First World War, the world price for coffee had been falling steadily: too much coffee was being produced in Brazil by wasteful and outdated methods. In order to keep the world price up, the coffee planters had persuaded the government to introduce a 'valorization' scheme, which involved the stockpiling of excess coffee by state agencies and the gradual release of the resultant coffee mountain on to world markets. In return, the planters would be tided over with loans from British and US banks worth up to 30 per cent of the value of reserved stocks.

Since valorization kept coffee prices artificially high, it cushioned producers against real demand and encouraged further overproduction. Buoyant world prices also acted as an incentive for Brazil's international competitors such as Colombia and the Central American countries to increase production. As real market forces exerted downward pressure on the world price, the Brazilian government had to borrow more money in order to subsidize the planters for the ever larger quantities of coffee that had to be stockpiled. The result was a growing foreign debt problem, which weakened the currency and fuelled inflation. By 1930, a third of the national budget went towards servicing the foreign debt.

Naturally, other Brazilian states and economic interest groups resented the valorization scheme because it served largely to guarantee profits for the coffee élite of São Paulo. Hence the new prominence of Rio Grande do Sul in national politics: its cattle-raising economy was geared to the production of jerked beef for the home market, and the inflation created by the coffee valorization scheme reduced the buying power of its domestic customers. The growing number of Brazilian industrialists – mostly concentrated in the city of São Paulo itself, and producing for the home market too – were jealous of the mounting resources which the state lavished on the coffee-growers. The urban classes too did badly from the inflation generated by the valorization scheme. Finally, the army became dissatisfied with a system which devoted so much of the nation's wealth to shoring up an export trade dominated by one state and its foreign business partners. Just as the empire, which had politically favoured the sugar barons of Rio de Janeiro and the north-east, came under threat when the coffee planters of São Paulo had achieved their ascendancy, so now the federal republic, which suited the Paulista coffee élite, began to crack under pressure from new social and economic forces.

It was the Wall Street Crash of 1929 that broke the back of the old republic. The coffee élite of São Paulo had been able to dominate national politics because they were the chief earners of foreign exchange in the country. But the Crash led to the collapse of world demand for coffee. Also, the loans needed to maintain the valorization scheme and to service the huge national debt became virtually impossible to obtain in the depressed US money markets. The situation was made worse by a misguided effort to prop up the Brazilian currency by maintaining its convertibility against gold or sterling – within weeks Brazilian reserves of foreign exchange were exhausted.

By the time of the presidential elections of 1930 the *café com leite* alliance had become unworkable. The coffee élite of São Paulo could no longer carry other vested interests with it. The outgoing president, Washington Luís, nominated as his successor Júlio Prestes, a Paulista like himself; this was in breach of a prior understanding with Minas Gerais that the next president would be a Mineiro. The choice of Prestes split the oligarchy of Minas Gerais along the lines of economic interest. Mineiro coffee growers were happy with Prestes, but the ranchers defected to a rival coalition led by the cattle barons of Rio Grande do Sul and comprising an assortment of nationalist interest groups – businessmen, industrialists, the middle classes and the *tenentes*.

This new coalition of opposition forces formed a Liberal Alliance to fight the election, choosing as its candidate the governor of Rio Grande do Sul, Getúlio Vargas, a wealthy cattle rancher. However, the election of 1930 was still a contest between two oligarchic machines, and, as it turned out, the São Paulo machine won. This time the opposition refused to accept the result with good grace. There followed several months of disputes and rising tension: Getúlio Vargas's running mate was assassinated and the *tenentes* staged rebellions in several state capitals.

These disturbances persuaded the military high command to depose the outgoing president. In effect, the armed forces had decided to put an end to the republic they had created in 1889: it was time once more to reshape the nation in the interest of progress. The military junta made the defeated Riograndense candidate, Getúlio Vargas, provisional president; but there would be nothing provisional about Vargas's rule: between 1930 and 1954 he was to govern Brazil for a total of nineteen years, relinquishing office only once in 1945–50.

Getúlio Vargas and the Estado Nôvo (1930–45)

The era of Getúlio Vargas was a watershed in Brazilian history. It marked the end of the hegemony of the São Paulo coffee interests and it redirected the economy from export-led growth to import-substitution industrialization guided by the state.

These changes came about gradually, almost fortuitously, for Vargas did not come to power with a new ideology, nor even with a specific programme for change. He was a veteran of the Riograndense oligarchy of big cattle ranchers, and his real interest was in redressing the balance of forces in the 'politics of the governors' to the advantage of his own state. His prime objective, therefore, was to break up the *café com leite* alliance and so deprive São Paulo of its political dominance. To this end the Riograndense bosses had seen fit to ally themselves with urban interests and nationalist groups.

For the first five years or so Vargas proceeded to wrest power away from São Paulo. Governing by decree, he sent 'interventors' to replace all state governors. Their job was to reduce the size of state militias and reorganize the political machine within individual states in order to build up a network of patronage in support of Vargas. Such a reordering of the machinery of federal patronage brought new social groups into the arena of national politics, namely, the relatively small class of industrialists and entrepreneurs, middle-class wage-earners, and, to some extent, the organized working class.

Predictably, the bosses of São Paulo did not willingly accept this rearrangement of the 'politics of the governors' which had worked so well for them. Provoked by the rather inept manœuvres of Vargas's interventor, they summoned the Paulista militia to an insurrection on 9 July 1932. Paulista resistance to centralization lasted some three months, but once federal troops had crushed the rebellion, Vargas had effectively overcome the main threat to his authority. On 16 July 1934 a constituent assembly produced a new constitution, which strengthened the president's hand and reduced the autonomy of individual states: São Paulo had thus been brought to heel. The constituent assembly then elected Getúlio Vargas to the presidency for a four-year term.

The new centralized regime existed, though, in an ideological vacuum. Ostensibly, the old liberal republic had been destroyed, but the 'Revolution of 1930' had in reality been an oligarchic manœuvre which São Paulo had failed to win. Now the victors needed to justify their power by gracing it with a set of political ideals. There were two willing purveyors of such a facility, and each took to fighting in the streets against the other for the chance to provide it: the Integralists were a fascist movement founded by the modernist writer Plínio Salgado in 1932; their rivals were the Aliança Libertadora Nacional (ALN), a popular front – which included socialists and radical liberals – formed in 1935 by the Brazilian Communist Party on instructions from Stalin's Communist International.

In November 1935 the ALN made the first reckless bid for power by trying to force Vargas's hand with a series of barracks rebellions by ALN supporters in the junior ranks of the army. This *pronunciamiento* failed to spread beyond Rio de Janeiro and a few cities in the north-east. It also failed in its main aim of persuading Vargas to buy peace by co-opting the ALN into his government. On the contrary, the president took it as an opportunity to smash the ALN, imprisoning the leader of the Communist Party, Luís Carlos Prestes, and countless left-wing militants.

The failure of the ALN left the field to the fascists. They saw a great opportunity to take over the state in 1938, for that was the year in which Vargas was constitutionally bound to call a presidential election at which he would not be eligible to stand himself. But Getúlio Vargas stole a march on Salgado's Greenshirts. In October 1937 a state of siege was declared to defend the state against an alleged communist plot. On 10 November Vargas suspended the constitution of 1934 which prevented him from continuing in office. In its place he proclaimed a different constitution which would give birth to a non-liberal 'New State', the *Estado Nôvo*. He offered a cabinet post to the fascist leader, Plínio Salgado, who turned it down. Then Salgado committed the error of trying to oust Vargas by a sudden strike. In May he led a few hundred Greenshirts in an attack on the presidential palace, but was held at bay until the army arrived to put down his hare-brained fascist putsch. Vargas now found himself with no organized opposition to his *Estado Nôvo*.

The creation of the *Estado Nôvo* was as much the result of economic crisis as of political calculation. In late 1937 coffee prices had slumped badly and Vargas had done little to check the flood of imports. The government had to contend with a massive deficit in the balance of payments, an unmanageable foreign debt and soaring inflation. In order to cope with the crisis quickly, Vargas assumed dictatorial powers, using the pretext of communist subversion to supersede the 1934 constitution with one of his own devising. It was this crisis too that persuaded Vargas of the need to encourage industrialization so as to compensate for the fluctuations of the coffee-based export-economy.

Getúlio Vargas's *Estado Nôvo* was one of the various authoritarian corporate states which appeared in several Latin countries in the 1930s. Civil rights were severely abridged, the press was censored, political parties banned and restraints on the police relaxed to the point of condoning torture. The government was authorized to intervene in the economy and society as the guardian of the national interest. Political representation was effected through the organization of economic interests in a National Economic Council, a forum in which conflicts would be harmonized for the sake of the well-being of the nation as a whole. Such a structure appealed strongly to the bureaucracy, to industrialists and to the armed forces. To bureaucrats it promised expanded powers to plan economic development. Industrialists were pleased because state protection meant a captive home market and good prices for subsidized Brazilian manufactures. The military welcomed it because it gave them further scope to develop an armaments industry run by themselves.

The *Estado Nôvo* therefore established industrialization as one of the overriding aims of policy. The state was to take an active role in stimulating industries such as mining, oil, steel, electricity, chemicals, motor vehicles and light aircraft. It intervened also in the export-economy in order to channel resources from agriculture to industry. Government agencies regulated the overseas sale of coffee and other commodities, adjusting the price structure so as to maximize state revenues. Foreign capital and transnational firms were welcomed under certain conditions as contributors to the process of modernization.

Relatively disadvantaged by Vargas's statism were the urban wage-earners, who had to put up with high prices for consumer goods made in Brazil, and the farmers, who received credits and subsidies from the state but faced government intervention on prices and production. The organized workers were also losers, even though 'social tranquillity' was a declared aim of the government. Labour laws conferred numerous benefits upon workers, such as an eight-hour day, paid holidays, security of employment, the right to strike, a minimum wage and good standards of health and safety. But in exchange for this legislation (not always observed in practice), trade unions lost their independence from the state and the right to free collective bargaining. Union finances, and even elections, were controlled by the ministry of labour. Special tribunals adjudicated wage claims, and in the 1940s real wages lagged behind the rising cost of living. The new labour code only really affected the urban industrial workforce; on the *fazendas* the age-old forms of coercive labour for the most part survived intact.

Though he turned decisively in the direction of economic nationalism, Vargas was a pragmatist, who well knew that most of the resources needed to set up an industrial base in Brazil would have to come from abroad. In the deteriorating world situation of the late 1930s, Vargas began to exploit the tensions between the USA and Nazi Germany so as to extract the maximum benefits for Brazilian development from the competing powers. Once war had broken out in Europe, it was the USA that proved the better market for Brazilian exports, as well as a ready source of loans and technical assistance for the crash programme of industrialization. Vargas allowed the USA to build military bases in northern Brazil for use against German U-boats in Atlantic waters and also for the co-ordination of the Allied invasions of North Africa. In return he got assistance with the construction of the giant steel mill of Volta Redonda, the show-piece of Brazil's industrial programme; together with generous credit for other investments in infrastructure. Although he hedged his bets until late in the war, Vargas finally plumped for the USA and declared war on Germany, sending a force of 25,000 men to fight in Italy with the US Fifth Army in 1944.

As the tide of war began to turn against Nazi Germany, Vargas realized that he must acquire democratic credentials to survive; the semi-fascist trappings of the *Estado Nôvo* had to be discarded. But to win an election – the one promised for 1943 had been suspended because of the war – Vargas needed a political base. He therefore allowed the formation of new political parties, creating two himself – the Social Democratic Party (PSD), which attracted industrialists and rural bosses, and a Labour Party (PTB), whose main support came from pro-Vargas trade unions. Economic liberals and the traditional export élites founded the National Democratic Union (UDN), which was opposed to Vargas. The Communist Party was legalized and its veteran leader Luís Carlos Prestes released from gaol.

As if two pro-Vargas parties were not enough, there appeared a mysterious movement dubbed the *queremistas* because of their ubiquitous slogan, *Queremos Getúlio* ('We want Getúlio'). To opponents of the regime this seemed a sign that Getúlio was none too keen to go to the polls on 2 December 1945 as promised. It looked as if Vargas might be trying yet again to wriggle out of an election by stirring up a movement like the *queremistas*, which would create an impression of widespread popular support and thus provide him with an excuse to remain in power. The USA, by now a vital contributor to Brazil's drive to industrialize, expressed its displeasure at the turn Brazilian politics were taking. The army became anxious that Vargas's personal ambitions might jeopardize the lucrative alliance with the USA. When Getúlio unexpectedly appointed his brother chief of police in Rio de Janeiro, the military high command intervened and asked the dictator to step down or be deposed.

On 29 October 1945 Vargas resigned and returned to his home state. Elections were duly held on 2 December and Eurico Dutra, one of the generals who had put pressure on Vargas to resign, won as the candidate of the PSD, a party that had Vargas's blessing. General Dutra, after all, had been one of the mainstays of the *Estado Nôvo*.

The Second Republic (1946–64)

The election of the new president ushered in the restoration of liberal democracy under a constitution drafted by a constituent assembly in 1946. The second republic was based on the liberal principles of the 1891 constitution, but incorporated much of the social legislation and the labour code of the *Estado Nôvo*.

Eurico Dutra also retained Vargas's commitment to industrial development through state planning. But the Vargas years had seen very high inflation and excessive borrowing. Dutra therefore had to deflate the economy to curb spending and bring prices down. At the same time he relaxed import and exchange controls in order to attract foreign capital and keep up the momentum of industrialization. Politically, he cracked down on the Communist Party – which was made illegal once more in 1947 – and tried to stifle the trade union reaction to the austerity measures by replacing militant union leaders with more malleable men.

Yet even though Dutra appeared more sympathetic to private enterprise than Vargas, he did not by any means renounce economic nationalism. On the contrary, he expanded the public sector by nationalizing most of the foreign-owned railway network; he pursued self-sufficiency in heavy industry, enlarging the Volta Redonda steelworks and pressing ahead with an ambitious scheme for hydro-electric power; and he kept up the dynamic of modernization by opening a new frontier of development in the vast Amazon territories.

Meanwhile, Getúlio Vargas remained politically active. He had been elected to the senate in two states and chose to sit for Rio Grande do Sul. He maintained a high profile in national politics and easily emerged as the combined PSD and PTB candidate in the 1950 presidential election, fighting on a highly nationalist and ostensibly pro-labour programme, which did not, however, deter the machine politicians of Rio Grande and Minas Gerais from backing him. Vargas's victory by a plurality of 48.7 per cent gave him his third presidency, though it was only his first by direct election.

Back in office, Vargas adopted his always pragmatic attitude to development and tried to continue the broad lines of Dutra's policies, including the new benevolence to private foreign investment. But he faced a problem which was largely political and one of his own making: he could not reconcile the nationalist and populist rhetoric which had captivated his supporters at the polls with a seriously inflation-prone and debt-ridden economy. The rapid industrialization favoured by nationalists required high levels of investment, which the state could finance only with foreign capital – of which the nationalists intensely disapproved – or by printing money, which caused even higher inflation and played havoc with economic planning and industrial relations.

For the next five years Vargas wrestled unsuccessfully with this dilemma. It brought him into repeated conflict both with the USA and the nationalists, especially as regards the profit remittances of foreign businesses and rights to oil exploration. Over the latter issue, Vargas fell out with congress. He wished to move ahead rapidly towards a solution of the country's energy shortage by creating a partnership between the state and US oil companies that could draw upon the capital and technical expertise required to undertake extensive and cost-effective drilling operations. However, after a protracted wrangle with congress, Vargas was compelled to set up an under-capitalized state monopoly so as to allay fears of US imperialist ambitions.

The year 1953 proved a turning-point for Vargas. A joint US–Brazilian commission set up by Dutra in 1949 had recommended a programme of development whose implementation required credits and loans from the USA. But the soaring inflation and worsening trade position led the US president, Eisenhower, to question the advisability of extending Brazil this financial aid. Harried by critics on the right, Vargas responded by appointing Oswaldo de Aranha, a long-standing associate, to the ministry of finance with a view to bringing inflation under control and stabilizing the economy. Aranha succeeded in reducing the trade imbalance and the level of debt, but was unable to get inflation down. His anti-inflation measures provoked a wave of strikes, and in early 1954 brought him into conflict with the labour minister, João Goulart; Aranha refused to raise the minimum wage, which had remained fixed for several years despite the high inflation. The division illustrated Vargas's problem over development: he had to decide whether to sacrifice his political support for a financially sound economy in which foreign investors would have the confidence to put in money. Vargas faltered and vacillated: in February 1954 he dismissed Goulart, but this incurred the wrath of the unions and the left. Then, at a workers' rally on 1 May, he conceded Goulart's point and announced unexpectedly that the minimum wage would be doubled. He was now attacked by industrialists for irresponsibility in handling the economy.

These political disputes took place against a background of rumours about corruption in the Vargas circle. A leading critic was Carlos Lacerda, the editor of a Rio de Janeiro newspaper which published accusations of financial irregularities. Without Vargas's knowledge, the chief of his bodyguard hired a gunman to murder Lacerda. In the event, the assassin's bullet missed the journalist, but killed an air force officer who had volunteered to protect him. This incident provoked a great national scandal. After the president's bodyguards had been clearly implicated in the officer's murder, the armed forces issued Vargas with an ultimatum to resign or be removed from office. On the night of 24 August 1954 Getúlio Vargas shot himself. A letter was found in which Vargas denounced the 'looting of Brazil' by traitors at home and capitalists abroad. This letter served to win Vargas a posthumous resurgence of popular sympathy, which worked to the advantage of nationalist politicians at the polls.

Development and Inflation

Vargas's successor as president was a former governor of Minas Gerais of Czech descent, Juscelino Kubitschek, who was narrowly elected on a nationalist ticket with João Goulart as his running mate. On taking office in January 1956, Kubitschek inherited a chaotic economic situation. Nevertheless, he decided against a programme of deflation, and opted instead to expand the economy regardless of rising inflation and appalling indebtedness, promising 'fifty years of development in five'.

The centre-piece of his development plans was the building from scratch of a new capital city 600 miles north-west of Rio de Janeiro in the virtually uninhabited state of Goiás. Brasilia, as the new capital was to be called, was intended as a spur to the exploitation of the hinterland, that massive unquantified resource that had lain virgin since the time of the European discovery. The city would be a symbol of Brazil's appetite for progress and economic power. Accordingly, its architecture was ultra-modernist and became famous the world over for the boldness of its design. In 1960, just four years after construction had begun, the dazzling capital was inaugurated. Over time, Brasilia would vindicate Kubitschek's vision inasmuch as it stimulated economic and population growth in the previously neglected states of Goiás and Matto Grosso, but in the short term it added hugely to the enormous burden of debt that successive Brazilian governments had contracted.

The deluge of economic problems left by Kubitschek brought down his successor Jânio Quadros after only seven months in office. Quadros, who had sought election in January 1961 as the man with the 'new broom' who would sweep away the endemic corruption in the government and the bureaucracy, found it impossible to make much headway against inflation. He managed to get a package of austerity measures through a hostile congress, and balanced these with a foreign policy which displeased the USA because of its support for Cuba and the renewal of links with the USSR and China. When opposition in congress finally led to deadlock, Quadros offered his resignation, probably in the expectation that he would be called back by a repentant legislature. But congress called his bluff, if such it was, by simply accepting his resignation.

Quadros's unexpected departure opened up a dangerous political crisis. According to the constitution, power now passed to the vice-president, who was the renowned populist João Goulart, the labour minister under Getúlio Vargas and a man greatly mistrusted by the armed forces and the parties of the right. A military coup seemed to be in the offing. Goulart, however, was a wealthy rancher from Rio Grande do Sul and enjoyed great influence in the political machine of this key state, where his brother-in-law Leonel Brizola was currently the governor. When the commander of the Third Army based in Rio Grande refused to join the military conspiracy against Goulart, the high command held back from launching a coup that might have split the armed forces. Instead, a compromise was devised which would keep Goulart in check by obliging him to share power with a prime minister and a cabinet who would be collectively responsible to congress.

João Goulart was thus controversially translated to the supreme office in September 1961 and left to cope with the difficulties of managing the Brazilian economy. Like his great mentor, Getúlio Vargas, he faced the dilemma of rectifying the nation's finances without alienating his nationalist supporters on the left. The times could scarcely have been less propitious for the introduction of a programme of economic austerity: the universities were in a ferment of revolutionary socialism after the recent success of Fidel Castro's revolution in Cuba; Trotskyist and Communist activists were organizing peasants into rival unions and encouraging illegal land occupations, which infuriated reactionary landowners; industrial strikes occurred frequently as high inflation ate up real wages; revolutionaries launched a campaign to give trade-union rights to the rank and file in the armed forces, a dangerously provocative tactic in view of the political record of the Brazilian officer caste.

At first, Goulart was careful not to alarm the USA. He was aware of the need for external aid and investment to finance the rapid economic growth which alone would keep politics from exploding into revolutionary violence. But Goulart had ridden to power on the back of the trade unions and the nationalists, and his debt to them could not easily be discounted. Like Vargas and Quadros, he found himself hamstrung on economic policy by a strongly nationalist majority in congress, which in August 1962 passed a law limiting remittances of profits by foreign companies to 10 per cent of investment capital. This measure resulted in a drastic fall in investment as foreign companies and investors quickly withdrew from Brazil. Since there were few other sources of finance, Goulart had to resort to printing money to fuel the by now formidable engine of Brazilian development. In 1962 the rate of inflation rose to an unprecedented 65 per cent; there was a run on the currency and the country experienced a new round of bitter strikes and food riots as the living standards of the working class and the urban poor were ravaged by the rocketing prices. The following year the USA cut by a half its aid to Brazil from a total of $355 million in 1962: the country was being made to suffer the consequences of its aggressively nationalist posture.

Goulart was under intense pressure from all sides to do something about the economy. In 1963 he managed to improve his political position. A plebiscite had convincingly backed the restoration of full presidential powers, and Goulart now brought in two very able men, both influenced by the economic theories of ECLA, to devise a stabilization plan: Santiago Dantas, a moderate nationalist, and Celso Furtado, an economist who was widely respected for his work to revitalize the depressed north-east. They produced a programme which combined conventional anti-inflation measures with political and economic reforms. To bring down inflation they recommended stringent wage controls and cuts in credit and public spending. But these deflationary policies were balanced by a series of structural reforms designed to redistribute wealth. Land tenure was to be revised so as to break up the inefficient *latifundia* and relieve landlessness among the peasants; income tax on high earners would be increased; and voting rights would be extended to illiterates so as to undermine the oligarchic machines that controlled the electoral system in the rural areas. The implementation of the plan required a package of financial aid of some $1.5 billion from the USA, the IMF and other sources. The Kennedy administration agreed to support it under the Alliance for Progress with credit instalments amounting to $400 million, even though reservations were expressed about its chances of success.

The Dantas–Furtado Plan was a reformist, democratizing programme, whose major flaw was that it pleased no one. It antagonized the left because of its deflationary elements, and the right because of its progressive reforms. Congress would not approve it since each of the three main parties had its reasons for voting it down. The pro-Goulart PSD, which represented domestic industrialists and the middle classes, united with the oligarchic UDN in opposition to radical reform. On the other hand, it joined with the other pro-Goulart party, the labourist PTB, against spending cuts and a credit squeeze. There ensued a political deadlock between the president and congress: Goulart was not allowed to go ahead with the Dantas–Furtado Plan, but congress could not produce a majority to impeach the president.

Goulart lacked sufficient depth of political support in the country to overrule congress. He therefore discarded the Dantas–Furtado Plan and set about creating for himself a mass base by embracing the positions of the radical nationalist left. As Goulart's rhetoric took on a revolutionary character, middle-class wage-earners and the industrial bourgeoisie – the bedrock of support for Getúlio Vargas's developmental nationalism – were scared into believing the right's warnings of communist subversion. In reality, Goulart's strident populism was destroying the substance of his actual support among the middle classes rather than strengthening it. In any case, he was far from being a revolutionary leader of the mettle required to transform a country as large and diverse as Brazil. For he was a big landowner and an inveterate wheeler-dealer whose career had been made in the oligarchic machine politics of Rio Grande do Sul.

By early 1964 political life had become dangerously polarized. There were calls from some state governors for military intervention. It was widely suspected that the army was conspiring against the president. Goulart responded by holding mass rallies. At one such in Rio de Janeiro on 13 March, he threw caution to the wind and provoked a confrontation with his enemies by signing before exultant supporters a number of decrees nationalizing the oil industry and expropriating large estates. Some days later he laid before congress a series of reform bills, which included the granting of the right to vote to enlisted men and the legalization of the Communist Party. In Rio de Janeiro there occurred a mutiny of sailors, and Goulart angered the armed forces by granting the mutineers a pardon.

By the middle of March the conspirators felt ready to act. The governors of São Paulo and other important states planned to set up an alternative government and call upon the USA for military aid. For its part the US embassy had made provision for supplying the rebels with guns and fuel in the coming conflict. On 31 March a military revolt broke out in Minas Gerais and spread to several other states. Troops marched on Rio de Janeiro, but to everyone's surprise Goulart's support melted away and the military took over the government on 1 April in what had turned out to be a bloodless *coup d'état*. The expected revolution had failed to materialize and João Goulart took refuge in Uruguay.

Military Rule (1964–84)

What made the 1964 coup a new departure in Brazilian history was not that it brought the armed forces into politics, but that it led to direct military rule for twenty years. The armed forces, after all, had effectively possessed a veto on politics from the time they had deposed Dom Pedro II in 1889. Monarchic legitimacy had then been destroyed and a constitutional republic created, but, as in other Latin American countries, the legitimacy of the republican order proved difficult to uphold. The army itself, though it regarded constitutional democracy as the norm, tended to resort to political intervention as a kind of hygienic measure required from time to time in order to rid the body politic of noxious elements that might threaten *ordem e progresso*. The coup against Goulart was no different:

with the country on the verge of insolvency and a civilian president unleashing forces he could barely control, the generals judged it necessary to step in once again.

The leader of the junta, General Humberto Castello Branco, was indeed a moderate and a constitutionalist among his brother officers; he was a man of great prestige, who in 1961, after Quadros's unexpected resignation, had urged a constitutional solution to the crisis by the acceptance of vice-president Goulart's succession. In 1964 the military were divided over how long to suspend the constitution. Castello Branco himself favoured an early return to constitutional government once the nation's finances had been sorted out. Other officers wanted a longer period of military rule in order to reconstruct the economy. Circumstances were to play into the hands of the latter group: the economy did not show any signs of health for several years, and when it did, the upturn coincided with a severe bout of political terrorism, which discouraged the military from handing over to civilian politicians.

Castello Branco's main concern was to restore financial discipline. In effect this involved revising the corporatist policies inherited from Getúlio Vargas's *Estado Nôvo*, and opening up the economy to market forces wherever it was expedient to do so. The man charged with this task was Roberto Campos, a former ambassador to the USA, who had resigned his post in protest at what he believed to be Goulart's financial recklessness. Campos introduced deflationary measures, cut back imports, gave incentives to exports and welcomed foreign investment. In particular, Campos created capitalist institutions, such as a stock market and a central bank, with a view to making the economy more responsive to the market than to the decisions of politicians and planners.

The economy, however, took several years to recover from the severe recessionary effects of Campos's policies. Political opposition to the junta gathered strength, for, understandably, the beneficiaries of Getúlio Vargas's *Estado Nôvo* and subsequent corporatist governments reacted fiercely to Campos's dose of liberal capitalism. Businessmen and industrialists resented the competition from more powerful foreign rivals and transnational companies which began to penetrate the domestic market, causing the bankruptcy of many previously protected native enterprises. The unions found their links with the state weakened by legislation which permitted firms greater freedom to hire and fire workers. Wage-earners in the middle and working classes were badly affected by mounting unemployment and the high cost of living. Strikes and demonstrations proliferated in the major cities.

In 1968 the phenomenon of urban guerrilla warfare appeared in Brazil, as it also did at this time in Argentina and Uruguay. A number of guerrilla groups commenced operations, mainly in the big cities, and the high point of their activities came in September 1969 after the ruling general, Artur da Costa e Silva, had suffered a stroke the previous month. The guerrillas took advantage of this temporary power vacuum to kidnap the US ambassador no less. It was a brilliant exploit, which the kidnappers used to bargain for the release of fifteen comrades from prison and for the publication of a revolutionary manifesto in the news media. But the extent of their success served to call forth a determined response from the armed forces. In November the most charismatic of the guerrilla leaders, Carlos Marighella, was killed in an ambush. Thenceforward, the guerrillas were ground down by harsh repressive methods, which included the systematic torture of suspects by the secret police and the use of shadowy paramilitary death squads to root out 'subversives'. By 1973 the insurgency was over: the guerrillas had failed to spark off the revolutionary uprising they were hoping for, despite the growing inequalities of wealth in a country where the bulk of the population continued to live in abject poverty.

The reasons for the failure of the guerrillas are complex. With their predominantly middle–class, university-educated cadres they were unable to break out of their political isolation – the clandestine Communist Party disapproved of the guerrillas' strategy and blocked their access to working-class organizations. The terrorist attacks on military targets precluded the emergence of any sympathetic groups within the armed forces who might have staged a *coup d'état*, this being the usual short cut to power for progressive movements in Latin America. But, decisively, the guerrilla campaign coincided with the long-awaited upturn in the economy. From 1968, while the guerrillas were robbing banks and bombing barracks, life was getting better for the middle classes and the skilled workers in the cities, which is where, in a rapidly urbanizing country, the political fate of the nation would be decided. In short, what finally put paid to the prospects of the urban guerrillas was the arrival of the Brazilian 'economic miracle'.

The Economic Miracle and Its Effects

As far as the generals were concerned, the 'miracle' obviated the need for an explicit political ideology to run the state. The tremendous popular enthusiasm generated by the idea of an economic miracle was manipulated by the junta to rationalize their continued suspension of full democratic rights. The economic upswing was 'miraculous' in that it seemed to be a sudden take-off into self-sustaining industrial growth, the hallmark of a modern economy.

Brazil was at last on its way to world-power status from the doldrums in which it had found itself for the best part of the 1960s.

The Brazilian rate of economic growth was indeed amazingly good: in 1968–74 the economy grew at an average yearly rate of between 10 per cent and 11 per cent. Even after the sudden rise in the world price of oil in 1973, which seriously damaged all the industrial economies, the Brazilian rate of growth averaged between 4 per cent and 7 per cent a year. By the mid-1970s the volume of exports had quadrupled since 1967. Far more significant was the fact that manufactured goods had replaced coffee as the major component of exports: the stubborn Latin American problem of monoculture – the dependence on the export of a single primary commodity – had been solved.*

Without doubt, a substantial industrial revolution had occurred in Brazil; and it had largely been engineered by technocrats sponsored by the armed forces. But this success was built on the programme of industrialization achieved over many years since the foundation of the *Estado Nôvo* by Getúlio Vargas in 1937. Underlying the intervening conflicts of parliamentary politics, there had been a remarkable continuity in the course of Brazilian development from the Getúlio Vargas era to the military governments of the 1960s and 1970s. Development continued to be based on a sustained drive for industrial growth largely financed by foreign loans and investment, but directed by the state. The military governments of the 1960s and 1970s kept all basic industries and utilities under state control; they largely retained the nationalist policy of import-substitution industrialization by selective tariffs; and they also preserved the core of the social welfare and labour legislation of the *Estado Nôvo*.

If the military coup of 1964 represented a break with the past, it was in the political sphere. Since the Second World War every Brazilian president had found it impossible to control inflation or attract foreign investment without provoking retaliation from the nationalists or waves of industrial unrest. After the war, when Getúlio Vargas had turned democratic populist, neither he nor any of his successors – Dutra, Kubitschek, Quadros or Goulart – had been able to reconcile state-led development, which depended on foreign investment and technology, with electoral politics. The demands on the state's patronage were too large and too varied for an elected president to meet; this failure proved fatal to the authority of successive elected governments. The state simply could not raise enough money to finance such intensive industrialization and yet cushion everyone against its adverse effects; the inevitable result was runaway inflation.

* For illustrative data on the structure of exports, see Statistical Appendix, table 8.

The fact was that the ideology of economic nationalism inherited from the late 1930s was in contradiction with the realities of industrial development in the 1950s and 1960s. By 1964 the country was faced with insolvency. The military then intervened to try and abolish the contradiction between nationalism and development: they suspended constitutional politics in the hope of giving technocrats a free hand to modernize the economy unhindered by nationalist pressures or high wage demands from organized labour. Paradoxically, the economic miracle was made possible by creating an authoritarian regime similar to those of Getúlio Vargas before the war, when political opposition was repressed and the state was able to follow a path of rapid industrialization with the blessing of the armed forces.

During the years of the economic miracle, industrialization raced ahead with massive injections of foreign capital. But the fruits of that development were far more unequally distributed than in previous decades. The gap between rich and poor – always very wide in Brazil – widened still further. In 1960 the richest 10 per cent of the population received 39.6 per cent of the national income; by 1980 they received 50.9 per cent, while the poorest 50 per cent received only 12.6 per cent. In São Paulo, which constituted the heart of the economic miracle, malnutrition, disease and high mortality ravaged the greater part of the population. In the *favelas* ringing the major cities, large numbers of the poor were housed in tin shacks lacking sewerage, running water and electricity. Blacks and mulattos in particular suffered these privations, for Brazil remained a society where social class coincided with racial stratification.

A good deal of this misery was caused by forces of industrial change which were very difficult for the state to control. As in all industrial revolutions, the growth of factory production attracted immense numbers of peasants to the cities. But however rapid the expansion of industry, Brazil's large and growing population could not be absorbed fully into the active workforce. Indeed, the desire to make the economy grow fast enough to mop up unemployment was a powerful incentive to press ahead with spending on development: the Amazon basin was opened to economic exploitation and peasant settlement, with consequent damage to the environment and a growing threat to the existence of the large numbers of nomadic Indian tribes that still lived in the extensive rain forests. The costs incurred by this massive drive to modernize were mounting foreign debts and a galloping inflation rate, which by the early 1980s had exceeded 100 per cent per annum.

The problem of inflation was apparently insuperable. Military governments were unwilling to deflate the economy too severely for fear of causing a major recession and slowing economic growth. The Brazilians therefore opted to live with high inflation: wages were indexed to the rate of rising prices, and an array of fiscal devices was employed to brake the accelerating cost of living. It was a highly unstable way to run an economy, and it produced enormous stresses and distortions. In the late 1970s the industrial heartland of São Paulo was a hotbed of strikes and labour unrest. As the currency depreciated, speculation, capital flight and corruption became rife among the propertied classes. Then in 1982 a rise in international interest rates made the burden of foreign debt too crippling to sustain; Brazil had to suspend interest payments on what had become the largest debt in the world, estimated at over $87 billion.

Brazil's armed forces had fallen victim to the juggernaut of development. In 1964 they had intervened in politics to restore the finances of the nation; by 1982 they presided over the worst financial mess Brazil had ever seen. Yet by that time the price of squeezing inflation out of the system and eliminating the foreign debt was an economic recession on a scale that was unacceptable even to military officers. Unwilling to embark on the kind of wholesale social repression that had occurred in Chile after the fall of Salvador Allende in 1973, the Brazilian generals decided instead to seek a legitimate form of government, whose authority would rest on a wide social consensus.

The Search for Legitimacy (1974–83)

Brazilian military governments had in fact been looking for such a consensus since the mid-1970s, when the rise in the world price of oil had produced a recession. But a genuine political consensus had always been very hard to come by in Latin America. The Brazilian generals found it difficult to fabricate even a semblance of one in the course of the 1970s. What they wanted was a measure of democratic credibility for their regime; what they actually got was persistent support for the civilian opposition.

When he became president in March 1974, General Ernesto Geisel introduced a phase of *abertura*, an 'opening' towards a freer society: press censorship was relaxed, torture suspended once the guerrillas had been defeated, and free elections for congress held in October 1974. But in these elections, as in subsequent municipal contests, the government-sponsored party lost heavily to the opposition. In 1977 Geisel introduced indirect elections and other devices calculated to secure majorities for the pro-government party. Even so, *abertura* was not abandoned; it continued on an erratic course. In 1979 Geisel's successor was chosen from two military candidates in an indirect election, which involved congress for the first time since 1964. The victor, General João Baptista Figueiredo, carried on the policy of *abertura*. Political exiles were allowed to return to the country. In November 1979 the two military-approved parties were dissolved and the formation of new independent parties was permitted (the Communist Party remained proscribed). Censorship of books and newspapers was abolished, but not of radio and television. Free trade unions and strikes were condoned, if not actually authorized.

Yet the process of 'redemocratization' was hazardous both for the military and for the civilian opposition. The great fear of the military rulers was that a return to free elections would simply mean going back to the bad old ways of populism, with professional politicians competing for power by making extravagant promises to the electorate with no reckoning of the economic consequences. Civilian politicians, for their part, realized that they could not push too hard for political reform without risking a reaction from military hard-liners. Nevertheless, the severity of the debt problem of 1982 propelled both sides towards a consensus of sorts: the armed forces wanted popular consent for the rigorous deflationary policies that would have to be adopted, while the civilian parties recognized the need for economic reconstruction.

In November 1982 free direct elections were held at municipal, state and federal levels. The opposition Party of the Brazilian Democratic Movement (PMDB) polled 44 per cent, the highest proportion of the vote, and did particularly well in the cities and in the economically advanced states. However, with 41.5 per cent, the government-approved party, the Partido Democrático Social (PDS) won the greatest number of seats, though it failed to control the lower house and the governorship of key states like São Paulo, Rio de Janeiro, and Minas Gerais. The PDS also won a majority of seats in the electoral college which was due to vote for a new president in January 1985.

The indirect election for president, however, did not go as expected. Disputes within the majority PDS resulted in the defection of a group of the party's electors in the college, and contrary to the wishes of the armed forces, the opposition PMDB candidate, Tancredo Neves (who had been prime minister under Goulart in 1961), was the victor. This surprising outcome boosted the process of redemocratization, for it spared the emerging parliamentary system from the taint of manipulation. The armed forces had to accept the result because of the risk otherwise of breaking the as yet fragile consensus which was needed to cope with the problem of the foreign debt.

The public euphoria that greeted Neves's victory in 1985 strengthened the general political will to undertake economic and political reforms. The 74-

year-old Neves, however, died before his inauguration and was replaced by his vice-president, José Sarney, a more conservative figure, who inherited the tremendous popularity of the deceased president-elect.

The Return to Democracy (1985–9)

On taking office, José Sarney tried to feel his way towards economic reconstruction without eroding his electoral support. His initial refusal to apply to the International Monetary Fund for assistance with the foreign debt pleased the nationalists; he decided instead to negotiate directly with the creditor banks. On the home front he launched the Cruzado Plan in February 1986 to tackle the inflation rate of 230 per cent per annum. The currency was reformed and a price freeze introduced; government spending was reduced in some areas and jobs shed in the overstretched public sector of the economy. To offset these disciplines – there were federal and state elections coming up in November – he allowed increases in real wages of between 15 and 34 per cent. The resultant consumer boom stimulated industrial output and took the edge off the debt-induced recession – at least for the middle classes.

Sarney's popularity in the opinion polls rose to 80 per cent. At the November elections his party, in coalition with the Liberals, won landslide victories. Backed by this solid support in congress, Sarney introduced two weeks later the second phase of the Cruzado Plan: indirect taxes were raised on a number of consumer goods in order to rein in demand and reduce imports, and thousands more jobs were cut in the state sector. However, subsidies on basic foods were retained in order to help the poor.

The difficulties of managing the debt-ridden economy without causing insupportable social hardship proved insuperable. Despite the fact that Brazil had been implementing painful austerity measures and privatizing large parts of its state sector since 1982, inflation continued to accelerate throughout the decade. The burden of debt repayments was too great for the country to bear. Even though the export sector had been revitalized, with industrial exports to new markets providing the main thrust of the recovery, Brazil's annual debt repayments consumed about one quarter of its export earnings. Given that new loans were difficult to negotiate, the democratic government could meet its social welfare obligations only by deficit financing, which fuelled inflation.

The continued austerity, combined with the rapidly rising inflation, eroded the authority of the Sarney administration. Attempts to redistribute land to help the 10 million landless peasants met with violent resistance from the big landowners, and the government was forced to retreat on an issue which had been seen as a test of democratic effectiveness. Instead, the government encouraged the resettlement of impoverished north-easterners in Amazonia. But this safety-valve provoked further conflict because the burning of the Amazon rain forests to make way for cattle-raising or subsistence farming threatened both the survival of Indian tribes and the ecological balance of the earth itself.

By the late 1980s food riots and widespread strikes were signs that the social consensus upon which the democratic restoration of 1985 had been based might be breaking down. Repeated efforts by Sarney to enforce wage and price freezes to control inflation came to nothing because of opposition from trade unions and industrialists. Attempts to create a social pact between the government, trade unions and employers met with limited success. At the municipal elections of November 1988, Sarney's party, the PMDB, lost crucial positions in the major cities to parties of the left led by a charismatic trade-union leader, Lula da Silva, and the veteran populist Leonel Brizola, a former governor of Rio Grande do Sul, who had called for popular resistance to the military coup of 1964 which unseated his brother-in-law, President João Goulart.

The PMDB had little prospect of winning the first direct elections to the presidency due to be held in November 1989: the country was in the throes of hyperinflation (it was running at a rate of over 1,000 per cent per annum), and yet the government was unable to muster support for a 'war economy' to defeat inflation despite appeals from José Sarney for Brazilians to join in a 'common task of national salvation'. The sheer weight of economic problems appeared to have overwhelmed the government, but it was the political establishment as a whole that shared the discredit. At the presidential election the PMDB candidate was defeated, but so was the pre-1964 populist Brizola and the radical trade-union leader Lula da Silva, who advocated expansionary policies and defiance of foreign creditors.

The new president was a forty-year-old independent Fernando Collor de Mello, who had promised 'to slay with a single shot the tiger of hyper-inflation'. Within hours of assuming office on 15 March 1990 Collor de Mello announced a 'shock' programme aimed at curing inflation – which had risen the month before to an annual rate of 2,700 per cent – and at wiping out the government's budget deficit. The cornerstone of the plan was a liquidity squeeze designed to rid the economy of excess money – for a period of eighteen months company assets would be frozen, a ceiling put on withdrawals from all private bank accounts, and wages and prices subjected to stringent controls. In addition, public spending would be cut, state companies privatized and public-service employment severely reduced. Collor sought popular backing for these Draconian measures by aiming a powerful propaganda campaign against the self-serving 'maharajahs' of the bureaucracy and the 'economic crimes' of businessmen and speculators. This populist tactic was intended to maintain the momentum of public support for the president so as to allow him to circumvent the obstructionism of a hostile majority in the congress. On the other hand, the risk was that public support might evaporate as a result of the deep recession induced by the free-market reforms. The success of Collor's strategy appeared to depend too much on fortune and circumstance, but the consequences of failure would be exceptionally grave, for Brazil's historic pursuit of progress would result in stagnation and uncontrollable financial disarray.

Brazil's extraordinary drive to modernize in the twentieth century produced a powerful industrial economy in the space of little over three decades. The costs were enormous: acute dislocations of regional economies, the destruction of virgin lands, an imbalance between the countryside and the cities, and deep cleavages between the working class, industrial capitalists and the middle classes. And yet, industry did not become productive enough to absorb the potential labour force, while the countryside remained underproductive and socially divided. Successive governments tried to force the pace of industrial development, as well as increasing spending on welfare programmes to alleviate the social misery. The results were vicious circles of inflation and budget deficits, which spiralled uncontrollably, robbing governments of authority. In 1964 the armed forces intervened to try to restore order, but by the late 1970s they too had been drawn into the spiral of inflation and debt; their historic pursuit of *ordem e progresso* had led, paradoxically, to a situation where economic progress had become the enemy of social order.

The Brazilian crisis of the 1980s was as much a crisis of the state as of the economy. In the medium term economic improvement might come through an upturn in the world economy combined with a successful anti-inflation programme and international assistance with debt relief. But a lasting settlement of the crisis would require the emergence of a legitimate democratic state, whose representative institutions could command the confidence of the nation as a whole.

12. Cuba: Dependency, Nationalism and Revolution

The Colonial Background

The history of Cuba was as exceptional for Latin America in the nineteenth century as it was in the twentieth. The largest island in the Caribbean, and one of the first to be settled by the Spaniards, it remained a Spanish colony until 1898. What made Cuba an exception was the rise and dominance of its sugar industry. Before the late eighteenth century, the island had been relatively poor, its main role being that of a meeting point and refuelling post for the Atlantic fleets. A small class of creole landowners raised cattle and grew some export crops like tobacco, coffee and sugar cane, but played no great part in the economy of the empire.

The first major boost to the economy occurred during the eleven-month occupation of Havana by the British in 1762–3, when Spanish restrictions were temporarily lifted and trade with England and North America opened the Cuban creoles' eyes to the economic potential of their island as a producer of commodities on the world market. However, the impetus for the island's development as a major exporter of sugar came in the 1790s, when massive slave revolts in the French Caribbean island of Haiti, following the French Revolution, dislocated what had been the most productive sugar industry in the Americas, and drove French planters to settle in nearby Cuba. Spanish trading restrictions were eased and no limits were placed upon the importation of African slaves. After 1793 Cuba developed into a large-scale slave society with a plantation economy powerfully geared to the export of sugar. The strong, though belated, growth of the Cuban economy made the creole élite largely indifferent to the question of political independence from Spain, and the great influx of African slaves discouraged political radicalism among the whites. For Haiti stood as an awful warning against any challenge to established authority in a slave society like Cuba's, where blacks by the 1820s already formed about a quarter of the population.

Still, there was dissatisfaction with Spanish colonial rule, and it expressed itself in the 1840s among a minority of planters who favoured Cuba's annexation by the USA; this prospect was also welcomed by influential politicians in the USA itself, which was already in the process of annexing Texas and other territories in the republic of Mexico. There were two reasons for wanting annexation: the USA had become Cuba's most important trading partner, and, with Britain pressing for the abolition of the slave-trade, Cuban slave-owners, anxious about the political weakness of Spain, began to perceive a common interest with the slave states of the American South. Annexationist revolts against Spain failed, but it was the defeat of the South in the American Civil War that finally ended support for annexation. After the abolition of slavery in the USA, the Cuban slave-owners sought political reforms that would give them greater autonomy within the Spanish empire; but as the intransigence of metropolitan governments in Spain weakened creole loyalties and the prospect of constitutional autonomy within the empire receded, independence appeared to many as the only way to advance creole interests.

On 10 October 1868 a creole landowner, Carlos Manuel de Céspedes, issued the *Grito de Yara*, a proclamation of independence and a call to arms. The war that followed caused widespread devastation; yet its length and bitterness served to forge a heroic sense of Cuban patriotism, and rev-olutionary heroes emerged such as Máximo Gómez and the mulatto com-mander Antonio Maceo, whose memory would continue to inspire generations of Cuban patriots. The Cubans, however, were unable to defeat the Spanish army and the Ten Years' War was concluded by the Treaty of Zanjón in 1878.

A major economic consequence of the war was the ruin of many Cuban sugar planters, which facilitated the extensive take-over of sugar mills and plantations by US interests. Also, the rise in the production of beet sugar in Europe at this time left the USA as the largest and most accessible market for Cuban sugar. Cuba thus entered into a contradictory situation in the 1880s from which she would find it virtually impossible to free herself: she was slipping into economic dependency upon the USA at the same time as she was acquiring a powerful tradition of revolutionary patriotism.

The War of Independence and US Intervention

After the failure of further attempts at autonomy within the Spanish empire, the cause of independence revived, and this time veteran leaders like Maceo and Gómez were joined by younger men, most notably by the radical liberal poet José Martí, who was to become the guiding light of Cuban nationalists in subsequent generations. In his voluminous writings, Martí, a supreme prose stylist and a powerful artistic voice, articulated the Cubans' yearning for nationhood, and warned of the dangers of absorption by the USA. He led the second major uprising against Spain in 1895, but soon met his death in battle. Antonio Maceo (who was himself killed in 1896) and Máximo Gómez continued the guerrilla struggle for independence, but once again it became bogged down in bloody stalemate against a large Spanish army ably commanded by the ruthless Valeriano Weyler.

The unending turmoil in Cuba alarmed the USA, not only because it feared for its economic investments in the island, but also because, with its plans for an interoceanic canal in Panama, it was already defining the Caribbean and Central America as a sphere of strategic interest. The USA declared war on Spain in 1898 when its battleship *Maine* was mysteriously blown up in Havana harbour killing 260 crewmen. Spain offered the Cuban insurgents a truce, but they opted instead to assist the USA in defeating the colonial power. The war was brought to a quick conclusion when the superior US navy sank a Spanish fleet as it tried to break out of a blockade of the port of Santiago.

It soon became clear that the USA had entered the war not so much to liberate Cuba as to secure its objectives as an emerging world power. The Cuban insurgents were entirely excluded from the peace negotiations and, as a result, Cuba was forced to accept independence on terms determined for her by a deal between an alien power and her colonial masters. Spanish property and capital on the island were protected, and the USA was allowed to set up a military government to oversee the reconstruction of the ravaged economy.

The US occupation of Cuba lasted from 1891 until 1903 and it provided an efficient administration which succeeded in eliminating famine and vastly reducing the incidence of disease through improved sanitation (the dreaded yellow fever was eradicated thanks to the scientific discoveries of a Cuban doctor, Carlos Finlay). A system of state education was established and the university modernized. The judiciary was overhauled in order to provide for its independence, and an electoral system for local and national government was put in place. In 1901 an elected assembly passed a liberal constitution which separated Church and state and guaranteed universal male suffrage. After Tomás Estrada Palma, the candidate of Martí's Cuban Revolutionary Party, had duly won the presidency in 1902, the US troops left the island; Cuba was now officially a sovereign state.

The USA, however, retained for itself a tutelary role in Cuba through the controversial Platt Amendment to the constitution, which gave it the right to intervene in the new republic's internal affairs for 'the maintenance of a government adequate for the protection of life, property and individual liberties'. The USA also reserved certain prerogatives over the conduct of Cuban foreign policy, and obtained a concession of land for US naval bases (an important base was built at Guantánamo). Moreover, the reconstruction of the Cuban economy had been undertaken largely through a massive influx of US capital; US companies acquired control of large parts of the sugar, tobacco and other industries.

The Limits of Independence

The manner in which Cuba had won her independence did not augur well for the future of the new republic. The intervention of the USA in the war, followed by the Platt Amendment, compromised the sense of nationhood which a post-colonial state must draw upon in order to build a legitimate authority. The ability of the USA so to dominate the island stemmed from the weakness of the Cuban landowning élites, many of whom had been ruined during the long abortive war against Spain in 1868–78. That conflict had led to the economic invasion of Cuban agriculture by US sugar companies. Spain's abolition of slavery in 1886 had further eroded the traditional basis of white authority in a society where up to a third of the population was black. Cuban society was therefore curiously fluid and amorphous: though an agrarian country, its traditional social leaders were not securely rooted in the land; constituted as a democratic republic, its people were nevertheless divided by the legacy of African slavery according to race, culture and religion; and, while Cuba was nominally independent, the prime source of wealth for the upper and middle classes lay in servicing an export-economy increasingly controlled by North American capital. Cuba, in short, was neither politically sovereign nor an integral part of the country upon which its economy was critically dependent.

There was no clear way out of this impasse. Annexation by the USA – the solution sought by the Cuban sugar planters in the middle of the nineteenth century – was precluded by the strong patriotic tradition forged in the course of the wars against Spain. On the other hand, the creation of a true national consciousness would be thwarted so long as sugar ruled economic life. Nationhood seemed a Utopian dream, but the alternative was a form of cultural suicide.

The sense of impotence arising from this impasse bred cynicism among

Cuban politicians. Constitutional democracy quickly degenerated into a venal spectacle in which populist *caudillos* vied with each other for the chance to divide the spoils of office among their respective clienteles. Elections became routinely fraudulent, provoking revolts by disappointed *caudillos*, which in turn led to intervention by the USA under the terms of the Platt Amendment. In 1906–9 Cuba was once again ruled directly by US proconsuls; between 1909 and 1921 US troops were sent to occupy the island on four occasions following unrest after corrupt elections. As a matter of course, politics were manipulated by US ambassadors intriguing with local politicians. Attempts by Cubans themselves to clean up public life fared no better, for whenever sugar boomed the rewards of office proved too tempting for even political reformers to resist.

The vulnerability of the sugar economy to fluctuations in the world price unsettled politics even further. From 1903 Cuba gained privileged access to the US market through a reciprocal trade agreement which reduced tariffs for sugar exports to the USA by 20 per cent in return for reductions of up to 40 per cent on a range of US imports to the island. Until 1920 the price of sugar held up well and the island enjoyed a period of growing prosperity. Other Cuban goods, such as tobacco, rum and nickel, found ready markets in the USA, while US investment in the island's economy increased. The golden age of reciprocal benefits peaked in the months between February and May of 1920, when the world price of sugar rose to a record 22.5 cents per pound and fortunes were made overnight in an exultant Cuba. This 'dance of the millions' encouraged many planters to borrow in order to expand, but overproduction on the world market caused the price of sugar to drop sharply to around 3.5 cents per pound by the end of 1920 and large numbers of Cubans were ruined. US companies were able to buy up the bankrupt mills and plantations, extending their dominance over the Cuban sugar industry even further. In 1914–23 overall US investment in the Cuban economy increased sixfold, and for the rest of the 1920s erratic world prices caused continual uncertainty; after the Wall Street Crash of 1929 the price of sugar slumped to below a cent per pound by 1932.

The faltering economy of the 1920s and the penetration of US capital stimulated the revival of nationalism, especially among students and intellectuals, who invoked the memory of José Martí and denounced the monoculture of sugar and the dependence on the USA. The focus of the nationalist struggle was the University of Havana, where students followed the example of the Córdoba University Reform Movement in Argentina and called for educational reforms; gradually the students' agitation broadened to include political and economic demands such as the nationalization of the sugar industry and the breakup of the large estates. A central demand of all Cuban nationalists was the repudiation of the Platt Amendment. The student protest was accompanied by an artistic and cultural concern with Cuban national themes, and by the appearance of an Afro-Cuban cultural movement. From this ferment there arose a small Communist Party in 1925.

The Machado Dictatorship and the Revolution of 1933

The election to the presidency of the Liberal Gerardo Machado in 1924 at first promised an end to the graft of the previous administration. Enjoying widespread popularity, Machado embarked on a programme of public works and measures to diversify the economy. But the fall in sugar prices of the late 1920s led him to repress strikes and protests, and when he got a controlled congress to grant him a further six-year term in 1928, he faced an explosion of anger from the student movement. As Machado's rule became increasingly repressive, students and middle-class intellectuals took to violence and terrorism. The students formed a Directorio Estudiantil, which was to play a continuing oppositional role in the island's politics. In 1931 there appeared a secret organization calling itself the ABC, whose members were young middle- and upper-class nationalists inspired by the Peruvian Haya de la Torre's APRA movement. ABC *pistoleros* resorted to assassinations and shoot-outs in the streets with Machado's brutal police. The unrest spread as labour unions joined the opposition to the dictator.

Reluctant to send in troops as in the past because of the nationalist agitation, Washington used its ambassador, Sumner Welles, to negotiate an end to Machado's rule. But the nationalists resented Welles's intervention and called a general strike in August 1933 (the Communist Party, fearing a US invasion, withdrew its support for the strike and tried to do a deal with Machado, which discredited it in the eyes of students and nationalists). Machado finally bowed to the pressure and went into exile. There followed an upsurge of revolutionary activity – occupations of factories and sugar mills by workers, looting of wealthy districts, and mob attacks on collaborators with the dictatorship.

The moderate government of Carlos Manuel de Céspedes, installed by the army in concert with Sumner Welles, was unable to control the situation. In September 1933 a revolt of non-commissioned officers – among whose leaders was a Sergeant Fulgencio Batista – unseated Céspedes and handed over power to a five-man committee chosen by the Directorio Estudiantil. The Havana students had succeeded in creating a nationalist revolution and, after some confusion, they chose one of their professors, the patrician Dr Ramón Grau San Martín, as provisional president. Workers now occupied sugar mills, in some cases demanding wage rises at gunpoint; strikes, riots and gun battles broke out all over the island. Grau's government passed a number of radical measures, such as the expropriation of a small number of US-owned sugar mills, some redistribution of land, the limitation of the working day to eight hours, restrictions on the employment of cheap non-Cuban labour from other Caribbean islands and the extension of the franchise to women.

Still, the revolution of 1933 was primarily the work of student agitation and, apart from the expected hostility of the USA and the Cuban business community, it was opposed by the Communists, the ABC nationalists and by ousted army officers, who staged a number of revolts. Four months later Grau's government was overthrown by a coup led by Fulgencio Batista, who effectively became the strongman of Cuba for the next decade, ruling at first through presidential stooges and then, from 1940, in his own right.

The First Batista Period (1933–44)

Batista was a military populist, a mulatto from a very humble background who had risen from the ranks and whose core constituency remained the enlisted men of the armed forces. As befitted a Latin American leader of the 1930s, he presented himself as a benefactor of the people, using the resources of the state for nationalist and redistributive ends. In 1934 the Platt Amendment was at last annulled, and a larger US quota for sugar helped raise production from the doldrums of the 1920s and early 1930s. Although Batista had the backing of US and Cuban business interests, he took steps to cultivate the trade unions, passing social welfare legislation, building houses for workers and creating employment through large public works programmes. A new labour confederation, controlled by a Communist leadership, was incorporated into the strongman's political machine. In the countryside, Batista redistributed some land and, following the example of the Mexican Revolution, initiated a programme of rural education, often staffed by army personnel.

Dismayed by the failure of the 1933 revolution, the students and radical nationalists formed a new party in memory of José Martí, the Partido Revolucionario Cubano-Auténtico, which became the principal opposition to Batista. Terrorism continued to be a habitual feature of political life, but by the late 1930s Batista felt secure enough to permit elections for a constituent assembly. In 1940 a new nationalist, social-democratic constitution was passed by a Batista-dominated assembly, which included universal suffrage, state rights over the subsoil, state 'orientation' of the economy and labour rights such as a minimum wage, pensions, social insurance and an eight-hour day.

The constitution of 1940 ushered in a period of legitimate democratic governments, though there was no weakening of the Cuban tradition of political gangsterism and corruption. Batista won a clean election in 1940 and continued to implement his populist programme in the improved economic climate fostered by the war and the consequent US aid. Yet radical nationalism reasserted itself in 1944; Batista lost the election – having forborne from rigging it – to Dr Grau of the Auténticos, and retired to the USA a wealthy man.

The Auténticos in Government (1944–52) and the Second Batistato (1952–9)

Expectations were high that Grau's return to the presidency by legitimate election would revive the ideals of nationhood and social justice associated with the frustrated revolution of 1933. But at the end of the Second World War sugar boomed mightily once more, and the hopes of reform and economic diversification were drowned in an orgy of corruption and violence by venal revolutionary gangs, which Grau looked upon with complaisance.

The sheer degeneracy of public life caused a split in the Auténtico Party: in 1947 Eddy Chibás, a charismatic young activist, broke away to form the Ortodoxo Party, pledged to the ideals of Martí and the revolution of 1933. Chibás contested the 1948 elections unsuccessfully against Grau's protégé, Carlos Prío Socarrás, another former revolutionary of the 1933 generation who was now, like so many others, involved in graft and intrigue, and whose government soon outdid Grau's for corruption. Chibás took to denouncing Prío on the radio every Sunday night until in despair he shot himself fatally in the stomach after a broadcast on 5 August 1951. With Chibás's sensational demise there appeared to have died too the chances of Cuban national regeneration. As political morality sank even further into the mire with the approach of the 1952 elections, a *coup d'état* by Fulgencio Batista was greeted with widespread relief.

The second Batistato (1952–9) put paid to constitutional politics on the island. Portraying himself as the guarantor of law and order, the dictator proceeded with some success to implement a programme of public works, economic diversification and 'Cubanization' – an attempt to get Cuban capital to invest in the sugar industry and other key sectors of the economy. Though growth was sluggish, there were signs of rising investment towards the end of the decade. Cuba was in the top three or four Latin American countries in the fields of education (it had a literacy rate of about 80 per cent), public health and social welfare. The average share of the national income that went to wage-earners was 65 per cent, a figure bettered only by Britain, the USA and Canada at the time.

Even so, this impressive state of development masked structural imbalances, mostly stemming from the predominance of sugar in the economy. In 1952 sugar still accounted for about a third of the national product (the proportion fell to about a quarter in the late 1950s), and represented over 80 per cent of exports. Though the share of Cuban capital in the sugar industry exceeded 55 per cent, the USA was still the largest market by far, and sugar exports remained at the mercy of world prices and import quotas fixed by the US congress. The pattern of sugar cultivation, together with generally weak external demand, produced high levels of seasonal unemployment and underemployment. Living standards in the countryside were therefore much lower than in the cities, where 56 per cent of the population lived. These imbalances were sufficient to keep alive economic nationalist aspirations among student groups and the Ortodoxos, who were agitated in any case by the political dead end which Batista's overthrow of the 1940 constitution represented in the development of the *patria*.

From this milieu of thwarted student nationalism emerged the mercurial and forceful figure of Fidel Castro in the early 1950s. A member of the left wing of Eddy Chibás's Ortodoxos while a law student at Havana University, and a fervent admirer of José Martí, the young Castro's appetite for leadership became evident in his revolutionary plan to topple Batista by attacking the Moncada barracks in Santiago. On 26 July 1953 a force of about 160 young people in their twenties attacked the barracks. Predictably, the action failed: most of the insurgents were gunned down or arrested. The 26-year-old Fidel Castro and his brother Raúl were able to escape, but were eventually caught. What saved them from torture and murder was the public outcry that followed the brutal treatment meted out by vindictive soldiers upon the first insurgents to have been taken prisoner. The quixotic Moncada attack and the official terror that it provoked served to turn Fidel Castro into a nationalist hero.

At his trial Castro defended himself with a now famous speech – known by its concluding line, 'History will absolve me' – in which he denounced the corrupt cliques that ruled Cuba and proclaimed the need to restore political freedom and economic independence. A composite of democratic, liberal values and patriotic aspirations derived from José Martí, this speech appealed to a wide spectrum of Cuban opinion. In the reconstructed version smuggled out of prison, a programme of reform was set out which echoed the aims of progressive movements all over Latin America: industrialization, redistribution of land, full employment and the modernization of education.

The text of *History Will Absolve Me* became the founding document of the 26 July Movement – so named after the date of the assault on the Moncada barracks – which Castro led after his release from prison in May 1955. Within a few months he departed for Mexico, where with other Cuban exiles he began to plot the overthrow of Batista. He was joined in Mexico by Ernesto 'Che' Guevara, a young Argentine doctor, who had recently undertaken a personal odyssey through Latin America to witness the condition of its people, and who had been confirmed in his revolutionary nationalism in 1954, when he witnessed the overthrow of the radical government of Jacobo Arbenz in Guatemala by an invasion force of US-backed rebels.

The Cuban Revolution (1956–9)

On 2 December 1956, after military training in Mexico, Castro and a company of eighty-two men sailed on the yacht *Granma* across the Gulf to Cuba. They landed at a beach in the south-eastern province of Oriente – a traditional starting-point of Cuban insurrections – close to the mountains of the Sierra Maestra. They were soon betrayed by peasants and ambushed by Batista's troops. Only twelve men survived this first military encounter. Escaping into the Sierra, the survivors regrouped to form the nucleus of a guerrilla force which gradually began to win small but telling victories against government troops and to expand as they were joined by peasants and members of the 26 July Movement.

Castro's rebellion had two prongs: the guerrillas in the Sierra Maestra, and the urban resistance led by Frank País in El Llano (the plain), where the struggle was conducted through propaganda, bombings, armed attacks on police and strike action. Still, for the whole of 1957 and until the middle of 1958, neither prong seemed capable of making much headway against the dictatorship. In the Sierra, the guerrillas, numbering some 160 men, were not able to establish a permanent base. In the cities, action was highly disruptive, but confused and ineffectual ever since a revolt in Santiago de Cuba, intended to coincide with the landing of the *Granma*, had been put down.

The militants of the 26 July Movement were in any case just one of several anti-Batista forces. There was the student organization, the Directorio Revolucionario, militant members of which attacked the presidential palace and narrowly failed to assassinate Batista. This organization also opened guerrilla fronts in the Sierra de Escambray and the Sierra de Trinidad. Then there were the established opposition parties such as the Auténticos and the Ortodoxos, who exerted pressure on Batista to call elections and eventually formed a tactical alliance with the 26 July Movement to oppose the dictator. Finally, the Communist Party was active in mobilizing labour against the dictator, but kept its distance from the 26 July Movement – about whose armed struggle it had serious misgivings – until mid-1958, when it sent the veteran Carlos Rafael Rodríguez to join Castro in the mountains. These campaigns in El Llano encountered serious reverses. On 5 September 1957 a naval mutiny by junior officers in the port of Cienfuegos was crushed by Batista. In April 1958 a general strike called by the opposition – a key test of its strength – won little support.

Yet even though Batista's army was keeping the rebellion in check, the dictator was losing the propaganda war. The brutality of his forces steadily alienated the Cuban public and horrified the Catholic Church, which was moved in February 1958 to call for a government of national unity. But more significant was the romantic image of Fidel Castro projected by the international news media after the American correspondent of *The New York Times*, Herbert Matthews, began in 1957 to publish a series of reports on his meetings with Castro in the Sierra Maestra. Opinion in the USA began to favour this young idealist who was fighting an obviously corrupt tyranny. In March 1958 Washington, concerned about Batista's counter-insurgency methods, imposed an arms embargo.

A critical turning-point for both sides was the failure of the general strike called for April 1958. Castro realized then that the struggle would be decided primarily through force of arms. For his part, Batista knew he must win a decisive victory over the rebels in the Sierra Maestra if he was to have any chance of regaining his credibility with the Cuban people and the US government. On 24 May 1958 Batista launched a major offensive against Castro's force of some 300 guerrillas. Fierce fighting continued for about three months, but Castro's superb qualities as a military leader, his intimate knowledge of the terrain and the agility of the guerrillas' strategy wore down Batista's troops. By the middle of August the offensive had foundered. Castro now sent Che Guevara and Camilo Cienfuegos with two columns to the province of Las Villas in the centre of the island. Once these guerrilla columns had won control of Las Villas, the island was cut in two, isolating the bulk of Batista's army at the eastern end.

The tide had turned against Batista. In a final bid to retain the backing of the USA, the dictator decided to go ahead with presidential elections due in November. His chosen candidate won, but there were massive abstentions. The fact was that the Cuban people had shifted their allegiance to a new charismatic leader, Fidel Castro. With Guevara and Cienfuegos fighting their way towards the capital in December, the dictator conceded defeat. On 1 January 1959 he fled with his entourage to the Dominican Republic. Che Guevara and his guerrillas entered the city, taking over key positions and calling a general strike in support of the victorious revolution. A week later Fidel Castro himself rode in triumph into Havana.

The Aftermath of Revolution (1959–62)

Castro had won an astonishing military victory and had toppled the dictator. Even so, the political influence of his 26 July Movement on Cuban society was very limited. In order to build up political strength Castro had in the latter stages of the war entered into a broad alliance with established parties of the opposition, ranging from the Auténticos to the Communists, and this had delivered to him the crucial support of the middle classes and organized labour. But Castro had grown to distrust professional politicians. Too many projects for reform had come to grief in Cuba – after all, Batista himself had first emerged as a revolutionary in 1933, and Grau of the Auténticos had similarly abandoned his principles when in office. By contrast, the lonely struggle in the Sierra Maestra had set the guerrillas apart from the old political class. Though the rebel leadership was bourgeois in origin, the privations of war had, according to Castro and Guevara, 'proletarianized' them. The alliance with the politicians of the cities was therefore regarded as a purely tactical necessity which, in Guevara's view, could not last beyond the time when it became a brake on revolutionary development.

The experience of the Sierra Maestra had transformed the guerrillas' view of what their revolution must achieve. An optimistic and Utopian strain had entered their thinking: not only should political sovereignty and social reform be their goals, but a new society and a New Man had to be created – a man free from material greed and individual ambition, one ready to share equally with his fellows in a just community. The puritanical fervour of such ideals may be explained to some degree as the reaction to the chronic venality which had characterized Cuban politics for so long. But it also recalled the millenarian zeal which had motivated the ascetic missionaries of Spain, who wanted to evangelize the Indians in order to build a New World free from the sins of the old. That millenarian impetus had never been entirely lost; it had surfaced in the Jesuit mission in Paraguay in the eighteenth century, and it also played a part in the ideals of the independence movements. Now it was reborn in Guevara's rousing, voluntarist declaration: 'We will make the man of the twenty-first century: we ourselves.'

The conviction that the guerrillas were the prototypes of the New Man gave Castro's revolution its sense of overriding legitimacy. Shortly after their victory, the guerrilla leaders started to concentrate power in their own hands. Officials of the Batista regime were put on trial in 'people's courts' and executed. The institutions of liberal democracy were either abolished outright or else allowed to wither away. Although promised, no new elections were held; the constitutional independence of the judiciary was limited when Castro assumed the right to appoint judges. The free press was either closed down or taken over by Communist-controlled unions. The trade unions themselves lost their independence from the government. Professional associations and private organizations were also deprived of autonomy, as was the University of Havana, the focus of opposition to earlier dictatorships.

These measures provoked opposition from liberal politicians and even from certain prominent guerrilla commanders whose reason for rebelling had been to restore the democratic constitution of 1940. The president chosen by Castro, a former anti-Batista judge, Manuel Urrutia, resigned as head of state in July 1959 in protest at the postponement of elections. A major figure in the revolutionary war, the *comandante* Hubert Matos attacked what he saw as the drift to communism and was arrested and imprisoned for treason in November of the same year. Many other Cubans, in what was to become a continuous exodus, began to leave the island for Miami. These were mostly middle-class professionals and property owners, who were dismayed at the radical changes being introduced by the revolutionaries. For although Castro seems not to have defined a precise political ideology at this stage, his intense nationalism made him determined to wrest the levers of the economy from foreign hands, while the awareness of rural misery gained from his experience in the Sierra had convinced him of the need to shift the basis of wealth and power in the country in favour of the peasants and the working class.

In fact, Castro saw that these goals were interdependent. The historic impasse between economic subordination to US sugar interests and Cuban aspirations to build a true *patria* could be broken only by making profound economic and social changes in the country. For if liberal democracy were to be restored without bringing the sugar industry under Cuban control, politics would again be blighted by a sense of impotence, which was the stubborn root of the corruption that pervaded Cuban public life. But to take over the export-economy and cut the ties of the Cuban bourgeoisie with US business required a new vision of society and the support of the mass of the population. Castro was still first and foremost a patriot, but the means of securing the *patria* were leading him in the direction of socialism.

Still, in the aftermath of victory, the Revolution was carried along more by enthusiasm than by ideology. A price freeze and large wage rises for workers boosted the popularity of the revolutionary government. An agrarian reform law was passed in May 1959, which authorized the expropriation of large estates and foreign-owned farms, and their conversion into co-operatives. Large companies, industries, banks and utilities were nationalized. These efforts to disengage the economy from its dependence on the USA brought confrontations with Washington, which in turn encouraged Castro to look for alternative markets and trading partners. In February 1960 the Soviet Union agreed to purchase 5 million tons of sugar over five years and granted Cuba a credit of $100 million with which to buy Soviet technology. In subsequent months other trade agreements were signed with Poland and China.

The developing crisis with the USA was brought to a head by the nationalization of American oil refineries when they refused to process crude oil from the Soviet Union. The US government retaliated by withdrawing its quota for imports of Cuban sugar; Castro responded by expropriating all US property; in October 1960 President Eisenhower placed a total embargo on US exports to Cuba. Given the atmosphere of Cold War that already existed between the USA and the Soviet Union, these confrontations, together with Castro's virulent anti-Yankee rhetoric, threatened to draw an essentially nationalist revolution on a smallish Caribbean island into the sphere of intercontinental geopolitics – with unforeseeable consequences.

The US embargo on trade increased suspicion in Cuba that an invasion was imminent. This furthered the militarization of the country, for in the vacuum that followed the suspension of the liberal–democratic constitution the pattern for social organization had been provided by the Rebel Army. Civilians were mobilized into militia and organized into neighbourhood 'Committees for the Defence of the Revolution', which served as units for civil defence as well as agencies for the supervision of the population.

The USA had indeed been preparing an invasion of Cuba, but instead of using its own troops, as in the days of the Platt Amendment, it was covertly training a force of Cuban exiles in Guatemala, which it hoped to use to spark off a general anti-Castro rebellion in the country. This strategy was misconceived; it underestimated Castro's popularity and military readiness, and it carried grave political risks in the tense atmosphere of the international Cold War. For this reason the new president, John F. Kennedy, refused to give official support to the invaders. When the invasion force landed at the Bay of Pigs on 15 April 1961, it suffered a crushing defeat at the hands of Cuban revolutionary troops. This humiliation of the USA boosted Fidel Castro's status as a patriot: he had convincingly exposed the neo-colonialist ambitions of the Americans. The Bay of Pigs episode also sharpened tensions between the superpowers, for the Soviet Union had previously threatened to defend Cuba from US aggression. Now it made good that threat by sending armaments to Castro.

In October 1962 a US spy plane revealed the presence of nuclear missiles on the island capable of hitting targets throughout the American continent. According to the Soviet leader, Nikita Khrushchev, these weapons were to be used solely for defensive purposes. But their presence on territory which lay only ninety miles from the US mainland was a clear provocation: on 22 October Kennedy ordered an embargo on all military systems bound for Cuba and demanded that the missiles be removed. A nuclear war seemed about to engulf the world in the days that followed until Khrushchev agreed to dismantle the Cuban missile installations in return for a US pledge not to invade the island. As a result of this international crisis, Cuba incurred the permanent hostility of the USA, its closest and most powerful neighbour, and became fully absorbed into the sphere of influence of the Soviet Union.

Building the Revolutionary State (1962–70)

The fundamental economic aim of the Revolution was to end the dependence on the sugar export-economy by diversifying agriculture and initiating a process of import-substituting industrialization. In this respect the Cuban revolutionaries shared the goals of other modernizing élites in Latin America. However, they proposed to achieve their aims by socialist methods. Under the direction of Che Guevara, who became head of the National Bank and later minister of industry, a Four Year Plan was drawn up, which proposed to restructure the economy by central planning. Workers would be motivated by 'moral incentives' and not by material benefits.

But the Cuban Revolution could not escape the developmental dilemma that faced other agrarian export economies: how to redirect resources towards manufacturing without damaging the export agriculture which earned the capital to finance industrial investment. In the aftermath of victory foreign-exchange reserves had been used up in large wage rises. The sugar export-economy had been neglected and production had fallen disastrously by 1962. With no foreign reserves and declining export earnings, there was little capital available to invest in developing a manufacturing sector. A further difficulty was that the US embargo on trade with Cuba cut off supplies of technology and finance needed for industrialization. Instead, Cuba had to turn to the Soviet Union for technical aid and financial credits. Inefficiency and lack of productivity also damaged the drive to industrialize: Guevara's insistence on moral incentives meant massive direction of labour by the state, but revolutionary commitment alone was not sufficient to generate the rates of productivity required to fulfil planning targets. Central planning was itself erratic since decisions were liable to be overridden by sudden changes of policy by a leadership which lacked economic expertise. By 1963 Soviet advisers were recommending the suspension of the industrialization programme and the revival of the sugar export-economy.

In the agricultural sector production had suffered as much from incompetence as from structural reform. Faced with the likelihood of expropriation, private farmers cut back production, and the Institute of Agrarian Reform aggravated the disruption through lack of a clear policy: at first it organized and administered peasant co-operatives, but the nature of the sugar economy, with its basis in huge plantations, dictated a more centralized structure; so the policy of co-operatives was replaced by collectivization in state farms, where peasants were paid wages and set production quotas. Many practical errors were committed too, causing shortages and dislocations: too many cattle were slaughtered to supply the demand for meat generated by the post-revolutionary wage rises; crop diversification failed for lack of adequate investment; basics such as sowing, planting and fertilizing were neglected or mismanaged. The inevitable result was an inability to supply foodstuffs to the population as a whole.

These obvious shortcomings, together with Soviet criticism of the quality of planning and decision-making, led to a debate within the leadership about the direction of economic policy. Che Guevara's attempts to create the New Man by subordinating all economic activity to the decisions of the guerrilla leaders were opposed by Communist planners who advocated a return to material incentives, wage differentials and a degree of reliance on market forces to allocate resources. In 1963 Fidel Castro accepted the basic Communist view on economic policy: industrialization would be subordinated to sugar production. The goal now was to develop sugar as never before: Fidel announced that a harvest of 10 million tons of sugar – the largest in Cuba's history – must be reaped by 1970. The aim was to make Cuba the largest producer of sugar in the world, so that she would be in a position to dictate the terms of her participation in the international economy. But the prospects did not look promising: the economy did not grow fast enough to compensate for the rise in population; sugar harvests lagged behind set targets; wages were kept low and consumption was cut back in order to maximize investment to achieve the 10-million-ton harvest in 1970.

Given the severe problems resulting from the radical restructuring of the economy, how did the Cuban people react to their new leaders? Thousands of middle-class Cubans opted to leave the country, settling mostly in Miami, which became a centre of anti-Castro conspiracies and propaganda. Castro allowed their departure because it was a painless way of eliminating internal opposition to the Revolution, even though a high price had to be paid in replacing professional and technical manpower. Despite many hardships, peasants and workers largely supported the regime. In the first three years of the Revolution wages rose by about 40 per cent but the demand generated by this huge increase in purchasing power exhausted the productive resources of the country, with the result that rationing had to be introduced. Rationing was to remain a permanent feature of daily life. But what ensured general support for the Revolution was the improvement in the living conditions of the mass of the people. They were regularly nourished, decently clothed and adequately housed. Unemployment and under-employment, the scourges of other Latin American countries, were eliminated by a programme of public works. A system of free medical care and social security was established. Free schooling and training opened up educational opportunities for the children of peasants and workers. The illiteracy rate dropped from 20 per cent to about 12 per cent in two years thanks to a campaign by young volunteers who went out to the villages to teach the peasants. Higher education was brought within the reach of all sectors of society.

There occurred too a revolution in attitudes and values. Racial equality was positively promoted in a country where up to 75 per cent of the population was black or of mixed race. Women were given equal rights at work and as citizens. Through education and propaganda, the government endeavoured to break down the prejudices of machismo in a strongly male-dominated society. Above all, the Revolution inspired in ordinary Cubans a deep sense of national pride, a belief that at last Cuba was beholden to no other nation – and certainly no longer prey to the contempt for Latins displayed by Anglo-Saxon Americans. In this regard Fidel Castro had struck a deep chord in the Cuban people. His ritual taunting of the Yankees, no less than their obvious impotence to topple him, became valuable and recurrent demonstrations of national independence.

These achievements were in large part due to the revolutionary idealism of leaders like Fidel Castro and Che Guevara. Their belief in the feasibility of creating a New Man buoyed up the Revolution through the treacherous currents of political struggle in the first decade after their victory. Fidel Castro saw the need to sustain the momentum of change by keeping this moral idealism constantly before the masses, and even after 1963, when economic errors forced him to heed the pragmatic counsels of the Communist planners, he continued to support Guevara's commitment to a moral revolution and to the exporting of the Cuban model of social development to other countries of Latin America and the Third World. Cuban radio stations broadcast to the rest of the continent and young revolutionaries came to Cuba to be trained in the techniques of guerrilla warfare. This internationalism bred unease among governments in Latin America. Cuba was expelled from the Organization of American States, and the Latin American republics followed the lead of the USA in breaking off diplomatic relations with Castro's government (with the exception of Mexico, which was concerned as ever to preserve its revolutionary image).

Che Guevara, after resigning from his official position in the government in 1963, chose to carry the torch of revolution to other countries. He led an expedition to help revolutionary forces in the Congo, but withdrew in disappointment from the labyrinth of Central African politics. He then went to Bolivia, where a socialist revolution in 1952 had been gradually undermined and its leaders overthrown by 1964, and tried to repeat the Cuban experience of the Sierra Maestra. But there too he met with failure. His nucleus of guerrillas did not prosper among the close-knit Indian communities of the Andean *altiplano*, and he lacked the full support of the Bolivian Communist Party, which remained sceptical about Guevara's voluntarist methods. In October 1967 he was captured and killed by Bolivian counter-insurgency forces. His death reverberated throughout the world and he became a heroic symbol of the revolutionary idealism which in the following year was to erupt in revolts against the established order by young intellectuals and students in many different countries.

Meanwhile, Fidel Castro had been urging Cubans to strain every sinew to reach the 10-million-ton sugar harvest by 1970. In the event only $8\frac{1}{2}$ million tons were harvested, which was a record in itself, but not enough to prevent a general sense of demoralization in the light of the crucial significance that Castro had attached to the figure of 10 million tons. Not only had the structure of the economy been badly damaged by the obsessive concentration on sugar, but the shortfall was a sign that the country was incapable of breaking out of the productive stagnation which had afflicted its economy since the 1920s. For the central economic aim of the Revolution had been frustrated: industrialization had had to be abandoned, and Cuba remained dependent on a one-crop export-economy in an international environment where demand for sugar was in long-term decline. Cuba's main trading partners were now the Soviet Union and the countries of the Communist bloc. In return for exports of sugar, Cuba received most of the imports she needed. The country had to rely excessively on Soviet goodwill; the Soviet Union, which supplied all of Cuba's oil, could, if it wished, bring the island to a standstill.

Pragmatism and Institutionalization (1970–90)

After the débâcle of the 1970 sugar harvest the Communist Party assumed a central role in the running of the state and the economy. However, the Peoples' Socialist Party, the old, rather discredited pre-revolutionary Communist Party, had dissolved itself in 1961 and its militants had joined Castroite organizations, where they exerted their ideological influence. In 1965 a new Cuban Communist Party was formed with Castroites dominant on the Central Committee and Fidel at its head. But the Party as such did not play a leading part in national life in the 1960s, for it was Castro who continued to rule in a direct, personal manner, and the guerrilla struggle of the Sierra Maestra was still the source of legitimacy for the new state. Yet from the early 1970s a process of 'building socialist legality' was initiated and the Revolution was institutionalized in accordance with Soviet models. The Communist Party was assigned the role of supreme organ of society and the Committees for the Defence of the Revolution, the bureaucracy, the judiciary and the local assemblies of 'people's power', as well as the national assembly, came under its direction. The revolutionary militia were disbanded and a military hierarchy was introduced into the Rebel Army, which developed into one of the largest and best equipped fighting forces in Latin America. In 1976 a constitution drafted by veteran Communist leaders, and based on that of the Soviet Union, was approved by a plebiscite.

Economic management now passed into the hands of Communist planners. Workers were organized into the state-controlled trade unions and regulated by labour tribunals. Pay differentials, performance bonuses and work quotas were introduced to improve output. In 1972 productivity rose by 20 per cent, and in 1971–5 GNP grew at an annual rate of about 16 per cent (though in the latter years of the decade it fell to below 4 per cent and in the 1980s failed to recover its peak rates). A small private sector in agriculture and services was tolerated so as to improve supply to the domestic market. Exports of sugar, tobacco and other commodities to capitalist countries were stepped up to earn the foreign exchange required to buy advanced technology. In later years tourism was also promoted as a means of earning precious hard currency. Loans were raised from foreign banks to finance development projects. In short, Cuba began once again to participate in the international capitalist economy (except for trade with the USA, which kept up its embargo), though it relied on the Soviet Union and the communist countries for aid and guaranteed exports.

Cuba adopted a new form of revolutionary internationalism in the 1970s and 1980s. After the killing of Guevara in Bolivia and the fall of Allende's Marxist government in Chile in 1973, less emphasis was placed on encouraging guerrilla struggles in Latin America. The new policy was rather to send combat troops or technical advisers to support embattled Marxist states such as Angola, where the government was threatened by a South African-backed guerrilla insurgency, or Ethiopia, which was at war with Somalia and later faced a separatist rebellion in Eritrea. After the Sandinista victory in Nicaragua in 1979, Cuban advisers and medical workers were sent to help the new regime. This kind of internationalism led to accusations that Castro was acting as an instrument of Soviet foreign policy. The USA became concerned when Cuba sent advisers and workers to help Michael Manley's socialist government in Jamaica and the Marxist government of Maurice Bishop in Grenada. In 1983 US Marines invaded Grenada and overthrew Bishop, expelling the Cubans from the island. Although this was a reverse, Cuba still asserted its right to aid revolutionary states abroad. For instance, some 20,000 troops fought in Angola until 1989 and up to 15,000 remained in Ethiopia after that date.

Some Cuban and Latin American intellectuals became disenchanted with the new communist political and bureaucratic disciplines of the 1970s. In 1971 the poet Heberto Padilla was arrested for cultural deviationism and allegedly obliged to confess his crimes against the Revolution before his fellow writers. Associates of Padilla suffered ostracism. In the years that followed a number of prominent Cuban writers and artists chose to go into exile, and criticized the intolerance of the official cultural establishment.

The Padilla affair divided the Hispanic cultural world. Writers of international stature like Octavio Paz and Carlos Fuentes (Mexico), Mario Vargas Llosa (Peru) and Juan Goytisolo (Spain), who had once welcomed the

Revolution, now denounced what they saw as a process of Stalinization. Other no less distinguished authors like Gabriel García Márquez (Colombia) and Julio Cortázar (Argentina) reaffirmed their loyalty to its ideals. The polemic over the character of the Cuban Revolution was of some moment in the Spanish-speaking countries because in the 1960s Fidel Castro's victory appeared to herald a new hope of overcoming poverty, dictatorship and corruption. But was the future of the Hispanic world to be Marxist or was liberal democracy still a feasible option? In the course of the 1970s the debate over artistic freedom widened to include questions about the degree of political freedom and civil rights allowed in Cuba. Castro's critics accused him of being a totalitarian *caudillo* who would brook no dissent. In a country shrouded in secrecy, accurate information regarding numbers of political prisoners, mistreatment of offenders, religious persecution or the punishment of homosexuals was difficult to establish.

However, evidence of growing dissatisfaction among ordinary Cubans with strict political controls and permanent rationing appeared in 1980, when the compound of the Peruvian embassy in Havana was overrun by nearly 11,000 people seeking political asylum. The Cuban authorities tried to defuse the situation by opening the port of Mariel to allow those who wished to emigrate to leave the island by sea. Some 125,000 embarked for Miami in small boats; their number included delinquents and mental patients whom Castro allowed to leave in order to embarrass the US government and claim that only misfits had voluntarily chosen exile. To counteract the bad publicity in the international news media, huge demonstrations were organized in Havana to proclaim loyalty to Fidel and the Revolution. Still, the mass exodus had its effect on daily life: Cubans were allowed to spend their spare money on food and clothes in 'free markets', which were permitted to operate alongside the official ration system.

Celebrating the twentieth anniversary of the Revolution in 1979, Fidel Castro warned that the present generation of Cubans would have to make further sacrifices so that future generations might live better. Indeed, the country's economic performance in the 1980s continued to deteriorate. Its fundamental problems were the historic ones of overwhelming economic dependency on a foreign power and the monoculture of sugar. The Soviet Union remained Cuba's largest trading partner; it effectively subsidized Cuba's monocultural export-economy by buying sugar at fixed prices well above the world price, and it supplied about 98 per cent of Cuba's oil needs and virtually all of its industrial and technological goods. With the US embargo still in force, Cuba was able to trade only with a limited number of capitalist countries such as Mexico, Spain, France, Canada and Japan, and this trade was heavily in deficit because there was little demand for sugar in such countries.

Like other Latin American states in the late 1970s, Cuba began to finance its development projects and cover its deficits by borrowing petrodollars from Western banks at favourable interest rates (this was in addition to the massive aid and subsidies it was already receiving from the Soviet Union). In 1982, after interest rates had gone up, Cuba was unable to make payments on its foreign debt to Western banks, which amounted to $3.5 billion, and had to negotiate the rescheduling of part of it with its capitalist creditors. In addition to this debt, Cuba also owed the Soviet Union over $7 billion for which it had to negotiate repayment from 1986.

These financial pressures forced the Party to exercise even firmer control over economic management and state spending. The 'free markets' that ran parallel to the state system were discontinued. There could be no easing of the regime of austerity that had marked the Revolution from the start, for wage costs had to be kept down while increasing the productivity of the labour force. Thus in the 1980s Castro revived Che Guevara's ideal of moral incentives rather than higher material rewards for labour; he once again exhorted the masses to volunteer for work without pay in order to build the revolutionary state.

Reduced earnings from foreign trade, slow economic growth and a rising population aggravated the problems of unemployment and inflation which Cuba had been experiencing since the 1970s, though neither approached the levels that existed in most other Latin American countries. Inflation fluctuated between 20 and 30 per cent, and though figures for unemployment were difficult to determine, Fidel Castro had declared as early as 1980 that the economy was suffering from excess manpower. This labour surplus was reduced by expanding the armed forces and sending troops, technicians and workers to give aid to other socialist countries in the Third World.

After three decades the Cuban Revolution had substantial achievements to its credit. It had eliminated the grave social and economic inequalities that characterized all the other countries of Latin America. Despite the austerity and the lack of individual freedoms, the population as a whole did not suffer hunger or material insecurity: rents were low, health services excellent and free; education was also free and accessible to all sectors of society. But perhaps the greatest achievement was the forging of a common national spirit, something that most other Latin American republics had failed to do. This achievement was the more remarkable in that before the 1959 Revolution Cuba's sense of national identity was one of the weakest in Latin America.

The Revolution might have saved Cuba from absorption by the USA, but had it found a way out of the country's historic impasse? So long as sugar – a commodity of declining value – continued to dominate the economy, Cuba would need preferential trade agreements with a foreign power, and this would inevitably set limits to its independence. Since 1960 it had been the Soviet Union and the communist countries of Eastern Europe that had replaced the USA as the island's principal overseas market, providing Cuba with a framework for subsidized trade. However, during 1989 these countries confronted an unforeseeable wave of anti-communist revolts that succeeded within a few months in bringing down the communist regimes of all the East European states and voting in democratic governments in their place; even the Soviet Union began to proceed rapidly towards dismantling the system of central planning and introduced elements of political democracy.

By early 1990 Fidel Castro was looking politically isolated and economically vulnerable: his socialist trading partnerships had disintegrated, and the Soviet Union had announced that Cuba would eventually have to pay the going rate for the oil and technology she received, while subsidized prices for sugar exports would have to be phased out. Without these economic underpinnings could socialist Cuba survive? Although Castro reaffirmed his commitment to the ideals of the Revolution, there were signs that a power struggle might be taking place within the top circles of the Cuban Communist Party: in 1989 General Arnaldo Ochoa, a hero of the Angolan campaign, had been unexpectedly charged with drug trafficking, tried in public and executed along with other military officers allegedly implicated in corruption.

The relatively sudden collapse of communism in Europe laid bare the fact that the Cuban Revolution had not resolved the island's historic impasse between acute dependency on a foreign power for its sugar exports and its intense desire for national sovereignty. The winning of economic autonomy remained a challenge yet to be overcome.

13. Argentina: The Long Decline

By the early decades of the twentieth century, Argentina had attained levels of prosperity and political stability comparable to the USA and leading European countries. Its economic success – reflected in an average growth rate of 5 per cent per annum between 1880 and 1914 – lay in the export of meat and grain to Europe. The wealth generated by this trade had created a consensus among the creole élites of landowners and merchants: regional *caudillismo* had been overcome and the country centralized under a constitutional democracy which guaranteed the political freedoms cherished by classic liberal republicanism. Argentina appeared to have fulfilled the aims of the leaders of its wars of independence – the 'barbarism' of the *caudillos*, no less than the obscurantism of Spain, had been overcome by modern 'civilization'.

Appearances, however, were deceptive. Progress had wrought great economic and demographic changes in Argentina, but it had not fundamentally changed the traditional culture of the country. By contrast with other successful post-colonial societies, such as the USA, Canada and Australia, the roots of Argentine society still lay in the sixteenth century. For the system of land grants following the conquest of the pampas from the nomadic Indian tribes in the 1870s had failed to produce the class of independent small farmers envisaged by liberal reformers. Instead, the pampas had been carved up into *estancias*, vast estates owned by cattle ranchers and wheat-growers, who perpetuated the seigneurial values of the Hispanic nobility.

As a result, the majority of poor immigrants from Italy, Spain and Eastern Europe failed to find a permanent living on the land; they remained locked up in the cities, particularly in Buenos Aires, where they found work in the great meat-packing plants, in the docks and railways, in trade, services and light industry, and in the expanding bureaucracy. Thus, what European immigration produced was not an agrarian revolution but a restive urban proletariat and an insecure lower middle class, neither of which felt any bonds of allegiance to the powerful lords of the pampas, in whose hands lay the economic and political power that had made Argentina rich. The developing conflict between the aristocratic landed interest and the masses in the cities was to put paid to the dream of the nineteenth-century creole liberals.

By the turn of the century, Argentina's oligarchic democracy was facing the challenge of incorporating the new urban classes into the political system. Armed revolts by the Radical Party – a coalition of dissident landowners and the urban middle classes, with some working-class support – eventually led to the passing of the Sáenz Peña electoral reform law in 1912, which granted universal male suffrage, secret ballots and compulsory voting. The urban masses were thus shortly able to wrest power from the *estanciero* class: the Radical Party was elected in 1916 and governed the country for a fourteen-year period until 1930.

The result, however, was an acutely lop-sided society, in which political authority no longer coincided with economic power. For Argentina's prosperity continued to depend on the export of meat and grain produced in the *estancias*, while the urban population was overwhelmingly employed in ancillary activities. After the electoral reform of 1912, Argentine politics became a matter of a clamorous majority of urban consumers using the democratic system to extract benefits from an entrenched élite of rural monopolists. Far from producing a national consensus that would reinforce the institutions of the liberal state, the extension of democracy, given the peculiar imbalance of Argentine society, led to a deadlocked conflict which was destined to tear the state apart.

The Rule of the Radicals (1916–30)

The political fortunes of the Radical Party under their great leader Hipólito Yrigoyen reflected the difficulties faced by Argentina in the first two decades of the twentieth century. Elected president in 1916, Yrigoyen sought to build up his party into a dominant national machine by enlisting the support of special interest-groups opposed to the established oligarchic parties. He extended generous subsidies and credit to the small farmers, he courted the trade unions by settling wage disputes in their favour, he backed the University Reform Movement that originated in the city of Córdoba in 1918 and won a following among intellectuals and the liberal professions. But the attempt to put together a coalition of interests spanning the middle and working classes started to go wrong when the Great War in Europe disrupted the export markets for Argentina's wheat and meat. Rising prices and unemployment provoked labour unrest, and Yrigoyen found himself having to crack down on the workers.

The Argentine trade unions were led by anarchists and syndicalists; many of these were Spanish or Italian immigrants who had brought with them from Europe a belief in direct action and the revolutionary general strike as the instruments with which to overthrow the bourgeois state. A series of bitter stoppages in 1918 culminated in a syndicalist general strike in January 1919. In one 'tragic week', bloody repression – accompanied by street-fighting between anarchists and militants of the right-wing Argentine Patriotic League – broke the strike, and the anarcho-syndicalist leadership with it. During the 1920s, with the war in Europe over, rising wages kept labour quiescent, and the leadership of the unions passed to the less combative socialists and communists. However, the memory of the Tragic Week of 1919 lived on: a tradition of labour militancy had been established in those anarcho-syndicalist years which would become a recurrent factor in the political struggles of the coming decades.

The labour troubles placed the Radicals in an awkward intermediate position between an intransigent agro-mercantile élite and a working class nursing revolutionary aspirations. After the crisis of 1919 Yrigoyen tried to rebuild the coalition of the middle and working classes by turning to public spending and the expansion of the bureaucracy to appease his urban constituencies. Yet the rise in living standards for the urban population was at the cost of inflation, which damaged the export-economy. The Radicals, therefore, came under pressure from the *estancieros* to restore financial discipline. At the 1922 elections the Radicals won again, but their new president, the patrician landowner Manuel Alvear, came from the right wing of the party and disapproved of Yrigoyen's populism. Alvear's administration gave priority to beating inflation by cutting state spending and raising import tariffs. The Radical Party, in fact, was experiencing the first stages of a conflict between the transfer of wealth to the urban classes and the need to keep the agrarian export-economy internationally competitive. It was a conflict that would be repeated time and again in the course of the twentieth century, and it plunged the country into a descending spiral towards economic chaos and political collapse.

Essentially a party of the urban middle class, the Radicals were unable to surmount the problem of inflation intact. Yrigoyen broke away in 1924, carrying with him the bulk of the middle-class membership to form the Yrigoyenista Radicals, and leaving behind him the patrician wing of the old party, whose members now became known as the Anti-Personalist Radicals. At the 1928 elections, Yrigoyen ran a populist campaign promising a return to the free-spending, job-creating bonanza of the early 1920s. He also played upon nationalist sentiment by advocating the nationalization of the oil industry. He won the election, but his policies soon aggravated the budget deficit and stoked up inflation. When Wall Street crashed, in 1929, his administration was doomed. A drought aggravated the effects of the financial crash upon the export-economy and unemployment soared. No amount of government spending could make up the loss of jobs. Once again, Yrigoyen, the great populist leader, found himself having to take on the proletariat. There were disturbing echoes of the Tragic Week of 1919 in the street-fighting that broke out between the Yrigoyenistas and their opponents – an assortment of militant workers, nationalist university students and, from the other side of the political spectrum, the right-wing bully-boys of the Patriotic League.

The fate of the Radical Party in 1930 epitomized the political problem faced by Argentina. There was no way out of the deadlock caused by the divergence between the economic power of the *estanciero* élite and the electoral weight of the urban bloc; for the middle classes constantly oscillated between the *estancieros* and the working class. When times were good, the middle classes responded to populist appeals and sided with the workers in order to wring concessions from the *estancieros*. But whenever the export-economy ran into trouble, they recoiled from the militancy of the workers and accepted the *estancieros'* recipes for correcting the country's finances. These swings of the political pendulum meant that, on the one hand, the export-economy kept being undermined by excessive urban demands, while, on the other, radical changes to the *estanciero* monopoly were out of the question so long as the middle classes broke their alliance with the proletariat, thereby weakening the power of the urban bloc. In short, neither revolution nor the status quo ante 1912 was possible; only periodic convulsions in an otherwise paralysed system.

As Yrigoyen's government faced growing economic and social disorder, the conservative *estanciero* interest saw its opportunity to move against it. In September 1930 Yrigoyen was overthrown by the armed forces in the first *coup d'état* of the century. In fact, the military were now beginning to act as an independent force in politics. Though predominantly middle class in origin, the officer corps had become a professional, self-regulating body that was not directly influenced by the interest of any particular social group. The primary concern of military officers was to ensure that Argentina made orderly progress towards the fulfilment of her presumed greatness. Yet despite repeated interventions in politics, the quality that was to characterize the behaviour of the armed forces in the course of the century was indecision. They lacked a coherent vision of the nation's destiny, and so, notwithstanding their firepower and their anxiety about order, they too became caught up in the swings and roundabouts of Argentine politics, siding now with the *estanciero* exporters, now with the middle classes, and for a while even with the urban proletariat.

In 1930 they were united only in their disgust with Yrigoyen, whom they blamed for jeopardizing the nation's prosperity with his demagoguery. But once they had taken over, they were not quite sure what to do with their power. A nationalist faction led by General José F. Uriburu wanted to set up a corporate state broadly similar to those of Mussolini in Italy, Primo de Rivera in Spain and Salazar in Portugal. The idea was to establish a state in which class politics would be subsumed under a strong executive authority capable of implementing the structural reforms necessary for the regeneration of the economy. A more influential faction, however, proved reluctant to break altogether with Argentina's liberal traditions; these officers hoped to turn the clock back to those halcyon days of civilized prosperity before Sáenz Peña's electoral reform had let in the Radicals. But short of scrapping the 1912 law, the only means of reinstating the politics of gentlemanly accords between *estanciero* parties was the systematic manipulation of the electoral process so as to exclude the lower classes. For a decade from 1932, Argentine government would be dominated by a coalition of conservatives and anti-Yrigoyen Radicals known as the Concordancia. The nationalist, corporatist remedy for Argentina's ills was postponed until 1943, when another military coup led to the rise of Juan Domingo Perón.

The Concordancia Governments (1932–43)

The fraudulent election of 1932 placed General Agustín P. Justo at the head of the first Concordancia coalition government, whose principal components were the conservative National Democrats, the Independent Socialist Party and the Anti-Personalist Radicals. The priority was to stabilize the economy – which was suffering as much from Yrigoyen's spending spree as from the world depression – by balancing the budget, servicing the foreign debt and reversing trade deficits. But there was also a concern to modernize the instruments of economic management, and important reforms were undertaken in this area, such as the introduction of income tax and the foundation of a central bank (its director-general was Raúl Prebisch, later to become a very influential theorist of Latin American economic dependency).

Given the depressed state of international demand, an urgent need arose to preserve the overseas markets of an economy which was so heavily geared towards exports. There was a particular danger of Argentina being shut out of her largest export market when Britain adopted a policy of Imperial Preference in 1932 – a trading agreement which accorded meat producers in Australia and South Africa preference over their competitors in return for privileged British access to their markets. The Argentine government succeeded in protecting her exports to Britain by concluding a similar deal in 1933. Under the Roca–Runciman Treaty, Argentine exports of beef to the British market would be sustained at their 1932 levels in return for a reduction in import tariffs on British goods and a range of concessions to British companies operating in Argentina.

During the period of the Concordancia governments domestic light industry expanded and replaced certain imports, particularly in textiles, electrical goods and processed foods. But this industrial growth was not the result of economic planning; it was stimulated by the rise in demand due to the recovery of the export-economy. The Concordancia's economic and fiscal policies followed orthodox liberal prescriptions – the exploitation of the country's 'comparative advantage' in agriculture, and the creation of a sound financial climate that would attract foreign capital to make up for the relative lack of interest among Argentine capitalists in investing in industry. These policies were based on an understanding of Argentina's role in the world economy that was shared by all the major political parties, including the Radicals and the Socialists, and they brought considerable well-being to the country in the 1930s at a time when the world depression was causing severe difficulties to most other Latin American republics.

Yet the 1930s have come to be known as the Infamous Decade. For, once again, economics and politics were out of kilter in Argentina and, however successful Concordancia governments might have been in running the economy, they could survive politically only through electoral fraud. In the long term, economic success is predicated on political legitimacy, and the Concordancia governments failed to win the allegiance of the urban classes. The latter were politically dissatisfied, for economic growth had boosted the strength of the trade unions and made them more combative, while spending cuts had accentuated middle-class *empleomanía* – the craving for white-collar jobs in the government service. In the cities, therefore, economic liberalism and financial orthodoxy were increasingly perceived as serving primarily the interests of the *estanciero* export-élite and foreign business. The result was a rise in nationalist sentiment among the middle and working classes.

Until the late 1930s nationalism had been a largely right-wing phenomenon. It arose from an anxiety about the ever fragile sense of Argentine identity, and was directed against putative threats to it from foreign influences such as the Protestantism of the British merchants or the corrupting egalitarianism inherent in democracy. Mass immigration had fuelled such fears. During the Tragic Week of 1919, young toughs of the Patriotic League had hunted down Jews, anarchists and Bolsheviks. However, in 1933 it was the Roca–Runciman Treaty which became the focus of great popular resentment against British 'imperialism'. A school of nationalist historians emerged who denounced the constant intervention of Britain in Argentine affairs since the early days of the republic, particularly its role in the secession of the province that became Uruguay and its seizure in 1833 of the Islas Malvinas (Falkland Islands). These historians chose as their hero the early nineteenth-century dictator, Juan Manuel de Rosas, long the bogey of Argentine liberals, whom they regarded as having defended the traditional way of life against European incursions.

The new cultural nationalism of the intellectuals found a sympathetic response in Buenos Aires among ordinary citizens angered at this time by the scandal of the transport monopoly operated by British companies. These companies became unpopular when they began pressuring the Argentine government under the terms of the Roca-Runciman Treaty to ban small individually owned buses that were competing against their appallingly inefficient trams. There was public outrage too over the monopolistic practices of foreign-owned meat-packing firms – accusations of tax evasion and exchange-control irregularities provoked heated quarrels in the senate (a member was actually shot dead in the chamber during a debate). As the Roca-Runciman Treaty and other issues, such as protectionism by the USA, exposed the constraints under which Argentina's export trade had to operate in the depressed world economy of the 1930s, nationalist feeling ran high and extended to economic affairs, undermining the political consensus on free trade, which all the major parties had subscribed to for over half a century.

The outbreak of the Second World War gave a further impetus to nationalism. Argentina's markets in continental Europe became largely inaccessible, and the flow of imports of technology and fuels needed for her industries was drastically reduced. Nationalists now argued for a policy of state-led industrialization to produce the goods that could no longer be imported and to lessen the economy's reliance on exports. The critical impetus, however, came with the conversion of the armed forces to economic nationalism as a result of a dispute with the USA over the creation of a pan-American alliance against the Axis powers. Under a treaty of 1941 the USA undertook to supply arms to several Latin American nations, but excluded Argentina because of its refusal to renounce its neutrality and join the anti-Axis alliance. This exclusion aroused fears in the armed forces that Argentina would be militarily weak in relation to Brazil, its historic rival in the region, which did receive US armaments. In 1941, therefore, the Dirección General de Fabricaciones Militares, a state-owned armaments industry run by the armed forces themselves, was set up, and became the forerunner of the state-run enterprises which proliferated in subsequent decades.

By 1943 the political authority of the Concordancia had worn away, despite the conservative coalition's considerable success in steering the economy through the world depression of the 1930s. Led by the right-wing Ramón Castillo, the government had been deserted by moderate conservatives; it had lost control of the congress to the Radicals, who had been agitating against ballot-rigging; and crucial social groups – the middle classes and organized labour – were frustrated with free-trade policies, which had, in any case, come under pressure from external factors in the world economy. But above all, the army, as in 1930, felt the time had come for another revolution to regenerate the fortunes of the nation. On 4 June 1943 Castillo was deposed.

Once again, however, the armed forces were unable to decide how to achieve national regeneration: whether to return to a more effective version of pre-1912 oligarchic politics – a dubious prospect after the experience of the Concordancia – or to install the authoritarian corporate state as envisaged in 1930 by Uriburu and as was currently being advocated by the Grupo de Oficiales Unidos, a hard-line nationalist faction of more junior officers. The latter option eventually prevailed. One of its leading proponents was a young colonel, Juan Domingo Perón, who, as minister of labour and later as vice-president of the military government, quickly built up a power-base from which to launch the nationalist project for a new Argentina.

The Rule of Perón (1946–55)

During 1943–5 Perón's basic strategy for winning power was to rally the urban classes, especially the proletariat, against the *estancieros* and foreign business. But the intense nationalism of Perón's movement attracted the support of groups from both the extreme right and left of the Argentine political spectrum, and this was to give Peronism a hybrid, not to say schizoid character, which would contribute to policy incoherence and internecine feuding, thereby preventing the movement from generating a truly unifying vision of national destiny.

To reinforce his rhetorical onslaught on the twin pillars of the free-trade export-economy, Perón used his position as minister of labour to settle industrial disputes in favour of the unions, so long as the leadership pledged its political allegiance to him. He also won enormous popularity by introducing a whole range of welfare benefits for trade unionists. As Perón's strength grew, the opposition to him from the established parties, which feared what they saw as a fascistic threat to the constitution and liberty, exerted pressure on the vacillating leaders of the military junta, who finally dismissed Perón and put him in gaol.

However, on 17 October 1945 the trade unions organized massive demonstrations in Buenos Aires and marched on the presidential palace to demand Perón's release. The military junta gave in, and Perón resumed his post in the government. He now had a mass movement behind him, which had succeeded, incredibly, in imposing its will upon the high command of the armed forces. In the presidential elections of February 1946 Perón won with 54 per cent of the vote. Once in power, he proceeded to purge the army leadership, raise officers' pay and give political posts to his military followers. The two foundations of his power were now in place: the trade unions and a privileged military establishment. Through them he could combine wide popular support with the executive force to impose economic change.

Perón had an additional political asset in Eva Duarte; she was a beautiful young woman from a poor background who had been an actress when she became Perón's mistress, but later assisted him in his rise to power, becoming his wife in 1945. Evita proved to be a populist of rare genius. She soon became the object of hysterical devotion for the *descamisados*, the 'shirtless' mass of urban workers who regarded her as the 'Madonna de América', their own special champion and protectress, the incarnate symbol of the yearning for 'social justice' which constituted the heart of Peronism. Evita's expert cultivation of her mystique gained her enormous personal power, even though she held no official position in the state. Her Eva Perón Foundation, funded by contributions from unions and business, and by state subsidies, was turned into a parallel welfare state, which provided hospitals, clinics, schools and many forms of charitable relief for the poor and the sick. She was also instrumental in binding the union movement to Peronism, taking a hand in the elimination of recalcitrant labour leaders and placing loyalists in key positions. It was also through her efforts that Argentine women won the vote in 1947. In short, Evita personified the traditional political culture of patronage and clientship, skilfully applied to modern conditions of mass politics.

Peronism can be regarded as a form of *caudillismo* of industrial society; its clients were, pre-eminently, workers who consented to being organized by the state into loyal unions in exchange for substantial social and economic benefits. Allegiance to their *Líder* had, therefore, a kind of feudal ferocity about it. Perón chose to conduct politics through the exploitation of his charismatic authority at mass rallies outside the presidential palace in the Plaza de Mayo. His ideology of *Justicialismo*, a vague eclectic creed appealing more to the emotions than to the intellect, was broadly corporatist, recalling aspects of fascism in its personality cult and in its authoritarian emphasis on the supremacy of the state over civil society, but also picking up native echoes of Yrigoyen's populist calls for harmony between the classes.

The principles of *Justicialismo* were eventually codified in the constitution of 1949, which enshrined a 'decalogue' of workers' rights and invested in the state rights over private property, land and natural resources, as well as the right to intervene in the economy. It also permitted the re-election of a president for any number of six-year terms, centralized power by allowing direct elections regardless of federal weightings, and increased the scope of presidential intervention in the affairs of the provinces. Yet there was a disabling flaw in the Peronist corporate state: it failed to include the *estanciero* élite, in whose hands lay the crucial levers of the economy; and so, far from bringing class harmony, *Justicialismo* simply deepened the cleavage that divided political authority from economic power in Argentina.

In 1946–8 all seemed to go well for Perón. Buoyant food exports to a ravaged post-war Europe ensured healthy economic growth and high revenues for the state. During these years the government nationalized the central bank, the telephone company, the railways and the docks. In 1947 the whole of the national debt was paid off, and a Declaration of Economic Independence was proclaimed. The export-economy was brought under a measure of state control with the creation of a government monopoly, IAPI, which bought domestic agricultural products at fixed low prices and sold them at high prices abroad. The profits were used to finance welfare projects and to subsidize domestic industrialists, whose products were protected from foreign competitors by high tariffs and stringent exchange controls. Internal demand was stimulated by large wage rises, and industrial output increased as a result. Until 1948, therefore, Perón's political power appeared impregnable, but thereafter the entire strategy of channelling resources from the export-economy to invest in domestic industrialization began to disintegrate.

The main cause of the crisis was a steep decline in export earnings as a result of foreign competition and errors in Perón's own policies. Wheat exports to Europe were being squeezed out by a reviving European agriculture and by North American cereals. The latter were subsidized by the provisions of the 1947 Marshall Plan, which was designed in part to stimulate US and Canadian agrarian exports to dollar-aided European markets to the detriment of Argentina and other world competitors. Since most of the imports for Argentine industry were bought in the USA, Perón found himself in an acute balance of payments crisis, with no dollars to pay for the American technology Argentine industry needed and little prospect of earning them on an American-dominated world grain market. In 1949 the USA granted Perón a 'credit' of $125 million (Perón refused to call it a loan so as not to compromise his much-vaunted economic independence).

The decline in beef exports, however, was due more to internal policy decisions. There was still demand for beef in Britain, Argentina's traditional export market, but large wage rises led to sharply increased consumption of beef in Argentina itself, which reduced exports and depleted foreign earnings. The problems of the export-economy were compounded by a severe drought in 1948, and by cut-backs in production as farmers reacted to unrealistically low prices imposed by the government. Finally, Argentina faced a shortage of energy as the needs of industry exceeded capacity to import oil and coal.

By 1949 the economy was in severe crisis: export earnings had dropped by 30 per cent on the previous year, dollar reserves were exhausted, industrial output was stagnant, unemployment rose, and inflation shot up to 33 per cent. Perón was now forced to revise his nationalist economic policies. He put additional resources and investment into agriculture in order to revive the export-economy. To cut inflation, he introduced an austerity package, which included a two-year wage freeze to be followed by a social pact on prices and incomes negotiated between unions and employers. At the same time, he wanted to maintain the drive to industrialize, but the counter-inflationary cuts in public spending left him with less money to invest in industry. To make up for this shortfall Perón turned to foreign investors. In 1952 the doors were opened to transnational companies. Perón needed them to relieve unemployment and to improve the balance of payments with their exports. Also, their presence would help modernize the industrial base with new technology and business methods. In 1954 he made a notorious deal with Standard Oil, which gave the US corporation the right to develop the oilfields of Patagonia. Perón was looking for a quick and efficient means of relieving the energy problem which was holding back Argentine industry, but ever since the time of Yrigoyen the oil industry had been a symbol of economic sovereignty for nationalists. Perón's new policies therefore carried a high risk of upsetting two of his key constituencies: organized labour and domestic industrialists.

For a time the situation improved, but the underlying problems remained. Agricultural exports failed to revive sufficiently to reverse the balance of payments deficit; state-protected industries continued to stagnate, crippled by mounting import costs and faltering energy supplies; inflation picked up and put acute pressure on wage controls. As the economy deteriorated and policy departed in practice from loudly proclaimed ideals, Perón took steps to tighten his grip on the country.

From 1950, when the economic crisis first started to make an impact on large groups in society, there had been a drive to 'Peronize' Argentina. Individual rights, political freedoms and the free institutions of civil society were steadily eroded by the Peronist state. Opponents, such as the Radical leader Ricardo Balbín and dissident trade unionists, were persecuted or imprisoned under a new law of *desacato* (contempt) for the authorities; the critical press was hamstrung by selectively rationed newsprint, while Peronist publications flourished; in 1951 the great liberal newspaper *La Prensa* was expropriated and handed over to the Peronist CGT labour confederation. Corporatism was taking a violent lurch towards totalitarianism in the name of '*La Comunidad Organizada*', which involved the extension of government control over independent unions, employers' organizations, professional associations, schools and universities.

Feverish propaganda and political theatre accompanied this push to Peronize the nation. When Eva Perón died at the age of thirty-three in July 1952, Peronism acquired a myth whose tragic associations gave it an almost hypnotic power over the urban masses. Less than a year later, in April 1953, as the shadows of disaster fell over the economy, Peronist frustration spilled over into ugly mob violence: the Jockey Club in Buenos Aires, the preserve of the *estanciero* élite, was set ablaze, as were the headquarters of the Radical and Socialist parties.

This growing malaise caused disquiet in the armed forces, despite Perón's efforts to placate the officer corps with various forms of patronage. Apart from a feeble coup attempt in 1951, the military remained divided as ever on political matters and held back from intervention, but when Perón took on the Catholic Church the army finally lost patience with him. Initially supportive, the Church turned hostile after Peronism began to encroach on its traditional domains of education, welfare and public morals. It regarded with distaste the pseudo-religious trappings of the Peronist personality cult, refusing for instance to support appeals by the *descamisados* to have the deceased Evita canonized by the Vatican. When in 1954 Perón legalized divorce and secularized education, relations with the Church reached break-ing-point.

As one of the last and the greatest of the autonomous institutions in a Peronized Argentina, the Catholic Church became the focus of resistance to Perón. Religious processions attracted large multitudes, larger than any counter-demonstrations that the Peronists were able to muster. Con-frontation led to open violence in June 1955, when military aircraft, in an attempt to spark a *coup d'état*, bombed the presidential palace during a mass rally of Peronists, killing several hundred people. This outrage inflamed the political atmosphere: the Peronists responded by putting many churches in Buenos Aires to the torch; violence and counter-violence broke out in the streets; finally, at a rally on 31 August, Perón exhorted his followers to take up arms and kill five opponents for every murdered Peronist; civil war appeared to be imminent. Two weeks later a series of army revolts succeeded in toppling Perón, who was allowed to escape to Paraguay.

The Return to Limited Democracy: Radical Governments after Perón (1955–66)

Needless to say, the ejection of the person of Juan Domingo Perón from the political stage of Argentina did not put an end to Peronism. For the next two decades, *El Líder* exercised a baleful influence over Argentine politics from his place of exile in Madrid. He had powerful resources at his command: a mass party of the urban lower-middle and working classes; the CGT, a trade-union confederation that utterly dominated the Argentine industrial labour force; the sacred myth of the dead Evita, once revered as the 'Spiritual Chief of the Nation'; and, not least, the messianic promise of his own second coming as the ultimate incentive to political action for his followers.

Perón also left another and more pervasive legacy in the structure of the Argentine state and economy: the state bureaucracy served a vast array of government monopolies and nationalized industries, which consumed huge amounts of public money and remained geared politically to satisfying urban interests regardless of the nation's overall economic performance. In effect, Perón had converted the state into a machine for producing budget deficits, trade imbalances and chronic inflation.

The outstanding problem for his successors, civilian and military alike, was how to bring this sprawling public sector under financial control without inducing a catastrophic urban recession, while at the same time finding measures to reverse the long-term decline in agricultural and industrial production. To make this problem worse, the Peronist apparatus was capable of being used as a political wrecking device to thwart repeated attempts at economic reconstruction. And so the split between political and economic power in Argentina continued to be as deep as ever: inflation and public deficits needed to be tackled in order to prevent further deterioration of the productive base of the economy, but any plans to solve these problems met with bitter opposition from the Peronists.

After the ousting of Perón, the armed forces had two principal alternatives for the regeneration of the country. The first was to try and bring political and economic realities as much into line with each other as possible – either by admitting the Peronist party and trade unions into the political system so as to win their compliance in the management of the economy, or by excluding the Peronists altogether and permitting other parties such as the Radicals to form governments with whatever measure of public support they might be able to summon. The second alternative was to suspend electoral politics altogether and install a technocratic military dictatorship which could attack the deep-seated problems of the economy without interference from political parties or civilian vested interests.

In 1955–66 there were several attempts to relaunch electoral politics, though with the Peronist apparatus restricted in some degree. Between 1955 and 1958 attempts by the military to organize 'Peronism without Perón' failed when the Peronists refused to be co-opted into the system while their leader was in exile. Then the Radicals were allowed to form a government, led by Arturo Frondizi, which managed to last from 1958 to 1962, eventually foundering on the rocks of Peronist opposition to its anti-inflation programme, nationalist attacks on concessions to foreign capital, and the hostility of domestic industrialists to high import prices resulting from the devaluation of the peso. Frondizi finally tried to appease the Peronists by legalizing their party, but when in 1962 they won the largest share of seats in the congress, together with several provincial governorships, the army chiefs compelled Frondizi to annul the elections. Within days he was ousted by a military coup.

Once more the armed forces tried to set up a civilian government. In 1962 the Yrigoyenista wing of the Radical Party was called to office under Arturo Illia, but even though he raised wages and held down prices, he too found it impossible to make much headway against the implacable campaign of strikes and occupations mounted by the Peronist CGT. Like Frondizi, Illia tried to conciliate the Peronists by legalizing their party, and once again they beat the Radicals in the congressional elections of 1965. By this time the economy was in a mess, with mounting inflation and an unmanageable public deficit. It was clear that democratic politics could not be conducted without the Peronists – they quite simply dominated all the elections they were allowed to contest – and yet neither could the economy be radically overhauled, in the view of the armed forces, with the Peronists in power. Given this dilemma, the military decided to try the second alternative for governing the country after Perón – the indefinite suspension of electoral politics and the establishment of a technocratic military regime. On 28 June 1966 Illia was overthrown and General Juan Carlos Onganía announced the coming of yet another *Revolución argentina*.

The Onganiato (1966–70)

Onganía intended to create a system which, like those in Brazil after the military coup of 1964 and in Franco's Spain in the 1960s, would rely upon the armed forces to maintain social order while technical experts got on with the business of economic modernization. Under his finance minister, Adalberto Krieger Vasena, a plan for financial stabilization, combined with export recovery, was put into effect. It differed from earlier stabilization plans introduced by both Perón and Frondizi in that it was designed to stimulate agricultural growth without creating urban recession. Inflation came down to 7.6 per cent in 1969, but exports remained steady and investment in energy and infrastructure climbed to a rate of 22 per cent a year in 1966–9. The Argentine 'economic miracle' appeared to be at hand. What is more, in the political sphere, Onganía seemed to have beaten the political parties into an unwonted submission: after the failure of a general strike in 1967, even the CGT, the Peronist confederation of labour unions, started to fragment.

The political calm, however, turned out to be superficial. In May 1969 an extraordinary uprising took place in the industrial city of Córdoba, the seat of a new motor-car industry. It was led by students and car workers in protest against cuts in university funding, job losses and other effects of Onganía's austerity programme. For two days the streets of the city were engulfed by rioting civilians. The *cordobazo*, as the uprising became known, led to a nationwide resurgence of militancy by the Peronist trade unions. It also fostered a belief among Marxist students and Peronist youth in the efficacy of direct revolutionary violence as a means of overthrowing the capitalist state. In this respect the *cordobazo* was in keeping with the spirit of the times: it can be regarded as the Argentine equivalent of the Paris *événements* of 1968 or the student protest movement in Mexico which had resulted in the Tlatelolco massacre. But when considered in this context, the *cordobazo* reveals the weakness of the Argentine state when compared to Gaullist France or the Mexico of the Institutional Revolutionary Party. After the traumas of Peronism and the miserable failure of truncated democratic government under the Radicals, Onganía's military junta had failed to muster the requisite political consent for its plans to regenerate the nation.

But lack of consent does not fully account for the swiftness of Onganía's fall after the Córdoba uprising. It was also caused by the endemic disunity of the Argentine armed forces, for ever since their first coup in 1930 they had been divided over the direction in which to take the country. At critical junctures, such as 1943, 1946 and 1955, they had not quite known how to exercise the power they had seized. This disorientation had allowed Perón to take over in 1946, because he at least offered an inspiring ideology. By contrast, Onganía had not succeeded in uniting the military behind a convincing vision of Argentina's future. After 1969, unnerved by continuing industrial unrest, riots in provincial cities, bad economic performance and, not least, the emergence of urban guerrilla groups, the generals wavered once again. When in March 1970 Peronist guerrillas kidnapped and murdered General Aramburu, a former president and a member of the junta which had ousted Perón in 1955, Onganía was overthrown. General Roberto Levingston, who replaced him, having failed to bring order to the country, was in turn deposed a year later by General Alejandro Lanusse.

In the meantime, the economy had cut adrift from the Krieger Vasena stabilization plan and was clearly heading for disaster: budget deficits climbed ever higher and the rate of inflation approached 60 per cent in 1972. Lanusse came to the view that military options for governing the country had been exhausted; not only had a controlled, semi-representative government failed, but so too had outright military technocracy; the nation, it appeared, was ungovernable without Perón, who alone could put an end to the escalating terrorism and reconcile political forces to the need for economic discipline.

A Second Chance for Peronism (1973–6)

Juan Perón had indeed proved that he was indispensable. But nearly two decades of exile had taken their toll. *El Conductor* was now an ailing 77-year-old; his wife, Isabel, a former nightclub dancer he had met in Panama, lacked the magnetism of Evita. Also, the Peronist movement itself had changed; it was riven by factionalism: at one extreme there were the unreconstructed militants, pledged still to the fascistic nationalism of the 1940s; in the middle ground, Peronism had mellowed into something akin to social democracy; while on its left, the movement had put out Guevarist shoots in the early 1960s among middle-class university students, who envisaged turning the struggle into a war of 'national liberation'. The Peronist youth, in fact, had nurtured a powerful guerrilla force called the Montoneros, who clashed repeatedly with the old-guard Peronist bosses for control of the trade unions.

The way for Perón's return was paved by the election to the presidency in March 1973 of Héctor Cámpora, a man on the traditionalist right wing of the movement. Perón's choice of Cámpora as a stand-in was a signal as much to the guerrillas as to the armed forces that Peronism was not in the business of installing the dictatorship of the proletariat. Indeed, Cámpora devised an anti-inflationary plan ratified by a social pact between employers and trade unions. A wide spectrum of Argentine opinion, from conservatives to traditional Peronists, felt this plan to be a last-ditch attempt to stave off chaos. But the social pact rested on a consensus of despair, and the urban guerrillas would have none of it. Both the Peronist Montoneros and the Trotskyite ERP (Revolutionary Army of the People) continued with their campaign of bombings, kidnappings and assassinations.

The deteriorating political situation persuaded Perón to return to Argentina straight away. The welcome he received at Ezeiza Airport in June 1973 amply illustrated the troubled state of the movement that bore his name. A gathering of about 500,000 supporters degenerated into violent confusion as Montoneros fought with armed trade-unionists, leaving several hundred people dead or wounded. A bare month after this incident Cámpora resigned and elections were called for September. Perón was duly swept into office with 62 per cent of the vote. His wife, Isabel, was elected vice-president.

With the return of Perón, history appeared to repeat itself. Though politics were in turmoil, external trade was experiencing a boom as high world prices boosted Argentina's exports of grain and beef. Cámpora's social pact, which Perón maintained, had by late 1973 brought inflation down to 30 per cent and increased real wage values by 13.3 per cent. These signs of imminent economic success buttressed Perón's popularity and encouraged him to implement the kind of nationalist and statist policies that he had tried in the 1940s. He nationalized banks and industries, subsidized native businesses and urban consumers, taxed and regulated the agricultural sector, revived the IAPI, and restricted foreign investment.

While he consolidated his position along these familiar lines, Perón began to attack the problem of the guerrillas. The Montoneros remained refractory within the wider Peronist movement: their blood feud with the trade-union leadership showed no sign of abating. In September 1973 they had gone so far as to assassinate José Rucci, the secretary-general of the CGT, the Peronist labour confederation. For its part, the ERP had intensified its attacks on the armed forces and continued to extort money through kidnaps and bank robberies. With the support of the army and the trade unions, Perón set out to crush the guerrillas. He openly repudiated the Montoneros, and passed harsher laws against political subversion. And yet he seemed to turn a blind eye to the activities of a secret organization calling itself the Argentine Anti-Communist Alliance – popularly referred to as the Triple A – which from early 1974 had commenced operations against the revolutionary left, abducting and killing known militants.

Perón's second attempt at regenerating Argentina was cut short by his death on 1 July 1974. By that time the prospects of success did not look very good. During 1974 there was a particularly sharp downswing in the economy, and by 1975 it seemed bound for catastrophe: inflation, for instance, soared to 183 per cent and continued rising at a rate of 30 per cent a month. After Perón's death the presidency passed to his wife, Isabel, who quickly proved unequal to the task of managing a stricken economy in the teeth of a ferocious guerrilla insurgency. The social pact collapsed and no further stabilizing measures could be made to prevail against the huge strikes organized by the trade unions against their own Peronist government.

In November 1974 a state of emergency was declared, which gave the army a virtually free hand to mount an offensive against the guerrillas. This it did with ruthless determination, resorting to clandestine operations to root out terrorism. In this so-called 'dirty war', which continued virtually until the end of the decade, the guerrilla armies were ground down by a strategy of lawless violence. The anti-subversive net widened arbitrarily to take in students, lawyers, journalists, trade-unionists and anyone suspected of aiding the guerrillas. These presumed subversives were spirited away in unmarked Ford Falcon cars to meet their fate at the hands of illicit death squads. Between 10,000 and 20,000 people were made to 'disappear'. The *desaparecidos* were taken to secret detention centres, where they were tortured or put to death. Meanwhile, the unfortunate Isabel Perón and her government were allowed by the army to hang on in office until March 1976, sufficient time for Argentina's second experiment with Peronism to destroy itself by its own brutal contradictions.

Military Government (1976–84)

When the armed forces took over the government in 1976, the only option that seemed available to them was to revive Onganía's technocratic dictatorship as a means of radically restructuring the economy. Military officers were appointed to run ministries, state enterprises and public bodies. The main aim was to return to a sound economy by conquering inflation and eliminating the budget deficit. This appeared to require the kind of 'iron surgery' that General Pinochet was applying in neighbouring Chile at the time: unbending repression of the left combined with neo-liberal economic policies. But Perón had created such a comprehensive network of state intervention and subsidy that in the late 1970s a programme of economic liberalization amounted to a declaration of war against urban society.

The economic programme of the new finance minister, José Martínez de Hoz, was designed in theory to roll back the frontiers of the state and reinstate the free market as the driving force of the economy. What occurred was a sudden, massive transfer of resources from the urban industrial sector to the agrarian export sector in a violent reversal of a trend that had dominated the Argentine economy for over thirty years. In 1976–7 real wages in industry fell by 50 per cent, the largest drop on record; food prices were raised and welfare subsidies withdrawn. These measures were accompanied by the attempted destruction of the labour movement. The Peronist CGT was abolished, strikes were made illegal and the death squads caused working-class activists to 'disappear' (a report on human rights in 1978 claimed that some 37 per cent of the *desaparecidos* were shop stewards or trade-union officials). Manufacturing industry contracted sharply during 1976 when tariff protection was removed, and collapsed internal demand led to falls in output and the shedding of up to 10 per cent of the workforce. On the other hand, market forces and government incentives boosted Argentina's ever resilient export-economy, producing a surplus of $900 million in the balance of trade in 1976 after a deficit of $1 billion the year before.

This programme of national regeneration was yet another attempt to remedy the split between economic and political power in Argentina; only this time the army was employing force to break the political organizations of the urban classes in order to withdraw the benefits they had obtained from the export-economy over several decades. But even though the military might have succeeded in destroying the political power of urban society, it could not hope to create a state that could exist other than by brute force. The divide remained: the success of the export-economy could not endure without political legitimacy, and yet the consent of the urban majority was required to legitimize the state. The problem of winning the consent of the urban classes was to preoccupy the military rulers in the late 1970s.

By 1978 the dominant military faction led by General Jorge Videla was unhappy with low urban wages and a depressed industry; they baulked at the prospect of the indefinite 'pauperization', as David Rock termed it, of the urban classes.* Martínez de Hoz was not allowed to continue with the privatization of the gigantic public sector, much of which was being lucratively run by military men anyway, and so it proved impossible to cut subsidies to state corporations and reduce government spending sufficiently to cut inflation for long; it remained at around 150 per cent, after having dropped from nearly 400 per cent in 1976. On the other hand, high interest rates attracted a large influx of speculative foreign capital. This led to an overvalued currency, which hit exports, and to very expensive credit for domestic industry, which kept output very low. As the balance of trade worsened, growth faltered. In 1980, external trade went sharply into deficit and there occurred a series of financial crashes accompanied by spectacular capital flight as investors lost confidence in the economy. In February 1981 a sudden devaluation designed to help exports led to a further massive run on the peso, resulting in an outflow of capital from the country of some $4.8 billion. Argentina's foreign debt had risen to $35.6 billion, with interest payments equivalent to 31.7 per cent of export earnings.

These multiple crises sowed discord in the armed forces. In March 1981 the leader of the junta, General Jorge Videla, handed over the presidency to another relative moderate, General Roberto Viola; the finance minister Martínez de Hoz resigned. Viola contemplated opening a dialogue with civilian politicians, and even making a deal with the Peronists in order to win some political support for the junta. But there was a hard-line faction, led by General Leopoldo Galtieri, for whom any accommodation with Peronism was out of the question. As the economic depression deepened, Galtieri staged a successful coup in December 1981. He then reinstated the original drive to rectify the economy by privatizing the state sector and reining in government spending (except for expenditure on armaments, which continued to rise).

Galtieri realized that he needed to broaden popular support for the junta if his economic policies were to have a chance of success, and so he decided to play the nationalist card. First, in January 1982, he revived an old territorial dispute with Chile over the Beagle Channel. Then, as the economy stumbled

* *Argentina: 1516–1982* (I. B. Tauris: London, 1986), p. 369.

ever deeper into crisis and political opposition to the junta strengthened, he came up with the idea of invading the sparsely inhabited Falkland Islands in the South Atlantic, whose sovereignty Argentina had claimed ever since Britain had occupied them in 1833. Perón had renewed the claim to the Malvinas in the 1940s and the issue had been on the Argentine foreign-policy agenda ever since. It was believed that a successful take-over of the islands – which were situated 8,000 miles from Britain and were therefore unlikely to be worth recapturing – would be a spectacular way of stealing the Peronists' nationalist clothes and distracting a restive populace from the tribulations of a renewed neo-liberal assault on the nationalized economy. Yet, contrary to expectations, the British government responded to the Argentine invasion of the islands of 2 April 1982 by sending a task force to the South Atlantic. Three months later, the British had retaken the Falklands, forcing the surrender of the 10,000 Argentine troops, most of them conscripts, which the junta had sent out to defend the islands.

The débâcle of the Malvinas destroyed the credibility of the armed forces as the ultimate guardians of the nation's interests. By this time the economy was in an appalling state: inflation exceeded 200 per cent, the peso had plummeted, and the ratio of export earnings to interest payments on the external debt had risen to over 54 per cent. Like other Latin American countries, Argentina had to suspend payments to its foreign creditors. As the inadequacies of the military government could no longer be concealed, Galtieri resigned and his successors promised to implement a phased return to constitutional democracy.

The Restoration of Democracy (1983–9)

The restoration of democracy in 1983 was greeted with euphoria; it marked a return to the principles upon which the republic had been founded. There was need of political as much as economic reconstruction, for if electoral manipulation had been commonplace under the Concordancia governments of the 1930s, and then again in the 1950s and early 1960s, the very principle of representative democracy based on consent and the rule of law had suffered a succession of shattering blows from Perón's quasi-fascist populism, from military authoritarians and from Marxist revolutionaries. Each of these anti-liberal alternatives had arisen in response to the fundamental problem of modernizing the Argentine economy. All of them had so far failed because they had been overwhelmed by the conflicts of interest that so deeply divided Argentine society. It was now hoped that the sheer scale of the catastrophe that had befallen Argentina would allow for a new political settlement under which a democratically elected government could win sufficient popular consent to undertake the restructuring of the economy.

In December 1983 Raúl Alfonsín of the Radical Party was elected president with the promise of healing the divisions of this much traumatized society. But Alfonsín had to embark on his programme of reform under the shadow of the crippling foreign debt, exceeding $45 billion and consuming over 50 per cent of export earnings in interest payments. He had little option but to accept an austerity plan from the IMF in return for further loans to pay interest. On the other hand, he had to win consent for his policies, particularly from organized labour, which was controlled as ever by the Peronists, the Radical Party's old enemies. The survival of democracy depended, therefore, on Alfonsín's success in reconciling economic and political interests. The inflation rate of over 1,000 per cent needed to be reduced, but growth had to be restored to urban society by stimulating the productivity of manufacturing as much as of agriculture.

A more direct threat to democratic institutions came from the opposition of the armed forces to the trials of military officers for breaches of human rights during the dirty war against the urban guerrillas in the 1970s. Public concern over allegations of systematic torture of detainees had been aroused by weekly demonstrations in the Plaza de Mayo in Buenos Aires, carried out in dignified silence by the mothers of those many thousands of young people who had been made to disappear in the previous decade. The cause of the *desaparecidos* became a kind of litmus test of the efficacy of the rule of law under the new democracy. Alfonsín was anxious to bring the offenders to book, but he had to consider the risk of provoking a *coup d'état*. For the armed forces persisted in justifying their counter-insurgency methods as necessary in a situation of internal war. They believed that their corporate honour was being insulted by one-sided accusations of brutality.

In June 1985 Alfonsín unveiled a package of reforms to cut runaway inflation and restore growth. Its centre-piece was the creation of a new currency called the austral to replace the worthless peso, and it was backed by a government resolution not to resort to printing money to finance public deficits. To reinforce the anti-inflationary drive, wages and prices were frozen indefinitely and public spending was to be cut back to eliminate waste. This new start for the nation was symbolized by the announcement that the Argentine capital would be moved from Buenos Aires to the small Patagonian town of Viedma. In addition, the government decided to privatize state industries and promote the export of manufactured goods to complement the traditional agricultural export-economy. The Austral Plan was meant to induce a psychological break with the past, and indeed Alfonsín sought to win popular consent by claiming that the survival of democracy depended on the success of his reform programme.

The Austral Plan seemed to work for a while, but it created a deep recession, output falling by over 4 per cent in 1985. Though growth resumed in the following year and inflation was brought down to about 50 per cent, economic austerity proved too difficult to maintain: social pressures forced up government spending, despite repeated efforts to streamline the public sector and avoid deficit financing. By 1987 the success of the Austral Plan was in the balance. Alfonsín needed to consolidate his authority to make his reforms stick; he hoped to win agreement for a social pact with the employers and the Peronist unions in order to improve the position of wage-earners without fuelling inflation. Nevertheless, there were already ominous signs that his authority was crumbling.

The most flagrant challenge to the authority of the democratic government came, predictably, from the army, which was aggrieved by the trials of former members of the military juntas and other officers involved in the dirty war, as well as by cuts in defence budgets. During the Easter weekend of 1987, a *pronunciamiento* led by a colonel at the main military base outside Buenos Aires was headed off by Alfonsín, who managed to enlist the support of the high command, though this raised public fears that he might have succumbed to military demands for the curtailment of human rights trials.

More seriously, the government began to lose the support of the general public, which was tiring of the constant appeals to tighten its belt and was frustrated with the erosion of wages by persistent inflation. Until 1987 there had existed a consensus between the Radicals and the Peronists over the imperative need to preserve democracy, and this had allowed Alfonsín to pass unpopular economic measures. This consensus had been facilitated by the fact that the leadership of the Peronists was in the hands of social-democratic moderates, called the *renovadores* because they wanted to shed the authoritarian image of the movement. But social discontent was altering this correlation of forces within Peronism and playing into the hands of the populist wing, which was dominated by the old-style *caudillos* of the trade-union machine, who called an increasing number of strikes.

The turning-point for Alfonsín came at the congressional and provincial elections in September 1987. The Radicals lost their majority in the chamber of deputies as well as sixteen of the twenty-one provinces, including Buenos Aires, to the Peronists. These losses convinced Alfonsín that he could not rule without the goodwill of the Peronist Party. He tried to put together a new social pact to see through yet another bout of austerity, but failed to persuade the Peronists, who organized a general strike in November (there were to be some thirteen general strikes during Alfonsín's term of office), and then blocked in the senate the passage of measures to cut the budget deficit. Despite a trade surplus in 1987, the worsening public deficits increased the costs of servicing the foreign debt, and there resumed political pressure on Alfonsín to seek a moratorium on repayments in 1988. The government was caught in a vice between the demands for austerity by the IMF and resistance to belt-tightening from unions at home. It had by now forfeited its authority in the management of the economy.

The impression of drift in government policy encouraged two further military rebellions in 1988, though neither succeeded. Terrorist activity revived: there were bombings by right-wing groups and, in January 1989, a force of sixty-nine left-wing guerrillas launched a surprise attack on an army barracks near Buenos Aires, holding it for thirty-two hours before being defeated by army units. The guerrillas claimed to have acted in defence of democracy by forestalling a military coup, but President Alfonsín later addressed the nation flanked by generals and praised the army for preserving the democratic system. Clearly, democracy was an ideal that everyone still supported, though many Argentines were becoming disenchanted with it in practice. One effect of the guerrillas' action was to restore some credibility to the historic claim of the armed forces to be the saviours of the nation. But the danger remained that if electoral politics failed to maintain public order, the military might decide once more that the nation must be saved from democracy itself.

The next presidential elections were due in May 1989, and the Radicals were rapidly losing popular support to the Peronists. Alfonsín tried to hold the line on inflation, but economic difficulties were getting the better of his administration: economic growth was sluggish and the budget deficit consumed over 10 per cent of GDP. Public services had broken down to the point of constituting a menace to health: at the height of the Argentine summer in January 1989, power cuts of up to six hours a day had to be imposed in the cities, with the risk of water shortages and epidemics breaking out in the insanitary shantytowns. During the election campaign, the government, clearly heading for defeat, lost the last vestiges of control over the economy; inflation shot up to an annual rate of well over 1,000 per cent.

The victor at the polls was the flamboyant Carlos Saúl Menem, a Peronist from the traditional wing of the party who appeared to hold emphatic nationalist views and had campaigned on the usual populist policies favoured by the Peronists, such as large rises to compensate wage-earners for soaring prices. In the months before Menem was due to take office, inflation rose to a compound annual rate of 28,000 per cent. The outgoing president, Alfonsín, declared a state of siege to cope with the food riots and looting that broke out in poorer districts of the cities. The survival of Argentine democracy hung on Menem's ability to recreate a consensus on the means of overcoming the appalling economic problems faced by the nation.

To everyone's surprise Menem attempted to achieve this consensus by throwing the weight of the Peronist movement's immense reserves of loyalty among the urban masses behind a radical programme of economic reconstruction involving deep cuts in state spending, reductions in the Argentine bureaucracy, the privatization of many loss-making companies in the huge public sector, and the opening of the economy to foreign investment. It was a balancing act fraught with risks, for it asked the Peronist masses to put up with the most radical by far of the many anti-inflationary programmes that the Peronist machine had been destroying regularly since 1955.

Menem persevered with his neo-liberal policies, but by mid-1990 they had split the Peronist movement, and militant labour leaders were calling strikes against the cut-backs in state industries and the drop in real wages. In spite of this, there was a great public awareness that the country was on the brink of complete collapse through hyperinflation and the burden of the foreign debt, and that desperate measures had therefore to be taken. There were also well-grounded fears of further military threats to the democratic system – a *coup d'état* could well result in the sort of blood bath the country had endured in the 1970s. However, if Menem were to succeed in curbing inflation and in making industry and agriculture more competitive in world markets, Argentina could begin to recover its economic wealth, and its democratic system might become permanently secure.

In the course of the twentieth century Argentina proved unable to modernize itself either by revolution or by reform. The export-economy, dominated still by a seigneurial élite, remained inefficient relative to its foreign competitors. Manufacturing industry was sustained by state protection and could not compete with foreign business without drastic overhaul. No regime was able to carry out the interrelated tasks of making the agricultural sector more productive and achieving self-sustaining growth in manufacturing. On the contrary, agriculture and industry remained at variance with each other, improvements in the one incurring costs in the other.

The decline from the great wealth of the first decades of the century eroded the foundations of the liberal state. For the conflict between the countryside and the cities destroyed the oligarchic consensus which had sustained constitutional government. Efforts to create a new non-liberal state failed. Juan Perón tried twice with a combination of populist nationalism and corporatism. In the 1970s Marxist guerrillas attempted the violent overthrow of the capitalist system, but were defeated. The armed forces intervened in government on numerous occasions; yet they too failed to regenerate the nation because they reflected the confusion of civilian politics rather than offering a coherent vision of their own. What eluded Argentina was a state-idea that could command general allegiance. For only a government with authority based on consent could succeed in restructuring the economy. And without such restructuring, Argentina, though rich in human and natural resources, was unlikely to recover the prosperity it had once enjoyed.

14. Chile: Democracy, Revolution and Dictatorship

The Parliamentary Republic (1891–1924)

Chile had emerged after independence as the most stable and economically dynamic of the Latin American republics. Its stability was built on the strong presidential regime established by Diego Portales in the 1833 constitution, and the system had been able to function so well because, thanks to its relatively centralized élites, the country had escaped the problem of regional separatism, which, under the guise of federalism, had caused so much havoc in its sister republics.

In the second half of the nineteenth century, these élites of landowners and merchants had been enlarged with the rise of capitalist mine-owners in the north, where extensive mining of copper and nitrates changed the character of the national economy. Success in the War of the Pacific against Peru and Bolivia (1879–83) yielded to Chile further deposits of nitrates, so that by the last quarter of the century the economy had come to rely on the export of these minerals to Europe, especially to Britain and Germany. The wealth generated by this export-economy had enormously enriched the élites, but it also led to the rise of an urban middle class and a significant proletariat in the capital city and in the mining towns of the north. Economic development produced social complexity, and with this came conflicts of interest which led eventually to the breakdown of the liberal order.

The first casualty of progress was the Portalian constitution. After a brief but bloody civil war in 1891 between two oligarchic factions of conservatives and liberals, the power of the presidency was curtailed by congress. There followed a 'parliamentary republic', in which a number of élite interest-groups dressed up as political parties vied for power and state patronage. In the words of Harold Blakemore, 'opportunism was the creed of most, and only the Conservatives and Radicals had a distinctive ideology, revolving around clerical issues'.* Yet if national politics was still largely concerned

* Cambridge History of Latin America, vol. 5, p. 524.

with patronage and the separation of Church and state, the first two decades of the new century produced a 'social question' which steadily began to interact with the parliamentary affairs of the privileged minority.

The 'social question' arose because the development of the mining export-economy created a deepening split between the countryside and the city. The rising urban population did not share the deferential attitude of the peasants to the great landowners who controlled the parliamentary system. These urban classes were more exposed to the fluctuations of the export-economy than were the peasants. The potential for unrest was greater in the cities, for in times of recession city people could not fall back on subsistence farming, and their wages were particularly vulnerable to the inflation which had become endemic since the 1880s.

The mass of wage-earners were excluded from political life by a restricted franchise and the machine politics of the established parties. The Chilean oligarchy, despite the success of the mining economy, remained profoundly traditional; their attitudes were still conditioned by seigneurial Hispanic values, which acted as a powerful brake on the development of a modern capitalist society, despite the free-trade philosophy to which they subscribed. The material aspirations of the middle and working classes ran up, therefore, against an arthritic structure of aristocratic privilege based in the countryside. From the early decades of the twentieth century, stable, prosperous Chile would slowly converge with the more troubled mainstream of Latin American republics, as the developing struggle between the new urban classes and the traditional agrarian society broke surface and churned up the politics of the parliamentary system. Even so, the historic strength of constitutional legality in Chile was to give this fundamental conflict a special character of its own.

Challenges to the Oligarchic Regime

Led by anarchist and syndicalist militants, the nascent working class sought improvements in living standards through strike action and revolutionary agitation. Between 1890 and 1910 over 250 strikes took place. During a 'Red Week' in October 1905 there were bloody clashes in the capital, Santiago, between rioting workers and upper-class youths of the Patriotic League; in 1907 a violent strike erupted in the northern mining town of Iquique, which ended in a massacre of workers by the army. Although unions were illegal, this labour agitation extracted some social legislation from the parliament on accident insurance, Sunday holidays and limited retirement benefits.

But living conditions for the working class otherwise remained harsh and insecure.

Labour unrest revived in 1917–19, when the anarchist unions mobilized great numbers of workers against the inflationary upsurge brought about by the First World War. The anarcho-syndicalist unions, however, began to lose influence to communist and socialist groups, especially after the failure of a general strike called in Santiago in September 1919. The great leader of the working class in these years was the printer, Luis Emilio Recabarren. Initially a member of the Workers' Federation of Chile (FOCH) founded in 1909 and encompassing socialists, anarchists and radical democrats, Recabarren moved it in the direction of Marxism and eventually linked it to the Communist Party, which he helped to found in 1922. Recabarren's great organizational skills would ensure that communism would displace anarcho-syndicalism as the dominant force in the Chilean labour movement. Indeed, the Chilean party was to become the most powerful of all the communist parties in Latin America.

By the late 1910s the impact of urban labour and the middle classes on national life was great enough to persuade the more radical liberals in the established oligarchic parties that their support would be useful in wresting power from their parliamentary rivals. A Liberal Alliance came into existence, which promised to bring the urban classes into the political system. By 1918 the Liberal Alliance had won enough support in the cities to gain a majority in the chamber of deputies. In 1920 its candidate, Arturo Alessandri, won the presidency.

Like the Radical president Yrigoyen in Argentina, Alessandri proposed to expand the economic role of the state by redistributing national income through labour and educational reforms, social welfare, and low-cost housing. But this interventionism of the state – exemplified also in Alessandri's proposals to nationalize banks and insurance companies – split the Liberal Alliance, and met with fierce opposition in congress. Ironically, the reforming populist Alessandri, finding himself thwarted by the power of congress, advocated the revival of a strong presidentialist regime like that created by the arch-conservative Portales. Chile was confronted with a political dilemma it would encounter repeatedly in the coming decades: to what extent was it possible to achieve reform without violating a democratic constitution which happened to favour the status quo?

The Military in Politics (1924–31)

On 5 September 1924 the armed forces – so often the agents of radical reform in Latin America – launched a *coup d'état* in favour of the progressive Alessandri, and suspended parliamentary politics. But Alessandri refused to rule by grace of the military and left Chile for Italy. A second military coup in January 1925 brought to power a group of young officers led by Carlos Ibáñez and Marmaduke Grove. Alessandri was invited back and he proceeded to frame a new constitution. The constitution of 1925, which was to remain in force until 1973, was intended to strengthen the hand of the president and enhance the powers of the state to intervene in the economy and in society. In fact, the staggering of elections for the presidency, senate and chamber of deputies meant that frequent elections and the resultant volatility of politics would continue to hinder the executive's room for manœuvre.

A more immediate problem was that the new constitution owed its existence to the intervention of the armed forces, a debt that the military revolutionaries were not prepared to cancel altogether. Falling world prices in the mid-1920s fuelled inflation and provoked renewed labour unrest. Friction with Carlos Ibáñez, the minister of war, who wanted to keep the labour movement on a tight rein (in June 1925 over 1,000 workers were machine-gunned by troops at La Coruña), led to the resignation of Alessandri. His successor also succumbed to Ibáñez, who eventually had himself elevated to the presidency by a rigged election in May 1927.

Ibáñez launched a programme of economic development through state intervention. He borrowed heavily from the USA and built roads, railways, irrigation systems and port facilities. He brought the state into partnership with US interests in a holding company for the nitrate industry, though with little success. Ibáñez might conceivably have evolved into a Chilean precursor of Getúlio Vargas in Brazil or Perón in Argentina; however, he did not create a political ideology, and his hostility to labour – and the strength of the Communist Party – precluded the elaboration of a corporate state which could have controlled industrial relations in times of recession. As a result, when the world depression hit Chile, Ibáñez had no political resources other than brute repression to cope with labour protests. Eventually, he was forced into exile in July 1931.

The fall of Ibáñez may have cut short one of the first experiments in authoritarian technocratic development in Latin America, but it did not altogether arrest the impetus towards state intervention. For between them, Alessandri and Ibáñez had changed the pattern of Chilean politics: the hold of the oligarchic parties over the electoral machine had been weakened, and new forces were gathering in the centre and on the left which would gradually extend the ideas of statism and economic nationalism into the mainstream of Chilean political life.

The world depression of the 1930s placed checks on this process. For a year Chile drifted without effective government. A 'socialist republic' under the leadership of Marmaduke Grove, Ibáñez's fellow conspirator in the military coup of 1925, lasted a mere thirteen days. However, it signalled the entry into politics of the Socialist Party, with a distinct Marxist orientation, as alternately a rival and an ally of the powerful Communists. This division on the left was to add a further complication to the political scene, although, paradoxically, it would prolong the agitated life of Chilean parliamentary democracy by making it more difficult for any one interest to dominate the state.

The Return to Democracy and the Rise of Economic Nationalism

The presidential election of 1932 returned Alessandri to office at a time when the country was undergoing the effects of the world depression. His finance minister, Gustavo Ross, applied orthodox measures to tackle the high inflation and revive the flagging export sector, on which the health of the rest of the economy depended. This entailed cutting public spending and dismantling some of the state bodies set up by Ibáñez. Although Ross made little impact on inflation, he succeeded in substantially reducing unemployment in a world where joblessness had become a scourge: the rate fell from over 250,000 unemployed in 1932 to below 16,000 in 1937. Real wages, however, could not keep pace with inflation and this led to the successful mobilization of labour by the Communists.

In 1935 Stalin's Communist International had directed communist parties to form alliances with socialist and left-of-centre bourgeois parties in popular fronts. In 1936 the Chilean Communists entered into an alliance with the middle-class Radicals, and two years later, with the Socialist Party. The prospect of forming a government through the Popular Front encouraged the left to increase pressure on Alessandri. From 1936 widespread industrial action threatened to upset Ross's plans for economic recovery. Alessandri's reaction was severe: he declared a state of siege, exiled labour leaders and called out the troops to break strikes in key services such as the railways. The political atmosphere became highly charged with the emergence of a Nazi party led by a Chilean of German stock, one Jorge

González von Marees, who led an attempted putsch in September 1938 just before the elections. The army put down the rebellion and Alessandri authorized the shooting of sixty-two young Nazis after they had surrendered. This lost him much public sympathy. Alessandri, the great populist leader of the 1920s, the man who had brought the urban classes into the political system and who had been a pioneer of state-led development, now found himself outmanœuvred by new forces on the left. In trying to cope with the world depression, he had lost touch with the middle classes and the workers.

It was the alliance of these two social forces in the Popular Front that pushed Chile once again towards state-led development and economic nationalism. At the presidential election of 1938 the Popular Front candidate, the Radical politician, Pedro Aguirre Cerda, beat Gustavo Ross, the liberal architect of the economic recovery of the 1930s, by a mere 4,000 votes. Under Popular Front governments, which lasted until 1946, the foundations of state capitalism were laid, its cornerstone being the Corporación de Fomento (CORFO), a government planning and investment corporation with wide-ranging powers, which was to spearhead the drive for industrialization for over three decades. Indeed, state-led development through protectionism and import-substitution was to become the unquestioned orthodoxy of successive Chilean governments until 1973.

Despite this basic continuity in the matter of industrialization and the guiding role of the state in the economy, political differences between the parties of left and centre would remain acute, and would sometimes issue in violence. For the combination of centre and left, which had produced the broad statist consensus in the first place, was itself highly unstable, since it could not agree on the limits and functions of state power as the agent of economic and social change.

After 1938, parliamentary politics divided into three broad blocs. In the centre, middle-class parties tended to favour a large state sector which could offer white-collar jobs to wage-earners and a wealth of subsidies to businessmen. But they baulked at any extension of state control that might threaten the property or security of the little man. On the left, Communists and Socialists agreed that the state should take over most of agriculture, finance and industry. They fell out, though, over questions of tactics and ideology, especially as regards the degree of compliance with constitutional legality. On the right, the old oligarchic parties representing landowners, large merchants and mine-owners remained very powerful, particularly in rural areas, but they were never able to recover their former dominance of the electoral system and were reduced to a strategy of parliamentary obstructionism, which sufficed, even so, to block radical reform.

What is striking about Chile is the absence of military interference in party politics during a period when the rest of Latin America saw a persistent meddling of the armed forces in government as many countries embarked on a course of economic nationalism through import-substituting industrialization. This was as much a reflection of the strength of the parliamentary tradition in Chile as of the general acceptance by the armed forces of the political consensus on the role of the state in fostering development. It was, after all, the military coups of 1924 and 1925 that had broken oligarchic liberalism and set Chile on the path of state-led development. So long as the military high command remained convinced that party politics were the best means of ensuring public order, and that nationalist policies would bring economic success, there would be no threat to democratic institutions.

Parliamentary politics in Chile, however, grew progressively more turbulent as the traumas of industrialization made their impact on a deadlocked party system. For the three political blocs on the right, left and centre were roughly equal in electoral strength; none of them, therefore, could alone command sufficient support at the polls to form a government without allying itself with another bloc. Given this balanced correlation of forces, the centre parties formed the hinge which determined the swings to the right or the left of any government. If the centre allied itself with the right, the parties of the left, which controlled the trade unions, were able to frustrate government policy through industrial action. On the other hand, if the centre joined with the left, the right would seek to obstruct legislation for fear of social reform. In any case, centre–left coalitions were prone to founder whenever the leadership of middle-class parties tried to curb the chronic inflation and public deficits with deflationary policies.

To make matters worse, the parliamentary system in Chile, with its staggered elections, tended to produce a majority in congress which was opposed to the policies of the incumbent president. An embattled executive, together with the fluidity of the political centre, made for bitter electoral competition between the parties. From the 1940s to the late 1960s Chile may have had a basic consensus on economic development through corporatist policies, but the tensions between capital and labour in a process of rapid industrialization grew steadily more acute.

Post-War Governments and the Advance of the Left (1946–64)

It was a split between the centre and the left which broke up the Popular
Front-type coalitions that ruled Chile in the 1940s. The third successive
Radical president, Gabriel González Videla (1946–52), at first enjoyed the
support of the Communist Party (though not of the Socialists). But when
he tried to impose a wage-freeze to reduce inflation he was faced with an
upsurge of strikes that turned violent in the teeth of fierce police repression.
González Videla then dismissed the three Communist ministers from his
cabinet, and declared a state of siege.

As the strikes and rioting continued, so did the rift between the Radicals
and the Communists deepen. In 1948 congress passed a 'Law for the Defence
of Democracy' which effectively outlawed the Communist Party. Communist militants went underground or fled into exile. It was during this
period, while on the run from González Videla's police, that the Communist
senator and Chile's greatest poet, Pablo Neruda, started to compose the
sequence of poems that became the famous *Canto general*. In that work he
expressed a vision of Latin America's historical destiny in which socialist
revolution was identified with genuine national independence from foreign
imperialists and indigenous traitors. The *Canto general* was to have an enormous emotional and psychological influence on Latin American nationalists,
shaping attitudes to progress and to the outside world in the post-war years.
It reflected also the mounting self-confidence of the Communist Party in
Chile, for despite its current persecution, it had made great advances in
municipal and parliamentary elections, and it was the dominant force in the
labour movement; now it was to make significant inroads into the intellectual
culture of the country.

Having fallen out so bitterly with the left, the Radicals and other centre
parties had nowhere to turn except towards the right. The next two presidents
emerged from the centre and right respectively, but they both failed to
alleviate Chile's economic problems, particularly as regards inflation, and so
were incapable of beating back attacks from the left. In 1952 the old populist
ex-dictator, Carlos Ibáñez, won the presidency. But he was unable to deliver
the prosperity he promised because a drop in the world price of copper after
the end of the Korean War produced a major upset in the balance of payments
and drove up inflation. Ibáñez, though a self-proclaimed nationalist, had to
go for assistance to the International Monetary Fund, which dictated an
austerity package to halt the rise in prices. This was denounced by the left
as a sell-out to imperialism, and Ibáñez's efforts to implement the IMF
stabilization plan were frustrated by strikes and riots.

The 1958 election gave a narrow victory to the right. Jorge Alessandri, the son of the old Liberal leader Arturo, had stood as the candidate of a coalition of the oligarchic Conservatives and Liberals, and he won because the vote for the centre had been split with the emergence of a Christian Democrat Party that drew away much of the Radicals' support. Alessandri had some initial success against inflation: the rate dropped from 39 per cent in 1959 to only 8 per cent in 1961, a very impressive performance in a part of the world where rapid inflation was threatening to become irreversible. But, once again, the export sector declined as a result of low world prices for copper; so the balance of payments remained in deficit, and the shortfall had to be made up by government borrowing, by encouraging foreign investment and by financial aid from the USA through the Alliance for Progress.

Although as a man of the right Alessandri was concerned with sound finance and with the need to attract foreign capital, he none the less went along with the broad policy of state-led development and import-substitution, such was the extent of the consensus on economic nationalism in Chile at this time. He introduced legislation designed to persuade the US-owned copper companies to base more of the refining process in Chile rather than abroad. But the result was disappointing; the scheme was attacked by the left, which wanted outright expropriation of the industry, and the mining companies themselves failed to respond with higher investments in the country. Indeed, the question of the nationalization of the copper industry would become one of the most acrimonious issues in Chilean politics in the 1960s. Alessandri also tried to tackle the very contentious issue of land reform. In 1962 he managed to pass, against the fierce opposition of members of his own oligarchic coalition, a law authorizing the expropriation of under-used land in large estates. Once again, despite the radical political import of such legislation, it was hindered and denounced by the left as a mere token reform.

What pushed Alessandri towards reform was the fact that by the early 1960s, Chile, like the more advanced Latin American countries, was experiencing the adverse effects of rapid industrialization and urbanization. As the flow of peasants into the cities continued at an ever increasing rate, the growth of shantytowns caused national concern about an economy that seemed incapable of providing work and a decent living to large sectors of the population. The stagnation of the economy was thought to be caused by the inequality of land distribution and by the domination of Chile's industry by foreign companies, which repatriated most of their profits and so drained the country of its resources.

Such perceptions gave a tremendous political boost to the parties of the left. At both the 1952 and 1958 elections, the Socialists, led by Salvador Allende, had formed an alliance with the Communists and had come very close to winning. This advance of the left reflected a disarray in the centre during the 1950s, for the Radicals, having been thrown into confusion after the bitter experience of González Videla's government, had lost much of their credibility. As the 1964 presidential election approached, it looked possible that the Socialist Allende might win power for the Marxist left in a democratic election.

In the event, this historic electoral breakthrough was denied the left by an extraordinary rally of the centre in the form of a new party, the Christian Democrats. It was formed only in 1957 as a result of a merger of splinter groups from the Radicals, the Conservatives, the Social Christians and a Catholic party originally founded in 1938 calling itself the National Falange. In fact, the victory of the Christian Democrat candidate, Eduardo Frei, at the 1964 presidential election was due in part to tactical voting by the right, alarmed at the prospect of Allende finally achieving the presidency. (At a congressional election in March 1964 the Socialists had won decisively and the right-wing candidate had come third, behind the Christian Democrat.) The parties of the right did not present any candidate for the presidential election and instead decided to support the Christian Democrat, Frei, who won the presidency with 56 per cent of the vote against Allende's 39 per cent and the Radical candidate's 5 per cent.

Although the centre and the right had outvoted Allende, it was clear that the left was steadily gaining ground over the right and centre. In fact, the fulcrum of Chilean politics had shifted to the advantage of the left, at least ideologically – the electoral programme of the Christian Democrats overlapped with that of the left as regards nationalization of industry, agrarian reform and the redistribution of wealth in favour of the working classes. However, underlying these shifts in the current of electoral politics there remained the sociological reality of a large and expanding urban middle-class interest without whose support no lasting change could come to Chile.

The Christian Democrat Government (1964–70)

The Christian Democrats promised a 'Revolution in Liberty', by which was meant the structural reform of the economy and society within the legal framework of existing parliamentary institutions. The party's ideology of 'communitarianism' envisaged a third way towards social justice that avoided the alleged extremes of free-market capitalism and communism. This was the rhetoric of corporatism adapted to the circumstances of Chile's liberal-democratic traditions. But the electoral programme of the Christian Democrats did have a genuinely radical edge: it would take the process of state intervention and income redistribution much further than any previous government, and it advocated extensive land and taxation reforms, measures which would have seriously affected the interests of the great landowners and the free-enterprise right; a radical shift in the balance of social forces was in the offing.

Political rivalries, however, militated against such a shift; for, to make its reforms work, the centre would have needed the tactical support of the left, as had occurred in the 1940s during the era of the Popular Front, when the foundations of economic nationalism and the welfare state had been laid. But by the early 1960s, centre and left had entered into a fierce competition which precluded such an alliance. This competition extended to the universities and trade unions, as well as the proliferating networks of neighbourhood associations, peasant leagues, youth and women's groups and other such grass-roots organizations which the Christian Democrats had been promoting with great success in an effort to increase participation in the political process. The idea of *poder popular* had caught on, and the left had to guard against being outmanoeuvred by the revitalized centre in this new mobilization of previously neglected social sectors. And yet neither bloc could achieve profound changes on its own. Indeed, the attempts of each to do so, successively, between 1964 and 1973 would result in the collapse of the democratic state, and a violent swing to the right at the hands of the armed forces.

What divided left from centre, despite the similarity of their short-term policy goals, was, therefore, acute ideological mistrust, compounded by intense competition at the grass roots to win the votes of new sectors of the electorate – particularly the peasant labourers on the great estates and migrants to the cities living in shantytowns. It was a classic instance of the rivalry of Marxists and Catholics, but during the 1950s it had taken on an intransigent quality arising from the international Cold War between the USA and the Soviet Union. Furthermore, after the success of Fidel Castro in Cuba, an optimistic Latin American left tended to look with disfavour upon gradualism and political compromise with bourgeois parties.

In the view of the Chilean left, the Christian Democrats were little better than tools of the Vatican and US imperialism. The Christian Democrats, for their part, feared that the Marxist parties would turn Chile irrevocably into a communist state within the Soviet empire. During the 1964 election campaign the Christian Democrats received funds from their West German and other European counterparts, and from US sources, including the CIA. What assistance, if any, the left may have received from external allies remains obscure. The outcome of these ideological and electoral rivalries was that Eduardo Frei could expect no backing from the left for his 'Revolution in Liberty'. On the contrary, the parties of the left often combined in congress with those of the right to thwart or discredit many substantial reforms proposed by the Christian Democrats.

Such was the fate of the drive to 'Chileanize' the copper industry. The plan was for the state to acquire a share in US-owned mining companies and to use this public investment to finance technical improvements that would increase efficiency and raise output. Denounced by nationalists of right and left as little more than a timid gesture, the legislation on the copper industry finally survived a troubled passage through congress in November 1965, but only after the Christian Democrats had made large gains at the congressional elections of the previous March. The policy of Chileanization, however, fell far short of its aim of increasing copper production twofold over five years. Though buoyant copper prices on the world market brought high export earnings, output did not rise significantly; the goal of revitalizing Chile's major industry in partnership with the foreign companies had not been fulfilled.

Another great reform in the Christian Democrat programme was the redistribution of land. The plan was to expropriate, with due compensation, parts of the massive estates in order to form agricultural co-operatives which would, it was hoped, provide land for up to 100,000 peasant families. The right predictably denounced the reform as an infringement of the right to private property. The parties of the left attacked it as not going far enough, and connived at illegal seizures of land organized by revolutionary peasant unions, which obliged the Christian Democrat government either to eject the squatters by force, and so tarnish its progressive credentials, or else to do nothing and risk being accused of tolerating lawlessness. This predicament gravely damaged the government's standing in the countryside and weakened the peasant leagues that the Christian Democrats had created in their pioneering and highly successful campaign to unionize the Chilean peasantry in the 1950s.

By 1969 the Christian Democrats had once again fallen short of their reformist goals. About 28,000 families had received land, a substantial number in historical perspective but far enough short of declared targets to give credibility to the left's attacks on the impotence of reformism. In other fields, such as in public health and education, and in the overhaul of the tax system, there were notable successes, but these were overshadowed by the relative failures of the copper and land reforms. What is more, from 1966 the economy had been performing badly, despite high copper prices, generous development loans through the Alliance for Progress and increased state aid to industry. Higher wages, both in rural areas and in the cities, sucked in imports and upset the balance of payments. As output in mining, agriculture and industry stagnated, the rate of inflation began to take off.

In the last years of Frei's six-year term of office an atmosphere of crisis enveloped Chile. Public dissatisfaction was reflected in electoral set-backs for the Christian Democrats, culminating in the loss of their majority in the chamber of deputies in 1969 after a fall in their share of the popular vote to about 29 per cent from the 43 per cent they had gained at equivalent elections in 1965. It was a crisis caused by rising expectations which exceeded the government's capacity to deliver. For the Christian Democrats had indeed put more money in the pockets of peasants and industrial workers, but the resulting increase in demand for goods and services could not be met by an economy that just did not produce or export enough. The inevitable result was inflation and, as prices shot up, the highly politicized, left-dominated trade unions intensified their attacks on the reformist government. In the end the 'Revolution in Liberty' failed because it lost the political consent of the people whose support it needed. This too would be the problem of the left when its turn came to attempt the restructuring of Chilean society on its own.

A short-lived *pronunciamiento* by the Tacna regiment near Santiago in 1969 pressing demands for better pay and conditions was one sign that Chile had returned to the situation of the mid-1920s, when important social groups had come to regard parliamentary democracy as a stumbling block to radical change. The leaders of the Tacna rebellion had sympathizers within the Socialist Party – a party whose origins went back to Marmaduke Grove's military intervention of 1931, when a 'Socialist Republic' was established for a few days. In 1969 each of the three political blocs had reason to feel frustrated with parliamentary politics. The right had seen the power of its traditional electoral machines in the countryside ebb away as the parties of the centre and the left made steady gains in recruiting the rural labour force to their ranks. The Socialists and Communists had always regarded parliament as the tool of the bourgeois state, and the election results of 1958 and 1964 persuaded them that only the vagaries of the electoral system kept them from victory. But crucially, by 1970, the centre, which had provided the hinge in electoral politics between the right and the left, was in a state of flux. The Christian Democrats, their reforms having been thwarted or curtailed, fell into disarray, a large faction advocating a move to revolutionary policies not much different from those of the Marxist left. As for the Radicals, their decomposition continued, as some groups defected to the right while others joined a new coalition of Socialists and Communists.

There was a general sense that the volatility of the parliamentary system had prevented a fundamental restructuring of an economy which had been in decline since the 1930s. By the late 1960s radical change seemed inevitable, but it was doubtful whether the liberal parliamentary system could survive such change intact. As in the time of Alessandri in the 1920s the question was: to what extent could change come about within the prevailing constitutional rules of politics? It was a question that neutered the Christian Democrats and would shortly divide and destroy the left. In the final reckoning it was to be the right that would show the greatest determination to impose the sort of radical change it wanted, regardless of the constitution.

Allende and the Chilean Road to Socialism (1970–73)

At the presidential election of 1970 the left proposed to move towards a full-blown socialist society. The Socialists and the Communists, together with splinter groups from the Christian Democrats and the Radicals, formed a coalition called Popular Unity with the veteran Socialist leader Salvador Allende as its candidate. According to Allende, the aim of his government would be to 'change the constitution by constitutional means'. The strategy was to win power legally through an election, while at the same time mobilizing the masses to transform the institutions of the liberal state into truly socialist ones. The obvious risk was that the representatives of the centre and the right might not acquiesce in the arrangements for their own demise.

Popular Unity's proposal to change the liberal constitution alarmed the middle and upper classes. The Christian Democrats, despite the similarity of many of their policies to those of Popular Unity, baulked at the 'Chilean road to socialism'. The parties of the right, led once again by Jorge Alessandri, registered an upsurge in support after their weak performance in 1964. Despite the perceived need for radical change across the political spectrum, disagreement over what kind of change was required and how it could be achieved reconstituted the rough electoral balance of left, right and centre. But given the deep economic crisis faced by Chile, this electoral balance amounted to a political impasse: the parliamentary system would not deliver the decisive majority that would have been required by any one political bloc for the deep structural changes each felt to be necessary.

Of the three blocs, the left held the decisive ideological advantage: there were relatively few Chilean voters who would have supported a return to free-market capitalism, discredited as it had been for the past half-century. A majority may have been sympathetic to the general aims of the left, but too many voters were held back by fears of destroying the constitutional system. Strategy was therefore crucial to the left. However, the strategy of 'changing the constitution by constitutional means' divided and weakened the left itself. The leadership of the Socialist Party, with the full backing of the Communists, saw this as the only way forward because it would not alienate the middle classes, whose support was judged to be indispensable for a successful transformation of the existing order. However, much of the Socialist rank and file argued for a rapid transition to socialism so as to pre-empt a reaction from the right. In this analysis they concurred with the influential Trotskyist groups to the left of Popular Unity – particularly the Movement of the Revolutionary Left (MIR), which enjoyed widespread support in the universities and among the young, and which advocated an armed struggle to overthrow the capitalist state. For the MIR a peaceful road to socialism was an illusion.

On 4 September 1970 Salvador Allende won a narrow plurality of the votes in the presidential election. (This slender margin of victory lengthened the odds against the success of the revolution by constitutional means.) Allende polled 36.3 per cent; Jorge Alessandri, for the right, 34.9 per cent; and Christian Democrat candidate, Radomiro Tomic, 27.8 per cent. Only a controversial deal with the reluctant Christian Democrats enabled Allende to be ratified as president by congress, as required by the constitution. Yet even before he was sworn in on 3 November, the far right started plotting to overthrow him. In October the commander-in-chief of the army, General René Schneider, was assassinated, very likely by right-wing extremists hoping to goad the army into staging a *coup d'état*.

Allende's government faced formidable opposition. The Popular Unity parties did not have a majority in either the chamber of deputies or the senate. Other institutions of the state – the judiciary and the civil service in particular – showed little enthusiasm for the government's policies. The powerful mass media were in the hands of the centre and the right. Against Popular Unity must also be counted the foreign companies in Chile – particularly North American – which feared expropriation. The US government too viewed the election of a Marxist with intense disquiet. It had seen how, soon after Fidel Castro had turned to communism, a dangerous confrontation had arisen with the Soviet Union over Cuba. Engaged as it still was in a seemingly unwinnable war against communists in Vietnam and

Cambodia, the last thing the USA wanted was another Latin American country to 'go communist'. From an early date the US government started a campaign to destabilize Chile by funding opposition groups and with-drawing credits and economic aid from the Allende government. (The Chilean armed forces, however, were still allowed access to US armaments and training.)

Despite the forces ranged against it, the aims of Popular Unity were revolutionary. In the political field they wanted to break the power of 'oligarchy', by which was meant the great landowners and monopoly cap-italists, and of 'imperialism', which referred to the US mining companies, foreign banks and transnational corporations. In their place would rise 'people's power', institutionalized in a one-chamber legislature and in a nationwide system of people's councils organized in neighbourhoods and workplaces. As regards the economy, Popular Unity proposed to attack 'underdevelopment' – whose cause was identified as Chile's dependence on the international capitalist market – by the nationalization of mining, industry and banking, as well as by the destruction of the system of large landholdings. Once the levers of the economy were held by the state, central planning would remove the chronic scourges of inflation and low growth which had dragged Chile down in recent decades, and would ensure full employment and rising living standards. (However, it was the severity of the economic crisis produced by Allende's short-term policies that gravely weakened his authority and eventually turned the tide of popular feeling against him.)

The Allende government's immediate aims were to reactivate the sluggish economy and to redistribute income more equally. Both objectives were to be achieved by massively increasing the purchasing power of the middle sectors, the working class and the poor. This would raise consumer demand and stimulate production in industry and agriculture, so mopping up unem-ployment. The obvious danger of inflation would be avoided by holding down prices, thus forcing producers to increase output in order to make up for declining profit margins. This policy of virtually unbridled expansion generated a tremendous boom, which lasted some twelve months. By the latter half of 1972 inflation had spun out of control: in one year it had shot up to 180.3 per cent, the highest rate in Chilean history. Public spending and the quantity of money in circulation had also increased beyond restraint. The government's policy of holding down prices proved inadequate as a means of coping with these intense inflationary pressures. Industry could not meet such a high volume of demand; there were bottlenecks in production and shortages of consumer goods. As the value of the peso slumped, imports became too expensive to make up for the shortages, and Chilean industry had to pay higher prices for imported materials and technology. The result was a flourishing black-market economy, which the government was unable to stamp out.

Conventional anti-inflationary measures were out of the question for an elected Marxist government: it was impossible to cut back public spending, reduce credit or keep wages below the rate of inflation. Added to these difficulties was the bitter opposition of landowners and businessmen to the government's policy of nationalization and expropriation. This opposition took the form of investment boycotts, capital flight, lockouts of the workforce and lagging production.

The policy of nationalization of industry also contributed to the short-term economic crisis. As businesses and factories were requisitioned by the state prior to takeover, or else occupied by trade unions in *de facto* expropriations, the process of production was inevitably disrupted and investment fell off, aggravating bottlenecks and shortages. Still, the government succeeded in nationalizing the major industries and private banks. The copper-mining companies were taken into state ownership with little fuss from congress. Many subsidiaries of transnational companies such as Ford or International Telephones and Telecommunications were also nationalized. But it was the lack of compensation for these expropriations, due largely to a depletion of foreign-exchange reserves, that most provoked the active hostility of US interests and provided the Nixon administration with the pretext for mounting an 'invisible blockade' against Chile by cutting off loans and credits from international agencies, thereby making the balance of payments worse and contributing to an already acute scarcity of the foreign exchange Chile badly needed in order to import technology for her nationalized industries.

The other great pillar of the revolutionary programme was land reform. Allende, conscious of his weakness in congress, availed himself of the legislation already passed by the Christian Democrats in 1967, which provided for the expropriation of estates over eighty hectares. The aim was to create a 'reformed sector' in agriculture consisting of small farms and co-operatives. But this legal instrument, inherited from the Christian Democrats, left quite large holdings in the hands of conservative farmers and helped only a fraction of the rural population to join co-operatives or acquire land. The great majority of the rural poor received little benefit from the reforms. Even so, in the first fourteen months of office the Popular Unity government had redistributed more land than the Christian Democrats had managed to do in six years.

The pace of land reform was very difficult to regulate. Awakened expec-

tations stirred the peasant leagues to increasing militancy. Illegal seizures
of land, actively encouraged by far-left groups, put pressure on the government to step up the rate of expropriations. Yet the revolutionary turmoil
in the countryside was contributing to a sharp decline in agricultural
output. Landowners decapitalized the estates that were threatened with
expropriation. Peasants on the new co-operatives preferred to work their
sizeable private holdings rather than communal lands, and they proved
resistant to the introduction of accounting systems by state officials.
The massive outlay in state credits and subsidies to the reformed sector was
not recouped in increased production. Agriculture made huge losses
and drained scarce resources away from other sectors of the nationalized
economy.

After the first year of the Popular Unity government, its major reforms
seemed in danger of being undermined by the worsening economic situation.
The crisis accentuated divisions within the left. There were renewed calls
from revolutionaries within the Popular Unity coalition, as well as from
MIR and the Trotskyist parties outside it, for the violent overthrow of the
state. But the staunchest opponents of this line were the Communists; they
preferred a gradual, constitutionalist approach for fear of provoking an
outright contest for state power against the centre and the right, which
would inevitably have brought in the army. What divided the left was the
question not of ends but of means, a division which reflected the
government's uncertainty as to its real strength in the country, for it was
unsure of its chances of success in an open conflict with the forces of bourgeois
society.

A key element in the Communist strategy for the peaceful transition to
socialism was the alliance of organized labour with the middle classes and
native businessmen. But the economic effects of the inflationary boom of
1971 began to alienate this bourgeois support. Black markets, shortages of
consumer goods, soaring prices and a worthless currency, no less than the
growing disorder in the streets, alarmed a sector of society which had no
overriding interest in revolution.

In the course of 1972 middle-class opposition to Allende became more
vocal and better organized. Thousands of women protested against rising
prices and scarcities of basic items by banging pots and pans in the streets.
There were strikes and demonstrations too from shopkeepers, white-collar
workers, students and professional associations. In the month of October
there was a concerted attempt by such groups to paralyse Chile after a very
damaging strike by road-hauliers which nearly brought the distribution of
goods in the country to a standstill. The transportation strike was ended by

the mobilization of the trade unions and the peasant leagues, but the more general October crisis was defused only after Allende had made crucial concessions to the middle-class interest-groups; he agreed to curtail the nationalization of medium and small businesses, and offered guarantees about the security of 'non-monopolistic' property rights.

After October 1972 the Communist strategy of inter-class alliances appeared less feasible; the middle classes were clearly moving towards the right. This led to redoubled calls from the revolutionary left to prepare for armed struggle. Allende resisted this course; if anything, his tactics at this juncture were to nail his colours to the mast of constitutionality, presumably in order to oblige the opposition to play by the democratic rules or else risk losing the moral debate by straying into lawlessness. What concerned Allende was the reaction of the army. In the wake of the middle-class strikes of October 1972, he brought three military commanders into his cabinet so as to pre-empt a *coup d'état* and reinforce law and order in the period leading up to the congressional elections of March 1973, when he would be able to gauge the strength of his support and modify his strategy accordingly.

The congressional elections were of great significance, as much for the opposition as for the government. Allende's enemies on the centre and right hoped to increase their combined strength to the two-thirds majority required for the impeachment of the president. For Allende, on the other hand, the elections provided an opportunity to win a Popular Unity majority in congress. This would allow him to change the constitution and introduce a unicameral 'people's assembly', which would boost his political authority and enable him to recover the faltering momentum of the transition to socialism. Each side, in other words, wanted to employ strict constitutional devices to neutralize the power of its opponents.

The results of the March elections proved inconclusive. On the surface they appeared to give a moral victory to the government, and so they were hailed by its supporters: the opposition majority in both houses of congress had been reduced slightly and Popular Unity's share of the vote had increased to 43 per cent from the 36.5 per cent that Allende had received on his election in 1970. But that 43 per cent in fact represented a fall from the 49.7 per cent that Popular Unity had polled in the municipal elections of September 1971, which had been held at a time when the euphoria created by the initial consumer boom had not yet been dissipated by runaway inflation. On the other hand, although the opposition parties of the centre and right had failed to win the two-thirds majority needed to impeach Allende, their total vote of 55.7 per cent was roughly the same as the vote that had given Eduardo Frei a landslide victory in 1964. The March results thus produced a political impasse; for neither side could make any progress towards overcoming the other without violating the constitution.

Inevitably, the deadlock that paralysed constitutional politics increased the polarization of the country. There was frustration in both camps. The centre and right launched themselves into further strikes and demonstrations. These were countered by mass rallies of trade-unionists and government supporters. The MIR stepped up its illegal occupations of factories, and the *cordones industriales* – organizations of revolutionary workers which had sprung up in the industrial belt round Santiago after the bourgeois strikes of October 1972 – began to arm themselves in preparation for a final reckoning with the forces of capitalism. Acts of sabotage and political terrorism by extreme groups on the right and left intensified the impression that Allende had lost control of the situation. A true revolutionary crisis seemed to be at hand.

Allende would not abandon his constitutionalist stand, despite insistent appeals from the revolutionary left. His authority, however, received a damaging blow in April 1973 when the workers at the El Teniente copper-mines – the aristocracy of the Chilean working class – came out on strike for higher wages. With inflation running at an annual rate of 600 per cent, even the most solid pillars of Popular Unity support seemed liable to crack under the strain. Condemned by the government, the miners' strike none the less continued for over two months, and was predictably exploited by the opposition parties.

Much depended now on the disposition of the armed forces. Even though the right was openly inviting the military to intervene, Allende still seemed able to count on the loyalty of the service chiefs in his cabinet, who included General Carlos Prats, the head of the army: on 29 June Prats put down a rebellion by a tank regiment in Santiago. But, in fact, Prats was losing the confidence of his colleagues, some of whom were calling for his resignation. Army units took to raiding the *cordones industriales* to confiscate the arms of the revolutionary workers, while overlooking the activities of right-wing paramilitary groups.

In an effort to shore up his authority, Allende tried to make a deal with the Christian Democrats. But it was very late in the day for any kind of centre–left alliance (such an alliance had actually been advocated by the Christian Democrat leader, Radomiro Tomic, before and after the 1970 election, but it had been rejected then by Allende). The Christian Democrats were reluctant to rescue a government consisting of parties which had helped to wreck their own reforms and whose administration was now so patently close to collapse. In July, Allende had to face another wave of strikes by road-hauliers and other commercial and professional interest-groups. These disturbances were used by the opposition parties in congress as a pretext to appeal to the army once again to step in and restore order. In August, General Prats was finally pressured to resign by his fellow officers; he was replaced as chief-of-staff by General Augusto Pinochet, who took his place in Allende's cabinet as minister of war.

On 11 September 1973 a military *coup d'état* planned by General Pinochet brought down the government. Allende himself, rejecting offers of safe conduct out of the country, chose to make a stand as the legitimate head of state and died during an aerial bombardment of the presidential palace, a martyr to Chile's unique experiment in making a socialist revolution by constitutional means.

General Pinochet and the Transition to the Free Market (1973–82)

The violence unleashed by the Pinochet coup was twofold. In the first instance, socialism had to be eradicated: members and active supporters of the Popular Unity government were rounded up and either imprisoned or sent into exile. To counter groups of armed workers and the entrenched guerrillas of the Trotskyist MIR, the military resorted to torture and killing. Within a year the Chilean left had been broken at a cost of several thousand lives and the exodus from the country of some 30,000 supporters of Popular Unity.

The second form of violence was less direct but far more protracted and diffuse. The military junta was determined to dismantle the state sector of the economy and impose financial discipline and free-market principles. But after forty years of state-led development and chronic high inflation, a sudden return to economic liberalism caused a slump in which millions were pauperized. The privatization of large parts of the public sector, which had been greatly expanded under both Frei and Allende, caused a massive shake-out of labour from nationalized industries and the bureaucracy. Other traditional features of the economic nationalism of the 1930s and 1940s – such as high import tariffs, state subsidies to domestic industry and resistance to foreign capital – were abandoned. Hence, with a new comprehensive tariff of only 10 per cent and an open-door policy towards foreign capital, over-protected Chilean companies lost out against foreign competitors and had to shed labour. In the countryside there was further disruption of agriculture as the land reforms undertaken by both Frei and Allende were reversed.

In 1975, at the lowest point of this massive depression, which was aggravated by the deep world recession resulting from the OPEC oil crisis, the GDP of Chile had fallen by 12.9 per cent and the rate of unemployment was approximately 17 per cent, three times the average rate of the 1960s. Given the virtual absence of unemployment benefit, the scale of hardship for the working classes was horrific.

The official justification for inflicting this trauma on the nation was that there was no alternative if Chile was to correct the alleged errors of decades and escape even worse disasters in the future. General Pinochet's economic advisers were young technocrats who adhered to liberal economic theories then enjoying a revival. Many had been trained at the University of Chicago under Professor Milton Friedman, a renowned advocate of the free market and of monetary control as a means of cutting inflation. According to these 'Chicago Boys', as the Chilean neo-liberals were derisively called by their opponents, persistent state intervention in the economy had produced distortions such as hyperinflation, huge budget deficits and stagnant production. Chile was to be the first country to attempt a return to the classic liberal economic principles which had been out of favour in Latin America since the late 1920s. The Pinochet regime therefore embarked on a drive to achieve a reconversion to free-market capitalism which was as ideologically committed as Allende's earlier transition to socialism had been. But unlike Allende, General Pinochet was under no illusions that such an ideological revolution could succeed other than by the violent destruction of the opposition.

Although the regime hoped that neo-liberal policies would lead to a quick recovery after an inevitable period of recession, the results of these policies were in fact very mixed. The years 1976–81 did show signs of a recovery after the economic trough the country had suffered after the coup. From a peak of over 600 per cent in 1973, inflation fell to 31.2 per cent in 1980 and only 8.9 per cent in 1981; the growth rate averaged 8 per cent a year; the export sector began to grow and to diversify away from its traditional reliance on copper-mining. But the unemployment rate did not come down much below 17 per cent and the real value of wages rose very slowly during the period.

The recovery, such as it was, was socially unequal. Over the period 1976–81 the richest 20 per cent of the population enjoyed the same level of consumption of basic foods as in 1969, while the consumption of the poorest 20 per cent fell by 20 per cent. Much of the new consumer spending generated by the recovery went on imports of luxury goods, which rose by about 300 per cent over the level for 1970; over a half of these imports were consumed by the richest 20 per cent. Thus the growth in the economy overwhelmingly favoured the upper classes and, to a lesser but significant extent, the middle classes. Large sections of the population continued to live in a state of acute deprivation. In any case, this highly uneven recovery was disrupted catastrophically by a new world recession, which in 1982–4 produced the worst slump in Chilean history.

Chile was particularly hard hit by the world recession of the early 1980s because its experiment in economic deregulation had made it extremely vulnerable to fluctuations in the international capital markets. Moreover, its efforts to control inflation had led it to maintain an artificially high exchange rate for too long. This had damaged export performance, sucking in imports and leading to a consumer boom which produced deficits in the balance of payments. The climate of financial instability encouraged capital flight, excessive borrowing and speculation instead of productive investment. It also encouraged the concentration of capital in a few large *grupos* – conglomerates which enjoyed favoured access to private foreign loans.

Indeed, the consumer boom enjoyed by the upper and middle classes in 1976–81 had been financed by huge levels of private borrowing from foreign banks. But in 1982, after international interest rates had gone up sharply, the Chilean financial sector crashed. Committed though it was to free-market economics, the government felt the need to nationalize banks and *grupos* in order to salvage the country's financial system. Thus the massive private debt was passed on to the state and Chile became one of the most indebted nations in Latin America with a foreign debt of $17 billion and interest payments amounting to 49.5 per cent of export-earnings. By nationalizing the foreign debt, the regime had effectively made it the collective responsibility of the people of Chile to pay off the mountain of credit amassed by the privileged conglomerates during the boom of the late 1970s. The regime implemented a harsh austerity programme, which reduced output by 12 per cent and drove unemployment above 20 per cent (in the shantytowns of Santiago unemployment remained at about 40 per cent for the rest of the decade).

The Search for Legitimacy (1983–9)

The social costs incurred by this erratic experiment in dismantling the machinery of economic nationalism could scarcely have been tolerated in a liberal democracy. Ironically, therefore, the liberalization of the Chilean economy had to be conducted under the most repressive military dictatorship the country had experienced. Soon after the coup, General Pinochet emerged as the undisputed strongman of the military junta, ruling by decree until

1980, when the economy, which had been improving since 1976, won passive middle-class support, persuaded the dictator to seek a limited degree of consent for his government.

The carefully controlled plebiscite of 1980 approved a constitution which entrenched Pinochet as president of the republic until 1989, with the possibility of a renewed mandate after that date. The regime, however, remained diplomatically ostracized abroad for its consistent violation of human rights. With the political parties still banned, the Catholic Church took upon itself the role of moral critic of the military government, denouncing the physical abuses perpetrated by the secret police against alleged subversives, and attempting to relieve the wretched conditions of the poorest groups in the shantytowns.

The economic slump of 1982–4 deprived Pinochet of the chance to normalize the regime; his authority continued to be perceived as anomalous and illegitimate. During 1983–4, as the effects of the depression made themselves felt among the middle classes as well as the working class and the poor, support for the clandestine political parties increased, and the resistance to Pinochet became open and violent. Strikes and days of protest unsettled the regime and led to the expectation that Pinochet might be overthrown or at least persuaded to stand down. The government declared a state of siege and intensified its repression of political and labour activists. The prevailing atmosphere of crisis encouraged the opposition; the Communist Party, for instance, tried to make Chile ungovernable through a policy of labour mobilization and armed struggle. Its military wing, the Manuel Rodríguez Patriotic Front, came very close to assassinating Pinochet in 1986, when guerrillas attacked his motorcade. The dictator, however, escaped with minor injuries and used this incident to give credibility to his claim to be the only bulwark against a return to Marxist rule.

After 1985 the possibility of overthrowing Pinochet began to recede. The opposition remained divided: the centre and the democratic socialists were chary of associating with the Communists and the revolutionary left, who were felt to be too identified with the Allende government, and whose policy of violent resistance alienated the middle classes. But what made the task of the opposition much more difficult was that the debt crisis had plunged the whole of Latin America into a period of depression and austerity; it no longer seemed convincing, therefore, to blame Chile's economic troubles exclusively on Pinochet and his Chicago Boys. What is more, the Chilean economy started to improve dramatically over the rest of the decade.

The appointment of a young technocrat, Hernán Büchi, as finance minister in 1985 marked the beginning of economic recovery. Büchi's strategy was to create the financial conditions for stable, export-led growth and to reorganize the productive structures of the export sector. Control of public spending, periodic devaluations, and incentives for domestic savings, foreign investment and the repatriation of capital gradually brought inflation down to 12 per cent by 1989, the lowest rate in Latin America. A vigorous campaign to sell parcels of the public debt to private investors in exchange for shares in Chilean industries reduced the nation's debt burden by over $4 billion. In the export sector, consistent growth was achieved by diversifying markets, improving distribution and marketing techniques, and increasing the mix of export products. Chile's historic dependence on copper exports fell from 70 per cent in 1973 to 45 per cent in 1989. Farming, fishing and forestry supplied a range of new exports to new markets in the Far East, Australasia and North America. In 1971 Chile exported 412 products to 58 countries; in 1988, 1,343 products were exported to 112 countries. Economic growth averaged between 5 per cent and 6 per cent in 1985–8, the highest rate in the region. In September 1988, a few weeks before a plebiscite was to be held to endorse General Pinochet's rule, the conservative newspaper *El Mercurio* declared: 'Good-bye Latin America. We no longer look to Argentina or Brazil as examples to emulate. On the contrary, our aim is to reach the standards of living of Australia, New Zealand or Taiwan.'

Opponents of the regime, on the other hand, pointed to the appalling human cost of these economic successes. Wage levels in 1988 were still 7 per cent lower than in 1981, and nearly half the population lived below the poverty line. Wealth was very unevenly distributed, with the top 5 per cent receiving over 80 per cent of the national income and per capita growth actually having declined by 2.5 per cent over the decade. (In contrast, Brazil, with over ten times the population, increased its per capita growth by about 4 per cent.) The government claimed to have cut unemployment by half from the 20 per cent recorded in 1982, but one in four Chileans still suffered great hardship, being forced to beg or peddle cheap articles on the streets.

Whatever the impact of the economic upturn on the standard of living, the fact remained that the so-called economic miracle failed to win Pinochet the general political consent he required to legitimize his rule. Presidential elections were due to be held in 1989 in accordance with the constitution; but Pinochet decided to hold a plebiscite in October 1988 to determine whether or not the people wished him to stay on as president until 1997. Pinochet lost the plebiscite, though he polled a substantial 42 per cent of the vote. He accepted the result with reluctance, but safeguards built in to the 1980 constitution would enable him to continue to preside over the National Security Council with powers to overrule the government on matters of national security. A third of the senate would be appointed by him and would be able to block most attempts to reform the 1980 constitution. Pinochet, in other words, was not minded to give up power entirely, and did not yet trust the democratic will of the people.

Achieving a majority of negative votes at the 1988 plebiscite was a great victory for the opposition, but it remained divided over the succession to Pinochet. On the left the Communists, Trotskyists, and the Marxist wing of the Socialist Party rejected any dealings with elements in the army and the regime. However, a Democratic Alliance led by the Christian Democrats, the party estimated to have the widest support in Chile, and which included the conservative Independent Democratic Union and the democratic wing of the Socialist Party, accepted negotiations with representatives of the government on the terms for the transition to democratic politics. There was support for such a transition within the army, the technocratic establishment and the business community, for it had become clear that Pinochet himself would never win the political legitimacy required to put Chile's economic recovery on a sound footing. For their part, the Christian Democrats, under Patricio Aylwin, their candidate for the presidency, accepted a mixed economy in which the state would encourage rather than intervene in private enterprise. At the elections held in December 1989 Aylwin was elected with 55 per cent of the votes.

At the end of the 1980s Chile was moving towards a consensus between the armed forces and the bulk of the civilian opposition on the economic and political principles upon which to build a modern democratic state. Under General Pinochet the neo-liberal Chicago Boys had tried to create a dynamic, free-market economy at great – some might say intolerable – human cost. But such economic modernization as had been achieved was unlikely to last without the underpinning of a legitimate state based on free, representative institutions and modern standards of welfare provision and social equality. Only then could Chile be said to have made good the boast that she was, uniquely in Latin America, on the point of becoming a developed nation.

15. Identity and Modernity: Literary and Cultural Developments II

Latin America entered the twentieth century on the defensive against US power and in a state of growing self-doubt. By the last quarter of the previous century the triumph of liberalism appeared to have resolved the ideological problems of nation-building; but these now threatened to re-emerge – particularly after the First World War, when the export-economies ran into difficulties in more troubled world markets, new social groups agitated for political rights and an intellectual backlash against scientific positivism divided the educated classes once again.

Having fought and largely won a bitter struggle against the privileged power of the Catholic Church, liberals were now to face a more diverse opposition. In addition to conservative Catholics, it comprised nationalists, anarchists, communists and fascists, all of whom attacked in some degree the European connection and were variously to take up the cause of the country-side against the city, the Indian communities, the blacks and mixed-bloods, the urban middle classes or the as yet small industrial proletariat. The classic liberalism of the ruling élites began to disintegrate under these pressures. There was, however, no persuasive ideology to replace it. Catholicism, though still strong, was in intellectual retreat; other ideologies did not yet command mass support. In effect, the first three decades of the new century marked a return to the confusing period which followed independence, when the projected destiny of the free nations was contradicted by the actual turn of events.

The breakdown of political consensus revealed how smug and exclusive liberalism had been as a ruling ideology. In contrast to the Catholic monarchy, it had failed to balance political unity with ethnic and regional diversity; nor had it taken root among the people as had Catholicism in traditional Iberian societies – on the contrary, there continued to exist a deep rift between the culture of the élites, based on the Enlightenment rationalism which had justified the struggle for independence, and popular culture, so richly varied in its melding of Hispanic, Indian and African traditions. Liberalism, and the scientific positivism which it spawned, had functioned in fact as the rationale for white oligarchy in Latin America.

Still, liberals had unequivocally espoused progress and modernization, and when liberalism came under attack, the issue of modernity itself became problematic. Anti-liberals viewed progress with suspicion: it was at best a form of aping Europeans; at worst it threatened the very soul of the nation. In consequence, Latin American intellectuals from the 1900s started upon a tortuous quest for their national essence – for *argentinidad, mexicanidad, peruanidad* and so on. By the 1920s that quest had led intellectuals to the discovery of popular traditions and ethnic lore, which came to be regarded as the touchstones of cultural authenticity. This current of nativism reinforced cultural nationalism, paving the way for the economic nationalism of the 1930s and the intensive state-led development of subsequent decades.

For virtually the whole of the twentieth century, then, the issue of national identity would dominate cultural life. But since identity and modernity were felt to be, if not mutually exclusive, certainly in tension with each other, the result was that the struggle against oligarchy and privilege became caught up in anti-democratic and even anti-progressive politics. Liberal ideas as such were dismissed as alien imports; electoral politics scorned as a bourgeois charade; the rule of law and respect for individual human rights subordinated to the general will of the community – as interpreted by a *caudillo*, a ruling party or a military junta. In short, the basic principles of liberal democracy became discredited by their association with oligarchy and positivism; on the whole, they were eclipsed by variants of authoritarian populism and, increasingly, by revolutionary socialism in the intellectual culture of Latin America.

The ferment that resulted from the demise of classical liberalism proved, however, to be immensely creative in the arts. The intellectual quest for some timeless national essence was the result perhaps of an illusory problem, but the preoccupation with identity which absorbed Latin American artists made for the broadening and deepening of cultural awareness: it was to win acceptance of hybridity as a positive reality; it helped to dignify the traditions of the Indians and the blacks; and it legitimized plebeian art forms, opening up creative channels between high culture and low.

In societies that were historically so fragmented and mixed, the artistic exploration of the question of cultural identity was therefore a means of groping towards some sense of unity, a common ground that could provide a solid basis for the genuine political consensus that had eluded the new states since independence. In fact, the search for identity may be regarded as part of the complex process of recovering in a modern context the qualities that had once made the Catholic monarchy so resilient and stable – the capacity to reconcile unity with diversity, and the cross-fertilization of élite culture with that of the common people.

Such a quest for identity gave the artist a major role in society. Under the Catholic monarchy, the clergy had acted as the ideological pastors of the people; in the independent republics, writers and intellectuals formed a kind of priesthood of the new national culture in the making. A successful creative writer in Latin America enjoyed a moral power and public status which he had rarely, if ever, been accorded in Europe. In the previous century there had been numerous instances of writers assuming high public office – the cases of Domingo Sarmiento or Bartolomé Mitre, both presidents of Argentina, being the most salient. The coming century would see a continuation of this pattern. The novelist Rómulo Gallegos was elected president of Venezuela in 1947; the poet Pablo Neruda was a senator in the 1940s and stood for the presidency of Chile in 1970. In Cuba, Fidel Castro appointed writers to important posts: the novelist Alejo Carpentier was ambassador in Paris in the 1970s, and the mulatto poet Nicolás Guillén occupied a number of influential positions at the ministry of culture. In Nicaragua, the revolutionary Sandinista government sought legitimacy in the 1980s partly by its association with creative writers – the minister of culture, for instance, was Ernesto Cardenal, a man famous both as a poet and a priest. José Sarney, elected in 1985 as the first president of a redemocratized Brazil, was a novelist and poet. In a Peru racked by debt, inflation and political terrorism, the country's greatest novelist, Mario Vargas Llosa, ran for the presidency in 1990.

The high public status of such men reflected the historical importance accorded to art and literature in Latin America. In times of great crisis the creative writer seemed best qualified to articulate the destiny of the nation. But that destiny could not be found by ignoring the issue of modernity, for the fundamental question was not so much the discovery of an authentic identity as the creation of a genuine national culture that would not be forever at odds with the modern world in which it had to exist.

The Appeal of Modernism

The catalyst of Latin American culture in the twentieth century was the modernist movement that began to emerge in Europe in the latter years of the First World War. That complex and multifaceted phenomenon was in many ways a reaction to the crisis of the classic liberal order: it arose from a sense of disillusionment with the idea of progress, with scientific rationalism and utilitarian ethics. Moreover, the rise of trade-unionism, the suffragette movement and nationalism appeared to give the lie to the liberal idea of the individual as the prime agent in politics; the Russian Revolution provided yet another powerful impetus towards forms of collectivism and the extension of the powers of the state.

European modernism registered both a general sense of cultural dissolution and a desire for an alternative order. For some artists that order was to be found in the recuperation of pre-liberal values, in a renewal of spirituality and religious awareness; others looked forward to a new society created by Marxism or fascism. In all cases modernism wanted to destroy established forms in order to recreate a more authentic experience or discover a new consciousness. It sought to disrupt logic and subvert common sense; to vindicate the instincts before reason, spontaneity before calculation, sexuality in the face of the prim morality of the bourgeoisie.

Modernism was above all experimental in form and technique, revolting against anything that appeared obvious or conventional. In poetry, it tended to distrust rhyme and metre, seeking rather to invigorate language through strange imagery and unexpected rhythms, including those of everyday speech. In the novel, it undermined realistic depiction of character and action by playing with time sequences, language registers and points of view. The plastic arts were revolutionized by the critique of representation itself and by the move away from the human figure as the central subject of the artist. This 'dehumanization' was seen too in music with the reaction against harmony through experiments with atonality and chromaticism. Relishing the eclectic and discordant, modernism was often fascinated by exotic cultures, and in this it diluted the sense of superiority generally felt by Europeans towards people from the traditional societies of Africa, Asia and, indeed, Latin America.

What was it, then, about the modernist revolution that attracted so many Latin American artists and released such creative energies? For the first time since independence the cultural situation of Latin America bore significant resemblances to certain aspects of the generally confused state of Europe from the 1910s to the mid-1940s: there occurred a reaction against classic political liberalism, a retreat from science and reason, a questioning of progress and a yearning to rediscover a sense of community by building a new society. These broad affinities placed Latin American artists in a position where they could profit from the experimental techniques and expressive innovations that were at the heart of modernism.

Yet despite this convergence of interests between Latin Americans and sections of the European intelligentsia, there remained important differences. On the whole, Latin America was still a traditional society in the very early stages of a transition to modernity, while European modernism arose from a disenchantment with a well-established modern civilization. In Latin America, a customary way of life was pervasive and familiar; in Europe, the population was mostly urban and industrial, and traditional lore had receded to a marginalized countryside. On the other hand, European artists could look back to classical traditions of high culture in the search for alternatives to modernity. But for the Latin Americans the disorientation was more profound: their Iberian heritage had been largely discredited by liberal intellectuals after independence and the pre-Columbian cultures were too remote to be meaningful.

In terms of high culture, Latin America seemed to exist in a void – cut off from a serviceable past yet threatened by a future outside its control. For this reason its reception of the techniques and themes of modernism – which tended to emphasize rupture, discontinuity and alienation – could not be purely imitative: these were soon transformed into original explorations of a unique situation – a state of isolation in time present, from where there were no clear avenues back to the past nor forwards into the future. Indeed, the great theme of the Latin American artist of the twentieth century was to be the condition of orphanhood (as his cultural isolation was often likened to), and the resultant search for ways out of what the Mexican poet Octavio Paz famously called 'the labyrinth of solitude'.

There were strains in European modernism that did not filter through to the Latin Americans. As ever, they got their modern culture from France: what Paris did not absorb, Mexico City, Buenos Aires, Rio de Janeiro and São Paulo failed to notice. Anglo-American modernism made little or no impact until the 1940s. T. S. Eliot, Ezra Pound and William Carlos Williams were hardly known before then; nor were James Joyce, D. H. Lawrence or Virginia Woolf, except to a tiny coterie in Buenos Aires, which, not surprisingly, included the young and iconoclastic Jorge Luis Borges. The Italian, German and Russian avant-gardes were encountered only in so far as they found influence in Paris. There were also currents in French modernism that did not greatly appeal. The cool neo-classicism of Paul Valéry's *poésie pure*, though it won followers in Spain, failed to attract the Spanish Americans. (In 1935–6, while living in Spain, Pablo Neruda edited a magazine in which he famously attacked *poésie pure* for its refusal to be sullied by contact with ordinary things.) The futurists' glorification of the machine and the rapid tempo of modern city life aroused limited enthusiasm among artists who tended to regard technology as a mortal threat. Cubism, pioneered by the Spaniard Picasso, did exert some lasting influence, notably on the great Mexican painter Rufino Tamayo and on the early poetry of the Chilean Vicente Huidobro, who provided a significant conduit for modernism through his theory of *creacionismo*. On the whole, avant-garde currents – futurism, cubism, imagism, Dada – reached Latin America in attenuated form via Spain, through the eclectic movement known as *ultraísmo*. One of its leading lights was Jorge Luis Borges, though he was to repudiate the avant-garde in the 1930s in order to pursue his strange, ironic reflections on the European cultural tradition, thereby laying the basis for his international reputation in the 1960s by anticipating what critics much later came to identify as the culture of post-modernism.

In general, Latin Americans were drawn to art that was passionate and irrational – to the legacy of Lautréamont and Rimbaud, to Apollinaire and, above all, to the surrealists. It is scarcely possible to exaggerate the influence of surrealism on Latin American poetry, fiction, painting and cinema. Surrealism, after all, fitted Latin American aspirations to perfection. To start with, it was anti-capitalist and anti-bourgeois, reaching into the unconscious in order to unlock the anarchic forces of dream and desire. The surrealists' almost mystical quest to repoeticize the modern world struck a deep chord in artists so recently dispossessed of religion. So too did the revolutionary imperative to recover a 'super-reality' in which the intellect would be integrated with the occluded parts of the psyche. For the prospect of finding 'communicating vessels', to use a phrase of André Breton's which had a particular resonance in Latin America, or of celebrating a 'communion' that would reassemble the fragments of human existence to make a new whole, held a particular fascination for young artists who came from countries lacking a sure sense of national identity and which were being disrupted by enormous social and economic changes.

Latin Americans also responded creatively to the modernist interest in primitive cultures. The fashion for African art and the Negro music of the United States drew attention to the formerly despised culture of the blacks in places like Cuba and Brazil. There was an element of modishness in this, but *negrismo* would lead to an immensely valuable injection of black music and poetry into the cultural mainstream in Latin America. Thanks to the work of intellectuals such as the anthropologist Fernando Ortiz and the anthologist Emilio Ballagas, black culture gained a certain respectability among whites, who would, for instance, come to accept Afro-American musical forms such as the rumba in Cuba, or indeed the samba in Brazil, as part of their general cultural patrimony. In the 1920s the white writer Alejo

Carpentier was one of the foremost musicologists concerned with black music in Cuba; his abiding interest in the African roots of Caribbean culture would combine with surrealism in the 1940s to produce his theory of the 'marvellous reality' of Latin America, the cornerstone of 'magical realism'.

Negrismo also brought the inflections of black speech into the repertoire of poetry as part of a general modernist tendency towards the demotic. But just as important, it encouraged blacks and mulattos to take pride in their culture. The mulatto poet Nicolás Guillén, a pioneer of Afro-Cuban poetry, declared:

> And now that Europe strips off
> to toast its flesh under the sun,
> and goes to Harlem and Havana for jazz and *son*,
> flaunt your blackness while the chic applaud,
> and to the envy of the whites
> speak out as a true black.*

In the Caribbean there appeared, in addition to Nicolás Guillén, other significant *negrista* poets such as José Zacarías Tallet of Cuba and Luis Palés Mato of Puerto Rico. White writers like the famous Venezuelan novelist Rómulo Gallegos and the Ecuadorian Adalberto Ortiz also wrote on Negro themes.

Modernist attraction to primitivism strengthened a developing interest in contemporary Indian communities. By the turn of the century a few intellectuals in Peru, led by the writer Manuel González Prada, had laid the foundations for *indigenismo*. The rise of disciplines such as anthropology lent intellectual respectability to this pro-Indian nativism. Yet it was modernism that finally allowed artists to perceive the creative possibilities of Indian culture. The key figure here was the Guatemalan writer Miguel Angel Asturias, whose anthropological researches in Paris and his contacts there with the surrealist movement revealed to him the cultural value of Maya myths and folklore. He began incorporating these into his own narrative fiction by the end of the 1920s, thus paving the way for the magical realism which was to attract so much international attention in the 1960s.

Modernist experimentation made for a more dynamic encounter with popular and native culture than was the case with social-realist or regionalist literature, which still remained close to nineteenth-century *costumbrismo*, with its picturesque and essentially condescending reflection of popular customs. It was in Brazil, where regionalism and a sentimental Indianism were well established, that the modernists went furthest towards upsetting complacent

---

* 'Oda pequeña a un negro boxeador cubano', *Sóngoro cosongo* (Havana, 1931), my translation.

notions about 'the primitive'. Brazilian modernism was initially centred in São Paulo, where it exploded sensationally on the cultural scene during the famous Week of Modern Art held in that city in February 1922, the centenary year of Brazil's independence. The leading modernist Oswald de Andrade, who had been impressed by the shock tactics of the futurists during a visit to Europe before the First World War, presented the Brazilian avant-garde with the liberating concept of *antropofágia*, inspired by the cannibalism of the Tupi Indians. Cannibalism was adopted as a metaphor of defiant barbarism, as an expression of scorn for bourgeois and capitalist values, but it also spoke of an anti-imperialist attitude to European civilization: the Latin American artist would no longer imitate European forms but would aggressively consume them for his own purposes, an act of destructive transformation that would result in 'totemic' and authentically Brazilian creations. The avant-garde products of *antropofágia*, rather ephemeral on the whole, foreshadowed the magical realism which would be more fully evolved in Spanish America.

Modernism also brought about a revaluation of Hispanic literary traditions, particularly as regards Renaissance and baroque poetry. Here it was the Spanish 'Generation of 1927' that led the way. The year 1927 was the tercentenary of the death of the great baroque poet Luis de Góngora, a controversial anniversary which these young poets chose to celebrate as a challenge to a rather pompous literary establishment. More seriously, these Spanish poets appreciated the fact that Góngora's dislocated syntax and complex metaphors could be adapted to the ends of modernist aesthetics. Additionally, and like Góngora himself, they turned to the rich Iberian traditions of popular poetry and song for evocative imagery and a metrical fluency that could deftly catch the natural rhythms of speech and could therefore also serve modernist purposes.

In the course of the 1920s and early 1930s Spanish American writers came into contact with the work of the 1927 group, comprising mainly poets such as Federico García Lorca and Rafael Alberti, but among whom one might also include their close friends and collaborators, the painter Salvador Dalí and the film-director Luis Buñuel. Lorca made celebrated visits to Buenos Aires and Havana in the late 1920s and early 1930s. In Havana, for instance, he met Nicolás Guillén and inspired him to write his Afro-Cuban songs in the popular Spanish mode. Alberti helped the young Pablo Neruda to find a publisher for his poetry, and he was later to reside for many years as an exile in Argentina. Neruda, who would become hugely influential throughout Latin America, lived in Spain between 1934 and 1938 and was a close friend of several of the 1927 poets. During the Spanish Civil War, he and other Spanish American poets, including César Vallejo and Octavio Paz, assisted the Republic and strengthened their personal ties with Spanish writers.

The first four decades of the century saw a cultural ferment throughout the Hispanic world. For in Spain as in America writers and intellectuals were faced with the challenge of modernity – not just the big city, machines and factories, but, more seriously for oligarchic societies, the advent of mass democracy and the materialism of the market. It is striking how the patrician anxieties that had been expressed by José Enrique Rodó in *Ariel* (1900) were echoed in the Spaniard José Ortega y Gasset's equally famous *La rebelión de las masas* ('The Revolt of the Masses', 1929). As part of their reaction to the modern world, the Spanish modernists looked back to neglected aspects of their tradition, especially the baroque, and in doing so pointed the way for the Spanish Americans to recognize their cultural affiliation with the Golden Age of Spain.

Modernist developments in Spain itself were cut short with the victory of Franco's Nationalists in the Civil War: Lorca had been murdered in 1936, and virtually all the major figures were dispersed by exile three years later. Spain, in consequence, was to languish in rigid isolation for some three decades, unable to benefit fully from the cultural ferment of the 1920s and 1930s. In Spanish America, however, the extremely stimulating modernist encounter with Hispanic traditions was able to evolve organically for the rest of the century, fertilizing narrative fiction as well as poetry, until it finally began to command international attention in the 1960s. Through contact with Spain, then, writers in America were able to reappraise the Spanish classics – Góngora, Quevedo, Lope de Vega, Cervantes, and indeed their own Gongorine muse, the Mexican nun Sor Juana Inés de la Cruz. The Spanish baroque had a general resonance in America; Alejo Carpentier would claim repeatedly that the Latin American sensibility was essentially baroque because of its love of excess, conceits and festive decoration. These qualities can be found to some degree in the writing of the major poets and novelists of the century, particularly so in Cuba, where a succession of writers – Carpentier himself, José Lezama Lima, Guillermo Cabrera Infante, Severo Sarduy – consciously evoked the Spanish baroque in their work. Playing as it did with disparate styles and ideas, the baroque offered artists a liberating self-recognition because it was incomparably suited to express *mestizaje*, the hybrid cultural reality of Latin America that liberal ideology had attempted to deny.

Spanish modernism also opened up a creative route to popular culture. Poets like Antonio and Manuel Machado, Lorca and Rafael Alberti were drawn to the traditional *cancionero* forms that still survived in popular song. In this they were seeking to revive a greatly admired feature of Golden Age culture which Alberti called *poesía en movimiento*, the phenomenon whereby highly cultivated poets such as Góngora and Lope de Vega would choose popular styles to compose ballads and songs that would find favour with the people and eventually flow into the mainstream of folklore. These cross-movements between *lo culto* and *lo popular* were to be seen increasingly in Latin America. Pablo Neruda was the moving spirit, and since the 1940s there has been a strong development of poetry and song written to be performed before a wide and often uneducated public. As a result, Latin American poetry managed to recover its place in the deeply ingrained Hispanic culture of the fiesta, as had been the case during the colonial period.

The interaction with Spanish modernism was an important factor in Latin America's slow and erratic struggle to emerge from the labyrinth of cultural solitude in which it had found itself since independence. But this encounter with the past was creative because it was not simply nostalgic: the past served to point to alternatives for a future which would otherwise lead to a modern society generally felt to be alien and threatening.

The Quest for a New Culture

Latin American modernists reacted against nineteenth-century optimism about progress. Many of them came from rural or provincial backgrounds – often from conventionally Catholic families – and they were shocked by the big city and the advancing wheels of the capitalist economy. Unable to withdraw into Catholic piety once again or to defend the patriarchal hacienda society of the countryside, they embarked on a search for new values, for a kind of society that would preserve the best of two worlds – the organic community of the old rural towns and villages they had once known, and the freedom and equality that romantic liberalism had seemed to promise after independence. Their great, haunting fear was of being denatured by the modern world, of seeing the familiar values destroyed and replaced by the impersonality of a mechanical and mercenary society. For writers like César Vallejo, who came from a large and intensely religious family in rural Peru, or Pablo Neruda, a railwayman's son from the deep south of Chile, personal integrity was bound up with a quest for cultural roots and national identity.

Not surprisingly, the modernist ferment was strongest in those parts of the continent that were modernizing most rapidly, and especially in Buenos

Aires and São Paulo, both very similar in that they were the two largest conurbations in Latin America, with a high proportion of immigrants from Europe (Mexico City would not emerge from the chaotic Revolution and its aftermath until the 1940s). The wealthy élites of these dynamic cities were highly receptive to cultural trends in Europe; the experiments of the avant-garde were avidly followed in artistic circles and repeated in the proliferating small magazines. Modernism in these centres retained a cosmopolitan quality, formal innovation and the constant interrogation of the process of creation being the prime interests of artists. Even so, the question of cultural identity did arise: the modernists of São Paulo, for instance, were effusively national-istic, even if their search for roots led them indifferently to praise *gaúchos* and *bandeirantes* as well as Indian cannibals; in Buenos Aires even the most avant-garde writers such as Borges were concerned also with creole values and the gauchesque heritage.

Indeed, the characteristic common to the various currents of modernism in Latin America was self-affirmation: the desire to turn the tables on Europe or at least to escape its tutelage and define a truly independent national culture. For what irritated the young generation who rebelled against the scientific positivism of the liberal élites was Eurocentrism, the assumption that Latin America must progress down the same path taken by Europeans since the Enlightenment. Not surprisingly, Oswald Spengler's book *The Decline of the West* (1926–8) had an immense influence, since it presented history as a process of cyclical growth and decay. This view made it possible, therefore, to turn the peculiar cultural features of Latin America into positive attributes. After the Mexican Revolution, José Vasconcelos was able to conceive of *mestizaje* – which liberal positivists had regarded as an obstacle to progress – as an advantage, since it provided the seed-bed for a future 'cosmic race'. The Cuban Alejo Carpentier came to believe that *mestizaje* made the Caribbean the cradle of a new civilization, just as the Mediterranean had once been the source of European civilization as a result of a similar mixing of races and cultures.

Another influential book was the North American Waldo Frank's *The Rediscovery of America*, published in New York in 1929. Frank took up Spengler's theme of European decline and argued that the organic decompo-sition of European civilization would lead to the growth of a new civilization in the Americas. An enthusiastic follower of Frank was Antenor Orrego, a Peruvian writer associated with the *indigenista* journal *Amauta* (in which extracts from Frank's book appeared in 1928, before its publication). He too spoke of the decomposition of European civilization and of the need to find a new 'integral' culture in America. But as a socialist and an *indigenista*, he accepted that such a view would entail a revaluation of the orthodox Marxist theory of the historical process.

Latin American intellectuals were quite prepared to rethink history. Orrego's fellow *indigenista*, Víctor Raúl Haya de la Torre, who founded the APRA party as a vehicle for the revolution that would liberate 'Indo-America', was inspired by Einstein's theory of relativity in the elaboration of a philosophy of history that would accommodate different conceptions of time depending on the particular conditions of a country:

> The history of the world, viewed from Indo-American 'historical space-time', will never be what the philosopher observes from the vantage-point of European 'historical space-time'. Likewise, we hold that what is 'last' in Europe may perhaps be 'first' in Indo-America.*

Haya de la Torre instanced imperialism, which European Marxists considered to be the last stage of capitalism, but which, in the historical experience of Indo-America, was the *first* stage of capitalist development. Efforts such as these to break down the scientific positivists' linear view of progress provided a stimulus to the creative imagination. There is an abiding preoccupation in twentieth-century Latin American literature with the nature of historical time – implicitly, in some of Borges's major fictions and essays, in Neruda's *Alturas de Macchu Picchu* ('Heights of Macchu Picchu'), in the prose and poetry of Octavio Paz, the novels of Miguel Angel Asturias, Alejo Carpentier, Carlos Fuentes, Gabriel García Márquez and many others; and the origins of such concerns are to be found in those first attempts by nationalist intellectuals of the 1920s and 1930s to develop a critique of Eurocentric historiography.

Yet if the rethinking of the historical process was intended to create a new space for Latin America, how was the new 'integral' culture to come about? Increasingly, it was Marxism that provided the guidelines for social transformation, and the most creative Marxist thinker was the Peruvian mestizo José Carlos Mariátegui, founder of *Amauta*, leading *indigenista* and author of the seminal *Siete ensayos de interpretación de la realidad peruana* ('Seven Interpretative Essays on Peruvian Reality', 1928). For Mariátegui, the Indian heritage was the source of cultural authenticity and, influenced still by the spirit of his Catholic upbringing and by *arielismo*, Mariátegui, like Orrego, looked for cultural wholeness – the integration of the spiritual and the material – through the regeneration of the indigenous communities and the

---

* *Espacio-tiempo histórico* (Lima, 1948), p. 13, quoted in Martin S. Stabb, *In Quest of Identity: Patterns in the Spanish American Essay of Ideas, 1890–1960* (University of North Carolina Press: Chapel Hill, 1967), p. 126.

revitalization of Indian traditions. Believing that the Inca state was a proto-type of a socialist society, Mariátegui argued that the Indian peasantry rather than the industrial proletariat were the true revolutionary class in Latin America.

Mariátegui died in 1930, too early for his passionate *indigenismo* to be synthesized with Marxist theory. But his readiness to reinterpret the historical models of European Marxism in the light of American experience anticipated and influenced the radical Marxist innovations of the 1960s in Latin America. The Cuban Revolution's moral idealism in striving to create a New Man and Che Guevara's subsequent emphasis on the peasantry as the revolutionary class owe a considerable debt to Mariátegui. The spirituality that still per-meates Mariátegui's thought provided an inspiration for radical theologians of liberation. His rejection of the Westernization of the Indian was to give added force to the Latin American left's struggle against imperialism and to its hopes of creating a socialist society unique to the continent. In Peru itself, a more concrete legacy can be found in the measures carried out by the military government of General Velasco Alvarado in 1968–75 – the dec-laration of Quechua as an official language and the radical land reform in which *ayllu* practice was adopted as a model for landholding. But Mari-átegui's vision was most directly influential in the 1980s, when the *Sendero Luminoso* guerrilla movement, with its mystical overtones and its unbending faith in the Indian community as the prototype of socialism, launched a revolutionary war against the capitalist state.

The vision of a restored 'organic community' or an 'integral culture' exercised an appeal well beyond Marxist circles – among nationalists, *indi-genistas, arielistas*, Catholics and indeed fascists. In Peru itself, there were conservative Catholic writers like Víctor Andrés Belaúnde who defended the rights of the Indian but also advocated the acceptance of the Hispanic legacy, criticizing Mariátegui and the left for their wholesale rejection of colonial culture. Even in Argentina, which had been the most successful liberal society in Latin America until the 1930s, nationalists like Ricardo Rojas, with his vision of 'Eurindia', or Ezequiel Martínez Estrada, whose *Radiografía de la pampa* ('X-Ray of the Pampas', 1933) was a famous denunci-ation of the ravages caused by economic development, were prominent in the reaction to the dominant liberalism that had transformed the national economy. From the 1920s, then, cultural nationalism – whether deriving from *indigenismo* or from an *arielista* defence of Latinity – rejected the course of European history since the Enlightenment, and showed an aversion towards technology and industrial capitalism. For at the root of this cultural nationalism lay a profound wish to find an alternative to the 'dehumanization' of the modern world.

Still, within the broadly nationalist ethos of the times, the old division between *americanismo* and *universalismo* persisted. The latter was most vigorously represented, as might be expected, in Buenos Aires, and best exemplified by the literary journal *Sur*, founded in 1931 by the wealthy patrician Victoria Ocampo. *Sur* had a crucial influence on the development of modern Latin American culture, and this was largely due to its policy of publishing contemporary European and North American literature in translation, which made it a major channel for the transmission of modernism to the continent. Pluralist and non-political, it acted as a forum for new ideas and styles, and though often accused of élitism, it nevertheless published the work of most of the important Spanish American writers of the century. *Sur*'s attitude to the question of cultural nationalism can be summed up in the observation of Borges, a writer closely associated with the journal: 'We can handle all the European themes, handle them without superstition, with an irreverence which can have, and already does have, fortunate consequences.'★ Thus, even among the cosmopolitans there was no deference to Europe. The real divide was between those, like the Peruvian *indigenistas*, who wanted to create a unique, non-Western culture for Latin America and others who sought a distinctive place within modern Western civilization.

The tensions generated by these divergent attitudes were most fully explored in post-revolutionary Mexico, where both *indigenismo* and the desire for modernization were strong. The result was the ambiguous and often contradictory ideology of the ruling Institutional Revolutionary Party (PRI), which presided over one of the most spectacular examples of economic growth in the continent, yet strongly promoted the Aztec heritage and contemporary Indian culture as sources of national identity. For instance, the archaeologist Manuel Gamio made a pioneering study of the culture of Teotrihuacan but also promoted the integral education of the contemporary Indian. He was made director of the newly founded Department of Anthropology in Mexico City in 1917 as part of an invaluable project to recuperate all aspects of Mexico's extremely rich and varied cultural legacy.

The question of *lo mexicano* had been at issue since the first decade of the century, when young *arielista* intellectuals like Antonio Caso, José Vasconcelos and Alfonso Reyes, founded the *Ateneo de la Juventud* in 1907 and led the intellectual opposition to the positivist *científicos* of the Porfirio Díaz regime. In the 1920s the Mexican muralists, influenced by the Russian

★ 'The Argentine writer and tradition', *Labyrinths* (Penguin: Harmondsworth, 1970), p. 218.

Revolution and the *indigenista* movement, depicted the Indian heritage as being in historic conflict with the Spanish. By contrast the writers and poets associated with the vanguard magazine *Contemporáneos* maintained the *arielista* openness to Spain and Europe.

It was José Vasconcelos who, as minister of culture under Obregón in 1921–4 and the early patron of the muralist movement, later sought to resolve these tensions by arguing that a true Mexican identity could arise only from *mestizaje*, a fusion of both Indian and Hispanic cultures. The influential *pensador* Samuel Ramos extended the concept of *mestizaje* to include foreign influences, observing that Mexican culture must ultimately be conceived as 'universal culture made ours'.★ Tensions between *indigenismo* and *universalismo* continued to mark the work of the country's best writers, such as Octavio Paz and Carlos Fuentes, but these men, even so, distinguished themselves by a readiness to make universal culture their own.

The result of these intellectual trends of the 1920s was that the cultural élite, comprising writers, artists, academics and clergy, was on the whole sharply opposed, in theory if not always in practice, to the governing élite of lawyers, businessmen, industrialists and, not least, military officers. For the rest of the century there would be no consensus about the general direction of Latin American development. This ideological conflict among the élites resulted in the weakening of the authority of the democratic state and its institutions, leaving a door open to dictatorship and the abuse of human rights. It also made for a highly charged political atmosphere, very conducive to populist manipulation, in which the framing of public policy for the common good was liable to be subordinated to powerful vested interests.

Modernism in the Visual Arts and Music

As occurred in the field of literature and ideas, the modernist revolution released new energies in the visual arts. Once again, the most creative centres were those where modernization was most advanced – Argentina, Chile, Brazil, Mexico and Cuba. Modernist styles came to Latin America during the 1920s largely as a result of visits to Europe by individual artists. On their return to their native countries these artists made contact with writers and intellectuals and participated in the general awakening to the cultural nationalism of the period by adapting modernist techniques to the exploration of indigenous cultural roots.

★ *El perfil del hombre y de la cultura en México* (Mexico, 1934), quoted in Stabb, op. cit., p. 192.

A key factor in the awakening of the visual arts was patronage. There now existed sufficient private wealth in the big cities to ensure a steady demand for paintings and artefacts. In post-revolutionary Mexico, however, the most influential patron was the state, which financed the muralists and would continue for the rest of the century to promote the arts and architecture. But as with writers and poets, tensions soon appeared between artists who searched for a national art and those who worked in international styles.

The creation of a national, public art was the common aim of the Mexican muralists. Muralism in Mexico antedated the Revolution: the painter and anti-Porfirista activist Dr Atl (Gerardo Murillo), who taught at the Academy of San Carlos, began experimenting with murals in the 1910s. His former pupils Diego Rivera, David Alfaro Siqueiros and José Clemente Orozco became the principal figures of the movement in the post-revolutionary period. Rivera moved from an early cubist phase towards a monumental, narrative style that depicted the struggles of the Mexican nation. His best work portrays the traditional way of life of the Indian peasants, but he was also fascinated with modern industry and found an effective visual language to convey the powerful promise of factory production. Siqueiros was concerned above all with advancing the socialist revolution, and he developed a style rooted in cubism and constructivism in which geometric masses were distorted by a kind of expressionist emotionalism that gave his frescoes a dramatic visual impact. Less politically committed, Orozco took his themes from pre-Hispanic mythology, Mexican history and the customs of ordinary people in order to represent the diverse cultural reality of modern Mexico. Juan O'Gorman, too, was less interested in promoting the class struggle than in celebrating the march of progress in serenely optimistic tableaux.

The mural movement in Mexico thus incorporated the conflicts between *indigenismo* and *universalismo*, between political commitment and personal values, that affected all the arts in Latin America throughout the century. A major painter like Rufino Tamayo – a Zapotec Indian of humble origins who started his career under the influence of Rivera and the muralists – became interested in surrealism in the 1930s and lived for most of his life in New York and Paris, treating Mexican themes in a lyrical, dreamlike style. Diego Rivera's wife, Frida Kahlo, was admired by André Breton: her work has an oneiric quality and boldly confronts her social and physiological condition as a woman. The photographer Manuel Alvarez Bravo created memorable surreal images, and worked in the cinema as a cameraman and director. Alberto Gironella turned away from political concerns to work in an international idiom, and in the 1960s he led a movement whose aim was to revive surrealism, a recurrent interest in Mexico, where many European avant-garde and surrealist artists – Luis Buñuel, Remedios Varo, Wolfgang Paalen, Leonora Carrington, Mathias Goeritz – settled in the 1940s.

Surrealism also left a deep impression on the Chilean Roberto Matta Echaurren after meeting André Breton in the 1930s; he was thereafter based mostly in Paris, although his painting, which was largely individual and universalist, bears traces of his native continent. Wilfredo Lam, a Cuban of Chinese-African extraction, was another outstanding surrealist painter. He too encountered the avant-garde in Paris but, while living in Cuba during the 1940s, he was greatly attracted to Afro-Caribbean culture, which continued to influence his style and themes after he moved back to Paris in the 1950s. The Cuban René Portocarrero was concerned with fantasy and magic, and inspired also by Afro-Caribbean culture. In Colombia, Fernando Botero invented a very original visual idiom that was often likened, in its satirical use of comically bloated, doll-like figures, to the magical realism made famous in fiction by his compatriot Gabriel García Márquez.

Artists in the River Plate republics, like writers, tended towards cosmopolitan styles, though Pedro Figari was noted in the 1920s for his evocations of creole customs. Xul Solar, variously influenced by Paul Klee, the surrealists and German expressionism, painted eerie landscapes suggestive of subconscious anxieties. The most notable artist in the non-figurative tradition was the Uruguayan Joaquín Torres-García, who returned to Montevideo in the 1930s after working in Catalonia with Antonio Gaudí and later in other centres, including New York, where he met Marcel Duchamp. He actively promoted abstract and constructivist styles, influencing the eclectic and fertile *Arte Madí* movement in Buenos Aires in the 1940s. The Argentine Roberto Aizenberg became a surrealist under his teacher Juan Batlle Planes in the 1950s, but his mature art combines fantasy, symbolism and an abstraction elaborated from constructivist principles.

Visual artists also contributed to the modernist upsurge of the 1920s in Brazil. The painter Emiliano di Cavalcanti was one of the organizers of the Week of Modern Art in São Paulo in 1922, where he exhibited along with Tarsila do Amaral and Anita Malfatti. Tarsila joined the vanguard movement associated with the poet Oswald de Andrade's journal *Antropofágia*, which attempted to combine modernist experiment with nationalist concerns; her revolutionary politics drew her to social realism, and in subsequent years she became one of the most respected artists of her country. Cândido Portinari was noted for his depiction of the life and customs of the Brazilian regions.

If the modernism deriving from the 1920s was broadly nationalist, by the 1950s questions of cultural identity had given way to unproblematic assimilation of international styles. It was in Brazil, which also saw the rise of an important movement of concrete poetry during the same period, that visual artists became most strongly committed to working in geometric abstraction and concrete-kinetic art. Notable artists were Lygia Clark, Hélio Oiticica, Sérgio Camargo and Lygia Pape. Cosmopolitanism flourished also in Venezuela, where Alejandro Otero and Jesús Rafael Soto explored colour, movement and geometric surfaces in compositions influenced by Marcel Duchamp and Mondrian in particular.

In these countries, and also in Mexico, the 1950s was a period of tremendous architectural vitality. Ambitious construction programmes for public buildings in the international modern style were sponsored by governments. Oscar Niemeyer and Lúcio Costa became world-famous for the remarkable buildings they conceived for Brasilia, the new capital of Brazil. The Venezuelan Carlos Raúl Villanueva designed the University City in Caracas, which included decorative work by international artists like Hans Arp, Alexander Calder, Vasarely as well as the younger Venezuelan abstractionists. Guido Bermúdez and Moisés Benacerraf contributed notably to modern public building in Caracas. The construction of a new campus for the National University of Mexico, with its famous Olympic Stadium and Central Library, gave rein to the talents of Juan O'Gorman, Gustavo Saavedra, Juan Martínez de Velasco and Félix Candela.

The fact that international modernism in architecture and the visual arts should have been espoused with such enthusiasm chiefly in Brazil, Venezuela and Mexico should cause no surprise. These were the richest countries in Latin America at the time – in Brazil and Mexico the state had embarked on a programme of intensive industrialization financed by foreign capital; Venezuela had set up a very lucrative export-economy based on huge reserves of oil. In all three countries, therefore, governments were prepared to celebrate their appetite for modernity in whimsical structures of concrete and glass. In Argentina, by contrast, economic and social troubles under Perón and the fragile Radical governments that followed him precluded a comparable exuberance.

After the Cuban Revolution, cosmopolitan idioms entered into a renewed tension with indigenist nationalism. This was most evident in the cinema. Faced with the power of Hollywood, domestic film production had always tended to be on a small scale and mostly financed or protected by the state. The standard fare for mass audiences was the historical epic – in Mexico the Revolution had been a favourite topic since the 1920s – or the romantic melodrama, a forerunner of the lachrymose *radionovelas* and television soap operas that were to win vast audiences in the 1950s and 1960s. Art films, based on work by serious writers, were being made by the 1950s: the exiled

Spanish director Luis Buñuel made some of his best films in Mexico after the War; in Argentina Leopoldo Torre Nilsson achieved distinction, as did Nelson Pereira dos Santos in Brazil. But the political cinema sponsored by the fledgling Marxist state in Cuba – directors such as Tomás Gutiérrez Alea, Santiago Alvarez and Humberto Solás won international regard – inspired film-makers in other countries to combine radical nationalist themes with the technical experiments of the contemporary French *nouvelle vague* directors. A number of revolutionary film-directors became well known on the international scene: Miguel Littín (Chile), Jorge Sanjinés (Bolivia), Fernando Solanas (Argentina), Ruy Guerra and Glauber Rocha (Brazil), the last being the most famous practitioner and theoretician of the Brazilian *Cinema Nôvo*, which came to prominence in 1962 during João Goulart's radical-populist presidency and which disappeared with it as a result of the military coup of 1964. Most revolutionary film-makers were to experience exile during the 1970s, and though a few succeeded in making films abroad, the radical cinema of Latin America had lost its momentum by the end of that decade. In the 1980s, mirroring what was to happen also in fiction, a number of women achieved a reputation as film-directors, notably María Luisa Bemberg (Argentina), whose features were successful on the international circuit.

Modernism, then, released new artistic energies, but the Latin American response was dual, tending to nationalism on the one hand and to cosmopolitanism on the other, though such tendencies were not, of course, mutually exclusive but depended on individual artists' own emphases and priorities. Cultural nationalism, which dominated the 1920s and 1930s, was superseded during the Second World War by universal styles, which in turn gave way to a new radical nationalism of the left in the 1960s as the preoccupation with indigenous identity revived.

The pattern is evident also in music: from the 1920s serious composers like Heitor Villa-Lobos (Brazil), Carlos Chávez (Mexico), Amadeo Roldán and García Caturla (Cuba) began to utilize themes from national folklore at a time when popular musical forms such as the samba of Brazil, the rumba, *son* and conga of Cuba and the tango of Buenos Aires were gaining international currency. A reaction to this folkloric nationalism came in the late 1940s and 1950s, as younger composers, chiefly Alberto Ginastera of Argentina and José Ardévol of Cuba, sought to assimilate more fully the modernist revolution in music; even some composers of the 1920s generation, such as Carlos Chávez, embraced *universalismo*. This current remained strong well into the 1960s and 1970s, but in that period musicians on the left (in Chile, Peru and other Andean countries, as in Cuba) developed a neo-*indigenista* style based on traditional popular music.

By the 1980s music, like all the other arts, had arrived at a situation of diversity and pluralism, in which the phenomenon of *mestizaje* or cross-cultural borrowing was itself a source of inspiration. New forms mixing popular and cultivated styles, foreign and traditional resources, appealed to a very large multinational public, not least because of the expansion of technology – radio, television, electronics – and the marketing know-how of the international recording and publishing industries. The most obvious instance is the international popularity of salsa music based on Caribbean rhythms but played on a combination of traditional and electrical instruments. But there were similar developments elsewhere, such as the fusion in Brazil of samba with rock and with Jamaican reggae music, the mixing of Mexican folk idioms with North American country music as in the Tex-Mex genre, or the crossing of tango and jazz by Argentines such as Astor Piazzola.

This new cross-culturalism stemmed from important social transformations that had occurred in Latin America between the 1960s and 1980s. An unprecedented phenomenon had been the mass migration of Latin Americans to the USA, either for economic or political reasons. Millions of Hispanic people, many of them of peasant origin, had to come to terms with Anglo-Saxon culture and modern liberal capitalism; the new genres had, therefore, a spontaneity and popular appeal which were lacking in the modernist experiments initiated by the more intellectual artists of the 1920s. For instance, the centre of salsa music was actually New York City, where large numbers of Puerto Ricans and Cubans had settled in the 1960s; in the 1970s and 1980s salsa became a kind of musical lingua franca for the Hispanic communities in the major cities of the USA and in the Caribbean basin. The other crucial transformation occurred within Latin America itself: this was the massive shift of population from rural to urban areas that took place in the 1950s and 1960s. (The migration to the big US cities from Mexico, Central America and Puerto Rico was a facet of this continentwide urbanization.) In the peripheral slums, country music was given an urban gloss and broadcast by the mass media; new genres tended to emerge from these vibrant plebeian milieux, such as the *chicha* music of the Lima shanty-towns, which by the 1980s had become more popular than either Andean or creole folklore.

Literature, of course, registered very clearly these oscillations between the desire to assert a unique identity and a passion for modernity within the broad revolution effected by modernism, for the resultant ambiguities and tensions formed the subject-matter of the best writers. In fact, a survey of the major literary works, themes and trends of the century can reveal the long-term significance of historical developments. In some respects the international 'Boom' enjoyed by Latin American literature from the mid-1960s masked the importance of the modernist ferment of the 1920s and 1930s. On the other hand, the Boom itself, and the pluralism of the 1980s in particular, anticipated a sea-change in the culture and society of Latin America, and therefore represented a phenomenon of great historical import for the continent.

Modernism in Poetry

In poetry the encounter with European modernism resulted from growing dissatisfaction with the limitations of *fin de siècle* Hispanic *modernismo*. Rubén Darío had failed to synthesize the ideal of art for art's sake with the new sense of *americanismo* fostered by José Enrique Rodó in *Ariel* and other essays. Younger poets and even major figures like the Argentine Leopoldo Lugones had tired of the contrived, mellifluous rhetoric of *modernismo*. The time had come to 'wring the neck of the swan', in the graphic phrase of the Mexican poet and *arielista* Enrique González Martínez, and write instead in plainer language about the local scene and about accessible human emotions.

The Mexican Ramón López Velarde, who published his first collection in 1916, the year of Darío's death, wrote about religious faith troubled by sensual longings, and looked for the quintessential Mexico in the everyday life of its provinces. His poem 'Suave patria' ('Gentle Fatherland') is one of the most widely known poems of his country. Several distinguished exponents of this poetry of emotional directness were women: Juana de Ibarbourou, the restlessly erotic Delmira Agostini and the early feminist Alfonsina Storni. But the most prominent was the Chilean Gabriela Mistral, the first Latin American writer to win the Nobel Prize (1945), who wrote sober, moving poetry about her condition as a woman and about the natural environment of America. The fact that these women came from Argentina, Uruguay and Chile, the most economically advanced countries, is an indication that modernization was eroding the conventions of traditional Hispanic society.

However, plain words and sincere expression were not sufficient to convey the confused and often violently negative reactions to life in the big cities. The real break with *modernismo* was produced by the revolution in form and style ushered in by the avant-garde. The 1920s was a time when manifestos and small magazines appeared in several cities, hailing the latest work of the European vanguard and publishing their own experiments in the new vein. In 1921 the mural-review *Prisma* was plastered on the walls of Buenos Aires;

the following year *Proa* was founded by Borges, who was also associated with the foundation of the magazine *Martín Fierro* in 1924; the São Paulo modernists published *Klaxon* in 1922; in Havana the *Revista de Avance* was founded in 1927; in Mexico City, the review *Contemporáneos* in 1928.

Borges was one of the chief agitators of the Argentine avant-garde, introducing *ultraísmo* to Spanish America. In 1921 he published an ultraist manifesto in Buenos Aires after returning from a long sojourn in Europe (1914–21), where he had latterly joined a group of very young anti-*modernista* poets in Madrid in founding the magazine *Ultra*. *Ultraísmo* was an eclectic movement, taking its cue from cubism, futurism and Dada; its real impetus came from a youthful desire to shock and experiment – to disrupt the complacent reveries of the *modernistas* and thrust poetry into the twentieth century. Some of Borges's *ultraísta* concerns are still evident in his earliest collections, such as *Fervor de Buenos Aires* ('Fervour of Buenos Aires', 1923), but in the 1930s he repudiated the avant-garde and rediscovered the value of metre and rhyme. Even so, his understanding of European modernism was profound, and it crucially shaped his prose fiction of the 1940s.

The most consistently provocative of the avant-garde poets was Vicente Huidobro (1893–1948), a Chilean who claimed to be the originator and presiding genius of the new Spanish American vanguard after having invented as early as 1915 what he called *creacionismo* – the doctrine that the poem must create its own reality, disclaiming any direct connection with the external world: the poet should 'make a poem as nature makes a tree'. This, of course, was one version of an aesthetic idea that was characteristic of modernism in general. Huidobro went to live in Paris in 1916, where he befriended Apollinaire, Tristan Tzara and Pierre Reverdy, and wrote poetry in French. Returning to the Spanish language, he was one of the first Hispanic poets to attack the logic of conventional discourse in order to involve the reader in the creation of poetic meaning. Once thought of as little more than an exhibitionist, he is nowadays acknowledged to be a substantial figure, whose masterpiece *Altazor* (1931, though written in 1919) expressed the outstanding theme of Hispanic poetry in the first half of the century – anguish at the loss of faith in a transcendent reality.

This theme pervaded the work of the most original poet of Latin America in the century, the Peruvian César Vallejo. Forsaking his rural Catholic background for city life, Vallejo was able to wrench his poetry out of its *modernista* carapace by the sheer force of his anguished imagination, with little if any prompting from the avant-garde. This phenomenon is already evident in *Los heraldos negros* ('The Black Heralds', 1918), but shortly afterwards Vallejo published *Trilce* (1922), one of the most remarkable poetic achievements of the century. The great theme of *Trilce* is the dislocation of language following a collapse of faith in the human soul. Vallejo's bewildered materialism is evident in the abrasive texture of the poems – ragged syntax, monstrous neologisms, commonplace phrases twisted into incoherence and hard scientific terms that are swept up by occasional flurries of misplaced lyricism. And yet the result is not cacophony; rather it is a weird, jangling music rising as from the depths of a tortured mind.

As a last refuge of human dignity in a senseless world, poetry became a way of life for Vallejo, who lived out the rest of his days in poverty after moving to Paris in 1923. In *Poemas humanos* ('Human Poems', 1939) he developed his idiosyncratic style with little debt to European modernism. Here he gropes for some kind of human solidarity, and yet, though he moved towards Marxism and was close to his compatriot José Carlos Mariátegui, he never found relief from his terrible existential dread. During the Spanish Civil War he wrote proletarian war poetry of great force, but the approaching defeat of the Republic caused him intense personal suffering, as can be inferred from the title of his long poem, *España, aparta de mí este cáliz* ('Spain, Take This Cup From Me'), published in 1938 shortly before his death.

Very different from Vallejo was Pablo Neruda, who had a lyrical imagination of rare inventiveness and was from the start a nature poet of commanding power. Even during his period of spiritual anguish, as recorded in the two parts of *Residencia en la tierra* ('Residence on Earth', 1933 and 1935), he wrote expansively, with a humour wrung from despair by the transformative richness of his metaphors. The famous *Canto general*, a long survey of the history of Latin America, was written between 1938 and 1950, much of it while he was in hiding after the banning of the Chilean Communist Party, which he had represented in the senate. The crucial section is *Alturas de Macchu Picchu* ('Heights of Macchu Picchu'), in which he describes with hieratic solemnity an ascent from a state of personal confusion to a new plane of understanding, having perceived a kinship with the exploited workers of the Inca past. In this revelation of historical meaning through collective solidarity Neruda found a role for himself as the voice of the common people, a vocation that allowed him to give free rein to his innate lyrical exuberance. His later work alternated between political verse and poetry exalting nature and the delights of love.

The first major Spanish American poets of the twentieth century – Borges, Huidobro, Vallejo and Neruda – all reacted against the *modernismo* associated with Rubén Darío. They initially drew on the experiments of the European avant-garde, but the rediscovery of both the baroque and the traditional popular lyric through the Spanish Generation of 1927 gave a distinctive

Hispanic quality to their work. The Spanish tradition was to remain potent throughout the century, but in the 1930s and 1940s French surrealism and the modernist poetics of the major North Americans – T. S. Eliot, Ezra Pound and William Carlos Williams – became crucial and lasting influences. The surrealists opened the door to the subconscious through free association; the Anglo-Saxons brought everyday experience, colloquial language and an empirical gaze to their poetry; both influences reinforced the image as the nerve-centre of meaning in a poem.

Neruda, like the Spanish poets Lorca and Alberti, assimilated surrealism for his own ends. A more faithful beneficiary was the prolific Octavio Paz, who befriended André Breton in Paris in the 1940s and found in the surrealist revolt against banal reality a source of enduring inspiration. Paz's concern was to find release from the solitude of the alienated individual immersed in the flow of time. He believed that fullness of being could be experienced in those rare instants of communion with others afforded by erotic love and poetry.

That belief remained constant throughout his work, though it underwent a number of variations. *Piedra de sol* ('Sun Stone', 1957) is a reverie on the vicissitudes of historical time, from which intermittent escape is found in the love of woman, the universal 'other'. During the 1960s he encountered oriental mysticism in India – the kaleidoscopic poem *Blanco* (1966) generates an interplay of images and rhythms in which conflict is transcended by ecstatic moments of fulfilment. His later poetry, such as *Pasado en claro* ('A Draft of Shadows', 1974), dwells movingly on the fragility of personal identity, but *Arbol adentro* ('A Tree Within', 1987) is possessed of a coltish humour expressed in an unforced, surrealist manner; the poet's death is conceived as an instant of communion which 'opens under my feet/and closes over me and is pure time'. Paz had an adventurous career that embraced a wide range of political and intellectual causes: he was close to Marxism in his youth, but was repelled by its intolerance when he was in Spain during the Civil War; by the 1970s he was a leading advocate of democratic liberalism. As a commentator and essayist, Paz became one of the most authoritative intellectual figures in Latin America (he was awarded the Nobel Prize for literature in 1990).

Octavio Paz, in fact, was nurtured in the rich poetic culture of Mexico in the 1930s. The journal *Contemporáneos* acted as the forum for a group of highly gifted poets such as Xavier Villaurrutia, José Gorostiza, Carlos Pellicer, Jaime Torres Bodet and Gilberto Owen, and it was notable for its openness to the new modernist currents both in Europe (especially France) and in the United States. Mexico continued to produce outstanding poets: Alí

Chumacero, Marco Antonio Montes de Oca, José Emilio Pacheco, Gabriel Zaid.

In direct contrast to the exalted poetics of a Neruda or a Paz, the Chilean Nicanor Parra inaugurated what he termed 'anti-poetry' – matter-of-fact, conversational and suspicious of histrionics. His downbeat, ironic tones had a salutary influence in the 1950s and 1960s, when writers felt under pressure to throw themselves into politics. Parra's fellow Chilean Enrique Lihn wrote with a disabused eye about personal relationships and also tackled political themes, but used anti-poetry to keep Neruda's exuberance at bay. Parra's work caught the attention of North American Beat poets like Allen Ginsberg and Lawrence Ferlinghetti, who translated his *Poemas y antipoemas* ('Poems and Anti-Poems', 1954).

The Beat Generation of the 1950s, in turn, were an important influence on the Nicaraguan Ernesto Cardenal, a Catholic monk who ran a community on the island of Solentiname, but who experienced a second conversion to communism after a visit to Cuba in 1970. Like Che Guevara, Cardenal believed that revolution would create a New Man in Latin America. His poetic style was called 'exteriorist', since it avoided introspection through objective imagery and everyday language, traits he derived from William Carlos Williams and Ezra Pound. His poems of the 1960s and 1970s are loose, polyphonic collages put together from a jumble of verbal materials: historical chronicles, Amerindian myths, the idioms of European love poetry and, not least, the linguistic rubble of city life – advertisements, newspaper headlines, shop signs, street talk. This heterogeneity is often exploited for comic and ironic effects, but in the end the jarring fragments are harmonized by the poet's faith in the revolutionary transfiguration of the complex into the simple: his Utopian dream of creating a 'City of Communion' (there is a clear affinity here with Octavio Paz's quest for 'communion') finally holds the world together and restores it to its primary innocence.

Though much of Cardenal's poetry was cosmopolitan in its forms and references, it was firmly rooted in the history of Nicaragua, and often depicted the life of the Indian peasantry – one of his masterpieces was the sequence of cantos *Homenaje a los indios americanos* ('Homage to the American Indians', 1969), in which he evokes indigenous America as a golden age of harmony and peace. After the overthrow of the dictator Somoza, against whom he had written virulent satires, Cardenal became minister of culture in the revolutionary Sandinista government. Other Nicaraguan poets of note were Joaquín Pasos (1914–47), who anticipated Cardenal with his conversational, wryly humorous style and his interest in the Indian peasants, and Pablo Antonio Cuadra, once a friend of Cardenal and an exteriorist like him, but who moved away from left-wing political commitment in the 1980s. Among younger politicized poets were Julio Valle-Castillo and Gioconda Belli.

In the 1960s and 1970s poets of the radical left took the political work of Neruda and Cardenal as their models. The guerrilla movements in various countries had their poets, of whom the most celebrated were Juan Gelman, a Montonero in Argentina, Javier Heraud of Peru, and the Central Americans Otto René Castillo and Roque Dalton (the last three of whom were killed in action). Cuba produced poets like Roberto Fernández Retamar, Pablo Armando Fernández and Fayed Jamis, who served the Revolution in their work. These committed poets wrote in a language shorn of modernist complexities in order to communicate directly with the masses. There occurred an associated development in folk music with the emergence of radicalized singer-poets, such as Mercedes Sosa of Argentina and Victor Jara of Chile, and groups like Quilapayún and Inti-Illimani, who set revolutionary lyrics to music played in traditional Andean styles. These folk-singers became world-famous at a time when international attention was focused on the guerrilla struggles taking place in many parts of the continent.

On the other hand, the tradition of cultivated, formal poetry, which Borges had salvaged from avant-garde experimentalism, continued to flourish in various ways. In Cuba a group which had been associated with the magazine *Orígenes* in the 1940s – José Lezama Lima, Eliseo Diego, Cintio Vitier – remained productive in the 1960s. Lezama Lima wrote a lush baroque poetry about spiritual quests and erotic transports. The Peruvian Carlos Germán Belli, though influenced by César Vallejo, invented a uniquely ironical and often comic style that fused baroque archaism with a modern idiom, as in the title-poem of his collection *¡Oh hada cibernética!* ('O Cybernetic Fairy!', 1971), where he prays to be freed by the fairy's 'electric brain and chaste antidote/from horrid human trades'. His younger compatriot Antonio Cisneros, whose language was plainer, was preoccupied with the historic *mestizaje* of Peru and, after a religious conversion, with themes of political and spiritual renewal. The Chilean Oscar Hahn made a tentative return to rhyme, metre and genre in his handling of the anxieties of the late twentieth century. The Argentine Alberto Girri was intensely subjective and his work was replete with classical allusions, as if he were seeking a desperate refuge from his own bleak nihilism, as well as the barbarism of modern society, in the civilizing myths of the ancients. A preoccupation with death and madness marked the work of the Argentine Alejandra Pizarnik, the major woman poet of the latter part of the century.

In Brazil, the modernist outburst of the 1920s was a reaction against the formality of the ruling Parnassian-symbolist aesthetic associated with Eurocentric liberalism. As in Spanish America, the quest for identity was the common concern of these modernists, but the movement was highly diversified in its response to modernization and big-city life. A strident nationalism – which crystallized in the notion of cultural *antropofágia* – characterized the work of Oswald de Andrade and his Pau-Brasil group (named after his collection *Brazilwood* of 1925). Members of the group included Manuel Bandeira, Raul Bopp, Mário de Andrade and Ronald Carvalho, whose Whitmanesque *Toda a América* ('The Whole of America', 1926) anticipated the breadth of Neruda's *Canto general*.

The most innovative writer of the group was Mário de Andrade. He is best remembered for his fantasy novel *Macunaíma* (1928), a precursor of magical realism, but his *Paulicéia Desvairada* ('Hallucinated City', 1922), published the same year as T. S. Eliot's *The Waste Land*, is a very early attempt to come to terms with the great metropolis: in a frenetic evocation of São Paulo, the clown-like poet, by turns appalled and excited by the swirl of modern life, tries on different masks and voices to fit his elusive and variable identity. An even more fervid nationalism was displayed by modernists associated with the magazines *Verde-Amarelo* ('Green-Yellow', the colours of the Brazilian national flag) and *Anta*, which appeared in the 1920s – writers like Menotti del Picchia, Cassiano Ricardo, Cândido Motta Filho and Plínio Salgado (this last, who appears to have been the original proponent of artistic cannibalism as a defence against foreign influence, went on to become the leader of Brazilian fascism in the 1930s).

However, as Mário de Andrade finally realized, Brazil was too diverse and mysterious to be unified by the creative will of the poet. For this reason, several major figures looked for a more manageable identity in their native regions, where personal experience could be more effectively placed within a larger social picture. Manuel Bandeira was to turn his gaze nostalgically to his native Recife in the north-east; Jorge de Lima wrote about the black culture of the north-east and was later drawn to Catholic spirituality, as was Murilo Mendes; Vinícius de Moraes was similarly inspired by Christian concerns and by the poor Negroes of the *favelas* in Rio de Janeiro (his *Black Orpheus* lyrics were to become world-famous), turning later to a direct, personal poetry of impressive power. The Rio poets who were associated with the magazine *Festa*, such as Cecília Meireles, Augusto Federico Schmidt, Tasso da Silveira, Adelino Magalhães, were indifferent, if not actually hostile, to the whole issue of identity, and remained universalist in outlook, writing personal poetry in the international style of modernism. Carlos Drummond de Andrade, a major modernist figure, began writing a poetry of plain statement in the 1930s, his ironic pessimism passing through a political phase but later developing a more personal accommodation with the world and a self-reflexive concern with poetry itself. João Cabral de Melo Neto represents the last phase of Brazilian modernism – the 'Generation of 1945', which tried to achieve a new sobriety of tone, returning cautiously to metre and a greater attentiveness to the textures of poetic language. There was a parallel here with Spanish American developments in the 1950s – the anti-poetry of Nicanor Parra and the *exteriorismo* of Ernesto Cardenal – but the influence of Carlos Drummond de Andrade was also important.

From this concern with form and texture Brazilian poetry in the 1950s developed, thanks in part to the theoretical writing of the young poet and critic Mário Faustino, towards concretism. The originators of concrete poetry in Brazil were Décio Pignatari and the brothers Haroldo and Augusto de Campos, all three associated with the magazine *Noigandres* (1952). Their inspiration came from oriental ideograms and the *Calligrames* of Apollinaire, as well as from the work of Ezra Pound and e. e. cummings; their general aim was to create a condensed, minimalist poetry by exploiting the material resources of printed language on the page. Hostile to rhetoric, concretism assimilated and reacted to non-verbal communication in other media – advertising, computers, abstract painting and atonal music. It exhibited a quasi-mystical fascination with outer space, high technology and the ephemera of consumer capitalism, anticipating in this the Pop Art of the 1960s.

Brazilian concrete poetry, in turn, exerted a wide influence abroad, stimulating analogous experiments in Britain and the USA. It was far less important in Spanish America (though it had an impact on Octavio Paz in the 1960s), and this reflects a constant difference between the two cultural spheres: Brazil from colonial times interacted more freely with the external world and has shown a more consistent appetite for modernization. There are parallels between concretism and the Parnassianism of the turn of the century (a literary movement which also had a more enduring influence in Brazil than in Spanish America): both were anti-romantic and aspired to modernity. Parnassianism had been associated with the progressive liberal republicanism that brought down the Brazilian monarchy; concretism emerged in the early 1950s at a time of rapid modernization under Getúlio Vargas and Juscelino Kubitschek, during the period when the new capital city, Brasília, was conceived and built in the international modern style.

This flowering of modernist architecture and concrete poetry in the 1950s and 1960s provides yet another example of the abiding Brazilian taste for impassive formalism – in marked contrast to Spanish American art, with its greater emotionalism and baroque complexity. However, in the 1970s and

1980s, after the Brazilian economic miracle began to falter and military dictatorship had clearly miscarried modernization, there was a return to the concerns of the 1922 modernists, and a belated, though partial, convergence with Spanish American writers, particularly as regards anti-imperialism and the quest for cultural identity. The poetry of Ferreira Gullar moved away from concretist experimentation towards social and political commitment, and Lindolf Bell attempted a synthesis of the Pop Art elements of concretism with the public poetry characteristic of Neruda and the folk-poets of Spanish America. Even the De Campos brothers sought to give concrete experimentalism a political edge; paraphrasing Mallarmé, Haroldo famously observed that the poet's task was to give '*un sens plus POUR au mots de la tribu*'. This engagement was evident in the work of younger poets like Leonardo Froes, Torquato Neto, Wally Salomão, Isabel Câmara and Paulo Leminski, which evinced a suspicion of modern technology and a desire to put down roots in the Brazilian soil.

The Prelude to Modernism in Fiction

In narrative fiction the effects of European modernism were not generally in evidence until the 1940s. The initial reaction against Hispanic *modernismo* took writers in the direction of regionalism and a naturalistic portrayal of social reality. The latter was a fairly new development, since the European realist novel of character and social analysis had made little impact in the nineteenth century.

The orientation towards realism was underscored by the political commitment of many writers in the 1930s, for whom social (or, indeed, socialist) realism was the correct way to deal artistically with the problems of Latin America. For instance, César Vallejo, who had virtually invented a modernist poetics for himself, published *Tungsteno* in 1931, an impeccable socialist-realist novel about the bleak lives of tin-miners in Peru. The exploitation of the tin-miners of Bolivia was the subject of novels by Augusto Céspedes, who also wrote about the calamity of the Chaco War. In Mexico, notable social realists were José Mancisidor and Gregorio López y Fuentes. Anarchist and Marxist writers of the Buenos Aires literary scene – Leónidas Barletta, Max Dickman, Enrique Amorim – were known as the Boedo group after a working-class district of the city, but their work was overshadowed by their modernist rivals. The exception was the eccentric Roberto Arlt, a Boedo writer of great imaginative gifts, whose fiction is still widely admired, portraying as it does the frustrations of lower-class urban characters in a grotesque expressionist style shot through with an absurdist humour.

Ecuador produced a talented school of mostly communist social realists in the port of Guayaquil, its second city and the centre of the country's export-economy. Enrique Gil Gilbert, Demetrio Aguilera Malta and the excellent short-story writer, José de la Cuadra, turned their attention to the dockers and plantation workers. The most famous of the Ecuadorians was Jorge Icaza, who blended social realism with *indigenismo* in the now classic *Huasipungo* (1934), a harsh novel about the expropriation of the lands of an impoverished Indian community by an unscrupulous landowner in league with a foreign oil company. Like Alcides Arguedas's *Raza de bronce* ('The Bronze Race', 1919), *Huasipungo* ends with a record of the Indians' failure to resist the incursions of the capitalist export-economy.

After Icaza, the *indigenista* novel became more politicized. The Peruvian Ciro Alegría, a supporter of the APRA party, published *El mundo es ancho y ajeno* ('Broad and Alien Is The World', 1941), which won international attention, and in which the themes of land expropriation and Indian survival under capitalism were also tackled. But the fundamental question remained whether the Indian world should resist economic development at all costs or else find ways of adapting to it. A major difficulty in deciding such a question was that *indigenista* writers were themselves educated Spanish speakers who could scarcely avoid imposing their own views on the Indians they wrote about. Could a modern writer penetrate the consciousness of an Indian? Even if this were possible, who would he be writing for? These were the problems that obsessed José María Arguedas, a Peruvian mestizo who was brought up speaking Quechua and spent his whole career struggling with the conflicts between Indian and Spanish culture. As a student of Quechua folklore, Arguedas was the first of the *indigenistas* to attempt a portrayal of the Indians on their own terms. In his collection of short stories *Agua* ('Water', 1935), he wrote a Spanish inflected with Quechua. The novel *Yawar Fiesta* (1941) incorporated Andean myths and rituals into the narrative. As far as a middle-class readership was concerned, this was mysterious and pleasing: it produced an effect of what was later to be called 'magical realism'.

Arguedas did not himself make the connection between *indigenismo* and European literary modernism in the 1940s. This was done by more experimental writers who had absorbed surrealism in Paris. In his later novels *Los ríos profundos* ('The Deep Rivers', 1958), *Todas las sangres* ('Everyone's Blood', 1964) and *El zorro de arriba y el zorro de abajo* ('The Fox Above and the Fox Below', 1970), Arguedas began to explore his own tormented relations with both Indian and Spanish culture, employing techniques that drew upon the discoveries of other writers.

Though modernism in Brazil made a powerful impact on poetry and the visual arts in the São Paulo–Rio de Janeiro axis, novelists reacted against liberal positivism by turning towards regionalism and social realism, a trend that was to continue until the end of the 1950s and which has remained an important feature of Brazilian literature. Regionalism was stimulated by the sociological and historical studies of Gilberto Freyre, who convened a regionalist congress at Recife in 1926, and whose work took the patriarchal plantation society of the north-east as the source of traditional Brazilian values and then described the loosening of racial and social bonds in the big city with the advent of the liberal republic. Freyre's influence was enormous; he performed for Brazil a function similar to that of the Mexican José Vasconcelos in Spanish America – his myth of racial tolerance in colonial slave society enabled his compatriots to dispel pessimism about race and to accept miscegenation as a positive phenomenon, as well as reconciling them in part with their Iberian heritage.

Writers of the 1930s like Raquel de Queirós, João Americo de Almeida and José Lins do Rego evoked the life of the sugar plantations with a combination of nostalgia for the paternalist order and a sense of outrage at the degradations of slavery and the pitiless hostility of the natural world. Jorge Amado became the best-selling novelist in Brazil by virtue of his strong narratives, which cleverly sentimentalized the oppressed culture of the blacks of the north-east and the impoverished peasants of the *sertão*. It was the *sertão* that provided the setting for the best of the regionalist novels, the classic *Vidas Sêcas* ('Barren Lives', 1938) by Graciliano Ramos, which described the tribulations of a peasant family in the drought-ridden backlands in tough, spare prose. Indeed, even after regionalism began to lose its force in the 1950s, the *sertão*, together with the north-east and the jungle, would remain the places to which Brazilian writers would imaginatively return in order to deflate the modernizing pretensions of the governing élites of São Paulo and Rio.

Modernism in Fiction

The modernist revolution was carried over from poetry to fiction in Paris, Buenos Aires and São Paulo. Argentines such as Borges, Macedonio Fernández, Roberto Arlt and Leopoldo Marechal had from the 1920s gone beyond technical experiment to question the assumptions of realism and authorship, introducing fantasy into their narratives to undermine the idea that fiction might simply reflect reality or that the writer could act as an authoritative source of truth. While living in Paris, two novelists who had previously written on nativist themes, the Guatemalan Miguel Angel Asturias and the Cuban Alejo Carpentier, came into contact with surrealism and saw how the use of primitive myths and beliefs could evoke a sense of the marvellous in fiction while also serving to represent the heterogeneous cultural reality of Latin America.

Yet the earliest experiment in what was to become known as magical realism occurred in Brazil. This was Mário de Andrade's remarkable novel *Macunaíma* (1928), in which a protean folk-hero's travels across Brazil are recounted in a strange, disjointed narrative interwoven with poetic fantasy and mythic suggestion. *Macunaíma*, however, was too far ahead of its time – Andrade was an urban writer with no direct experience of the Brazilian interior, and so his work came across as an outlandish literary fantasy; it had few successors in Brazil and attracted limited attention outside the vanguard until the 1970s, when the influence of magical realism from Spanish America revealed the historic significance of *Macunaíma* to a younger generation of Brazilian writers, who were captivated by its fundamental theme of multiple identity.

A major influence on modernist developments in fiction was the work of North American writers of the 1920s and 1930s. From John Dos Passos Latin Americans learned narrative devices modelled on cinematic techniques and newspaper reportage which would reflect the dislocated experience of big-city life. Hemingway showed them how to pare down rhetorical flourishes to achieve a hard, colloquial style. A more substantial and enduring influence was William Faulkner, whose work helped to introduce multiple points of view, the interior monologue and stream-of-consciousness narration. Faulkner's sombre and complex vision of a racially divided, patriarchal society in decay, struck a deep chord with writers all over Latin America – from the Uruguayan Juan Carlos Onetti, the Mexicans José Revueltas, Agustín Yáñez and Juan Rulfo, to the young Colombian Gabriel García Márquez and the Peruvian Mario Vargas Llosa. Translations of Faulkner's work began to appear from the late 1930s in the literary magazines of Buenos Aires, and especially in *Sur* (Borges translated *The Wild Palms* in 1940), and through these magazines too, earlier North American writers, such as Herman Melville and Henry James, who had been unknown until then, exerted an influence on the new writing.

Perhaps the greatest single modernist influence in the long run was James Joyce. In the 1920s and 1930s he was known to only the most cosmopolitan writers – Borges and his Buenos Aires circle, Carpentier and Asturias in Paris – but he was rarely imitated. Only after 1945, when a Spanish translation of *Ulysses* appeared (inevitably, in Buenos Aires), can a direct influence be found. It is clearly evident in Leopoldo Marechal's *Adán Buenosayres* (1948), which used a mythic structure – derived from Dante's *Inferno* – to tame the unruliness of the urban environment. It was not until the 1960s that typical Joycean features – mythic underpinnings, stream-of-consciousness narration and intensive wordplay – would be used by many talented Latin Americans to express, and yet hold together, in 'total novels' their experience of the chaotic urbanization which was so prevalent during that period.

By the mid-1940s the technical resources of the Latin American storyteller had been enriched by these influences, and certain key works were published over the next decade: Borges's collections of stories and spoof essays *Ficciones* ('Fictions', 1944) and *El Aleph* (1949); Leopoldo Marechal's urban epic, *Adán Buenosayres* (1948); seminal magical realist or historical novels such as Miguel Angel Asturias's *El señor presidente* ('The President', 1946) and *Hombres de maíz* ('Men of Maize', 1949), and Alejo Carpentier's *El reino de este mundo* ('The Kingdom of this World', 1949) and *Los pasos perdidos* ('The Lost Steps', 1953); Juan Rulfo's Faulknerian dystopias, *El llano en llamas* ('The Burning Plain', 1953) and *Pedro Páramo* (1955), this last a bitterly ambivalent study of patriarchal dependency. In Brazil, João Guimarães Rosa's *Sagarana* (1946) and *Grande Sertão: Veredas* ('The Devil to Pay in the Backlands', 1956) were acclaimed as masterpieces of modernist writing. All these works summed up and reformulated the major themes of the preceding century, while setting patterns for most of the fiction that was to follow.

Of all the great Latin Americans, Jorge Luis Borges was the most eccentric and yet the most modern. His work at first appears utterly remote from the Americanist concerns of his fellows, aspiring instead to converse on equal terms with the classics of the European tradition. Rooted in the childhood reading of exotic adventure stories in English – G. K. Chesterton, Robert Louis Stevenson, Kipling – his imagination was strangely stimulated by the philosophy of Berkeley and Hume, Schopenhauer and Nietzsche. From Berkeley and Hume he took his basic premise – the subjective nature of all knowledge and experience; from voluntarist thinkers like Schopenhauer and Nietzsche he derived his sense of the fragility of personal identity, as likely to be the product of self-assertion as a mere conceit of some cosmic intelligence. Lacking objective truth, man was condemned to play in a game of no fixed rules and no specific end; for if the existence of beings other than oneself was uncertain, the presence of God or some hidden demiurge could not be ruled out. The act of writing was a paradigm of existence: the author might invent characters and plots, but was he the true source of his inventions, or did they simply reflect patterns repeated endlessly throughout universal literature? In the face of such radical uncertainties, the reader was invited to question personality, meaning and, ultimately, reality itself.

Borges's chosen medium, other than poetry, was the *ficción* – a short story or pseudo-essay whose brevity gave him the opportunity to condense mental play into reverberating images and situations. The early *ficciones* were philosophical fantasies in which, for instance, the universe was compared to a well-ordered but limitless library that refused to disclose its overall design, or the hazards of chance and meaning likened to a lottery run by a shadowy panel of judges. Without ever losing their philosophical dimension, many *ficciones*, especially the later ones, were given Argentine settings. An obsessive theme was the duel, the clash for supremacy between two rivals – mostly he chose gauchos or adventurers, but he could also write teasingly about contests between society ladies, writers and even the two great Liberators Bolívar and San Martín at Guayaquil. The duel, in fact, becomes a metaphor for an eternal human yearning to assert identity by eliminating a rival (though Borges liked to show how the victor in the end was a mirror image of his victim).

In Borges's fiction dualities constantly resolve themselves into unities only to unravel into further dualities, and so on to infinity. Because he resigns himself to this process, he is universally modern; but the obsession with unity and identity reveals him to be as Latin American as his contemporaries. After all, most of the *ficciones* for which Borges is celebrated were written in the late 1930s and the 1940s, a period which saw the collapse of classic liberalism in Argentina – the nation's destiny was becoming enigmatic even before the country entered a historical labyrinth under Juan Perón.

With his contemporaries Borges shares a nostalgia for the past (though not the same version of it), and a desire for unity and order; like most of them, too, he was white and middle class. But what makes him an exception is that he did not entertain the hope of finding an 'integral culture' unique to Latin America. This, precisely, was the aspiration of Miguel Angel Asturias, a writer who, white and patrician though he was, tried to penetrate the mentality of the Indians of his native Guatemala in order to discover a unified consciousness that would act as an antidote to capitalist alienation.

Asturias began his career by writing *Leyendas de Guatemala* ('Legends of Guatemala', 1930), in which he recreated tales of the colonial and pre-Hispanic past. However, his first novel, *El señor presidente* ('The President', 1946), was actually started in 1922 and written mostly in Paris, where he lived from 1923 until its completion in 1933. Immensely original in language and structure, it is an assault on a modernizing Liberal dictator (like Guatemala's Estrada Cabrera or Mexico's Porfirio Díaz), which is set in a nightmare city where all human relations have been debased by capitalism and oppression. Against these forces of modern darkness the protagonists find refuge in the 'light' of rural community – the intricate symbolism being organized around dualities which serve to bind the loose, phantasmagoric episodes into a coherent whole.

Hombres de maíz ('Men of Maize', 1949) enlarges upon Asturias's central theme of the destruction of an organic culture by capitalist development. The originality of this novel was its use of Maya myths as much to structure the story as to provide a spiritual defence for the Indian community against its white exploiters. This made it one of the first works of magical realism, because it introduced non-rational material into the fabric of the novel as a valid expression of an alternative mentality. In subsequent work Asturias gave a socialist answer to problems of the nation and continued to write in a magical realist style. He was awarded the Nobel Prize in 1967.

Asturias's encounter with surrealism in Paris in the 1920s enabled him to revolutionize the form and matter of the *indigenista* novel. The other great originator of magical realism, Alejo Carpentier, was also inspired by surrealism in Paris, where he lived from 1928 to 1939. But it was a visit to Haiti in 1943 and his reading of Spengler that led him to dismiss the 'literary tricks' performed by European surrealists in their quest of *le merveilleux* and point instead to the real marvels that were to be found everywhere in Latin America. The writer must capture *lo real maravilloso*, the marvellous-in-the-real, evident in the splendour of the natural world and especially in the magical consciousness preserved in the many ethnic cultures of the continent.

Yet what distinguished Carpentier crucially from Asturias was that he presented the pursuit of a unified consciousness as a problem. Carpentier was not wholly opposed to the modern world: he valued the rationalist humanism of the Enlightenment, realizing that it was a force for freedom which had justified Latin American independence. His entire work, therefore, represents a search for a point of synthesis between reason and instinct, matter and spirit. *El reino de este mundo* ('The Kingdom of this World,' 1949), a novel about the process of Haitian independence, portrays the voodoo culture of a slave community as a liberating agent, yet concludes by showing its impotence to resist rationalism. *Los pasos perdidos* ('The Lost Steps', 1953) describes a quixotic journey into the outback of a Latin American country by an alienated modern artist in quest of the Holy Grail of a timeless, integrated consciousness. It ends, however, with a return to the city and an acceptance that the clock cannot be put back. His very ambitious novel *El siglo de las luces* (1963), translated in English as 'Explosion in a Cathedral', is set during the 'Age of Enlightenment' (its original title in Spanish), and explores the impact of the French Revolution on three characters in the Caribbean, striving in its very structural arrangement to find a pattern of history that might accommodate both a spiritual and a material dimension to experience.

After this novel, Carpentier, who had returned to live in Cuba after the Revolution, did not publish any major work for over a decade. The fiction that appeared in the 1970s was influenced by Marxism, although Carpentier remained a modernist writer, fundamentally interested in the individual consciousness as opposed to social reality. His *Recurso del método* ('Reasons of State', 1974) is a novel about a typical dictator, who admires Europe and feels contempt for the 'barbarism' of his own country, which he rules with a rod of iron until his overthrow by a Communist-led uprising. *La consagración de la primavera* ('Rite of Spring', 1978) attempted to bring together in a grand synthesis all his major themes so as to show how they were resolved positively with the triumph of the Cuban Revolution.

The output of the Mexican Juan Rulfo, by contrast, was very meagre – one novel and a collection of short stories – but in form and subject-matter it proved to be of major significance. In *Pedro Páramo* (1955) he invented a fictional world which exposed the ambivalence of Latin patriarchy – hateful for its oppression of the individual spirit, yet craved for because it affords protection and a kind of social identity. The characters are all dead, inhabiting the narrative as a medley of voices and echoes that recalls the rule of the eponymous *caudillo* in the town of Comala. Written well after the Revolution had been institutionalized by a modernizing élite, its bitter pessimism reflects a sense of betrayal: the post-revolutionary order has failed to bring freedom and justice; paternalist authority persists, but in a perverted form which makes the social community a shadow of hell rather than a microcosm of God in his heaven. In fiction of great technical brilliance and economy, Rulfo caught the situation of Latin America in the mid-century – strung out between a rural society in crisis and a modern world terrifying in its unfathomable progress.

These early magical realists portrayed rural communities in conflict with an invading capitalism. In the two great cities of the River Plate – Buenos Aires and Montevideo – the terrors of urban capitalism had to be confronted by writers who no longer had an escape route to rural community. Eduardo Mallea wrote about anguish and solitude in a world that had lost its spiritual bearings. Ernesto Sábato explored states of madness and evil, portraying individuals alienated by the scientific rationalism of the modern world. In the works of both novelists, the psychological condition of the characters can be regarded as a microcosm of the larger malaise afflicting Argentina in the 1940s and 1950s. The Uruguayan Juan Carlos Onetti invented a strange fictional world where characters are oppressed by existential anguish, having lost their faith in any form of truth. With *La vida breve* ('A Brief Life', 1950) Onetti inaugurated his celebrated Faulknerian cycle, the 'Saga of Santa María', a series of novels – of which *El astillero* ('The Shipyard', 1961) and *Juntacadáveres* ('Corpsecollector', 1964) are reckoned the best – set in an imaginary provincial river port inhabited by individuals desperate to live by an illusion that will compensate for the meaninglessness of existence.

Fiction in Brazil remained broadly regional and realist. However, João Guimarães Rosa, the outstanding writer of the post-war years, applied modernist techniques to the great regionalist theme of the *sertão*, the wild backlands of the Brazilian interior. Rosa's first published collection of stories *Sagarana* (1946) established him as a writer of rare inventiveness, combining poetic prose with metaphysical speculation in his evocation of a trackless region populated by adventurers and illiterate peasants. Ten years later he brought out seven narrative pieces, under the title *Corpo de Baile* ('The Dancing Troupe'), which were set against the same background, though the experimentation with language and technique was carried at times to the point of hermeticism. In the same year he published his masterpiece *Grande Sertão: Veredas* ('The Devil to Pay in the Backlands', 1956), a Joycean epic of the outback which intriguingly inverted the point of view of Euclides da Cunha's turn-of-the-century masterpiece *Os Sertões* ('Rebellion in the Backlands', 1902): instead of the civilized urban liberal moved to perplexity by the superstitious hordes of the *sertão*, we have Riobaldo, an inhabitant of the barbarous interior of Minas Gerais, who addresses his narrative to an implied listener, an educated city-dweller, representing perhaps the modern 'civilized' reader. Rosa thus assumes the voice of a man living effectively in a traditional world peopled by cowboys, bandits, millenarian preachers and other outlandish figures, all of them dwarfed by the overmastering emptiness of the *sertão*, the symbolic space in which they seek their destiny and their salvation, and into which the reader is imaginatively drawn.

As critics have observed, the multifarious narrative, written in a poetic prose full of neologisms, syntactical distortions and regional vocabulary (a glossary has been published for native speakers of Portuguese), recalls the genre of medieval romance, but even though these questing knights errant of the *sertão* undergo endless trials, they can find no sure destiny – everything remains ambiguous, dual, unresolved. We have before us a traditional world deranged by doubt – Riobaldo is uncertain whether or not he has made a pact with the devil, whether God exists, where his life is leading him. If this is a latter-day romance, it has been infiltrated by a modern agnosticism and thus functions as a literary analogue of contemporary Brazil – a confusingly diverse country, fundamentally traditional yet unsettled by an incursive modernity, for as a nation it must try to encompass cultural extremes, skyscrapers as well as Stone Age jungle tribes.

Subsequent Brazilian fiction oscillated between these poles, but the *coup d'état* of 1964, which established a military dictatorship for some twenty years and imposed censorship for most of that time, caused the impoverishment of cultural life. Clarice Lispector, an accomplished writer who rose to prominence in the early 1960s with novels such as *Laços de Família* ('Family Ties', 1960), *A Maçã no Escuro* ('The Apple in the Dark', 1961) and *A Paixão Segundo G. H.* ('The Passion According to G. H.', 1964), looked to the urban environment as a setting for existentialist probings of the consciousness of mainly female protagonists. Autran Dourado confronted the country and the city in novels like *Uma Vida en Segrêdo* ('A Hidden Life', 1964), *Opera dos Mortos* ('The Voices of the Dead', 1967) and *O Risco do Bordado* ('Pattern for a Tapestry', 1970), set in his native region of Minas Gerais. Antônio Callado got into trouble with the authorities for his novels *Quarup* (1967), which described the effects of the military coup on the poor north-east, and *Bar Don Juan* ('Don Juan's Bar', 1970), a satirical attack on police repression as well as the terrorism of the guerrillas in the late 1960s.

Satire and parody were favourite weapons of a younger generation of writers living under the military government of the 1960s and 1970s. In 1967 a São Paulo company staged Oswald de Andrade's play *O Rei de Vela* ('The Candle King', 1937), which led to the rediscovery of the modernism of the 1920s. (This was a selective revaluation: it celebrated the Pau-Brasil writers but ignored the ultra-nationalist Verde-Amarelo group, tainted as it was by the fascism of Plínio Salgado, one of its founders.) Mário de Andrade's *Macunaíma* (1928) was made into an influential film in 1969 by Joaquim Pedro de Andrade (no relation). This vogue for the *antropofágia* of the 1920s led to magical realism and to parody. João Ubaldo Ribeiro made a promising debut with *Sargento Getúlio* ('Sergeant Getúlio', 1971), though his magical realism would not blossom fully until the monumental ¡*Viva o Povo Brasileiro!* ('An Invincible Memory', 1984). Ivan Angelo's *A Festa* ('A Celebration', 1972) recorded with bitter humour the migration from the country to the city by peasants fleeing the drought-stricken north-east. Márcio Souza's *Galvez, Imperador do Acre* ('The Empire of the Amazon', 1976) was a satire on imperialism set in the jungle. The rain forests of the Amazon basin were the location of powerful works by the anthropologist Darcy Ribeiro, who analysed the equivocal attitudes of modern Brazilians to the Indian aborigines in *Maíra* (1977) and *Utopia Selvagem: Saudades da Inocência Perdida* ('Savage Utopia: Longings for a Lost Innocence', 1982).

The Spanish American Boom: Fiction in the 1960s and 1970s

From the early 1960s Spanish American literature received international acclaim, and the work of some of its best writers was recognized as being of world class. Yet the Boom, as it was called, was fairly uneven in its attention to the range of accomplishment in Latin America. Deservedly, Borges won international recognition after he shared the French Prix Formentor with Samuel Beckett in 1961, and, of the poets, Pablo Neruda and Octavio Paz found fame outside the Hispanic world, but few writers of earlier decades became quite so well known – neither Carpentier, who continued to write in the Boom years, nor Asturias, despite being awarded the Nobel Prize in 1967. The figures at the centre of the Boom were a number of young novelists – Julio Cortázar, Carlos Fuentes, Gabriel García Márquez and Mario Vargas Llosa – whose work was generally admired for its power and originality. Other novelists were drawn into the magic circle but none reached the heights of fame of these four. What caused such unprecedented interest in Latin American writing?

To some extent it marked the entry of Spain's top publishing houses into the international book market. The firm of Seix Barral in Barcelona, the city in which Vargas Llosa and García Márquez were living in the early 1960s, was particularly active in promoting the new novelists. Borges's discovery by French critics at a time when France was fascinated by its own experimental *nouveau roman* and the structuralist *nouvelle critique* of Roland Barthes stimulated interest in Latin American writers such as Julio Cortázar, who had been living in Paris for many years. Then the Cuban Revolution of 1959, with its charismatic young leaders Fidel Castro and Che Guevara, won support from intellectuals throughout the world as a successful example of the anti-imperialist struggle of underdeveloped countries. The Cuban missile crisis of 1961 made Latin America a region of vital strategic concern for the USA, and focused the attention of the international media on Latin American affairs. But the Boom was more than a triumph of publicity; it served to highlight the inherent quality of the work being written in a part of the world which had been overlooked for too long.

Julio Cortázar wrote boldly experimental novels, of which the most influential was *Rayuela* ('Hopscotch', 1963), and excellent short stories with which he first made his name in the 1950s. (A short story of his was filmed by the Italian director Michelangelo Antonioni as *Blow-Up* 1966, which became famous as a picture of London in the hedonistic Swinging Sixties.) Influenced by surrealism, Cortázar regarded bourgeois life as one-dimensional, and modern culture as rationalistic and repressive. By ingeniously incorporating fantasy into his fiction he pointed to the 'other side' of the mind, a suppressed reality, to which erotic desire had largely been banished. Following his compatriot Borges, he interrogated the literary process itself, dismantling the conventions of narrative in flamboyant gestures designed to eroticize the act of storytelling by encouraging the reader to penetrate his half-open texts in pursuit of an ever-delayed fullness of meaning.

Bourgeois alienation from the erotic was a major theme of Carlos Fuentes, but he was also a perceptive analyst of the new Mexican middle classes, comfortably off thanks to the rapid development of the 1950s and 1960s. *La región más transparente* ('Where the Air is Clear', 1958) surveyed the chaotic multiplicity of Mexico from the central viewpoint of Ixca Cienfuegos, an unhappy combination of the Spanish and the Aztec, as his name suggests. Fuentes here revealed two abiding and interrelated concerns – the search for cultural identity and the sacrifice of integrity to material ambition. In *La muerte de Artemio Cruz* ('The Death of Artemio Cruz', 1962), the novel that made his international reputation, he created a powerful account of the rise of a great magnate of the Revolution, born an illegitimate mestizo. Fuentes put his finger on the tragic paradox of modernization: Artemio Cruz may be an odious embodiment of the Revolution betrayed, but he is also a figure of pathos, who has opted to survive his dreadful origins by clawing his way to the top at the expense of personal integrity. In subsequent work, notably *Cambio de piel* ('A Change of Skin', 1967), Fuentes displayed vast ambition in his readiness to explore the labyrinth of the middle-class psyche in relation to the history of Mexico. *Terra Nostra* (1975) was a dazzling fictional summation of three centuries of Hispanic history no less, in which Fuentes searched for a synthesis between the repressive unity of Philip II's Spain and the pluralistic freedom which it denied.

The exuberance of Carlos Fuentes's imagination was matched by Mario Vargas Llosa, who in 1963 at the age of twenty-six won a major literary prize for *La ciudad y los perros* ('Time of the Hero', 1962) a novel about a military school which renders the complex relations between the social classes in Lima with all the verve and suspense of a thriller. Vargas Llosa's superlative gifts as a narrator, his Flaubertian dispassion, which merely sharpens the poignancy of his characters' hopeless predicaments, and the originality of his technique of polyphonic construction, made him the outstanding social and political novelist of Latin America.

In *La casa verde* ('The Green House', 1966) and *Conversación en la catedral* ('Conversation in the Cathedral', 1969) – two brilliant studies of the multifaceted reality of Peru, a country splintered by geography, race and class – he employed techniques which departed from the linear constrictions of the realist novel the better to convey the sweep and ironic density of a *comédie humaine*. And even though he portrayed Peruvian society as corrupt from top to bottom, he was able to write comic novels like *Pantaleón y las visiltadoras* ('Captain Pantoja and the Special Service', 1973) and *La tía Julia y el escribidor* ('Aunt Julia and the Scriptwriter', 1978), in which his themes of corruption, hypocrisy and misplaced idealism were treated in a lighter, satirical vein.

The most famous of all these novelists, and one of the greatest narrative artists in Latin America, was Gabriel García Márquez. A journalist by profession and at one time a student of film-making in Rome, he gained a reputation in the late 1950s and early 1960s as a writer of accomplished novellas and short stories. Noted for their spare, dispassionate style and set mostly in the fictional town of Macondo, a tropical backwater on the Caribbean coast of his native Colombia, these early works revealed a world where moral values were intensely felt yet were none the less strangely vulnerable to shifting perceptions, as if at the mercy of some existential kaleidoscope turned irregularly by the hand of fate. García Márquez's themes emerged from deep within the Hispanic tradition – thwarted love, quixotic idealism, honour, loyalty and the force of destiny. A central preoccupation was with the condition of failure, and more precisely, with the moral stance that should be taken towards it, his characters tending to veer between escapist nostalgia and a stoical affirmation of personal integrity.

All these themes were masterfully subsumed in *Cien años de soledad* ('One Hundred Years of Solitude', 1967), probably the greatest and certainly the most celebrated Latin American novel ever written. It recounts in a pseudo-mythic narrative the foundation, growth, decline and destruction of the town of Macondo as experienced by successive generations of the Buendías, its founding family. Though Macondo is the result of a rebellion against superstition and received authority, its patriarch comes nevertheless to resign his quest for 'civilization' and 'the benefits of science' and succumbs instead to a powerful nostalgia for the past, setting a fateful pattern for his progeny, whose rebellions and indulgences invariably result in a terrible isolation. Stalked by the spectre of incest, the family's growing estrangement from reality issues finally in an act of passion between two Buendías that brings down an ancestral curse upon the house.

The novel reads as a grand metaphor of failure, the failure of Latin America's independent history. But at the same time it is a comedy of errors surveyed with godlike detachment by an overmastering narrator. Ultimately, the novel is a triumph of style – an extraordinary blend of baroque exuberance and measured irony. Its narrative manner won fame the world over as the foremost example of magical realism; but this was magical realism very much in the comic mode, slipping indifferently between fact and fantasy so as to render the naive bemusement of characters confronting a world they fail to comprehend. But its humour is never patronizing; it expresses, rather, a sense of compassion, as if the author himself had shared in that strange condition but had just managed to avoid its consequences. The novel, in fact, relates the timely flight from Macondo of one Gabriel Márquez; his liberation allows him to look back and narrate the process by which the Buendías sealed themselves in a cycle of fate that brought them to the point of destruction. And so, towards the end we have evidence of a release, an inkling of freedom, but it is a very hard-won freedom, whose highest testimony is the realized achievement of this majestic work of art.

García Márquez's work was not entirely typical of the new writing. His fictional world was rural and provincial, portraying a traditional society beginning to feel the impact of modernity. In this respect it represented a culmination of the fiction produced between the 1930s and the 1950s, both modernist and regionalist. But the writing of the Boom was predominantly based in the big city, and its mentors were Cortázar and Carlos Fuentes, with the unsolicited tutelage of Borges. Joycean experimentation and linguistic games were the order of the day. The bias against modern capitalism was still ostensibly strong, but, unlike the writers of the 1930s and 1940s, the novelists of the Boom looked for an integral consciousness not in rural community or *indigenismo*, but in the 1960s counter-culture of sexual liberation, rock music and individual revolt. Their favourite targets were the old landowning oligarchies and the modernizing élite of business executives and technocrats, whose dissident offspring many of them were.

José Donoso analysed the bad faith of the Chilean upper classes, using fantasy and literary reflexivity in acclaimed novels like *El obsceno pájaro de la noche* ('The Obscene Bird of Night', 1970) and *Casa de campo* ('Country House', 1978) to reproduce the evasions of uneasy bourgeois consciences isolated in a chaotic inner world that at times verged on madness. His compatriot Jorge Edwards also criticized the tormented hypocrisies of the upper classes cut loose from the moorings of traditional values. The Peruvian Alfredo Bryce Echenique extracted a certain glum humour from the social antics of the Lima *haute bourgeoisie* in *Un mundo para Julius* ('A World for Julius', 1970) and *Tantas veces Pedro* ('So Often Pedro', 1977).

In the mid-1960s Mexico produced *La Onda*, a 'new wave' of experimental writers – Gustavo Sainz, José Agustín, Fernando del Paso, Salvador Elizondo – who, as beneficiaries of the unwonted post-revolutionary stability, were given to writing ambitious novels *à la* Carlos Fuentes, characterized by comic irony, word-games and Joycean mythification; these were attempts to grapple with the monstrosity of Mexico City, by now a sprawling, partially rich metropolis with equivocal ties to the country's violent past.

It was, however, the Argentine Manuel Puig who emerged as the most original novelist after the major figures of the 1960s' Boom. Puig was the first Hispanic writer to have made a conscious use of a camp sensibility to parody and yet exploit the resources of mass culture. Novels like *La traición de Rita Hayworth* ('Betrayed by Rita Hayworth', 1968), *Boquitas pintadas* ('Heartbreak Tango', 1969) and *The Buenos Aires Affair* (1973) are full of allusions to soap operas, thrillers, popular songs and the cinema. Puig's characters indulge in romantic fantasies as a refuge from an unbearable reality. His most representative novel is *El beso de la mujer araña* ('The Kiss of the Spider Woman', 1976), made, fittingly, into a prize-winning Hollywood film by the Argentine director Hector Babenco. It is the story of a homosexual who shares a cell with a Trotskyite urban guerrilla, whom he eventually seduces and betrays to the authorities. As with human relations, so with literary genres: Puig's assimilation of the vulgar is as much an act of love as a parodic betrayal, for the camp author is an avatar of the Spider Woman – he sets out to entangle popular romance in complex, knowing fictions but finds himself fatally drawn to its soothing simplicities.

Puig established a connection between serious fiction and modern popular culture which was extremely fruitful, opening up new fields of interest for the contemporary novelist. For in the expanding cities literature was confronted with other, more potent media – radio, TV, movies, pop music, magazines and comics. From roughly the 1950s, serialized melodramas on radio and television – *radionovelas* and, later, *telenovelas* – became the staple cultural diet of the mass of city people all over Latin America. This was a manifestation of the new urban capitalism under which most of the population now lived – consumer-driven, shamelessly vulgar, and little different from popular culture in other parts of the world. Puig had discovered a way of sharing in these modern cultural phenomena while reflecting critically upon them. Other novelists began to see similar possibilities in the course of the 1970s and 1980s, including Boom writers like Vargas Llosa, Carlos Fuentes and even García Márquez.

Strangely enough, ludic brio was the hallmark of Cuban writing. Here the homosexual element was very marked. José Lezama Lima, Catholic, homosexual and a poet, wrote a narrative extravaganza called *Paradiso* (1966), a novel that defies description – plotless, discursively poetic, full of symbolism and erotic pursuits of a transcendent unity. Guillermo Cabrera Infante was recognized as a major figure with the publication of *Tres tristes tigres* ('Three Trapped Tigers') in 1967, a comic recollection of pre-revolutionary Havana, in which the narrator's manic punning evokes a world of anarchic fun and sexual escapades. The same world is celebrated in the semi-autobiographical *La Habana para un infante difunto* ('Infante's Inferno', 1979). A third important figure was Severo Sarduy, who, resident in Paris, was taken up by Roland Barthes and the *Tel Quel* intellectuals; homosexual and baroque like Lezama, he regarded art as virtually purposeless, its only function being to advert to the void that underlies the apparent permanence of things. Wilfully camp and profuse in erudite allusions, Sarduy's major works – *Gestos* ('Gestures', 1963), *De dónde son los cantantes* ('From Cuba with a Song', 1967), *Cobra* (1972), *Maitreya* (1978) – are the quintessence of the aestheticizing self-reference which was a feature of so much writing during the Boom.

This Cuban literature of polyvalency and play was produced by exiles or dissidents from Castro's regime, a reaction no doubt to the conformity demanded by the commissars of the Revolution. It was often meant to be subversive: Cabrera Infante started out as a functionary of the state, but growing dissatisfaction caused him to leave Cuba and eventually settle in London, from where he aimed his puns at the Castroite monolith. A more galling defection was that of Reynaldo Arenas; the son of peasants, he was an uncompromising homosexual with an invincible pessimism about the human condition. His magical-realist novel *El mundo alucinante* ('Hallucinations', 1969) displeased the regime and contributed to his subsequent exile in New York. It is a fictional account of the career of the Mexican friar and leading advocate of independence, Servando Teresa de Mier, describing his disillusionment with the Enlightenment ideals of liberty and reason, which result in grotesque distortions when transplanted in Spanish America. Another major novel, *Otra vez, el mar* ('Farewell to the Sea'), was published in 1982 from a manuscript smuggled out of Cuba after years of harassment. It is a frankly anti-revolutionary work recounting the collapse of a poet's faith in communism.

In Cuba itself, Edmundo Desnoes received international attention with *Memorias del subdesarrollo* ('Memories of Underdevelopment', 1965), a novel about an intellectual's reluctant acceptance of the Revolution, which was made into an admired film by Tomás Gutiérrez Alea. Other significant works appeared from Jesús Díaz, Pablo Armando Fernández, Miguel Barnet and Roberto Fernández Retamar, though none achieved lasting interest outside the island.

The growing division over the Castro regime was not confined to the Cuban literary world. Throughout the 1960s there had existed a broad consensus of moral support for the Revolution among Latin American writers and intellectuals. This was not just evidence of anti-US nationalism; it ran far deeper than this: the Cuban Revolution was felt to provide the answer to the questions of identity and modernity that had fuelled the modernist movement in Latin America since the 1920s – it appeared to be the last exit to an 'integral culture' from the great freeway that was sweeping Latin America towards modern capitalism.

Yet the modernist experimentalism that characterized the Boom was essentially individualistic, predicated on the right of the artist to creative freedom: how could such individualism be reconciled with revolutionary commitment? The question would become increasingly difficult to avoid after the disastrous failure of Cuba to meet the 10 million-ton target for the 1970 sugar harvest, when Fidel Castro decided to hand over the running of the economy to orthodox Soviet planners, and the state itself was consolidated according to the East European communist model. This tightened discipline dispelled many romantic illusions about creating a free, egalitarian society unique to Latin America.

The 1970s: Freedom, Authority and the State

The question of artistic freedom came to a head in 1971 with the arrest in Cuba of the writer Heberto Padilla for producing ideologically unsound work, and his subsequent public confession that he was guilty of deviationism. Fidel Castro's angry condemnation of 'bourgeois liberal' intellectuals in April of that year drew a line between loyal supporters of revolutionary authority and those who put their personal freedom above the concrete problems of the masses.

The result was a split in the ranks of Latin American writers. Before this episode there had been intermittent debates about political commitment and artistic freedom. Writers like García Márquez, Vargas Llosa, Fuentes and Cortázar had expressed their support for revolutionary change in Latin America, but insisted on the artist's right to follow his own imagination; García Márquez's famous dictum was that 'the supreme duty of the writer is to write well'. After the Padilla affair there came an acrimonious parting of the ways. Cortázar and García Márquez were the most prominent defenders of the Cuban Revolution and, later, of the Nicaraguan Revolution of 1979, while Vargas Llosa, Octavio Paz and Carlos Fuentes began to distance themselves.

These disputes over the freedom of the individual artist took place against a very sombre background: the overthrow of the democratically elected Marxist government of Salvador Allende in Chile in September 1973, which was followed by the horrific repression under General Pinochet; the chaotic return of Juan Perón to Argentina in the middle of an escalating 'dirty war' between the army and urban guerrillas; military dictatorships in most republics, which resorted to the use of death squads to keep down workers' discontent.

The creative response to authoritarianism first came from the left. In the mid-1970s there appeared a number of novels about dictators which took up the line originated by the Spaniard Ramón del Valle-Inclán in his novel about a Latin American tyrant, *Tirano Banderas* (1926), and continued by Miguel Angel Asturias's *El señor presidente* ('The President', 1946). These novels invariably presented dictatorship as a right-wing phenomenon, a reactionary defence of privilege, of which there were countless examples in Latin American history. Alejo Carpentier, like his coeval Asturias, saw it as a manifestation of classic *caudillismo*. His *Recurso del método* ('Reasons of State', 1975) portrayed dictatorship in personalist terms, as part of the traditional dialectic between 'civilization' and 'barbarism', which made the novel seem rather out of touch with the brutal military technocracies of the 1970s. In *El otoño del patriarca* ('The Autumn of the Patriarch', 1975), García Márquez elaborated a magical-realist discourse that embraced the whole mentality of patriarchy, showing brilliantly through the orchestration of narrative voices how the people themselves colluded with their oppressor in a diseased symbiosis that paralysed the body politic.

But the most highly regarded of these dictator novels was *Yo el supremo* ('I, the Supreme', 1974) by Augusto Roa Bastos, who, as an opponent of General Stroessner, the ruler of Paraguay since 1954, was sadly well placed to analyse tyranny. The dictator in question was no other than Dr Francia, the great Paraguayan despot of the post-independence period. Having written a fine *indigenista* novel, *Hijo de hombre* ('Son of Man', 1960), Roa Bastos was able to profit from the experiments of the 1960s Boom to extend his critique of authoritarianism to the very notion of authorship itself.

During the 1970s those writers who had broken with Castro remained in a state of ideological disarray. This in itself was an index of the pervasive discredit suffered by liberal and democratic ideas among the Latin American intelligentsia since about the 1920s: after disillusion with revolutionary social-ism there seemed nowhere to go but into parody and the subversive play of language. Such was the path taken by Cuban dissidents like Cabrera Infante, Arenas, Sarduy and Lezama Lima while Vargas Llosa, by far the most gifted realist writer in the continent, withdrew from social criticism into comedy and gentle satire, writing witty novels like *Captain Pantoja* (1973) and *Aunt Julia* (1977). Carlos Fuentes and the writers of *La Onda* were also drawn to literary play and psychological exploration, though in *Terra Nostra* (1975) Fuentes obliquely approached the question of despotism and intolerance by relating it to the alleged obscurantism of Counter-Reformation Spain.

It was in Mexico that an intellectual search for an ideological alternative to revolutionary socialism was begun in the early 1970s. Its origin can be traced to the revulsion caused by the Tlatelolco massacre of students in 1968. The poet Octavio Paz, who at the time was ambassador to India, resigned his post and eventually returned to Mexico. There he founded the journals *Plural* (1971–6) and *Vuelta* (1976–), and embarked upon a quest for a new political ethic for Latin America. He initiated a critique of the all-embracing state, notably in his collection of political essays, *El ogro filantrópico* ('The Philanthropic Ogre', 1971–8), a term which aptly described the intrinsically corrupt but benevolent corporatism of the Mexican state under the PRI. This critique of unaccountable state power was taken up in various ways by younger Mexican intellectuals: Enrique Krauze, Gabriel Zaid, Carlos Monsiváis and campaigning journalists like Julio Scherer García.

However, it became clear that criticism of state power could not be confined to Mexico: it was a phenomenon with deep roots in Hispanic political culture – and, moreover, not all ogres were as philanthropic as the Mexican: in the 1970s state terrorism grew to scandalous proportions in the military dictatorships of Argentina, Chile, Brazil, Uruguay and many other republics. Even Cuba, still the great hope of the left, could not be exempted from the charge of authoritarianism, for in the wake of the Padilla affair there emerged more evidence of a systematic denial of basic civil rights, of persecution of homosexuals and political dissidents, and of other restrictions on individual liberties.

As the 1970s drew to a close, there was a rising tide of popular feeling in favour of democracy throughout Latin America. By this time, after the systematic abuse of human rights had become commonplace in many parts of the continent and guerrilla struggles had almost everywhere led to a violent dead end, the basic principles of political liberalism were widely seen, even on the radical left, to possess a certain value – guaranteed civil rights, the rule of law, free elections and, above all, the accountability of governments to the people they were meant to serve.

This general popular movement in favour of democracy exerted considerable pressure upon the military dictatorships of the continent and contributed to their downfall in the early 1980s. But the bankruptcy of Latin American authoritarianism was not just political, it was also economic. Military dictatorships fell because they could no longer run the economy: fifty years of forced, state-led development had resulted in unproductive industries, chronic unemployment, the rapid decline of traditional rural society and acute overcrowding in cities. The explosive mix of inflation and stagnation was something that no government of whatever ideological hue seemed able to cope with, much less eliminate.

Since the 1920s the labyrinth had been a recurrent device of the Latin American modernists, serving as an image of personal disorientation. In the course of the inflationary 1960s and 1970s, state and society had themselves become increasingly labyrinthine: social relations had been wrenched from their traditional frame and scrambled by rapid industrialization and big-city life; political loyalties began to lose meaning when all options appeared to lead to farce or tragedy; even ordinary language had become suspect after decades of mendacious rhetoric from *caudillos* and military juntas. How could writers make sense of such dislocated societies?

In the circumstances, novelists resorted to fantasy to express the prevailing sense of disorder and unreality. The literary interrogation of language itself became a therapeutic exercise, because, in the interests of truth, it was important for writers to reflect upon their own medium of communication. Thus, the writing of the 1960s and 1970s was heavily influenced by the self-referential, ludic works of Borges and James Joyce. This was not in all cases a sign of bourgeois escapism, as some of the more rigid Marxist critics alleged, but evidence of a vital need to deal with, if not to exorcize, a perplexing reality that seemed to lie beyond the full grasp of the individual imagination.

The 1980s: The Decline of Patriarchy?

It is perhaps not surprising that Mario Vargas Llosa was the writer most actively in search of new political values for Latin America in the 1980s. Twenty years earlier he had been the most powerful social realist in the continent, having invented strikingly effective narrative techniques for capturing the labyrinthine reality of his native Peru. During the terrible decade of the 1970s he withdrew into a more personal sphere, but by the early 1980s his writing had recovered its social and political cutting edge. Under the influence of Karl Popper, Isaiah Berlin and, to some extent, Friedrich von Hayek, he rediscovered the principles of liberalism, which were enjoying a revival throughout the Western world in the late 1970s and 1980s.

His novel *La guerra del fin del mundo* ('The War of the End of the World', 1981) was highly significant in being a retelling of the crushing in 1897 of the Canudos rebellion in the impoverished north-east of Brazil, the subject of Euclides da Cunha's masterpiece *Os Sertões* ('Rebellion in the Backlands', 1902). Da Cunha, though a liberal and a positivist, had displayed an ambivalence towards the 'barbarous' messianic rebels who were rejecting the liberal republic. Vargas Llosa, while maintaining that ambivalence, nevertheless opted for progress and modernization. This was an extremely radical stance to take in Latin America in the 1980s, for Vargas Llosa was vindicating the political heritage of nineteenth-century liberalism, and implicitly rejecting the nationalist, anti-liberal ideology which had been the norm since the 1920s and which had formed the barely questioned background to Latin American modernism.

New-found radicalism replenished Vargas Llosa's powers as a novelist of direct social and historical concerns. In *Historia de Mayta* ('The Real Life of Alejandro Mayta', 1984) he turned his attention to the strategy of revolutionary war espoused by his own generation, which had so greatly contributed to the bloody conflicts of the 1960s and 1970s and which Peru itself was currently undergoing in the insurgency of the *Sendero Luminoso* guerrillas. In *El hablador* ('The Storyteller', 1988) he tackled the complex question of Indian welfare and modernization, a highly sensitive topic in Peru, the stronghold of radical *indigenismo* since the time of Mariátegui. The novel cast a critical eye on the old Latin American anxiety about cultural roots and national identity, the central figure being a Peruvian Jew who flees modern society and becomes a shaman and storyteller to an Indian tribe in the Amazonian jungle. An argument is created in favour of plurality and open-endedness in the approach to complex cultural realities.

Despite the revival of liberal ideas, there remained a vigorous Marxist culture with a continuing commitment to armed struggle. Writers like Augusto Roa Bastos (Paraguay), Mario Benedetti (Uruguay), David Viñas (Argentina) and Eduardo Galeano (Uruguay) pursued this anti-imperialist line. In the 1980s Galeano, the author of a best seller on economic and cultural dependency, *Las venas abiertas de América Latina* ('The Open Veins of Latin America', 1971), brought out a trilogy, *Memoria del fuego* ('Memory of Fire', 1982–6), which denounced Latin America's exploitation by imperialist powers after the Spanish Conquest and charted her quest for an authentic identity. This radical perspective was particularly fruitful in Central America, where the Nicaraguan Revolution was under attack and guerrilla wars in El Salvador and Guatemala remained unresolved. The poet Ernesto Cardenal produced an important new poem-cycle, *La música de las esferas* ('The Music of the Spheres', 1989), and other Central American writers became internationally known. Radical political fiction appeared from Omar Cabezas, Sergio Ramírez (the vice-president of Nicaragua) and Manlio Argueta of El Salvador.

Even so, in the 1980s Marxism as an ideology was in deep crisis in Latin America, as in the rest of the world. It was not just that the armed struggles of the 1960s and 1970s had produced few successes, or that Cuba and Nicaragua were obviously stuck in an economic rut; the whole system of state planning was at issue, and this revision was occurring in both China and the Soviet Union no less, where market principles were being introduced and foreign investment from the USA, Japan and Europe encouraged. By the end of the 1980s political liberalization in the East European communist states and even in the Soviet Union itself was creating a movement towards some form of democracy, based on free elections and civil liberties. How would this process affect Cuba and Nicaragua? To what extent would it force a rethinking of the standard Marxist analysis of Latin American history based on the theory of dependency? In fact, the general political culture had reached a kind of stalemate, for the usual stock of ideas appeared to be worn out, while new recipes like free-market liberalism seemed too dangerous to apply.

The result was a sense of drift and fragmentation, with the dominant mood being one of sobriety: it was a time to reckon the losses and bear witness to the horrors of recent decades. A more realistic, testimonial literature had already begun to appear after the Pinochet coup of 1973 and its horrifying sequel – most notably Antonio Skármeta's *Soñé que la nieve ardía* ('I Dreamt the Snow Was Burning', 1975) and *Ardiente paciencia* ('Burning Patience', 1985), and Ariel Dorfman's *Viudas* ('Widows', 1981) and *La última canción de Manuel Sendero* ('The Last Song of Manuel Sendero', 1982). Much of this testimonial work was produced by socialist writers in exile. A number of skilful Argentine writers started to assess, in fiction of a largely documentary character, the traumas resulting from their country's weird obsession with Peronism since the 1940s: Ricardo Piglia, *Respiración artificial* ('Artificial Respiration', 1980); Osvaldo Soriano, *No habrá más pena ni olvido* ('A Funny, Dirty Little War', 1980); Mario Schizmann, *A las 20.25 la señora entró en la inmortalidad* ('At 8.25 Evita Became Immortal', 1981); Marta Traba, *Conversación al sur* ('Mothers and Shadows', 1981); Luisa Valenzuela, *Cola de lagartija* ('The Lizard's Tail', 1983); the ex-Montonero Miguel Bonasso's account of the dirty war against the guerrillas, *Recuerdo de la muerte* ('Memory of Death', 1984); Tomás Eloy Martínez's *La novela de Perón* ('The Peron Novel', 1985), an analysis of the career, mystique and legacy of the great *caudillo*.

This trend towards greater realism was noticeable even among writers who had themselves been deeply influenced by the experimentalism of the Boom. Authors like Severo Sarduy, Gustavo Sainz and Manuel Puig moved away from complex Joycean fictions towards novels with an accessible story, drawing upon the cinema, television and rock music. Though critical of mass culture, these writers were also fascinated by its drawing power. In fact, the new realism of the late 1970s and 1980s may be regarded as an attempt by serious writers to tackle the profound changes that the major Latin American societies had been through since the 1950s, but without falling back on the nationalist and socialist nostrums that had been current since the 1920s. And because cultural nationalism had been so closely associated with modernism in Latin America, breaking out of ideological stereotypes also involved a revaluation of the modernist heritage. For instance, Manuel Puig, whose novels of the 1970s already evinced a post-modernist ambivalence towards the culture of the masses and a suspicion of radical political solutions, wrote *Sangre de amor correspondido* ('Blood of Requited Love', 1982), a novel about a Brazilian stonemason in Rio de Janeiro, derived largely from tape-recordings of interviews with the man in question. It takes the form of a monologue which betrays the acute psychosexual disorientation of a peasant who has migrated to the big city and whose traditional values – sexual as much as social – have fallen to pieces, leaving him floundering in a private world of fantasies and self-deception.

Similarly, the Mexican Elena Poniatowska developed a style which applied the techniques of fiction to documentary narratives concerned with the impact of great events upon the lives of ordinary people. Works like *Hasta no verte, Jesús mío* ('Until We Meet Again', 1969), which related the testimony of a peasant woman who had had first-hand experience of the changes undergone by Mexico from the Revolution to the development of the post-war years, *La noche de Tlatelolco* ('Massacre in Mexico', 1971), on the Tlatelolco outrage, *Nada, nadie* ('Nothing, No one', 1988), about the 1985 earthquake, were far removed from the social-realist novels of the 1930s in that they imposed no preconceived ideological scheme but tried instead to capture historical reality as it affected individuals. A correspondence can be found with the phenomenon of the 'new social movements' which appeared in many countries after the debt problem of 1982. These grass-roots movements, running local campaigns for better housing and conditions, represented a pragmatic assertion of rights by common people outside totalizing ideologies and populist parties; this was a democratic pluralism in action, not yet formalized by a state machine nor co-opted by *caudillos*. By analogy, Poniatowska relinquished the author's privilege of narrative control from above, as it were, and allowed ordinary people to make themselves heard from below. The thrust of her objective, pluralistic style was anti-authoritarian and, in the context of Latin America, anti-patriarchal, for it was no accident that Poniatowska was a woman and that her principal subjects were also women.

Indeed, another significant cultural trend of the late 1970s and 1980s was the rise to prominence of women writers. The Brazilian Clarice Lispector had established her literary reputation in the 1960s, but her most popular work was *A Hora da Estrela* ('The Hour of the Star'), which appeared in 1977, the year she died, and explored the reactions of a poor country girl from the north-east to the consumer society of São Paulo. In the 1980s, Nélida Piñón became well known for her reworking of issues such as the historical roots of the Brazilian identity crisis, but from the female experience.

In Spanish America, the vitality of female writing was highlighted by the international success of Isabel Allende's *La casa de los espíritus* ('The House of the Spirits', 1982), a magical-realist novel that traced the history of twentieth-century Chile through four generations of women, culminating in the protagonist's incarceration after the military coup of 1973. It was a denunciation of the violence inflicted by men on the country and, as a love story, it looked forward to a new dawn of reconciliation, whose symbol was the unborn child carried by the heroine while in prison. Other famous women writers came from countries which had experienced brutal military repression in the 1970s, and had themselves gone into exile – notably, Luisa Valenzuela of Argentina and Cristina Peri Rossi of Uruguay, both of whom, like Allende, wrote in a magical-realist mode, illuminating political issues with fantasy.

The importance of women writers in the 1980s awakened interest in earlier female authors such as Victoria and Silvina Ocampo, Alejandra Pizarnik (all of Argentina) and the Mexican Rosario Castellanos, whose novel *Balún-Canán* ('The Nine Guardians', 1957) was an original study of the crumbling of the white, patriarchal order from the perspective of the young daughter of a great landowning family. Well before the rise of feminism in the 1960s, Castellanos intuited the connection between the subordination of women in traditional society and the economic and ethnic oppression which sustained that same social structure.

Indeed, the prominence of women's writing in the years following the Boom may well point to the true historic significance of the general flowering of Latin American literature since the 1920s – modernism gave writers the means to come to terms with the passing of the patriarchal authority of traditional Hispanic society. The first effects of the modernist revolution were to be seen in lyric poetry, for the reaction to modernity was initially an expression of individual anguish. From the 1940s, however, modernism began to transform narrative fiction as the pace of industrial development quickened and the bonds of a still largely rural society began rapidly to dissolve in the growing cities. This process culminated in the Boom of the 1960s, when young writers started to reflect in their work the fluid social relations characteristic of modern urban culture.

Yet even though the advance of consumer capitalism quickly destabilized social hierarchies in the cities, the patriarchal ethos was so deeply embedded in politics through patronage and clientship that it resulted in authoritarian developmental states run from the 1940s by civilian governments and military juntas alike. The conflict-ridden 1970s finally saw this kind of neo-patriarchal state enter into a terminal crisis of authority, its bankruptcy revealed in the foreign-debt catastrophe of the early 1980s. Retrospectively, then, it can be appreciated that from the late 1960s the writers of the Boom and the post-Boom had been registering the progressive impotence of Hispanic patriarchy – in the subversive language games of novelists (many of whom were homosexual), in the dictator novels of the mid-1970s, in the new fascination with the egalitarian ethos of international mass culture, in the literature that bore testimony to the repressions of the authoritarian state, and finally, in the burgeoning of women's writing.

Patriarchal authority was being displaced by cultural pluralism, just as white oligarchy had earlier been undermined by a revaluation of *mestizaje* and ethnic diversity. But, equally, the evolving pluralism of urban culture was converting the quest for an 'integral culture' – the basis of that essential identity that had so preoccupied nationalists and modernists until the 1960s – into an irrelevance. In the course of the century Latin America had been forced to recognize itself in its diverse forms of *mestizaje* and now, finally, it became impossible to deny the ultimate and most painful *mestizaje* for nationalists to accept – the admixture of foreign influences, a major phenomenon of the modern world.

Unquestionably, the demise of patriarchy would represent a profound sea-change in Latin America, marking the emergence of a truly modern culture. For patriarchy had been the universal principle of the Iberian Catholic monarchies, as of the pre-Columbian Indian societies before them; patriarchy had also pervaded the attempts at modernization in the Iberian world from the eighteenth century until the 1920s, when even most liberals advocated reforms from above by a strong state; and patriarchy, too, had deeply marked the period of economic nationalism, with its populist *caudillos* and military oligarchies. Only after the rapid urbanization of the mid-twentieth century had the general democratization of culture begun. Indeed, in the 1980s there was an awakening to the possibility that Latin America had arrived at the end of an era.

This sense of an ending was powerfully displayed in Brazil in a remarkable historical novel by João Ubaldo Ribeiro, *Viva o Povo Brasileiro!* (1984), a work which surveyed the span of Brazilian history and exhaustively re-examined the theme of national identity, only to show it up as a mirage when set against the multiplicity of the country. The original title in Portuguese – 'Long Live the Brazilian People!' – parodied the sham of populist nationalism, yet expressed also the desire for a true consensus as the basis of national identity, an ambivalence that informs the entire novel. Its apocalyptic ending occurs in the late 1970s (precisely the time when the military dictatorship was facing up to its own failures), and describes a storm that brings the unifying 'Spirit of Man' from across the ocean to hover, as yet unseen, above the people of Brazil.

The influence of García Márquez's fiction on Ribeiro's work was noted by critics, and the Colombian writer himself – a past master of the literary apocalypse – published another magnificent novel in 1985, which captured the mixed feelings that accompanied the dying days of patriarchy. *El amor en los tiempos del cólera* ('Love in the Time of Cholera') is a love-song to traditional Spanish American society. (García Márquez once described himself as a failed writer of sentimental songs like the *bolero*, and indeed likened *One Hundred Years of Solitude* to a *vallenato*, a genre of popular Colombian song.) Set in 'the city of the viceroys', a former Caribbean slaving-port modelled on Cartagena de Indias, the novel describes the thwarted passion of an old-fashioned young poet for a well-to-do girl who marries a patrician Liberal doctor instead.

The work is self-consciously anti-modern in spirit, romantic love being likened to cholera, a disease the enlightened doctor wants to stamp out. Yet, against all the odds, love triumphs right at the very end, as the original sweethearts, ravaged by old age, travel dreamlike on a quarantined boat up and down the Magdalena River; theirs is a 'floating fiesta' on the waters of time, a sanctuary beyond the destructive reach of modern development. Carrying the reader as it does along a knife-edge between parody and self-indulgence, the novel may be termed a post-modernist romance, for it is as if all the themes of the Spanish romantic tradition – honour, glory, virginity, impossible love – were being caressed one last time before being put away for good by an author who can so richly idealize the values of a patriarchal society because he knows they cannot survive for long in reality.

The demise of patriarchy would appear to leave Latin American culture defenceless against the claims of the modern world. Yet this, in fact, may be more of a historic opportunity than a disaster, for it would create the conditions to realize the great dreams of the Liberators for the first time since independence. As we have seen, what brought to grief the ideals of Bolívar and other revolutionary liberals was the sheer strength of Hispanic patriarchy in its many guises, from *caudillismo* and authoritarian rule to the pseudo-democratic regimes that appeared repeatedly all over the continent. If the literature of the 1970s and 1980s began to signal the end of an era, it might well have been pointing to a new beginning for the Enlightenment values that inspired the leaders of the independence movement. Popular sovereignty, liberty, equality, the rights of man, the spirit of free inquiry and critical reason – all of these were adopted as positive ideals by Bolívar and his successors throughout the nineteenth century, even though such ideals, as it turned out, could have no enduring purchase on reality so long as patriarchal values pervaded Latin American society.

Once again, it was García Márquez who intuited the relevance of the ideals of the independence period to the situation of Latin America in the 1980s. His novel *El general en su laberinto* ('The General in His Labyrinth', 1989) described the last days of Simón Bolívar as he made his way to exile in failing health after the collapse of his authority in Gran Colombia, the independent republic he himself had brought into being. His recurrent obsession is with the idea of Spanish American unity, and he constantly decries the anarchy into which the continent has been plunged after having severed its ties with Spain. As the great hope of uniting the Spanish American world fades, Bolívar senses that the new republics are entering a labyrinth – a long history of turmoil in which national identity and modern culture would appear to be violently at odds with each other. But what a man like Bolívar understood was that a stable national identity could not be achieved other than on the basis of a unifying political ideal. In his efforts to preserve Gran Colombia and in his dream of a pan-American federation, he was striving to rediscover in modern political conditions the fundamental quality that had made the Catholic monarchy of Spain (and indeed Portugal) so stable and resilient – namely, its capacity to reconcile political unity with cultural diversity.

Under the Catholic monarchy the integrative principle was found in religious orthodoxy, which served as the binding-force of a global empire because it legitimized royal authority. That unifying principle was lost at independence and was never to be recovered, despite repeated efforts by conservatives. In the nineteenth century liberal republicans had tried to establish new principles of political unity based on the ideas of the European Enlightenment, particularly the sovereignty of the people under the rule of law. But they failed to achieve a consensus, not least because they left out of the national idea the ethnic and regional multiplicity of Latin America.

It was the rich and multifaceted experience of modernism in the twentieth century that enabled Latin America to take the measure of its own diversity, of its deeply rooted *mestizaje* of Iberian, Indian and African traditions, and of the enduring strengths of its popular culture. This long exploration of a complex heritage and its relations with the outside world was perhaps a necessary process before a genuine democratization of culture and society could take place. Latin America appeared to be approaching such a condition in the last decades of the century, when the critique of patriarchal authority prompted a reassessment of the liberal-democratic values inherited from the European Enlightenment, that great storehouse of modern ideas that had been the inspiration of Simón Bolívar and the liberators of the continent. This critique of patriarchy, in short, may point to an eventual reconciliation of Latin American national identities with the inescapable pluralism of modern culture.

Statistical Appendix

TABLE 1
Population and Projected Growth

	Population (millions) 1988	2000	2025	Life expectancy at birth (years) 1988
Argentina	32	36	44	71
Brazil	144	178	236	65
Chile	13	15	19	72
Mexico	84	105	142	69
Cuba	10	12	—	76
Colombia	32	38	50	68
Peru	21	26	37	62
Nicaragua	4	5	9	64
El Salvador	5	6	10	63
Bolivia	7	10	16	53

Source: World Development Report 1990, table 26

TABLE 2
Urbanization

| | Urban population | | | |
| | As a percentage of total population | | Average annual growth rate (per cent) | |
	1965	1988	1965–80	1980–88
Upper income				
Argentina	76	86	2.2	1.8
Brazil	50	75	4.5	3.6
Chile	72	85	2.6	2.3
Mexico	55	71	4.4	3.1
Cuba	58	74	—	—
Middle income				
Colombia	54	69	3.7	3.0
Peru	52	69	4.3	3.1
Lower income				
Nicaragua	43	59	4.7	4.6
El Salvador	39	44	3.2	1.9
Bolivia	40	50	3.1	4.3

Source: World Development Report 1990, table 31

TABLE 3
Economic Growth

| | GDP Average annual growth rate (per cent) | | GNP per capita | |
	1965–80	1980–88	Dollars 1988	Average annual growth rate (per cent) 1965–88
Upper income				
Argentina	3.5	−0.2	2,520	0.0
Brazil	8.8	2.9	2,160	3.6
Chile	1.9	1.9	1,510	0.1
Mexico	6.5	0.5	1,760	2.3
Middle income				
Colombia	5.8	3.4	1,180	2.4
Peru	3.9	1.1	1,300	0.1
Lower income				
Nicaragua	2.6	−0.3	N/A	−2.5
El Salvador	4.3	0.0	940	−0.5
Bolivia	4.5	−1.6	570	−0.6
Developed economies				
United Kingdom	2.4	2.8	12,810	1.8
USA	2.7	3.3	19,840	1.6
Japan	6.5	3.9	21,020	4.3

Source: World Development Report 1990, table 2

TABLE 4
Inflation

| | Average annual rate of inflation (*per cent*) | | |
	1960–70	1970–78	1980–88
Upper income			
Argentina	21.80	120.40	290.5
Brazil	46.10	30.30	188.7
Chile	32.90	242.60	20.8
Mexico	3.50	17.50	73.8
Middle income			
Colombia	11.90	21.70	24.1
Peru	9.90	22.20	119.1
Lower income			
Nicaragua	1.90	11.00	86.6
El Salvador	0.50	10.30	16.8
Bolivia	3.50	22.70	482.8
Developed economies			
United Kingdom			5.7
USA			4.0
Japan			1.3

Source: World Development Report 1980, table 1; World Development Report 1990, table 1

TABLE 5
Total External Debt Disbursed (End-of-year balance in US $ billion)

	1978	1979	1980	1981	1982	1983	1984[a]
Latin America	150.8	181.9	221.0	275.4[b]	315.3[b]	340.9[b]	360.1[b]
Oil-exporting countries	64.3	77.5	92.3	118.9	135.6	145.6	153.4
Bolivia[c]	1.7	1.9	2.2	2.4	2.3	3.0	3.2
Ecuador	2.9	3.5	4.6	5.8	6.1	6.6	6.8
Mexico	33.9	39.6	49.3	72.0[d]	85.5[d]	90.0[d]	95.9[d]
Peru	9.3	9.3	9.5	9.6	11.0	12.4	13.5
Venezuela[e]	16.3	23.0	26.5	29.0	31.0	33.5	34.0
Non oil-exporting countries	86.5	104.3	128.7	156.4	179.6	195.2	206.7
Argentina	12.4	19.0	27.1	35.6	43.6	45.5	48.0
Brazil[f]	52.2	58.9	68.3	78.5	87.5	96.5	101.8
Colombia	4.2	5.1	6.2	7.9	9.4	10.4	10.8
Costa Rica	1.8	2.3	3.1	3.3	3.4	3.8	4.0
Chile[g]	6.6	8.4	11.0	15.5	17.1	17.4	18.4
El Salvador	.9	.9	1.1	1.4	1.6	2.0	2.3
Guatemala	.8	.9	1.0	1.4	1.5	1.7	1.9
Honduras	.9	1.2	1.5	1.7	1.8	2.0	2.2
Nicaragua[c]	.9	1.1	1.5	2.1	2.7	3.3	3.9
Panama[c]	1.7	2.0	2.2	2.3	2.8	3.2	3.5
Paraguay	.6	.7	.8	.9	1.2	1.4	1.5
Dominican Republic	1.3	1.5	1.8	1.8	1.9	2.5	2.8
Uruguay	1.2	1.6	2.1	3.1	4.2	4.5	4.7

Source: ECLAC on the basis of official information; Brazil and Venezuela: ECLAC, on the basis of data from the Bank for International Settlements

Notes:

a. Provisional figures. b. Figures not comparable with those previous to 1982, owing to the inclusion of the Mexican commercial banks' debt. c. Public debt. d. Including commercial banks' debt. Estimates on the basis of data supplied by the Secretariat of Finance and Public Credit. e. Including the public debt plus the non-guaranteed long- and short-term debt with financial institutions reporting to the Bank for International Settlements. f. Including the total medium- and long-term debt plus the short-term debt with financial institutions reporting to the Bank for International Settlements.

g. Short-, medium-, and long-term debt, excluding the debt with the IMF and short-term credits for foreign trade operations.

TABLE 6

Ratio of Total Interest Payments to Exports of Goods and Services[a]

	1977	1978	1979	1980	1981	1982	1983	1984[b]
				Percentages				
Latin America	12.4	15.5	17.4	19.9	26.4	39.0	35.8	35.0
Oil-exporting								
countries	13.0	16.0	15.7	16.5	22.3	32.0	31.0	33.0
Bolivia	9.9	13.7	18.1	24.5	35.5	43.6	49.3	57.0
Ecuador	4.8	10.3	13.6	18.2	24.3	30.1	26.0	31.5
Mexico	25.4	24.0	24.8	23.1	28.7	39.9	36.7	36.5
Peru	17.9	21.2	14.7	16.0	21.8	24.7	31.2	35.5
Venezuela	4.0	7.2	6.9	8.1	12.7	21.0	20.3	25.0
Non oil-exporting								
countries	11.9	15.1	18.8	23.3	31.3	46.6	40.7	36.5
Argentina	7.6	9.6	12.8	22.0	31.7	54.6	58.4	52.0
Brazil	18.9	24.5	31.5	34.1	40.4	57.1	43.4	36.5
Colombia	7.4	7.7	10.1	13.3	21.6	25.0	21.7	21.5
Costa Rica	7.1	9.9	12.8	18.0	25.5	33.4	41.8	32.0
Chile	13.7	17.0	16.5	19.3	34.6	49.5	39.4	45.5
El Salvador	2.9	5.1	5.3	6.5	7.5	11.9	14.2	15.0
Guatemala	2.4	3.6	3.1	5.3	7.5	7.8	7.6	4.0
Honduras	7.2	8.2	8.6	10.6	14.5	22.4	17.7	19.0
Nicaragua	7.0	9.3	9.7	15.7	15.5	33.2	19.3	18.5
Paraguay	6.7	8.5	10.7	14.3	15.9	14.9	24.3	19.0
Dominican Republic	8.8	14.0	14.4	14.7	10.5	22.6	24.9	23.5
Uruguay	9.8	10.4	9.0	11.0	13.1	22.4	27.6	31.5

Source: 1977–83: International Monetary Fund, *Balance of Payments Yearbook*; 1984: ECLAC, on the basis of official data
Notes:
a. Interest payments include those on the short-term debt.   *b.* Provisional estimates subject to revision.

TABLE 7
Structure of Production

| | Distribution of GDP (per cent)[a] | | | | | | | |
| | Agriculture | | Industry | | Manufacturing[b] | | Services | |
	1965	1988	1965	1988	1965	1988	1965	1988
Upper income								
Argentina	17	13	42	44	33	31[c]	42	44
Brazil	19	9	33	43	26	29	48	49
Chile	9	N/A	40	N/A	24	N/A	52	N/A
Mexico	14	9	27	35	20	26	59	56
Middle income								
Colombia	27	19	27	34	19	20	47	47
Peru	18	12	30	36[c]	17	24[c]	53	51[c]
Lower income								
Nicaragua	25	21[c]	24	34[c]	18	24[c]	51	46[c]
El Salvador	29	14	22	22	18	18	49	65
Bolivia	23	24	31	27	15	17	46	49
Developed economies								
United Kingdom	3	2[c]	46	42[c]	34	27[c]	51	56[c]
USA	3	2[c]	38	33[c]	28	22[c]	59	65
Japan	9	3	43	41[c]	32	29	48	57[c]

Source: World Development Report 1990, table 3
Notes:
a. GDP and its components are shown at purchaser values. *b.* Manufacturing is included in the figures for the industrial sector, but its share of GDP is also shown separately. *c.* These figures are for years other than those specified.

TABLE 8
Structure of Imports and Exports

	Percentage share of imports							
	Food		Fuels		Other primary commodities		Machinery & transport equipment	
	1965	1988	1965	1988	1965	1988	1965	1988
Upper income								
Argentina	6	4	10	8	21	7	25	43
Brazil	20	14	21	28	9	7	22	25
Chile	20	2	6	6	10	2	35	46
Mexico	5	16	2	1	10	8	50	36
Middle income								
Colombia	8	9	1	4	10	7	45	37
Peru	17	19	3	1	5	4	41	44
Lower income								
Nicaragua	12	25	5	11	2	3	30	17
El Salvador	15	15	5	8	4	4	28	19
Bolivia	19	15	1	3	3	3	35	52
Developed economies								
United Kingdom	30	10	11	5	25	8	11	37
USA	19	6	10	10	20	5	14	43
Japan	22	17	20	21	38	20	9	13

Source: World Development Report 1990, tables 15 and 16

| | Other manufactures | | Percentage share of exports | | | | | | | |
| Other manufactures | | Fuels, minerals, metals | | Other primary commodities | | Manufacture & transport equipment | | Textiles & other manufactures | |
1965	1988	1965	1988	1965	1988	1965	1988	1965	1988
38	38	1	5	93	70	1	5	5	20
28	26	9	21	83	31	2	18	7	30
30	44	89	67	7	18	1	3	4	12
33	38	22	38	62	7	1	33	15	22
35	43	18	26	75	49	0	1	6	24
34	33	45	58	54	20	0	3	1	18
51	44	4	2	90	89	0	0	6	9
48	53	2	3	81	68	1	3	16	26
42	27	92	89	3	8	0	1	4	2
23	41	7	10	10	8	41	39	41	43
36	36	8	6	27	17	37	47	28	31
11	30	2	1	7	1	31	65	60	33

Bibliographical Essay

Abbreviations

CHLA   Cambridge History of Latin America
HAHR   Hispanic American Historical Review

The historiography of Latin America is vast; the following list is intended as a select guide to further reading. It is confined largely to standard works and scholarly articles (in English for the most part), but includes some more specialized items which point to major developments in the main areas of scholarship in recent decades. References are organized with regard to subject-matter rather than in alphabetical order. Further bibliographical information can be found in the annual *Handbook of Latin American Studies* (Texas University Press: Austin, 1936–   ). Bibliographical guidance is also available in the leading academic journals devoted to the history of Latin America: *Hispanic American Historical Review*, *Journal of Latin American Studies*; and in the following research reviews: *Latin American Research Review*, *Bulletin of Latin American Research*. See too the bibliographies on specific topics or individual countries in the ten-volume *Cambridge History of Latin America*, edited by Leslie Bethell (Cambridge University Press: Cambridge, 1984–92). A useful work of reference is *The Cambridge Encyclopedia of Latin America and the Caribbean*, edited by Simon Collier, Harold Blakemore and Thomas Skidmore (Cambridge University Press: Cambridge, 1985).

Part One: *The Age of Empire*

General

Charles Gibson, *Spain in America* (Harper & Row: New York, 1966), is a masterly brief survey of the colonial period. Guillermo Céspedes, *Latin America: The Early Years* (Alfred A. Knopf: New York, 1974), is a concise survey with stimulating insights.

James Lockhart and Stuart B. Schwartz, *Early Latin America: A History of Colonial Spanish America and Brazil* (Cambridge University Press: Cambridge, 1983), is an important and dispassionate synthesis that focuses on social–structural factors and ethnic relations, and makes illuminating comparisons between the Spanish and Portuguese experiences. Lyle N. McAlister, *Spain and Portugal in the New World, 1492–1700* (Oxford University Press: Oxford, 1984), is objective and informative. The *CHLA*, vols. 1 and 2 contain general essays by specialists on colonial America.

A reliable demographic survey is Nicolás Sánchez-Albornoz, *The Population of Latin America: A History* (University of California Press: Berkeley, 1974).

Older standard surveys are still useful; see J. H. Parry, *The Spanish Seaborne Empire* (Penguin Books: Harmondsworth, 1973), and the companion volume by C. R. Boxer, *The Portuguese Seaborne Empire* (Penguin Books: Harmondsworth, 1973). For a good account of colonial institutions, see C. H. Haring, *The Spanish Empire in America* (Oxford University Press: Oxford, 1947).

A useful compilation of primary sources on the colonial period is Benjamin Keen (ed.), *Latin American Civilization*, vol. 1, *The Colonial Origins* (Houghton Mifflin: Boston, 1974). A number of influential scholarly essays have been anthologized in Peter J. Bakewell, John J. Johnson and Meredith D. Dodge (eds.), *Readings in Latin American History*, vol. 1, *The Formative Centuries* (Duke University Press: Durham, NC, 1985).

Chapter 1: Discovery and Conquest

On discovery and exploration, see *European Expansion in the Later Middle Ages* (North-Holland: Amsterdam, New York and London, 1979), in which Pierre Chaunu discusses Columbus's voyages against the background of earlier Iberian maritime enterprises; J. H. Parry, *The Age of Reconnaissance: Discovery, Exploration and Settlement, 1450–1650* (Weidenfeld and Nicolson: London, 1963), sets the Portuguese voyages and Columbus's enterprise in the context of a wider survey of European overseas exploration. Samuel E. Morison, *The European Discovery of America: The Southern Voyages, 1492–1619* (Oxford University Press: New York and Oxford, 1974), is a thoroughly researched study by a naval authority.

For the standard biography of Columbus, see Samuel E. Morison, *Admiral of the Ocean Sea: A Life of the Admiral Christopher Columbus* (2 vols., Little, Brown: Boston, 1942); see also Christopher Columbus, *Journal of the First*

Voyage. Diario del primer viaje, 1492, ed. and trans. B. W. Ife (Aris and Philips: Warminster, 1990), a bilingual text with a discussion of Las Casas's edition of the original.

J. H. Elliott, *The Old World and the New, 1492–1650* (Cambridge University Press: Cambridge, 1970), is a collection of essays on the impact of the discovery on the European mind; the intellectual repercussions of the discovery are more fully discussed in A. R. Pagden, *The Fall of Natural Man: The American Indian and the Origins of Comparative Ethnology* (Cambridge University Press: Cambridge, 1982).

For accounts of the Conquest, see Hernán Cortés, *Letters from Mexico*, ed. and trans. A. R. Pagden (Oxford University Press: Oxford, 1972); Franscisco López de Gómara, *Cortés: The Life of the Conqueror by His Secretary*, trans. Lesley Byrd Simpson; Bernal Díaz del Castillo, *The Conquest of New Spain*, trans. J. M. Cohen (Penguin Books: Harmondsworth, 1963); Agustín de Zárate, *The Discovery and Conquest of Peru*, trans. J. M. Cohen (Folio Society: London, 1981). William H. Prescott's *History of the Conquest of Mexico* and *History of the Conquest of Peru* (first appeared in 1843 and 1846 respectively, but many editions since) are highly readable, classic narratives, though out of date in some respects. John Hemming, *The Conquest of the Incas* (Macmillan: London, 1970), is an informative chronicle of the overthrow of the Inca empire and subsequent resistance to Spanish rule; F. A. Kirkpatrick, *The Spanish Conquistadores* (A & C Black: London, 1934; 3rd edn, 1963), provides an overview of the entire process of conquest in the New World.

Mario Góngora, *Los grupos de conquistadores en Tierra Firme, 1509–1530* (Universidad de Chile: Santiago, 1962), and James Lockhart, *The Men of Cajamarca* (University of Texas Press: Austin, 1972), are two important studies of the background and motives of Spanish warrior bands in Panama and Peru respectively.

Miguel León-Portilla, *The Broken Spears: The Aztec Account of the Conquest*, trans. Lysander Kemp (Beacon Press: Boston, 1961), is an anthology of indigenous reactions to the Conquest, and *El reverso de la conquista. Relaciones aztecas, mayas e incas* (Universidad Nacional Autónoma de México: Mexico, 1964). Nathan Wachtel, *The Vision of the Vanquished* (Harvester Press: Brighton, 1976), is a controversial work which attempts to analyse the ideological impact of the Conquest on Peru.

Chapter 2: Indians and Iberians

Indians

William M. Denevan (ed.), *The Native Population of the Americas in 1492* (University of Wisconsin Press: Madison, 1976), is a collection of essays on demography which reflects the controversies surrounding the subject. Friedrich Katz, *The Ancient American Civilizations* (Praeger: New York, 1972), is an authoritative survey. On Middle America, see Ignacio Bernal, *The Olmec World* (University of California Press: Berkeley, 1969); René Millon, *Urbanization at Teotihuacan, Mexico* (University of Texas Press: Austin, 1973), part 1, vol. 1, which contains a summary of current knowledge about this obscure civilization; Nigel Davies, *The Toltecs: Until the Fall of Tula* (University of Oklahoma Press: Norman, 1977), *The Aztecs* (Macmillan: London, 1973), and *The Ancient Kingdoms of Mexico* (Penguin Books: Harmondsworth, 1983); Michael D. Coe, *The Maya* (Thames and Hudson: London, 1987). On Andean societies and the Incas, see the pre-Conquest chapters in Magnus Mörner, *The Andean Past: Land Societies and Conflicts* (Columbia University Press: New York, 1985); Alfred Métraux, *The History of the Incas* (Pantheon Books: New York, 1969); John V. Murra, *The Economic Organization of the Inka State* (JAI Press: Greenwich, Conn., 1980), a seminal anthropological study of the rationale of the Inca empire; and John V. Murra (ed.), *Anthropological History of Andean Polities* (Cambridge University Press: Cambridge, 1986). Geoffrey W. Conrad and Arthur A. Demarest, *Religion and Empire: The Dynamics of Aztec and Inca Expansionism* (Cambridge University Press: Cambridge, 1984), argues that religion was a major cause of both the rise and the fall of the native empires.

Iberians

Standard works on the Iberian powers are: Stanley G. Payne, *A History of Spain and Portugal* (2 vols., University of Wisconsin Press: Madison, 1973); Harold Livermore, *A New History of Portugal* (Cambridge University Press: Cambridge, 1966); Angus Mackay, *Spain in the Middle Ages* (Macmillan: London, 1977); Charles Julian Bishko, 'The Peninsular Background of Latin American Cattle-Ranching', *HAHR*, 32 (1952), pp. 491–515; J. H. Elliott, *Imperial Spain, 1469–1716* (Edward Arnold: London, 1963); John Lynch, *Spain under the Habsburgs* (2 vols., Blackwell: Oxford, 1964, 1969); Bernice Hamilton, *Political Thought in Sixteenth-Century Spain: A Study of the Political Ideas of Vitoria, De Soto, Suárez and Molina* (Oxford University Press: Oxford,

1963); A. R. Pagden, *Spanish Imperialism and the Political Imagination* (Yale University Press: New Haven, 1990).

Chapter 3: Spain in America

For the characteristics of the early Spanish colonies, see Peter Boyd-Bowman, 'Patterns of Spanish Emigration to the Indies until 1600', *HAHR*, 56 (1976), pp. 580–640; Peggy K. Liss, *Mexico under Spain, 1521–1556: Society and the Origins of Nationality* (University of Chicago Press: Chicago, 1975), which studies the attempts by Crown officials to impose law and order in the early post-Conquest period. The role of Cortés after the Conquest is studied by G. Michael Riley, *Fernando Cortés and the Marquesado in Morelos, 1522–1547: A Case Study in the Socioeconomic Development of Sixteenth-Century Mexico* (University of New Mexico Press: Albuquerque, 1973); and F. V. Scholes, 'The Spanish Conquistador as Businessman: A Chapter in the History of Fernando Cortés', *New Mexico Quarterly*, 28 (1958), pp. 1–29. For the role of the *encomendero*, see José Miranda, *La función económica del encomendero en los orígenes del régimen colonial* (Universidad Nacional Autónoma de México: Mexico, 1965). J. H. Parry, *The Audiencia of New Galicia in the Sixteenth Century* (Cambridge University Press: Cambridge, 1948), examines the earliest attempts to establish royal government in a frontier region of Mexico in the post-Conquest period.

The early years of colonial Peru are ably synthesized in James Lockhart, *Spanish Peru, 1532–1560* (University of Wisconsin Press: Madison, 1968), a portrait of a post-Conquest society in the making. For an anthology of first-hand testimonies of life in Spanish America, see James Lockhart and Enrique Otte (eds.), *Letters and People of the Spanish Indies, Sixteenth Century* (Cambridge University Press: Cambridge, 1976).

Charles Gibson, *The Aztecs under Spanish Rule: A History of the Indians of the Valley of Mexico, 1519–1810* (Stanford University Press: Stanford, 1964), is an important work that opened up a new field of study. Other important works in this field are: Ronald Spores, *The Mixtec Kings and Their People* (University of Oklahoma Press: Norman, 1967), which shows how an Indian kingdom in Mexico adapted to the Spanish Conquest; Nancy M. Farriss, *Maya Society Under Colonial Rule: The Collective Enterprise of Survival* (Princeton University Press: Princeton, 1984); Steve J. Stern, *Peru's Indian Peoples and the Challenge of Spanish Conquest: Huamanga to 1640* (University of Wisconsin Press: Madison, 1982), which deals with the ways an Indian society coped with Spanish rule; Karen Spalding, *Huarochirí: An Andean Society*

Under Inca and Spanish Rule (Stanford University Press: Stanford, 1984), an influential monograph that stresses continuities as well as ruptures. Nathan Wachtel, *The Vision of the Vanquished* (Harvester Press: Brighton, 1976), is a work that concentrates on the destructive effects of the Spanish Conquest on Inca society and the Andean world-view. Magnus Mörner, *The Andean Past: Land, Societies and Conflicts* (Columbia University Press: New York, 1985), is a wide-ranging synthesis of the history of this region.

C. H. Haring, *The Spanish Empire in America* (Oxford University Press: Oxford, 1947), is an informative general survey of government institutions. Mario Góngora, *El estado en el derecho indiano* (Universidad de Chile: Santiago, 1951), is the standard work on the principles underlying Spanish imperial government, of which portions are included in the author's *Studies in the Colonial History of Spanish America* (Cambridge University Press: Cambridge, 1975). J. Lloyd Mecham, *Church and State in Latin America: A History of Politico-Ecclesiastical Relations*, rev. edn (University of North Carolina Press: Chapel Hill, 1966), is an authoritative study which first appeared in 1934.

John Leddy Phelan, *The Millennial Kingdom of the Franciscans in the New World* (University of California Press: Berkeley, 1956), discusses the ideas and motives behind the Franciscan mission to the Indians. Robert Ricard, *The Spiritual Conquest of Mexico: An Essay on the Apostolate and the Evangelizing Methods of the Mendicant Orders in New Spain, 1523–1572*, trans. Lesley Byrd Simpson (University of California Press: Berkeley, 1966), is a classic study first published in French in 1933. Pierre Duviols, *La Lutte contre les réligions autochtones dans le Pérou colonial* (Editions Ophrys: Paris, 1971), studies the systematic campaigns undertaken by the colonial Church between 1532 and 1660 to eradicate native religions.

J. H. Parry, *The Spanish Seaborne Empire* (Penguin Books: Harmondsworth, 1973), includes a useful survey of the transatlantic link. However, Pierre and Huguette Chaunu, *Séville et l'Atlantique, 1504–1650* (8 vols., Librairie Armand Colin: Paris, 1955–9), is a standard work which consists of an exhaustive review of all aspects of the maritime trade with America, with ample statistics and graphs. See also, William L. Schurz, *The Manila Galleon*, 2nd edn (E. P. Dutton: New York, 1959), a monograph of enduring value.

Mario Góngora, *Studies in the Colonial History of Spanish America* (Cambridge University Press: Cambridge, 1975), contains excellent essays on the principles of Spanish imperialism; J. H. Parry, *The Spanish Theory of Empire in the Sixteenth Century* (Cambridge University Press: Cambridge, 1940), is rather dated but still useful as an introduction. Colin M. MacLachlan, *Spain's Empire in the New World: The Role of Ideas in Institutional and Social Change*

(University of California Press: Berkeley, 1989), deals with the imperial culture of the Habsburgs and argues that it was undermined by Bourbon ideology; A. R. Pagden, *Spanish Imperialism and the Political Imagination* (Yale University Press: New Haven, 1990), is the most thorough discussion to date.

On the status of the Indians, see Lewis Hanke, *The Spanish Struggle for Justice in the Conquest of America* (Little, Brown: Boston, 1965), and *Aristotle and the American Indians,* 2nd edn (Indiana University Press: Bloomington, 1970); Juan Friede and Benjamin Keen, *Bartolomé de las Casas in History* (Northern Illinois University Press: De Kalb, 1971); and Philippe-Ignace André-Vicent, *Bartolomé de Las Casas: Prophète du Nouveau Monde* (Editions Tallandier: Paris, 1980).

On the founding principles of the *encomienda*, see Silvio Zavala, *La encomienda indiana* (Centro de Estudios Históricos: Madrid, 1935); and Lesley Byrd Simpson, *The Encomienda in New Spain: The Beginning of New Mexico* (University of California Press: Berkeley, 1950).

Alistair Hennessy, *The Frontier in Latin American History* (Edward Arnold: London, 1978), is an illuminating study of the dynamics of frontier regions.

Chapter 4: The Spanish Indies

On the economy, see Woodrow Borah, *New Spain's Century of Depression* (University of California Press: Berkeley, 1951), which takes demographic decline as a sign of economic depression. However, John Lynch, in vol. 2 of *Spain Under the Habsburgs* (2 vols., Blackwell: Oxford, 1964, 1969), argues that certain regions and economic sectors in the Indies flourished as a result of the sharp drop in exports of silver to Spain. On forms of land tenure, see François Chevalier, *Land and Society in Colonial Mexico: The Great Hacienda,* trans. Lesley Byrd Simpson (University of California Press: Berkeley, 1963), a standard work that is now somewhat dated and restricted; Lesley Byrd Simpson, *The Encomienda in New Spain* (University of California Press: Berkeley, 1950); Elman R. Service, 'The Encomienda in Paraguay', *HAHR,* 31 (1951), pp. 230–52; James Lockhart, 'Encomienda and Hacienda: The Evolution of the Great Estate in the Spanish Indies', *HAHR,* 49 (1969), pp. 411–29, an incisive study that cuts through much confusion about colonial landholding; William B. Taylor, *Landlord and Peasant in Colonial Oaxaca* (Stanford University Press: Stanford, 1972), an influential work which revealed survival into the late colonial period of extensive Indian land tenure. For a survey of labour and labour relations, see Juan A. Villamarín and Judith

E. Villamarín, *Indian Labour in Mainland Colonial Spanish America* (University of Delaware Press: Newark, 1975).

On textile manufacturing, see Richard E. Greenleaf, 'The Obraje in the late Mexican Colony', *The Americas*, 23 (1966–7), pp. 227–50; John C. Super, 'Querétaro Obrajes', *HAHR*, 56 (1976), pp. 197–216. Richard J. Salvucci, *Textiles and Capitalism in Mexico: An Economic History of the Obrajes, 1539–1840* (Princeton University Press: Princeton, 1988), surveys the colonial textile industry and concludes that the *obraje* was not 'a factory in embryo'; it declined steadily and was wiped out by foreign competition in the 1840s.

On mining, see Peter J. Bakewell, *Silver Mining and Society in Colonial Mexico: Zacatecas, 1546–1700* (Cambridge University Press: Cambridge, 1971), a standard work; David A. Brading and Harry C. Cross, 'Colonial Silver Mining: Mexico and Peru', *HAHR*, 52 (1972), pp. 545–79, a masterly comparative synthesis; Robert C. West, *Colonial Placer Mining in Colombia* (Louisiana State University Press: Baton Rouge, 1952).

Research into colonial Hispanic society has increased enormously since the 1970s. See James Lockhart, 'The Social History of Colonial Spanish America: Evolution and Potential', *Latin American Research Review*, 7 (1972), pp. 6–46. The theoretical principles underlying the division of colonial society into two 'republics' are discussed in Mario Góngora, *Studies in the Colonial History of Spanish America* (Cambridge University Press: Cambridge, 1975). The dynamics of colonial society are ably studied in a pioneering work by J. I. Israel, *Race, Class and Politics in Colonial Mexico, 1610–1670* (Oxford University Press: Oxford, 1975).

On the formation of the creole élites, see Richard Konetzke, 'La formación de la nobleza en Indias', *Estudios Americanos*, 3 (1951), pp. 329–60; Stephanie Blank, 'Patrons, Clients and Kin in Seventeenth-Century Caracas: A Methodological Essay in Colonial Spanish American Social History', *HAHR*, 54 (1974), pp. 260–83; Fred Bonner, 'Peruvian Encomenderos in 1630: Elite Circulation and Consolidation', *HAHR*, 57 (1977), pp. 633–59; Peter Marzahl, *Town in the Empire: Government, Politics and Society in Seventeenth-Century Popayán* (Institute of Latin American Studies, University of Texas: Austin, 1978); Mario Góngora, 'Urban Social Stratification in Colonial Chile', *HAHR*, 55 (1975), pp. 421–48; Louisa Schell Hoberman, 'Merchants in Seventeenth-Century Mexico City: A Preliminary Portrait', *HAHR*, 57 (1977), pp. 479–503.

On women's position in society, see Asunción Lavrin (ed.), *Latin American Women: Historical Perspectives* (Greenwood Press: Westport, 1978); Asunción Lavrin (ed.), *Sexuality and Marriage in Colonial Latin America* (University of Nebraska Press: Lincoln, 1990); Asunción Lavrin and Edith Couturier,

'Dowries and Wills: A View of Women's Socioeconomic Role in Colonial Guadalajara and Puebla, 1640–1790', *HAHR*, 59 (1979), pp. 280–304.

On Indian society, see Charles Gibson, *The Aztecs under Spanish Rule: A History of the Indians of the Valley of Mexico* (Stanford University Press: Stanford, 1964); William B. Taylor, *Drinking, Homicide and Rebellion in Colonial Mexican Villages* (Stanford University Press: Stanford, 1979); John H. Rowe, 'The Incas under Spanish Colonial Institutions', *HAHR*, 37 (1957), pp. 155–99; Nicolás Sánchez-Albornoz, *Indios y tributos en el Alto Perú* (Instituto de Estudios Peruanos: Lima, 1978); James Lockhart and Stuart B. Schwartz, *Early Latin America: A History of Colonial Spanish America and Brazil* (Cambridge University Press: Cambridge, 1983).

On Africans and the slave trade, see Philip Curtin, *The Atlantic Slave Trade: A Census* (University of Wisconsin Press: Madison, 1969); Frederick P. Bowser, *The African in Colonial Peru, 1524–1650* (Stanford University Press: Stanford, 1974); Colin A. Palmer, *Slaves of the White God: Blacks in Mexico, 1570–1650* (Harvard University Press: Cambridge, Mass., 1976).

For an overview of ethnic questions, see Magnus Mörner, *Race Mixture in the History of Latin America* (Little, Brown: Boston, 1967), and Magnus Mörner (ed.), *Race and Class in Latin America* (Columbia University Press: New York, 1970).

On colonial culture, see Mariano Picón-Salas, *A Cultural History of Spanish America: From Conquest to Independence*, trans. Irving I. Leonard (University of California Press: Berkeley, 1964); Irving I. Leonard, *Books of the Brave* (Harvard University Press: Cambridge, Mass., 1949), and *Baroque Times in Old Mexico* (University of Michigan Press: Ann Arbor, 1959), two classic works on literature and culture; Jacques Lafaye, 'Literature and Intellectual Life in Colonial Spanish America' in *CHLA*, vol. 2, pp. 663–704, and *Quetzalcoatl and Guadalupe: The Formation of Mexican National Consciousness* (University of Chicago Press: Chicago, 1976).

On particular individuals, see Octavio Paz, *Sor Juana Inés de la Cruz: Her Life and Her World*, trans. Margaret Sayers Peden (Faber and Faber: London, 1988), a literary biography that sheds light on a whole culture and society. *A Sor Juana Anthology*, trans. Alan S. Trueblood (Harvard University Press: Cambridge, Mass., 1988), is a bilingual edition of selected poems. Rolena Adorno, *Guaman Poma: Writing and Resistance in Colonial Peru* (University of Texas Press: Austin, 1986), studies the Peruvian mestizo's fusion of Spanish Renaissance cultural models of writing with traditional Andean concepts in his chronicle. Margarita Zamora, *Language, Authority and Indigenous History in the 'Comentarios Reales de los Incas'* (Cambridge University Press: Cambridge,

1988), is an analysis of the Inca Garcilaso de la Vega's adaptation of Renaissance culture for the purpose of justifying the Inca empire.

For other forms of artistic expression, see George Kubler, *Mexican Architecture in the Sixteenth Century* (2 vols., Yale University Press: New Haven, 1948); Damián Bayón, 'The Architecture and Art of Colonial Spanish America' in *CHLA*, vol. 2, pp. 709–46; Robert Stevenson, 'The Music of Colonial Spanish America' in *CHLA*, vol. 2, pp. 771–98.

On the 'patriarchal' character of the Spanish American empire and state, see Richard M. Morse, 'The Heritage of Latin America' in Louis Hartz, *The Founding of New Societies* (Harcourt, Brace and Jovanovich: New York, 1964), pp. 123–77, and 'Towards a Theory of Spanish American Government', *Journal of the History of Ideas*, 15 (1954), pp. 71–93. See also Timothy E. Anna, 'Spain and the Breakdown of the Imperial Ethos: The Problem of Equality', *HAHR*, 62 (1982), pp. 254–72, which provides interesting contemporary evidence of the patriarchal conception of imperial relations held by creoles.

Chapter 5: Colonial Brazil

Cáio Prado Júnior, *The Colonial Background of Modern Brazil* (University of California Press: Berkeley, 1967), is a useful survey by a distinguished Marxist historian. See also Dauril Alden (ed.), *Colonial Roots of Modern Brazil* (University of California Press: Berkeley, 1973).

For some major factors in the creation of Brazil, see John Hemming, *Red Gold: The Conquest of the Brazilian Indians, 1500–1760* (Macmillan: London, 1978), a wide-ranging and readable survey; Charles E. Nowell, 'The French in Sixteenth-Century Brazil', *The Americas*, 5 (1949), pp. 381–93; Richard M. Morse (ed.), *The Bandeirantes: The Historical Role of the Brazilian Pathfinders* (Alfred A. Knopf: New York, 1965), a collection of essays on the activities of the slave-hunters who opened up the interior of Brazil to the Europeans; Philip Curtin, *The Atlantic Slave Trade: A Census* (University of Wisconsin Press: Madison, 1969).

C. R. Boxer's books offer an unrivalled conspectus of Brazil's place within the Portuguese empire. See *The Portuguese Seaborne Empire* (Penguin: Harmondsworth, 1969); *Portuguese Society in the Tropics* (University of Wisconsin Press: Madison, 1965); *Salvador de Sá and the Struggle for Brazil and Angola, 1602–1686* (Athlone Press: London, 1952); *The Dutch in Brazil* (Oxford University Press: Oxford, 1957).

On government and society, see Stuart B. Schwartz, *Sovereignty and*

Society in Colonial Brazil: The High Court of Bahia and Its Judges, 1609–1745 (University of California Press: Berkeley, 1973) and Dauril Alden, *Royal Government in Colonial Brazil* (University of California Press: Berkeley, 1968), a study of the implementation of Crown policy in the eighteenth century.

Gilberto Freyre, *The Masters and the Slaves: A Study in the Development of Brazilian Civilization*, trans. Samuel Putnam (Alfred A. Knopf: New York, 1956), is a famous book which seeks to get to grips with Brazilian society's multiracial origins and its experience of slavery; the somewhat rosy picture it paints should be contrasted with C.R. Boxer's *Race Relations in the Portuguese Colonial Empire, 1415–1825* (Oxford University Press: Oxford, 1963). The whole subject of social and ethnic relations has been transformed by the sound empirical research in Stuart B. Schwartz, *Sugar Plantations in the Formation of Brazilian Society: Bahia, 1550–1835* (Cambridge University Press: Cambridge, 1985). C.R. Boxer, *The Golden Age of Brazil, 1696–1750* (University of California Press: Berkeley, 1962), is the standard account of the impact of gold-mining on the economy and society.

A.J.R. Russell-Wood, *Fidalgos and Philanthropists: The Santa Casa da Misericórdia of Bahia, 1550–1775* (University of California Press: Berkeley, 1968), places in its social context the Bahian branch of the major charitable institution of the Portuguese colonies. An unusual but important perspective on colonial life is provided by Susan A. Soeiro, 'The Social and Economic Role of the Convent: Women and Nuns in Colonial Bahia: 1677–1800', *HAHR*, 54 (1974), pp. 209–32. James Lockhart and Stuart B. Schwartz, *Early Latin America: A History of Colonial Spanish America and Brazil* (Cambridge University Press: Cambridge, 1984), skilfully systematizes most of what is known about social structures and relations in colonial Brazil.

J.B. Bury, 'The Architecture and Art of Colonial Brazil' in *CHLA*, vol. 2, pp. 747–70, is a learned and well-written survey.

Part Two: The Challenge of the Modern World

Chapter 6: Reform, Crisis and Independence

Richard Herr, *The Eighteenth-Century Revolution in Spain* (Princeton University Press: Princeton, 1958), is a standard work on the impact of the Enlightenment. For the Bourbon reforms in the Indies, see John Lynch, *Spanish Colonial Administration, 1782–1810: The Intendant System in the Vice-*

royalty of Río de la Plata (Athlone Press: London, 1958); John R. Fisher, *Government and Society in Colonial Peru: The Intendant System, 1784–1814* (Athlone Press: London, 1970).

On the ideological impact of the Bourbon reforms, see A. P. Whitaker (ed.), *Latin America and the Enlightenment* (Cornell University Press: Ithaca, New York, 1961); Mario Góngora, *Studies in the Colonial History of Spanish America* (Cambridge University Press: Cambridge, 1975); Magnus Mörner (ed.), *The Expulsion of the Jesuits from Latin America* (Alfred A. Knopf: New York, 1965); Antonello Gerbi, *The Dispute of the New World: The History of a Polemic, 1750–1900*, trans. Jeremy Moyle (University of Pittsburgh Press: Pittsburgh, 1973).

For studies of the leading creole classes and their socio–economic role, see Doris M. Ladd, *The Mexican Nobility at Independence (1780–1826)* (University of Texas Press: Austin, 1976); David Brading, *Miners and Merchants in Bourbon Mexico, 1763–1810* (Cambridge University Press: Cambridge, 1971); John E. Kicza, 'The Great Families of Mexico: Elite Maintenance and Business Practices in Late Colonial Mexico City', *HAHR*, 62 (1982), pp. 429–57, an important article that shows how the top creole families still prized honour and status above all else, even though they continued to engage in transatlantic trade; see also his *Colonial Entrepreneurs: Families and Business in Bourbon Mexico City* (University of New Mexico Press: Albuquerque, 1983); John R. Fisher, *Silver Mines and Silver Miners in Colonial Peru, 1776–1824* (University of Liverpool: Liverpool, 1977); Susan Migden Socolow, *The Merchants of Buenos Aires, 1778–1810: Family and Commerce* (Cambridge University Press: Cambridge, 1978); Javier Cuenca Esteban, 'Statistics of Spain's Colonial Trade, 1792–1820: Consular Duties, Cargo Inventories, and Balances of Trade', *HAHR*, 61 (1981), pp. 381–428.

The role of the military is discussed by Lyle N. McAlister, *The 'Fuero Militar' in New Spain, 1765–1800* (University of Florida Press: Gainesville, Florida, 1957). Leon G. Campbell, *The Military and Society in Colonial Peru, 1750–1810* (American Philosophical Society: Philadelphia, 1978), shows how inadequate funding of the armed forces made Tupac Amaru's rebellion difficult to suppress.

On Tupac Amaru and other late colonial revolts, see Lillian E. Fisher, *The Last Inca Revolt, 1780–1783* (University of Oklahoma Press: Norman, 1966); John Leddy Phelan, *The People and the King: The Comunero Revolution in Colombia, 1781* (University of Wisconsin Press: Madison, 1977); Anthony McFarlane, 'Civil Disorders and Popular Protests in Late Colonial New Granada', *HAHR*, 64 (1984), pp. 17–54, and 'The "Rebellion of the Barrios": Urban Insurrection in Bourbon Quito', *HAHR*, 69 (1989), pp. 283–330, which, like Phelan's study, show that the 'cluster of rebellions' in the last fifty years of colonial rule were reactions to Bourbon fiscal pressures and not early bids for independence.

On Brazil, see Dauril Alden, *Royal Government in Colonial Brazil* (University of California Press: Berkeley, 1968); A. J. R. Russell-Wood (ed.), *From Colony to Nation: Essays on the Independence of Brazil* (Johns Hopkins University Press: Baltimore, 1975), an anthology of essays on the impact of the Enlightenment and on the process of Independence; Kenneth R. Maxwell, *Conflicts and Conspiracies: Brazil and Portugal, 1750–1808* (Cambridge University Press: Cambridge, 1973), discusses the strained relations between the colony and its metropolis.

On the events leading to independence and the revolutionary wars, see R. A. Humphreys and John Lynch (eds.), *The Origins of the Latin American Revolutions, 1808–1826* (Alfred A. Knopf: New York, 1965); John Lynch, *The Spanish American Revolutions, 1808–1826* (W. W. Norton: New York, 1973); O. Carlos Stoetzer, *The Scholastic Roots of the Spanish American Revolution* (Fordham University Press: New York, 1979); Jorge I. Domínguez, *Insurrection or Loyalty: The Breakdown of the Spanish American Empire* (Harvard University Press: Cambridge, Mass., 1980). Timothy E. Anna, *Spain and the Loss of America* (University of Nebraska Press: Lincoln, 1983), argues that Spain's strategic policy errors were decisive factors in the process of independence; see also his 'Spain and the Breakdown of the Imperial Ethos: The Problem of Equality', *HAHR*, 62 (1982), pp. 254–72, which sheds interesting light on creoles' conception of imperial relations. Charles C. Griffin, 'Economic and Social Aspects of the Era of Spanish-American Independence', *HAHR*, 29 (1949), pp. 170–87, is an essay that has become a classic. Reliable lives of the two main Liberators are Gerhard Masur, *Simón Bolívar* (University of New Mexico Press: Albuquerque, 1969), and J. C. J. Metford, *San Martín the Liberator* (Longmans: London, 1950).

Chapter 7: The Quest for Order: Conservatives and Liberals in the Nineteenth Century

David Bushnell and Neill Macaulay, *The Emergence of Latin America in the Nineteenth Century* (Oxford University Press: New York and Oxford, 1988), discusses the main developments to 1880, but focuses also on individual countries, while eschewing dependency theory and 'neo-colonialism' as analytical tools. Tulio Halperín-Donghi, *Historia contemporánea de América Latina* (Alianza Editorial: Madrid, 1969), is a synthesis based on dependency theory; see also his *The Aftermath of Revolution in Latin America* (Harper & Row: New York, 1973). Peter J. Bakewell, John J. Johnson and Meredith D. Dodge (eds.), *Readings in Latin American History*, vol. 2, *The Modern Experience* (Duke University Press: Durham, NC, 1985), is a collection of important scholarly articles on the national period.

J. Lloyd Mecham, *Church and State in Latin America: A History of Politico-Ecclesiastical Relations* (University of North Carolina Press: Chapel Hill, 1966), is a good study of the vexed relations between Church and state after independence. On the ideology of modernizing élites in the latter half of the century, see the anthology edited by Ralph Lee Woodward, Jr., *Positivism in Latin America, 1850–1900* (D. C. Heath: Lexington, Mass., 1971), and Frank Safford, *The Ideal of the Practical: Colombia's Struggle to Form a Technical Elite* (University of Texas Press: Austin, 1976), which shows how technical education was held back by chronic political instability and government neglect until the export-economy started to expand.

On economic developments, see Roberto Cortés Conde and Stanley J. Stein (eds.), *Latin America: A Guide to Economic History, 1830–1930* (University of California Press: Berkeley, 1977); Roberto Cortés Conde and Shane J. Hunt (eds.), *The Latin American Economies: Growth and the Export Sector, 1880–1930* (Holmes and Meier: New York, 1985), essays on the link between exports and internal development; Bill Albert, *South America and the World Economy from Independence to 1930* (Macmillan: London, 1983), a concise survey of problems of economic dependency and modernization.

On Brazil, see E. Bradford Burns, *A History of Brazil* (Columbia University Press: New York, 1970). On the slave-based society, see the two classic works by Gilberto Freyre, *The Masters and the Slaves: A Study in the Development of Brazilian Civilization*, trans. Samuel Putnam (Alfred A. Knopf: New York, 1956), and *The Mansions and the Shanties: The Making of Modern Brazil*, trans. Harriet de Onís (Alfred A. Knopf: New York, 1963); and the masterly study by Stanley J. Stein, *Vassouras: A Brazilian Coffee County, 1850–1900: The Roles of Planter and Slave in a Plantation Society* (Princeton University Press: Princeton, 1985). On the struggle to abolish slavery, see Leslie Bethell, *The Abolition of the Brazilian Slave Trade: Britain, Brazil and the Slave Trade Question, 1807–1869* (Cambridge University Press: Cambridge, 1970); Robert Brent Toplin, *The Abolition of Slavery in Brazil* (Atheneum: New York, 1972); Robert Conrad, *The Destruction of Brazilian Slavery, 1850–1888* (University of California Press: Berkeley, 1973). Emília Viotti da Costa, *The Brazilian Empire: Myths and Histories* (University of Chicago Press: Chicago and London, 1985), is a comprehensive survey of the period up to the fall of the monarchy. Robert M. Levine, '"Mud-Hut Jerusalem": Canudos

Revisited', *HAHR*, 68 (1988), pp. 525–72, argues that the anti-republican rebels were not crazed fanatics but orthodox Catholics fighting for social justice. The consequences of rapid export expansion are studied in Richard Graham, *Britain and the Onset of Modernization in Brazil, 1850–1914* (Cambridge University Press: Cambridge, 1968). Warren Dean, *The Industrialization of São Paulo, 1880–1945* (University of Texas Press: Austin, 1969), shows how the export–economy stimulated industrial development.

On Chile, see Jay Kinsbruner, *Chile: A Historical Interpretation* (Harper & Row: New York, 1973); Simon Collier, *Ideas and Politics of Chilean Independence, 1808–1833* (Cambridge University Press: Cambridge, 1969); Arnold J. Bauer, *Chilean Rural Society from the Spanish Conquest to 1930* (Cambridge University Press: Cambridge, 1975); Harold Blakemore, *British Nitrates and Chilean Politics, 1886–1896: Balmaceda and Lord North* (Athlone Press: London, 1974).

On Mexico, see Michael C. Meyer and William L. Sherman, *The Course of Mexican History*, 3rd edn (Oxford University Press: New York, 1987); Charles A. Hale, *Mexican Liberalism in the Age of Mora, 1821–1853* (Yale University Press: New Haven, 1968), an incisive study of liberal and conservative ideologists; Michael P. Costeloe, *Church Wealth in Mexico: A Study of the Juzgado de Capellanías in the Archbishopric of Mexico, 1800–1856* (Cambridge University Press: Cambridge, 1967); Jan Bazant, *Alienation of Church Wealth: Social and Economic Aspects of the Liberal Revolution, 1856–1875* (Cambridge University Press: Cambridge, 1971); Laurens B. Perry, *Juárez and Díaz: Machine Politics in Mexico* (Northern Illinois University Press: De Kalb, 1978); John Coatsworth, *Growth Against Development: The Economic Impact of Railroads in Porfirian Mexico* (Northern Illinois University Press: De Kalb, 1980).

The attractions of monarchy were greatest in Mexico, but in fact endured throughout Spanish America. This has begun to receive proper attention very recently. See, for instance, Mark J. Van Aken, *King of the Night: Juan José Flores and Ecuador, 1824–1864* (University of California Press: Berkeley, 1989), a biography of the first president of the republic, a low-born mestizo and later a *caudillo* of the wars of independence, who in the 1840s plotted with another leading *caudillo* of the independence struggle in Bolivia, Andrés Santa Cruz, and with Spain, to set up monarchies in Ecuador, Peru and Bolivia. See also Ana Gimeno, *Una tentativa monárquica en América: El caso ecuatoriano* (Banco Central del Ecuador: Quito, 1988).

On Paraguay, see Harris Gaylord Warren, *Paraguay: An Informal History* (University of Oklahoma Press: Norman, 1949); *Paraguay and the Triple Alliance* (University of Texas Press: Austin, 1978).

On Argentina, see David Rock, *Argentina: 1516–1982: From Spanish Colonization to the Falklands War* (I. B. Tauris: London, 1986); James R. Scobie, *Argentina: A City and a Nation*, 2nd edn (Oxford University Press: New York and Oxford, 1971); Carlos Díaz Alejandro, *Essays on the Economic History of the Argentine Republic* (Yale University Press: New Haven, 1970); Miron Burgin, *The Economic Aspects of Argentine Federalism, 1820–1852* (Harvard University Press: Cambridge, Mass., 1946); James R. Scobie, *Revolution on the Pampas: A Social History of Argentine Wheat* (University of Texas Press: Austin, 1964), and *Buenos Aires: Plaza to Suburb, 1870–1910* (Oxford University Press: New York and Oxford, 1974); John Lynch, *Argentine Dictator: Juan Manuel de Rosas, 1829–1852* (Oxford University Press: Oxford, 1981); Allison W. Bunkley, *The Life of Sarmiento* (Princeton University Press: Princeton, 1952).

Chapter 8: 'Civilization and Barbarism': Literary and Cultural Developments I

The classic statement of Latin American liberalism is Domingo Sarmiento's *Facundo*, which is available in English as *Life of the Argentine Republic in the Days of the Tyrants: Or, Civilization and Barbarism*, trans. Horace Mann (Gordon Press: New York, 1968). José Enrique Rodó's *Ariel* has been edited with a good introduction by Gordon Brotherston (Cambridge University Press: Cambridge, 1967). Euclides da Cunha, *Rebellion in the Backlands*, trans. Samuel Putnam (University of Chicago Press: Chicago, 1957), is a literary classic which reflects the self-doubt of the Latin American positivists at the turn of the century.

Charles A. Hale, *Mexican Liberalism in the Age of Mora, 1821–1853* (Yale University Press: New Haven, 1968), is good on the ideological problems encountered in one of the older viceroyalties after independence; his *The Transformation of Liberalism in Late Nineteenth-Century Mexico* (Princeton University Press: Princeton, 1990) discusses the rise of positivism and Social Darwinism.

William Rex Crawford, *A Century of Latin American Thought*, 3rd edn (Harvard University Press: Cambridge, Mass., 1963), is a useful review of the major *pensadores* with generous quotations from their works. See also Leopoldo Zea, *The Latin American Mind* (University of Oklahoma Press: Norman, 1963), and *Positivism in Mexico* (University of Texas Press: Austin, 1974). For a broader perspective on positivism, see the anthology edited by Ralph Lee Woodward, Jr., *Positivism in Latin America, 1850–1900* (D. C.

Heath: Lexington, Mass., 1971). On obstacles to the implementation of modern ideas, see Frank Safford, *The Ideal of the Practical: Colombia's Struggle to Form a Technical Elite* (University of Texas Press: Austin, 1976). The importance of foreign influences is illustrated by Richard Graham, *Britain and the Onset of Modernization in Brazil, 1850–1914* (Cambridge University Press: Cambridge, 1968). An excellent brief synthesis is provided by Charles A. Hale, 'Political and Social Ideas in Latin America, 1870–1930' in *CHLA*, vol. 4, pp. 367–441.

On Brazil, see Samuel Putnam, *Marvelous Journey: Four Centuries of Brazilian Literature* (Alfred A. Knopf: New York, 1948); Erico Verissimo, *Brazilian Literature* (Macmillan: London, 1945); David Haberly, *Three Sad Races: Racial Identity and National Consciousness in Brazilian Literature* (Cambridge University Press: Cambridge, 1983).

For Spanish America, see Gerald Martin's surveys, 'The Literature, Music and Art of Latin America, from Independence to 1870' in *CHLA*, vol. 3, pp. 797–839, and 'The Literature, Music and Art of Latin America, 1870–1930' in *CHLA*, vol. 4, pp. 443–526; Jean Franco, *The Modern Culture of Latin America: Society and the Artist* (Penguin Books: Harmondsworth, 1970), and *An Introduction to Spanish American Literature* (Cambridge University Press: Cambridge, 1969).

Part Three: The Twentieth Century

Chapter 9: Nationalism and Development: An Overview

Of the general histories, the best are Benjamin Keen and Mark Wasserman, *A Short History of Latin America* (Houghton Mifflin: Boston, 1980), which is well-written and informative, and is influenced by the theory of dependency (see below for selected texts), which in the 1960s and 1970s provided the basic conceptual framework for most Latin Americanists across the range of specialisms, from economic history to literary criticism. Tulio Halperín-Donghi, *Historia contemporánea de América Latina* (Alianza Editorial: Madrid, 1969), is a reliable history by a leading scholar, whose interpretation is also based on dependency theory. Thomas E. Skidmore and Peter H. Smith, *Modern Latin America*, 2nd edn (Oxford University Press: New York and Oxford, 1989), first appeared in 1984 and offers a 'modified dependency approach'. The *CHLA*, vols. 4–9, contains chapters on general developments and individual countries between *c.* 1870 and *c.* 1990.

For an informative history of Central America, a region which attracted much international attention in the 1980s, see Ralph Lee Woodward, Jr., *Central America: A Nation Divided* (Oxford University Press: New York and Oxford, 1985), and James Dunkerley, *Power in the Isthmus: A Political History of Modern Central America* (Verso: London, 1988), which adopts a radical class-based approach. For an economic analysis, see Victor Bulmer-Thomas, *The Political Economy of Central America since 1920* (Cambridge University Press: Cambridge, 1987). See also the relevant chapters in *CHLA*, vols. 5 and 7, with their corresponding bibliographies.

For republics like Bolivia, Colombia, Peru and Venezuela, which are dealt with only tangentially in this chapter, see the individual chapters in *CHLA*, vols. 5 and 8 on these countries and others, and their respective bibliographies.

For data on economic and social developments, see the *Economic Survey of Latin America*, published annually by the United Nations' Economic Commission for Latin America and the Caribbean (ECLAC), Santiago, Chile. A comparative international perspective is provided by the data published annually in the *World Development Report* of the World Bank. The *Latin America Weekly Report* (Latin American Newsletters: London) is a reliable digest of current affairs; *Latin America Regional Reports* are also available.

On 'dependency theory', see André Gunder Frank, *Capitalism and Underdevelopment in Latin America: Historical Studies of Chile and Brazil* (Penguin Books: Harmondsworth, 1969), one of the most influential texts; Fernando Henrique Cardoso and Enzo Faletto, *Dependency and Development in Latin America*, trans. Marjory Mattingly Urquidi (University of California Press: Berkeley, 1979); Stanley and Barbara J. Stein, *The Colonial Heritage of Latin America: Essays on Economic Dependence in Perspective* (Oxford University Press: New York and Oxford, 1970). A useful anthology is Ronald H. Chilcote and Joel C. Edelstein (eds.), *Latin America: The Struggle with Dependency and Beyond* (Halstead Press: New York, 1974). The validity of dependency theory is debated in the specialist essays in Christopher Abel and Colin M. Lewis (eds.), *Economic Imperialism and the State: The Political Economy of an External Connection during the 19th and 20th Centuries* (Institute of Latin American Studies, University of London: London, 1984). See also André Gunder Frank, *Critique and Anti-Critique: Essays on Dependence and Reformism* (Macmillan: London, 1984). Bill Albert, *South America and the World Economy from Independence to 1930* (Macmillan: London, 1983), offers a succinct and impartial review of the issues.

The literature on political and social developments is overwhelming; much of it relates to individual countries, and further guidance is available in the bibliographies for subsequent chapters. The following works are included for the purpose of general orientation. On rural development and peasant movements, see Alain de Janvry, *The Agrarian Question and Reformism in Latin America* (Johns Hopkins University Press: Baltimore, 1981); Rodolfo Stavenhagen, *Agrarian Problems and Peasant Movements in Latin America* (Doubleday: Garden City, New York, 1970). Richard Gott, *Guerrilla Movements in Latin America* (Thomas Nelson: London, 1970), is a good survey, which concentrates on rural guerrillas. On urban growth, see Jorge Hardoy (ed.), *Urbanization in Latin America: Approaches and Issues* (Doubleday: Garden City, New York, 1975). George Philip, *Oil and Politics in Latin America: Nationalist Movements and State Companies* (Cambridge University Press: Cambridge, 1983), deals with the important question of the political pressures behind state intervention in a crucial sector of the export-economy.

Attempts to theorize about Latin American politics have generated much controversy. The following represent three major trends: John J. Johnson, *Political Change in Latin America: The Emergence of the Middle Sectors* (Stanford University Press: Stanford, 1958), is a standard work of reformist liberal 'modernization' theory of the 1950s and early 1960s, which underpinned President Kennedy's Alliance for Progress. It was largely eclipsed in the 1960s and 1970s by reformist or revolutionary versions of the 'dependency theory' referred to above. The predominance of military dictatorships from the mid-1960s to the early 1980s prompted much analysis, of which the most influential on the left was the theory of the 'bureaucratic-authoritarian state' as an uneasy alliance of the dominant élites with the armed forces for the purpose of repressing labour mobilization; its best formulation is in Guillermo O'Donnell, *Modernization and Bureaucratic Authoritarianism: Studies in South American Politics* (Institute of International Studies, University of California: Berkeley, 1973). By contrast, US political scientists in particular tried to explain the relative absence of stable liberal democracies in Latin America by looking for distinctive traditions in the political culture and analysing their rationale. The notion of 'corporatism' was employed to give a cultural explanation for the interventionism of the state in the period from the 1930s to the early 1980s; see Howard J. Wiarda, *Corporatism and National Development in Latin America* (Westview Press: Boulder, Colorado, 1981).

For surveys of the development of the Latin American economy in different periods and countries, see the essays by diverse specialists in *CHLA*, vols. 4–9. Rosemary Thorp and Laurence Whitehead (eds.), *Inflation and Stabilization in Latin America* (Macmillan: London, 1979), is an informative collection of essays by economic historians surveying the problem of inflation in the major countries during the 1970s. For accounts of the fortunes of economic liberalism, as applied in the 1970s and early 1980s, see Alejandro Foxley, *Latin American Experiments in Neoconservative Economics* (University of California Press: Berkeley, 1983), and Joseph Ramos, *Neoconservative Economics in the Southern Cone of Latin America, 1973–1983* (Johns Hopkins University Press: Baltimore, 1986), both of which are generally unsympathetic. For a monetarist critique of government policy by an influential financial expert, see T. G. Congdon, *Economic Liberalism in the Southern Cone of Latin America* (Trade Policy Research Centre: London, 1985).

The 1980s debt crisis generated a good deal of comment and analysis. See Pedro-Pablo Kuczynski, *Latin American Debt: A Twentieth Century Fund Book* (Johns Hopkins University Press: Baltimore, 1988), a lucid exposition of the problem by a former Peruvian finance minister and international banker; Rosemary Thorp and Laurence Whitehead (eds.), *Latin American Debt and the Adjustment Crisis*, Macmillan Press Series (Macmillan: London, 1987), a survey of the impact of debt and inflation on policy-making in different countries. Carlos Marichal, *A Century of Debt Crises in Latin America: From Independence to the Great Depression, 1820–1930* (Princeton University Press: Princeton, 1989), showed that the problem was not new.

The debt crisis also led to a reassessment of development strategies. Stephany Griffith-Jones and Oswaldo Sunkel, *Debt and Development Crisis in Latin America: The End of an Illusion* (Oxford University Press: Oxford, 1986), is a critical analysis of what went wrong with inward-looking policies by two ECLA-influenced economists. The stimulating essays in Esperanza Durán (ed.), *Latin America and the World Recession* (Cambridge University Press: Cambridge, 1985), constitute a post-mortem on Latin American development strategies by regional experts of various persuasions, reflecting some of the new thinking about the continent's problems in the context of the experience of other developing countries. David Lehman, *Democracy and Development in Latin America: Economics, Politics and Religion in the Postwar Period* (Polity Press: Cambridge, 1990), tackles the difficult task of relating economic and political developments in a turbulent period.

Chapter 10: Mexico: Revolution and Stability

The best survey is Michael C. Meyer and William L. Sherman, *The Course of Mexican History*, 3rd edn (Oxford University Press: New York, 1987). A well-written assessment of the country can be found in Alan Riding, *Distant Neighbors: A Portrait of the Mexicans* (Alfred A. Knopf: New York, 1985) [British title: *Mexico: Inside the Volcano* (I. B. Tauris: London, 1987)]. For developments since 1930, see *CHLA*, vol. 7.

The Revolution has attracted most attention. See the two classic works by

Frank Tannenbaum, *Peace by Revolution: Mexico After 1910* (Columbia University Press: New York, 1933), and *Mexico: The Struggle for Peace and Bread* (Alfred A. Knopf: New York, 1950). A fascinating record is provided by Anita Brenner, *The Wind That Swept Mexico* (University of Texas Press: Austin, 1987), which contains 184 'historical photographs'. On the ideological background, see James D. Cockroft, *Intellectual Precursors of the Mexican Revolution* (University of Texas Press: Austin, 1968). For an evaluation of the debate on whether the events in Mexico constituted a genuine social revolution, a great rebellion or a contest between power-seeking oligarchs, see David M. Bailey, 'Revisionism and the recent historiography of the Mexican Revolution', *HAHR*, 58 (1978), pp. 62–79. John Womack, Jr., *Zapata and the Mexican Revolution* (Alfred A. Knopf: New York, 1968), is a celebrated study of the agrarian revolt by Indian communities; see also his excellent survey, 'The Mexican Revolution, 1910–1920' in *CHLA*, vol. 5, pp. 79–154. An influential study is Ramón Eduardo Ruiz, *The Great Rebellion, Mexico 1905–1924* (W. W. Norton: New York, 1980). For the effect of the Revolution on different regions and the role of *caudillos*, see David A. Brading (ed.), *Caudillo and Peasant in the Mexican Revolution* (Cambridge University Press: Cambridge, 1980). One of the best and most comprehensive studies is Alan Knight, *The Mexican Revolution* (2 vols., Cambridge University Press: Cambridge, 1986), which argues that the Revolution was a genuine mass movement with radical social objectives. This line is pursued by John Mason Hart, *Revolutionary Mexico: The Coming and Process of the Mexican Revolution* (University of California Press: Berkeley, 1987), which reveals how deeply the USA had penetrated Mexico's economy and the political influence it exerted on *caudillos* of all factions.

Robert E. Quirk, *The Mexican Revolution and the Catholic Church, 1910–1929* (Indiana University Press: Bloomington, 1973), studies an important and hitherto neglected subject. Jean Meyer, *The Cristero Rebellion* (Cambridge University Press: Cambridge, 1976), reveals the extent and gravity of this Catholic revolt.

Roger Jansen, *The Politics of Mexican Development* (Johns Hopkins University Press: Baltimore, 1971), is a penetrating study of the one-party state. Peter H. Smith, *Labyrinths of Power: Political Recruitment in Twentieth-Century Mexico* (Princeton University Press: Princeton, 1978), studies the basis of the PRI's power.

On the economy, see Clark W. Reynolds, *The Mexican Economy: Twentieth-Century Structure and Growth* (Yale University Press: New Haven, 1970).

Chapter 11: Brazil: Order and Progress

Rollie E. Poppino, *Brazil: The Land and The People* (Oxford University Press: New York and Oxford, 1968), and E. Bradford Burns, *A History of Brazil*, 2nd edn (Columbia University Press: New York, 1980), are sound general surveys. An overview of economic development is provided by Werner Baer, *The Brazilian Economy: Growth and Development*, 2nd edn (Praeger: New York, 1983). For developments since 1930, see *CHLA*, vol. 9.

For general political and economic changes in the early part of the century, see Gilberto Freyre, *Order and Progress: Brazil from Monarchy to Republic*, trans. Rod W. Horton (Alfred A. Knopf: New York, 1970); Richard Graham, *Britain and the Onset of Modernization in Brazil, 1850–1914* (Cambridge University Press: Cambridge, 1968); Warren Dean, *The Industrialization of São Paulo, 1880–1945* (University of Texas Press: Austin, 1969).

The rule of Getúlio Vargas was crucial in promoting the industrialization of Brazil. See Robert M. Levine, *The Vargas Regime: The Critical Years, 1934–1938* (Columbia University Press: New York, 1970); John D. Wirth, *The Politics of Brazilian Development, 1930–1954* (Stanford University Press: Stanford, 1970). Richard Bourne, *Getúlio Vargas of Brazil, 1883–1954: Sphinx of the Pampas* (Charles Knight: London, 1974), has written a sound biography.

The sharp swings between military and civilian governments in the course of Brazilian modernization have been much analysed. See Thomas E. Skidmore, *Politics in Brazil, 1930–1964: An Experiment in Democracy* (Oxford University Press: New York and Oxford, 1967); Alfred Stepan, *The Military in Politics: Changing Patterns in Brazil* (Princeton University Press: Princeton, 1971); Alfred Stepan (ed.), *Authoritarian Brazil: Origins, Policies and Future* (Yale University Press: New Haven, 1973); Thomas E. Skidmore, *The Politics of Military Rule in Brazil, 1964–85* (Oxford University Press: New York and Oxford, 1988). Peter Flynn, *Brazil: A Political Analysis* (Ernest Benn: London, 1978), is a class-based interpretation of modernization and the role of the military. See also the following attempts at an overview of the whole process: Luiz Bresser Pereira, *Development and Crisis in Brazil, 1930–1983* (Westview Press: Boulder, Colorado, 1984), and John D. Wirth and others (eds.), *State and Society in Brazil: Continuity and Change* (Westview Press: Boulder, Colorado, 1987).

Chapter 12: Cuba: Dependency, Nationalism and Revolution

Hugh Thomas, *Cuba or The Pursuit of Freedom* (Eyre & Spottiswoode: London, 1971), is a massively documented political history that has become the standard work. For developments since 1930, see *CHLA*, vol. 7.

Accounts of Cuba before 1959 tend to be influenced by a desire to identify the historical roots of Castro's Revolution. However, for a well-researched and balanced study of the struggle for Cuban independence and its aftermath, see Louis A. Pérez, Jr., *Cuba: Between Empires, 1878–1902* (University of Pittsburgh Press: Pittsburgh, 1983). For subsequent struggles against US domination, see Robert F. Smith, *The United States and Cuba: Business and Diplomacy, 1917–1960* (College and University Press: New Haven, 1960); Luis A. Aguilar, *Cuba 1933: Prologue to Revolution* (Cornell University Press: Ithaca, New York, 1972); James O'Connor, *The Origins of Socialism in Cuba* (Cornell University Press: Ithaca, New York, 1970). An attempt to assess the extent of the change wrought by the Revolution can be found in Jorge I. Domínguez, *Cuba: Order and Revolution* (Harvard University Press: Cambridge, Mass., 1978). For a supportive view of Castro and the Revolution by the US journalist who famously interviewed him in the Sierra Maestra, see Herbert L. Matthews, *Revolution in Cuba* (Scribners: New York, 1965), and his *Castro: A Political Biography* (Penguin Books: Harmondsworth, 1969). Another positive, and well-illustrated, account is Lee Lockwood's *Castro's Cuba, Cuba's Fidel* (Random House: New York, 1969). A negative view is offered by a former comrade of Castro, Carlos Franqui, *Family Portrait with Fidel* (Random House: New York, 1984). For a more rounded picture, see Tad Szulc's biography, *Fidel: A Critical Portrait* (William Morrow: New York, 1986).

On the guerrilla struggle, see Che Guevara, *Reminiscences of the Cuban Revolutionary War* (Penguin Books: Harmondsworth, 1969). A useful brief synthesis of Guevara's career and ideas, though rather dated now, is Andrew Sinclair, *Guevara* (Fontana: London, 1970).

On the political system, see Theodore Draper, *Castroism, Theory and Practice* (Praeger: New York, 1965). The aims and policies of the revolutionary state are favourably surveyed in Leo Huberman and Paul M. Sweezy, *Socialism in Cuba* (Monthly Review Press: New York, 1969), while K. S. Karol, *Guerrillas in Power* (Hill and Wang: New York, 1970), gives a critical account from the perspective of the left. On the economy, see Carmelo Mesa-Lago (ed.), *Revolutionary Change in Cuba* (University of Pittsburgh Press: Pittsburgh, 1971), and Carmelo Mesa-Lago, *The Economy of Socialist Cuba: A Two-Decade Appraisal* (University of New Mexico Press:

Albuquerque, 1981). Cuba's economic difficulties in the 1980s and the policy of 'rectification' are sympathetically discussed in Jean Stubbs, *Cuba: The Test of Time* (Latin American Bureau: London, 1989).

Chapter 13: *Argentina: The Long Decline*

David Rock, *Argentina, 1516–1982* (I. B. Tauris: London, 1986), and James R. Scobie, *Argentina: A City and a Nation*, 2nd edn (Oxford University Press: New York and Oxford, 1971), are good syntheses. On the economy, see Carlos Díaz Alejandro, *Essays on the Economic History of the Argentine Republic* (Yale University Press: New Haven, 1970). For developments since 1930, see *CHLA*, vol. 8.

For the dynamics of political history, see Robert A. Potash, *The Army and Politics in Argentina, 1928–1945* (Stanford University Press: Stanford, 1969), and *The Army and Politics in Argentina, 1945–1962* (Stanford University Press: Stanford, 1980); Peter H. Smith, *Politics and Beef in Argentina* (Columbia University Press: New York, 1969), and also his influential study, *Argentina and the Failure of Democracy: Conflict among Political Elites* (University of Wisconsin Press: Madison, 1974).

For the first period of Peronism, see George I. Blanksten, *Perón's Argentina* (University of Chicago Press: Chicago, 1974), a standard work. For an account of the later period of Peronist government by one of his ministers, see Guido di Tella, *Argentina Under Perón (1973–1976)*, Macmillan Press Series (Macmillan: London, 1983). Joseph A. Page, *Perón: A Biography* (Random House: New York, 1983), is a well-researched assessment of the great *caudillo*.

Guillermo O'Donnell, *Modernization and Bureaucratic Authoritarianism: Studies in South American Politics* (Institute of International Studies, University of California: Berkeley, 1973), argues that the élites allied themselves with the military in order to contain the 'threat' of labour militancy. Gary W. Wynia, *Argentina: Illusions and Realities* (Holmes and Meier: New York, 1986), correlates economic policy and types of government. Joseph Ramos, *Neoconservative Economics in the Southern Cone of Latin America 1973–1983* (Johns Hopkins University Press: Baltimore, 1986), is informative, if rather technical, about the free-market experiments of the military juntas.

Chapter 14: Chile: Democracy, Revolution and Dictatorship

Useful surveys are Jay Kinsbruner, *Chile: A Historical Interpretation* (Harper & Row: New York, 1973), and Brian Loveman, *Chile: The Legacy of Hispanic Capitalism* (Oxford University Press: New York and Oxford, 1979). On the economy, see Markos J. Mamalakis, *The Growth and Structure of the Chilean Economy from Independence to Allende* (Yale University Press: New Haven, 1976). On the growing role of trade unions before the election of Allende, see Alan Angell, *Politics and the Labour Movement in Chile* (Oxford University Press: Oxford, 1972); see also, James Petras, *Politics and Social Forces in Chilean Development* (University of California Press: Berkeley, 1969). For developments since 1930, see *CHLA*, vol. 8.

J. Ann Zammit (ed.), *The Chilean Road to Socialism* (Institute of Development Studies, University of Sussex: Brighton, 1973), gives the proceedings of a conference held in March 1972 and contains outlines of the economic, agrarian and social policies of the UP government by some leading figures, including Salvador Allende and Radomiro Tomic. Stefan de Vylder, *Allende's Chile* (Cambridge University Press: Cambridge, 1976), is a balanced evaluation of the Allende government's achievements and errors by a sympathetic economist. A lucid critique of Allende from a sympathizer of the Christian Democrats is Paul E. Sigmund's *The Overthrow of Allende and the Politics of Chile, 1964–1976* (University of Pittsburgh Press: Pittsburgh, 1977). Ian Roxborough, Jackie Roddick and Philip O'Brien, *Chile: The State and Revolution* (Macmillan: London, 1977), criticizes Allende from the standpoint of the revolutionary left. Edy Kaufman, *Crisis in Allende's Chile: New Perspectives* (Praeger: New York, 1988), is a comprehensive account which focuses on Allende's errors. On Pinochet, see J. Samuel Valenzuela and Arturo Valenzuela (eds.), *Military Rule in Chile: Dictatorship and Oppositions* (Johns Hopkins Press: Baltimore, 1986).

Chapter 15: Identity and Modernity: Literary and Cultural Developments II

The ideas of the *pensadores* and intellectual history in general have been relatively neglected, but see *CHLA*, vol. 9. Seminal texts available in English are José Carlos Mariátegui, *Seven Interpretative Essays on Peruvian Reality* (University of Texas Press: Austin, 1971), the classic Marxist exposition of *indigenismo*, and Octavio Paz, *The Labyrinth of Solitude: Life and Thought in Mexico*, trans. Lysander Kemp (Grove Press: New York, 1963), a famous essay that explores the cultural anxieties of a nation facing the modern world.

For a review of the major *pensadores*, see William Rex Crawford, *A Century of Latin American Thought*, 3rd edn (Harvard University Press: Cambridge, Mass., 1963); Martin S. Stabb, *In Quest of Identity: Patterns in the Spanish American Essay of Ideas 1890–1960* (University of North Carolina Press: Chapel Hill, 1967), is illuminating on the emergence and development of nationalist ideology. For an interesting study of the influence of eccentric ideas on nationalist mass movements, see Frederick B. Pike, *The Politics of the Miraculous in Peru: Haya de la Torre and the Spiritualist Tradition* (University of Nebraska Press: Lincoln, 1986). The most impressive brief survey is Charles A. Hale, 'Political and Social Ideas in Latin America, 1870–1930' in *CHLA*, vol. 4, pp. 367–442.

Jean Franco, *The Modern Culture of Latin America: Society and the Artist* (Penguin Books: Harmondsworth, 1970), offers a useful overview of the dominant trends; see also, Germán Arciniegas, *Latin America: A Cultural History*, trans. J. Maclean (Alfred A. Knopf: New York, 1966). Gerald Martin, 'The Literature, Music and Art of Latin America, 1870–1930' in *CHLA*, vol. 4, pp. 443–526, is a knowledgeable and stimulating survey of *modernismo*, modernism and the differences between them; the corresponding chapters in subsequent volumes bring the survey up to the period of the so-called Post-Boom. An interesting compilation of avant-garde material can be found in Nelson Osorio (ed.), *Manifiestos, proclamas y polémicas de la vanguardia literaria hispanoamericana* (Biblioteca Ayacucho: Caracas, 1988). John King, *'Sur': An Analysis of the Argentine Literary Journal and Its Role in the Development of a Culture, 1931–1970* (Cambridge University Press: Cambridge, 1986), is an important study of Latin America's most influential journal.

Dawn Ades, Guy Brett, Stanton Loomis Catlin and Rosemary O'Neill, *Art in Latin America: The Modern Era, 1820–1980* (Yale University Press for the South Bank Centre: London, 1989), is the lavishly illustrated catalogue of an exhibition at the Hayward Gallery, London, with excellent essays on the major artists and developments, mostly in the twentieth century. See also Oriana Baddeley and Valerie Fraser, *Drawing the Line: Art and Cultural Identity in Contemporary Latin America* (Verso: London, 1989).

John King, *Magical Reels: A History of Cinema in Latin America* (Verso: London, 1990), is a valuable survey of an area which is attracting scholarly interest.

Jean Franco, *An Introduction to Spanish American Literature* (Cambridge University Press: Cambridge, 1969), is perceptive and comprehensive but now somewhat dated; David Gallagher, *Modern Latin American Literature* (Oxford University Press: Oxford, 1973), contains well-handled introductory essays on the most famous writers. Gordon Brotherston, *Latin*

American Poetry: Origins and Presence (Cambridge University Press: Cambridge, 1975), is one of the best introductions to the subject; see also his *The Emergence of the Latin American Novel* (Cambridge University Press: Cambridge, 1977).

The most wide-ranging essays in English relating twentieth-century fiction to major cultural issues are to be found in John King (ed.), *Latin American Fiction: A Survey* (Faber and Faber: London, 1987), which includes pieces by novelists of the first rank such as Mario Vargas Llosa, Augusto Roa Bastos, Manuel Puig and Guillermo Cabrera Infante, and which also, exceptionally, covers Brazilian fiction. Gerald Martin has written a good survey, *Journeys Through the Labyrinth: Latin American Fiction in the Twentieth Century* (Verso: London, 1989). Philip Swanson (ed.), *Landmarks in Latin American Fiction* (Routledge: London, 1990), is a collection of essays on some of the major texts of the Boom and Post-Boom, with an excellent introduction. Jean Franco's *Plotting Women: Gender and Representation in Mexico* (Verso: London, 1989) is a pioneering study of women's writing.

Historians and critics have long been absorbed by the question of cultural identity, and have tended to neglect the Latin American aspiration to modernity. For a discussion of these issues, see Edwin Williamson, 'Coming to Terms with Modernity: Magical Realism and the Historical Process in the Novels of Alejo Carpentier' in John King (ed.) *Latin American Fiction*, pp. 78–100, and 'Magical Realism and the Theme of Incest in *One Hundred Years of Solitude*' in B. McGuirk and R. Cardwell, *Gabriel García Márquez: New Readings* (Cambridge University Press: Cambridge, 1987), pp. 45–63, which shows how the historic conflict between identity and modernity is mythologized in this key novel.

Brazilian literature is not particularly well served by up-to-date literary histories in English: the two standard surveys are Samuel Putnam, *Marvelous Journey: Four Centuries of Brazilian Literature* (Alfred A. Knopf: New York, 1948), and Erico Verissimo, *Brazilian Literature* (Macmillan: London, 1945). Gerald Martin's *Journeys Through the Labyrinth*, and his chapters in the *CHLA*, help to remedy this lack.

Many works of Latin American literature are available in English; see Jason Wilson, *An A–Z of Modern Latin American Literature in English Translation* (Institute of Latin American Studies, University of London: London, 1989), and Gerald Martin, *Writers from Latin America* (Book Trust: London, 1990). Latin American writers have excelled at the short story; see Nick Caistor (ed.), *The Faber Book of Contemporary Latin American Short Stories* (Faber and Faber: London, 1989), which includes several younger writers of the 1980s.

Maps
=

THE DIVERSITY OF THE AMERINDIAN WORLD
BEFORE THE EUROPEAN INVASIONS

Area not dealt with

High civilizations (Empires)
Theocratic and militaristic chiefdoms
Semi-sedentary peoples in tropical forests or savannahs
Semi-sedentary peoples in desert territory
Nomadic hunting, fishing and gathering peoples

PAPAGO
PIMA
SERI
OPATA
GUAICURA CONCHO
TARAHUMAR
YAQUI
PERICU
COAHUILTEC
ZACATEC TAMAULIPEC
ŠAYULTEC OTOMI HUASTEC
TOTONAC
AZTEC
TARASCA MIXTEC
ZAPOTEC ZOQUE MAYA
MAYA
CHOL
CHORTI PAYA
LENCA
PILPIL
MATAGAL MOSQUITO
ULVA
OROTINA
BORUCA
GUAYMI CUNA
CHOCO
CHIBCHA
CAYAPA
COLORADO
JIVARO
CHIMU
CAMPA
CHANCA
CHINCHA INCA
COLLA
AYMARA
ATACAMA
DIAGUITA MATARA
ARAUCANIANS
COMECHINGON
QUERANDI
HUARPE MINUAN
CHIQUIYAMI
PUELCHE
MAPUCHE PEHUENCHE HET
POYA
CHILOTE
CHONO NORTHERN TEHUELCHE
SOUTHERN TEHUELCHE
TEUESH
ALACALUF
ONA
YAHGAN

CUBAN
CIBONEY LUCAYO
SUBTAINO TAINO
IGUAYO
HAITIAN
CIBONEY

CARIB

GOAJIRO QUETIO
MOTILON PALENQUE CHAIMA
YARURO CARIB WARRAU
MAPOYE CARIB
ACHAGUA
WITOTO WAICA MACUSI
TUCANO ARAWAK APARAI
BORA MACU
OMAGUA MURA ARAWAK ARUA TUPINAMBA
CATUKINA ARARA TEMBE TREMEMBE
IPURINA MUNDURUCU
NORTHERN TIMBIRA
CAWAHIB CAYAPO POTIGUARA
NAMBIKWARA AKWE SHERENTE JAICO
CHIQUITO SHAWANTE ACRO AETE
BORORO SOUTHERN TUPINAMBA
CHIRIGUANDO CAYAPO
MBAYA BORORO
PAYAGUA BOTOCUDO
CHOROTI GUARANI
ABIPON CAINGANG
GUARANI
GUENOA
ARACHANE
CHARRUA

ATLANTIC OCEAN

Equator

PACIFIC OCEAN

ARAWAK

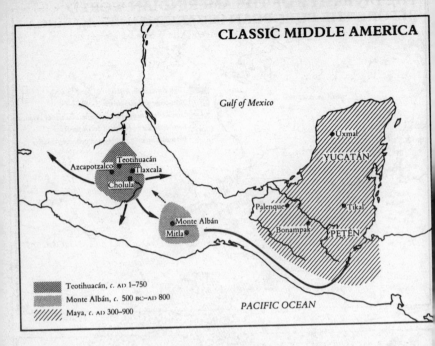

CLASSIC MIDDLE AMERICA

Gulf of Mexico

Azcapotzalco · Teotihuacán · Tlaxcala
Cholula

Monte Albán
Mitla

Uxmal

YUCATÁN

Palenque

Tikal

Bonampak · PETÉN

PACIFIC OCEAN

▨ Teotihuacán, *c.* AD 1–750
▨ Monte Albán, *c.* 500 BC–AD 800
▨ Maya, *c.* AD 300–900

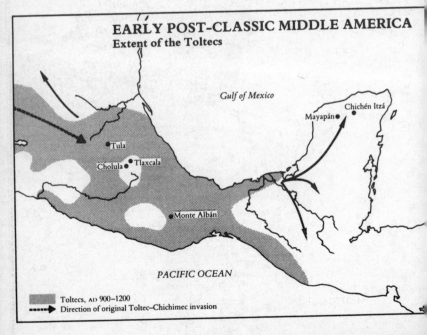

EARLY POST-CLASSIC MIDDLE AMERICA
Extent of the Toltecs

Gulf of Mexico

Chichén Itzá
Mayapán

Tula
Cholula · Tlaxcala

Monte Albán

PACIFIC OCEAN

▨ Toltecs, AD 900–1200
▸ Direction of original Toltec–Chichimec invasion

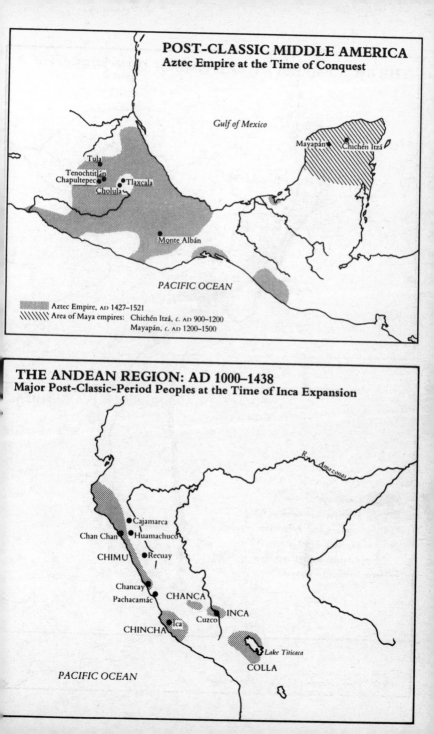

POST-CLASSIC MIDDLE AMERICA
Aztec Empire at the Time of Conquest

Gulf of Mexico

Tula

Tenochtitlán
Chapultepec
Cholula
Tlaxcala

Mayapán
Chichén Itzá

Monte Albán

PACIFIC OCEAN

Aztec Empire, AD 1427–1521
Area of Maya empires: Chichén Itzá, *c.* AD 900–1200
Mayapán, *c.* AD 1200–1500

THE ANDEAN REGION: AD 1000–1438
Major Post-Classic-Period Peoples at the Time of Inca Expansion

R. Amazonas

Cajamarca
Chan Chan
Huamachuco
CHIMU
Recuay

Chancay
Pachacamác
CHANCA
INCA
Cuzco
CHINCHA
Ica
Lake Titicaca
COLLA

PACIFIC OCEAN

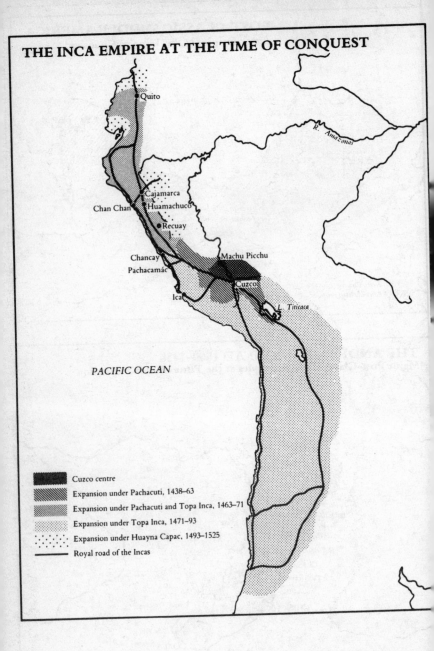

THE INCA EMPIRE AT THE TIME OF CONQUEST

Quito

R. Amazonas

Cajamarca
Chan Chan
Huamachuco
Recuay

Chancay
Machu Picchu
Pachacamác
Cuzco
Ica
L. Titicaca

PACIFIC OCEAN

- Cuzco centre
- Expansion under Pachacuti, 1438–63
- Expansion under Pachacuti and Topa Inca, 1463–71
- Expansion under Topa Inca, 1471–93
- Expansion under Huayna Capac, 1493–1525
- Royal road of the Incas

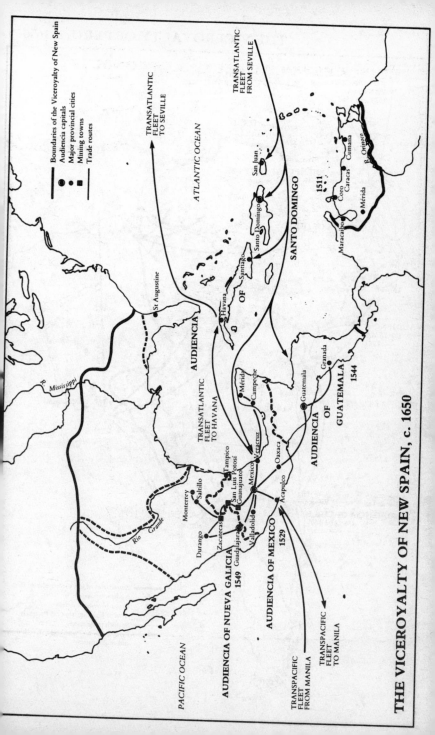

THE VICEROYALTY OF NEW SPAIN, c. 1650

Boundaries of the Viceroyalty of New Spain
Audiencia capitals
Major provincial cities
Mining towns
Trade routes

PACIFIC OCEAN

ATLANTIC OCEAN

TRANSATLANTIC FLEET TO SEVILLE

TRANSATLANTIC FLEET FROM SEVILLE

TRANSATLANTIC FLEET TO HAVANA

AUDIENCIA OF SANTO DOMINGO

AUDIENCIA OF GUATEMALA

AUDIENCIA OF NUEVA GALICIA

AUDIENCIA OF MEXICO

TRANSPACIFIC FLEET FROM MANILA

TRANSPACIFIC FLEET TO MANILA

St Augustine

Mississippi R.

Rio Grande

Durango

Monterrey

Saltillo

Zacatecas

Guadalajara

San Luis Potosí

Guanajuato

Valladolid

Mexico

Tampico

Veracruz

Acapulco

Oaxaca

Mérida

Campeche

Guatemala

Granada

Havana

Santiago

San Juan

Santo Domingo

Maracaibo

Coro

Caracas

Cumaná

Mérida

Orinoco R.

1549

1529

1544

1511

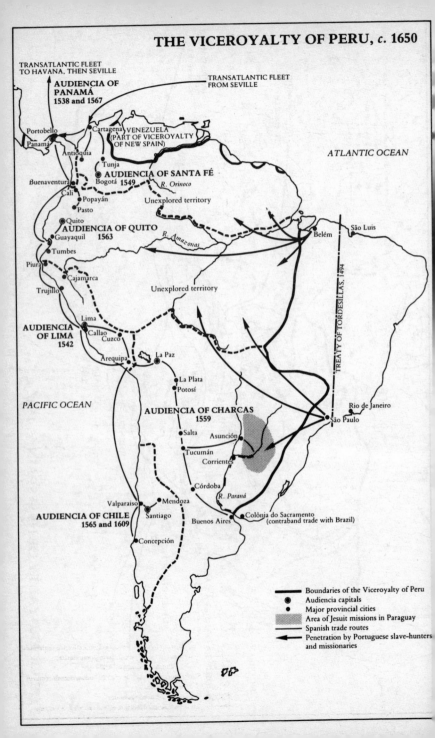

THE VICEROYALTY OF PERU, c. 1650

TRANSATLANTIC FLEET
TO HAVANA, THEN SEVILLE

TRANSATLANTIC FLEET
FROM SEVILLE

AUDIENCIA OF
PANAMÁ
1538 and 1567

Portobello
Panamá
Antioquia
Cartagena
VENEZUELA
(PART OF VICEROYALTY
OF NEW SPAIN)

ATLANTIC OCEAN

Tunja
Buenaventura
Cali
Bogotá 1549
AUDIENCIA OF SANTA FÉ
R. Orinoco
Popayán
Pasto
Unexplored territory
Quito
AUDIENCIA OF QUITO
1563
Guayaquil
R. Amazonas
São Luis
Belém
Tumbes
Piura
Cajamarca
Trujillo
Unexplored territory

Lima
AUDIENCIA
OF LIMA
1542
Callao
Cuzco
Arequipa
La Paz

La Plata
Potosí

PACIFIC OCEAN

AUDIENCIA OF CHARCAS
1559

Salta
Asunción
Tucumán
Corrientes

Córdoba
R. Paraná

Rio de Janeiro
São Paulo

TREATY OF TORDESILLAS, 1494

Valparaíso
Mendoza
AUDIENCIA OF CHILE
1565 and 1609
Santiago
Buenos Aires
Colônia do Sacramento
(contraband trade with Brazil)
Concepción

Boundaries of the Viceroyalty of Peru
Audiencia capitals
Major provincial cities
Area of Jesuit missions in Paraguay
Spanish trade routes
Penetration by Portuguese slave-hunters
and missionaries

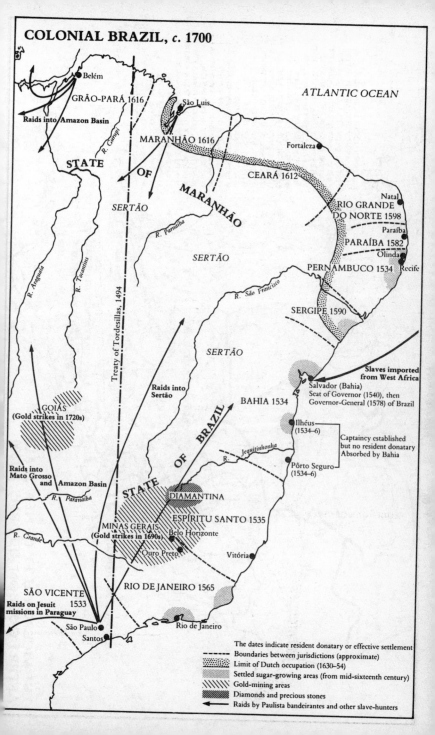

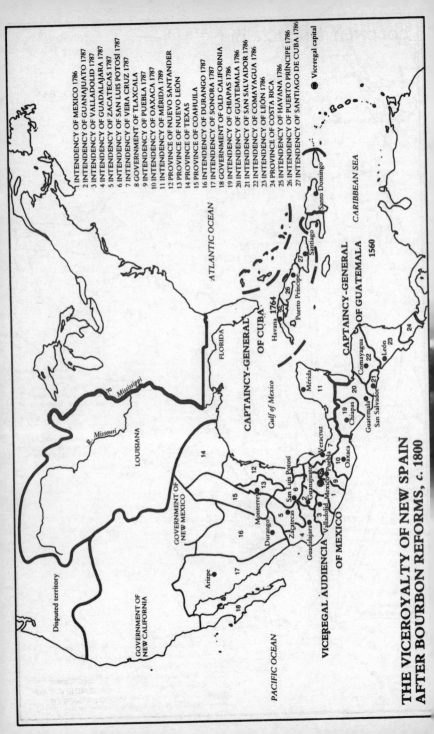

THE VICEROYALTY OF NEW SPAIN
AFTER BOURBON REFORMS, c. 1800

1 INTENDENCY OF MEXICO 1786
2 INTENDENCY OF GUANAJUATO 1787
3 INTENDENCY OF VALLADOLID 1787
4 INTENDENCY OF GUADALAJARA 1787
5 INTENDENCY OF ZACATECAS 1787
6 INTENDENCY OF SAN LUIS POTOSI 1787
7 INTENDENCY OF VERA CRUZ 1787
8 GOVERNMENT OF TLAXCALA
9 INTENDENCY OF PUEBLA 1787
10 INTENDENCY OF OAXACA 1787
11 INTENDENCY OF MÉRIDA 1789
12 PROVINCE OF NUEVO SANTANDER
13 PROVINCE OF NUEVO LEÓN
14 PROVINCE OF TEXAS
15 PROVINCE OF COAHUILA
16 INTENDENCY OF DURANGO 1787
17 INTENDENCY OF SONORA 1787
18 GOVERNMENT OF OLD CALIFORNIA
19 INTENDENCY OF CHIAPAS 1786
20 INTENDENCY OF GUATEMALA 1786
21 INTENDENCY OF SAN SALVADOR 1786
22 INTENDENCY OF COMAYAGUA 1786
23 INTENDENCY OF LEÓN 1786
24 PROVINCE OF COSTA RICA
25 INTENDENCY OF HAVANA 1786
26 INTENDENCY OF PUERTO PRINCIPE 1786
27 INTENDENCY OF SANTIAGO DE CUBA 1786

● Viceregal capital

SPANISH SOUTH AMERICA AFTER BOURBON REFORMS, *c.* 1800

Cartagena

Caracas • Cumaná

CAPTAINCY-GENERAL OF VENEZUELA
1777

• Bogotá

VICEROYALTY

• Popayán

OF NEW GRANADA

• Quito

1717 AND 1739

• Guayaquil

I. TRUJILLO 1784

Trujillo •

I. TARMA 1784

VICEROYALTY

I. LIMA 1783

Lima •

OF PERU

I. HUANCAVELICA
1784

• Cuzco

1542

I. HUAMANGA 1784

P. MOJOS

I. CUZCO 1784

I. PUNO 1783

Arequipa •

La Paz •

I. AREQUIPA 1784

I. COCHABAMBA 1783

I. LA PAZ 1784

I. CHARCAS 1783

P. CHIQUITOS

I. PARAGUAY 1783

I. POTOSÍ 1783

PACIFIC OCEAN

VICEROYALTY

• Salta

Asunción •

I. SALTA 1783

P. MISIONES

Tucumán •

Corrientes •

OF RIO DE LA PLATA

ATLANTIC OCEAN

I. SANTIAGO

I. CÓRDOBA
1783

P. MONTEVIDEO

Santiago •

Buenos Aires •

CAPTAINCY-GENERAL

1776

Montevideo •

Concepción •

I. BUENOS AIRES 1783

OF CHILE

I. CONCEPCIÓN

1778

P. THE MALVINAS ISLANDS

● Viceregal Capital
I. = INTENDENCY OF
P. = PROVINCE OF

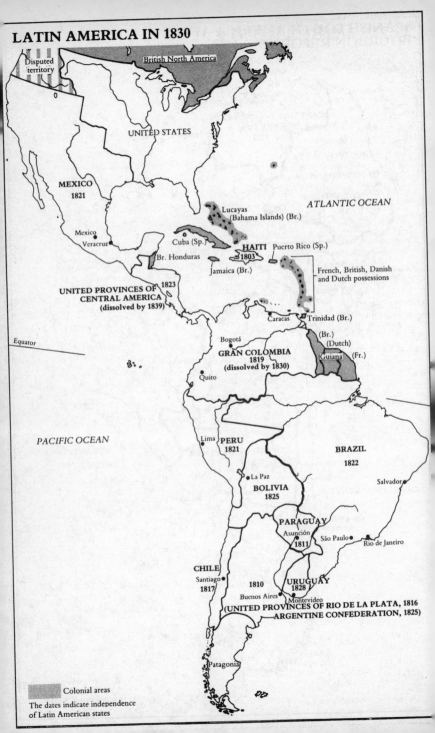

LATIN AMERICA IN 1830

Disputed territory

British North America

UNITED STATES

ATLANTIC OCEAN

MEXICO
1821

Mexico
Veracruz

Lucayas
(Bahama Islands) (Br.)

Cuba (Sp.)

HAITI
1803

Puerto Rico (Sp.)

Br. Honduras

Jamaica (Br.)

French, British, Danish
and Dutch possessions

UNITED PROVINCES OF   1823
CENTRAL AMERICA
(dissolved by 1839)

Caracas

Trinidad (Br.)

Equator

Bogotá

GRAN COLOMBIA
1819
(dissolved by 1830)

(Br.)
(Dutch)
Guiana (Fr.)

Quito

PACIFIC OCEAN

Lima

PERU
1821

BRAZIL
1822

La Paz

BOLIVIA
1825

Salvador

PARAGUAY

Asunción

1811

São Paulo

Rio de Janeiro

CHILE

Santiago

1817

1810

URUGUAY
1828

Buenos Aires

Montevideo

(UNITED PROVINCES OF RIO DE LA PLATA, 1816
ARGENTINE CONFEDERATION, 1825)

Patagonia

Colonial areas

The dates indicate independence
of Latin American states

LATIN AMERICA (POLITICAL)

CANADA

UNITED STATES

ATLANTIC OCEAN

MEXICO
Mexico City

Havana

THE BAHAMAS

CUBA

HAITI   Santo Domingo
Port-au-Prince   **DOMINICAN REP.**

Puerto Rico (to U.S.)

BELIZE
Guatemala
HONDURAS JAMAICA

ST KITTS-NEVIS   ANTIGUA & BARBUDA

GUATEMALA   DOMINICA
EL SALVADOR   ST LUCIA
San Salvador **NICARAGUA** ST VINCENT   BARBADOS
Tegucigalpa   GRENADA
Managua   TRINIDAD & TOBAGO
COSTA RICA
San José   Panamá   Caracas

PANAMA   **VENEZUELA**

Equator   GUYANA
                                 SURINAME
                Bogotá   Fr. Guiana
        COLOMBIA

ECUADOR Quito

PACIFIC OCEAN

PERU
Lima

BRAZIL

La Paz
BOLIVIA   Brasília

PARAGUAY
Asunción

Santiago   **URUGUAY**
CHILE   Buenos Aires
            Montevideo
       ARGENTINA

Areas not independent

The capitals of independent Latin American
states are represented only

Falkland Islands (to U.K.)

Index of Subjects

===

absolutism, 59–60, 63–4, 70, 75, 196, 202–3, 205, 273, 375
see also, Catholic Monarchy; regalism; 'right of resistance'; tyranny
Africans, 141–4
see also slavery
agriculture,
pre-Columbian, 39, 41, 43, 47, 48–9, 54
colonial, 82, 119–20, 123–5, 181, 187–8
twentieth-century, 335–6, 337–8
see also, land reform; sugar
Alliance for Progress, 349–51, 425
Amazon, discovery of, 32
America
discovery of, 3–5
population in fifteenth century, 38
americanismo, 163, 287, 288, 305, 524, 534
see also, universalismo
anarchism, anarcho-syndicalism, 316–17, 328, 380, 461, 486–7
Andes region, development of civilization, 39–42
Aragon, 60–61
architecture
Brazil, 191
eighteenth century, 163
seventeenth century, 157–8
sixteenth century, 157–8
twentieth century, 528
Argentina, 33, 246
Buenos Aires, British invasions of, 204–5
colonial period, 124, 131, 142, 163, 198, 199, 204–5
Concordancia governments, 463–6
conquest of, 35
'dirty war' against guerrillas, 355–6, 476–7, 480
economy, 462–78, *passim*; 480–1, 483
immigration, 459–60
independence, 218–20, 221
literature and culture;
nineteenth century, 287–93, 303–4, 306–7, 309–10;
twentieth century, 523–7 *passim,* 532, 539–40, 543–4, 547, 550, 553–4, 561
military intervention, 462–3, 471, 472–3, 484
military government, 351, 477–9
nineteenth century, 274–80
nationalism, 465–71 *passim*
Onganiato, 473–4
Peronism, 466–72, 475–7, 482–3
Radical governments, 460–63, 472–3, 480–83
rebellion against Spanish rule, 218–20
redemocratization in 1980s, 479–83
twentieth century, 459–64
see also, state, corporate
arielismo, 305, 327, 329, 519, 523, 524, 531
audiencias, 14, 21, 92–3, 94, 240–41
Aztecs, 17–21, 41, 42–6
and Spanish, 36

religion, 45–6
society, 44–5

bandeirantes, 176–7, 185–6
Belize, 322
Bolivia, 245
colonial (Upper Peru), 28, 92, 104, 123, 124, 126, 130, 198
independence, 219, 231, 241
literature and culture, 308
republican period, 256, 258, 270, 274, 325, 337, 362, 453
silver, 105, 126, 127–8, 129, 131
tin, 321
Tupac Amaru rebellion, 200, 202
Bourbon monarchy, 162, 163, 196–7
institutions of, 197
Bourbon reforms,
in America, 198–205
in Spain, 196–8
Brazil, 33
architecture, 191, 423
Canudos rebellion, 304, 305–6, 412
colonial period, 167–92
Communist Party, 414, 417, 420, 428, 432
discovery of, 167
economy, colonial, 183–8; nineteenth-century, 251–2, 281; twentieth-century, 414–5, 425, 427–31, 434–5
eighteenth-century
Pombaline reforms, 205–9
Estado Nôvo, 416–20

of Portugal, 74, 168–9, 178–
83, 208–9
comparison, 74, 178–9, 208
see also, colonial institutions;
imperialism
state, republican, 205, 255–6,
258, 259, 265–73 *passim,*
279–80, 313–14, 318, 328,
351–2, 364, 371
legitimacy of, 234, 341–2,
345, 348–9, 372–3, 376–7,
392, 478
weakness of, 342, 345, 348–9,
350, 364, 374–5, 525
sugar, 179
Brazil, 184–5
Cuba, 453–4
syncretism, religious, 101–2,
139, 143

Tenochtitlán, 20, 21, 42–3
Texas, 261–3
textiles, *see obrajes*
theatre, seventeenth century,
155–6
Toltecs, 40–41, 46
towns, early, 78–9, 81–2
tyranny, 60, 63–4, 70, 162, 202–
3, 221, 272, 273, 287

United States of America
(USA), 203, 204, 208, 217,
291, 305–6, 310, 314, 320–

23, 332, 334, 346, 353,
357–8, 365–6, 369–70, 372,
515, 516, 530, 534, 535,
542–3
and Argentina, 466, 469
and Brazil, 410, 419–20, 424,
425–6
and Chile, 488, 496, 499–500,
501
and Cuba, 323, 324, 325, 437,
438–9, 440, 449–50, 452–3
and Guatemala, 325, 353
and Mexico, 259, 261–3, 380,
385–6, 388, 394, 408
see also, Alliance for Progress;
imperialism; Monroe
Doctrine; Roosevelt
Corollary; Texas
universalismo, 524, 525, 526, 529
see also, americanismo
University Reform Movement
(Argentina), 318, 440, 460
Upper Peru, *see* Bolivia:
colonial
urbanization, 335, 338, 339–41,
359
urban guerrillas, 356–7, 427–8
Uruguay, 204–5, 219, 249, 274,
276, 335, 342, 350, 367,
371, 376
Batlle reforms, 318
literature, 308, 527, 547
urban guerrillas, 356

Venezuela, 244–5, 335, 340,
349, 361, 365, 367, 368,
372, 373, 376, 513
colonial, 78, 101, 124, 126,
131, 142, 198–9, 203
conquest, 31
economic growth, 335
independence, 213, 217–18,
222–3, 228, 231, 240, 241
literature and culture, 287–8,
309, 528
Tierra Firme, 11, 16
Vilcabamba, neo-Inca state of,
30
visual arts
modernism, 525–9
seventeenth century, 159

women,
black, 144, 145
in convents, 160–61
early migrants, 83
Indian, 145, 168
mestizas, 146
as slaves, 144, 145
writers, 160–61, 531, 562–3
working class, 314–17, 353, 355,
376, 380, 424, 461, 467–8,
486, 487, 500, 505–6
see also, labour

yanaconas, see labour systems
Yucatán, 16, 34, 101, 139, 263

Index of Names

Index of Names